6.50

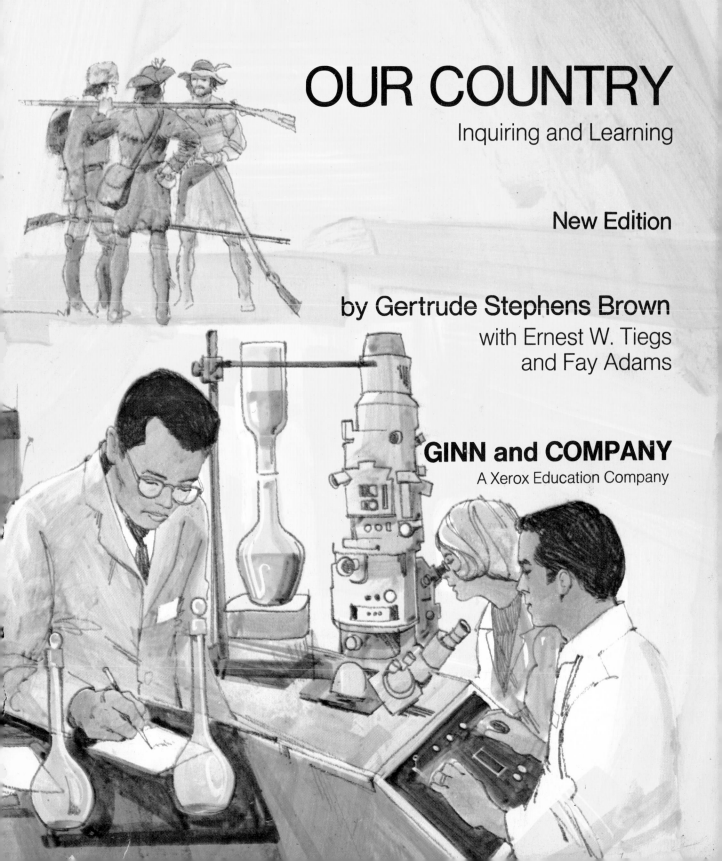

The Tiegs-Adams Series

OUR COUNTRY
Inquiring and Learning

New Edition

by **Gertrude Stephens Brown**
with Ernest W. Tiegs
and Fay Adams

GINN and COMPANY
A Xerox Education Company

Contents

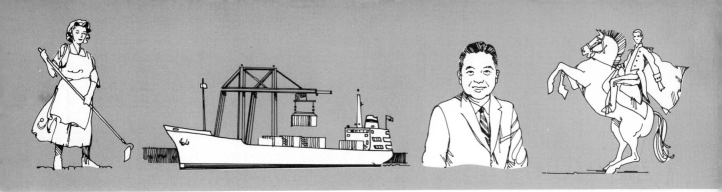

5

Maps in This Book

UNIT ONE
Our Beginnings

1 · Finding and Exploring the New World

The First Americans Meet Columbus

A Story · Huge Gray Birds and Strangers

It was early morning on the island. Two young Americans from a nearby village were on their way to fish in the ocean. Their path through the tall grass was shaded by palm trees.

Suddenly the younger boy stopped. "Look!" he cried. "Huge gray birds sit on our waters! Why have they come?"

"I don't know!" replied the older boy, staring across the water. "But they look very queer. I think they bring visitors. See! Strangers are climbing down into small boats."

"Who are they?" cried the younger boy.

"They're not dressed like warriors," replied his friend. "Perhaps they are gods from heaven."

"But they're coming to shore! I'm afraid! Let's run away!"

Columbus makes friends with the first Americans. Why did he call them Indians?

"No!" insisted the older boy, bravely. I'll stay here and watch. I can hide behind the trees. You race to our village and bring back others."

Very soon, a group of Americans collected near the beach. They watched the strangers row closer and closer to their shores. It is not surprising that these Americans were puzzled. They had never seen large sailing ships before. Nor did they know that the strangers were from Europe, far across the sea. You may have guessed that these strangers were sailors led by Columbus.

Soon, the visitors stepped ashore. The white-haired leader threw himself on the sand and kissed it. He kneeled and raised his hands to the Great Spirit. After this, his followers crowded around him and also fell on their knees. The Americans wondered if the leader were a god. But his followers called him Columbus.

Columbus claimed the new land for Spain. He pushed his shining sword into the sand. Then he raised a handsome flag and spoke words. He *claimed* the island for his king. This meant that it now belonged to Spain. Do you think that Spain had a right to this island?

Columbus named the island San Salvador. It means "Holy Savior" in Spanish.

Soon the villagers lost their fear. Probably this was because the white-haired leader was smiling and holding out gifts. Sparkling glass beads! Bright red caps! And tiny bells! At once he began to make friends with the Americans.

Columbus called the Americans "Indians." He thought he had reached a part of the rich lands known as the Indies, you see. Since Columbus's time, the name *Indians* has always been used for these first Americans.

The Indians were the first Americans. They were the first people to live in America. For thousands of years they had lived on the continents of North and South America and on nearby islands such as San Salvador. A *continent*, remember, is a huge body of land. Find the two continents of North and South America on the global map on page 10. Also, locate the island of San Salvador where Columbus landed.

There were many tribes of Indians. A *tribe* was a large group of people who lived together in villages or wandered together from one area to another. The people of a tribe were somewhat like a large family. They had much in common. They spoke the same language. They hunted and fished with each other. They shared other work.

Our Earth is nearly round like a great ball.
A small model of our earth is called a *globe*. A globe shows correctly the sizes and shapes of the bodies of land and oceans on our earth. When you look at a globe you can see only half of our earth. The global map above shows you almost half of it.

Find the *continent* of Europe on this global map. Europe is sometimes called "the Old World." It was the home of the explorers who discovered America, or "the New World." America was a new world to people from Europe. West of Europe stretches the Atlantic Ocean. Find it on the global map above.

People in Europe had no way of knowing that across the Atlantic were two great bodies of land, or *continents*. Then, bold explorers sailed west across the Atlantic and found this "New World." Christopher Columbus led the way. Find the route which his three small ships took across the ocean.

A few years later, Cabot made a voyage to America for the English. Find his route. What part of our continent did he discover? Neither Columbus nor Cabot realized how large the New World was. Many years passed before the Europeans explored most of the land along the coasts of North and South America.

10

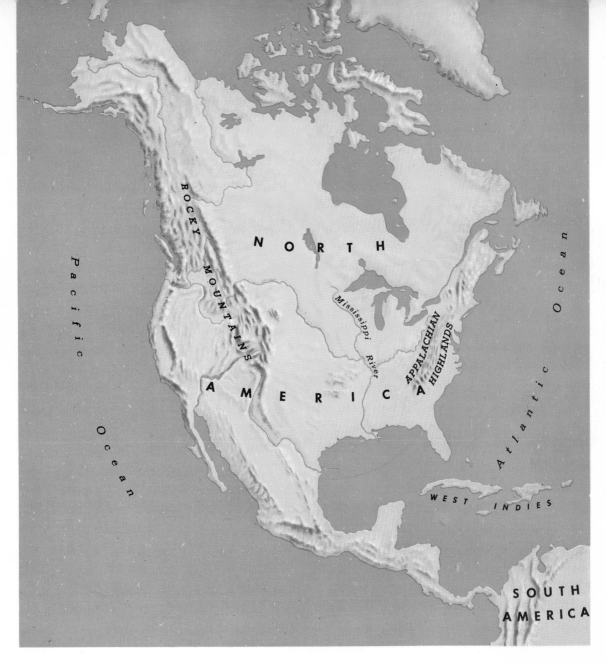

On this map notice how the continent of North America reaches from the Atlantic to the Pacific Ocean · Find the long Mississippi River that flows through the middle of the land. Where are the mountains?

North America is the continent to which the English and other early settlers came long ago. It is the continent on which we live.

The map above is different from the global map on the opposite page. Maps like the one above are usually more useful than a globe when you study a part of the earth. If you look for the United States on a globe you will see that it appears very small. The map-maker would not be able to show all the rivers, mountains, and cities in such a small space. He would need a huge globe to show even some of these things. Therefore he makes a map which is flat, to show the United States. You will find that most of the maps in this book are flat.

But a map cannot show the exact shape of a body of land or water. That can be done only on a globe. The continents and oceans do not look quite the same on a map as when they are drawn on a globe. If we press the rind of half an orange out flat, the edges break and it flattens out. It looks different. The same thing happens when we make a map.

These Indians had not learned how to make tools and weapons from iron. Instead, they made them from wood, stones, and bones. Many Indians were skilled craftsmen. They made useful and attractive clay pots and dishes. They wove fine cloth and handsome baskets. Some of them built strong canoes.

Not all Indian tribes were alike. This was partly because of geography. Not all tribes settled on the same kind of land. A tribe that lived in a forest area, for example, could build houses of logs and planks. Wild game and fish were usually plentiful near their homes.

But life was very different for tribes that settled in dry regions. Such a region had few trees. So the people had to build homes of other materials. Some used dirt and brush. Others made bricks of adobe soil. Still others carved their homes out of cliffs.

Some tribes lived simply. They were content to hunt and fish and perhaps to raise a few vegetables. They made most of the things which they needed from materials they could find close at hand.

Other tribes built powerful "nations." They laid out large cities and put up splendid palaces and temples. Some of their people were skillful farmers, weavers, or artists.

Like some Europeans, some tribes went to war. Others were friendly and peace-loving. Columbus was welcomed by friendly Indians, as you know.

But of course these Indians wondered why he had come to their land. Why had he landed on their shores, anyway? What did this stranger want? To answer that question we need to go back even earlier in time.

How a New Route Led to a New World

Wanted! Treasures from the Indies! Columbus and his sailors were from the continent of Europe. Find this continent on the global map on page 10. For many years, people in Europe had known about the Indies. The name *Indies* was given to lands in Asia far to the east of Europe. The Indies meant the rich lands of India, China, and the Spice Islands. Can you find these lands on the global map on page 24? They had wonderful goods to trade. Spices to make food taste better! Beautiful shining silks! Sparkling gems and wondrous gold and silver articles.

In Europe, kings and wealthy nobles wanted these goods from the Indies. But they were very expensive. One small box of pepper cost a great deal of money, for example. Also, such goods were scarce. Merchants could not get enough for their customers. Can you think why?

Goods from the Indies were brought a very long distance. Trains of mules carried the goods over mountain trails. But caravans of camels hauled them across the hot deserts. There were no good roads or fast ways of travel in those days. It took months to journey from one city to another. But that wasn't all! There was often great danger along the way from robbers who lay in wait.

Part of the journey was by sea, but it was also dangerous. Some ships were lost in storms. Others were seized by pirates. So, trade with the Indies was very difficult.

A new route was needed. By the 1400's, people in Europe began to dream of a shorter, safer route to Asia. Merchants wanted it. Kings and queens became interested in finding it. The country of Portugal sent ships south to search for a route around the coast of Africa.

But one daring man thought that a new route to the Indies could be found in another direction. That man was a sea captain from Italy, Christopher Columbus.

Columbus believed the shortest route to Asia crossed the Atlantic. He knew that the earth was round and thought he could sail west to reach the Indies in the east. He had spent many years studying such a route. But he did not have the money to make his dream come true. He could not hire sailors and pay for ships and supplies for a long journey. Only kings and nobles could afford this enormous expense.

Over and over, Columbus asked for help. But each time he was turned away. Finally, after many years, the captain was ready to give up hope. Then suddenly Columbus was called back to a splendid Spanish palace. The King and Queen of Spain had decided to help him, after all.

Columbus set sail one sunny day in August, 1492. His three small ships left a busy harbor in Spain. It is said that one of the pilots who helped to guide his ships was a black. The global map on page 10 shows the route. It led south and west across the Atlantic Ocean.

In those days, many people called this ocean the Sea of Darkness. But not Columbus! He had learned much about it and its winds and currents. A *current* is a flow of water. Columbus knew that a

Captain Columbus uses a compass to direct his ships.

current flowed westward across the Atlantic from the coast of Africa. He had learned that winds blew westward above it. *Winds* are currents of air that move over the earth. Columbus felt sure that these currents of wind and water would help to carry his ships west.

Columbus kept a careful record of each day's happenings on this voyage. Some days, the sea was calm and the weather was delightful. But other times, storms blew up and sent huge waves crashing across the decks. After several weeks many of the sailors became discouraged and frightened. Never before had they lost sight of land for so long a time.

They feared they never would find their way back to Spain.

These sailors complained bitterly. They begged their captain to turn back. He refused. He persuaded them to be patient just a little longer. Finally, they saw land very early on the morning of October 12, 1492.

Columbus discovered the New World. But he did not know this when he landed on San Salvador. He believed the earth to be much smaller than it is. Also, he did not know that between Europe and Asia lay two great continents. Therefore, he thought he had reached lands near Asia. That is why he spoke of them as the Indies.

Today, San Salvador and its neighbor islands are called the *West* Indies. Find them on the global map on page 10. Now locate them on the map on page 188. Notice what a long distance they are from India and China.

When Columbus returned to Spain, he was welcomed as a hero. The king and queen were delighted that he had reached the Indies. Columbus promised that soon ships could sail west to the lands of gold, pearls, precious stones, silks and spices.

Columbus made three other voyages west. While on these voyages, he discovered other islands in the West Indies. He also touched the coast of South America. He never found the riches he was seeking. But he always believed that he had discovered lands off the coast of Asia.

Columbus failed to reach the Indies. We know that he had made a much more important discovery. He had found a world that was new to Europeans.

He had shown great courage and skill. He had conquered the Sea of Darkness. He had trained sailors for long voyages across the Atlantic. Indeed, Columbus led the way for many explorers. He also started the first Spanish settlement in the West Indies.

How this New World was named. During Columbus's time, there lived a seaman and writer named Americus Vespucci. Several years after Columbus's first voyage, Americus made some voyages along the northeast coast of South America. He wrote letters about the lands he had seen to important people in Europe. In his letters, he claimed that he had discovered a New World. A teacher read a copy of one of these letters. He was writing a book about geography. In this book he suggested that these new lands across the Atlantic be called "America" for Americus.

Later on, the name *America* was given to both continents in the New World. Do you think that this was fair? Why?

Many Spaniards Followed Columbus to the New World

Other explorers sailed west from Spain. Like Columbus, they hoped to find a waterway to Asia, claim new lands, and win great treasure.

A number of blacks from Spain and North Africa journeyed to the New World with these explorers. In fact, there were Africans in nearly every exploring party which visited North and South America.

At one time Africans had ruled a large part of Spain. They had ruled it for about 500 years.

The Spaniards took with them guns, cannon, and horses. The Indians had never seen horses. They were worried when riders galloped toward them. They were frightened by the thundering guns and cannon. Usually the Indians tried to get along with their visitors.

"We want gold!" the Spaniards said in sign language. The Americans answered by shaking their heads or by pointing to distant lands. They hinted that gold might be found far away. This encouraged the Spaniards to search and search.

Ponce de Leon searched for gold and a magic fountain. By this time, there were Spanish settlements in the West Indies. Ponce de Leon was the governor of one. He had been handsome and strong. Now he had grown old and tired. Then, one day, he heard of an island to the north and west with a wonderful Fountain of Youth. It was said that anyone who drank of its waters would become young and strong again. Besides, there was gold hidden nearby, said the Indians.

The governor and his men found some lovely green islands. But they did not find the amazing fountain or any treasure. So they sailed on. Soon, they landed on the shore of a low flat land. They had discovered the southeastern tip of what is now our country. They saw many beautiful flowers and graceful palm trees and pine forests. They gave this land the name *Florida*, a Spanish word for flowers.

The adventurers tasted the water of many a Florida lake and stream. But alas! They did not grow any younger. Just as disappointing, they did not find gold. At last, they gave up and returned to the West Indies. Still, they had claimed a large new land for Spain.

Cortes was a successful treasure hunter. He was a bold Spanish leader. Cortes guided several shiploads of soldiers from the West Indies to Mexico. He had many exciting adventures. In time, he conquered the powerful Indians, the Aztecs, who ruled the heart of Mexico.

Ponce de Leon looks for the Fountain of Youth in Florida.

THE SPANIARDS EXPLORE THE NEW WORLD

- •••••• Coronado
- •—•—• Cortes
- – – – De Soto
- +—+—+ Ponce de Leon
- ········· Future state boundaries

The Spaniards explored the southern part of what is now our country. Notice how far they travelled on foot and on horseback.

The Aztecs had rich gold and silver mines. Cortes was able to seize from them vast stores of treasure. He sent shipload after shipload of gold and silver back to Spain. Gold from the New World was helping Spain to become a very rich country. Still, the hunt for more gold continued.

A search for gold led to a mighty river. The Spanish leader, De Soto, had helped Spain to conquer lands in South America. Then, he became a governor in the West Indies. But he was not satisfied to remain there. Instead, he planned a treasure hunt.

Indians captured by the Spaniards had told of rich cities to the north. De Soto decided to find and conquer these cities.

He sailed for Florida with 600 soldiers and helpers, and many horses. Slowly the men pushed inland through the thick

16

forests and around the low wet lands, or *swamps*. Little by little, they picked their way across Florida. Follow their route on the map on page 16. You can see that they marched northward through what are now our states of Georgia and South Carolina. Of course these future states were wilderness then. The Spaniards travelled on through present-day North Carolina, Tennessee, Alabama, and Mississippi.

As the months passed, many of the men became ill and died. Others were killed in battles with the Indians. At last the exhausted party came to the banks of a wide river. They had discovered the mighty Mississippi. It was the largest river De Soto had ever seen. Still, he was not as excited as one would expect. He had hoped to discover gold, remember. He had been hunting for it for three long years.

De Soto made camp on the banks of the Mississippi. There the men built boats to row across the river. Later, the Spaniards wandered on west into what is now Arkansas. They saw many Indians and vast new lands but no signs of gold. Finally, they turned back. By the time they reached the Mississippi, De Soto was very ill. Before long he died and his followers buried him in the great river which he had discovered.

About this time, another treasure hunt was going on, farther west. Again the cry was "Gold! Gold! Where is the GOLD?"

Tales of riches led the Spaniards to our Southwest. You know that the Spaniards had seized Mexico's riches. They had begun to rule this land which they named New Spain. Now, they heard that there were seven gold cities of Cibola to the north and west. Two parties set out to find them.

The first group was led by a black, Estevanico. Earlier, he had explored parts of our present-day Southwest while hunting for these cities.

This time, ambitious Estevanico guided his party across what is now New Mexico. One day, he saw a shining city in the distance. Estevanico eagerly hurried toward it. But before he reached it, unfriendly Indians killed him.

Other explorers discovered that this wondrous city was an Indian village carved out of bright-colored cliffs. The sunlight had made it shine like gold.

Find Coronado's route on the map on the opposite page. He led a party of more than a thousand men north from New Spain. They travelled across miles of mountains and *deserts*.

After many weeks, Coronado noticed dazzling buildings some distance away. "Ah! See!" he shouted. "A rich city of Cibola! I'm sure of it!"

The excited party galloped closer. But alas! The "city" was another small Indian village made golden by the sunlight. Still, Coronado did not give up. Now, he divided his party into several groups. He sent each group to search in a different direction.

Coronado led his men east over present-day Texas and north into what is now Kansas. Another group travelled west. It discovered the beautiful Grand Canyon of the Colorado River. But none of the groups found gold.

Coronado and his men returned to New Spain empty-handed. However, they had claimed for Spain enormous lands north and west of Mexico.

The French Wanted Their Share of the Riches

France sent Cartier to the New World. Spain was not the only country interested in the new lands. The French king also wanted a share of the lands and riches of the New World.

Cartier was an experienced French sailor. In 1534, the king of France sent him across the Atlantic. He was to claim lands for France and also to search for a waterway to Asia.

Remember! Many countries in Europe were still eager to locate an easy route to the Indies, to gain more wealth and power for themselves. They hoped that a waterway led through or around the New World.

Cartier was in charge of two ships. He landed on the shores of what is now eastern Canada. There he planted the French flag, and claimed the land for France. The next year, he returned and sailed far up a great river. You can follow his voyage on the map on page 19. He named this river the St. Lawrence and wondered if it was the magic waterway. But it wasn't! He finally reached *rapids*, swift, churning waters that tumbled over rocks. So he could go no farther.

After spending the winter on the St. Lawrence, Cartier returned to France. Though he made several other voyages, he failed to find gold or the magic waterway.

For about seventy years, the French almost forgot Canada. Then they became interested all over again. They saw Spain settling much of the New World and decided they must start a colony of their own. A *colony* is a group of settlers called

La Salle claims for France the land of the great Mississippi River Valley. He had travelled all the way down this great river to its mouth.

THE FRENCH EXPLORE
THE NEW WORLD

- - - - Cartier's second voyage
———— Champlain
+-+-+ La Salle

The French explored a large part of the New World, as this map shows. Notice how they followed inland waterways westward and then southward.

colonists who go to live in another land owned by their country. Champlain was in charge of the colony in New France.

Champlain became known as "the Father of New France." He was a well-trained leader and explorer. He started the first successful French colony beneath cliffs far up on the St. Lawrence. He called the settlement Quebec.

Champlain helped the colonists to build a fort and plant food crops. He also encouraged them to trade with the Indians for furs. You see, furs could be shipped to Europe and sold for high prices.

Champlain was the governor of the colony but he spent much time away. His first love was exploring and mapping new lands and waterways. On one trip he explored two of the Great Lakes—

Huron and Ontario. On another trip he discovered and named Lake Champlain. Find these lakes on the map above.

The fur-trading business attracted more and more young Frenchmen to New France. One was twenty-three year old La Salle, the son of a nobleman.

La Salle was a wise dreamer. He started a trading post on the banks of the St. Lawrence near an Indian village. There he built up a good fur trading business with the Indians. But before long, he became more interested in their tales than their furs. They told of a great river to the south and west. La Salle hoped that it might be the dreamed-of-waterway through America. He wondered if it could lead to the Pacific Ocean and decided to find out.

19

La Salle and his exploring party travelled as far as the Ohio River. Later he made a still more remarkable journey. He led his party all the way down the Mississippi River to its mouth. The *mouth* of a river is the place where it empties into the sea.

This Mississippi River, with two of its branches, is shown on the map on page 19. Locate its mouth. Near this area, La Salle raised the French flag and claimed the entire Mississippi Valley for France. He named it Louisiana in honor of his king.

Wisely, La Salle dreamed of building many settlements in this huge valley. He started two in what is now Illinois and planned for another at the mouth of the Mississippi. He did not live to see all of his dreams come true. However, he had led the way. Other French explorers and settlers followed to learn about this Louisiana region and build settlements.

Another country in Europe was also interested in the race to the New World. The next section will give you an idea of how it gained a foothold there.

The Dutch Claimed a Small Share of the New World

By 1600, the Dutch were looking westward with longing eyes. The Dutch people live in a small European country called the Netherlands. It is located next door to France. See if you can find it on the map on page 188. The Dutch made a great deal of money as traders and merchants. Like other traders, they were interested in finding a better route to the Indies.

The Dutch sent Henry Hudson to search for a waterway through the New World. Hudson was a skillful English seaman. An important Dutch company hired him to sail across the Atlantic. His orders were to search for the mysterious waterway leading through America.

The busy Dutch settlement of New Amsterdam.

Captain Hudson had many adventures, but one journey is especially interesting to us. He sailed about 140 miles up the river that now bears his name, the Hudson River. He hoped it would lead him to the Pacific, but of course he was disappointed.

You can understand why if you locate this river on the map on this page. It flows through our state of New York but not to the Pacific. Still, because Henry Hudson explored it, the Dutch claimed the lands that surrounded the Hudson River.

The Dutch started a colony, New Netherland. Soon, Dutch traders arrived and built trading posts along the Hudson River. They hoped to get rich in the fur business and were eager to trade with the Indians.

The Dutch named their main settlement after the largest city in their homeland. It was called New Amsterdam and was built on the southern tip of an island located at the mouth of the Hudson River. Peter Minuit had bought the island from the Manhattan Indians. He paid them with about twenty-four dollars worth of axes, kettles, knives and bright-colored beads.

This land became known as Manhattan Island, the name it still has today. On it, the Dutch built a fort, a mill, and some little houses. Because of its good harbor and excellent location, New Amsterdam grew steadily. You can see a picture of it on the opposite page.

Long before the Dutch arrived, still another European country, England, had shown an interest in the New World. Indeed, this interest dated back to the days of Columbus. Soon after the first voyage of Columbus, an English ship sailed west.

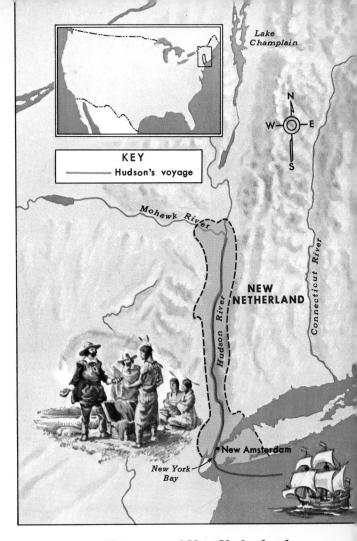

This map of New Netherland shows many things · The green area shows the land the Dutch called New Netherland. Find the Hudson River. What other rivers do you find? What do the pictures tell you? Look at the small map, or inset, in the upper left-hand corner. Can you find New Netherland on it? The inset shows in what part of our country New Netherland was.

John Cabot claims the north-eastern part of North America for England.

The English in the New World

In 1497, the King of England sent John Cabot to the New World. Cabot was from Italy but had been living in England. In fact he had taken an English name. Like Columbus, Cabot believed that he could sail west to reach the Indies. But he said he could find a shorter route than the famous captain had followed. Trace Cabot's voyage on the map on page 10. Notice that he sailed almost straight west of England.

One summer day, this explorer reached the cool rocky shores of a large island along the northeast coast of North America. He thought he was near China. Still, he did not see any splendid cities with shining gold towers. Nor were there any camel caravans loaded with silks and spices.

Cabot did find a different kind of wealth, however. He noticed that the shallow waters off the large island were alive with fish. Indeed, there were so many fish that they could be scooped up in baskets. But no wonder! These were the richest fishing grounds in the world. Many Europeans depended on fish as a main food. So Cabot knew that fishermen would welcome news of these fishing grounds. Also, he could boast that he had claimed a great deal of land for England.

The king was pleased with Cabot's reports, especially the news that he had almost reached China. So a second voyage was planned. This time, the captain was to guide five ships west. This time he promised that he would lead them all the way to China to be loaded down with gold and other treasures.

Of course, the ambitious captain could not keep his word. He reached the east coast of North America, but it was nowhere near China, as you know. He did explore farther, however, and claimed for England much land along the Atlantic coast.

Later, this claim to land in America became very important to England. Do you know why? Here England's thirteen colonies were to grow up. In fact, our own United States began here, as you will learn in the next chapter. But now let us read how the two earliest English colonies were started in America.

The colony that gave up and the Lost Colony. In the late 1500's, three shiploads of Englishmen sailed to America. They started a colony on an island off the coast of what is now North Carolina. They suffered many hardships in the lonely new land and lived in fear of the Indians. After a year, they gave up and returned to England.

Soon, another group of settlers arrived on the island. This group of 150 men and women was in charge of an able governor. How proud he was when, a few weeks

All that the governor found of the little colony was the word "Croatan" carved on a tree.

later, he became the grandfather of a baby girl. She was the first English child born in America and was given the name of the new colony, Virginia.

Before long, supplies ran low and the governor returned to England to get what was needed. But his country was now at war and he was not allowed to sail back to the little colony. Finally, after three years, he was able to return. But he found the small village in ruins and no signs of the colonists.

Had the people starved to death or been attacked by Indians? The sad governor could not tell, but he did notice the word *Croatan* carved on a tree. This was the name of a friendly Indian tribe so he decided that perhaps the settlers had gone to live with its people. Still the mystery was never solved, and to this day we think of these settlers as the *Lost Colony*.

A few years later, another Virginia colony was started on our shores. It became the first permanent English colony in our land. You will learn about it in Chapter Two.

See If You Remember

1. Why did European merchants want to find a better trade route to the Far East?

2. What plan did Columbus have for finding a new route to the Far East?

3. Why did Columbus call the people who lived on San Salvador, Indians?

4. What European country led the race to claim lands in the New World?

5. What were some rivers and lakes which the French explored?

6. Where was New Netherland?

7. Why was Cabot's voyage important?

Find the Missing Words

From the list below, choose the word or words to complete each sentence correctly. On a paper, write the sentence numbers and the correct missing words.

1. __?__ discovered the New World.

2. Coronado led Spaniards to our __?__.

3. __?__ conquered Mexico.

4. The Mississippi River was discovered by __?__.

5. Cartier claimed eastern __?__ for __?__.

6. __?__ started the first successful __?__ colony in Canada.

7. __?__ explored the Mississippi and claimed the lands it drained for France.

8. __?__ explored along the Hudson River for the Dutch.

9. __?__ claimed much land along the Atlantic coast for England.

10. The English failed when they tried to start a colony on an island that is now a part of the state of __?__.

List

John Cabot	La Salle	Cortés
Ponce de León	Canada	Hudson
Northwest	Columbus	France
Champlain	De Soto	North Carolina
Southwest	French	Spanish
Mexico	England	South Carolina

Let's Think Together

1. You read about many famous explorers. In what ways do you think they were alike?

2. What does the word *goal* mean? *Courage* helped Columbus reach his goal. What other qualities do you think he showed?

3. Where are men exploring today? What

are some ways their problems are different from those faced by explorers long ago?

4. Indian ways of living were influenced largely by the kind of area in which a tribe lived, remember. How does the geography of your region affect your ways of living?

About Directions

Let's review directions. The four main ones, remember, are north, south, east, and west. *North* is always toward the north pole on any part of the globe. *South* is always toward the south pole.

Find north and south on the maps on page 24. As you face toward the north pole, east is at your right. West is at your left.

On a wall map, north is also toward the north pole. If your class has a wall map, find north on it. Where are the other three directions on this map?

Learning from Maps and Globes

Maps can tell us many things. They have a language all their own—a language of lines, "signs," and colors.

Our Country contains dozens of useful maps. They can help you understand much about places, events, and topics mentioned in a chapter. They can, that is, if you study them carefully.

On page 24 are two global maps. Each one shows a half of the world, or a *hemisphere*. The one at the left shows the *Western Hemisphere*. The one at the right shows the *Eastern Hemisphere*. Use these maps to help you answer the following questions:

1. In which hemisphere do you live? In which one is the Old World? From which did Columbus sail?

2. Locate the north pole. You cannot see the south pole on these global maps. Halfway between the poles is the *equator*. The equator is an imaginary line around the earth, halfway between the north and south poles. Point to it. Does the equator run through our country?

3. The largest bodies of land are *continents*, remember. There are seven continents: Asia, Africa, North America, South America, Europe, Australia, and Antarctica. Which six continents are shown on the global maps? On which one do you live? From which one did John Cabot sail? Which one lies south and east of our continent?

4. The largest bodies of water are called *oceans*, as you know. Which is the largest one? Point to the Atlantic, the second in size. Which ocean is nearest your home? Locate the Indian Ocean. Is it in the Eastern or Western Hemisphere? Find the smallest ocean, the Arctic. Which pole does it surround? It is interesting to remember that seven tenths of the earth's surface is covered by ocean water.

Let's Meet the Vikings

1. Columbus and his men were not the first Europeans to find the New World. Bold Vikings were. They reached the eastern shores of Canada about the year 1000. Lief Ericson was one of their leaders. Read in another book about him and other Vikings. Share what you learn.

2. Draw and color a Viking ship.

3. On the global map on page 188–189 locate: the Viking lands of Norway, Sweden, and Denmark in northern Europe; the islands of Iceland and Greenland where some Vikings settled; and eastern Canada which the Vikings called *Vinland*.

2 · Building the Thirteen English Colonies

A Freedom That Began Long Ago

A Story ·
A Burgess Ex-
plains a Very
Important
Freedom

Ten-year-old Ann sat in the shade. She pushed her sewing aside and exclaimed, "It's too hot to do anything."

"August is always hot!" said her older brother. "But think of Father at Jamestown!"

"What does a Burgess do?" asked Ann.

"You can ask him tonight if you want!" replied Robert, staring across the fields. "Look! There he comes!"

Ann hurried into the house to get their mother. In a few moments they came out together.

They watched a galloping horse bring its rider nearer and nearer. Moments later, Father pulled his horse to a stop. Then he swung down to greet his family. It seemed that everyone was talking and laughing at once.

Finally Mother said to her husband, "My! My! You look dreadfully tired."

"Never mind! It was worth it. Think of our fine new freedom," Father exclaimed proudly.

"What is it, sir?" asked Ann.

"A very important freedom, my girl. The freedom to help make our own laws!"

The first meeting of Virginia's House of Burgesses. What was a Burgess?

Ann was listening to every word. "Oh!" she spoke up. "Is that what a Burgess does? Were you making laws?"

Father nodded. "Indeed so. And for that right we give God thanks."

Ann knew that laws were "rules." She had heard her father say that laws helped people do what is best.

"What laws did you make?" asked Robert. "Will you tell us about some?"

"Aye, after supper is over." Then the happy Burgess led his family into the house.

Ann and Robert lived in the colony of Virginia long ago. Their father owned a large piece of land. Such land owners were called *planters*, and their lands were *plantations*.

Most planters were raising excellent crops. The land was flat and there was plenty of rain and hot sunshine. But there were no machines to use in the fields. So each plantation needed many workers. They lived in cabins close together on one part of the plantation.

The colony was in charge of a governor sent from England. At first, leaders in faraway England made all the laws for the settlers. Then in 1619, this right was also given to the colonists themselves.

Two men from each settled district were chosen to be lawmakers. Such a lawmaker was called a *Burgess*. He was to *represent*, or act for, the people of his district. Therefore, he was their *representative*.

Father was one of the two Burgesses from his district. On July 30, 1619, all of the Burgesses gathered at Jamestown to hold their first meeting. This group was called the *House of Burgesses*. Its meetings went on for six days. But wait!

Let's listen to the story Father told on that long-ago summer evening.

"The Burgesses met at the church. We gathered there every morning when the drum signal sounded, soon after sunrise. The weather was very hot. But we wore our coats and hats as lawmakers in England do.

"We talked about what laws were needed. Every Burgess had a chance to speak his mind. Anyone who interrupted could be fined 100 pounds of tobacco. That's worth quite a sum, you know."

Father continued, "We made laws for the good of our colony. One says that healthy men must work and idle ones will be punished. Another says people must not give guns or gun-powder to the Indians. Several are about crops. We decided that each planter must raise enough food for his family and workers. We must not just grow tobacco that sells well in England. Then we passed laws about worship. Everyone must attend church services twice on Sunday unless excused."

"I guess a Burgess is an important person!" exclaimed Ann.

"Yes, lass!" replied Father. "But remember! The Burgesses represent the people. The people are free to tell us what laws are needed. They have chosen us." Then he added, "It is wonderful being free to help make our laws. I hope we shall always use this right wisely." Thus the proud Burgess finished his story.

The freedom to govern ourselves in this country had begun. The House of Burgesses was the first group of its kind in America. Its meetings at Jamestown helped lead the way to our government today. Let's learn more about Jamestown and the surrounding lands.

How the Southern Colonies Were Settled

Jamestown was the first successful English settlement in America. It was started by some English leaders. They formed the London Company. This company arranged to send three shiploads of adventurers and soldiers to America. They were to start a colony and hunt for gold and silver. Also, they were expected to raise crops for the company.

Early in 1607, the ships set out. The long trip across the Atlantic took four months. But finally the ships sailed into Chesapeake Bay, and up a quiet river. The leaders named this the James River in honor of their king. He had given a large piece of land for the colony.

It was May and Virginia seemed a very pleasant land. It was blooming with flowers and green with trees and grapevines. There were grassy meadows, too, and patches of wild strawberries. Deer, bears, foxes, and other wild animals roamed through the woods. And the weather was delightful.

The tired colonists eagerly left their boats. They settled on a low swampland that extended out into the river. They named this place Jamestown. There they cut down trees and built a rough fort and a few huts.

Soon, however, the men realized that Jamestown was a poor place for a settlement. Its weather was damp and unhealthful. Its water was bad, and the whole place was alive with mosquitoes.

Still, few of the colonists were willing to work to improve conditions. The men did not bother to build sturdy houses. They drank the smelly swamp water rather than dig wells for pure water. They were not even willing to raise crops for food. You see, most of the men had come from families of wealth. They had never learned to work with their hands.

Soon the food supplies ran low and there was not enough to eat. Many men became ill and a large number died. It seemed that the whole colony would starve to death. Then Captain John Smith took command.

Captain John Smith became the leader of Jamestown. He made friends with some Indians nearby. He arranged to trade with them for corn. He ordered the men to give up their search for gold and to plant crops instead. He insisted that all men must work if they wanted to eat.

Captain Smith had many exciting adventures with the Indians. One is said to have taken place when he was captured and taken before the Indian chief, Powhatan. Powhatan decided that the captain was a dangerous enemy. He must die. But Powhatan's lovely daughter, Pocahontas, begged her father to spare the captain's life. Her wish was granted. Captain Smith was allowed to return to Jamestown. Later, Pocahontas married one of Smith's friends and went to live in England.

Jamestown had many problems. Even Captain Smith could not get things to run smoothly. Because there were so many dreadful problems, the men were discouraged and homesick. Finally they decided to give up and return to England.

The colonists boarded ships and started down the river. On their way, however, they met other ships from England. They were loaded with supplies and had many new colonists. The Virginians turned their ships around and led the way back to Jamestown. Soon there was also other good news. No longer were the colonists to work entirely for the company. Instead each settler was to be given land to farm himself. This was such cheering news that the colonists worked much harder.

In time, the Jamestown settlers became successful farmers. They learned from the Indians how to grow corn and tobacco. They raised corn to eat and to feed their animals. They also began to grow tobacco and some other crops to sell to England. Tobacco brought such a good price in England that it became known as a "money" crop.

However, tobacco was a soil robber. It took much goodness from the soil and wore out the fields very quickly. Men did not know then, how important it is to put plant foods back into the soil. They did not spread fertilizer over the land as farmers do now. Instead, they used new land. They cut down the trees and planted new fields of tobacco.

In time, some men owned huge farms. They were called plantations, as you read earlier. Most plantations were located along the banks of rivers. Each of these had its own river front and wharf where boats could unload supplies from England and take on tobacco.

A planter could not farm his plantation by himself, remember. It was too large. But it was hard to find enough helpers. Men did not care to work for others when they could own lands themselves. Some planters began to buy slaves to work in the fields and do the housework.

Each plantation was like a busy little village. It had a large house where the planter lived with his family. Some distance away were the small, plain cabins of the workers from Africa. Then there were barns and stables. And there was the blacksmith shop where iron tools were made. Near the large house were storerooms, spinning and weaving rooms, the laundry, and sometimes several kitchens.

The planter's home was the largest building on the plantation. It was usually built on a rise back from the river with a view of the countryside. It had attractive gardens and spreading shade trees.

The homes of the richest planters had many rooms. Almost every room had a

Plantations were built along rivers. Rivers were the only highways at that time. Each plantation had its own wharf, as this drawing shows.

fireplace to provide heat during the winter. Such homes were furnished with furniture and drapes brought from England. Food was served on lovely English china.

Of course, these homes lacked many conveniences we enjoy today. They had no bathtubs, plumbing, cookstoves, or electric lights. For light, the people used candles or lamps which burned whale oil. Cooking was done over fireplaces.

Life was pleasant for the planter's family. The men managed their plantations. The women ran their homes. They planned the meals and directed the spinning, weaving, and sewing. They arranged "company" dinners, dances, and other parties.

The slaves did most of the work on these plantations. Some were house servants. Others were expert carpenters, bricklayers, mechanics, and shoemakers. But the largest number of slaves worked in the fields. They raised such crops as tobacco, rice, and sugar cane.

PLANTER'S HOUSE · WEAVING SHED · SPINNING SHED · KITCHEN · ORCHARD · TANNERY · VEGETABLES · WHEAT · STABLES · WORK-SHOPS · BARN · BLACKSMITH · TOBACCO · TOBACCO

Virginia and her neighbors became known as the Southern colonies. Other colonies were started along the southern part of the Atlantic coast. The map on page 36 shows them. Read the legend under the map. What does it tell about the key? Use the key to locate and name the five Southern colonies. What colony was farthest south?

These colonies occupied a wide strip of low flat land along the Atlantic coast. Such low, flat land is called a *plain*. When it extends along a seacoast, we speak of it as a *coastal plain*.

The southern coastal plain reached inland for many miles. Its nearly level land was thickly forested. Wide lazy rivers wandered through it. One was the James River which was mentioned earlier.

Many settlers came to live in the Southern colonies. Some laid out plantations. They had heard about the long hot summers and plentiful rainfall. So settlers discovered that fine crops could be raised. Some were crops that could not be grown in England, such as rice and indigo for blue dye. Farming soon became the leading industry of this region. That is, most settlers made a living as farmers.

Many settlers could not afford to own a large plantation. They moved "back" from the coast. They started small farms in the wilderness of the "back" country. They had to do their own work. They cut down trees, built their cabins, and began raising crops.

Other colonists preferred to live in towns. One of these towns was Williamsburg. It became the capital of Virginia in place of Jamestown. Find Williamsburg on the map. In South Carolina, Charleston became a busy seaport. Look for it on the map on page 36. Later Savannah, Georgia was started.

Now use this map for a different reason. Study the key again. What does brown show on this map? What does it tell you about the Northern colonies? Next we shall read about them.

31

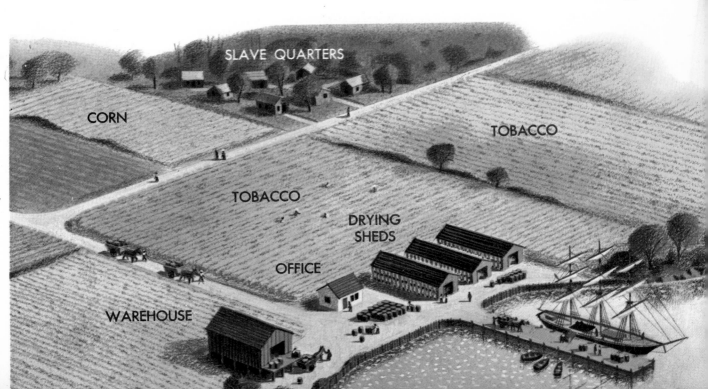

SLAVE QUARTERS

CORN

TOBACCO

TOBACCO

DRYING SHEDS

OFFICE

WAREHOUSE

The Indians taught the settlers how to plant corn.

How New England Was Settled

The Pilgrims were the first New Englanders. We must go to England to learn their story. A new law ordered every Englishman to attend the Church of England. Some people refused to obey this law. They wanted to worship God in their own way. So they held meetings in secret. When the king learned of this, he was angry. He had the meetings broken up and their leaders thrown into prison. This made the people so unhappy that as many as could moved to the Netherlands. There they could worship as they pleased. They became known as the Pilgrims.

The Pilgrims lived in the Netherlands for several years. But, as their children grew, they began to speak the Dutch language and follow Dutch customs. "This will never do," said their parents, sadly. "We are still English at heart. We must leave the Netherlands."

"Let us journey to America," suggested some of the leaders. "In the New World, we can worship God as we choose, yet live like Englishmen."

So, after months of planning, a band of courageous Pilgrims set out across the Atlantic. They sailed in a small ship, the *Mayflower*. The long voyage took many weeks. But at last, one cold wintry day in 1620, the Pilgrims reached the northeast coast of America. Before they went ashore, the people agreed that they would make fair laws, and that everyone would obey them.

The Pilgrims called their first settlement Plymouth. They said, "Here we shall build our homes and a new England. It shall be a strong new England for our children and our children's children." Even today, the northeast corner of our country is known as New England.

During the first winter in New England, the Pilgrims suffered terrible hardships. The weather was bitterly cold. There were no houses. Trees had to be cut down and "make do" shelters built. Food supplies ran so low that the people almost starved to death. Nearly everyone got sick and half of the people died. Those who survived were discouraged and homesick. Yet they did not give up. They remained in the lonely new land to conquer the wilderness. They were determined to build a strong Plymouth colony.

In the spring, friendly Indians taught the Pilgrims how to plant corn and vegetables. The colonists hunted game in the forests and caught fish in the sea. As time passed, the men built more comfortable homes. Slowly Plymouth grew.

Plymouth began the custom of celebrating Thanksgiving. Its people set aside a time in the fall to feast and give thanks for their harvest. Today, we, too, have a day for giving thanks. Our Thanksgiving Day is celebrated on the fourth Thursday of each November.

The Puritans also came to New England. Unlike the Pilgrims, the Puritans wanted to be members of the Church of England. But they did not agree with all of its ideas. Because they wanted to make it more "pure," they became known as Puritans.

Many Puritans had been leaders in England. Yet the king would not allow them to change the rules of their church. He insisted that they worship according to the rules already laid down. This made the Puritans very unhappy and many sailed to America so they could worship in their own way. They brought quantities of tools, seeds, and household furnishings as well as cattle and horses.

The Puritans started the Massachusetts Bay Colony. They founded Boston. Locate it on the map on page 36. Boston had one of the best harbors on the Atlantic coast. It soon became a busy seaport and trading center.

Within a few years, thousands of Puritans joined the first settlers. Some of them started little villages near Boston. It was in one of these villages that Andrew Courageous grew up, later on.

The Pilgrims march up the hill to attend church in the building which was both a fort and a meeting house.

A story about Andrew in Massachusetts Bay Colony. Andrew Courageous Hopkins lived in Massachusetts more than two hundred years ago. His comfortable home was shared by his parents, five sisters, three brothers, and a grandfather.

Families were large then. They worked hard, too. They frowned on lazy people. Indeed, they thought that wasting time was a sin. Even the young children were taught to do their share of the work.

Everyone in the Hopkins family was busy on this gray afternoon in November. Grandfather was carving legs for a chair. Father was cleaning his hunting gun. Andrew's oldest brother was sawing logs. John and David were driving the cows and sheep home from the pasture. Mary was weaving cloth on the loom. Another sister was spinning thread on the spinning wheel. Anne was knitting woolen stockings while she rocked the baby's cradle with her foot. And two girls were helping their mother prepare supper.

But ten-year-old Andrew had the pleasantest job of all. He also was helping with the supper. He turned the spit to keep the roast of deer meat from burning. It was browning over the flames in the huge stone fireplace. Nearby a big iron kettle of vegetables hung over the log fire cooking.

After supper, Father read from the Bible and said the evening prayers. Soon it was bedtime. You see, New England families usually went to bed early.

Andrew and his brothers shared a small room upstairs under the eaves. It was crowded but they seldom complained. When they did, their father said, "See here. None of that! Our home is very comfortable compared to the early ones in Massachusetts."

That was true. Indeed many kinds of changes had come in this colony in which Andrew lived.

Massachusetts Bay Colony grew larger and larger. In time, it swallowed up the smaller struggling Plymouth Colony. Together, the two became known as Massachusetts.

Some people in Massachusetts disliked the way Puritan leaders ran the colony. They allowed only church members to vote. They made strict rules and required that these be obeyed. One rule was that everyone must attend the Puritan church. The Puritans had wanted to worship God in their own way. But they were not willing to give this freedom to others.

In time, several other colonies took root in New England. One was Rhode Island. Find it on the map on page 36. As you can see, it is southwest of Boston.

Rhode Island was started by a brave young minister named Roger Williams. Williams felt that the Puritan leaders were unfair. He thought the people should be allowed to have whatever religious beliefs they wished. He also argued that the laws should be made by the people rather than by a few leaders of the church.

Williams preached these ideas in his church. But he soon got into trouble for doing so. The Puritan leaders were so angry with him that they decided to drive him out of Massachusetts. One cold winter night friends warned him that he was to be arrested. So that very night brave Roger Williams set out.

He stumbled through the snow-covered forests to a village where friendly Indians lived. There he spent the winter.

The next spring, Williams paid the Indians for a fine stretch of land on a beautiful bay. There he started a colony of his own. He believed that God had provided a good place for his settlement. So he named it Providence. Soon many other people moved to this village. Find Providence on the map on page 36. Today, it is Rhode Island's capital and largest city.

Other settlers built the colony of Connecticut, west of Rhode Island. Locate Connecticut on the map on page 36. As you can see, it is cut into two parts by the Connecticut River. The wide valley which follows along this river attracted wagonloads of colonists. One town which they laid out was named Hartford. Later, it became the capital of Connecticut.

Some colonists moved north. They started villages in present-day New Hampshire and Maine. Some settled along the coast. Others dared to go farther inland.

Settlers from Massachusetts travel to the Connecticut Valley to start new homes.

New England's early settlers lived in little villages. This seemed like a good plan. Most of the settlers had lived in villages in England.

A family lived on its narrow lot in the village. A family built their house on the front. Back of it they planted a garden and fruit trees and put up a cowshed. But they planted crops in fields which they had cleared at the edge of the village. There they grew such crops as corn, wheat, barley, and hay.

Some houses faced the square grassy field called the *common*. It was a public pasture owned by all of the villagers in common. There, in the center of the village, the cattle could graze peacefully. They were protected from the wild animals by homes and other buildings.

In time, many villages had a school, a blacksmith shop, an inn, and a grist mill. In the grist mill the farmers' wheat was ground into flour. The meeting house was very important. There, the people held meetings. They talked over and passed laws for their village. And there they chose their leaders. Find the meeting house in the drawing on page 37.

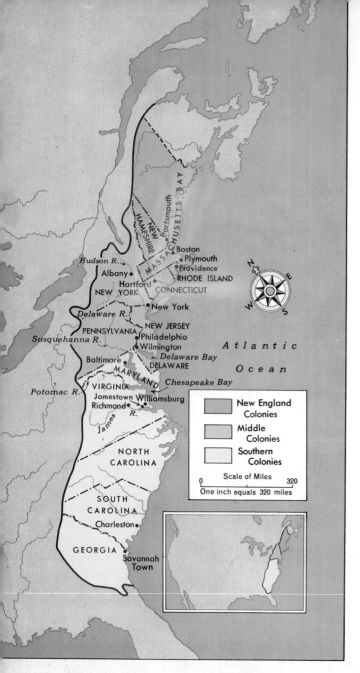

The Thirteen English Colonies · How are the three groups of colonies shown? Study the key to find out.

Look at the small inset map of North America. It shows where the colonies were on the continent of North America. The inset also tells something about how the colonies compared in size with all of North America.

New Englanders had a share in making laws for their colony. They had the right of electing representatives to their colony's law-making body, or *legislature*. But the king chose the governors and certain other leaders for Massachusetts. So its people did not have as much say about their laws as they wished. This made them unhappy and led to quarrels with the king's leaders. But that is another story.

At first, the people tried to make a living by farming. But this was hard to do. In much of New England, the soil was thin and rocky. Long, long before, rivers of ice, called *glaciers*, had moved across the land. They had shaved off mountaintops and dug away tons and tons of good earth. They had left behind millions of rocks sticking up through the thin soil. Only the river valleys still had rich fertile areas.

Also much of New England was covered by hills and low mountains, as the picture on page 35 suggests. Many of the valleys between were small and narrow.

Furthermore New England did not have the climate for growing crops which could be sold in England. Deep snow blanketed the ground for long months at a time and spring was usually quite late in arriving. So the growing season was short. The *growing season* is the part of the year that is warm enough to grow crops. It begins when the heavy frosts of spring are over and lasts until killing frosts come in the fall. New England's growing season was about like that in England. So both areas grew about the same kinds of products. Therefore, New England's farmers could not sell crops to their mother country.

New Englanders managed to grow most of their food and raise sheep to provide wool for warm clothing. But when they could not raise crops to sell, they lacked money for buying tools, gunpowder and other things they needed. To earn a better living, many men turned from farming to other occupations.

Some began to earn a living by lumbering, shipbuilding, or fishing. New England was covered with thick forests. Some settlers went into the woods to cut down timber. The logs were floated down the swift streams to sawmills and sawed into lumber. Shipping lumber to England became a good business. Tall straight pines in New Hampshire and Maine were cut down for ship masts.

Along harbors and on the banks of rivers, men also began to build ships. The shipyards welcomed workmen who were skillful with tools.

The seacoast provided other opportunities for making a living. Some colonists became fishermen. Many fishermen settled along the coast. This coast has dozens of bays. Arms of the sea have

Early New England towns looked something like this.

New England grew and grew. More and more people settled along its rocky coast and on its valleys and hills. By 1700, three thriving colonies shared its lands. They were Massachusetts, Connecticut, and Rhode Island. The settlements which had sprung up in New Hampshire and Maine were governed by Massachusetts for a long time. In 1741, however, New Hampshire became a separate colony. The Maine settlements continued to be a part of Massachusetts, as the map on page 36 shows you.

During the years New England was growing, thousands of people were also settling other lands along American shores. Many flocked to the lands south of New England, along the Middle Atlantic coast. We think of these lands as the Middle colonies.

Some settlers earned a living
as ship builders.

reached into the land to carve out these bays. They provide shelter for boats. Fishermen found the coastal waters of New England rich with cod and other fish. The fish could be dried or salted. Then they could be stored for a long time. Fish sold well in Europe and also in the colonies. So fishing became an important industry.

(1) Fish were (2) cleaned, (3) salted, (4) spread out to dry.

People from Many Countries Settled the Middle Colonies

The Middle colonies were New York, Pennsylvania, Delaware, and New Jersey. Look on the map on page 36 and find each one. Which one bordered New England? Which one was largest? Which was farthest south?

Only one Middle colony, Pennsylvania, was founded by Englishmen. New York, Delaware, and New Jersey were started by people from other countries. The first settlers in this middle region were hard-working Dutch people from the Netherlands.

New York began as the Dutch colony of New Netherland. The Dutch built fur trading posts, forts, and farms along the Hudson River.

Some Dutch people were farmers, and others were fur traders, carpenters, or merchants. They were thrifty people and worked hard. But they were fun-loving too. So they planned many good times. Ice skating and sleighing were favorite sports in the winter.

One of the merriest holidays was celebrated in December. Then Saint Nicholas arrived with his pack of gifts for all who had been good. The Dutch handed down to us the custom of welcoming Santa Claus at Christmas time.

The Dutch settlements prospered for a number of years. Then, one day, the king of England said that this colony was occupying English lands. He sent ships to New Amsterdam to demand surrender. Most of the Dutch were farmers and traders. They had only a few soldiers and could not protect themselves. Without firing a single shot, the Dutch gave up.

New Netherland's name was changed to New York and New Amsterdam was given the name New York City. Can you locate this city on the map on page 36?

New York City grew rapidly. But this is not surprising. Located on Manhattan Island, at the mouth of the Hudson, it had one of the finest harbors in the world. It was also close to rich farmlands. Soon, ships from many parts of the world were calling at its port to take on lumber, furs, and grain. As the years passed, it hummed with the business of buying and selling. New York City is now the largest city in our country.

Delaware's earliest settlers came from Sweden and Finland in northern Europe. The Swedes and Finns were strong outdoor people. Since they had always lived near thick forests, they were clever woodsmen. They were used to building their homes of logs. When they came to the New World, they put up the same kind of log cabins they had enjoyed in Europe. These were the first real log cabins in America.

Other settlers admired these strong, warm log houses. Because they were easy to build and comfortable to live in, many settlers began to put up such homes. In time, thousands of log homes dotted the colonies.

The English took the lands that became the colonies of Delaware and New Jersey. Swedish settlers also came to the area just north of Delaware where a few Dutch had settled. Later this area became the colony of New Jersey. When the English seized New Netherland they also took the lands to the south. Soon English people joined the Swedes and Dutch in starting farms and building settlements in these colonies of Delaware and New Jersey.

Pennsylvania was settled by English people called Quakers. Like the Pilgrims, they objected to attending the Church of England. Still, when they worshiped in their own way, they got into trouble. Some of them were put in prison and others were fined large sums of money. You can imagine, then, how glad the Quakers were when the king gave land in America to their leader, William Penn.

The first group of Quakers sailed a hundred miles up the broad Delaware River. They named their village Philadelphia

A tree-shaded street in Philadelphia. Penn planned this city carefully.

which means "City of Brotherly Love." William Penn planned Philadelphia very carefully so that it would have straight wide streets and many parks and gardens.

Within a few years, Philadelphia grew into a busy town. Many ocean-going ships visited its safe quiet docks. They unloaded goods from England and carried away crops, lumber, and other products.

Philadelphia also became one of the most beautiful towns in all of the colonies. The people were proud of its tree-shaded avenues and its neat red brick homes with shining marble steps.

Many people in the Middle colonies were farmers. In Europe, their ancestors had farmed the land for hundreds of years. So the new settlers were pleased when they found their region had miles and miles of good farmland.

Broad lowlands spread over New Jersey and Delaware. Rich deep soil covered the wide valleys that reached back along the rivers of the Middle colonies. The summers were warm and long, and plenty of rain fell. So large crops of fruit, barley, corn, and wheat could be grown. Soon, so much corn and wheat was raised that this region became known as the "bread

basket of America." It shipped many boatloads of grain to Europe.

Some settlers chose other occupations. They had learned special trades in their homelands. When they moved to America, they found jobs as carpenters, painters, and bricklayers. Indeed, some of these men knew how to build entire houses out of brick.

Other settlers earned a living as traders, shopkeepers, and businessmen. Some of them took charge of the goods that were sent to Europe. Men who liked to push into the wilderness became fur traders. They paddled far up the streams to trade with the Indians. The furs they brought back sold quickly to wealthy people in Europe.

The Middle colonies prospered. Their people worked hard, but they liked life in America. They enjoyed owning their own farms or having businesses or other ways to earn a living. And they were proud of their opportunity to take part in the government.

You see, people in the Middle colonies also chose representatives to help make their laws. Each of these colonies had a legislature elected by the people. This privilege was greatly prized throughout the thirteen English colonies.

In time the people of the thirteen colonies began to think of themselves as Americans. Although most of them had come from England, others were from the Netherlands or Sweden, for example. For a while, newcomers felt close ties with their native land. But gradually this feeling changed, and their main interests were centered in the new land. Then they began to call themselves *Americans*.

Of course there was no United States of America in those days. Not yet! Just thirteen colonies, each trying to go its own way. They had many similar problems, but they had hardly begun to work together. What were some reasons why?

Some Problems of the Colonies

Wide distances separated the thirteen colonies. As you may remember, these colonies reached from Maine on the north to Georgia on the south. They were strung out along the Atlantic coast for about sixteen hundred miles. We can tell this by using the scale of miles on the map on page 36. A *scale of miles* helps to measure distances from one place to another.

See how well you can use the scale of miles on this map. Pretend that you lived near the coast in New Hampshire, long ago. About how many miles to the south was the colony of Georgia? Let's find out by placing a ruler on the map. As you can see, the distance between Georgia and New Hampshire is almost three inches. On this map, one inch is equal to about three hundred miles. Three inches would be equal to nine hundred miles. We know, then, that Georgia was about nine hundred miles south of the colony of New Hampshire.

You may recall that Andrew Courageous lived in the colony of Massachusetts. Use your ruler and the scale of miles to learn about how far it was to his Uncle's home in Savannah, Georgia.

The colonies had different kinds of lands and climates. As you may know, *climate* is the kind of weather a place generally has through the years. You remember that New Englanders had settled on hilly, rocky lands. Their winters were long and cold with a short growing season, so farming did not pay very well. Still, thick forests covered the hills and mountains and there were millions of fish in the waters off the coast. This is why many men became fishermen, lumberjacks, or shipbuilders.

The Middle colonies had more nearly level lands and much rich soil. Their growing season was long enough so a variety of crops could be raised successfully. Furthermore, the deep rivers and good harbors encouraged trading and shipping.

The Southern colonies had wide, flat lands. Their warm climate and long growing season were excellent for raising tobacco, rice, and other money-making crops. So men laid out plantations and farms. Agriculture was the leading occupation in this southern region.

These early Americans had many different kinds of problems to solve. Most of the people were very busy earning their own living. They had little time to learn about the problems in other colonies.

The settlers did not always understand each other. Not many had visited the other colonies. Travel was slow and it was neither safe nor comfortable. One could take a sailing vessel from one seaport to another. One might also go by stagecoach for short distances and ride horses the rest of the way. But a long trip took many weeks. Most people had neither the time nor the money for travel. They had little chance to see how settlers lived in other areas.

There was no dependable way to get news. There were no telephones, daily papers, nor regular mail service. So most people knew little about life in other colonies. But word had spread about the systems of *indenture* and *slavery*.

Many colonists had indentured servants. Such a servant had been too poor to pay his way to America. A well-to-do colonist had paid it. In return, the servant had to work for that master a certain number of years. Finally he earned his freedom. Then he was also given clothing and a little money or land.

Some indentured servants were white and some were black. The first slaves were treated as indentured servants. But soon this changed and the slave system began.

Slavery was a special problem. Slaves had not chosen to live in America. They were forced to come from Africa. Also, most of them were owned for life.

There had been slavery in many parts of the world for thousands of years. Some slaves were captured in Europe. Some were from Asia and some from Africa. At the time the colonies were settled, a few Europeans owned slaves from Africa.

The Southern colonies and those in the West Indies needed many workers on plantations. More and more blacks from West Africa were brought to America as slaves.

Most West Africans were farmers or raised cattle. They knew how to care for crops and cattle in a warm climate. These skills were very useful in the West Indies and the Southern colonies.

Slaves were owned in all of the colonies. But gradually this system was given up in New England and nearby areas. It did not pay. The lands, climates, and ways of living were different from those in the Southern colonies. Differences between the Northern and the Southern colonies were going to cause serious problems.

Many of the blacks in Africa were skilled craftsmen. Some were fine artists. This beautiful head was carved from ivory.

Even with differences, the colonists had much in common. They enjoyed living in America. They liked owning their farms and plantations and helping their towns to grow. Best of all, they were free to take part in their government and to work things out for themselves.

But these new Americans were unhappy when England tightened her hold. They were alarmed when some of their freedoms were threatened. Then, they decided to work together to defend their precious way of life.

You will learn in the next chapter how a courageous struggle for freedom led to the birth of our nation.

Can You Remember?

1. What three groups of English colonies were established in our country?

2. When and where was the first permanent English settlement started? What were some problems its settlers faced?

3. Why did the Pilgrims come to America?

4. How was New York settled? How did the colony of Pennsylvania begin?

5. What was the House of Burgesses? Why is it important to us today?

Some Other Things to Do

1. Learn who represents your area in your state's legislature, and how he is chosen.

2. List some ways the colonists earned a living. Make a check (√) before each one which is shown in a picture in Chapter 2.

3. On your outline map, color the New England colonies light green, the Middle colonies yellow, and the Southern colonies orange. Make a key something like the one on the map on page 36.

Fun with Maps

Use the map and legend on page 36 to help you answer the questions below:

1. Which of these is the *title* of the map?
a. An Inset Map
b. The Thirteen English Colonies

2. How many groups of colonies does the *key* tell about?

3. Point to the *direction finder* on the map. What does N stand for? Which of the thirteen colonies extended farthest north? Draw a direction finder on a paper and write the letters of the four main directions in the correct places.

4. There are *four in-between directions*. Northeast is in-between north and east.

Southwest, of course, is between south and west. What are the other two in-between directions? In which direction is Boston from Philadelphia?

5. Point to the *Scale of Miles*. How many miles does 1 inch stand for on this map? Review the sentences on page 42 about a scale of miles and be ready to measure some distances. About how many miles is it
a. from New York City to Richmond?
b. from Boston to New York City?
c. from Philadelphia to Boston?

Learning More about Your Text

1. Turn to the *Contents* on page 4. It shows how your text is divided into six parts, or *units*. What is the title of Unit One?

See how each unit is divided into chapters. Point to the title of Chapter 1. What is the title of the chapter you will read next? On what page does this chapter begin?

2. In the front of your book is a list of maps. On what page is it located? Turn to it when you need to use a special map.

3. The *Index* is another helpful part of your text. Is it in the front of the book or in the back? Notice that it covers several pages and contains the names of people, things, and places, listed in alphabetical order.

Look in the *J* section for *Jamestown*. What page numbers follow the word, Jamestown? Find *Captain John Smith*. Be sure to turn to the *S* section, for an index always lists a person's last name first, as does a telephone book. What pages follow Smith's name?

4. Your text contains many interesting and helpful pictures. Each one can provide much valuable information when you study it and its legend carefully. Which picture in Chapter 2 did you enjoy most? What important information did it contain?

3 · How the Thirteen Colonies Won Their Independence

The Colonists Quarreled with England

A Story · Unwanted Tea

It was midnight. A small group of men sat in a little candlelit room not far from the Boston water front. They were members of a group that called themselves the *Sons of Liberty*.

"The tea ships are still in the harbor!" complained one.

"And they'll stay!" grumbled another. "The governor refuses to send them back to England. He says the tea will be unloaded."

"We'll not buy it nor pay one penny tax on it!" declared their leader, Samuel Adams, pounding the table.

"That's the truth!" agreed a third man. "But what can we do?"

"We must decide tonight!" said Adams fiercely. "We must get rid of the tea."

That night these Sons of Liberty agreed on a daring act. They planned an astonishing "tea party."

The Boston Tea Party. On a cold December night in 1773, more than forty colonists dressed as Mohawk Indians. They smeared bright war paint on their faces and stuck feathers in their hair. Then they rushed down the dark streets to the wharf and boarded the tea ships.

"King George won't collect a tax on this tea," declared these colonists. They tossed more than 300 chests of tea overboard into Boston Harbor.

With loud war whoops, the excited "Mohawks" went to work. Using their sharp hatchets, they ripped open dozens of chests of tea and tossed them overboard. Before long, more than three hundred and forty chests had been dumped. As the chests splashed into the water, they spilled thousands of pounds of costly tea into the harbor.

When England's King George heard about the Boston Tea Party, he was furious. "The colonists shall be punished," he stormed. "I shall send General Gage and an army to Boston to close their port to all ships. He shall remain there to govern Massachusetts. He'll teach those colonists a lesson! I'll force them to pay for every pound of tea they have destroyed!"

British tea ships had also been unwelcome in some other harbors in the colonies. They had not been allowed to land in Philadelphia or New York. In Charleston, South Carolina, the tea had been seized and stored in damp cellars to spoil.

The trouble over tea was caused by a quarrel over taxes. A *tax* is money paid by people to the government to help run it. England felt it had the right to tax the colonies. So a tax had been added to each pound of tea sold in America. This made the colonists angry. For a long time, England and the thirteen colonies had disagreed about taxes. By 1773, these disagreements had grown into a bitter quarrel. To understand why, we need to go back many, many years.

For years, England had let the colonies do much for themselves. They had not seemed very important. Also they were located three thousand miles across the Atlantic Ocean. To get in touch with them required a long sea voyage. Indeed, it took three or four months to send word and get an answer back. It seemed easier to let the colonies depend on themselves for most things.

Each colony's governor was appointed by the king in England. However, its laws were made by a legislature which its people elected. The legislature even made the tax laws for its colony.

As the years passed, the colonies continued to run most of their affairs. They did more and more things as they pleased. This was freedom, and they liked it. They enjoyed doing things in their own way.

The colonies were proud, too, that they were growing stronger and more prosperous. But, in the meantime, England's feelings about them had begun to change.

England tried to gain more control of the colonies. The king and his advisors said that the colonies owed England a great deal. England had given them their land in the first place. England had protected them from being seized by other countries. The king and his advisors said that England was the mother country and the colonies were her children. It was their duty to help England as she had helped them.

By this time, the colonists were raising fine crops and trapping many animals for furs. They were taking lumber from the forests and fish from the sea. And they were making money by trading with other countries. The king and his friends believed that England should have a share of this wealth and they thought of a way to get it.

The English government passed Trade Laws. Under these laws, the colonists were supposed to ship only to Eng-

In New England the colonists discussed many problems at town meetings.

land such goods as tobacco, furs, and lumber. The colonists were to buy manufactured goods from the mother country. She would send them such things as tools, nails, buttons, and fine woolen cloth. If the colonists manufactured these things themselves they would be punished. Also, the colonists were not to buy goods directly from other countries. Such goods had to be sent to England first where a tax was added.

At first the colonists were very unhappy with these new Trade Laws. They had been used to trading with whatever country they pleased. They had made many articles in small shops as well as in their homes. They did not want to buy all their manufactured goods from England. That would cost much money plus the extra tax.

Within a short time, however, the colonists realized that they might not have to obey the Trade Laws. England was so far away that she could not control their trade. So the colonists paid little attention to the Trade Laws. They carried on a good business with other countries for many years.

By 1763, England decided the colonists must obey the Trade Laws. England had been fighting a long war with France and it had cost a huge amount of money. The English people were already paying high taxes. So Parliament felt that the colonies should pay their share. *Parliament* is the legislature which makes the laws for England.

A part of the French war had been fought in America, west of the Appalachians. Find these mountains on the map on page 65. France had held a string of forts up and down the Mississippi and Ohio rivers. Do you see them on the map west of the mountains? England had sent a large army to capture these forts and protect the colonies. You will read more about that war later.

But this is important to remember now. England believed that the colonies should be taxed to help pay for the English army in America. So, Parliament demanded that the old Trade Laws be obeyed.

This was bad news for Americans. It meant an end to their trade with other countries. It also meant paying high prices for British goods. Then, to make matters worse, Parliament passed a new law.

In 1765, Parliament passed the Stamp Act. It said that a special stamp must be put on each newspaper printed in the colonies. Stamps were required also on calendars and other important papers. They had to be bought from the

British government. Actually, the money they cost was a tax.

When the colonists heard about this law, they were very angry. For a hundred years they had been making their own tax laws. They feared that if Parliament had the right to pass the Stamp Act, it would pass other tax laws. This would take away much of the freedom which they prized very dearly.

The colonists sent a special message to the king. They asked that their own representatives be allowed to help make the tax laws. But the king refused to listen.

Then the Americans became very bitter and complained, "This is taxation without representation. That isn't fair!"

Soon, colonists were fighting the Stamp Act. Some called themselves "Sons of Liberty" and organized "clubs." They held meetings and planned ways to work against the Stamp Act. Indeed, some of them rushed to the stamp offices and destroyed many stamps. You can see a picture of this below.

Colonists joined to fight the Stamp Act. These angry colonists are setting fire to a stamp office. Why did they do this?

Colonial merchants refused to buy English goods. Before long, this began to hurt England's business. It is not surprising, then, that its merchants begged Parliament to give up the Stamp Act.

Some leaders in England had also believed that this law was unfair. One was the famous British law-maker, William Pitt. Although he was sick, he left his bed and spoke in Parliament against the Stamp Act. Finally Parliament agreed to do away with or repeal it.

Later on, England placed taxes on tea and other goods. This time, the king was determined that the tax laws would be obeyed. Special tax officers were put in charge and told to punish anyone who broke the laws.

This stirred the alarmed colonists to new action. In dozens of towns and villages, the Sons of Liberty persuaded the settlers not to buy the taxed goods. The tea companies and some other businesses soon felt the sting of hard times. It is little wonder then, that they pleaded with Parliament to repeal these laws.

After a time, Parliament removed the taxes on most goods. But the tea tax remained. It was a reminder that England still had the power to tax the colonists.

Business soon improved for most English merchants, but the biggest English tea company was losing money. To help this company, Parliament allowed it to sell tea in the colonies at a very low price. But the colonists were still required to pay the tax on this tea. Angrily they refused. Instead they caused much trouble for the company's tea ships in several harbors.

You read earlier about the Tea Party in Boston harbor. You remember that when this happened the angry king sent General Gage to rule Massachusetts. And an army of soldiers was sent to help him.

England insisted that she had the right to tax her colonies as she wished. And the colonists were just as determined to have their way. They said that making their own tax laws was a part of their freedom. The king and many leaders in Parliament did not realize how much the settlers prized this freedom.

As the months passed, England and the colonies grew farther and farther apart. At the same time, the colonies seemed to draw closer together. Many colonists were beginning to think of themselves as "Americans."

The Colonists Began to Work Together

Newsletters helped to draw the colonists together. In those days, remember, there were no telephones or radios, and only a few newspapers. But some men found a way to pass along the news, just the same. They organized groups of men to write "news letters." Such groups were called Committees of Correspondence.

Bold Samuel Adams had organized the first Committee of Correspondence in Boston, Massachusetts. Within a short time, other committees were at work in several colonies.

The committees met regularly to discuss the latest news and talk over problems which faced the colonies. Then they wrote all the information they could in newsletters.

Carrying newsletters for the Committee of Correspondence.

General Gage's stern rule in Massachusetts alarmed all of the colonies. For one thing, he sent the members of its legislature home. Then he began to govern the colony himself. He boasted, "I'll teach these hot-headed Americans to obey orders!"

Gage also closed Boston's harbor. This was a sad event for the busy seaport. Many people depended on shipping and fishing for a living. With ships idle, hundreds of men had no jobs.

Boston suffered other hardships, too. Some of its people were required to let British soldiers live in their homes. You can see some soldiers in the picture below. They wore handsome uniforms with bright red coats and high leather boots, as you will notice. The colonists called them "Redcoats," and some made fun of the soldiers behind their backs.

But other colonists were quite polite and accepted the Redcoats. They still felt loyal to England and were spoken of as *Loyalists* or *Tories*. They said, "We came from England and these are English colonies. So we must obey the King."

Daring young men galloped over roads and trails to deliver the letters. They rode from village to village in all kinds of weather. At each stop, a friendly welcome awaited the messengers. And no wonder! Young and old were eager to hear the latest news.

The Committees of Correspondence had already warned that General Gage and his troops were landing in Boston. Now Boston's own committee sent out word of the strict British rule there.

After Boston's Tea Party, Redcoats arrived to close the port.

Of course, Samuel Adams was not a Tory. He was a proud *Patriot*. So were many other colonists who objected to unfair tax laws and Boston's loss of freedom.

They were furious that General Gage had seized control of Massachusetts and had closed Boston's port. They declared angrily, "If the British can take away Massachusetts' freedom, the other colonies are in danger, too. We must talk together and see what can be done."

Soon the First Continental Congress was held. It began in September, 1774, in Philadelphia. Find Philadelphia on the map on page 65. As you can see, it was about halfway between the northern and southern colonies.

Fifty-six able men attended this important meeting. They were called *delegates* and represented every colony but faraway Georgia. Some delegates had traveled to Philadelphia by boat. Others had made the journey by stagecoach. But a few had ridden several hundred miles on horseback.

Some delegates are shown in the picture at the right. Notice how excited they were as they chatted outside their meeting place, red-bricked Carpenter's Hall. Nearly all were dressed in their Sunday best. They wore ruffled blouses, short knee breeches, and handsome long coats. And look at their long white stockings and silver buckled slippers. Powdered wigs tied back with ribbons were stylish in those days, too, as you know. How different the colonial styles were from those of today.

The meeting of the First Continental Congress was important for many reasons. It was the first time that so many leaders from so many colonies had gathered to-

Colonial leaders gathered at Carpenter's Hall for the meeting of the First Continental Congress. What had they come to discuss?

gether. Remember that the thirteen colonies had been acting quite independently, each one like a small nation. Each one had its own government and took care of its own affairs. By 1774, however, the colonies were beginning to think more alike. Now they had sent delegates to discuss together the problems with England.

The delegates to the Congress knew why they were meeting. But no one could guess what might be decided. So excitement was in the air as they sat down together. Samuel Adams was there, and George Washington, Patrick Henry, and many other leading colonists.

"I am not a Virginian, but an American," Patrick Henry declared.

Patrick Henry was a member of Virginia's House of Burgesses and a fearless Patriot. The delegates were not surprised when he spoke out boldly against England. He pleaded for the colonies to stand together. He urged that they defend their rights and freedoms. But he warned that this might lead to war.

One could see that the delegates were opposed to war. When it was mentioned, many shook their heads and muttered, "No! No! Not that!" One man whispered to his neighbor, "Surely we can settle things with England without war!"

The meetings of the First Continental Congress lasted for seven weeks. During that time, many matters were discussed. Finally, the delegates agreed that they felt loyal to England. But they made it clear that they could not give up their rights. Furthermore, they declared that they would not buy goods from England or ship goods to her until certain laws were repealed. Also, this Continental Congress decided to meet again in May, 1775.

Most of the delegates returned to their homes, hoping that the quarrel with England could be settled by peaceful ways. They wanted the right to make their own laws. They wanted the right to trade freely with other countries. But many wanted to remain citizens of England. Others, however, did not agree.

Some Patriots began to work for independence. These brave men had begun to hope that someday the colonies would form a new nation. One of these men was the ever busy Samuel Adams. He was persuading dozens of colonists to help work for freedom.

Another was his friend, John Hancock, who had become a rich merchant. A third was Paul Revere, who earned his living making beautiful articles of silver. These men lived in Massachusetts. Already, they had had their fill of unpleasant experiences with British Redcoats.

Patrick Henry of Virginia was also speaking out for freedom. One day in March, 1775, he addressed a group of Virginians who had gathered in St. John's Church in their capital city, Richmond. You can see a drawing of this occasion above. His stirring words rang out, "Gentlemen may cry peace! peace—but there is no peace! The war has actually begun!"

Later on in his speech, Patrick Henry spoke the words which have become famous, "Is life so dear, or peace so sweet, as to be purchased at the price ... of slavery? ... I know not what course others may take; but as for me, give me liberty, or give me death!"

In the meantime, Boston buzzed with excitement as it prepared for more trouble. Quietly, Patriot leaders arranged for men in many towns and villages to drill together during their spare time. They were called *minutemen* and were to be ready to fight at a minute's notice. A picture of these minutemen is shown on pages 54 and 55. They were training in secret almost under General Gage's nose. Secrets are not kept easily, though, and soon this news leaked out.

A search for two Patriot leaders and hidden arms. General Gage heard that two of the boldest Patriots were Samuel Adams and John Hancock. They had stirred up much bitter feeling against England, and were working for independence. The King called them dangerous rebels and ordered them arrested. It was whispered that they might be sent to England and hanged.

General Gage learned that Adams and Hancock were staying at the village of Lexington, a few miles northwest of Boston. You can find Lexington on the map on this page. Gage also heard that Patriots had hidden guns and ammunition at Concord, near Lexington. Do you see Concord on this map?

The British general sent nearly a thousand British soldiers to Lexington and Concord. They were to capture Adams and Hancock and destroy the colonists' supply of arms.

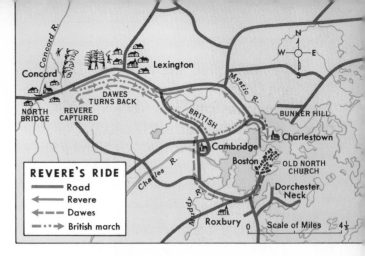

This map shows the routes which Paul Revere and William Dawes took to warn the colonists. Where was the first shot of the Revolutionary War fired? What happened at the North Bridge?

The Redcoats set out one April evening. Little did they dream that their plans had been discovered. They did not realize that brave minutemen were watching and would warn the colonists of their march.

Two midnight riders spread the news of the British march. One was Paul Revere. As you know, he earned his living as a silversmith. But he was also a skilled horseman and could ride like the wind. He had offered to gallop through the countryside and awaken the people.

On the night of April 18, Revere waited anxiously for a special signal. He stood with his horse in the shadow of a tree at Charlestown, across the bay from Boston. Revere's eyes were glued on the tall tower of Boston's North Church. There a Patriot was to hang a lantern. One light was the signal that the Redcoats would march by land. Two lights would mean the British were crossing by water.

Suddenly, two lights shone from the distant tower. Revere leaped into his saddle and raced away toward Lexington and Concord. He drew up in front of one farmhouse after another and shouted to the sleeping people, "Wake up, everyone! Wake up! The British are coming across the river! To arms!" Another expert horseman, William Dawes, helped Paul Revere sound the alarm.

A story poem called "The Midnight Ride of Paul Revere" has been written by the poet Henry Wadsworth Longfellow. Here are some of its lines:

A hurry of hoofs in the village street,
A shape in the moonlight, a bulk in the
    dark,
And beneath, from the pebbles, in passing
    a spark
Struck out by a steed flying fearless and
    fleet:
So through the night rode Paul Revere;
And so through the night went his cry of
    alarm.

Excited colonists rushed from their beds. They lighted candles and dressed quickly. Friends helped Adams and Hancock mount horses and escape through the darkness to Philadelphia.

Meanwhile, minutemen seized their guns and hurried to Lexington Green, the village common. There were only about seventy of these Patriots. But they had courage and spirit and were ready to prove it. Their captain warned them not to fire first. "Wait until we are fired on!" he ordered. "But, if the British mean to have a war, let it begin here!"

A shot at Lexington began a war. At dawn, hundreds of Redcoats marched into Lexington. There the small band of colonists were waiting. The surprised British captain commanded the minutemen to lay down their arms. But the Americans refused. Then a shot was fired. It began a long war. Because the colonies were revolting, this was called the *Revolutionary War*. It is also known as the *War for Independence*.

The handful of Patriots fought bravely. But they were no match for a thousand trained soldiers. So, after several of their men were killed, the Patriots gave up and scattered.

Expecting no further trouble, the British marched on to Concord to search for guns and gunpowder. But news of their coming had spread. Four hundred Patriots attacked them at North Bridge.

News of the fighting stirred many minutemen to action. Some were plowing when they got the word. But they did not finish their furrows. Nor did they stop to unhitch their animals from the plows. Shouldering their guns, they hurried off to join other Patriots.

Many of these men lined up along the road that led back to Boston. They hid behind trees, fences, and buildings in

Minutemen drill together.

Indian fashion. Then they peppered the returning Redcoats with gunfire and rocks. Dozens of British soldiers fell by the roadside. Others stumbled wearily on. But General Gage had to send fresh troops to their rescue.

That night, many campfires burned brightly around the edge of Boston. From a distance, they seemed to twinkle like harmless fireflies. But actually, they meant trouble for General Gage and his soldiers. They were Patriots camped round about Boston. Some blocked the roads so the British could not leave to get food. And some Patriots were watching the movements of British ships in the harbor. But a few men were mischievous as well as daring. They ventured to the very door of General Gage's home. There, they tacked up this bold message, "Come out and fight!"

Within a short time, colonists from New Hampshire to Georgia had heard about events in Massachusetts. Some sided with the Massachusetts minutemen. But others felt that they had been too eager to fight. Still, few people knew how to solve the increasing problems.

Could the colonies persuade England to deal with them fairly? Or should they become independent? The colonists were trying to answer these questions. To decide what was wisest, they sent their leaders to another meeting of the Continental Congress.

The Colonists Declared Their Independence

The Second Continental Congress met in Philadelphia in 1775. Again, the ablest leaders of the colonies gathered together. George Washington was there, and so was John Hancock, who became the President of the Congress. Other delegates included Benjamin Franklin, Samuel Adams and his cousin, John Adams, Thomas Jefferson, and Patrick Henry. This time, the meeting place was the brick building called the State House.

This Congress made one more attempt to settle the differences with England. It sent a message to the king, but he refused to receive it. Instead, he called the colonists rebels and announced new plans

55

for punishing them. So, hope for peace faded. Then the Congress decided that the colonies must prepare to defend themselves. It voted to have an army.

The Continental Congress chose Washington to head its army. They asked him to be the commander-in-chief of it. The picture on page 55 shows him taking command of the troops near Boston.

Washington was a trained soldier and officer. He was also a respected leader who was deeply interested in the affairs of the colonies. Congress believed that he could inspire soldiers from the different colonies to work together. How had he become such a respected leader throughout the land?

George Washington: surveyor and young soldier. George Washington was born on a plantation in Virginia. When he was sixteen, he finished school. He liked arithmetic and enjoyed working in the out of doors. So it is not surprising that he turned to surveying. A surveyor measures lands. Young Washington was hired to survey wilderness lands in the Appalachian Mountains.

Beyond the Appalachians is the Ohio River. Find it on the map on page 65. It flows through a wide valley of rolling hills and fertile plains. Both England and France claimed this vast region. Indeed, the English king had given much of it to Virginia years before.

England's colonists wanted the rich Ohio Valley so they could settle there and farm it. And the French were just as eager for it. They began to build a chain of forts from Lake Erie to the Ohio.

This news alarmed Virginia's British governor. He asked young Washington to carry a message to the French. By this time, Washington had become an officer in the Virginia army and was proving himself a wise leader.

One cold mid-winter day, Washington and a small party set out. For weeks, the men tramped west over ranges of lonely, snow-covered mountains. Finally, they reached the French fort.

The commander was polite to his visitors. But when he read the governor's letter, he was angry. "No! No!" he thundered. "We shall never leave! These lands belong to His Majesty, the King of France. We shall never give them up!"

This answer worried young Washington. He knew that it would cause trouble. He probably did not guess, then, however, that this problem would lead to a war in which he would serve.

Washington and the French and Indian War. Soon, Washington was sent West again. This time, he led a band of soldiers. His men were to build a fort where the Allegheny and Monongahela rivers join to form the Ohio River. Find this place on the map. It was a splendid location for a fort because it was a natural gateway to the Ohio River Valley. The country that controlled this "gateway" could control the Ohio River Valley.

Unfortunately, Washington and his men reached their goal too late. French soldiers were already camped there, and had begun to build Fort Duquesne. A force of French soldiers and some Indians met Washington's men and sharp fighting began. Finally, the colonists were forced to surrender. This battle began England's war with the French and Indians.

The news of the trouble with the French and Indians spread quickly. In a few months, England sent General Braddock and many soldiers to fight the French west of the Appalachians. George Washington became one of Braddock's officers.

General Braddock had a large army as well as heavy cannon and supply wagons. He intended to attack Fort Duquesne. But it was more than two hundred miles inland across rugged mountains. There was no road through the wilderness. So one had to be built!

A group of sturdy colonists began this back-breaking task. Day after day, for weeks they chopped down trees. Braddock's soldiers followed along behind the workers. But the long lines moved very slowly.

At last, as the soldiers approached the French fort, a terrible thing happened. Sharp cries rang through the forest and arrows and bullets whizzed through the air. Hiding behind trees, the French and Indians shot down hundreds of British soldiers. As more Redcoats came up, they fired their guns. But they could not see the enemy. Washington had several narrow escapes, but was not wounded. General Braddock refused to let his soldiers break their lines, so many of them were mowed down. General Braddock was killed and this battle ended in a crushing defeat for the British.

Later on, however, George Washington helped the British capture this fort. And in time, the British won the war.

After the war, Washington and other colonial soldiers returned to their homes with new feelings. They had learned how to defend themselves in war. They had also become friendly with soldiers of other colonies. In time, such friendships helped the colonies draw closer together.

Washington: planter and statesman. With the war over, Washington went back to Virginia. He married a charming woman, Martha Custis, and took her to live on his large plantation, Mount Vernon. The picture of it, below, may give you some idea of its beauty. Mount Vernon is located on the Potomac River. Thousands of people now visit it every year. Perhaps you will go to see it some day.

Washington spent much time managing his plantation. But he also served as a

Mount Vernon faces the Potomac River · George Washington worked hard to improve the lovely house shown here. Also, he did much to improve the crops raised on the plantation.

member of the Virginia legislature, the House of Burgesses. Later, he was elected a delegate to the meetings of the First and Second Continental Congresses, as you have read. He had become a respected leader throughout all of the colonies.

In 1776, the Continental Congress made plans to declare independence. Conditions were growing steadily worse. The British refused to give the colonies the rights which they demanded. Several bloody battles had been fought. One, called the Battle of Bunker Hill, broke out near Boston. To make matters worse, the king had hired German soldiers to fight against the colonies. This made the Americans furious.

By June, 1776, many members of Congress believed that the colonies should be free. One man, Richard Henry Lee, of Virginia, declared boldly, "That these United Colonies are, and of right ought to be, Free and Independent States." Quick as a flash, some delegates agreed

with him. Others wanted more time to think about breaking away from their mother country. Still, the Congress appointed a committee of five men to plan and write an important document, or paper. This was called the *Declaration of Independence.*

Thomas Jefferson was named chairman of the committee. He was a tall, sandy-haired young lawyer from Virginia. He had studied government and was a fine thinker and writer. He wrote most of the Declaration of Independence. Other members of the committee were Benjamin Franklin, John Adams, Roger Sherman, and Robert Livingston.

Franklin was one of a family of seventeen children. Though he went to work when he was ten years old, he studied before work in the morning and after work, late at night. Franklin became a printer, writer, and inventor. He had also served as postmaster for the colonies.

John Adams was a lawyer from Massachusetts. Roger Sherman was from Connecticut. He had been a shoemaker. But by studying nights, he became a fine lawyer and judge. Robert Livingston was a young statesman and lawyer from New York.

The Declaration of Independence is read to the Continental Congress. What important news did it announce?

The Declaration of Independence.
On July 2, 1776, the members of the Congress gathered in the State House. It was time to vote on Lee's statement on independence. Each colony was allowed one vote and twelve colonies voted for it.

Then one delegate leaned over and whispered to his neighbor, "The Declaration is finished. Soon we shall hear it."

A hush fell over the room as the Declaration was read. It said "that all men are created equal" and have the right to "Life, Liberty, and the pursuit of Happiness." It explained that a fair government was needed to help men have these rights. But when a government was unfair, it was time to seek a new one.

The Declaration then listed many ways in which England had been unfair to her colonies. It announced that "We, therefore, ... declare, That these United Colonies are ... Free and Independent States."

When the Declaration had been read, the audience cheered. Some men rushed up to praise Thomas Jefferson and some shook hands with the other members of the committee. Then, as the delegates became quiet, each part of the daring Declaration was talked over carefully.

On July 4th, the delegates from twelve colonies voted to accept the Declaration. Soon, the other colony sent a messenger with its vote for the Declaration.

Many townspeople gathered outside the State House to hear the Declaration read. Afterwards they shouted, "We're free! We're free!" Then a large bell high in the tower rang out the good news.

The State House soon became known as Independence Hall. It is still standing and is visited by thousands of people

FLAG

ADOPTED

IN 1777

every year. Its huge bell is called the Liberty Bell and is now shown in Independence Hall.

The Fourth of July is called Independence Day. It is celebrated as the birthday of our country and is a national holiday.

Copies of the Declaration of Independence were printed and rushed to all of the colonies. Congress wanted everyone to hear it read as soon as possible. After the Declaration of Independence was signed, the colonies became known as states. Name the first thirteen states of our country. The map on page 65 will help you.

In 1777, the Continental Congress adopted a flag for our country. A picture of it is shown above. As you can see, it had thirteen red and white stripes, and a circle of thirteen stars on a field of blue. Each star stood for one of the thirteen states. This flag took the place of the Continental Army flag which had been flown in some places in 1776.

Our American flag is sometimes called The Stars and Stripes. How many stars does it have? Why does it have more stars than were on the flag of 1777?

By this time, Americans knew that their fight for freedom had just begun. But they did not realize that it would take a long time to win that freedom.

How Our Country Won Its Independence

A long war began. Actually, it had started in 1775, at Lexington and Concord. After that, the bitter battle of Bunker Hill was fought near Boston. The Americans finally lost this battle because they ran out of ammunition. The British suffered the heaviest losses. But they remained strong enough to hold this important seaport.

Then, Washington took command of the Continental Army. Month after month, his soldiers caused trouble for the British in Boston. Finally, the Redcoats boarded ships and sailed away to Canada.

Soon, George Washington led his soldiers to New York City. But his army was too small to defend this city against the British. So, the Americans marched southwest into New Jersey. Meanwhile, Washington needed a spy to find out what the British would try next. The young soldier who volunteered for this dangerous errand was Nathan Hale. He had been a schoolteacher.

Nathan Hale served our country bravely. He dressed as a Dutch teacher and wandered across the British lines. He talked with the Redcoats and laughed at their jokes. They liked him so much that they talked freely of their plans. They did not dream that they were giving away secrets to an enemy.

About the time Hale was ready to leave, a Tory recognized him. The Tory hurried to the British general and Hale was captured. The British tried to buy off the young American. They offered him money and a chance to be an officer in their army. But Hale remained loyal. When he was led out to be hanged, he was asked if he had anything to say. Calmly, he made a remarkable speech. It ended with these words, "I only regret that I have but one life to lose for my country."

Washington's troops finally captured Trenton. After Hale's errand failed, the British chased the small American army back, mile after mile, through New Jersey. Then the Americans crossed the Delaware River into Pennsylvania. Meanwhile, some of the British set up camp at Trenton, on the Delaware. Find Trenton on the map on page 65.

That December in 1776, the fight for independence seemed hopeless. Still Washington had a daring plan. Christmas was near, and he knew that the enemy would celebrate with holiday par-

Nathan Hale gave his life for his country.

ties. So he decided to attack when it would be least expected.

One night, the hopeful general led about 2,000 soldiers to the banks of the Delaware. There, in a cold stinging rain, they crowded into open boats. Skilled fishermen guided the boats across the river. They had to steer their way carefully to avoid the broken chunks of ice that floated down the current.

When the men landed on the other side, snow was falling. Even so, they began their nine-mile march to Trenton. When the shivering troops reached the city, they found the enemy asleep after a merry feast. Surrender came quickly. Also, the daring Americans won large stores of ammunition and food.

This Christmas victory inspired the Patriots with new courage. They did not know, then, that 1777 would bring many dark hours and only one important victory.

Victory at Saratoga. British troops had captured New York City and had won many battles. Now, their leaders hoped to end the war with one crushing blow. General Burgoyne's Redcoats were camped in Canada. But they were to march south through New York. Other British troops were to move in from the west. Still others were to sail up the Hudson River from the south. Together, these British armies would close in on the Americans like the jaws of a huge trap. Thus they would conquer New York.

New York State extends south of New England, as the map on page 65 shows. New York was a "key" state. By conquering it New England would be cut off from the other states. The British believed this would end the war.

In time, Burgoyne's troops headed south. But they traveled very slowly. There were many unfriendly Indians along the way. Then, too, the land was a vast wilderness with thick forests and dozens of lakes and swamps. There were no roads over which to move a large army and its food and ammunition.

When Burgoyne's men finally reached the middle of New York, they did not meet other British troops. Instead, near Saratoga, American soldiers surprised them. Fierce fighting began and lasted for days. Finally the British general surrendered his large army of nearly five thousand soldiers. This victory was very important to the colonies. But it was not enough to win the war.

Washington's men spent a terrible winter at Valley Forge. Find Valley Forge on the map on page 65. It was located about twenty miles from Philadelphia. The British were camped in this city in comfortable homes and inns.

The Continental Army was crowded into small wooden huts like those in the picture on page 62. The weather was bitterly cold. And the icy winds piled snow in deep drifts around the cabins.

The Congress had sent Washington little money or food. So his army suffered many hardships. The men were half-starved. There were no beds and only a few blankets. There was not enough warm clothing. The shoes of some soldiers were worn through and their bruised feet left bloody tracks on the snow.

Some soldiers died and many others were sick with fever. Yet those who were able, drilled faithfully all winter long. They still hoped that someday they would win the war.

During the long, cold winter of 1777-78, Washington and his soldiers camped at Valley Forge.

Many times, Washington was discouraged. But he did all he could for his men. He spent his own money to buy food and supplies for the army. He also wrote to other leaders asking for help.

Slaves and freed men joined in the fight for independence. About 5000 blacks took part in the Revolutionary War. The first to die in this war was a former black slave, Crispus Attucks.

Some blacks fought at Lexington, Concord, and Bunker Hill. Two black Minutemen, Peter Salem and Salem Poor were heroes in the Battle of Bunker Hill. A number of blacks were with Washington at Valley Forge.

There were many black soldiers in the New England troops. Rhode Island had a whole regiment of them. Other blacks served in the navy. Some were spies or guides, or with the supply wagons.

People from other countries helped in the war. Two army officers came from Poland, a country in Europe. They were Count Pulaski and Thaddeus Kosciusko. Another, Count von Steuben, was from Germany. Two rich friends came from France. They were Baron de Kalb and the young Marquis Lafayette.

Lafayette joined General Washington's army at Valley Forge. Lafayette was a wealthy red-headed Frenchman. He had been trained as a soldier in France. He believed in the Americans' fight for freedom and admired their courage.

"Let us help these brave Americans," said the young nobleman to some of his friends.

But few of Lafayette's companions

were interested. So he made plans to act by himself. "I shall sail to America," he declared. "I will join Washington's army. It will be a great privilege to serve under him."

When the king of France learned of Lafayette's ideas, he was astonished. "No!" he commanded. "That young dreamer must not leave France! I forbid it!"

But Lafayette had made up his mind. He bought supplies and a ship. He kept the ship hidden in a quiet Spanish harbor until he was ready to sail west. He was afraid to cross France in his coach, however. So he dressed as a poor messenger. He galloped ahead of his carriage and finally reached Spain. Soon he sailed to America.

Lafayette offered to serve in the Continental Army without pay. He was made a general and joined Washington at Valley Forge.

France decided to help the Americans. A few months earlier, Benjamin Franklin had sailed to France to ask for help. France was still bitter about losing the recent war with England. So the French king listened to Franklin. But he was not ready to say yes. The king did not think that the Americans could win a war with England.

Then came the news of the important victory at Saratoga. Now the king changed his mind. He invited Franklin to a big celebration in the royal palace. There, he announced that France was a friend of the American states. He even agreed to help them in their fight for independence.

In a short time, General Lafayette returned to France. He arranged for many soldiers and quantities of supplies to be sent to America.

One American general, Benedict Arnold, turned traitor. A traitor is one who betrays his country or tells its secrets. Arnold had served as a brave officer in the Continental Army for several years. But he had lost some battles and had been blamed when things went wrong. This had hurt him very deeply.

Arnold also worried about things at home. His wife was a Loyalist and tried to get him to join the British. Finally, Arnold was deeply in debt. Then he stooped to a shameful way of earning money. He sold some of his country's army secrets.

Arnold was in command of the soldiers at the fort of West Point. This fort was located on the Hudson River, fifty miles north of New York City. It controlled much of the Hudson River. Also many military supplies were stored there.

Arnold arranged to surrender his army to the British. But his plans failed. Watchful Patriots caught his helper, the young British spy, Major André. Major André's papers proved that Arnold was a traitor. Then Arnold feared for his life and fled to the British headquarters at New York City.

During the rest of the war, Arnold led British troops. So of course he was hated by all Patriots. Later on, he sailed to England, where he spent the rest of his life. But he was always lonely and unhappy. Probably he could never forget that he had betrayed his country.

George Rogers Clark seized British forts in the West. Another American officer, George Rogers Clark, is remembered for his courage and loyalty. This daring leader fought for independence in the western wilderness. After the French and Indian War, the English had taken over the French forts west of the Appalachians. British soldiers were stationed at these forts. They caused much trouble for the pioneers who had settled in this region. Tall, red-headed Clark had heard about this when he was surveying in the wilderness.

One day, Clark visited the Governor of Virginia, Patrick Henry. Said he, "Pioneers in the West are being attacked by British soldiers and Indians! This should be stopped! I can raise a force of 200 men to seize their forts! But I shall need money for supplies."

"You are a man of courage!" said Henry. "And you know the wilderness well! Virginia will provide the money for your plan. And may good fortune be with you!"

Clark gathered his men together. They boarded boats and floated down the Ohio River for many miles. Then they hid their boats and marched across the rolling plains of Illinois. They were headed for Fort Kaskaskia, on the Mississippi River. Locate this fort on the map on page 65.

After dark, Clark's men stole up to the fort and attacked. The surprised British surrendered without firing a shot. This victory gave Americans the oldest settlement west of the Appalachians.

Clark hoped to capture other British forts in the West. But they were many miles apart. So it was necessary to make careful plans and to win the friendship of the Indians. Clark visited their campfires. He proved to the chiefs that he was a fair but bold man. He persuaded them to smoke the peace pipe with him.

Clark and his men suffered great hardships on their march from one fort to another. They tramped across the snowy plains during bitterly cold weather. And they pushed through swift icy streams swollen by melting snows. Their clothes became thin and ragged. Often there was not enough food. Some men became sick and died. But those who could moved on. In time, Clark's brave band captured many British forts. This gave the Americans the "Northwest."

In the meantime, other men served in the Continental Navy. Perhaps John Paul Jones was the most famous one.

Captain John Paul Jones fought bravely at sea. As a boy, John Paul had lived on the west coast of Scotland. Scotland is a part of Britain, as the map on page 188 shows. John Paul saw many ships come and go. He dreamed of the day that he would be a sailor on one of them. Just think! That day came when he was twelve years old.

Some of John Paul's trips at sea took him to America. One day, he decided to settle here. About this time, he added Jones to his name. From then on, he was called John Paul Jones.

When the Revolutionary War began, Jones offered to serve at sea. At first, the states had no navy. But Congress helped to form one. It had guns placed on some trading ships and fishing vessels. This "navy" was very small and was no match for England's fine ships. But its men were brave fighters.

Captain Jones took part in many sea battles. A very famous one was fought between his ship, the *Bonhomme Richard*, and the English vessel, the *Serapis*. His ship was old and clumsy and the English

CANADA

L. Superior

L. Michigan

L. Huron

L. Ontario

L. Erie

Ft. Dearborn (Chicago)

Missouri R.

Ft. Kaskaskia

Ohio R.

Mississippi River

CLAIMED BY SPAIN AND U.S.

SPANISH TERRITORY

New Orleans

St. Lawrence R.

CLAIMED BY ENGLAND AND U.S.

SARATOGA

N.H.

NEW YORK

Hudson R.

West Point

Allegheny R.

PENNSYLVANIA

Ft. Pitt (Ft. Duquesne)

Monongahela R.

Delaware R.

N.J. New York

TRENTON

Philadelphia

VALLEY FORGE

MD.

DEL.

Potomac R.

Mount Vernon

WASHINGTON THE FUTURE CAPITAL

Chesapeake Bay

Richmond

York R.

YORKTOWN

VIRGINIA

APPALACHIAN HIGHLANDS

NORTH CAROLINA

SOUTH CAROLINA

Charleston

GEORGIA

Savannah

MASSACHUSETTS

LEXINGTON AND CONCORD

Boston

CONN. R.I.

BUNKER HILL

Atlantic Ocean

THE NEW NATION

Thirteen original states

Lands gained from England at the close of the Revolution

■ Early forts   ✕ Battle

0   Scale of Miles   205

One inch equals 205 miles

The Thirteen States during the War for Independence.

ship was fast and heavily armed. The two vessels shot at each other for hours. Finally Jones's ship caught fire and began to sink. It looked hopeless, but still the brave captain refused to surrender.

Instead, he shouted, "I have not yet begun to fight!" Jones brought his ship close to the English vessel. Then his men tied the two ships together. They climbed aboard the English ship and forced its crew to give up. Thus, Captain Jones led his men to victory.

War's end: Cornwallis's surrender to Washington. In October, 1781, the Americans won the most welcome victory of all. It took place at Yorktown where General Cornwallis had led his Brihtis troops. Yorktown is on the York River, back from Chesapeake Bay. Locate it.

When Cornwallis set up camp, Lafayette moved his men in to cut off escape by land. A daring young Negro spy, James, helped to make Lafayette's move a success.

Meanwhile, Washington's army had marched south to help bottle up the British. French ships blocked Chesapeake Bay to prevent their escape by sea.

Fighting went on for three weeks. But Cornwallis realized that his army was surrounded and he was trapped. So he surrendered.

This ended the war. The states had won their long, hard struggle for freedom!

Soon a peace treaty was made. In it, the British agreed that the thirteen "colonies" were free and independent. Also the British gave the thirteen states all of the British lands west to the Mississippi River. This meant that the thirteen independent states reached from Canada to Florida and from the Atlantic to the Mississippi.

By this time, the states often called themselves the United States. During the war they had banded together. But they had not planned for a strong United States government. Why, do you suppose? And how did our national government begin? You can find out in the next chapter. And there, also, you can learn more about what government is.

At 10 o'clock on an October morning in 1781, a British drummer boy drums out an important message. The British army at Yorktown is ready to surrender!

Some Questions about This Chapter

1. What taxes did the colonists refuse to pay to England?

2. What is the Declaration of Independence? Did it give the colonies their independence? If not, how was that won?

A Matching Game

On paper, write the numbers 1 to 9 and the words in List A. After each item, copy the phrase from List B which belongs with it.

List A

1. Parliament
2. Freedom
3. Washington
4. First Continental Congress
5. Tories
6. Defeat of the British at Saratoga
7. Mount Vernon
8. John Paul Jones
9. Patrick Henry

List B

Commander-in-chief of the Continental Army

The group of representatives who meet to make England's laws

"Give me liberty or give me death"

Encouraged the French to help the Patriots

The right to think and make choices

Colonists who remained loyal to England

The American hero of many sea battles

Washington's home

A meeting of leaders representing the colonies in 1774

Reviewing Some Map Language

Turn to the map on page 65 and use it. Study the *key*. What color shows

a. the first thirteen states?

b. the unsettled lands west of the Appalachians, gained from England?

As you know, a *symbol* is a kind of sign, or tiny drawing, which stands for something else. What symbol on the map on page 65 stands for

a. a fort?

b. a city?

c. a place where a battle was fought?

What Is Your Opinion?

1. Why do people want to govern themselves?

2. What do you think these words mean— "taxation without representation"? How do we have taxation *with* representation in our country today?

3. What is meant by the words "price of freedom"? What price did the Americans pay?

Some Other Things to Do

1. Use your index to find the names of the famous men listed below. On a paper, write the names and the page numbers that tell about them.

George Washington   Thomas Jefferson
Nathan Hale   Lafayette
Benjamin Franklin   George Rogers Clark

2. Think of the meaning of each word below and prove that you understand it by using it in a sentence.

wilderness   Patriot
representative   tax
nobleman   delegate
repeal   minutemen
independence

4 · How the Thirteen States Became the United States

Government: A Guide to Help People Work Together

"Government" on a baseball field. Two teams of fifth graders were warming up for a baseball game. Bill was umpire. It was his job to see that the players obeyed the rules.

"Batter up!" called Bill.

Jean tested her bat and stepped to the plate. As a fast ball crossed the plate, she swung hard. She sent a fly toward left field where it was caught. Jean had raced to first base but of course she was called out. She knew she would be. She knew that when a fly is caught, the batter is out. That is the rule.

Next Joe Miller went to bat. He missed the first ball which whizzed by. The umpire called "Strike one!" Joe chopped at the second ball but missed again. This was strike two. Joe let the third pitch sail by because it looked high. But the umpire didn't think so. He called it strike three. The batter was out!

Now Joe was angry. He shook his bat and shouted, "That ball was a mile high!"

Then two other players reminded him that an umpire's word goes. That was also a rule. So he accepted the umpire's decision with an "O.K.!"

The ball game went on. It was an exciting game, played fairly. The members of both teams knew the rules and tried to play as they should. The rules told them how to play. The umpire helped the players to keep them in mind. In a way, the umpire was enforcing the rules. Together,

the umpire and the rules provided a kind of government for the baseball game.

Government is partly rules or laws. Our laws tell us what we may do and what we may not do. They guide our actions and help us to have safe and helpful ways of living. They encourage good citizenship and protect us from many dangers. There are rules to guide us at home and at school. But those for our states and nation are called laws.

We help to make our laws. Boys and girls usually have a say in planning at home and at school. In a different way, grownups have a part in making the laws. They can vote for, or choose, the leaders who pass our laws. They may also tell their leaders what laws they think are necessary.

Our government, therefore, is run by the people, and is called a democracy. The word, democracy, means "the people govern." We call this self-government.

Government is a kind of steering wheel. You know how a person uses a steering wheel to guide an automobile. Government guides groups of people. It helps them to work together in an orderly way.

During the Revolutionary War, the states began to call themselves the United States, remember. At that time, the Congress acted as the "steering wheel." It helped the states draw closer together. But then, they had a very precious goal in common. They were working for the independence they all wanted.

After the war, it was a different story. The new nation faced more problems than ever. But its government was weak and seemed almost a failure. It did not have the power to act as a strong steering wheel.

How Our United States Government Began

Thirteen steering wheels and trouble. With the war over, the states paid little attention to their nation. Instead, they thought more about their own selfish interests. Some were printing their own money, and some threatened to make their own treaties. They could not agree about boundary lines. They argued about trade and the use of rivers. And small states complained that their larger neighbors were becoming too powerful.

You see, the thirteen states were being guided by thirteen different steering

A farmer's wagon is stopped at the boundary between two states. This farmer will have to pay a tax before he can take his produce into his neighboring state.

The Constitutional Convention met to plan a national government. Sometimes the leaders argued bitterly. How did Franklin help at these times?

wheels. This caused many quarrels and threatened serious trouble.

"We cannot go on like this," declared wise leaders. "Our states are not united. A way must be found to help them work together for the good of all. We need a strong nation to handle our common problems. Something must be done."

Many leaders favored a change. Among them were Washington, Franklin, and Jefferson. They believed that a stronger national government was needed.

The Constitutional Convention planned a new government. Early in 1787, word went out that a special meeting would be held in Philadelphia's State House. Each state was asked to send delegates to this important convention.

The delegates gathered late in May. All of them were respected leaders and most of them had had experience in government. A number had been members of the Congress and had worked together. They knew each other well.

George Washington was elected chairman of the convention. Before long, the delegates began to disagree. Some were afraid that a strong national government would have too much power. And what about the states? Would the large states have more say in the new government than the small ones? "No! No!" declared those from the smaller states. "This must not be!" But others insisted that the states with the largest number of people had the right to the most representatives in the new government.

And who would head the new nation? Some said that a President should be in charge. But others feared a President might become another powerful King George. Strangely enough, one delegate suggested that a President hold office for life. But so many delegates shouted out against this idea that Washington had to rap for order.

Planning went on through the long hot summer, but time after time there were arguments. Fortunately, wise Benjamin Franklin knew how to calm the storms. He was now eighty-one years old but was still a sharp thinker and clever story teller. He was loved by everyone and his stories often set the delegates to laughing. He earned the nickname they gave him, the "Peacemaker of the Convention."

Finally in September, the new plan of government was finished. It was called the *Constitution of the United States*. Soon, it was signed by most of the delegates. Then it was sent to each state to be voted on. Some states were not completely happy with the new Constitution. But in time, enough voted for it to make it the law of the United States.

Still, some people complained! They were afraid that a strong national government might take away their rights and freedoms. So, in 1791, some additions, or *amendments*, were made. These ten amendments to the Constitution are called the *Bill of Rights*. They describe certain rights, or freedoms, as, for example, the freedom to worship as we please. They promise that the government will not take away these freedoms.

The Constitution provided for three branches of government. This was to make sure that no person or group was given too much power. The three branches are the *executive*, the *legislative*, and the *judicial*.

The *executive* branch is in charge of our country's affairs. It sees that the laws are enforced. Indeed, an executive is a kind of manager. The President is the Chief Executive of the United States. He is elected by the voters of our country.

The *legislative* branch makes the laws. It is called the Congress. Its members are also elected by the people.

The *judicial* branch decides what the laws mean and when people are breaking them. Its members are appointed, or chosen, by the President. The judges chosen by the President must also be approved by Congress.

George Washington became our country's first chief executive, or President. But this was not surprising. Think how well he had already served his people. He had been a member of the Houses of Burgesses and later of the Continental Congress. He was the Commander-in-Chief of the Army during the long war. By this time, he was such a hero that all the bells in Philadelphia were rung when he arrived for the Constitutional Convention. There, he was elected its chairman, you remember. He had guided the delegates through a long difficult summer. So everyone respected and trusted him, and hoped he would be elected President.

The election for our first President was held in 1789 and Washington received every vote. Actually, he had not wanted this office. He was weary from his years of service and longed for a quiet life at Mount Vernon. But he gave up his own plans to serve his country once more.

One early spring day, he left Mount Vernon in a handsome coach pulled by four horses. He was on his way to New York City, the new capital of the United States. As he traveled through towns and

villages, thousands of people lined the streets to cheer him. Some had closed their shops, and farmers had left their fields. Children were out of school. And everyone was dressed in his best clothes for this special holiday.

Many people threw flowers in front of Washington's coach. One mother wrote in her diary:

I helped daughters Virginia and Anne gather a few of the first blossoms of spring today. They tossed them in the path of General Washington as he passed through our village. He is indeed a great man.

New York made special plans to honor Washington. A boat was sent to carry him across the bay. It was rowed by thirteen men, representing the thirteen states. Above is a picture of this exciting event.

When Washington reached the shore, he was greeted by a mighty welcome. Cannons boomed! Bands played! Church bells rang! While people cheered, the tall, quiet leader walked down a path covered by a long red carpet.

Washington became President of our country on April 30, 1789. This was *Inauguration Day*, the day that the President took the oath of office. Standing on a small upper porch of New York's City Hall, Washington placed his hand on an open Bible. Then he promised to serve his country faithfully and see that its laws were obeyed.

Many people listened as Washington took the oath of office. Members of Congress and other leaders stood nearby in the City Hall. In the street below, thousands of excited Americans gathered to cheer for their new President.

Some Americans spoke of calling Washington, "Your Highness" or "Your Majesty." But others objected. They said, "No! We fought a war to be rid of kings." It was decided that "Mr. President" was a friendly title. From that day to this, Americans have addressed their chief as "Mr. President."

Washington was President for two terms of four years each. Soon after he was elected, Congress decided that New

York City was too far north to be the nation's capital. Before long, Philadelphia was made the capital. It was ninety miles farther south.

In the meantime it was decided that a new capital would be built. It was to rise on the banks of the Potomac River. The land for the capital was given by Maryland and Virginia.

Washington guided plans for the new national capital. He hired a skilled French builder. This man had come to America to serve in the Revolutionary War. He suggested that the first government building, the *Capitol*, be the heart of the new city. It would be at the center, with wide avenues extending from it like spokes in a wheel. This plan was used.

The black scientist and inventor, Benjamin Banneker, also helped. He helped measure the land for the streets and buildings of the new capital.

Congress named the new capital in honor of Washington.

George Washington died at his Mount Vernon home. He was sixty-seven years old. Because of his long and splendid service to the United States, this great leader is often called the *Father of Our Country*.

Many years have passed since Washington's time. And how ways of living have changed! But, as always, Americans prize their freedoms. Being free is very important to us. So is the right of self-government. Let's look at our United States government today.

Our National Government Today

The Constitution is still our country's plan of government. Yet it was written more than 175 years ago. Also, it was planned when the United States had a small family. Only thirteen states! But that family has grown! How many states does our country have today? It's remarkable, then, that the Constitution written so long ago still serves our country well.

Let's review some things you learned earlier. The Constitution divided the powers of government among three

Benjamin Banneker and the French builder work on plans for the capital.

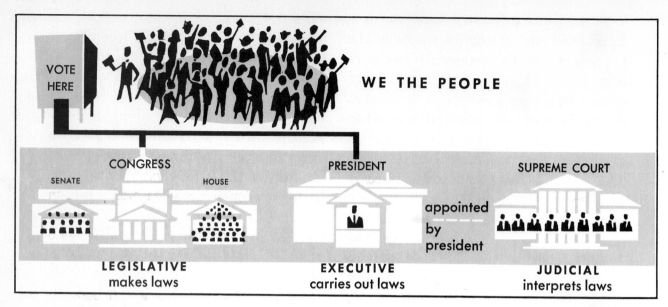

VOTE HERE

WE THE PEOPLE

CONGRESS

SENATE   HOUSE

PRESIDENT

SUPREME COURT

appointed by president

LEGISLATIVE
makes laws

EXECUTIVE
carries out laws

JUDICIAL
interprets laws

branches. They are the executive, the legislative and the judicial, remember. Each of these branches is shown on the chart above.

Notice that we choose most of our leaders. How is this done? Which ones do we elect? Which ones are appointed by the President?

The President is the head of our national government, you recall. Then what branch does he represent? Why do we call him the Chief Executive? Perhaps you know that he is elected for a term of four years. But he may also be re-elected for a second term.

The President is a very busy man and works hard many hours a day. He is in charge of enforcing the laws, remember. Then too, he is the Commander-in-Chief of the Armed Forces. These include the Army, Navy, and Air Force.

Our Chief Executive must be ready to serve the United States any hour of the day or night. Because his job is such a big one, however, he has many helpers. Some, called *Secretaries*, serve as members of the President's *cabinet*. Each secretary is the head of a special department under

the President. For example, the Secretary of State heads the Department of State. It is in charge of our foreign affairs, our business with other countries.

Congress makes the laws for our country, as you have learned. It can declare war on another country. Also, some of its members serve on special committees to study conditions in our land. They advise the President about ways of solving some of the nation's problems.

Congress is made up of the *Senate* and the *House of Representatives*. Each state sends two Senators to the Senate. They are elected by the people and hold office for a term of six years. They may be elected again.

Representatives are also elected by the people of their state. They serve for a term of two years and may be re-elected. The number of Representatives which a state may send to Congress depends on its population. Some states like California and New York have a large population. So they may send from thirty to forty or more Representatives to Congress. The states with a small population send fewer

Representatives. Congress meets in the beautiful Capitol shown at the bottom of page 77.

The Supreme Court heads the judicial branch of our government. This highest court of the land is made up of nine *justices*, or judges. They are appointed by the President and may serve for the rest of their lives.

The Supreme Court settles questions about laws which have been passed by Congress and the states. The Supreme Court may decide that a law does not agree with the Constitution. Then it is no longer a law.

The meetings of the Supreme Court are held in a gleaming white marble building. It looks something like a splendid Greek temple, as the photograph on page 77 shows. The justices wear long, flowing robes and sit in large leather chairs on a raised platform. Indeed, these judges look very dignified and solemn as they listen to important cases.

Washington, D.C. is the center of our national government. As you know, this city is the capital of the United States. Find it on the map on page 504. What symbol is used to show our national capital?

Perhaps you are wondering about the letters "D.C." after Washington. They stand for the words, *District of Columbia*. This district is not a part of any state and is governed mainly by Congress.

Thousands of Americans visit Washington, D.C. every year, and many people from other lands also come. Some are sent on business for their countries. Everyone enjoys seeing this exciting city and its many attractive buildings. Let's pretend we are sightseers there.

A Look at Our National Capital

First, let's look at Washington from the "air." We can do that from the top of the Washington Monument. This tall slender building was built in honor of George Washington. It rises 555 feet above the ground and is covered with white marble. Find it on the map on page 76.

In just seventy seconds, an elevator whisks us to the top. Then, beneath us, the city of Washington spreads out in all directions. It looks like a giant picture map come to life.

We see broad tree-lined avenues and crowded business streets. There are schools and churches, and block after block of homes. There are green parks, large and small, some of which follow along the winding Potomac River.

But especially interesting are the splendid government and memorial buildings. Several look out on the long parkway called the Mall. Find the Mall on the map on page 76. Notice that it extends both east and west of our viewpoint, the Washington Monument. Let's use the map, now, to help us locate and name some famous buildings. The most thrilling one, of course, is the Capitol.

Our beautiful Capitol sits on the east end of the Mall. It is an enormous building with a wing on each end, and is crowned by a huge white dome. Notice how the Capitol is the "hub" of this area with many avenues extending out from it. One is important Pennsylvania Avenue and another, Constitution Avenue.

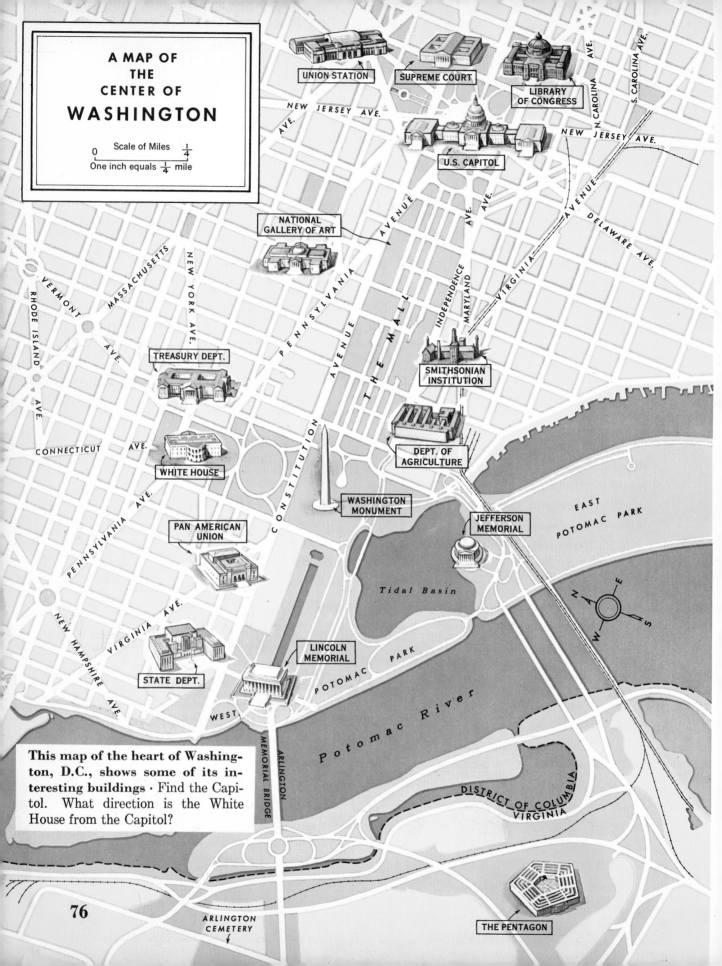

A MAP OF THE CENTER OF WASHINGTON

Scale of Miles 0   ¼

One inch equals ¼ mile

UNION STATION

SUPREME COURT

LIBRARY OF CONGRESS

U.S. CAPITOL

NEW JERSEY AVE.

N. CAROLINA AVE.

S. CAROLINA AVE.

NEW JERSEY AVE.

DELAWARE AVE.

NATIONAL GALLERY OF ART

AVENUE

INDEPENDENCE

MARYLAND

VIRGINIA

MASSACHUSETTS

NEW YORK AVE.

VERMONT AVE.

RHODE ISLAND AVE.

PENNSYLVANIA

AVENUE

THE MALL

SMITHSONIAN INSTITUTION

TREASURY DEPT.

CONNECTICUT AVE.

CONSTITUTION

DEPT. OF AGRICULTURE

WHITE HOUSE

PAN AMERICAN UNION

PENNSYLVANIA AVE.

WASHINGTON MONUMENT

JEFFERSON MEMORIAL

EAST POTOMAC PARK

Tidal Basin

POTOMAC PARK

VIRGINIA AVE.

NEW HAMPSHIRE AVE.

STATE DEPT.

LINCOLN MEMORIAL

WEST

MEMORIAL BRIDGE

ARLINGTON

Potomac River

DISTRICT OF COLUMBIA

VIRGINIA

N E S W

This map of the heart of Washington, D.C., shows some of its interesting buildings · Find the Capitol. What direction is the White House from the Capitol?

ARLINGTON CEMETERY

THE PENTAGON

76

Three government buildings in Washington. Below, our Capitol where many of our laws are made. Above, the White House, home of the President. At the right, the Supreme Court building.

The handsome Supreme Court Building faces Constitution Avenue. Nearby is the Library of Congress. It is one of the largest libraries in the world and has millions of books on its shelves.

Now, look north from the Monument. There you can see the White House, the official home of our President. It is often called the Executive Mansion. Can you explain why? What other important building is just east of the White House?

As we look west, we see the impressive Lincoln Memorial. It was built in honor of Abraham Lincoln and looks out on a lovely long pool. This building contains an immense statue of Abraham Lincoln. Nearby is another fine building, the Jefferson Memorial. It honors an earlier President of our country, Thomas Jefferson. He also wrote the Declaration of Independence, you remember.

Across the Potomac is the huge Pentagon. It has five sides and is the largest office building in the world. More than 25,000 people work there. It contains the main offices of the Defense Department, the Army, Navy, and Air Force of our country.

You learned earlier who serves the United States as Commander-in-Chief of our Armed Forces. And you have just had an "air" view of his home. Would you like to learn more about this Executive Mansion?

A closer look at the White House. This stately mansion is surrounded by velvet green lawns dotted with tall trees and lovely flower gardens.

The White House is almost as old as our nation. Builders began work on it in 1792, three years after our country became the United States. Washington chose its location. But it was not finished in time for him to live there. Part of it was ready to be occupied by our second President, John Adams. As time has passed, many additions and changes have been made in this fine mansion.

Just think! The White House has more than a hundred rooms, and dozens of halls and bathrooms. But they are not all used by the President and his family. Some are "company" rooms where special guests are entertained.

Special dinners and receptions are held in the large rooms on the first floor. One is known as the East Room. The huge Blue Room is richly decorated with blue silk hangings. The Green Room has stately green and white hangings.

The Capitol is Washington's most inspiring building. Its marble dome rises 300 feet into the sky. Glance again at the picture of this huge building on page 76. Notice how many steps lead up to the tall columns at its entrance ways. The entrance in the right wing leads to the Senate Chamber where the Senate meets. In the left wing, is the large auditorium where the House of Representatives gathers.

Visiting this building is thrilling. Here the laws of our country are made, you recall. Here many of our leaders have worked together to make our country great. If you go to Washington, try to spend some time at the Capitol. Then stand on its steps and think how much we owe the leaders who have represented us there.

Many leaders serve us in another level of government. They represent us in our state. Suppose we find out how state government is carried on.

How Our States Are Governed

Thinking about our states. Most of us live in one of the fifty states of our country. In which one is your home? How much do you know about your state?

There are many things to learn. Some information is waiting for you in the Tables for Reference on page 499. And you can find out much more by using the encyclopedia. Discover who the first settlers were and when they came to your region. Find out how the people lived in those early days and what kind of government they had.

Two services provided by state governments. Wide new highways are built. Also, state highway patrols help keep these highways safe.

Each state has its own constitution. Some states used the Constitution of the United States as a pattern. But this was not true of the first thirteen states. Why, do you suppose?

Most state constitutions contain a "Bill of Rights." Also they provide for three main divisions of government, the executive, the legislative, and the judicial.

Each state has a capital and a governor. The *capital* is the city in which the main part of the state's government is carried on. What city is the capital of your state?

The *governor* is the chief executive of the state and is elected by the people. He may serve for a term of two or four years, depending on his state's plan of government. It is his duty to see that the state laws are enforced. He tries to keep the affairs of his state running smoothly. Who is the governor of your state?

Each state has a lawmaking body elected by the people. It is the legislative branch. In many states, it is called the legislature. What is it called in your state? This group makes some laws that may be especially interesting to you.

For example, there are state fishing laws. Does your father go fishing sometimes? If he does, he probably knows about these laws. One may require that a fisherman have a fishing license. Another law may tell when the fishing season begins and when it ends. You see, fishing is allowed only a part of the year. Can you think why?

Do your parents own an automobile? If they do, they are familiar with the automobile laws of your state. One requires that a person pass certain tests in order to get a driver's license. Another says that an automobile must have the latest state license plates. Of what use are they? Some laws are made to help avoid automobile accidents.

Some other state laws provide for building highways and bridges. There are many laws about schools. Still others provide for state hospitals, parks, and camping areas. And there are laws that require the testing of milk and other foods. You see, they prevent unhealthful foods from being sold. Our state, then, does many things to encourage better living conditions for its people.

Each state has a flag of its own. Can you describe your state flag? You may be interested in learning more about it. Does it fly over your school? If so, it flies below the flag of the United States.

Each state is represented by a star on our national flag. It is this flag that we salute, no matter in what state we live. And it is the one that is displayed in our schoolrooms.

Self-Government at School

Many boys and girls help to govern themselves at school. They suggest some of the rules and choose their class officers. Their president takes charge of class meetings and may help enforce class rules. The secretary may write down some class business.

Members of the safety committee also perform certain duties. They may help to keep order in the halls, or in the cafeteria. They may direct students across streets, or help to keep playgrounds safe.

Class officers serve in many important ways. It is a good idea, then, to choose the most able pupil for each office. What kind of citizens should they be? Could you "measure up" for an office?

A class that elects its leaders and makes some rules is learning about self-government. Does your class help to govern itself? If so, has it ever had any problems to work out? Has your safety committee had any experiences like this one?

Self-government at Pleasant Hill School. The twelve-o'clock-bell rang loud and clear. "Lunch time! Lunch time!" it said to many pupils.

When the fifth grade was excused, two boys pushed ahead. Jack, a safety officer, stopped them. "Why the rush?" asked Jack. "It's against the rule to push."

"We can't wait all day!" complained Joe.

"Naw! We're hungry!" grumbled Jim.

"Maybe so," agreed Jack. "But you mustn't push others out of your way. Remember the safety rules."

"You can't tell us what—"

"Look!" interrupted Jack. "I'm supposed to see that our rules are obeyed. Please help me. If you don't like my ways, you can vote for someone else next month."

By this time, the other pupils were eating under a big tree. The two who were in such a hurry were last, after all. Do you think the safety officer handled his problem wisely?

Practicing democracy at school helps to prepare us for duties later on. The boys and girls of today will be tomorrow's citizens. Some of them will be its leaders.

In time, you may hold an office in your community, or perhaps in your state. Indeed, some of you may serve in high places in our nation. And you will be

Committees elected by pupils in a Chicago school help work out class problems.

able to vote. So you will have a part in choosing many leaders.

The privilege of self-government is still a precious one. But a democracy is only strong if everyone does his part. Find out all you can about how you can serve. Let's keep our country free, strong, rich, and beautiful!

Can You Tell?

1. What is government and when and how was our government planned?

2. What was the new plan of government called? What three divisions were planned? What does each do?

3. What is the Bill of Rights and why was it added to the Constitution?

4. What city was our first capital and where and why was a new one laid out? What do the letters *D. C.* stand for?

5. What is the President's main job?

In What Order?

Below is a list of important events about which you have read. On a piece of paper, write them in the order in which they happened.

a. George Washington was inaugurated.

b. Our country had grown to fifty states.

c. Washington was elected President.

d. The Constitutional Convention was held.

e. The War for Independence was fought.

Choose the Correct Ending

Three endings are given for each of the nine incomplete sentences below. Write the numbers 1 to 9 on paper. After each number write the letter of the ending which completes the sentence correctly.

1. At the close of the Revolutionary War, the colonies (a) worked together. (b) argued with each other. (c) were ruled by England.
2. One central government was needed (a) to unite the states. (b) to give more power to each state. (c) to reduce taxes.
3. The Constitutional Convention elected as its leader and chairman (a) Benjamin Franklin. (b) Thomas Jefferson. (c) George Washington.
4. The new plan of government was called (a) the Bill of Rights. (b) the Constitution of the United States. (c) the Federal organization.
5. The purpose of the legislative branch was (a) to make laws. (b) to enforce the laws. (c) to punish lawbreakers.
6. The United States is (a) a democracy. (b) an autocracy. (c) an empire.
7. The lawmaking body in most of our states is called (a) the Supreme Court. (b) the executive body. (c) the legislature.
8. The city of Washington was planned by (a) a French engineer. (b) George Washington. (c) General Lafayette.
9. The laws of our country are made by (a) Congress. (b) the states. (c) the President.

Some Questions to Talk Over

1. What is a democracy?
2. What rights do the people of a democracy enjoy? What responsibilities must they take to keep their government a democracy?
3. Would you rather live in a democracy or in a country with some other form of government? Why?
4. What can we do to improve our kind of government?

Some Other Things to Do

1. See if your class can elect officers. Discuss the duties of each office and help the class choose the most able "candidates."
2. If you live in a city, find out how it is governed. See if your teacher can arrange a class trip to your City Hall.
3. Learn more about your state. Read in a library book about its early settlers. Use the Tables for Reference to find out when it entered the Union. Locate your state capital on the map on pages 504–505. Tell who is your governor. Find out all you can about your state flag. Learn how many Representatives and Senators your state sends to Washington and the names of these leaders.
4. Pretend you are guiding some friends on a tour of Washington, D. C. List places you will visit and an important fact about each one. Look for helpful pictures in this chapter. What map will you use?

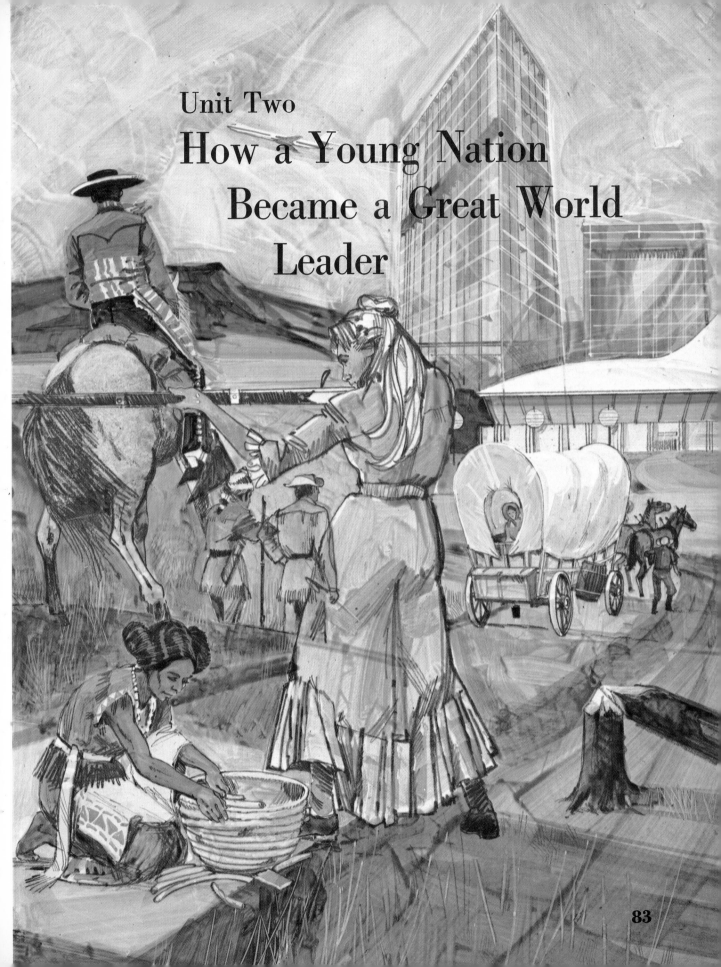

Unit Two

How a Young Nation Became a Great World Leader

5 · Our Wonderful Country

Learning about Our Beautiful Country

The day a famous song was born. It was a pleasant summer day in 1893. A wagon crawled slowly up a steep mountain road. It carried happy sightseers.

"It's a lovely day!" exclaimed one member of the party.

The guide nodded. "We're lucky since we're heading for the peak."

"Will we go all the way to the summit?" asked a man.

"Yes, to the very top, sir," answered the guide. "And today's so clear and bright you'll see far and wide."

"How exciting!" a woman chimed in.

The travelers were on their way up Pikes Peak. This magnificent mountain towers high in the Rocky Mountains.

When the sightseers reached the summit, they were thrilled, indeed. The air was so clear that they could see many miles in every direction. To the east, golden wheat fields carpeted the plains. To the west were purplish mountain slopes and peaks patched with snow. Above were endless blue skies.

"Oh, beautiful! Beautiful!" exclaimed one woman, Katherine Lee Bates. Then she wrote on a paper, the words of the stirring song, *America the Beautiful*.

Through the years this hymn has become a favorite of Americans everywhere. How often we sing its inspiring words. They begin this way, as you may know:

"O beautiful for spacious skies,
For amber waves of grain,
For purple mountain majesties
Above the fruited plain.
America! America!
God shed His grace on thee,
And crown thy good with brotherhood
From sea to shining sea!"

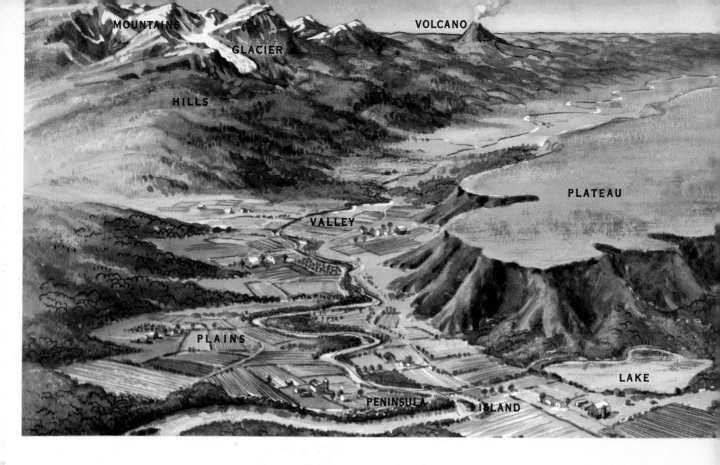

Our country is "America the Beautiful." It has wide plains and fertile valleys. It has rolling hills and majestic mountains. It has winding rivers and sparkling lakes, large and small. It has cool thick forests and hot empty deserts. And it has hundreds and hundreds of miles of shores washed by the seas.

We are very fortunate to live in such a beautiful, varied land.

Where is our country located? The song just mentioned gives us one clue, "From sea to shining sea!" The United States extends from the Atlantic into the Pacific. Most of it is in the Western Hemisphere on the continent of North America.

Most of our country has a pleasant "middle" location, as the inset map on page 86 shows. Forty-eight of our states share the middle part of North America.

This picture shows some kinds of land forms found in our country. Which two kinds are shown on pages 88 and 89?

There, the climate is neither too hot nor too cold. This fine location and favorable climate have helped our country become a great nation.

The United States is very large. Only three nations in the whole world are larger. They are the Soviet Union in Europe and Asia, China, and Canada. Can you locate these countries on the map on page 188?

Many nations are much smaller than ours. Our country is nearly seventeen times the size of France. It is 178 times the size of the Netherlands.

The United States stretches miles and miles from east to west and from north to south. In some places, the distance

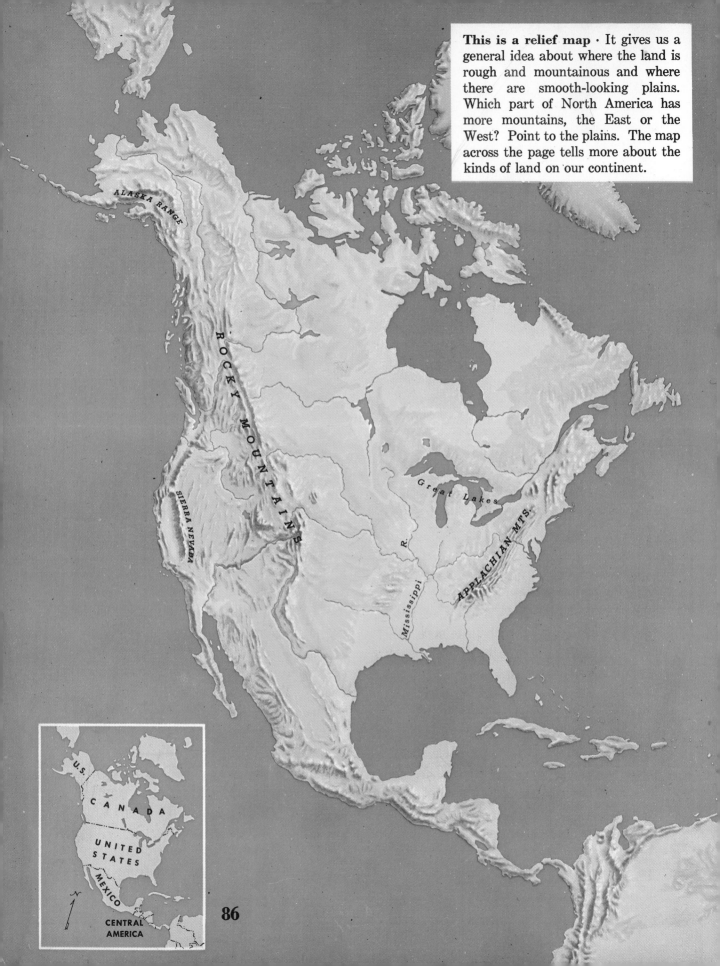

This is a relief map · It gives us a general idea about where the land is rough and mountainous and where there are smooth-looking plains. Which part of North America has more mountains, the East or the West? Point to the plains. The map across the page tells more about the kinds of land on our continent.

ALASKA RANGE

ROCKY MOUNTAINS

SIERRA NEVADA

Great Lakes

APPALACHIAN MTS.

R.

Mississippi

U.S.

CANADA

UNITED STATES

MEXICO

CENTRAL AMERICA

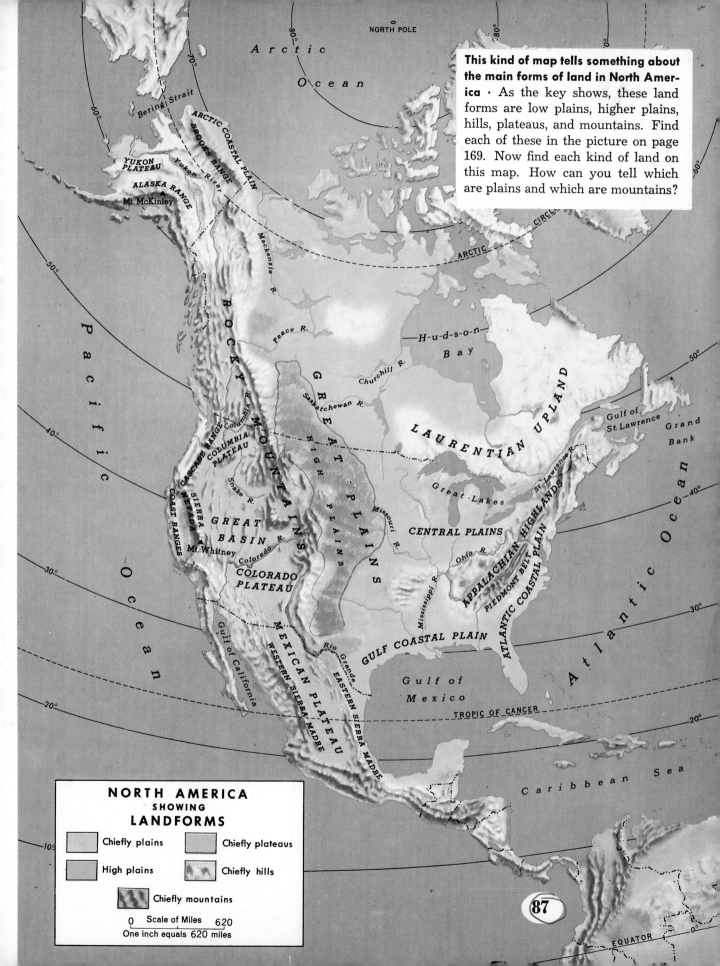

NORTH POLE

Arctic

Ocean

Bering Strait

ARCTIC COASTAL PLAIN

**YUKON
PLATEAU**

Yukon River

BROOKS RANGE

ALASKA RANGE
▲Mt. McKinley

Mackenzie R.

Peace R.

H-u-d-s-o-n
Bay

Churchill R.

ROCKY MOUNTAINS

G R E A T   P L A I N S

Saskatchewan R.

CASCADE RANGE
Columbia R.
COLUMBIA
PLATEAU

Snake R.

High Plains

Missouri R.

L A U R E N T I A N   U P L A N D

Gulf of
St Lawrence

Grand
Bank

Great Lakes

CENTRAL PLAINS

COAST RANGES
SIERRA NEVADA
GREAT
BASIN
▲Mt. Whitney
Colorado R.

COLORADO
PLATEAU

Ohio R.

APPALACHIAN HIGHLANDS

St Lawrence R.

PIEDMONT BELT

ATLANTIC COASTAL PLAIN

Mississippi R.

Rio Grande

GULF COASTAL PLAIN

MEXICAN PLATEAU
WESTERN SIERRA MADRE
EASTERN SIERRA MADRE

Gulf of California

Gulf of
Mexico

TROPIC OF CANCER

Pacific Ocean

Atlantic Ocean

Caribbean Sea

EQUATOR

This kind of map tells something about
the main forms of land in North America · As the key shows, these land
forms are low plains, higher plains,
hills, plateaus, and mountains. Find
each of these in the picture on page
169. Now find each kind of land on
this map. How can you tell which
are plains and which are mountains?

NORTH AMERICA
SHOWING
LANDFORMS

Chiefly plains

Chiefly plateaus

High plains

Chiefly hills

Chiefly mountains

Scale of Miles
0   620
One inch equals 620 miles

87

from the Atlantic to the Pacific is nearly three thousand miles. It is about fifteen hundred miles from Canada on the north to Mexico and the Gulf of Mexico on the south. The United States is so large that it has many different kinds of lands.

Our country has high lands and low lands. You can see this very plainly on the map on page 87. The highest places are its tallest mountain peaks. One of these is Pikes Peak about which you just read. It rises in the Rockies, you remember. Point to the Rockies on the map on page 87. Other towering peaks are also found in the Rockies, and in the Sierra Nevada, and the Alaska Range. Look for these mountain ranges on the map.

The height of land above the level of the sea is called *altitude*. Mount Whitney, in the Sierra Nevada, is 14,495 feet above sea level. So we say its altitude is 14,495 feet. Mount McKinley in Alaska soars very much higher, however. Its altitude

Many miles of plains reach across the heart of our country.

is 20,300 feet. It is the highest point in the United States.

Another word for altitude is *elevation*. Elevation figures appear on certain road signs. For instance, if you were driving into Chicago, you might see this sign, "Chicago, elevation 610 feet." It tells us that Chicago is 610 feet above sea level.

An elevation sketch extends across the map on pages 90 and 91. It shows the elevation of lands located along an imaginary line across our country. Notice that this line reaches from Chesapeake Bay on the east coast to San Francisco on the west.

Large areas of our country are plains. You probably remember that *plains* are low lands which are mostly level. Look at the plains in the picture below. Now find the plains on the map on pages 90 and 91. The map key will help you. Notice that two kinds of plains are shown on this map. What are they? What color stands for low plains?

Find the plain that follows along the Atlantic coast. What is it called? What plains lie between the Appalachian

Mountains and the Mississippi River? Which plains are the highest? Look on the elevation sketch and see. Find these high plains on the land-form map. What color is used to show them?

Plains are usually easy to farm. Most of them are fertile and can produce large amounts of food. Plains are also easy to travel across. Thousands of miles of rails and highways reach across them.

Some parts of our land are plateaus. A *plateau* is a broad area of land too high to be called a plain. A plateau may be partly flat and partly hilly and have steep slopes on one or more sides. Notice the plateau in the picture on page 85. How is it different from the plains?

On the map on page 91, what color stands for a plateau? Locate some plateaus. Those in the western part of our country are generally very dry lands and are not easy to farm. In some places cattle and sheep graze on them.

Hills extend through many sections of our country. *Hills* are rolling lands that are lower than mountains. Look at the hills above. Notice how rounded they are. Hills are rounded because rain, wind, snow, and ice have been wearing them down for millions of years. You can understand, then, where we get the saying, "It's as old as the hills." When a person says that, he means something is very old.

Hills are usually difficult to farm. But they are often wooded and beautiful. Some of our loveliest hills are in New England. Use the map on page 91 to help you locate them. What color is used to show hills on this map? Notice that the northeastern part of our land is almost covered by hills.

Our country has range after range of mountains. *Mountains* are much higher than hills, as the picture on page 85 suggests. Old mountains like the Appalachians are quite rounded. But young mountains like the Rockies and Sierra Nevada have high, sharp peaks like the ones in the picture on page 96.

89

UNITED STATES
SHOWING
LANDFORMS

Chiefly plains	Chiefly plateaus
High plains	Chiefly hills
Chiefly mountains	

Scale of Miles

0   230

One inch equals 230 miles

Pacific Ocean

WASH.

COLUMBIA

Columbia R.

OREG.

COLUMBIA PLATEAU

COAST RANGES

CASCADE RANGE

MONT.

N. DAK.

ROCKY

Missouri

S. DAK.

IDA.

Snake R.

BLACK HILLS

CALIF.

NEV.

GREAT

NEBR.

SIERRA NEVADA

CENTRAL VALLEY

Great Salt Lake

GREAT

BASIN

UTAH

COLO.

WYO.

HIGH

Platte R.

KANS.

COAST RANGES

▲ Mt. Whitney 14,495 ft.

MOUNTAINS

COLORADO

▲ Pike's Peak 14,109 ft.

Arkansas

PLAINS

Colorado River

PLATEAU

N. MEX.

Gila R.

ARIZ.

OKLA.

TEX.

Rio Grande

San Francisco

Colorado Springs

Pacific Ocean
Sea level

SIERRA NEVADA

CENTRAL VALLEY

GREAT BASIN

COLORADO PLATEAU

Pike's Peak

ROCKY MOUNTAINS

HIGH PLAINS

GREAT PLA

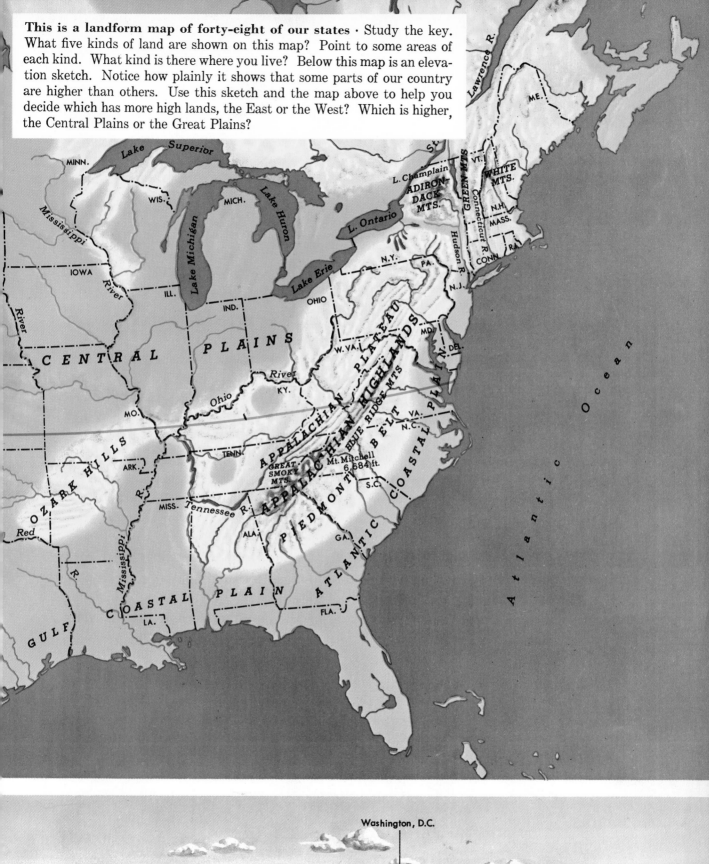

This is a landform map of forty-eight of our states · Study the key. What five kinds of land are shown on this map? Point to some areas of each kind. What kind is there where you live? Below this map is an elevation sketch. Notice how plainly it shows that some parts of our country are higher than others. Use this sketch and the map above to help you decide which has more high lands, the East or the West? Which is higher, the Central Plains or the Great Plains?

MINN.

Lake Superior

WIS.

MICH.

Lake Michigan

Lake Huron

IOWA

Mississippi River

ILL.

IND.

Lake Erie

OHIO

L. Ontario

N.Y.

PA.

N.J.

L. Champlain

ADIRON-DACK MTS.

GREEN MTS

WHITE MTS.

VT.

N.H.

MASS.

Connecticut R.

CONN.

R.I.

Hudson R.

ME.

St. Lawrence R.

C E N T R A L   P L A I N S

MO.

Ohio River

KY.

W. VA.

PLATEAU

APPALACHIAN HIGHLANDS

MD.

DEL.

OZARK HILLS

ARK.

TENN.

APPALACHIAN HIGHLANDS

GREAT SMOKY MTS

BLUE RIDGE MTS

Mt. Mitchell 6,684 ft.

VA.

N.C.

BELT

ATLANTIC COASTAL PLAIN

Red

R.

MISS.

Tennessee R.

ALA.

PIEDMONT

S.C.

GA.

Mississippi R.

GULF   C O A S T A L

LA.

P L A I N

A T L A N T I C

FLA.

A t l a n t i c   O c e a n

Washington, D.C.

Atlantic Ocean

Sea level

OZARK HILLS

CENTRAL PLAINS

APPALACHIAN HIGHLANDS

ATLANTIC COASTAL PLAIN

I N S

The Columbia River flows through the Cascades on its way to the Pacific Ocean.

What color on the map stands for mountains? Locate the Appalachian Mountains. Now point to the Rockies. Which are higher? Use the elevation sketch to help you answer.

Fertile valleys lie between some ranges of hills and mountains. The picture on page 85 will remind you what a valley is like. Let's locate one on the map. Look for the valley running north and south through much of California. It lies between the Sierra Nevada and the coastal mountains. What is it called?

Many valleys have been carved out by rivers rushing down from mountains and hills toward the sea. Mountains, hills, and river valleys are nature's drainboards. Most kitchen drainboards slope toward the sink so water will run off. Likewise, water drains off of mountains and hills. This water from rain and melting snows pours into many little streams that cut their way down the slopes. The streams form little valleys. Then they make larger, lower valleys as they hurry to join a larger stream or river.

A large valley may look quite flat. Actually, however, it slopes down toward the middle. So water drains off into the river that flows through the valley. What river drains the Mississippi Valley?

Many rivers drain our lands. Some begin in the Appalachians and flow eastward as the map on page 91 shows.

Two of the largest rivers in the eastern part of our country are the Hudson and the Connecticut. They flow southward from mountains and hills which are a part of the Appalachian Highlands. *Highlands* are just what the word tells you, lands that are high. They may include hills, plateaus, and mountains. The Appalachian Highlands have a plateau, ranges of hills, and low mountains. In what mountains of the Appalachian Highlands does the Hudson River begin? In what ranges does the Connecticut River start?

Some other rivers which rise in the Appalachians flow westward. They join the Mississippi River and are a part of the *Mississippi River System*. A large river together with all of its branches is called a *river system*.

Point to the Mississippi on the map. Notice that it flows southward through the Central Plains. Into what body of water does it empty? The Indians gave this wide, mighty Mississippi its name. It means "Father of Waters." The Mississippi is one of the largest rivers in the world.

The map shows why the Mississippi is such a giant. See how many rivers pour into it! They flow from the east and from the west. The largest eastern branches are born in the Appalachians. One is the famous Ohio River. Some important western branches begin high in the Rockies. The longest one is the winding Missouri. It wanders across our land for about 2,700 miles before it joins the Mississippi. It dumps so much brownish mud into the Mississippi that it is nicknamed the "Big Muddy."

The twisting Columbia drains lands far to the northwest. It begins in high snow-capped mountains in Canada. On the map, see how it flows southwestward. Into what ocean does it empty?

Another western river, the Colorado, rises in the Rockies. Locate it on the map. Now look for the Rio Grande which also starts in the Rockies.

There are dozens of other wonderful rivers in our country. Some serve as waterways. Some provide water for irrigation and power for making electricity. Rivers are among nature's most useful and beautiful gifts to us. We should care for them wisely.

Five Great Lakes extend along part of our northern boundary. Locate and name the Great Lakes. Four of them are shared with Canada. Which one lies entirely within our country?

The Great Lakes were formed by glaciers. A *glacier* is a large body of ice that moves very slowly over the land. Long ago, huge glaciers moved down from the far north. They carved enormous hollows out of the land. When the ice melted, the hollows filled with water. They became known as the Great Lakes.

Cleveland grew up on one of the Great Lakes, Lake Erie.

The Rio Grande starts high in
the Rockies as a small stream.

The Great Lakes reach hundreds of
miles inland. Indeed, Lake Superior extends almost to the middle of our continent. The Great Lakes are a part of a
very valuable waterway. See how they
empty into connecting rivers and finally
into the St. Lawrence River. Notice that
this large river flows into the Atlantic.
Later on, we shall learn about this very
important waterway.

**Pictures and maps have told you
some things about our beautiful
country.** But your study has just begun.
You can learn much more in the chapters
which follow. And you could have a
bird's-eye view of some parts if you flew
across our country. Let's pretend we are
taking such a trip on a fine spring day.

Enjoying a
Bird's-Eye View:
Flying Across
Our Country

Starting our trip. You know what an
exciting city Washington, D. C. is. You
visited it in the last chapter. Suppose we
begin our plane journey from our national
capital. We shall board our plane, then,
at the busy Dulles International Airport
nearby.

Maps are especially useful when one is
traveling. They help us to understand
what we are seeing. The map and elevation sketch on pages 90 and 91 contain
much helpful information for us. Let's
refer to them often as we travel westward.

Turn to these pages now. Notice the
red line that extends across the map. It
gives a general idea of the route we shall
take. The sketch below the map tells
something about the elevation of the lands
along this route.

**Westward across the Appalachian
Highlands.** How thrilled we are as we
board our jet. Soon, the giant plane taxis
down the runway. At the right moment,
it roars ahead with a tremendous burst of
speed. Soon, we are in the air and climbing steadily.

As we look out, we have a wonderful
view. To the east is the broad blue Chesapeake Bay. Find it on our map. Beyond
it, both north and south, stretches a wide
sweep of plains. Our map shows that this
is a part of the fertile Atlantic Coastal
Plain.

Scattered over this plain are many towns and cities. In between them, lie thousands of farms connected by roads. The roads seem to be narrow ribbons crisscrossing the countryside. And the automobiles look to us like tiny bugs crawling along. Why do they seem so small?

Now we are above hilly lands. Gradually they rise to meet the forested Appalachians. You will read much about these mountains in the next chapter. A wide belt of hilly lands extends west of the mountains. Its hills are green with woods, croplands, and pastures.

Across the heart of our country. Farther on, the land begins to flatten out. But this is not surprising! According to the map, we are now above the eastern part of the Central Plains. Before the white men came, forests blanketed this area. Today, there are patches of woods here and there. But most of the trees have been cut down to make room for farms and cities. Some cities are quite large but dozens of others are small.

Many farms share the fertile lands of the Central Plains. Their fields look like squares on a giant checkerboard. Some are green pastures where cattle graze. But many are planted in corn and other crops.

Before long, we catch glimpses of the mighty Mississippi. Our map shows that it divides the rich Central Plains. In what direction does it flow?

Above the Great Plains. We speed farther and farther west. As the land stretches out under us, it becomes flatter until it is almost as level as a floor. Now we are looking down on the Great Plains. Do you see them on the map? Their neat green squares are mostly wheat fields. By July, the ripening wheat will turn to a golden color, and be ready to harvest.

As the Great Plains extend west, they rise to meet the Rockies. Notice how your elevation sketch shows this. Indeed, the lands at the foot of the Rockies are quite high. The city of Colorado Springs, on our route, is 5,900 feet above sea level. So it is more than a mile high.

On across our vast West. Speeding on, we cross above the Rockies. We see beautiful snow-capped Pikes Peak and its lovely neighbor peaks, and range after range of mountains. Their lower slopes are dark with thick forests. Now and then, we see jewel-like lakes in deep valleys. Sometimes, we catch glimpses of silvery streaks. They are falls and streams tumbling down through the canyons.

Beyond the mountains, we come to plateau country. As your map shows, much of the West is made up of this kind of land. On these plateau lands are some bare, rugged mountains as well as forested slopes. Also there are some patches of irrigated fields. But much of the land seems to be a dry and empty desert.

At the western edge of the plateau lands are snow-capped mountains. They are a part of the Sierra Nevada, or "snowy range." As we fly over them, we see dense forests on their lower slopes. Many lakes shine like mirrors hidden among the trees of the valleys.

On west we fly, over the fertile Central Valley in California. Beneath us are fruit orchards, fields, and some towns and cities. Soon, we see San Francisco and the shores of the Pacific. We have flown "from sea to shining sea" across our beautiful country.

Ours is a beautiful and varied land. We have high mountains like the Grand Tetons in the Rockies and wide plains like those of Nebraska.

Our large and beautiful country has many kinds of natural resources. *Natural resources* are nature's "gifts." Air and water are valuable natural resources. So are soils, climates, forests, fish, coal, and oil.

We cannot live without air. We must breathe air to stay alive. Plants and all living things must also have air — clean air. But clean air is becoming scarce in some parts of our country.

We are polluting our precious air. We are pouring into it enormous quantities of gases, smoke, and other wastes. *Air pollution* is caused by automobiles, buses, trucks, and planes. Also waste from factories and electric-power plants pollutes the air.

Air pollution is thickest in and around our large busy cities. Sometimes air pollution becomes so bad that it makes people ill. It has even killed people.

Sometimes winds carry pollution far over the countryside. There it can damage crops and animals and kill trees.

Water pollution is another serious problem. Clean water is also necessary to us. Without it we would die. Without it plants and animals would die. We drink it. We use it for cooking and washing. We use it to carry away wastes and put out fires. Farms must have it.

Factories use tremendous quantities of water. It is used in making almost everything we use. Water is used in making the food we eat, the clothing we wear, the T.V. sets we watch.

We are using more and more water every year because there are more people every year. Also, we want more "things." The more "things" we have, the more water is used in making them.

Many factories dump tons and tons of dirty wastes into our lakes and rivers. So do the sewers from some cities. These harmful wastes pollute the water. They can make it unsafe for people and poisonous for fish.

Our supply of clean fresh water is running short. You see, most of the earth's water is in the oceans. It is too salty to drink or to use in farming or manufacturing. We depend mainly on streams, lakes, and rivers for our water supply. Yet we are polluting most of them. This is very dangerous!

We must think and work together to protect our beautiful country. We must find ways to prevent air and water pollution. We should keep our streets clean, and protect our parks, beaches, and mountain trails. Everyone must help to keep our country beautiful.

Careless use of some natural resources began long ago. A part of that story is told in Chapter 6.

What Key Words Are Missing?

Write the numbers 1 to 7 on a piece of paper. After each, write the word or words needed to complete the sentence.

1. Only __?__ nations are larger than the United States.

2. Our country is about __?__ times the size of the Netherlands.

3. __?__ of our states share the middle lands of North America.

4. The __?__ Mountains form a great wall through the heart of our country.

5. The five __?__ are a part of a very valuable inland waterway.

6. Nature's gifts such as climate and soil are called __?__.

7. Elevation means height or __?__titude

Using Pictures

1. Study the picture on page 85. On a paper draw and label: a plain, hill, mountain range, and plateau.

2. Find some interesting pictures showing different parts of our country and be ready to share them. See if the most attractive ones can be exhibited on the bulletin board.

3. Help your class plan a picture file. Arrange for a suitable box, and a folder for each chapter of the text. Be sure to write the title and number of each chapter on its folder. Talk over ideas to keep in mind in collecting helpful pictures. Choose a committee to sort and file the pictures.

4. Use pictures and maps together. On the map on pages 90–91, locate the area shown in each picture on pages 88, 89, 92, 93, and 94.

Using Maps

Use the maps on pages 86, 87, and 90–91 to help you answer the following questions.

1. On which page is the relief map?

2. Which page has the landform map of our country? Locate on this map, where you live. What is the main kind of landform in your area?

3. Which page shows an inset map?

4. Where do you find an elevation sketch?

5. Where is the landform map of our continent located?

6. On which pages are there maps with keys?

7. On which page would you look to study landforms in Canada?

Drawing to Scale

Many maps have a scale of miles. This means that they have been drawn to scale.

Let's draw a map of your classroom to scale.

1. Measure your room. How long is it? How wide?

2. Suppose you use the scale 1 *inch* = 1 *foot*. How many inches long will your map be? How many inches wide?

3. Draw your map on the board, exactly to scale. Write the scale in one corner.

Comparing Is Fun!

Comparing is deciding how things are alike and how they are different. Probably you have compared things or places many times.

Pictures are useful in making some comparisons. Let's use the pictures on pages 88 and 89, to prove this. Which picture shows

a. flatter land?

b. the more thickly-wooded land?

c. hills?

d. better farm land?

It is often interesting to compare areas on maps. Turn to the map on pages 90–91. Does the eastern half or the western have

a. more plains?

b. the larger plateau area?

c. more high mountains?

d. more hills?

Such comparing requires sharp eyes and clear thinking. But you will find it fun and also useful in helping you to learn.

What Do You Think?

1. What are some ways we can learn more about our country?

2. In which part of the United States would you prefer to live? Why?

3. Why do we say that our country is rich in natural resources?

4. Why do you think we have more and more pollution?

5. How can we help to stop pollution?

6 · The Pioneers on the March

Daniel Boone Explored a Wilderness

Daniel Boone: a fearless hunter and pioneer. Daniel Boone stood on a cliff above a rushing river. He looked across at wide green meadows. They were favorite hunting grounds of the Indians.

"That's pretty country," he said to himself. "The Indians call it Kentucky. Someday I'll settle there."

Already, white men were pushing into Indian lands. They were hunting the wild game the Indians needed for food. Because Boone was one of these hunters, the Indians planned to capture him.

Suddenly the bushes moved. Boone knew that Indians were near and jumped. He landed part way down the cliff in a crooked old tree. Quickly, he leaped into the river and swam across, disappearing from sight.

Daniel Boone was born in a small cabin on a Pennsylvania farm, fifty miles from Philadelphia. There were no schools nearby, but his aunt taught him to read and write. He did not learn to spell very well, as you can see from this sentence he carved on a tree:

D. Boon cilled a BAR on this tree, 1760.

Young Daniel loved to spend long summer days in the woods, hunting and exploring. He learned about the trees and the plants. He trained himself to glide silently through the forest like the Indians. He practiced the calls of birds and of animals. He discovered that some hoots were not the calls of owls. Nor were all "gobble-gobble-gobbles" those of wild turkeys. They were sometimes the calls of clever Indian hunters. The Indians lured wild game closer in this way.

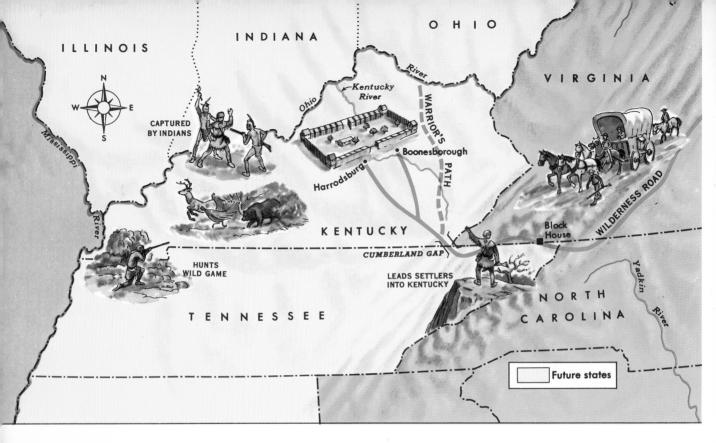

This map shows some of Daniel Boone's adventures west of the Appalachians. He had many scrapes with the Indians and was captured twice. But each time he escaped. He started the fort settlement of Boonesborough. Find it on the map on page 109.

By the time Daniel was twelve, he was tall and strong. His father gave him a gun. Daniel practiced steadily and became such a fine marksman that he was called "a dead shot." This meant that he could kill an animal with a single bullet.

When Daniel was fifteen, his family set out for North Carolina, five hundred miles to the south. The wagons were loaded down with household furnishings, food, clothing, and farm tools. Daniel and his brothers drove the cattle behind the wagons. So the Boones traveled slowly. Be-

sides, there were only a few miles of good road. The rest of the way led over rough trails through the wilderness.

Now and then, the Boones camped for several days. Then Mrs. Boone and her older daughters did the washing while the younger children herded the cattle. But Daniel spent his spare time hunting to provide meat for the family.

After many weeks, the Boones reached the Yadkin Valley in North Carolina. There, they cut down trees and built a log cabin. As soon as the crops were planted, Daniel wandered off to explore the wooded hills nearby. With him he took his two best friends, his dog and his long rifle.

Later, Boone married the daughter of a neighbor and decided to be a farmer. But he soon changed his mind and turned back to hunting. This was the life he loved best.

One day, another hunter told Daniel Boone some wonderful tales about Kentucky. This new land was located west of the Appalachian Mountains. Find it on the map on page 100. Kentucky's rivers were rich with fish. Deer and elk roamed its rolling plains. Bears, panthers, wildcats, beavers, and muskrats lived in its forests. Wild turkeys and wild geese nested in its trees. "I'll tell you, Kentucky's just made for hunters!" said Boone's friend.

"Must be a mighty fine place!" answered Boone with shining eyes. "I'm going to see for myself, someday."

Boone and his friends journeyed to Kentucky. In 1769, Boone and several other hunters headed west into the wilderness country. Packed on Boone's horse was a warm bearskin blanket, gun powder, a small kettle, some salt, and a few other supplies. He carried his trusty rifle.

The men crossed range after range of tree-covered Appalachian Mountains. Point to the Appalachians on the map on page 109. After weeks of hard travel, they reached Cumberland Gap. A *gap* is an opening or low place through a mountain range.

Boone and his friends made their way north into Kentucky on the Warriors' Path. Locate it on the map on page 100. Hunters had given this name to the trail that led to Kentucky. This land was the hunting ground of several different tribes.

Kentucky was all that Daniel Boone expected. Its rolling hills were clad in thick forests. It had many pleasant valleys, and green meadows carpeted with tall, waving grass. Long before, the Indians had burned off the trees in the meadows so that more grass would grow. This encouraged deer and other animals to graze there.

Kentucky: a new frontier. Boone and his hunter friends made camp. They shot and trapped many animals and were able to collect a large number of furs and skins. But, within a few weeks, all but Boone were killed by the Indians. Why do you think that some Indians had become angry with the pioneers?

Still, this fearless pioneer was not ready to give up and return home. Alone, he explored wide stretches of the wilderness. He found that much of the soil was rich and fertile. He knew that the land would grow good crops. The forests would

Setting beaver traps. Hunters were the first to explore west of the Appalachians.

furnish plenty of wild game for hunting and trapping. Perhaps someday he would lead settlers to this new frontier.

Boone realized that it would not be easy to settle in Kentucky. It was a lonely wilderness. There were no roads leading to it. And it was far from towns and cities. Furthermore, many Indians lived in this wild region. They would probably fight to protect their lands. Here, life would be dangerous as well as hard.

Yet some pioneers might face dangers and hardships willingly. They longed for new lands. Do you know why?

The Frontier Was Being Pushed West

The first frontier had stretched along the Atlantic coast. You read about it in Unit One. It was the wilderness to which the earliest settlers had come. It, too, had been a lonely land of dangers and hardships. Yet it had offered so many new opportunities that colonists had remained to settle it. These settlers had laid out towns and farms along its coast, remember.

As the years passed, there were more and more people living along this coast. Many Americans had large families. Also thousands of new settlers came from Europe. As the sons of the colonists grew up, many of them started their own farms. By the time of the Revolutionary War, most of the best land along the Atlantic coast was being used. The good land that was left was too expensive for most people.

Then there was another problem. Much of the land had been farmed for a long time. Tobacco and some other crops had taken so much plant food from the soil that it was worn out. In places, farmers could hardly make a living on their poor soil. People had to move farther west to find fertile land that they could afford. The widest areas of rich-soiled new lands lay beyond the Appalachian Mountains.

The Appalachians had kept back the earliest settlers. The Appalachians are made up of a group of mountain ranges. They are known as the *Appalachian Mountain System*. The map on

page 109 shows that they run north and south through the eastern part of our country. Use the scale of miles on the map. About how many miles west of the Atlantic coast are they?

Explorers and hunters found that the ranges of Appalachians rose like high walls, one beyond the other. Because these mountains were very old, their peaks had been gently rounded and worn down by rain, snow, and streams. But the slopes were steep and covered with thick forests. And there were few gaps in the ranges, as the photograph on page 102 shows. Trails that crossed the mountains had to wind in and out across valleys and slopes.

Hunter pioneers were the first colonists to cross the Appalachians. They were often on the move looking for wild animals, so they found out much about a region. They learned about the Indians. They discovered the easiest places to cross rivers. They found the Indian trails and located the gaps through the thickly-wooded Appalachian Mountains.

Boone and his men cut a trail 300 miles long through the wilderness. It became known as the Wilderness Road.

Some frontiersmen hunted out the best routes to the West. They marked cuts, or blazes, on trees along the way. Such men were called trail blazers. Daniel Boone was one of the most famous trail blazers.

Boone and a party of brave pioneers carved out a route to Kentucky. Boone rode ahead to show the way and blaze the trail. Slowly the workmen followed, swinging their mighty axes to chop down trees and clear underbrush. The picture above shows them at work.

Building a route through the Appalachians was very difficult. But day by day, the workmen pushed farther into the wilderness. They cleared trails through valleys and up and down mountain slopes. Finally, the 300-mile pathway was finished. It was narrow and rocky and

Near the end of the Wilderness Road Boone and his friends built Boonesborough.

cluttered with tree stumps. But it became known as *Wilderness Road*. Locate it on the map on page 100 and on the map on page 109. As these maps show, the Wilderness Road led to the heart of Kentucky to the Kentucky River. Near this river, Boone's party camped. There the men planned to build a settlement.

Boone and his friends built Boonesborough. Find it on the maps. To protect it from the Indians, Boonesborough

was constructed like a fort. Study the picture of it above. Strong log cabins were lined up around a center yard. Notice that they were joined together by a heavy wall of logs called a *stockade*. They had no doors or windows in their rear walls.

The huge log gates that led into the fort were closed at night and during times of danger. Each evening the pioneers drove their cattle, horses, and other livestock inside the stockade. This was the safest place for the animals during the night.

At each corner of the stockade stood a stout two-story blockhouse with narrow windows. When the Indians attacked, the pioneers fired their guns through these windows.

For further protection, settlers cleared away the hiding places close to the fort. The picture on page 104 shows that most trees around the stockade had been cut down. But one old elm was left standing. On hot days, it spread cooling shade for nearly a hundred feet. This friendly elm served as a kind of town hall for the settlers. Under this tree the people discussed their problems and plans. There, they made the laws for their settlement.

Planning together was the American way of life, even long ago. Working things out together is a part of what we call democracy. As you read earlier, *democracy* means that people govern themselves.

The Taylors lived in a log cabin they had built themselves in western Virginia. How is this home different from yours?

Many Pioneers Flocked to Kentucky and Tennessee

Tales of Kentucky spread. Some were told by the hunters and trappers who had returned from west of the Appalachians. These men held their listeners spellbound as they described buffalo hunts and other exciting adventures. But even more welcome was information about the fine fertile land. Many people were beginning to think about moving west. So they were eager to learn more about the land there. One such family was the Taylors.

The Taylors lived in Virginia on a tobacco farm, but they were poor people. Their land was worn out and produced only small crops. Mr. Taylor was often tempted to give up and move elsewhere.

One evening, a weary traveler knocked at the Taylors' cabin. "I'm traveling back

Everyone helped on moving
day. The Taylors were "going
West" to Kentucky.

from the West," he explained. "Could
you let me stay here for the night?"

Mr. Taylor nodded and invited the
stranger in. While the two men talked,
Mrs. Taylor and her daughters prepared
supper. Supper was the light meal of the
day. This evening, it was corn-meal mush
topped with honey and milk. The hot
mush was bubbling in a large iron kettle
that hung over the fire in the fireplace.

After supper, the Taylors and their
bearded guest sat around the cheery fire.
He told the family many interesting
things about Kentucky.

Kentucky had lands for sale! The
hunter said these lands were selling for
about two dollars an acre. When a man
bought land, he was given a *deed*. It was
the special paper to prove that he owned
it. "Of course," remarked the stranger,
"some people think that frontier land

should be free. So they don't bother to
buy it. They settle where they please and
clear the land and plant crops. But they
are squatters. They are living on land
they don't own or rent. This is against
the law."

"What happens to squatters?" asked
curious Matthew.

"Oh, they're forced to move, once the
Government finds out about them," answered the hunter. "The smartest folks
buy the land and get a deed for it."

**Many ambitious settlers soon pre-
pared to move West.** Among them were
the Taylors and some of their neighbors.
They bought land near Boonesborough
and received deeds.

After months of planning, Mr. Taylor
said to his wife, one winter evening, "Well,
it's all settled, now. When spring comes,

106

we'll head West. There'll be about fifty of us going together."

Packing up was a big job. There were so many things to take to a new home! Clothing! The soft mattress-like feather beds! The churn for making butter! The useful spinning wheel. The table and chairs! Dishes and iron kettles! Supplies of tea, salt, sugar, flour, corn meal, and bacon! Seed corn and seed potatoes for planting in the new fields! And guns and gun powder!

But not everything could be moved west, Mr. Taylor had explained, "The trail over the mountains is rough and steep. We can't take wagons so we'll have to pack all our belongings on the horses."

"Everything?" asked Matthew.

"Everything we take," answered Mr. Taylor. "Better give away all the things we can do without. That tall chest, for instance, and most of our large furniture."

"But, Mother, that tall chest of drawers was a wedding present from your grandmother!" objected Ella. "I was hoping I'd have it some day."

"I wish you could," answered Mrs. Taylor. "I love that chest. My grandmother brought it from England when Virginia was still a young colony. But it's too heavy to load on the horse. Let's give it to poor Widow Allen."

Over the Wilderness Road to Kentucky. At last, the Taylors and their friends set out for the lands west of the mountains. They were led by a hunter-guide. He had been over the trail several times. The women and children rode on horses, but the men and older boys walked. Some drove cattle. Others carried their rifles over their shoulders and kept an eye out for unfriendly Indians.

At night, the travelers camped beside a stream and cooked their meals. Wrapped in blankets, the pioneers slept under the stars while several men and their dogs stood guard.

The slow, tiresome journey took many weeks. But finally the travelers arrived at the little settlement of Boonesborough. They stayed there until they could build a fort and homes of their own, nearby. They and other brave pioneers helped to settle the Kentucky wilderness.

The Kentucky wilderness became a territory and then a state. A *territory* of the United States is a section of the country which is not a part of any state. When enough people have settled in a territory, it can have its own legislature. You remember that a *legislature* is a group of leaders elected by the people to make their laws. The governor and other officers of a territory are chosen by the President of the United States and Congress. When a territory has a large enough population, it may ask to become a state.

At one time, your state may have been a territory or a part of one. This was true of all but the first thirteen states. When did your part of our country become a state? Turn to page 499 and find out.

Kentucky became a state in 1792. It was the first territory west of the Appalachians to join the Union, the United States. After it was a state, its people had more say in their government. They could vote for the President of the United States. They could also elect some leaders to represent them in Congress.

Many pioneers settled on the rich lands of Tennessee. Find Tennessee on the map on page 109. In which direction is it from Kentucky?

Pioneers travel in a Conestoga wagon to the Ohio. Then many traveled down this river by boat.

James Robertson encouraged many pioneers to settle in Tennessee. As a young man, he had traveled west from North Carolina. Alone, with his horse and dog, he had journeyed to this frontier. He was delighted with its fertile lands.

Robertson led many families across the mountains into Tennessee. Hundreds of other settlers also poured into this region. Soon, Congress voted Tennessee a state.

Settlers Streamed into the Ohio Valley

North of Kentucky and Tennessee stretched the Northwest Territory. Find it on the map. As you can see, it was separated from Kentucky by the crooked Ohio River. Notice that this vast territory stretched west all the way to the Mississippi River.

In Chapter 3, you read how these lands were won. George Rogers Clark and his men took them from the British during the Revolutionary War. Clark captured British forts on some of the rivers in this western wilderness.

The wide wilderness north of the Ohio River had thickly-wooded hills and gently rolling plains. And it had plenty of fertile land for farming. But it was not an easy frontier to settle. Powerful and unfriendly Indian tribes lived there.

Angrily the Indians had watched the white man move into their Kentucky hunting grounds. They had seen him scare away the game. They knew settlers were chopping down forests and laying out farms. But the Indians did not intend to give up the Ohio country. They said, "Never shall white men plant their corn north of the Ohio River." So when the earliest settlers ventured into Ohio country, they faced great danger.

Indian warriors crept up on lonely settlements and attacked them. The Indians stole goods and burned down cabins. They scalped some settlers and carried away others.

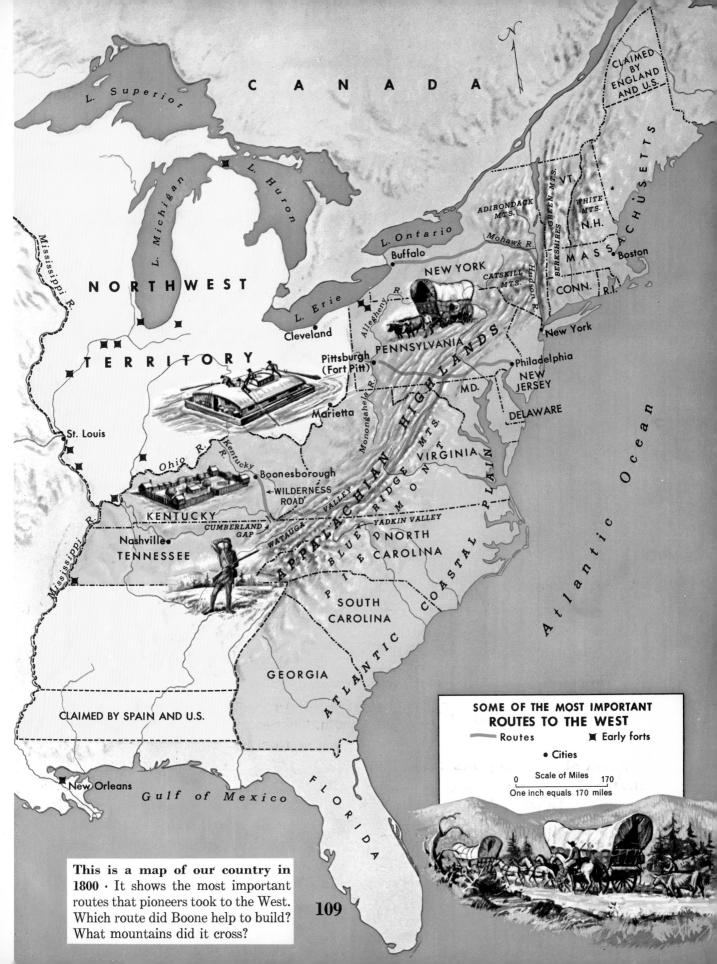

C A N A D A

L. Superior

L. Michigan

L. Huron

NORTHWEST

L. Ontario

Buffalo

NEW YORK

ADIRONDACK MTS.

Mohawk R.

CATSKILL MTS.

VT.

GREEN MTS.

N.H.

WHITE MTS.

BERKSHIRES

MASSACHUSETTS

Boston

CONN.

R.I.

Hudson R.

L. Erie

Cleveland

TERRITORY

Pittsburgh (Fort Pitt)

PENNSYLVANIA

New York

Philadelphia

NEW JERSEY

MD.

DELAWARE

Mississippi R.

Allegheny R.

Marietta

Monongahela R.

APPALACHIAN HIGHLANDS

VIRGINIA

PIEDMONT

St. Louis

Ohio R.

Kentucky R.

Boonesborough

←WILDERNESS ROAD

WATAUGA VALLEY

BLUE RIDGE MTS.

YADKIN VALLEY

NORTH CAROLINA

ATLANTIC COASTAL PLAIN

KENTUCKY

CUMBERLAND GAP

Nashville

TENNESSEE

SOUTH CAROLINA

Atlantic Ocean

Mississippi R.

CLAIMED BY SPAIN AND U.S.

GEORGIA

ATLANTIC

CLAIMED BY ENGLAND AND U.S.

N

New Orleans

Gulf of Mexico

FLORIDA

SOME OF THE MOST IMPORTANT ROUTES TO THE WEST

Routes — Early forts

• Cities

Scale of Miles
0 — 170
One inch equals 170 miles

This is a map of our country in 1800 · It shows the most important routes that pioneers took to the West. Which route did Boone help to build? What mountains did it cross?

109

Finally, the United States government sent an army to help the pioneers. After it defeated the Indians, tribal leaders gathered around a council fire to sign a peace treaty with the Government. The Indians agreed to move farther west and let the white man settle what is now southern Ohio and Indiana.

Meanwhile, Congress had sold several million acres of Ohio land to land companies. They were to survey and advertise it and sell it cheaply. Soon, many pioneers had settled in the Ohio country. They were so pleased with it that they sent enthusiastic letters to their friends "back East." One settler wrote:

I am delighted with Ohio. Wild game is plentiful here and the climate is fine and healthful. Land is cheap and the soil is rich and grows wonderful crops. Come West and see for yourself and you'll be eager to settle here, too. But hurry! People are pouring into this Ohio country.

By the way, we have good news from Congress about this region. As you know, the Ohio country is a territory at present. But Congress has passed a law to divide it into states as soon as it is settled. The new states are to have the same rights as the other states. Isn't that splendid?

Soon thousands of pioneers were on the march west to "Ohio." The map on page 109 will show you three routes they traveled. Many from Virginia tramped over the winding Wilderness Route through Cumberland Gap. But people from New England and the Middle Atlantic states used routes farther north.

Two northern routes led west. The one which began in New York followed the Hudson and Mohawk rivers. It led to the

PITTSBURGH

RAFT

plains country near Lake Ontario and Lake Erie.

Another route drew land-hungry pioneers west across Pennsylvania. Locate it. Over it creaked hundreds of covered wagons like the one in the picture on page 108. Conestoga wagons were often painted red and bright blue and had white canvas tops. Usually they were pulled by teams of horses or oxen. But some pioneers could not afford teams. They pulled their own small wagons.

The Pennsylvania route led across the forested Appalachians to Pittsburgh. Look for this settlement on the map. About how many miles west of Philadelphia was it? You can find out by using the scale of miles. Pittsburgh was sometimes called Fort Pitt. It had grown up around a fort begun by the British in 1759.

Pittsburgh was the gateway to the Ohio River Valley lands. Notice this on the map. It was located where the Allegheny and Monongahela rivers meet to

KEELBOAT

FLATBOAT

form the Ohio. From Pittsburgh, it was easy to float down the Ohio to the lands of the new West. Thousands of pioneers passed through this town on their way to the Ohio Valley. Many stopped to rest and to buy supplies. Boat building was one of Pittsburgh's chief industries. It had small boats and large ones for sale.

Hunters and trappers preferred canoes. But farmers bought or built flatboats, rafts, or keelboats. Study the picture above carefully and notice how these kinds of boats differed from each other.

Some families built their own boats. The Smiths were one such family. Mrs. Smith wrote in her diary about their experiences.

July 25: Father and James, John, and Franklin, have been busy for two weeks building a large raft. It is eighty feet long.

July 30: The cabin on the raft is done. We don't need to hurry our journey down the river. We will be comfortable in the cabin.

August 1: We are loading the raft to-morrow. We will store our food, clothing, and furniture in the cabin. The raft is also large enough to carry our covered wagon and our livestock.

August 2: At last we are on our way! We are drifting down the river with the current. Father and the boys take turns guiding us with long sweeps. (A sweep was a long oar used to push and to steer boats.)

August 4: We had trouble today! Our raft got stuck in the sand. We must always watch lest we scrape against rocks or buried logs and brush.

August 6: It is hot! Even so, Mary has spent an hour every day sewing on her sampler. She does cross-stitching neatly for an eight-year-old. Mattie and I have been busy spinning and weaving.

August 8: Father has been sharpening his tools today and mending harness. We must be ready to go to work when we reach our land in Ohio.

August 10: The haystack on our raft is getting smaller and smaller. But no wonder! Our team of horses and the cow eat hay all day.

August 18: We are almost at our journey's end. Tomorrow Father and the boys will roll the wagon off the raft and load it once more. Before we go on, they will spend some time taking our raft apart. Every nail and piece of sawed lumber is precious. We will use them to build our new home.

What Happened to the Indians?

Sequoia holds a chart showing his Cherokee alphabet.

The Indians of the south lost their lands. Two of the large tribes in the south were the Creeks and the Cherokees. The Creek Indians had about fifty towns in Georgia and Alabama. Most of them were several hundred miles inland from the coast. Generously the Creeks gave up some lands along the coast when Europeans started the colony of Georgia.

Later on, more and more settlers from the United States moved into Creek country. They took more and more of the Creek land. Then the Creeks began to fight back.

The Cherokees lived in western North Carolina and Tennessee. They helped many white settlers. Some of them also tried to change their own ways of living. They built roads and schools. A Cherokee leader, Sequoia, developed a system of writing in the Cherokee language. A printing press was bought. A newspaper was printed every week. The Cherokees even set up a government much like that of the United States.

But the white settlers continued to take Indian lands. Some Cherokees gave up and moved west of the Mississippi River. Many refused to leave.

After a time, the United States told the Creeks, Cherokee, and other Indians of the south that they must move far to the west. The Indians fought against the order. But they lost. Those who held out the longest, suffered the most. Over one fourth of the Cherokee died on the way west to the lands of what became Oklahoma.

The Indians of the north also suffered. About the same time, they were also losing their lands to other settlers from the United States.

The Indians of Ohio badly defeated an army set against them. But another army arrived. It forced them to give up a large share of their lands.

The Indians tried to hold the lands they had left. They tried to stop the settlers by force. They were defeated. They too had to move far to the west.

112

We should not forget these brave people who suffered because the pioneers settled on the frontiers. The proud descendants of these Indians are an important part of our people today.

More and more people moved west. By 1803, so many people had settled in Ohio that it was allowed to become a state. It was the third state west of the Appalachians to join the Union.

As time passed, many settlers travelled even farther west. They journeyed to lands which are now a part of Indiana and Illinois. Other pioneers from the south settled the region west of Georgia. Find these new frontiers on the map on page 109. Pioneers pushed the frontiers farther and farther west. Their farms and villages sprang up all the way to the Mississippi.

Some Study Questions

1. What did Daniel Boone do?
2. Why did Boone think that Kentucky was a good place to settle?
3. How did hunter-pioneers help to settle the West?
4. What was the Wilderness Road? Why was it important? How was it different from our roads today?
5. Why did people find it hard to settle the Ohio Valley?
6. How is a territory of the United States different from a state? When can a territory become a state?

To Help You Dramatize

It is fun to make a play about some event in our lessons. We call this dramatizing. It is a good idea to keep such plays very simple. Therefore, it is not necessary to make scenery or costumes or to memorize parts.

First, help your class choose an event to dramatize. Then quickly get all the information you can about that event. Read the story material carefully and study helpful pictures. While you are doing this, pretend you are one of the "characters" and think what you would do and say in the play. A good actor always tries to be the character he is playing.

A Choosing Game

Here are some sentences with several endings. Choose the correct ending for each sentence.

1. The Cumberland Gap was a low place in the (a) Rocky Mountains. (b) Appalachian Mountains. (c) White Mountains.
2. Boone and his friends built a fort and village called (a) Pittsburgh. (b) Big Lick. (c) Boonesborough.
3. The American way of working things out together is a part of what we call (a) business. (b) territory. (c) democracy.
4. To prove that a man owned the land on which he settled, the United States government required him to have (a) a cabin. (b) a deed. (c) tools.
5. People who settled on land which they did not own were called (a) settlers. (b) fur traders. (c) squatters.
6. The first territory west of the Appalachians to become a state was (a) Kentucky. (b) Ohio. (c) Tennessee.
7. Fort Pitt was the gateway to (a) Kentucky. (b) the Ohio Valley lands. (c) the lands along the Hudson River.

Some Questions to Discuss

1. Many pioneers traveled on rivers to reach new lands in the West. The map on page 109 shows that these were the long routes. Why didn't the pioneers follow shorter routes?

2. The pioneer leaders took the Indians' lands without paying for them. Why did they think this was right? How would you have felt about this if you had been a pioneer? How would you have felt if you had been an Indian? Have the Indians ever been paid for their lands?

Some Other Things to Do

1. Imagine that you are Daniel Boone. Tell your class about your adventures while hunting in the wilderness.

2. Make a sketch of one of these:

    A log cabin.

    A blockhouse.

    A stockade.

3. Help your class compare "moving day," as shown in the picture on page 106, with moving today.

4. Find out all you can about Conestoga wagons. Draw one.

5. Plan with your class to dramatize the story on pages 105–107.

Working with Others

You probably have noticed that the exercise, "Some Other Things to Do," usually lists some things for you to do by yourself and some to share with your classmates. Group activities give you a chance to show how well you can work with others. Working with others in the classroom is just as important as it is on a baseball team. Here are suggestions to keep in mind when working together:

1. Decide what jobs are to be done and list them on the board.

2. Choose a committee to complete each big job.

3. Elect a chairman for each committee.

4. Co-operate with the chairman and others.

5. Be ready to share materials.

6. Work quietly, quickly, and well.

7. Be ready to share what you have done with the other members of your class.

Fun with Maps

Turn to the map on page 109. This is a *political* map. Such a map shows into what countries, states, and territories a land is divided. Notice that this political map shows the United States in 1800. How many states did it have then? What ones had been added to the first thirteen? You may wish to look back at the map on page 65.

Your map also shows relief. How can you tell? Does the Appalachian Highland region look smooth or wrinkled?

Another thing, this is a *route* map. Prove this by reading its title. What symbol stands for a route? Trace, with your finger, the route that led north along the Hudson River. What two towns did it connect? What symbol is used to show a town?

Look at the route which crossed Pennsylvania. To what fort did it lead? What is the symbol for fort?

What route led to Kentucky? To what settlement? Compare these three routes. Which led farthest inland? On which one could pioneers travel farthest by boat?

7 · How Our Country Gained the Louisiana Territory and Florida

Americans Were Interested in New Orleans

By 1800, thousands of pioneers had settled west of the Appalachians. The farmers raised corn, wheat, and other crops as well as cattle, hogs, and sheep. Some men roamed the woods, trapping wild animals and collecting furs. Others started sawmills for sawing logs into lumber. So Westerners had crops, meat, wool, hides, furs, and lumber to sell.

The people of the East were eager to buy the West's products. But there were no good roads for sending these products east. The Wilderness Road was too steep and rough for heavily-loaded wagons. Another route had to be found.

Soon, the pioneers began to use the Mississippi River as a highway. Find this river on the map on page 117. One of its chief branches is the long, crooked Ohio River. Point to the place where the Ohio River joins the Mississippi. Boats could float down the Ohio to the wide waters of the Mississippi. Then they could continue down the Mississippi to New Orleans.

At New Orleans, Spanish soldiers stopped American boats and forced their owners to pay a duty, or tax, on their goods.

Crops were shipped on slow clumsy flatboats. Usually, boatmen guided their boats to the middle of the river and let them drift southward with the current. Finally, they reached New Orleans.

As the years passed, more and more flatboats traveled up and down the Mississippi River. They were the chief cargo carriers for the Ohio and Mississippi valleys. They carried millions of dollars' worth of goods.

Shipping on the Mississippi helped New Orleans to become a busy port. Indeed, this port was the West's gateway to the sea and to the eastern United States. The boatmen unloaded their goods at New Orleans and stored them. As soon as possible, they were taken aboard ocean-going vessels. From New Orleans they were shipped to cities along the Atlantic coast, the West Indies, and parts of Europe.

Still, many Americans were worried about sending their goods to New Orleans. It did not belong to the United States and was sometimes an unfriendly place for Americans, as the following story shows.

Trouble at New Orleans. One cool November day, Judson Smith galloped into the little village of Four Corners on the Ohio River. He drew up in front of the country store and dashed in.

"'Morning, Jud," said the storekeeper. "You look upset! What's happened?"

"Plenty!" replied Jud. "Remember Joe Green and Jim Larsen?"

"Why, yes! Those young chaps own a flatboat and move goods down the river!" exclaimed the storekeeper. "They left Four Corners with grain and lumber way last spring."

"That's right," answered Jud. "They reached New Orleans but they had a bad time there. Their goods and boat were seized and they were marched to prison."

"Well, I never!" exclaimed the storekeeper. "Who told you?"

"Joe! He's back! Escaped and walked all the way from New Orleans. He's fighting mad about things down there. Says farmers better look for another route to send their goods East."

"Fiddlesticks!" declared the storekeeper. "The Mississippi's the best route. But we won't stand for bad treatment!" he added, pounding the counter.

"I should say not!" answered Jud. "The United States should buy New Orleans and be done with it."

Many Americans felt as Jud did. You may agree when you have read more about conditions there.

The early story of New Orleans and the Louisiana Territory. You learned how La Salle led a party down the Mississippi. He claimed for France all of the lands drained by this river, remember. He named this enormous region Louisiana. Some years later, the French started the settlement of New Orleans.

After the French and Indian War, France was forced to give England its lands east of the Mississippi. At the close of the Revolutionary War, as you know, these lands became a part of our country. They reached from the Appalachians to the Mississippi.

Spain had helped France during its long war. So, as payment, France gave Spain New Orleans and all of its remaining Louisiana lands. This area was west of the Mississippi River. It became known as the *Louisiana Territory*. As the map below shows, it stretched through the very heart of America. It reached from the Gulf of Mexico all the way to Canada and west to the Rocky Mountains. Its capital and most important settlement was New Orleans.

New Orleans remained under Spanish rule for a number of years. During this time, American boats had to get permission to load and unload goods at New Orleans. Furthermore, for this privilege, they had to pay a special tax.

By 1800, conditions for trade down the Mississippi looked very discouraging. A bold French general named Napoleon had become the ruler of France. He forced Spain to give back New Orleans and the Louisiana Territory.

This was disturbing news to Americans. They knew that the ambitious Napoleon had made France a powerful nation. He had conquered much of Europe. He had even sent soldiers to take over parts of the West Indies. The Louisiana Territory was at our back door. What would Napoleon do with it?

Now, farmers hardly dared to send crops to New Orleans, unless . . . . unless it could be bought. That was the answer, President Jefferson and Congress decided.

This map shows how the Louisiana Purchase increased the size of the United States. How many states did the United States have in 1803?

Purchased: A Seaport and a Huge Territory

A big bargain: The Louisiana Purchase. In 1803, two of our statesmen met with Napoleon's officials in Paris, France. The Americans were ready to offer two million dollars for New Orleans.

During the talks, one important French leader asked, "Why doesn't the United States buy the whole Louisiana Territory? We will sell it and New Orleans for $15,000,000."

The two Americans were astonished at this surprising offer. The Louisiana Territory covered over a million square miles. They had not dreamed of buying so much land. Furthermore, they did not have the Government's permission to do so.

Still, there was no way to talk over the matter with President Jefferson and Congress. Nor was there any way to rush messages across the sea. The telegraph and the telephone had not yet been invented, remember.

Our statesmen did not send a letter to ask what to do. They dared not wait several weeks for an answer. Instead, they decided themselves to accept France's offer. This business deal became known as the *Louisiana Purchase.*

The Louisiana Purchase added a huge area to our young country. It extended our borders west to the Rocky Mountains. It gave the United States the entire Mississippi River as well as the busy port of New Orleans.

The Louisiana Purchase pleased some people but not others. The farmers in the West were especially de-

delighted. Hunters, trappers, and some daring pioneers were happy about it, too. The new lands provided a wide area for adventure and settlement.

But many Easterners complained bitterly. They grumbled that fifteen million dollars was too much for an empty wilderness. They did not realize that the territory cost only about three cents an acre. Neither did they know how rich and fertile it was.

No one guessed then, that someday thirteen proud states would be carved from this vast region.

Soon, the United States gained still more frontier lands. They were the lands of Spanish Florida.

How Florida Became a Part of Our Country

Spain had owned Florida. Ponce de Leon claimed it for Spain early in the 1500's, you may recall. The Spaniards started the fort and little village of St. Augustine there in 1565. It was Florida's first permanent settlement. Just think! It was founded more than forty years before Jamestown began.

The Spaniards kept their hold on Florida for about two hundred years. But then, a change was made. After the French and Indian War, this land was given to England.

Florida under the English. The English divided this southeast region into two parts, East Florida, and West Florida. Find them on the map on page 117. In which one is St. Augustine located?

Notice that West Florida extended eastward from the Mississippi River along the Gulf of Mexico. This strip of land was from eight to forty miles in width. What territory of the United States lay north of West Florida?

Now locate East Florida on the map. See how far south it extended. Just as interesting, it was mostly a peninsula. A *peninsula* is a body of land which is almost surrounded by water.

Unfriendly Indians lived in the Floridas. Many had come to the Floridas from farther north. They had been driven off their lands by white settlers. But England found ways to keep peace with them in Florida. Also, it encouraged planters to settle on the rich-soiled lands. Some families came from neighboring Southern colonies. When the Revolutionary War broke out, many Loyalists fled to East Florida. There, they believed they could live happily under English rule.

Then Spain gained the Floridas back. Spain could not keep order. These lands became hiding places for thieves and other lawbreakers. Robbers roamed about, attacking, stealing, and killing. No plantation or settlement was safe and settlers lived in constant fear. Nor did they dare to ship crops down the rivers. Thieves lay in wait to seize boats and cargo.

In 1810, West Florida was added to the United States. For several years, many Florida settlers had wished for this. So had the pioneers who lived in the Mississippi Territory, to the north. No longer could they send their crops down the rivers. Nor were their plantations safe from attack. Robbers and Indians wandered across the border and threatened their lives.

The United States knew that it must protect its settlers. To make sure this was done, it offered to buy West Florida. When Spain refused to sell, our country took this region. Later on, its lands were divided among three new states, Louisiana, Mississippi, and Alabama.

Spaniards and blacks built St. Augustine around a fort.

Our country bought East Florida in 1819. Serious problems had developed here, also. Robbers and angry Indians stole across the border into Georgia and raided settlements there. Our government asked Spain to stop these attacks. But little was done. Finally, in 1819, Spain agreed to give up the peninsula. In return, the United States paid five million dollars.

East Florida is now occupied by our state of Florida. St. Augustine is located in this area, remember. Therefore, Florida can boast of having the oldest city in the United States.

During the early 1800's, other problems were disturbing our young country. Some of them got us into a war.

A War,
Then a Rush to
New Frontiers

France and England were at war with each other. Both countries needed meat, grain, and cotton from the United States. They were willing to pay high prices for these goods. But of course, neither country wanted such cargo to reach its enemy's ports. So there was much trouble at sea. The French captured many American ships that were on their way to England. The English navy seized an even larger number of American ships bound for France.

But another problem was even more serious. The English were searching our ships for sailors. Sometimes, American sailors were seized and put to work on English ships. England said that these sailors had been born in England and were therefore English citizens. England claimed that they had left the English navy for American ships where the pay was higher.

The United States demanded that the English stop searching our vessels. But the English government paid no attention to this request. Instead, more and more American ships and sailors were seized. Finally, the United States declared war on England.

The War of 1812 was fought between the United States and England. It lasted about two years. During that time, many battles were fought on land and on sea. One took place when Fort McHenry was fired on. Fort McHenry was important because it protected the city of Baltimore on Chesapeake Bay. During the battle to capture this fort, the words of "The Star-Spangled Banner" were written.

A young American lawyer, Francis Scott Key, had boarded a British ship in the bay. His business was to arrange for freeing a captured American friend. Because the battle raged so furiously, Key had to remain on the English vessel all night. He saw English gunfire pound the fort and bombs bursting against the dark sky. So he feared that the Americans would be forced to surrender.

But the first light of dawn brought good news. Key saw the American flag still floating proudly above the battered fort. He was so stirred that he wrote the inspiring words we now sing as our national anthem. As you may remember, they begin like this:

"Oh! say, can you see!"

Oh! say, can you see by the dawn's early light
What so proudly we hailed at the twilight's last gleaming?

The war ended in 1814. It was really a "tie," for neither side had won. But both countries were tired of fighting and agreed to sign a peace treaty.

Looking westward. Even before the war, many settlers had heard the call of the West. Some had left southern states to move into the Mississippi Territory. Thousands of others had settled in the Ohio country.

Still earlier, however, a few hunters and trappers wandered beyond the Mississippi River. They brought back amazing tales. They told of enormous grassy plains and huge herds of buffalo grazing there. They described towering mountains and rushing rivers, as well as strange Indian tribes.

Pioneers on the frontiers heard these tales first. They pieced together the bits of information and passed the "news" along. Still, no one seemed to know very much about this vast region west of the Mississippi. After the Louisiana Purchase, President Jefferson persuaded Congress that these lands should be explored. The next chapter will continue this story.

Do You Know?

1. Why the United States wanted to buy New Orleans?
2. How our country got Florida?
3. Why the War of 1812 was fought?

Can You Match Them?

Eleven descriptions are in List A. Write the numbers 1 to 11. Find the item in List B which matches each numbered description and write it after that number.

List A

1. A seaport on the Mississippi River
2. Land bought from France
3. Our President in 1803
4. A famous French general
5. The business deal with France
6. The price paid for this deal
7. The oldest city in the United States
8. Land nearly surrounded by water
9. When we gained West Florida
10. Lands added to our country in 1819
11. Author of our national anthem

List B

1810	New Orleans
James Monroe	East Florida
Spain	1812
peninsula	Louisiana Territory
Napoleon	England
island	Francis Scott Key
St. Augustine	Thomas Jefferson
$20,000,000	Louisiana Purchase
$15,000,000	West Florida

Some Things to Talk Over

1. Is the Mississippi River as important a water highway today as it was in the early part of the nineteenth century? Give reasons for your answer.

2. If the United States were buying the Louisiana Territory today, it would cost a great deal of money. Why? Why could it be purchased for about 3 cents an acre in 1803?

3. Why do countries fight wars?

Some Other Things to Do

1. Learn more about one of the following:
New Orleans   Napoleon   St. Augustine
The Louisiana Purchase   Francis Scott Key

2. Use the Geography Dictionary and the drawing on page 502 to review the meaning of the term *peninsula*. Draw a peninsula, coloring the land green and the water blue.

3. Draw a picture about some event described in Chapter 7. Write a legend beneath it. Have a committee choose the most attractive drawings to exhibit on the bulletin board.

4. Learn the words of "The Star-Spangled Banner" and discuss their meaning with your class. Sing this famous song together.

Thinking and Problem Solving

By this time, you know that there are several "thinking and problem solving" questions at the end of each chapter in your text. Probably your class has been talking over such questions.

Actually, all of us have problems to think through every day, and also many questions to answer. How well can you do this?

Here are some examples of questions;

1. How can we help to make our playground a safer place?

2. How should a person plan before going on a hike in a strange area?

3. Why aren't all rivers used as water highways?

Let's try to answer the last question. Read it over again. Then think of some reasons. Two might be:

1. Some rivers have falls and rapids and are too dangerous.

2. Water transportation may be too slow for some goods.

Now, copy Question 3, above, on a paper. Under it, write all the possible answers you can think of. Next, read them over carefully. Are you certain they are correct? And have you thought of all the reasons?

Some ways to check on your information and also get more are:

1. Read in books.
2. Ask people you know.
3. Study helpful pictures and maps.
4. Observe things around you that might suggest answers.

What you have done is called "Solving a Problem." It is a good way to help a person answer important questions.

8 · How the Oregon Territory Was Added

Lewis and Clark Explored the Northwest

Planning a great adventure. One day, President Jefferson sent for his secretary, Captain Meriwether Lewis.

"Captain Lewis," began the President, "You know that I have been eager for our country to explore the lands west of the Mississippi."

Captain Lewis nodded. "Yes, Mr. President. You've often mentioned this. And you want a trail blazed all the way to the Pacific."

"I do, indeed," replied Jefferson. "You are the man to explore this region. You have proven yourself a good leader and soldier. You have had experience in dealing with Indians and know the ways of the wilderness. I want you to lead a party west."

"That would be a big task, Mr. President. But I'm as anxious as you to see this job done," answered Captain Lewis.

"Good!" exclaimed Jefferson. "Then suppose you prepare for the venture. Choose a group of strong frontiersmen to go along, and be ready to leave next spring. Make plans to bring back reports and maps of the lands you see. We'll

The Lewis and Clark party traveled upstream from St. Louis on the Missouri River. Soldiers stood guard. Why was this done?

Many kinds of supplies were collected for the trip.

want you to explore the Missouri and other important rivers. We want to know if there is a water route to the Pacific. Also, we desire records about the plant and animal life. And you should collect as much information as possible about the Indian tribes."

"I shall do my best, Mr. President," answered Captain Lewis.

Jefferson asked another soldier and frontiersman, William Clark, to be Lewis's partner. The two men were close friends. Clark was a younger brother of daring George Rogers Clark. He had captured English forts west of the Appalachians during the Revolution, you remember.

Twenty-eight frontiersmen were chosen. Some were soldiers and skilled hunters and two were experienced boatmen. One was a blacksmith and several were expert builders. One was a cook. Another could speak the languages of several Indian tribes. Two men agreed to take

along their fiddles to provide music when there was spare time.

During the winter, the men prepared for the strenuous trip. They took long hikes and practiced shooting. Some arranged for supplies. In strong boxes they packed guns and gun powder, buckskin clothing, and warm blankets. Corn meal, flour, salt, and tea were also carefully packed. And notebooks for sketches and reports! Also dozens of bracelets, looking glasses, and other small presents for the Indians.

In May, 1804, the Lewis and Clark party set out for the Northwest. By this time, there were forty-five men in the group. One was a black named York. The men left from the small frontier settlement of St. Louis. Find it on the map on page 117. It is on the Mississippi River near the mouth of the muddy Missouri.

The explorers moved up the wide, twisting Missouri in three boats, a large keelboat and two long narrow canoes. The party traveled slowly, for the men were rowing upstream against swift currents.

At night, the explorers camped by the river's edge. By the light of their campfire, Lewis and Clark wrote reports of what they had seen. One man said in his diary:

Many mosquitoes and tiny gnats are swarming about us. Will they never stop? We are miserable with them.

Another wrote:

We have stumbled over many tough, thorny plants which we call the prickly pear. Some people call this the cactus. Its thorns are as sharp as needles.

Often the men stopped to explore. They saw deer, elk, bears, wolves, and foxes in the woods that reached back from the river. There were rabbits, squirrels, porcupines, and badgers. And beaver lived along the streams.

By November, the explorers had pushed up the crooked Missouri River for about a thousand miles. They had reached the wind-swept plains of what is now North Dakota. The weather was growing colder and snow was falling! So the men decided not to travel farther until spring.

The explorers camped on the northern plains for the winter. There they built a stout log shelter and called it Fort Mandan. Look for Fort Mandan on the map. The Mandans were friendly Indians who lived on the Dakota plains. They brought the white men gifts of beans, corn, pumpkins, and squashes.

During the winter, the Indians told the explorers many interesting stories. Some were about western mountains so high they nearly scraped the sky. We know that these were a part of the great Rocky Mountain System.

Other stories were about the Pacific Ocean. The Indians called it "Everywhere Salt Water." The Mandans also told of many rivers. But their tales of the "Mighty River of the West" interested Lewis and Clark the most. The explorers were sure there was such a giant river. They knew it emptied into the Pacific Ocean. They had heard how its wide mouth had been discovered nearly ten years before by an American sea captain. The captain had named it the Columbia River, using the name of his ship.

Lewis and Clark asked the Mandans many questions about the Columbia. Where did it begin? Through what kinds of lands did it flow? Where did it empty into the sea? But the Indians did not know the answers. "White man go west, find out," said the Mandan chief with signs. That was just what the explorers intended to do when spring came.

That winter, Lewis and Clark became acquainted with a French trapper and his Indian wife, Sacajawea. Several years before, young Sacajawea had been

Sacajawea watches the boats being loaded. Lewis and Clark are preparing to continue their journey up the Missouri after spending the winter near the present city of Bismarck, North Dakota.

125

kidnapped from her tribe and sold to the trapper. She knew some parts of the West well. So Lewis hired her and her husband as guides.

In April, when the snows began to melt, the party set out. Its smallest member was Sacajawea's tiny black-eyed baby boy. She carried him strapped to her back.

The explorers paddled north and west up the narrowing Missouri River. You can tell by the map that they crossed present-day Montana. As the river cut through the hills and low mountains, its currents became swifter. It was much harder to row the boats. One man wrote in his diary:

Our boats tipped over today, and we saw our records sink out of sight! It seemed for a moment that they were lost forever, but Sacajawea was quick to act. She dove into the cold water and rescued our valuable reports. How thankful we were!

One morning, the travelers reached thundering falls. Now they had to leave the river and tramp overland around the falls and the rapids. To carry their boats, they built carts with slices of logs for wheels. On the narrowing river again, the men rowed farther and farther. Finally, they came to the place where three different rivers joined the Missouri. The Indians called this place "Three Forks." It was at Three Forks that Sacajawea had been stolen, so she felt sure that her people lived nearby.

By this time the Rockies loomed higher and higher. Lewis and Clark knew they must soon leave their boats behind. They needed horses to carry the supplies, but they did not know where to get them.

Then the explorers met a group of Shoshone Indians. Sacajawea recognized the leader as her brother, the chief of his tribe. He greeted her warmly. In exchange for trinkets he gave the party some supplies, a dozen ponies, and a guide.

West across the Rockies and the "top of our continent." The explorers tramped on through the mountains. But they had many discouraging experiences. From one diary we learn:

We have been making our own trails. So many rocks push through the rough ground that our moccasins are worn through and our feet are cut and bleeding. The nights are cold and sharp. We are very hungry, but can find almost no game here.

The Rocky Mountains rise higher and higher. A heavy snow fell today. Slippery paths caused us to have a bad accident. Several of our horses fell down the mountainside and we could not rescue them. Our men must now carry more supplies.

After many weeks, the men reached the snow-covered "top of our continent." It is spoken of as the *Continental Divide.* It is called a "divide" because it forms a dividing line between the streams that flow eastward from the mountains and the streams that flow westward. Those on the east side flow toward the Mississippi River, whose waters finally reach the Gulf of Mexico and the Atlantic Ocean. Most of the streams on the west side hurry toward the Pacific. One of these is the Columbia River which you can locate on the map on page 117. Notice how the Columbia twists and turns on its way to the ocean.

Standing on the Continental Divide, the explorers looked west. They saw

Climbing higher and higher, the explorers finally reached the Continental Divide.

mountains stretching on and on, range after range! The map shows this mountainous region. Find the rugged Bitterroot Mountains.

The explorers had neither maps nor compass to guide them. They were weary and nearly starved; yet they pushed on. After many days, they tramped down the last steep slopes. Ahead were low green hills, pleasant meadows, and a shining river. On its banks, the men camped and rested. There they built five sturdy canoes.

Down winding rivers to the Pacific. As the adventurers paddled far down the river, they discovered that it joined a broader waterway. It was the Snake River. Find this twisting Snake River on the map. They followed it for many days until they reached a place where it poured into a wide river. "Surely this is the 'Mighty River of the West,'" declared Lewis. "This is the Columbia! I know it!"

Now the men had to guide their canoes through swirling rapids and rough waters. Finally, Captain Lewis knew they were approaching the Pacific. The air had a salty flavor and a thick ocean fog hung low. Indeed, when this thick curtain lifted, the explorers saw white-capped waves breaking against the shore.

At last, after about a year and a half, the brave band had reached its goal. With glad hearts, the men gave thanks for this victory. One leader wrote in his diary: *"The ocean is at last in view. Oh, what joy!"*

During the winter of 1805–1806, the explorers camped near the Pacific. For shelter, they built cabins surrounded by a strong stockade. After repairing the guns, much time was spent hunting. Deer and elk were plentiful and provided meat as well as skins for new moccasins and clothing. Many days were also spent exploring. Though this region was a rainy one, it had fine fertile valleys and the hills were covered with tall straight trees. The Oregon country looked like a good land for fur traders and settlers.

The next spring, the explorers started east. Their notebooks were full of interesting reports, sketches, and maps. In addition, they carried samples of skins, furs, and rocks tied in bundles. Finally, in September, the weary men reached St. Louis, their starting point. Their travels had taken nearly two and a half years. But no wonder! They had traveled about 8,000 miles, through all kinds of rugged wilderness country.

Lewis and Clark helped our country in many ways. Their explorations gave the United States a claim to the Ore-gon lands west of the Louisiana Territory. Find these lands on the map on page 117. The Oregon country stretched from California to Alaska, and it extended about 800 miles inland from the Pacific Ocean.

Lewis and Clark brought back much valuable information about the vast lands west of the Mississippi. They described plains, mountains, rivers, and trails they had followed. They told about Indian tribes and plentiful wild game.

These reports stirred up much interest. Hunters and trappers were especially happy about news of fur-bearing animals. Soon some of them ventured westward.

Lewis and Clark and their party see the Pacific Ocean for the first time. Imagine how excited they must have been! It had taken them about a year and a half to reach this spot.

These Mountain Men have caught a beaver in one of their traps. Notice the beaver lodge in the stream.

Traders and Trappers Journeyed to Oregon

Since 1787, American trading ships had visited Northwest harbors. They sailed around South America and up the Pacific coast to the Oregon country. There, they traded with the Indians.

When a trading ship entered a harbor, many canoes raced to meet it. But the Indians could not always be trusted. So a captain allowed only one or two on board ship at a time. The Indians had velvet-like sea otter skins and other rich furs to "sell." These were traded for pieces of bright cloth, glittering glass beads, and shining knives. The Indians did not realize how valuable their beautiful furs were. They did not guess what large fortunes fur traders made selling the furs in the East.

One famous fur trader built a trading post in Oregon. His name was John Jacob Astor. This New York businessman had become wealthy buying and selling furs. One day, Astor heard about the many fur-bearing animals Lewis and Clark had seen in the Northwest. "I shall build a fur-trading post there," said he.

Astor sent one group of traders and trappers overland to Oregon, and another group by boat around South America. At the mouth of the Columbia River, Astor's men built the settlement of Astoria. Can you find it on the map on page 130.

Astoria was not a successful trading post. Furthermore, it was seized by the British during the war of 1812. Still, it helped to strengthen our claim to Oregon lands.

Within a few years, dozens of daring Americans ventured into the vast Northwest. At first, most of them were fur traders and trappers.

Traders and trappers helped to conquer the Northwest. They roamed far inland to set traps and trade with the

Indians. They explored rivers and valleys and found passes through the mountains. So, they were sometimes called mountain men.

They were pathfinders and trail blazers, too. They discovered where the rivers were easiest to cross. They located and marked the easiest routes across the plains and mountains. The information they gathered opened the way for pioneer settlers.

Kit Carson was one famous mountain-man trail blazer. He had learned much about the West while trapping, hunting, and guiding parties.

James Beckwourth, was a daring black pathfinder. He, too, had wandered through the mountains searching for beaver. While exploring in northern California, he discovered the lowest pass in the Sierra Nevada. Today, it is known as Beckwourth Pass.

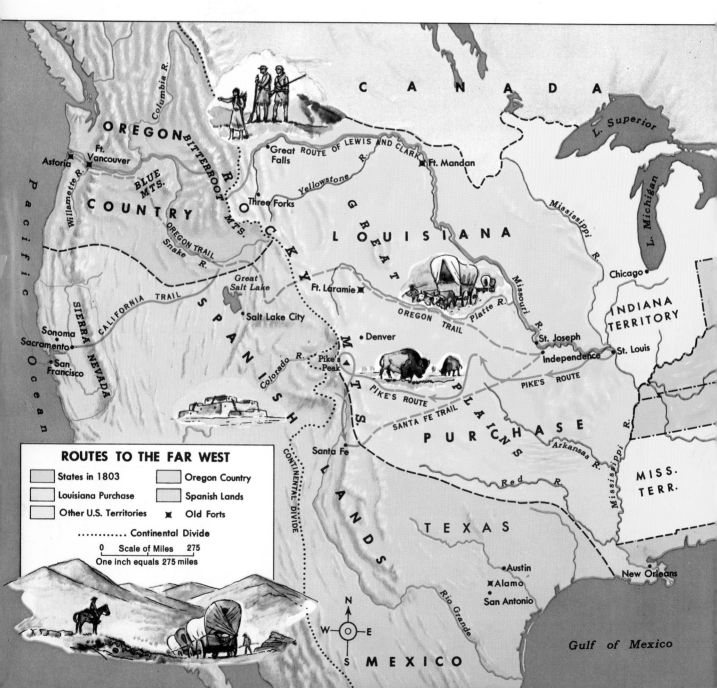

ROUTES TO THE FAR WEST

States in 1803
Louisiana Purchase
Other U.S. Territories
Oregon Country
Spanish Lands
✖ Old Forts
.... Continental Divide

0   Scale of Miles   275
One inch equals 275 miles

The First Settlers Traveled to the Oregon Country

Missionaries were the first settlers in Oregon. In 1834, Jason Lee and his helpers journeyed west with a group of trappers. Lee settled in the green Willamette Valley to work among the Indians. Locate this valley on the map on the opposite page. Two years later, a missionary doctor, Dr. Marcus Whitman, went west to what is now the state of Washington. His wife and several friends also made the journey. Mrs. Whitman wrote:

The Indians thought we women were a very strange sight. They had not seen white women before, I suppose. We rode our horses side saddle as is the fashion for women. But we noticed that the Indian women rode like men.

Oregon's first settlers encouraged others to move west. They wrote letters East, praising their new homeland. When Lee and Whitman returned East for workers and supplies, they bragged about the rich Oregon country. Soon other settlers journeyed West. They, too, wrote encouraging letters about Oregon, letters like this:

Truly we have come to a wonderful land! The soil is very rich and grows crops all the year round. We raise tall wheat and large fruit. The pastures are high with grass. There is more than enough to feed many horses, herds of cattle, and flocks of sheep.

Huge forests of oak, pine, cedar, and fir grow here. We are cutting trees and putting up cabins as fast as we can. Salmon swim up the Columbia. They are fine to eat. The climate is pleasant and mild. It never gets very cold, although we have plenty of rain.

We find this country delightful and hope that many of our friends will someday come here to live.

Such letters were passed around from one family to another and even printed in newspapers. Thousands of people heard about the faraway Oregon country. Some, like the Conwells of Massachusetts, decided to move there. They made plans to follow the Oregon Trail.

The Oregon Trail began at Independence, Missouri. Find Independence on the map on page 130. This settlement was located in the western part of present-day Missouri on the Missouri River. Now look for the Oregon Trail and trace it west. See how much shorter and more direct it was than the route Lewis and Clark took.

People from many states journeyed to Independence in their covered wagons. They camped there until forty or fifty wagons were ready to go on together. A group of wagons was called a *wagon train.*

The long trip to Oregon took nearly five months. So it was necessary to carry large quantities of food and some other supplies. These things could be bought at the warehouses in Independence.

Among the foods which the Conwells purchased were flour, sugar, smoked meats, coffee, salt, and dried fruit. Also they bought such articles as extra shoes and boots, seed potatoes, spare wheels and other wagon parts, and ammunition. From their home they had brought feather beds, blankets, dishes, and other household belongings.

Sometimes rafts were used to float the wagons across deep rivers.

West on the Oregon Trail

Headed West. May seemed the best month for starting west. By that time, the days were sunny and warm, and fresh new grass covered the plains. The pioneers depended on grass for food for their cattle, sheep, oxen, and horses.

A wagon train often hired a mountain man as its guide. He knew the trails and the easiest places to cross the rivers. Also he could locate the best camping places. Each wagon train chose one man as captain and leader. Mr. Conwell was chosen captain of his wagon train. But a committee of several men was elected to help the captain make the rules.

Nearly everyone in a wagon train had a special job or two. Some men guided the wagons and some drove the livestock. Blacksmiths kept the wagons in good repair and their wheels greased with bear or wolf fat. Skilled marksmen shot game for meat and kept watch for unfriendly Indians. These guards rode horses as you can see in the picture on this page.

The women cooked meals and did the washing when they could. Also, they cared for the children and the sick. Even the children had some chores. They gathered firewood and helped to care for their younger brothers and sisters.

On the trail, the day began very early. At four o'clock in the morning, guards fired their guns to awaken everyone. Soon the women were busy cooking breakfast over the campfires. Meanwhile, the men and boys rounded up the horses and cattle.

After breakfast the bedding was put away. Then the wagons were loaded and the oxen hitched to them. Most wagons were pulled by teams of oxen. These big patient animals were stronger than horses.

About seven o'clock, a shrill bugle blew the starting signal for the day's march. Then, one by one, the wagons creaked down the trail. What clouds of dust they stirred up! At noon the travelers stopped for a quick lunch while their animals grazed and rested nearby. Soon, though, the long line of wagons were rumbling onward again. By late afternoon, the pioneers guided their wagons into a large circle. Within this protected circle, they built campfires and cooked the evening meal.

After supper, the children played and the older people talked. Some evenings many pioneers sang and danced while a few played violins. Just before bedtime, when the campfires burned low, the travelers often sang a hymn.

The pioneers crossed wide plains. They found that these stretched west from the Mississippi to the Rockies. The plains nearest the Mississippi were gently rolling lands patched with trees. They were carpeted with tall grass and were known as *prairies*.

West of the prairies, the pioneers came to drier lands, the Great Plains. Find them on the map on page 90. Little rain fell in this region. By early summer its short coarse grass began to burn in the sun's scorching heat.

Some rivers cut through the plains. The Oregon Trail followed one, the Platte, for many miles. Do you see the Platte on the map? There were no bridges over the Platte or any other river in the West. When the water was shallow, the oxen and other animals splashed through it easily. But crossing a deep river was harder. Sometimes, the men chained each team of oxen to the wagon in front as well as to its own wagon. The oxen then swam across the river, pulling the floating wagons.

If the river was very deep, the pioneers built rafts to carry their wagons. Now and then, a raft tipped over.

One woman wrote in her diary:

I am sad tonight. My beautiful marble-topped mahogany table slipped off the raft today. It was soon swallowed up in the quicksands at the river's edge. I prized this table so! It was a wedding gift from Aunt Ann.

At the river's edge, the travelers often saw wild animals drinking. Among them were deer and antelope. But the buffalo were the animals the pioneers feared.

Enormous herds of buffalo roamed the plains. Millions of them fed on the grass of the plains. When they were frightened, they charged across the land. This was known as a buffalo stampede and was dreaded by every pioneer.

One day, Mr. Conwell's wagon train watched a stampede. While the pioneers were eating breakfast, they noticed huge clouds of dust sweeping towards them.

"It's a buffalo stampede!" shouted Dan Conwell. "Women, children, into the wagons! Men, get your guns! Hurry!"

As the clouds of dust rolled closer, the thunder of hoofs shook the ground. The great dark animals charged forward bellowing angrily.

Watching the stampede was a terrifying experience. Some pioneers had been killed during such stampedes. Fortunately for the Conwells and their friends, the animals were frightened off by the men shooting their guns. The buffalo herd swung to the right as it approached the wagons.

A few animals stumbled and fell, but the others plunged ahead. Finally, the last ones thundered by. Then the men went out to count the dead animals. They found enough to provide hides for many robes, and meat for days and days.

To keep the meat from spoiling, the pioneers cut it into long thin strips. Then they dried it over a bed of coals. The dried meat was called jerky. Long before, Indians had taught pioneers how to preserve meat in this way.

In time, white men killed most of the buffalo. Unfortunately, some frontiersmen became buffalo hunters. Bold young William F. Cody was just such a hunter. He was hired to supply buffalo meat for workers, when a railroad was built across the plains in the 1860's. He shot so many of the big clumsy animals that he was nicknamed "Buffalo Bill." Other frontiersmen killed these beasts chiefly for their hides. Buffalo hides sold for good prices in the days of the pioneers.

The plains Indians were also skillful buffalo hunters. They valued these animals especially for their meat and hides. The Indians made tents, moccasins, and robes from buffalo hides. They fashioned cups and spoons from the horns, and tools from the bones. Strong bow strings and thread could be made from the muscles.

Indeed, the plains Indians depended on the buffalo for their living. But white men destroyed these animals by the thousands. This made the Indians so angry that they often went on the warpath.

In time, so many buffalo were killed that less than a thousand could be found in all of our country. Finally, laws were passed to protect the few that were left. Today, there are about 5,000 in the United States. Most of them roam over protected areas in our western plains region.

Women faced loneliness, hard work, and danger on the frontier.

Women shared the dangers and hard work with the men. They dried and prepared the meat of animals that were killed. They collected and prepared

Buffalo products made by the Indians.

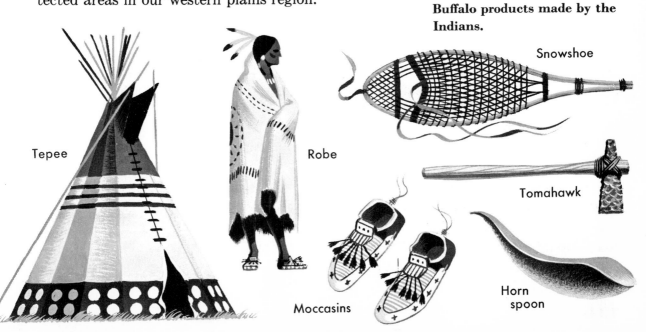

Tepee

Robe

Snowshoe

Tomahawk

Moccasins

Horn spoon

plants for medicines. They cooked the food and made the clothing. They cared for the children and often taught them to read and write. They looked after the sick.

When farms were started on the frontier, the wife worked as hard as her husband. She usually made her own soap and candles. She dried meats and fruits, prepared corn, and churned the butter. Often she spun the yarn and wove the cloth from which she made the family's clothing. Also she often helped with the farm work.

And always she shared the dangers and the loneliness of moving westward and living on the frontier.

Beyond the plains, towered the snow-peaked Rockies. The Indians called them "the Shining Mountains," because their snowy peaks shone in the sun. As the map on page 130 shows, these mountains stretch from Canada into Mexico. They extend through lands that are now parts of Montana, Wyoming, Colorado, Utah, and New Mexico.

The pioneers thought the Rockies were well-named. Even though they were patched with snow, their steep, high slopes were bare and rocky. The Rockies are young mountains, remember. They have not yet been worn round and smooth by weather as have the Appalachian Mountains.

The highest slopes in the Rockies have no timber. There, the weather is too cold for trees to grow. The place where the trees stop growing is called the *timber line*. The pioneers could see where this timber line began. But they noticed, too, that the lower slopes were thickly covered with forests.

The Oregon Trail led through a pass in the Rockies. The map on page 130 shows where it crossed the mountains. Indeed, as higher peaks loomed up ahead, eleven-year-old John Conwell became worried. "How can our wagons climb those steep mountains?" he asked.

"Never fear, my boy!" replied the guide. "We will not cross the high peaks. There is a better way through a wide pass! We will climb a little at a time. Up some 'hills' and down! Through a pleasant high valley. Then up more 'hills' and down! Sometimes we will crawl along slowly; but we'll manage!"

After many weeks, the pioneers reached the Continental Divide. "We are crossing through the top of our continent," exclaimed the guide. Far to the west stretches the Oregon country."

"Way over there?" asked John. "Is all that land the Oregon country?"

"Indeed it is," replied the guide. "It extends for hundreds of miles from here to the Pacific Ocean. It's still a two months' journey to the Willamette Valley where you will settle."

Steep hills sometimes cost the pioneers many belongings. One day, the Conwell party rested at the bottom of a steep slope. "Look, Mother," exclaimed John. "There's a plow rusting over there!'

"And a bedstead!" added Susan Conwell. Why were they left here?"

"To make the wagons lighter, I suppose," answered Mrs. Conwell. "The hills ahead are rough and steep."

At that very moment, Mr. Conwell called to his wife, "We're in trouble, Nora. The wagons are too heavy."

"That's a pity," answered Mrs. Conwell. "We've nothing to spare."

"Half of our seed potatoes, maybe," suggested Mr. Conwell. "And the mahogany bed and dresser."

Mrs. Conwell's eyes filled with tears, but she was a brave pioneer. "I suppose so," she said, "but it grieves me deeply."

The other wagons also unloaded some goods. Then the men yoked the cows with oxen to help pull the wagons. The picture above gives a hint of this hard climb.

Farther on, stone cliffs rose above a river. As the travelers rested here, they realized that many other pioneers had passed this way. Some had carved their names on the rocks. John and his friends decided that they, too, would leave their names on a large rock.

The long journey west was full of hardships. You already have learned about some of them. Months of crawling along rough, dusty trails! Long hot days of blistering summer heat! Dangerous rivers and high mountains to cross!

Sometimes Indians attacked and stole horses and other goods. Some days there was only a little water to drink. At times, all that could be found was bitter and made many pioneers sick. Also the travelers had to eat the same kind of foods, day after day. Often, they felt like seven-year-old Alice Conwell. She said, "I'm tired of eating fried meat and corn cakes!"

"So am I, dear," agreed her mother. "But there is little else." Then, with a twinkle in her eye, she added, "To-night, we'll have corn cakes and fried meat."

There were no doctors to take care of the sick or of babies born on the long journey. And nothing could be done for the thin, dying animals who dropped along the trail.

Thousands of brave pioneers bore hardships willingly. Most of these people were farmers. They knew that in Oregon they could buy fine fertile land very cheaply. Still, they were always glad when journey's end was near.

Journey's end. One cool October evening, the Conwells and their friends sat about their crackling campfire. How excited they were! Captain Conwell had just announced that the party would reach Willamette Valley in a few days.

As the campfires died down, Captain Conwell began to speak. "The land of promise is very near," he said. "Let us thank God for our safe journey."

Two days later, John Conwell felt a new tingle of excitement. "Whoopee!" he shouted. "We made it to Oregon!"

His mother smiled, "Yes! And I hope by the time you grow up, Oregon will be a state!"

One day, Mrs. Conwell's dream came true. Let's learn how that happened.

How Oregon Became a State

More and more pioneers moved to the Oregon country. Some went to hunt and trap, but the largest number were settlers. They built villages and laid out farms.

But their land was not a state. They could not vote for the President of the United States or for members of Congress. They could not choose their governor. Indeed, they were citizens of a poorly-governed region. They wanted their land to become a state as soon as possible.

Both the United States and England had claimed the Oregon country. And each nation had good reasons for its claim. England's famous Sir Francis Drake had visited the Oregon coast many years before. Then during the American Revolution, Captain Cook had claimed Oregon for England. In addition, the English had built trading posts in the Columbia River Valley.

Still, the United States believed it should have Oregon. The American seaman, Captain Gray had visited it and discovered the Columbia River. Lewis and Clark had led a party of explorers through

part of it. John Jacob Astor had built the trading settlement of Astoria in Oregon. American fur traders had explored it. Furthermore, many American pioneers were settling in Oregon.

Neither country was willing to give up its claim. So some leaders felt that the matter should be settled by a war. But others urged a wiser way, talking things over at a conference, or meeting. Finally, in 1846, a conference was held.

The United States and England decided to divide the Oregon country. Representatives of the two countries met together and agreed on a *compromise*. In a compromise, each party gives up a part of what he at first wanted.

England agreed that the United States should have the land south of what is now the boundary line of Canada. Find this southern part of the Oregon country on the map on page 139. As you can see, it contained land which now forms the states of Oregon, Washington, and Idaho, and parts of Wyoming and Montana.

The United States agreed that Great Britain should have the northern part of the Oregon country. This part is now called British Columbia. It is a very important part of Canada.

In 1859, Oregon became a state. At last, Congress allowed it to join the Union. How the brave settlers welcomed this news! They celebrated with loud cheers and singing.

Meanwhile, many other Americans had moved to lands far south of Oregon. For a long time, this region had been called the *Spanish Southwest*. One part of it had been explored while Jefferson was President. Captain Zebulon Pike was sent to map its lands, as you will learn later.

This map shows how the Oregon Country was divided between the United States and Canada · What States or parts of states came from the area taken by our country? Now find our part of the Oregon Country on the map on page 151.

Some Review Questions

1. Why were Lewis and Clark sent on an expedition?

2. What route did Lewis and Clark take? Why did the expedition take so long a time?

3. What was the Oregon country? Why was it called a rich hunting ground?

4. How did missionaries help to settle the Oregon country?

5. What were some hardships the pioneers faced on their travels west?

6. How was the Oregon country divided between Britain and the United States?

Is It True?

Write the numbers 1 to 10 on paper. Read the following sentences carefully. If a statement is true, write *yes* after its number. If it is not true, write *no*.

1. The Lewis and Clark Expedition set out in 1804. *yes*

2. The Lewis and Clark Expedition followed the Mississippi River. *no*

3. Sacajawea was a faithful Indian guide. *yes*

4. Lewis and Clark finally reached the Pacific Ocean. *yes*

5. A large group of covered wagons is called a wagon train. *yes*

6. Only the United States had good reasons for claiming the Oregon country. *yes*

7. The United States and England went to war to decide who would have the Oregon country. *no*

8. John Jacob Astor built the trading post of Astoria in Oregon. *yes*

9. The trip overland to Oregon took about two months. *no*

10. The route which led to the Northwest was called the Oregon Trail. *yes*

Thinking with Your Class

1. How do we use the Oregon Trail today? What would you see along it? How would a trip on it be different from the Conwell's journey?

2. What does the phrase, "conquering mountains" mean? How have we conquered the mountains of our country?

3. Why is a compromise often a wise way to settle a quarrel?

4. Lewis and Clark did not turn back, even though they suffered many hardships and were often discouraged. Do you keep trying when you are tempted to give up? Why is this important?

Things to Do

1. Read a book about William F. Cody.

2. Learn all you can about buffaloes. How does our Government now protect these animals?

3. Write a short story about one of the following:

Captain Lewis   Buffalo Bill
Captain Clark   Jason Lee
Sacajawea   Dr. Marcus Whitman

4. Among the dances and games which the pioneers enjoyed were

Pop Goes the Weasel
Here We Go 'round the Mountain
Sandy Land
Captain Jinks
Little 'Liza Jane

Ask your teacher if you may sing and play some of them.

5. Help your class make a mural. A *mural* is a long band of pictures extending across a wall. See if your class can make a mural showing pioneers traveling to Oregon.

Use a wide strip of heavy wrapping paper or the back of a roll of wallpaper. Fasten the paper along a blackboard in your classroom. Plan what will be shown on the mural and arrange for groups to sketch the main ideas on paper. Sketch the best drawings on the mural. Draw them with chalk and color with crayons, water colors, calcimine, or poster paints.

Let's Measure Distance

Turn to the map on page 130. How many miles does one inch equal on it? Use this scale to measure some distances.

1. How many miles is it from St. Louis to Independence? Place the end of your ruler on the symbol for St. Louis. The distance between the two settlements measures a little less than one inch. How many miles is one inch on this map? Independence, then, is about 250 miles west of St. Louis.

2. How far is it from St. Louis to Fort Laramie? Measure this distance with your ruler. Is it about three inches? Then let's multiply 3 times 275 to get the distance.

3. Find the distance from St. Louis to San Francisco.

More about Problem Solving

Here are some other suggestions to remember after your problem-solving research:

1. Be ready to take part when it is your turn.

2. Stick to the main points of the question or problem.

3. Be sure to share only accurate information.

4. Be ready to share materials which may help to solve a problem or answer a question. You may wish to:

a. Read a helpful sentence or two from a book.

b. Point out certain details in a picture or on a map.

c. Report information gained from talking to experts.

5. Base your final opinion or ideas on facts rather than on guesses.

6. Be courteous and helpful even though you disagree with the information or opinions of others.

9 · Texas and the Spanish Southwest Become Part of Our Country

From Frontier Boy to Explorer

Zebulon Pike grew up in wilderness country. His father was an army officer on duty west of the Appalachians. Captain Pike helped to protect pioneers who were settling on the frontier.

Zeb's family moved often, so he had little chance to attend school. Still, he learned to read, write, spell, and do arithmetic. Just as important for those days, Zeb learned how to live in the rough wilderness country. Many wild animals such as rabbits, squirrels, and deer lived near his home. Also there were panthers and wildcats roaming about, and wolves and bears. Zeb knew he must learn to shoot well and practiced target shooting month after month.

The wilderness was Indian country, too. Zeb got acquainted with some of the Indians. He learned to talk with them and understand their ways. How he admired the strong daring braves!

Zeb longed to be strong and tall, but he was small. Still, he was wiry and quick and faced danger like a hero. But then, someday he intended to be a soldier.

The boy's dream came true when he was fifteen. He joined the United States Army and served under his father.

Later on, Pike became an explorer. He led a group to the northern part of the Louisiana Territory. The weather was bitterly cold and the party suffered many hardships. But he did his job well. Some months later, he was asked to explore lands in the southwestern part of the Louisiana Territory.

Pike learned useful skills from the Indians.

Pike Learned about Southwestern Lands

Captain Pike set out from St. Louis in July, 1806. In his party were twenty-two soldiers and a doctor. Many of the men had traveled with Pike on his earlier journey. They volunteered to go with him again.

The countryside was green and beautiful. Grassy plains stretched as far as the eye could see. As you know, gently rolling plains extend from the Mississippi west to the Rockies. Wild life was plentiful on these grasslands. Frequently, the men saw herds of buffalo, as well as deer and antelope. Also there were thousands of strange little prairie dogs.

Pike's orders were to explore along the Arkansas and Red Rivers and find the source of each one. The *source* of a river is the place where it begins.

Pike crossed the plains and the Rockies. You can trace his route on the map on page 130. Notice that finally the party came to the Arkansas River. By this time, winter had begun.

One day, Pike saw a strange-looking blue "cloud" in the distance. Soon he realized that the "cloud" was a huge snow-crowned mountain. It was a part of the Rockies. Its peak stood out because it towered so high.

Later, Pike and his men set out to climb the lofty peak. But there was no trail and the weather was dreadfully cold. Deep snow covered the peak's steep rocky slopes and blocked the way. Pike finally turned back. Still his attempt was not forgotten. Today, this magnificent mountain is named Pikes Peak. Just think! It is nearly two and a half miles above sea level.

For many weeks, Pike searched for the source of the Arkansas River. Snow fell day after day and icy winds blew. The horses were starving and the men had to carry their own supplies through snowdrifts. Hunting was poor and the explorers were often hungry as well as half frozen.

Finally, the men found the headwaters of the Arkansas in a canyon in the Rockies. There, it was just a small swift stream tumbling down over rocks.

Soon, the explorers began a search for the Red River. They wandered southwest. The map on page 130 shows where they went. They entered a part of New Spain. Americans called it the *Spanish Territory*, or the Spanish Southwest. Locate it on the map. See how it extended all the way to the Pacific and north to the Oregon country. Coronado's party from Mexico had claimed these lands long before.

With Pike in the Spanish Southwest. In these sunny lands Pike and his men found desert-like plains and ranges of mountains. In some sections were huge bright-colored cliffs. From a distance they appeared to be splendid castles.

Pike's party learned that many Indians lived in the Southwest. Some lived in villages of apartment-like buildings of mud brick, or adobe. These buildings had thick walls and were several stories high. The top of each story served partly as a porch for the story above.

Such buildings had many rooms. Each room was occupied by a different family.

Each room had a firepit for cooking food. The smoke escaped through a hole in the roof. The rooms at the ground level usually had no doorways. Can you think why? To enter such a room, a person climbed up a ladder to his roof. Then he went down another ladder through a hole in his roof. When there was danger, the ladders could be removed.

The Spaniards called these villages pueblos. *Pueblo* is the Spanish word for village. So we call these people Pueblo Indians.

These Indians were farmers and sheep herders. They grew small patches of corn, beans, and pumpkins. They raised sheep and goats to provide meat and wool for clothing. They wove beautiful baskets and handsome blankets and made pottery.

Other Indians lived in houses built of earth and logs. But they often moved from one place to another. They raised a few sheep and were expert buffalo hunters.

While Pike and his men were exploring, Spaniards spotted them. They decided that the explorers were spies sent by the United States. So the Americans were arrested and taken to the Spanish city of Santa Fe. Find Santa Fe on the map.

Pioneers from Mexico

Santa Fe began before the Pilgrims came to America. It was started by Juan Onaté. He led a large party north from Mexico to start a colony. In his party were his wife and family and nearly 130 other families. There were also soldiers, missionaries, and a large number of skilled workmen.

Many of the colonists rode horses. Mules and carts carried supplies and even

Pike explores the Southwest.

The Palace of the Governors.

dishes and books. More than 7000 animals were driven behind the carts. There were extra horses and mules, as well as cattle and sheep. Onaté had planned carefully for this new colony.

The colony became known as New Mexico. The Mexicans made friends with some of the Indians. They taught them how to build carts and weave cotton cloth. They showed the Indian farmers how to grow crops like wheat, peas, and onions. They helped them to start apple, peach, and pear trees. The Indians shared their foods. They showed the colonists where to find honey and nuts.

Santa Fe became the capital of New Mexico in 1610. It is the oldest capital in our country. Santa Fe's most famous building is the *Palace of the Governors,* shown above. For many years, the work of government in New Mexico was carried on here. It is the oldest government building in the United States.

The Palace of the Governors is partly Spanish-Mexican in style and partly Indian. The colonists used ideas from their Spanish ancestors. One was adding covered walkways along a building.

Notice how round logs extend beyond the walls. They support the roof. The Pueblo Indians used logs in this way. They did not cut them off at the wall. Instead they saved them for use on a larger building if needed later on. Big logs were scarce in this dry land. The clever Indians were careful not to waste them. They continued to build in this way when they worked for the Mexican colonists.

So a charming Spanish-Mexican-Indian style of building grew up. It is popular today in many parts of the Southwest.

Pike and his men were brought to this Spanish-Mexican capital, Santa Fe. After they were freed, they returned to the United States. You can imagine how much interesting information they had to share.

Other Americans Became Interested in the Southwest

Hunters, trappers, and traders were especially interested in Pike's reports. The plucky young explorer brought back news of much wild game. He told of finding rivers where beaver and otter might be trapped.

Another thing, Pike believed that Santa Fe's people needed American goods. He said that a successful trader might make money in this lonely settlement. He warned, however, that traders might be jailed. Santa Fe was a part of Mexico and was governed by Spain. Spain did not want its people to trade with outsiders.

Then in 1821, Mexico won its freedom. After that, some frontiersmen began to do business in the Southwest.

Trading drew Americans to Santa Fe. The first hardy traders loaded goods on mule pack trains and set out from Missouri. After traveling southwest about 900 miles they reached Santa Fe.

As the traders led their mules into the town's *plaza*, or center square, people crowded around. They pushed and shouted for goods. They bought cloth, nails, tea, salt, tobacco, knives, ribbon, and many other articles! And they paid well in silver, gold, and hides. In fact, this business proved so successful that some Americans made plans to take large wagon trains to Santa Fe. "A wagon train could make a fortune!" exclaimed one hopeful trader.

Other frontiersmen shook their heads. "You couldn't travel to Santa Fe with a wagon train," they declared. "The trail is too dangerous." But the adventurers were determined. They blazed the *Santa Fe Trail.*

The people of Santa Fe were eager to buy the goods of American traders.

The Santa Fe Trail became the chief route to the Southwest. Find this route on the map on page 130. It started at Independence, Missouri. It crossed plains cut by deep rivers. It led across hot desert lands dotted with thorny cactus and gray-green sagebrush.

Along the Santa Fe Trail, men saw herds of buffalo and antelope as well as many rattlesnakes and long-tailed lizards. At night, the cries of hungry wildcats and the sharp yips of coyotes echoed across the land.

Sometimes robbers attacked the traders. There were also other dangers on the long, hard journey. But the men dreaded especially the sixty-mile stretch of hot, dry, sun-baked desert. On it, they could not find water for themselves or their animals. Crossing this blistering land was almost unbearable. Still, some traders continued to guide their wagons over the Santa Fe Trail, year after year.

Many Americans started farms in southern Texas.

Meanwhile, exciting events were taking place in the part of the Southwest known as Texas. Find Texas on the map on page 130. Although Texas was ruled by Mexico, it was attracting thousands of daring American settlers.

Many Pioneers Flocked to Texas

Moses Austin opened the way for pioneers in Texas. He had been trading with Spaniards and Indians in Texas. Traveling through this wide land, he had crossed lonely rolling plains. In the north, wild horses and wild game roamed here and there. And there were a few scattered tribes of Indians.

Farther south, Spanish priests had built churches called *missions*. There, Indians were taught the Christian religion as well as trades. Forts were put up near the missions and small settlements grew up

close by. One of the most important was San Antonio.

Austin had found southeastern Texas much to his liking. It received plenty of rainfall. Its mild climate and rich soil seemed just right for growing cotton and other crops. "This is a fine place for pioneers to settle!" declared Austin. "There is room for thousands of families. I must bring Americans here."

This ambitious adventurer then persuaded the Mexican Government to give him a large grant of land. Soon after his return to the United States, however, Austin became seriously ill. "I cannot live much longer," he said to his son, Stephen. "You must carry on my work."

Stephen Austin encouraged many pioneers to settle in Texas. He made speeches and wrote letters praising Texas as the finest region in the whole world. He promised that good land could be bought very cheaply. For just twelve and a half cents an acre!

Many pioneers hurried to Texas. Austin himself led hundreds of families to the new frontier. He named his first settlement Austin. You can find it on the map on page 504. Today, Austin is the capital of Texas and Stephen Austin is often called "The Father of Texas!"

Thousands of Americans set out. Left behind on their homes were signs like these: "Gone to Texas" and "Starting from Scratch in the Southwest."

Many people traveled in covered wagons. Fathers and older sons rode ahead as scouts. They carried long rifles to shoot turkeys, deer, and other wild game. They also kept watch for Indians.

By 1835, almost 30,000 Americans had poured into Texas. They came from nearly every state in the Union. But the largest number were from the South. They planned to grow cotton, rice, and sugar.

Some Texas pioneers had a hard life. One settler wrote this letter to his brother back home in Virginia:

Dear Brother John,

At last we are settled in the Southwest! But it was a long journey. As you know, we came through the Cumberland Gap to Kentucky. At the Ohio River, we hired a flatboat to bring our covered wagon and horses down the Mississippi.

I took the wheels off of the wagon and braced it so it would not roll off. North of New Orleans, we left the flatboat and came across the plains by wagon.

We are twenty miles from a village. Once every two or three months I go to the general store to get supplies. This trip takes me several days.

But I hurry back as fast as possible. I am always worried about Maggie and the children, for there are unfriendly Indians not far from our home.

We have built a comfortable cabin and have planted vegetables and corn. Next year I will plant some cotton. Farming is hard, slow work. I have only a hoe and a big stick for tools. When I left my heavy iron plow with you, I intended to buy more tools here. But they are very scarce.

Of late, we have had plenty of wild honey and corn bread. We crush our corn into meal with a hammer and stones like Mother did when we were boys.

We do not have schools yet, so Maggie will teach the children their "three R's."

We are well. This is good, as the nearest doctor is sixty miles away.

My regards.

Your brother,
Martin

Being a Texas pioneer required courage and hard work. But in Texas these pioneers were no longer citizens of the United States. They were governed by Mexico. This caused serious problems.

How Texas Became an Independent Nation

The pioneers were unhappy under Mexico's rule. They spoke a different language from the Mexicans. The pioneers had helped to make their laws and choose their leaders in the United States. But in Texas, they were not allowed to decide such things for themselves. They were no longer living in a democracy.

Still, more and more settlers flocked to Texas. So many came that Mexico feared they would become too strong to govern.

To prevent this, the Mexican government passed stricter laws for its colonists. One law forbade any more pioneers to enter Texas. Another raised taxes, and a third demanded that the people give up their guns.

"Give up our guns?" exclaimed the disgusted settlers. "Then how can we hunt game for our tables? How can we protect ourselves?"

Disputes with Mexico increased. Stephen Austin went to Mexico to see what could be done. His errand failed and he was held in jail many months. When he was released, he hurried back to Texas.

After the settlers heard Austin's story, they were very angry. They were even more aroused by other news. Cruel General Santa Anna had made himself the dictator of Mexico. A *dictator* is one who seizes all the powers of government for himself. The settlers from the United States knew Santa Anna would treat them badly. So they declared, "It is time to act! We must protect our rights!" They demanded their independence. They were joined by some of the Mexican settlers.

The Texan's fight for independence began in 1836. Santa Anna refused Texas its freedom and made plans to punish the daring rebels. With several thousand soldiers he set out for the north.

When news of Santa Anna's plans leaked out, worried Texans prepared to defend themselves. One group carried ammunition and other supplies to San Antonio's old Spanish mission, the Alamo Though its roof had fallen in, it made a strong fort. It had high walls nearly three feet thick.

148

More than 3000 Mexican soldiers attacked the Alamo. Less than 200 Texans defended it.

The Battle of the Alamo. Santa Anna led more than 3,000 soldiers against the Alamo. As the picture on this page shows, they hammered the fort with gunfire.

Santa Anna commanded the Texans to surrender. But they answered boldly, "No! It's victory or death! We'll fight it out to the last man!"

Santa Anna expected an easy victory but he had a surprise in store. Day after day the brave Texans held the fort, though they had less than 200 men. One brave defender was James Bowie, inventor of the Bowie hunting knife. Another was Davy Crockett, the famous frontiersman from Tennessee.

The daring Texans were able to hold the Alamo for twelve days. But at last the struggle became hopeless. Storming the walls, Santa Anna's troops finally broke into the fort. They captured the five weary Texans who remained alive. Santa Anna ordered them shot.

The Battle of the Alamo ended in defeat for the Texans. Yet it also led to final victory. While this battle was being fought, other Texans were organizing an army. With the words "Remember the Alamo!" ringing in their ears, farmers, stockmen, and adventurers united. Now, they were more determined than ever to fight. Their leader was Sam Houston.

Sam Houston was elected the commander-in-chief of the Texas army. Sam was born in Virginia. But he soon moved with his family to Tennessee. Though he disliked school, he loved to read. When he was sixteen, Sam went to work in a store. But he soon ran away to live with a tribe of nearby Indians. The Indian chief became fond of Sam and adopted him as his own son.

Sam lived with the Indians for nearly three years and learned their language and ways of living. In later years he often tried to protect the Indians when they were treated unfairly.

149

After serving in the United States army for a time, Houston became a successful lawyer. At the age of thirty-four, he was elected the governor of Tennessee. But his home life was unhappy, and as soon as he could, he started west. He settled in Texas, where he became an important leader.

Houston's soldiers won freedom for Texas. Driven on by the memory of the Alamo, the Texan army quietly tracked down Santa Anna's troops. The Mexican army was camped in the woods preparing supper.

Suddenly the Texans rushed forward shouting "Remember the Alamo!" The Mexican troops were so surprised that they were easily defeated. General Santa Anna was taken prisoner and was forced to sign the paper which gave Texas its freedom. At last, Texas could plan its own government.

Texas became an independent republic. It organized a government patterned after that of the United States. Then Sam Houston was elected its first president. Because its flag had one star, Texas was nicknamed the "Lone Star Republic."

The Republic of Texas occupied a larger area than present-day Texas does. As the map on page 151 shows, it reached north over part of the lands now occupied by Oklahoma, Kansas, and Colorado. It also included a part of New Mexico.

Texas was a republic for more than nine years. But during that time, many of its settlers longed to be citizens of the United States once again. This desire led to statehood for Texas and new lands for our country. That story follows.

The Southwest Was Added to the United States

In 1845, Texas joined the Union. It became our twenty-eighth state. This caused bad feelings in Mexico. Mexico had not agreed to the independence of the Texas republic. It complained bitterly when Texas became a state. Mexico felt that our country had taken over a huge area of land that did not belong to it.

Mexico was a weak and divided country. The Mexican government therefore also feared that the United States would try to take away the Spanish, or Mexican, Southwest.

Furthermore, Mexico quarreled with Texas over its Rio Grande boundary. Mexico insisted that it owned the lands on both sides of this river. This boundary dispute started a war.

The Mexican War broke out in 1846. Fearing trouble, the President of the United States sent troops to Texas. Soon, war was declared. Some battles were fought in Mexico and some took place in the Southwest. An American army followed the Santa Fe Trail to New Mexico and easily conquered that area. Other Americans won California.

After two years, our country defeated its neighbor. A peace treaty was signed, but bitter feelings remained. Indeed, because of it, Mexico felt unfriendly toward the United States for a long time.

The peace treaty gave our country the vast Southwest. It pushed our boundaries south to the Rio Grande and

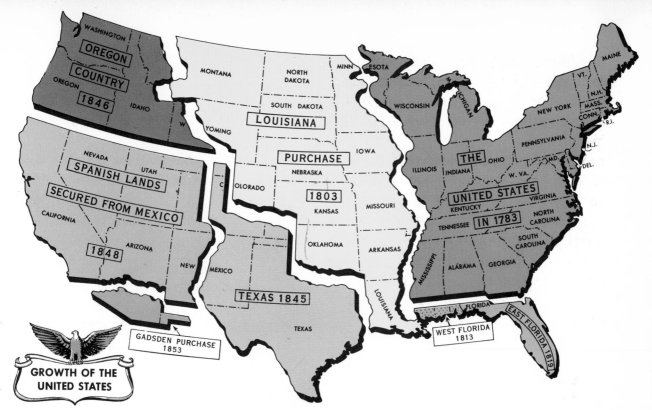

Labels on map:
WASHINGTON · OREGON COUNTRY 1846 · OREGON · IDAHO · MONTANA · NORTH DAKOTA · MINNESOTA · SOUTH DAKOTA · WYOMING · W · MAINE · VT. · N.H. · MASS. · CONN. · R.I. · NEW YORK · MICHIGAN · WISCONSIN · LOUISIANA · IOWA · PENNSYLVANIA · N.J. · NEVADA · UTAH · SPANISH LANDS · SECURED FROM MEXICO · CALIFORNIA · ARIZONA · 1848 · NEW · MEXICO · C · COLORADO · PURCHASE · NEBRASKA · KANSAS · MISSOURI · 1803 · THE · OHIO · MD. · DEL. · ILLINOIS · INDIANA · W. VA. · UNITED STATES · VIRGINIA · KENTUCKY · IN 1783 · NORTH CAROLINA · TENNESSEE · SOUTH CAROLINA · OKLAHOMA · ARKANSAS · MISSISSIPPI · ALABAMA · GEORGIA · TEXAS 1845 · TEXAS · LOUISIANA · GADSDEN PURCHASE 1853 · FLORIDA · WEST FLORIDA 1813 · EAST FLORIDA 1819 · GROWTH OF THE UNITED STATES

west to the Pacific. It gave us an enormous region of about 500,000 square miles.

Look on the map above and locate these lands. This region is our great Southwest. From it have been carved parts of Wyoming, Colorado, New Mexico, and Arizona and all of California, Nevada, and Utah. The Mexicans of this region became citizens of the United States.

We paid Mexico $15,000,000 for this Southwest. A few years later, the United States bought from Mexico a strip of land which is now occupied by the southern parts of Arizona and New Mexico. This area was known as the Gadsden Purchase. Locate it on the map above.

The northwestern part of the lands which Mexico gave up included Great Salt Lake. Find it on the map. Near its shores, a daring group of pioneers called Mormons had gone to live even before the Mexican War ended.

This map shows how the United States grew until it reached the Pacific Ocean · What states or parts of states came from the lands won from Mexico?

The Mormons Settled Utah

The Mormons were looking for a new home. They were members of a religious group organized by a young man named Joseph Smith. At first, they had lived in New York State. But because their beliefs and ways of living were different from those of most people, they were treated unkindly. Finally they were run out of the community.

The Mormons were determined to worship God in their own way so they moved west to Ohio. But still they had no peace.

After a few years, they went on to Illinois and later to Missouri. Always the story was the same. Yet they would not give up their religion. Instead, they journeyed farther west.

The Mormons traveled to Utah. Led by wise Brigham Young, 143 pioneers set out from Missouri. Across the plains and mountains, they guided ox-carts and heavily-loaded covered wagons. With them they took cows, horses, mules, dogs, and chickens.

Finally, one hot summer day, the travelers reached the western side of the Wasatch Mountains, one of the ranges of the Rockies. The tired people looked

The Mormons dug ditches to bring water to their fields from nearby mountains.

down on a broad sun-baked land and the shining waters of Great Salt Lake. Then they heard their leader say of the land near the lake, "This is the Place! Here we shall build our homes."

The new land did not look inviting. It was nearly surrounded by mountains and sage-covered hills. It was a dry, brown desert. Indeed, one woman wrote in her diary:

Truly I am broken-hearted. I had hoped we would settle in a peaceful green valley. But our good leader says that this dry land is where we will build our homes. I cannot see how we can raise crops here.

Still, the Mormons had faith in their leaders. This faith was rewarded as the months and years passed. The hard-working pioneers turned their dry sandy lands into fine, successful farms.

The Mormons laid out farms and planted crops. Little rain fell. But the men flooded their fields with water by damming streams that rushed down from the mountains. In some places, ditches were dug to lead water to crops. This system of supplying water to dry land is known as *irrigation*.

The Mormons had many discouraging experiences. One happened in the spring when new crops had just come up. Millions of hungry crickets swept down. They began to eat every green thing they could find. Heartsick men, women, and children fought the swarms of insects, but their work seemed useless.

Then suddenly, there was a flurry of wings. Thousands of seagulls swooped down and gobbled up nearly every cricket. You can imagine how thankful the pioneers were. In honor of the seagulls, two

This monument to the helpful seagulls is in Salt Lake City near the Mormon Temple.

handsome monuments were put up. One can see them today in Salt Lake City.

The Mormons built many settlements in Utah. Their first and most important one was Salt Lake City, named for the large salty lake nearby. Within a short time, several thousand Mormons settled in Salt Lake City. Today, it is Utah's beautiful capital. Locate it on the map on pages 504–505. In time, many towns grew up in other parts of Utah. Some of these are now busy cities.

After the Mexican War, Utah was made a United States territory. The main wagon route west passed through the Utah territory. Hundreds of pioneer families traveled through it on their way to California.

The Gold Fields Called Many Pioneers to California

California lay far to the west. Find it on the map on page 130. It stretched for more than a thousand miles along the Pacific coast. For nearly three hundred years, California belonged to Spain. Then, in 1821, when Mexico won its independence from Spain, California became a Mexican territory. After the Mexican War, it became a part of our country, as you know.

But wait! We are getting ahead of our story. Let's turn back the pages of history to a long-ago day in 1542.

In 1542, California was discovered by a Spanish sailor named Cabrillo. Sailing into beautiful San Diego Bay, Cabrillo went ashore and claimed the land for Spain.

As the years passed, other Spaniards visited the land. They named some of the bays and islands along the coast. But none of them attempted to settle there for a long time.

In 1769, pioneers from Mexico began to build missions in California. This work was in charge of a brave priest, Father Junipero Serra, and a skilled soldier, Portola. Helping them were other priests, a number of soldiers, and some Indians.

The first mission was put up at San Diego. In time, the Mexicans and their Indian helpers built a chain of twenty-one missions. These reached from San Diego north to Sonoma. Find these two cities

153

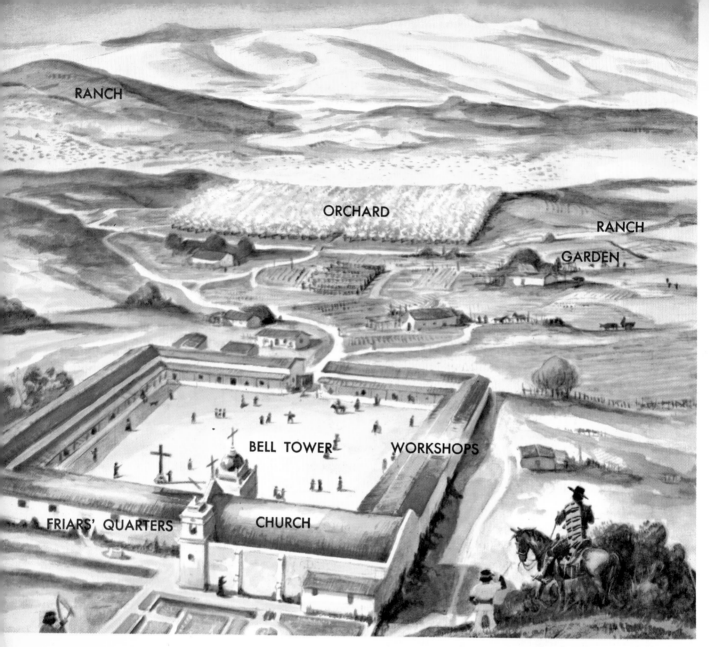

RANCH

ORCHARD

RANCH

GARDEN

BELL TOWER

WORKSHOPS

FRIARS' QUARTERS

CHURCH

Most missions in Spanish California were built around a central courtyard.

on the map on page 277. The missions were about a day's journey apart. They were connected by a trail known as *El Camino Real*, or "The King's Highway."

At the missions, the priests taught the Indians the Christian religion and helped them to live more like the Spaniards. The picture above suggests what a mission was

like. Each one had thick adobe and stone walls and red-tiled roofs.

As you can see, a mission was often built around a central courtyard. One building was the church with its high bell tower. Another provided living quarters for the *friars*, or priests. Still another was a workshop. In it, Indian girls were taught such things as spinning, weaving, how to make soap, and how to dip candles. Indian boys were trained to make furniture, boots, and saddles.

Beyond the missions, large ranches were laid out. They were called *ranchos*. Some ranchos belonged to soldiers who had helped to build the missions. As pay, the soldiers had been given large grants of land.

Life was pleasant and unhurried on the ranchos. Most families lived in low, one-story adobe houses. Indians helped raise the crops and tend the cattle and sheep that roamed the hills. So the settlers had plenty of time for picnics, dances, and activities at their nearby mission.

As time passed, other settlers were given land grants. One of these men was an American named Captain John Sutter. His 97,000 acres of land lay in the beautiful Sacramento Valley and reached back to the wooded slopes of the Sierra Nevada. Point to these mountains on the map.

Sutter's ranch was a prosperous one. It had wide grasslands where thousands of cattle grazed, and fertile soil where fine crops were raised. And hidden in its stream beds, unknown to anyone, was a fortune in shining gold.

Gold was discovered on Sutter's ranch. Captain Sutter had hired James Marshall and other workmen to build a sawmill on a stream in a wooded canyon. One chilly morning in 1848, Marshall noticed bits of yellow gravel glistening in the stream bed. Curious, he picked up a handful of the bright pebbles. "This looks like gold," he said to himself.

The next morning, Marshall mounted his horse and galloped off. He rode through a pouring rain to show Captain Sutter what he had found.

"Captain Sutter!" he called out when he drew his horse to a stop beside the ranch house. "Captain Sutter!"

"Yes!" answered the captain. "Oh! It's you, Marshall! Come in! You're wet and out of breath! What happened?"

"I've special news! But news to keep a secret!" replied Marshall, excitedly, as he locked the door. Handing Sutter a dark bottle, Marshall continued, "Look what's in there! It's gold! I'm sure!"

"Gold!" exclaimed Sutter, examining the soft heavy bits of rock. "We must be certain!"

The two men tested the metal and finally Sutter declared, "You're right! This is gold! Where did you find it?"

"It's from the stream near the sawmill," answered Marshall. "There's lots more! You will be a rich man, sir!"

The two men agreed to keep their discovery a secret. But the news soon leaked out among Sutter's men. Excited farm workers quit their plowing and the stockmen left their cattle to hurry to "the magic stream bed." Meanwhile, the gold news spread south to San Francisco.

The Gold Rush began! One day, a man dashed down the muddy streets of San Francisco. Waving a bottle of fine gold sand, he shouted, "This is gold! Pure gold! Sutter's ranch is rich with gold!"

When this startling news spread over the town, strange things began to happen. Businessmen locked their offices. Merchants closed their stores. Sailors deserted the ships anchored in the harbor. Soon, only a few people remained in San Francisco. Hundreds had hurried to the newly-found gold fields in the Sacramento River Valley.

The Gold Rush brought the "Forty-Niners" to California. Before long, the news of the gold fields traveled across our country. Newspapers printed glowing tales of how much gold a man could pick up in a day. Men everywhere began to dream of making a fortune out West. By 1849, thousands of people were heading for the gold fields. Those who traveled west that year became known as "Forty-Niners."

Many "Forty-Niners" who lived along the Atlantic crowded on ships bound for California. Ships sailed south around South America and then north along the Pacific coast. Sometimes, this voyage took six months. There were days and days of stormy weather and sickness. Sometimes supplies ran low and there was not enough fresh food or drinking water. But what did hardships matter if one reached the gold fields?

Some "Forty-Niners" traveled overland. They loaded their belongings in covered wagons painted with signs that said, "Californy or Bust." They followed the long dangerous trail west toward the setting sun. Find the California Trail on the map on page 130.

The gold hunters found many hardships in California. In the gold fields, there were no comfortable houses. So people pitched tents or built rough shacks for shelters. A loaf of bread cost a dollar, and eggs sold for three dollars each. Sugar cost three dollars a pound, and a chicken might bring as much as ten dollars.

Sending mail was expensive, too. There was no regular mail service to or from California. So people had to send letters by boat or with travelers. It sometimes cost as much as five dollars to send one letter back East.

More and more people moved to California. Many came to hunt for gold, but only a few made fortunes. Soon the easy riches were gone. Then people had to find other ways of making a living. Some became ranchers. Some found jobs in the villages and towns that had sprung up.

But nearly everyone stayed on in California. Within a year, California had a population of nearly a hundred thousand people. It became a state in 1850.

A gold-mining camp in the Sierra Nevada.

Most Mexicans who were living in California stayed. They had become citizens of the United States by the treaty of peace with Mexico.

Mexican and Spanish ways of living remained a part of California life. Spanish-style houses were built by some newcomers from other parts of the United States. Mexican ways of cattle and sheep raising were copied by ranchers. California farmers grew many plants brought from Mexico in earlier days. For example Mexicans brought with them lemons, olives, and avocados. Most names of places in California are Spanish. So are thousands in other parts of the Southwest. Mexican-Americans can be proud of their many gifts to our country.

Do You Remember?

1. What did Pike learn about the Southwest?

2. Why is Sam Houston remembered?

3. How did the United States get its lands in the Southwest?

4. Why did the Mormons settle in Utah?

5. Why did many people go to California in 1849?

Which Are Partners?

Each word or phrase in List A tells something about a word or phrase in List B.

Write the numbers 1–12 on a paper. After each one, write the correct "partner" from List B.

List A

1. Zebulon Pike	7. Father Serra
2. Sam Houston	8. Santa Fe Trail
3. Santa Fe	9. Cabrillo
4. Mormons	10. Stephen Austin
5. irrigation	11. Forty-Niners
6. Brigham Young	12. James Marshall

List B

a. led Mormons to Utah
b. discovered California
c. discovered gold on Sutter's ranch

d. led Texas' fight for independence

e. founded the first California missions

f. explored the Spanish Southwest

g. called "Father of Texas"

h. a system of watering lands

i. a city built by Spaniards in the Southwest

j. settled Utah

k. went to California during Gold Rush

l. chief route to the Southwest

For You to Decide

1. How are all pioneers alike?

2. What is a republic? Is the United States a republic? Give the reasons for your answer.

3. Americans did not enjoy living under the flag of Mexico. Why? We live in a democracy. How do you think it is different from some other kinds of government? What rights do we have in the United States which we might not have as citizens of some other countries?

Let's Review Map Symbols

Copy the numbers in Column I. Find, in Column II, the meaning for each symbol in Column I. Write it after the correct number.

Column I		Column II
1.	....	branches of a river
2.	▲	state boundary line
3.	———	fort
4.	•	mountain peak
5.	∿	mission
6.	⚑	route
7.	–·–·–	international boundary line
8.	⚓	city

Other Things to Do

1. If there is an Indian reservation near your home, learn all you can about it.

2. If someone you know has lived in another country, have him explain how his life there was different from what it is in the United States. Tell your class what you learn.

3. Show that there are two sides to a question. Divide the class into two groups. Let one group give reasons why we took the Spanish Southwest. Let the other group tell reasons why this was unfair.

4. Read in another book more about the "gifts" and know-how which Mexican-Americans have brought to our country.

5. Study the paragraphs about "Using an Encyclopedia" on this page. Look in the correct volume and find information about one of these topics:

a. California Missions   c. The Alamo

b. California Gold Rush   d. Salt Lake City

Using an Encyclopedia

An *encyclopedia* is usually a set of many books, or volumes, as you probably know. Each volume contains information about many subjects. This is arranged alphabetically. For example, if you wish to read about bicycles, you look in the B volume. It is important to look carefully at the volume letter. Sometimes a volume may contain two or three letters.

Here are some good ideas to remember when it is your turn to use an encyclopedia:

1. Read your material carefully.

2. Study the pictures and the picture legends about your topic.

3. Take brief notes about the most important information.

4. Finish with your study as quickly as you can. There are never enough copies of volumes to go around in a class.

5. Return your volume to its correct place on the shelf.

10 · How the North and South Fought a War

From Indenture to Slavery

The first Afro-Americans were indentured servants. A Dutch ship brought them to Jamestown, Virginia one August day in 1619.

"That ship flies a strange flag!" exclaimed a settler as he watched it anchor. "I wonder why it has come."

Soon the reason was plain. The Dutch captain wished to exchange some of the Africans he had on his ship for needed supplies. Could the Virginia colony use more workers to clear the forested lands and take care of the crops?

The settlers had some indentured servants but they were eager for others. Such servants worked several years for a master. Then they were set free, remember.

Quickly a trade was arranged. Twenty black people were brought ashore to begin their terms of service. In time, the blacks were freed. Some became landowners themselves.

As the planters prospered, they needed many workers. But workers were hard to find. They decided that owning them was the answer. Slave ships began bringing more black people to our shores. Now these Africans were being bought for life. Thus slavery began in our land.

Virginians watch a Dutch ship anchor at Jamestown in 1619. What cargo did it carry?

Skilled black craftsmen help to build the lovely homes of their owners.

At that time, owning slaves was common in many parts of the world. Earlier many slaves had been captured in Europe and Asia. Later on most slaves were taken from Africa. All of the European countries allowed slavery in their colonies. It is not surprising, then, that many planters in America adopted this custom.

The custom of owning slaves spread. In time, slaves were held by some families in each of the thirteen colonies. By 1790, when Washington was President, there were thousands of slaves in our country. But the largest number were held in the southern part.

The Southern states had many large plantations. So hundreds of planters had bought slaves to help with the work.

Black women were trained to do the housework and cooking and to look after the children. Many black men toiled in the fields, planting, hoeing, and harvesting the crops. Others were skillful carpenters or blacksmiths or bricklayers.

Many people in both the Northern and the Southern states thought that owning slaves was wrong. Some remembered that the Declaration of Independence said, "all men are created equal." But so long as some people owned others as slaves, it was hard to see how all people were created equal.

The Declaration of Independence also said that all men have such rights as "Life, Liberty, and the pursuit of Happiness." The thirteen colonies had fought for independence because of their love of freedom. Yet their slaves had no freedom.

Many Americans in both the Northern and the Southern colonies disliked slavery. They hoped that it would soon die out. Benjamin Franklin had spoken out against it. Later on, Thomas Jefferson encouraged Congress to pass a law forbidding further slave trade with Africa. George Washington arranged to free his slaves at Mount Vernon. And in time, other slave owners in both the northern and southern parts of our country freed their slaves.

However, many Southerners said that they needed slaves. "Without them, how could large crops of tobacco, rice, and sugar be raised?" planters asked. It was very hard to find free men who would do such work. So, most Southerners decided that slavery was necessary. At the same time, slavery was disappearing in the northern part of the United States.

Differences Divided Our Country on the Slavery Problem

There wasn't much need for slaves in the Northern states. Most farmers raised cattle, sheep, grain, and vegetables. The work could be done by the owner and his family. In the North, too, the growing season was quite short. During the long cold winters, there was not enough work to keep slaves busy. Yet they had to be cared for all the year round. So owning slaves did not pay.

Furthermore, farming was just one of the ways of making a living in the North.

Factories and mills were built in many New England villages. This did not happen in the South. Why?

Many New Englanders had turned to fishing, remember. Others were employed in the lumbering and shipbuilding industries. In the Northern states, too, there were dozens of towns and cities. Thousands of people earned their living in businesses or in factories.

The Northern states had many factories and mills. One, a cotton mill, is pictured below. As time went on, more people gave up farming and went to work in manufacturing industries.

Others who took jobs in the factories were immigrants. *Immigrants* are people who come from other countries to live in our land. Thousands of immigrants moved to our country. Most of them were poor and eager for jobs. Some journeyed west to start farms. But many went to work in factories and mills in the Northern states.

The Northern states had plenty of labor and did not need slaves. Furthermore, factory owners did not want slaves to feed, clothe, and shelter. But conditions were different in the South.

With the cotton gin a man could clean much more cotton than he could by hand.

Farming was the main industry in the Southern states. This had been true from the earliest days. These states had a fine climate for growing many different crops. *Climate* is the weather a place has year after year. The South's climate was especially favorable for producing tobacco, sugar cane, rice, and cotton.

Planters owned slaves to do their work. The planters furnished food, clothing, and cabins for their slaves. They believed that this cost less than finding and hiring other workers.

Cotton was becoming the most important crop in the Southern states. After spinning and weaving machines were invented, planters could sell large quantities of cotton. Mills bought all the cotton they could get. They could hardly

weave goods fast enough to supply eager housewives.

Plenty of cotton could be grown; but preparing it for the mills was another matter. You see, when cotton is picked, it contains many small seeds, as the picture on page 243 shows. Before cotton can be used at the mill, these seeds must be removed. Once, this was a long, slow job because it had to be done by hand. It took about eight hours for one slave to clean a single pound of cotton. Therefore, many workers were needed to prepare large amounts of cotton for the mills.

Later on, a young schoolteacher invented a faster way to remove seeds. You will read about his cotton gin in Chapter 14. The main thing to remember now is that such a gin could remove seeds from as many as fifty pounds of cotton a day. Later on, the cotton gin was improved so that it could clean a thousand pounds a day. It now paid planters to raise large fields of cotton. But this required even more workers.

After the early 1800's, many planters flocked west. They settled on the broad, fertile plain that reached across Alabama, Mississippi, Louisiana, and into Texas. This region also had a long growing season, hot summers, plenty of rain, and rich soil. So it was well suited to raising large crops of cotton. In time, so much cotton was grown in the Southern states that they were called the "cotton kingdom."

Because cotton brought in the most money, people said that it "ruled" the South. It was "King Cotton." It was raised on small farms as well as on large plantations. Indeed, each Southern farmer dreamed of the day when he could grow even more cotton.

The number of slaves in the Southern states increased. The children of slaves were also slaves. When they were old enough, they were trained to do their share of the work. Sometimes they were sold to another master.

By 1850, there were more than three million slaves in the Southern states. Though many families had but one slave each, other families owned large numbers. The slave system in the Southern states seemed to grow stronger every year. At the same time, the North was becoming more opposed to slavery.

The words *North* and *South* came to refer to two large sections of our country. You can locate them on the map on page 166.

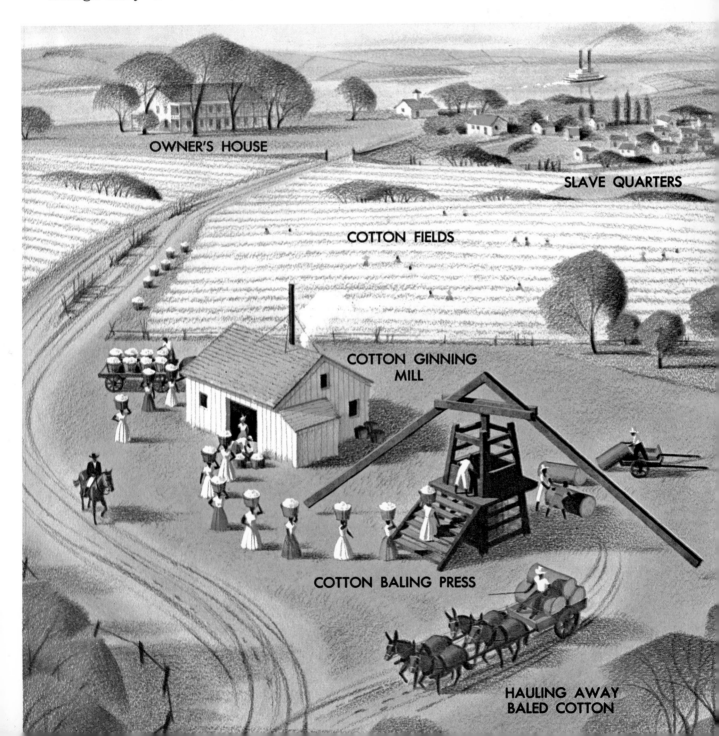

OWNER'S HOUSE

SLAVE QUARTERS

COTTON FIELDS

COTTON GINNING MILL

COTTON BALING PRESS

HAULING AWAY BALED COTTON

Many people, white and black, worked against slavery. Some people said that slavery should not be allowed anywhere in our country. Those who opposed it most strongly were called Abolitionists. They wanted to abolish or do away with it at once. They made speeches and wrote articles against it.

One leading Abolitionist was Frederick Douglass, a former slave. As a boy, he could not attend school. But he learned to read and write, anyway. He became a stirring speaker and writer and worked full time against the hated slave system.

Douglass and many others, black and white, helped a bold "freedom" plan to succeed. It was nicknamed the *Underground Railroad*. It helped large numbers of runaway slaves to escape to free states in the North. Some blacks fled all the way to Canada.

As you know, a railroad has conductors and stops at stations. The Underground Railroad's "conductors" directed slaves along secret routes. The "stations" were homes along the way where friends provided food and clothing and shelter.

One of the most daring conductors was Harriet Tubman, a runaway slave herself. Again and again she stole into the South and conducted slaves to freedom. To prevent capture, they crept northward at night. They slept by day, hidden in the woods or in a cave or barn or attic. This frail black woman led more than 300 slaves from the South. Among these were her own parents.

Thousands of slaves escaped. This loss and the frightening uprisings of some slaves against their masters worried the South. There was increasing bitterness against the North.

The Slavery Problem Led to many Quarrels

The North and the South quarreled about the slave problem in new states. Some territories were being settled rapidly. One by one, they were asking to join the Union. The question was, would they be slave-holding states or free ones?

Many people in the North wanted Congress to forbid slavery in the new states. But the South thought each one should have the right to decide for itself whether it would be "slave" or "free." The South wanted our country to have as many slave states as free ones.

Each state sends two Senators to Congress to help make laws. The North had more people than the South, as well as more industry. But as long as there were as many slave states as free ones, the South had the same number of Senators as the North. This meant that the Southern Senators could keep the North from passing laws harmful to the South.

The North and the South also disagreed about the rights of states. Most Northerners said that a citizen's first loyalty should be to his whole country. But many Southerners felt differently. They thought one should be loyal first of all to his own state. They even felt that a state had the right to leave the Union if it had a good reason.

About this time, California asked to enter the Union as a free state. The South opposed this, as it would make sixteen free states to fifteen slave states. Congress quarrelled bitterly over this problem.

Some Southerners said that their states should leave the Union. It seemed that war might break out. Could Congress prevent such a terrible mistake?

Two wise statesmen worked for peace. They were Daniel Webster and Henry Clay. They had been members of Congress for many years and had proved very able leaders.

Webster was a Senator from New England, and was known for his fine speeches. Because they were often about the Constitution, Webster became known as the "Defender of the Constitution."

Henry Clay came from Kentucky. He had many friends and was well-liked. His friendly smile and quiet manner helped him smooth out many quarrels in Congress. So he earned the title of "the peacemaker." His attempt to iron out the trouble over California resulted in a famous compromise. In a compromise, remember, each side gets part of what it wants, but also gives up some things.

The Compromise of 1850. One day in the Senate, Clay rose and addressed his fellow lawmakers. He suggested a compromise. To please the North, California was to be admitted to the Union as a free state. To please the South, the new states to be made out of the territories of New Mexico and Utah were to decide for themselves about slavery. Another thing, runaway slaves were to be captured and returned.

Many leaders were not entirely satisfied with this compromise. But Webster gave a stirring speech for it and it became a law. The Union was saved for a time.

But alas! The Compromise did not do all that Clay had hoped. Many Northerners refused to return runaway slaves. In fact, some Northerners were helping more and more slaves escape. This made the Southerners very angry.

After 1850, the North and the South drifted farther apart than ever. The North did not try to understand the feelings of the South. The South no longer trusted the North. Feelings between them grew more bitter with every passing month.

Harriet Tubman leads slaves to freedom.

This map shows which states remained in the Union and which joined the Confederate States of America.

In 1860, Abraham Lincoln was elected President of the United States. At the age of nineteen, he had worked on a river boat on the Mississippi. In New Orleans, he had seen men buying and selling slaves. He made up his mind, then, that slavery was wrong and often after that, spoke against it.

The South knew how Lincoln felt about slavery. Indeed, some of its leaders warned that if he were elected President, their states would leave the Union. Soon after Lincoln's election, several states did withdraw from the Union. We shall read further about that later. But now, let's learn more about this tall, homely backwoodsman who became the chief executive of the United States.

Lincoln's early life. Abraham Lincoln was born in Kentucky on February 12, 1809, in a dark one-room log cabin. His parents were very poor, but they did the best they could, clearing the land and raising crops between the tree stumps. Later on, they moved to Indiana.

When Abe was nine, his mother died. The next two years were sad and lonely ones for Abe, his sister Sarah, and his father. Then, one day, his father rode away to Kentucky. Soon he returned with a new wife and a wagon filled with her furniture. "Here's your new mammy," Abe's father called out.

The new Mrs. Lincoln greeted the tall slim boy with a smile. He soon discovered that she was a good friend and an understanding mother. She encouraged him to learn all he could. She watched him proudly as he studied by the light of the flickering fire on the hearth.

While Lincoln was growing up, he worked at many kinds of jobs. For a time he was a clerk in a country store. He was also a rail splitter as the picture above shows. But he always dreamed of being a lawyer. So with part of his earnings he bought books and studied law. Finally, his dream came true.

Lincoln settled in Springfield, Illinois, where he practiced law. Later he held several offices in his state government.

In November of 1860, Lincoln was elected President. This made the South very unhappy for the new chief executive was against slavery.

Eleven Southern states left the Union. Soon after the election, South Carolina said that it was no longer a part of the United States. Within a few weeks, six other states also left the Union. They set up a government of their own and called it the *Confederate States of America.* Later, four more states joined the Confederacy. Jefferson Davis was elected President of the Confederacy.

Look on the map on page 166 and name the 11 Confederate states. Which slaveholding states remained in the Union?

Most Americans were very unhappy and worried. It was not easy to see the United States divided into two republics. But what could be done? How would Lincoln handle the sad situation?

Lincoln worked hard at all of his jobs. Above, splitting rails. Below, riding to court as a lawyer.

The North and the South at War

In 1861, Lincoln became the President of a divided United States. He took his oath of office before crowds of people in front of the Capitol in Washington, D.C. He was dressed in a black suit and a stiff white shirt and carried a cane with a gold handle. Because he was six feet four inches tall, and wore a high silk hat besides, he looked like a giant.

As Lincoln stepped forward, he placed his left hand on an open Bible. Raising his right hand, he said:

I do solemnly swear that I will faithfully execute the office of President of the United States, and will, to the best of my ability, preserve, protect, and defend the Constitution of the United States.

People probably wondered how their new President would "preserve, protect, and defend the Constitution." Several states had already denied it by leaving the Union. Would Lincoln decide that they should be punished? And what would he say about slavery?

Lincoln did not answer all these questions in his Inaugural Address. But he loved the Union and was determined to do all in his power to save it. He said:

I hold that . . . the Union of these States is perpetual (lasting) *. . . no State upon its own mere motion can lawfully get out of the Union. . . . In your hands, my dissatisfied countrymen* (the South), *and not in mine, is the momentous* (very important) *issue of civil war.*

As the weeks passed, it was plain that war was near. Indeed, it broke out only a few weeks after Lincoln became President.

Fighting began at Fort Sumter. This fort was located on a small island in the harbor of Charleston, South Carolina. Find Fort Sumter on the map on page 166. It belonged to the United States government. Union soldiers were stationed there. Because South Carolina was now a part of the Confederacy, Fort Sumter was ordered to surrender. When it refused, its food supply was cut off.

Lincoln ordered food shipped to Fort Sumter. This made Confederate leaders angry. Early on one April morning, Southern soldiers began to fire on the fort. Fort Sumter fired back, and a fierce battle raged for many hours. Finally, the fort surrendered and the Confederates took it over. This was the first battle of the Civil War.

Many women helped to care for wounded soldiers. As the war went on, hundreds of battles were fought. There were thousands of sick and wounded soldiers but not enough hospitals, nurses, medicines, or bandages. Some women volunteered to help and made bandages and prepared food in their homes. Some like Clara Barton worked as nurses in hospitals and on the battlefields. Because they were so kind to the soldiers, the nurses were often called "the angels of mercy."

On January 1, 1863, Lincoln freed the slaves in the Confederate states. For some time, people in the North had felt that the slaves should be freed as soon as possible. Now, Lincoln thought the time was right. He announced that all slaves living in the Confederate states were emancipated, or freed. This order is called the *Emancipation Proclamation*.

Southerners did not pay any attention to this Proclamation. So most slaves were not freed until after the war.

Many blacks fought bravely for freedom. Some who became soldiers or sailors had always lived in the North. Others had escaped from their masters before the war began. But thousands had fled from the South after the fighting started. Altogether about 186,000 black men served in the Union forces.

The war lasted four long, sad years. Both sides had hoped that it would end quickly. But instead, it dragged on and on. Each side won some important battles.

Union vessels tried to stop ships from entering or leaving Southern ports.

As the months passed, the North developed a plan for defeating the South. One part of this plan was to blockade, or block, the South's ports. To do this, the North sent ships to guard the coast and block the harbors from Virginia to Texas. Because the South had few factories, it was now buying most of its clothing, shoes, ammunition, and guns from Europe. A blockade would prevent these goods from reaching Southern ports.

The blockade worked! The Union ships were so alert that few supply ships got through it.

Another part of the North's plan was to win control of the Mississippi. This would cut the South into two parts: the states on the east side of the Mississippi and Arkansas, Louisiana, and Texas on the west side. This would prevent the states east of the Mississippi from getting food raised in Texas, Louisiana, and Arkansas.

During the three-day battle of Gettysburg over 7000 men were killed.

One by one, the main cities along the Mississippi were captured by Northern forces. The last important one was Vicksburg. Do you see it on the map on page 166. When the army of General Grant captured it, the North controlled the whole river.

One of the most important battles of the war took place near the small crossroads village of Gettysburg, Pennsylvania. The Battle of Gettysburg lasted for three long days. Finally, the Union forces drove the Confederate troops back. Because so many soldiers fell here, Gettysburg was made a National Cemetery. A *National Cemetery* is a place where many of our country's soldiers are buried.

President Lincoln helped to dedicate the National Cemetery of Gettysburg. A special service was held to honor the men who had died there. Two great leaders were invited to speak at the service. One was Edward Everett, famous for his fine speeches. The other was President Lincoln.

Edward Everett was introduced first and talked for two hours. When he had finished, people clapped loudly, but hardly anyone could recall what he had said.

Then Abraham Lincoln stood before the solemn crowds of people. He gave the speech which is now known as Lincoln's Gettysburg Address. The tall, sad-faced President began:

Four score and seven years ago our fathers brought forth on this continent, a new nation, conceived in Liberty, and dedicated to the proposition that all men are created equal.

There was more to Lincoln's speech. But, altogether, it had only about three hundred words. It was over in less than five minutes. Yet he had said so much so well that today Lincoln's Gettysburg Address is known and loved by millions of Americans.

170

General Grant served as general-in-chief of the Union troops. He had been trained as an officer in the United States army and had fought bravely in the Mexican War. After the capture of Vicksburg, Grant was given the command of all of the Union forces. Later on, Grant became President of the United States.

General Robert E. Lee served as leader of the Confederate troops. He was a kind and brave man who was honored and loved by all who knew him.

When the war began, Lee could hardly decide whether to remain loyal to the United States government or help his state of Virginia. He did not believe slavery was right, nor did he approve of states leaving the Union. Still, after days of prayer, he chose to serve Virginia. Later, he acted as general-in-chief of all the Confederate forces.

The Confederate troops surrendered in the spring of 1865. The Confederacy had suffered one defeat after another and lost many soldiers. In addition, most of its ammunition and food were gone. Confederate leaders knew it was useless to fight on. So Lee agreed to meet Grant to discuss the terms of a surrender.

One April morning, General Lee rode off on his faithful horse, Traveler, to meet General Grant. Lee looked sad, but splendid, too, in his neat gray uniform and shining black boots. At his side hung the beautiful jeweled sword which Virginia had given him as a present. With his white hair and snowy white beard, Lee was indeed a handsome leader.

The two generals met in a little town called Appomattox Courthouse, in Virginia. They shook hands and then sat down to talk about surrender and peace. After a time, General Grant said, "Your officers may keep their swords and tell all of your men to keep their horses and mules. They may be needed for spring plowing."

General Grant then decided that food must be sent to Lee's men. He knew that they were half-starved. The food that Lee was waiting for had been captured by Northern soldiers.

"Thank you with all my heart," answered Lee, gratefully. Then he mounted his horse and rode back to talk to his troops. As he left, Union soldiers began to cheer, but Grant stilled them.

Lincoln ended his Gettysburg address saying, "government of the people, by the people, for the people, shall not perish from the earth."

"No!" said Grant sternly. "Do not cheer! Let us just be glad in our hearts that the war is over. And let us remember that the Southerners are once again our countrymen."

Later, when Lee talked to his soldiers, tears filled his eyes. He praised them for their courage in many battles and then told them their cause was lost. He had surrendered. He assured them that none would be put in prison, and that they could keep their swords and their horses. And he asked them to go back to their homes and do the best they could to make our country strong and united again.

Lee, himself, set a good example. He became the president of a university. He did much to encourage friendship between the North and the South. He proved himself a great American who was even greater in defeat than in victory. Meanwhile another great American was trying to pave the way for a happy peace.

Abraham Lincoln was re-elected as President of the United States. After he took the oath of office, he made an address which has become very famous. In it he said,

With malice (hard feelings, or bitterness) *toward none, with charity* (goodwill) *for all, with firmness in the right . . . let us strive* (work) *on to finish the work we are in, to bind up the nation's wounds, . . . and cherish* (encourage) *a just and lasting peace among ourselves. . . .*

Lincoln hoped that the Confederate states could be treated as though they had never left the Union. He had already made some plans to help the North and the South work together again. However, he was not able to carry them out.

Lincoln was shot! The war had been over only a few days. One evening, President and Mrs. Lincoln attended a theater in Washington. The play had just begun when Lincoln was shot by a half-crazy actor.

Friends carried the wounded President to a nearby house. Skilled doctors rushed to his bedside and watched over him all night long. But he died early the next morning.

Soon telegraph wires flashed the tragic words, "Lincoln is dead," to the East, West, North, and South. Then, Americans everywhere realized that they had lost a sincere friend and a great leader.

Peace Brought Many Problems

Some very unhappy years followed the Civil War. President Abraham Lincoln was dead. In his place as President was the kind but weak leader, Andrew Johnson. Johnson had served as Vice-President while Lincoln was President. If the President of our country dies, the Vice-President becomes the new President.

President Johnson wanted to carry out Lincoln's plans not to punish the South. He hoped that leaders of both the North and the South would sit down together and discuss ways of rebuilding our country.

But Northern leaders in Congress were stronger than Johnson. They would not agree to his plans. They insisted that the South must be punished.

Conditions in the South were very discouraging. When Confederate soldiers returned to their plantations, they found them deserted and their buildings in ruins. Their furniture had been stolen. Their tools and livestock were gone. Most of their freed slaves had fled. Their fields were overgrown with weeds, and their families were scattered.

The southern people needed to rebuild their homes and plant crops. They also needed to rebuild railroads and bridges. Yet this work required much money and they were now very poor. They did not know what to do or where to get help. As the months went by, they became more and more discouraged. And no wonder!

Union soldiers were sent to the defeated states to help set up new governments. The right to vote and hold public office was taken from many Southern leaders. Instead, selfish and untrained people were allowed to hold office. Among them were the carpetbaggers.

Carpetbaggers were given their name because they carried their belongings in small traveling bags made of pieces of bright carpet. You can see some of these bags in the picture on this page. Many carpetbaggers were dishonest. They had flocked to the South from all over the country. They hoped to make money in the new governments being set up. They knew that if they could hold important government offices, they could govern the South as they pleased. They could steal money for themselves.

The carpetbaggers were usually elected to office by persuading poor white Southerners and ex-slaves to vote for them. Also the carpetbaggers put some of these people in government jobs. Many poor white Southerners lived on small farms tucked far back in the mountain land of the South. They had no training for important government jobs. Nor did most blacks. Only a small number had learned to read and write.

"Carpetbaggers" arrive in the defeated South.

Indeed, the South's worries seemed endless. And what about the several million blacks who had just been freed? They were homeless and jobless. What were they to do?

Freedom brought new problems to the blacks. At first freedom seemed wonderful. Many left their plantations to look for a better life. But even after one day's travel, they realized that they had no place to go. They had no homes. They had no way to earn money for food or clothing.

The blacks had no jobs. They had no land to work, no tools, no one to help them. They lacked training and education except for the little they had received on the plantations. Yet they must now find ways to support themselves.

Some went north to look for jobs in the big cities. But many others realized they could do little but farm. So thousands went to work for their former masters or for other landowners.

Booker T. Washington teaching at Tuskegee. He started this school to help his people get an education.

The planters needed help badly but could not afford to pay wages. So they worked out a plan called share cropping. Under this plan, the ex-slaves tended and harvested the crops. In return for work, they were provided with cabins, food, mules, plows and other tools, seed, and the use of the land. In addition, they were given a share of the crops.

Training and education helped the blacks to improve their way of life. Many wanted other kinds of jobs. They wanted to become mechanics, government workers, doctors, or teachers. But they needed education for such jobs. Schools and colleges were started to help educate them. Whenever possible, they eagerly enrolled in these new schools.

Education and hard work made it possible for many ex-slaves to make a better life for themselves. They not only helped themselves but their country. They helped to build a better and stronger United States.

The North and the South began to work together again. In time, the army and the carpetbaggers left. Southerners were allowed to elect their own leaders. Gradually, they were able to rebuild their bridges, railroads, and roads. They began to raise more tobacco, cotton, and sugar cane than ever before. They also began to grow many other kinds of crops. At the same time they built many different kinds of factories. In fact, so many changes were made, that Americans began to call this part of our country "The New South."

Slowly the North and the South learned to be friends again. Together, they looked ahead to a happier future in our fast-growing country.

174

Some Study Questions

1. How did slavery begin in our country? Why did men want slaves?

2. Why did the North and the South quarrel over slavery?

3. What was the Compromise of 1850? Why didn't it work?

4. Why did the South leave the Union when Lincoln was elected President?

5. How did the Civil War begin? How did Lincoln feel about this war?

6. Why did the South finally surrender? What two great generals met to draw up the terms of surrender?

Some Sentences to Complete

Read each of the following incomplete sentences. Then, from the list below, choose the word or group of words to complete each sentence. Write each correctly completed sentence on a sheet of paper.

1. The first blacks brought to the colony of Virginia were __?__.

2. By 1775 some people in each of the __?__ colonies owned slaves.

3. The document called the __?__ said "all men are created equal."

4. The first battle of the Civil War was that of Fort __?__.

5. The __?__ freed slaves in the Confederate States.

6. __?__ was one of the great Northern generals.

7. Robert E. Lee was the commander of the __?__ army.

8. The Civil War started in the year __?__.

9. The __?__ cut off supplies for the South and helped to end the war.

10. __?__ are people who come from other countries to live in our land.

List

Henry Clay	Confederate
Emancipation Proclamation	thirteen
Vicksburg	1861
Declaration of Independence	Sumter
	Ulysses S. Grant
	Robert E. Lee
blockade	1756
immigrants	1860
indentured servants	peace
Underground Railroad	Union

What Do You Think?

1. What do you think it means to say that "all men are created equal"? Is it true?

2. Do we now pledge our first loyalty to our state or to our country? Why?

3. Lincoln was one of the great leaders of our country. Why do you think he became a great man? Name some other great leaders. How are they alike?

4. Why do we say that education can improve our way of life?

Some Other Things to Do

1. Review the paragraphs, "Using an Encyclopedia," on page 158. Read in the correct volume about one of the leaders listed below. Be ready to share what you learn.

Abraham Lincoln	Robert E. Lee
Ulysses S. Grant	Clara Barton
Frederick Douglass	George Washington Carver

2. Dramatize an interesting event in Lincoln's life.

3. Ask your teacher to read and explain Lincoln's Gettysburg Address to your class.

4. Study the paragraphs, "Taking Notes," on page 176. Read in another book on the Underground Railway and take notes on the main facts.

5. Find out all you can about the Red Cross. List ways it helps people in war and in peace. Ask someone from the Red Cross to talk to your class. Try to have your class join the Junior Red Cross.

6. From what countries have people come who live in your community? Show these countries on a world map.

Using a Political Map

Turn to the map on page 166. Use it to help you answer these questions:

1. What is the title of the map?
2. Notice that color is used to show three different groups of states. What are these groups? What part of the map names them?
3. Why is this a political map?
4. Does this map show relief, or not?
5. Does it have an inset map?

The names of some states on this map are written in abbreviated, or shortened, form. Point to Massachusetts. Notice that its abbreviation is *Mass.* Vermont's is *Vt.*

On a piece of paper, copy the names of the states below. Then write the correct abbreviation after each one. You may want to refer to page 499 in the Tables for Reference.

| California | Illinois | Michigan |
| Connecticut | Wisconsin | Ohio |

State abbreviations are often used on maps and letters. So it is a good idea to learn as many of them as you can. Remember that an abbreviation is always followed by a period.

When and in What Order?

Below are some important events about which you read in Chapter 10. Copy the sentences. Write the order in which these events happened before each sentence. After each one, write the year the event took place.

In what order	Important Events	Year
_?_	The war ended.	_?_
_?_	Lincoln was born.	_?_
_?_	Lincoln freed the slaves.	_?_
_?_	The Compromise was passed.	_?_
_?_	Lincoln was elected President.	_?_

Taking Notes

We often need to remember important facts we have read. One way to help our memories is to take notes. Here are some hints for simple note-taking.

1. Read each paragraph carefully.
2. Write down the main word or words that tell the important facts.
3. Keep notes as brief as possible.
4. Use abbreviations whenever you can.

From now on, why not take notes on information you need. They may prove very useful when you make a report.

11 · Our Changing Country

When Our Youngest States Were Born

Hawaii's torch for statehood. In the Pacific Ocean lies Hawaii, a group of lovely islands. Find them on the map on page 178. For years and years, many people had wanted Hawaii to be a state of the United States.

One February evening in 1959, a strange yellow flame danced high above a wooded hill on one of these islands. Thousands of people feared that a dangerous fire had broken out. Firemen and police raced to the hilltop and curious crowds followed.

Much to everyone's surprise, the "fire" proved to be a safe one. It was a fire with a message. It was a tall gas torch burning brightly.

"This is a torch for statehood!" explained the people standing near it. "We shall keep it burning day and night until Hawaii is made a state."

This time, the islanders did not have long to wait. In March, Congress gave them their wish. When the thrilling news reached Hawaii, the celebrations began. Whistles were blown and firecrackers set off! Church bells were rung! Cheering crowds filled the streets of the cities, and parades and speeches were planned. At last, Hawaii had joined our family of states. In 1959 it became the fiftieth state of the United States.

A few months earlier, Alaska had been voted into the Union. How proud its people had been! "Our state is the largest one in the whole United States!" they boasted. And indeed this was true. Find it on the map on page 178.

Hawaii's torch for statehood.

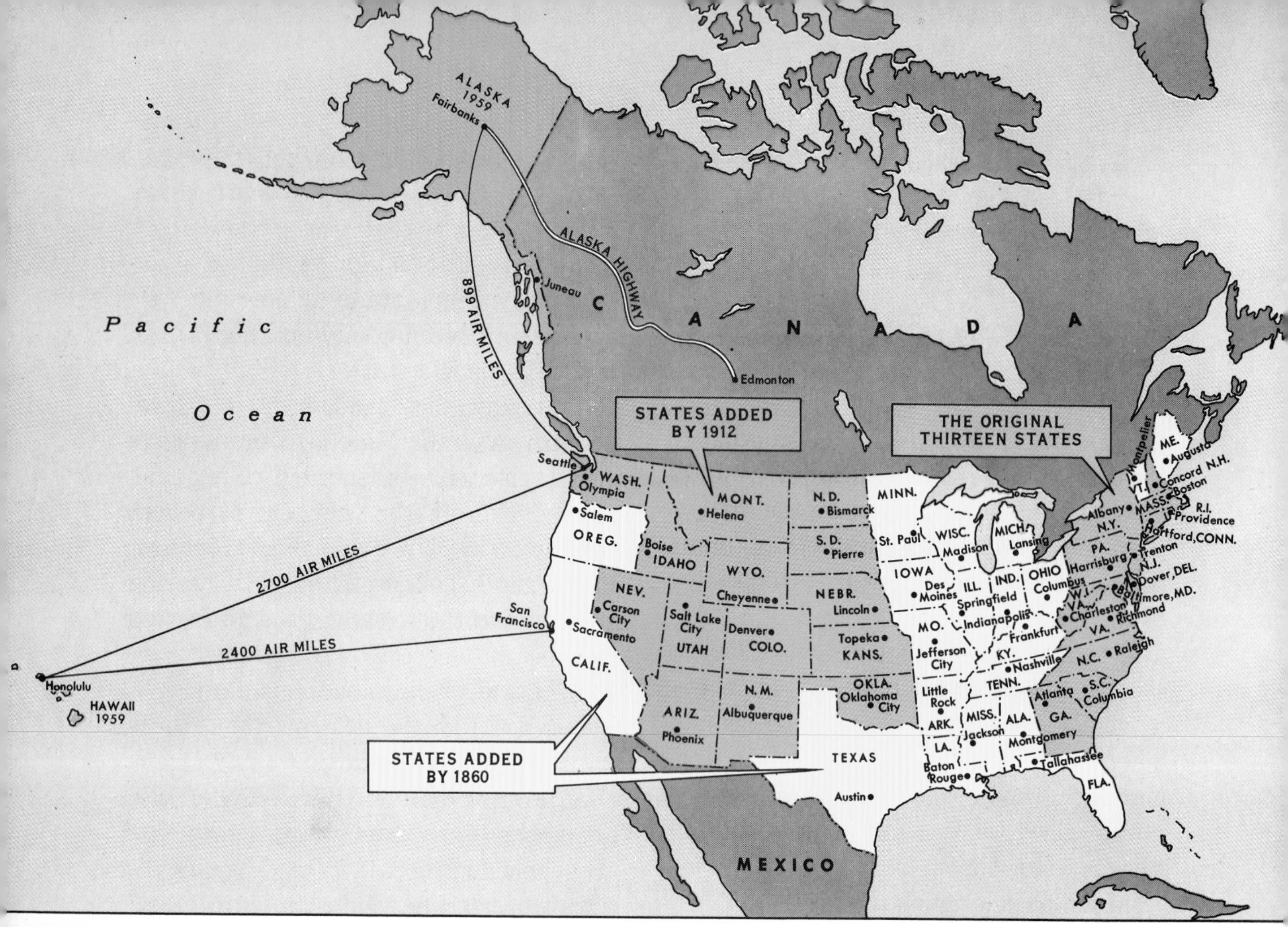
Pacific
Ocean
ALASKA
1959
Fairbanks
ALASKA HIGHWAY
899 AIR MILES
Juneau
C A N A D A
Edmonton
STATES ADDED
BY 1912
THE ORIGINAL
THIRTEEN STATES
Seattle
WASH.
Olympia
Salem
OREG.
Boise
IDAHO
MONT.
Helena
WYO.
Cheyenne
N.D.
Bismarck
S.D.
Pierre
NEBR.
Lincoln
MINN.
St. Paul
WISC.
Madison
MICH.
Lansing
IOWA
Des Moines
ILL.
Springfield
IND.
Indianapolis
OHIO
Columbus
PA.
Harrisburg
N.Y.
Albany
VT.
Montpelier
ME.
Augusta
N.H.
Concord
MASS.
Boston
R.I.
Providence
Hartford, CONN.
Trenton
N.J.
Dover, DEL.
Baltimore, MD.
W.V.
Charleston
VA.
Richmond
2700 AIR MILES
San Francisco
Sacramento
NEV.
Carson City
Salt Lake City
UTAH
Denver
COLO.
Topeka
KANS.
MO.
Jefferson City
KY.
Frankfort
2400 AIR MILES
CALIF.
Nashville
N.C.
Raleigh
TENN.
Honolulu
HAWAII
1959
OKLA.
Oklahoma City
N. M.
Albuquerque
ARIZ.
Phoenix
Little Rock
ARK.
MISS.
Jackson
ALA.
Montgomery
GA.
Atlanta
S.C.
Columbia
STATES ADDED
BY 1860
TEXAS
Austin
LA.
Baton Rouge
Tallahassee
FLA.
MEXICO

This map shows how our country grew from Thirteen to Fifty States. In 1959 two new states joined the Union. What are their names?

Later on, we shall learn more about this giant state of Alaska and Hawaii, its sister in the Pacific.

Today, our country has fifty states, as you probably know. All of them are shown on the map on this page. In which one do you live? Find it on the map above. Did it become a state before or after the Civil War? You can find out by looking back at the map on page 166 and then comparing it with the map on pages 504 and 505.

Let's go back to these earlier years. As you know, Chapter 10 told the story of the Civil War. But what important events have happened in the hundred years since then? For one thing, our family of states has grown.

From Territories to States

Gold and silver "rushes" helped to settle the West. You read how people had headed for California during its Gold Rush. Other parts of the West also had some exciting "rushes."

Even before the Civil War, some gold and silver was discovered in the Rocky

Mountains. It was found in present-day Colorado. This attracted thousands of people who hoped to get rich. Valuable deposits of silver and gold were also found farther west in Nevada. So adventurers and miners hurried to its "diggings." Then fortune-hunters flocked to the "silver and gold lands" of Montana, New Mexico, Idaho, and South Dakota. All of these states were then territories.

Mining camps sprang up in these lands. For a few years they were as busy as beehives. But soon, the easy-to-mine riches were gone and most miners gave up. Many drifted away, but a few turned to other occupations.

By this time, some men were beginning to farm these lands. Others grazed livestock on the Great Plains. Find these plains on the map on page 90.

Cattle were raised on the Great Plains. The cattle-raising industry had started on the Texas plains. It became an important business because the fast-growing cities in the East needed large quantities of meat.

Before long, this industry spread north. Herds of cattle were raised from Texas all the way to Montana. The cattle were shipped east on the railroads that were being built westward. When they were ready for market, cowboys drove them far across the plains to these railroads.

Railroads also helped to settle the West. By 1869, a railroad connected the West with the East. In fact, it extended to California, as a later story will explain.

The main loading points along the western railroads grew into small settlements. Some people called them "cow towns." They became bustling little trading centers when more people started homes on the plains. These railroads also brought farmers and other settlers to the West.

Gradually, more farmers moved to the western plains. Some settled on the western Central Plains. Others were attracted to the Great Plains. Many went to live on homesteads. Congress had passed the Homestead Law which allowed a pioneer to occupy 160 acres of free land. After five years, the land was his if he had worked on it, built a house, and lived there.

Other pioneers bought land from the railroads. Companies had spent fortunes building railroads across the West. To help meet this huge expense, the Government gave them land. Then these companies offered much of it for sale.

Cowboys round up cattle on the Great Plains.

Immigrants travel on a train
that crosses the western
plains.

The railroads sent glowing reports of their lands far and wide, even to some countries in Europe. They boasted about the wonders of the West. They praised the pleasant climate and fine rich soil. Best of all, they said, was that the new lands could be bought very cheaply.

Many farm families in northern Europe welcomed such information. Their countries were crowded and there was not enough good land to go around. Besides, the best land was owned by wealthy people. Poor people could not afford the high taxes or other expenses. In these countries, there were few opportunities to get ahead. Surely, life in America would be more promising. Surely America was the place to go.

Many immigrants helped to build our country. Among those who settled on the plains were people from Sweden, Norway, Denmark, and Germany. Find these countries on the map on page 189.

Even before the railroads advertised their land, however, immigrants had poured into our country. Many of them were from Ireland. Some had started homes in the cities. Others had helped to build our railroads.

These "new Americans" brought with them their skills and a willingness to work hard. They knew how to be thrifty and make their opportunities count.

The western plains were settled slowly. Indians tried to stop the newcomers from taking their lands. Too, the northern winters were long and cruel. Even more important, the plains seemed too dry to grow most crops. However, farmers learned that wheat could be grown. After a wheat-harvesting machine was invented, more settlers decided to sow this crop. They began to lay out wheat farms on these wide flat lands.

In time, new states and cities were formed. You can name the states if you use the Tables on page 499. Which ones had been a part of the Louisiana Territory? The maps on pages 117 and 151 will help you decide. Which ones were carved from lands won from Mexico? Use the map on page 151 to see.

Small trading centers were started here and there in the West. Some grew into busy towns as did some of the mining centers. Denver, Colorado began as a mining town. Today, it is a bustling and lovely city. Today, there are also dozens of other cities scattered over these western lands.

Cities throughout our country have grown very fast in recent years. And how they have changed since they began! Why? See if you can find some answers to that question as you read on.

Our Cities Grew as Manufacturing Increased

Through the years, many people moved from farms to cities. Perhaps some of them thought that cities would offer an easier life. Farm work was hard and farm life was often lonely. But mainly, people thought they could earn a better living in a city. There, one might have a choice of jobs. True, the "pay" was small, but at least, one received it every Saturday night.

"Pay" on the farm was quite a different matter. A farmer's chief income was from his harvest, once a year. As you may know, *income* is the money that a person receives or earns during a year. Often, after storms or long dry spells, the crops were very poor. Then, there was hardly enough money to pay the bills, or perhaps none at all. A farmer could never be sure how much income he would have. But things looked more hopeful for city work, whether in factories or other kinds of business.

Many factories had been started. After the Revolutionary War, mills and factories were built in our country. The first were cotton and woolen mills. In these mills, machines were used to spin thread and weave cloth. Then as time went by, machines were invented to do other kinds of manufacturing. They made things more quickly and cheaply than people could by hand.

At first these factories were small and were owned by one family. An owner who hired workers was the *employer* and the workers were the *employees*.

In the early days, an employer had so few employees that he knew them all. But as businesses grew larger, more of them were owned by groups of men. Some large companies hired thousands of employees. The owners no longer knew their employees nor even much about their working conditions. Usually, they paid low wages. And some allowed very unpleasant and unhealthy working conditions. Dark uncomfortable rooms! Not enough fresh air! Dangerous machines! No safety helps! Furthermore, most employees had to work twelve hours a day, six days a week, without a vacation.

Now and then, a few brave employees complained. But generally, little was done to improve things, and sometimes complaints cost a person his job. Workmen felt, therefore, that they must "unite" to get what they deserved.

Workmen joined together to help each other. They formed organizations called *labor unions*. Some labor unions persuaded employers to raise wages and agree to shorter hours and better working conditions. But often such agreements came only after the union members went on strike. In a *strike*, all of the union members stopped working at the same time.

In time, labor unions became more and more powerful. But even before this, many businesses had grown larger than ever. The giant companies were spoken of as "big business."

Together, business and labor produced more goods than ever before. For one thing, remarkable machines had been invented to help to speed up work. Also, our country was producing more crops. And it was "harvesting" larger quantities of wonderful natural resources, such as oil, timber, and iron ore. All of these products are *raw materials*. These raw materials were changed into useful products in many kinds of factories.

Furthermore, more railroads had been built. At this time, we depended mostly on railroads and ships to move goods. They hauled raw materials to factories and carried finished goods to market.

Our cities hummed with industry. More factories and mills were built. Nearly all of them were built in or near a town or city. Soon, manufacturing became our largest industry. No wonder, then, that it created many jobs for city-dwellers. Many towns became cities, and cities grew even larger.

All of these manufacturing industries needed people. Workmen were needed not only in the factories but also in the mines and on the railroads. Other people were needed to direct all of these businesses and to sell all the goods that were produced. Many of the people who helped build these industries and businesses were "new Americans."

People from many lands settled in our cities. Some of them had come to the United States as immigrants. Others were the children or grandchildren of immigrants.

When you stop and think, all of us are immigrants or come from immigrants. We do, unless our people were Indians, the first Americans, you remember. The Jamestown settlers and the Pilgrims were immigrants, for they came to our shores from another land. Since their times, millions of immigrants have streamed to our country.

People from other lands have not only helped our country to grow. They have made our lives richer in many ways. They have brought us their art and music and some delightful customs. They have brought a love of freedom and a willingness to work hard. Large numbers have found jobs in our factories or in other industries. Some have become leaders in such fields as government, business, education, science, music, and art.

Many blacks have moved to cities from the farms of the South. Like other Americans, blacks are employed in every industry. Some are doctors, lawyers, teachers, storekeepers, or nurses. Others are on duty as firemen or policemen in our cities.

The population of our cities has grown. The word *population* means the number of people living in a place or region. On page 184 is a population map. Study the key and legend beneath it. What does the lightest color show on the map? What does the darkest color tell?

See if you can find about where you live on the map. Is it a thinly-settled region or a thickly-settled one? In which kind of region are cities located?

New York is our largest city. Find it on the population map. Three other enormous industrial centers are Los Angeles, Chicago, and Detroit. Locate them.

Large cities have many difficult problems. Among them are traffic jams, dirty air, slums, and crime.

Thousands of automobiles, trucks, and buses share crowded streets. Much of this traffic is caused by people who live in the suburbs of the cities. These people depend on automobiles and buses to carry them to and from their work.

Heavy traffic adds greatly to another problem, dirty air or *smog*. The engines of automobiles, trucks, and buses pour out smelly fumes that increase this *air pollution*. When the wind is quiet, a blanket of smog may hang over a city for days. Smog can cause headaches and watery eyes; it is unpleasant and unhealthful.

Slums are old, overcrowded neighborhoods. Their buildings have become ugly and rundown, with rusty plumbing and even broken windows, and doors that don't lock. Rats and bugs seem to be everywhere. People live in slums because they are too poor to move elsewhere, perhaps because they are out of work. Many of our black Americans have become trapped in such slums. Life may look empty and discouraging to such people; these feelings are partly to blame for increased crime and riots.

Thinking Americans know that talking things over and working together is the way to solve problems. Much is being done to provide better opportunities for poor people. Job-training centers have been opened. Many businesses employ unskilled workers for "earn while you learn," on-the-job, training. Young people are being helped to remain in school.

Many cities are working on *urban renewal*. Clearing away slums is part of urban renewal. But clearing them all away will take years and tremendous sums of money.

ST. GAUDENS – IRELAND

BELL – SCOTLAND

BERLIN – RUSSIA

TOSCANINI – ITALY

DR. JULIAN – U.S.A.

RIIS – DENMARK

SIKORSKY – RUSSIA

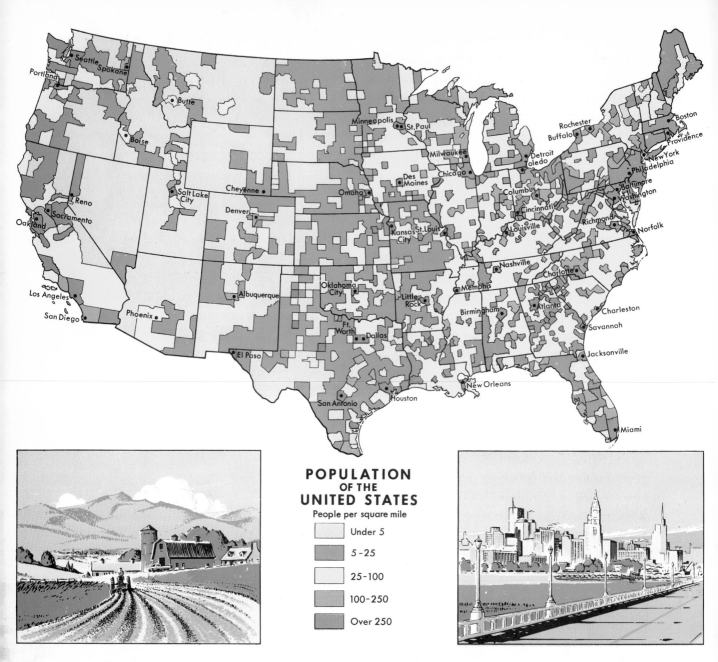

POPULATION
OF THE
UNITED STATES

People per square mile

	Under 5
	5 - 25
	25 - 100
	100 - 250
	Over 250

**This map shows where most of the people in forty-eight of
our states live** · This kind of map is called a population map.
The darkest color on the map shows where the most people live.
The lightest color shows where the fewest live. By 1970 about
205 million people were living in the United States.

This kind of population map tells the number of persons living
on a square mile of land. A square mile is the area of a square
a mile long, and a mile wide. In the key find the color that stands
for areas having less than two people to a square mile. What
parts of the forty-eight states have the fewest people. What
parts have the most people?

184

Have you ever wondered why some towns became cities? The key reason is that each one had a favorable location. Some cities were near plenty of raw materials needed by factories. Also, they are transportation centers. Atlanta, Georgia grew because it was on a railroad. Today, transportation centers are connected to other cities by railways, highways, airways, and perhaps waterways. How does this encourage a city's growth?

Port cities are doubly fortunate. They are connected by waterways with port cities of the world. Some like St. Louis and Kansas City are river ports. But many, located on the seacoast, are busy seaports. New York and Los Angeles are examples of seaports.

Most of our cities have had an important share in helping our country develop world trade. But our port cities have had a special part. From their docks, raw materials and manufactured goods have been shipped to every country on the globe. To these docks come raw materials needed by the factories and the people of our country.

How Our World Trade Grew and Changed

All of us are traders. Your parents and neighbors are traders, and so are you. Trade is exchanging one thing for another, and buying and selling. How many times did you trade yesterday?

You may trade a baseball for a knife, or a box of crayolas for a pencil set. At the store, you may trade a dime for an ice cream cone. And perhaps you exchange money for a lunch in your school cafeteria.

Your parents trade money for groceries and for clothing and furniture. Probably, they traded money for many things in your home as well as for an automobile or boat.

Remember! Trade has two parts, getting, and giving in exchange. You probably do some trading every day. It often means buying and selling.

Many different products are loaded and unloaded at our busy ports. This freighter is docked at the port of Philadelphia.

We trade to get things which we do not make or raise ourselves. We can do this if we produce more of some things than we can use. For example, a farmer sold his crops to get money; but he could sell them because he raised more than he could use himself. Keep these ideas in mind as you read on about world trade.

World trade is carried on between nations. The main reasons for it are similar to those you have just read. A country needs certain materials which it lacks. It sells the goods which it can spare, and uses the money to buy the goods which it needs.

Today, all countries large and small take part in world trade. But the leading traders include the United States, Canada, Great Britain, France, Germany, Italy, Argentina, Brazil, and Japan. Can you locate each of these countries on the map on page 189?

The United States began its world trading long ago. In those days, it *exported* mostly raw materials such as timber, and cotton, and tobacco. *Exports* are goods which are shipped out of a country. At that time, we had only a few factories, so we *imported* many manufactured goods. *Imports* are goods which are shipped into a country.

Today the picture has changed. Today, we manufacture far more goods than we can use. We try to sell our "extra" goods to other nations. We export large quantities of machinery and tools, for example. We also export many shiploads of such farm products as wheat, corn, and soybeans.

We buy such crop goods as coffee and bananas. Why, do you suppose? We also purchase large quantities of tin and rubber and some other raw materials that we do not have in this country. Indeed, fifteen different kinds of raw materials are imported to make the telephones which serve us so faithfully. Also we use more and more raw materials. So we import lumber, oil, iron, and other minerals.

Ships from many different nations visit our harbors. They may bring us perfume from France, or silks from Italy. They may unload coffee from Brazil or bananas from Costa Rica, or iron ore from Venezuela. A cargo of tin may have come from the East Indies, or some fine china and woolen articles from Great Britain. Canada sends us huge quantities of paper for printing newspapers and books.

Sometimes, however, carrying on world trade has led to serious problems. In a way, it helped to lead our country into a world war.

How We Fought in Two World Wars

In 1914, a terrible war broke out in Europe. In this war Germany and her partners fought against the Allies. The Allies included Britain, France, Russia, Belgium, and several other countries.

For nearly three years, the United States stayed out of this war. During that time, we traded with the countries of both sides. But this was not easy. Each side tried to prevent our goods and supplies from reaching its enemy.

The United States entered this war. British vessels stopped many of our ships on the way to Germany and seized our cargo. At the same time, German submarines roamed the seas. As you know, a submarine is a specially-designed vessel that can travel beneath the waves. Germany's submarines sunk many enemy ships and even several that carried passengers. One was the huge British ocean liner, the *Lusitania*. When it went down, nearly 1200 people lost their lives. More than a hundred of them were Americans.

This sad event angered Americans. Some declared that we must go to war against Germany. They urged that we join the Allies immediately! But our President still hoped that war could be avoided. However, he informed Germany that we would not stand for further loss of American lives.

Germany made no promises. Soon the Germans sunk several American ships. So, the United States entered the war against Germany in April, 1917. In the months that followed, two million Americans were sent to Europe to help the Allies.

The war ended on November 11, 1918. On this day the Germans asked that fighting be stopped. They realized that they had lost the war. Today, in our country Veteran's Day is a holiday in October. It honors our veterans who have served in the Armed Forces.

Because so many countries fought in this war, it was spoken of as a world war. It is now called World War I.

In 1939, the Second World War broke out. It began in Europe. Germany seized a small neighboring country and then attacked another one next door. When this happened, Britain and France declared war on Germany. Italy and then Japan joined Germany. Then later, the

The *Lusitania* was sunk by a German submarine. Over one hundred Americans lost their lives.

Soviet Union, or Russia, declared war on Germany.

This Second World War was a terrible battle of machines as well as of men. Thousands of planes fought in the air. Some dropped bombs from the sky. The bombs were aimed at railroads and factories where war supplies were being made. But at the same time, whole blocks of cities were smashed and thousands of people were killed.

The United States sent aid to Britain and the other Allies. As the war went on, Americans feared for the future. They believed that our country would be in danger if Germany, Japan, and Italy won. Our factories ran day and night to manufacture goods that were needed by the Allies. And our farmers shared with the Allies crops that they harvested. Shipping these goods across the seas was

COUNTRIES OF
OUR WORLD

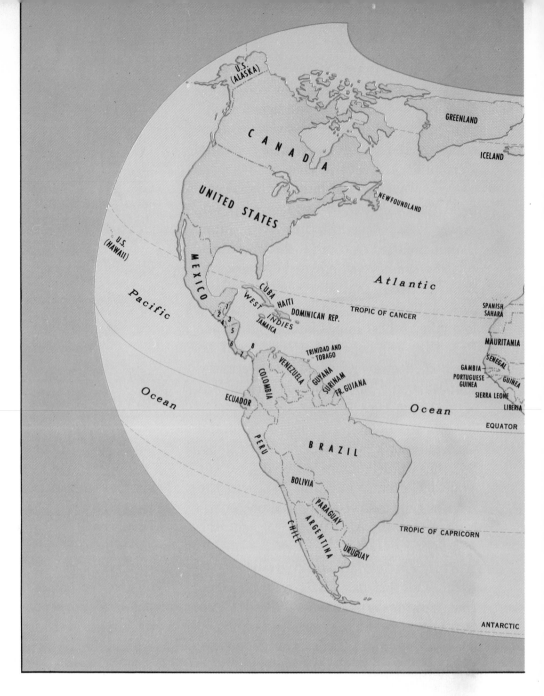

dangerous business, of course. But we knew that the Allies needed help and continued to sell goods to them.

Then suddenly, we found ourselves fighting in the war. But for us, this began on the other side of the world.

Japan attacked several American bases. On the quiet Sunday morning of December 7, 1941, Japanese planes sneaked in to bomb our military bases in Hawaii. At that time, Hawaii was a United States territory. Its Pearl Harbor was the home of a part of our navy. Nearby was a United States air base.

The Japanese bombs killed hundreds of Americans. They sunk or damaged many ships, and destroyed more than 100 planes. Japanese airmen also attacked our bases on the Philippine Islands. Locate these islands on the map on this page.

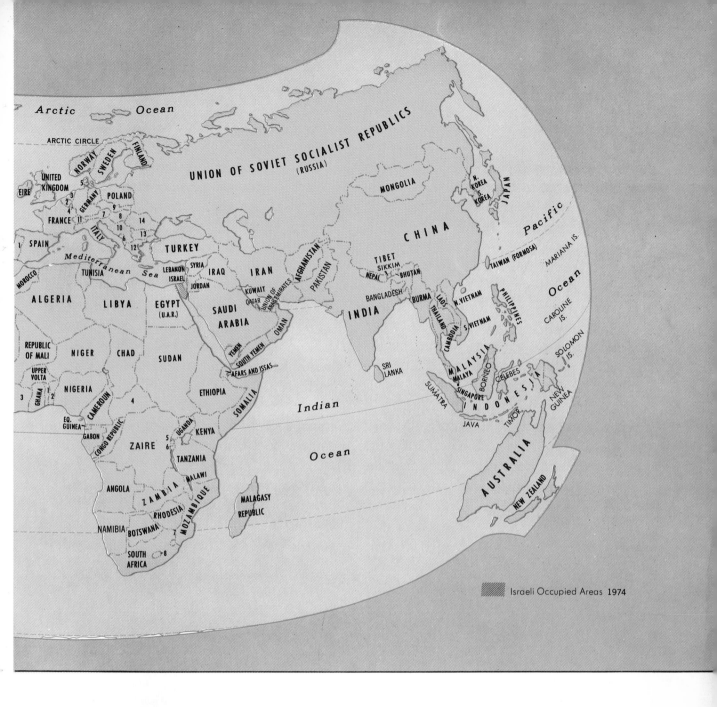

Israeli Occupied Areas 1974

This political map shows the countries of our world · However, our world is changing rapidly. There may be some countries in Africa that have become independent since the map was made.

On this map most of the countries of Europe and Central America are too small to be named. Instead each of these countries is numbered. The key to these numbers is to the left of the map. For example the key tells you that number 11 in Europe is Switzerland. What is number 1 in Europe? What is number 6 in Central America?

Notice that they are quite close to Asia and the island country of Japan.

The United States joined the Second World War. Now the United States had to defend itself. Our country declared war on Japan. Then Germany and Italy began to fight the United States.

The Second World War went on for several more years. Bitter battles were fought all over the world. In Europe! In the Atlantic and Pacific oceans! And in North Africa and Asia!

World War II ended in 1945. It had killed millions of people. It left other millions crippled. It ruined homes, farms, factories, and cities. It cost billions of dollars! Nearly everyone felt that such a war must not happen again.

Leaders of the United States and other countries met. They talked over ways for nations to work together. They planned for an organization to work to keep the peace. It was called the *United Nations*.

The United Nations was started in 1945. At first 50 countries belonged to it. Today more than 130 countries are members. Most meetings are held at the U.N. headquarters in New York City.

The U.N. has many goals. One is to cut down air and ocean pollution around the world. Another is to help people all over the world to raise more food and improve their living conditions. But its most important goal is to prevent wars.

Some wars have broken out, however. The United States has had a part in two —one in Korea and one in Southeast Asia. Other wars have been fought near India, in Africa, and in the Middle East.

All of us need to work for peace. We can begin by trying to understand other peoples. We can learn more about them in books, newspapers, and on TV. We can enjoy their art and music.

We can learn from other countries and they learn from us. We can share discoveries in medicine and other sciences. We can work together in exploring space!

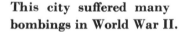
This city suffered many bombings in World War II.

Our Newest Frontier: Space

We are beginning to explore and work in Space. Space begins about 100 miles beyond the Earth's surface. Our planet, Earth, travels through Space. It travels around the sun. So do eight other planets. One is Mars. Another is huge far-distant Jupiter. Our earth and these planets are satellites of the sun. A *satellite* is a "body" which travels around another larger "body."

Astronomers have told us some things about Mars, Jupiter, and other bodies in Space. They have studied them through powerful telescopes. Now we can get more information, thanks to some wonders of our *Space Age*.

People-made satellites are helping us. Some of these spacecraft carry a crew. Those with no crew aboard are *unmanned* satellites.

Weather satellites are unmanned craft. They circle the earth, gathering information for us about the weather.

Communications satellites are also unmanned satellites. They send "messages" to far places around the world. They pass along telephone calls, and radio and T.V. programs across the seas. They can bring us the latest happenings in Japan, or England, or Israel.

Other unmanned satellites serve as explorers. They can venture much farther into space than men have dared to go. *Mariner 9* flew around the planet Mars. It photographed about 7000 pictures of Mars. *Pioneer 10* raced nearly 400 million

A weather satellite.

miles out into space. It traveled past the giant planet, Jupiter, and sent back useful information.

These satellites are at work because skilled engineers, scientists, and trained workers helped build them. They also built and equipped remarkable space ships for our astronauts.

The astronauts: our daring spacemen. The brave crews aboard space ships are astronauts. The word, *astronaut*, means "sailor among the stars."

Astronauts have to pass many kinds of difficult tests. Many are experienced pilots. Some are scientists. All are

191

thoroughly trained before taking off into Space. They study and practice in teams. They try to learn ahead of time how to solve problems in Space.

Our country's Space trips began in 1961. The first lasted fifteen minutes. Alan Shepard went alone on this important beginning trip. John Glenn was the first American to travel around the earth. In 1962 he flew around the earth three times in his spacecraft, the *Friendship 7*.

Other flights followed. As with the first ones, there were exciting moments of countdown. Then there was the thundering roar and lift off. The mighty rocket engine pushed the craft at its top into the sky.

At flight's end, the returning craft coasted down over the ocean and splashed into the waves. A helicopter then snatched the astronauts up. It flew them to a United States Navy ship waiting nearby.

Each flight was a little longer. On each one, the astronauts learned more about how to live and work in Space. Some took space walks and did repair jobs outside the ship, firmly attached to it, of course. Sometimes, serious problems threatened. But the men were trained to think calmly and find answers. They could talk over problems with experts at the Control Center at Houston, Texas. Its amazing equipment could correct most problems if the astronauts couldn't.

These early astronauts faced hardships and dangers proudly. They were blazing the trail for our first trip to the moon. They were pioneers.

On to the moon! In 1968, the *Apollo* flights began. The Apollo ships were larger and equipped for longer trips.

A Saturn rocket carrying the Skylab 4 Astronauts takes off in November 1973.

A busy day in the city. More and more of us each year live in cities and their suburbs.

Apollo 7 traveled around the earth for nearly eleven days as its astronauts studied space problems.

Other Apollo flights traveled toward the moon. It is more than 240,000 miles away. The moon is a satellite of the earth. It has no air, water, or weather. Nothing lives there.

Some Apollo astronauts traveled around the moon. They photographed it, but they did not land. That was planned for a later flight.

Exploring on the moon. In July, 1969, two astronauts separated their small landing craft from *Apollo 11*. The landing craft carried them down to the moon's surface. They were the first people ever to land there.

As Neil Armstrong stepped on the moon, he said, "That's a small step for man, but a giant leap for mankind." What do you think he meant?

Soon astronaut Edwin Aldrin also stepped out on moon soil. The two explorers planted an American flag on this new "land." But they represented all peoples of the world. It has been agreed that no country can claim the moon.

The visitors from earth took many pictures. They gathered samples of rocks and moon dust to bring back. After two days of exploring, the men fired the small rocket that lifted them into Space. Soon, they joined *Apollo 11* with Commander Collins on board.

Since this historic landing, there have been other successful flights to the moon. And new space ventures are taking place. But only a few of us can be space travelers. Most of us may never set out in a space ship. We will remain on earth living and working in our own wonderful country.

Working Together

We live in an urban country. Cities and the suburbs around cities are called *urban areas*. Over 150 million people in the United States now live in urban areas. That is about three-fourths of our people.

Working together on our problems. Young people help to clean up a river. Adults meet to discuss ways to solve urban problems.

People live in urban areas because they can find work there. Urban areas can be interesting and pleasant places to live. But some sections are unpleasant and unhappy areas of slums! They are ugly with unhealthy run-down buildings. No one wants to live in a slum. But some people cannot find jobs that pay enough for them to move elsewhere.

Urban areas often have air pollution. As you read earlier, air pollution is caused by factories of all kinds and by automobiles, trucks, and buses.

Most urban areas have transportation problems. During work-travel hours, the streets and freeways are crowded with traffic. It may take hours for people to travel to and from their jobs. What other problems can you think of in urban areas?

People create the problems. It is people who let buildings run down. It is people who cause air pollution. It is people who cause water pollution. We are the ones who throw trash on the sidewalks and streets. We are the ones who are greedy for more and more things.

But it is people who also build parks and playgrounds in cities. They plant trees and flowers. They help neighbors. They work together to solve problems.

It is people who build handsome buildings and pleasant apartments and houses. It is people who take part in the government of their urban area. They plan schools, hospitals, museums, and ball parks. People make problems. People can solve problems.

We are using more and more natural resources in our country. There are more of us every year. Also we want more things. Almost everything we use comes from natural resources such as soil, water, trees, coal, iron, and oil, remember.

Think of the many ways we use oil, for example. Farmers use it to raise the food we eat. They use it to run many kinds of machines. Machines prepare the fields, plant seeds, and get rid of weeds. Machines harvest crops and milk cows. Trucks and railroads that take the farmers' crops to market use fuel from oil.

Factories use huge amounts of oil. Oil is used to make the electricity that heats and lights many factories. This electricity also runs the machines that make the products. And many chemicals, plastics, and fibers for cloth are made from oil.

Think of the oil that is used to run autos, trucks, airplanes, railroads, and ships! And of course, oil is used to make the electricity that heats and lights many homes. Every year there are more of us using up more products from oil.

What products can you think of that are made of steel? Every year there are more of us using more products from steel. Steel is made from iron, coal, and other natural resources. These are resources that cannot be replaced once they are used up. Some of these raw materials must be imported from countries all over the world.

We must work together to solve our problems. We must stop polluting our water and air. We must clean up our lakes and rivers. We need to learn to use our natural resources more wisely. We must find ways to improve our growing urban areas. We should make them healthy and pleasant for all who live there.

We all share these problems. We must think together. We must plan together. We must work together to solve them.

Keeping our country beautiful is a big job! It is an exciting job. But we can do it if we all work together. IT'S UP TO YOU AND ME!

Some Questions about This Story

1. How did railroads help to settle our country?

2. How did the growth of manufacturing cause cities to grow?

3. What are labor unions? Why were they formed?

4. What problems did "big business" bring?

5. How have immigrants helped our country?

6. What does it mean to *trade*?

7. What do people trade? What do nations trade? Why do they trade?

8. Why do we say that we live in the Space Age?

9. What are some problems of urban areas?

10. Why must we use natural resources more wisely?

What Is Your Idea?

1. Would you rather work for a small company or a large one? Give your reasons.

2. Did you ever sell anything? Did you make a profit? Why must companies have a profit to stay in business?

3. Why is it said that business could not get along without labor? Do you think labor could manage without business? If not, why?

4. Why does it take courage to be an immigrant?

Some Other Things to Do

1. Talk to someone who owns a small business. What are some of his problems?

2. Talk to an employee of a large company. What does he like about his work?

3. Read about a leader in this chapter. Take notes to help you make a report.

4. Find out about one of the following:
>   weather satellites
>   communications satellites
>   one of the Apollo flights

Be ready to share what you learn.

5. Have a "Can you locate it?" contest. Use a world map and a map of the United States. Divide into two teams. See which team can earn the most points locating the places named in this and earlier chapters.

Using a World Map

Use the map on pages 188–189 to help you answer the questions below.

1. What ocean is nearest to your state? Do you live near another large body of water? If so, point to it and name it.

2. What continent lies southeast of us? Many of its countries trade with us. Name and locate those mentioned in Chapter 11.

3. Find and name the largest continent. What country named in Chapter 11 is a part of this continent? What ocean would we have to cross to reach it?

Let's Review Maps

1. On what page did you find a population map? What does color show on this map? What can you study to find out what each color stands for?

2. Use the map on pages 504–505 to check up on symbols. What symbol is used to show:
   a. the capital of a state?
   b. our national capital?
   c. a state boundary line?
   d. an international boundary?

3. What kind of a map is shown on pages 188 and 189? Is it a political map? What on the map tells you?

4. What continents are shown on this map?

5. Notice the key at the left of the World Map. Let's practice using it. Point to the list of European countries. What number is before the name, Netherlands? Find that number on the map. What number stands for Greece? Locate Greece.

UNIT THREE

Looking at Our Great Nation

12 · New England: From Textiles to Electronics

An Electronic Wonder that Serves Us

A machine that does arithmetic. A computer is an electronic wonder. It makes use of the power of moving electrons, or electricity. It uses this electric power to do many wonderful things. For example, a computer can add and subtract as well as multiply and divide.

Such a machine can work difficult arithmetic problems as quick as a flash. Just think! A large one can do several thousand additions in a single second! But not by itself! No, indeed! A computer cannot think. Trained experts must "tell" it what to do. They must feed it certain information before it can go to work.

One computer is shown in the picture below. Read what the legend tells about it. What does this machine do?

Some large computers can do many kinds of jobs. They may be used in stores, banks, and other businesses. Some sort mail in post offices. Some work for

This computer makes calculations from information fed to it about a satellite in orbit.

airlines or help run trains. Each one can do the work of many people in a few seconds. Smaller ones do special jobs such as helping to guide spacecraft at a control center or on board a craft.

The "grandfather" of these computers was planned in England. A clever mathematics teacher designed it more than a hundred years ago. He had in mind a machine that could add much faster than a person. He put together a mass of wheels, screws, levers, and other parts.

This early computer was never finished successfully. Its inventor gave up when his money was gone. But there were other reasons for giving up, also. In those days, there were no large factories or engineers ready to help him. Nor could his computer be run by electricity. Why not, do you suppose?

This strange machine was soon forgotten. But many years later, Americans became interested in it all over again. They learned much from it.

In the 1940's, a New England professor built a computer. It was a success and could solve many difficult problems rapidly. Since then, engineers and factories have built many other computers. Each year, such machines have been improved. The latest models are more simple in design, and can work at lightning speed, faster than ever.

Today, many computers are manufactured in New England. This part of our country also turns out other remarkable electronic equipment, as well as many other kinds of goods. You see, manufacturing is its leading industry. See if you can find some reasons why as you read about New England's geography.

A Look at New England

Six states make up New England. Look at this region on the political and inset maps on page 200. The inset map reminds you that New England occupies the northeast corner of our country. This map also shows that New England is a small region. It is the smallest of the main regions of our country. In fact, if you placed New England on the map of Texas, only one fourth of this large southern state would be covered.

What states make up New England? Look on the political map and see. Name each one. Which is the largest? Which is the smallest? Which reaches farthest north? What state has no coast line?

Most of New England is hilly or mountainous. The map on page 201 shows this plainly. Notice that New England is one of the hilliest parts of our whole country. Along its coast are low hills. Some have rocky cliffs that border the sea. Inland, the hills are higher.

Western New England has many mountains. They stretch in long chains from north to south. What ranges do you see on the map on page 201? New England's hills and mountains are a part of the Appalachian Highlands. Can you explain what high lands are? Why do you think this land would be difficult to farm?

Forests carpet much of New England. If we flew over this region, we would see acres and acres of lovely trees. There are oaks, maples, birches, and other hardwood trees as well as evergreens. The hardwood trees are a beautiful sight in

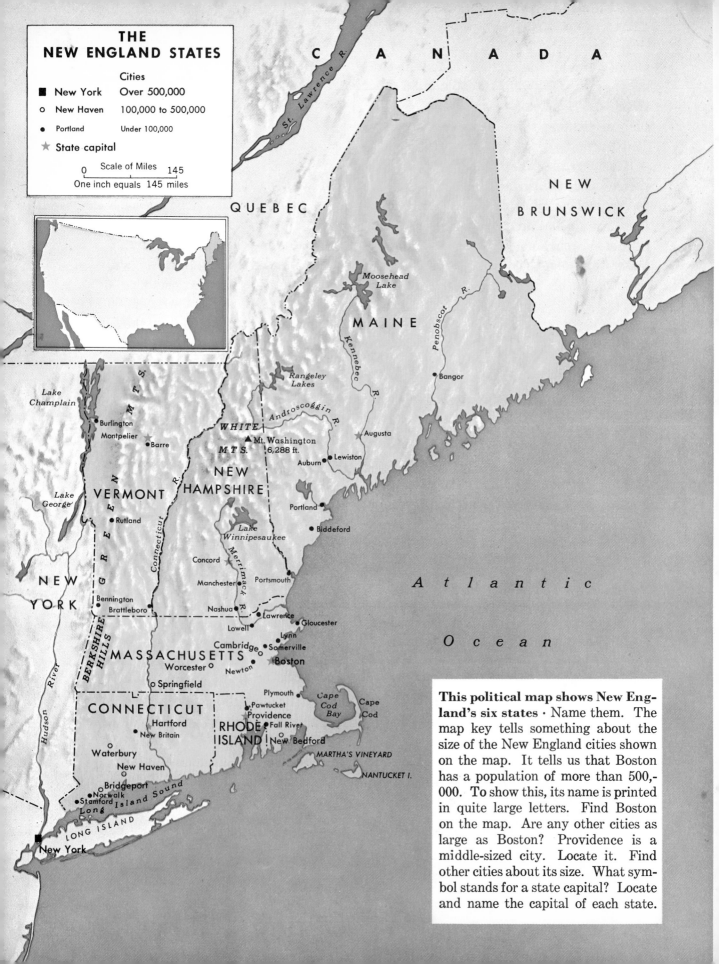

THE NEW ENGLAND STATES

Cities

■ New York   Over 500,000

○ New Haven   100,000 to 500,000

● Portland   Under 100,000

★ State capital

Scale of Miles
0 ——————— 145
One inch equals 145 miles

CANADA

St. Lawrence R.

QUEBEC

NEW BRUNSWICK

Moosehead Lake

MAINE

Penobscot R.

● Bangor

Kennebec R.

Rangeley Lakes

Androscoggin R.

Lake Champlain

● Burlington
Montpelier ★
● Barre

GREEN MTS.

WHITE MTS.
▲ Mt. Washington 6,288 ft.

★ Augusta

● Auburn ● Lewiston

NEW HAMPSHIRE

Lake George

VERMONT

● Rutland

Connecticut R.

Lake Winnipesaukee

● Portland

● Biddeford

Concord ★

Merrimack R.

NEW YORK

Bennington ●
● Brattleboro

BERKSHIRE HILLS

Manchester ●
Nashua ●
Lowell ●

Portsmouth ●

Lawrence ●
● Gloucester
Lynn ●
Cambridge ○ ● Somerville
Boston ★
Newton ●

MASSACHUSETTS
Worcester ○

○ Springfield

Plymouth ●

Cape Cod Bay

Cape Cod

CONNECTICUT

Hartford ★
● New Britain

Pawtucket ●
★ Providence
RHODE ISLAND
Fall River ●
New Bedford ●

Hudson River

○ Waterbury

New Haven ○

● Bridgeport
● Norwalk
● Stamford
Long Island Sound

LONG ISLAND

■ New York

MARTHA'S VINEYARD

NANTUCKET I.

Atlantic Ocean

This political map shows New England's six states · Name them. The map key tells something about the size of the New England cities shown on the map. It tells us that Boston has a population of more than 500,-000. To show this, its name is printed in quite large letters. Find Boston on the map. Are any other cities as large as Boston? Providence is a middle-sized city. Locate it. Find other cities about its size. What symbol stands for a state capital? Locate and name the capital of each state.

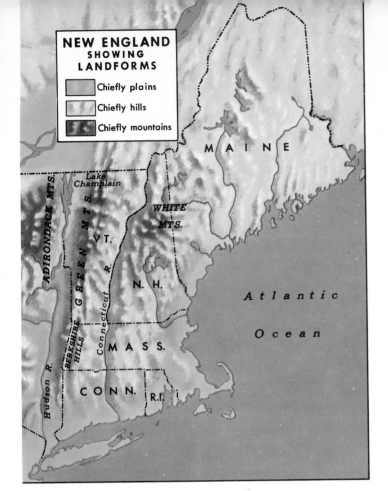

NEW ENGLAND
SHOWING
LANDFORMS

Chiefly plains
Chiefly hills
Chiefly mountains

ADIRONDACK MTS.

Lake
Champlain

MAINE

WHITE
MTS.

GREEN MTS.

VT.

N. H.

BERKSHIRE HILLS

Connecticut R.

Hudson R.

MASS.

CONN.

R.I.

Atlantic

Ocean

You learned in Chapter 5 about five different kinds of land found in our large country · This map shows you which kinds of land New England has. Which does it have more of, hills or plains? Which are easier to farm?

What are some of the main occupations in New England today? You can find out if you study the map at the right. What color is used to show agriculture, or farming? What symbol is used to show manufacturing centers? Notice how many of these centers are along rivers.

Which of New England's occupations do you think depend on this region's natural resources? Which of these occupations is important in your community?

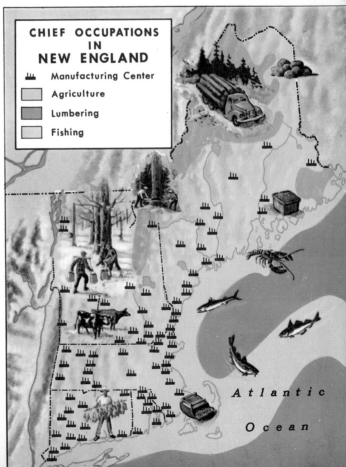

CHIEF OCCUPATIONS
IN
NEW ENGLAND

Manufacturing Center
Agriculture
Lumbering
Fishing

Atlantic

Ocean

201

A lighthouse on a rocky point
along New England's coast.

the fall. Then their leaves turn brilliant shades of yellow, red, and orange. Soon these leaves fall. The trees are bare all winter, but in the spring they leaf out in bright new shades of green.

The softwood trees include pines, firs, spruces, and hemlocks. We call them "evergreens," for they are clad in green the whole year round. They have needles instead of broad leaves.

New England has hundreds of lakes and streams. Look on the map on page 200 and see how many you can count. Notice what interesting Indian names some have. But the largest one, Lake Champlain, is named for a French explorer who visited Vermont in the 1600's.

Many lakes are too small to show on the map. But they, together with the larger ones, began thousands of years ago when glaciers covered this region. The glaciers hollowed out basins, large and small. Then, as they melted, water filled the hollows and created lakes. Today, lovely sparkling lakes help to make New England a favorite vacationland.

The lakes are fed by many small streams that drain the hill and mountain areas. From the lakes flow other streams that come together to form rivers. In New England, rivers need not go far to reach the sea. But, as they rush down through the rough hilly lands, they tumble over rocks and form rapids and falls. The rivers are swift and powerful.

The winding Connecticut is the largest river in this region. Look on the map and notice how it begins in New Hampshire's mountains. Follow it south. See how it marks the boundary line between Vermont and New Hampshire. It flows on through Massachusetts and Connecticut to empty into Long Island Sound. A *sound* is a long and somewhat narrow body of water. Some sounds separate one or more islands from the mainland. Notice how Long Island Sound separates Long Island from the mainland of the United States.

New England has a rocky coast. It is dotted with lighthouses that warn ships away from the dangerous points. The oldest lighthouse was built just two years after Washington became President.

This rocky coast is a ragged one, as the map shows. It has thousands of little inlets and coves, and many islands. Fine summer homes are located on some islands. These islands are another part of New England's inviting vacationlands. Indeed, New England has a climate that attracts vacationers, summer and winter.

Let's review some things about climate. Some people think that climate is weather. They are partly right and partly wrong. You see, when we mention weather, we are talking about conditions on a single day, or for a short time. So, when an icy wind blows and we shiver,

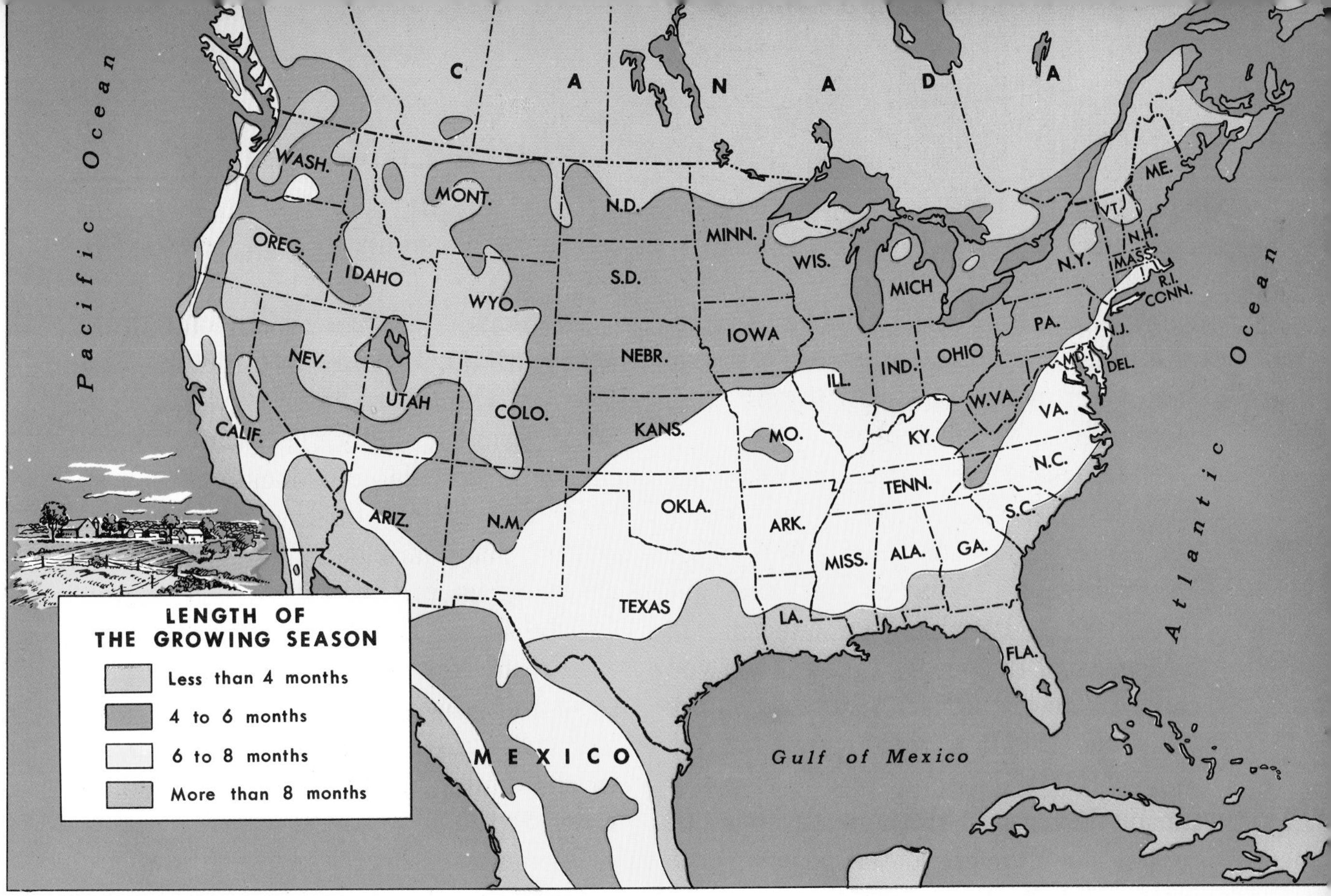

This map shows the length of the growing season in different parts of forty-eight of our states · Find the parts where the growing season is less than four months. Notice that a large area in the West has a growing season as short as the most northern parts of our country. Why? The map on page 90 will help you decide.

we may exclaim, "B---r! This is cold weather!" Or, think of mid-summer when the hot sun beats down and the heat is sizzling. Then we may complain, "This weather is roasting hot!"

But when we talk about climate, we mean the weather in a place the whole year round. Climate is the kind of weather a place usually has over a long period of time.

Lands far to the north generally have a cooler climate than those which are near the equator. Also, high lands have a cooler climate than low lands in the same area. Therefore, we can expect lands far to the north and high lands to have a short growing season.

Remember that the growing season is the length of time crops can grow. It begins when the killing frosts of early spring are over. It lasts until the frosts come again in the fall or winter.

Another thing to keep in mind is that rainfall is an important part of climate. You will find a helpful rainfall map on page 220 of your book.

What is New England's climate like? The map on this page gives some clues. Notice that a part of northern New England has a growing season of less than four months. We know, then, that its winters are long and cold, and that spring comes very late. About how long can plants grow in the southern part?

Snow may begin falling in early November in New England. This region often has a "white Christmas." It can expect icy winds and snowstorms from December to March or April.

A famous New England poet, John Greenleaf Whittier, wrote a long poem about his winter experiences. It is called "Snow-Bound." What do you think this title means? Perhaps your teacher will read parts of the poem to you. Then you can talk over whether or not people are "snowbound" often, today.

New England's summers are pleasantly warm. But generally the weather is not as hot as in many other parts of the United States. For one thing, New England is located quite far north. Also, it is often cooled by ocean breezes.

And what about rainfall in this region? How much can it expect a year? Turn to the rainfall map on page 220 and find out. This is plenty of rain for growing crops.

Earning a Living from the Soil and the Sea

Some New Englanders are farmers. Many of them raise food for the city dwellers who live in this crowded region. Some farmers supply city markets with chickens, turkeys, and ducks, as well as eggs. Others grow fresh vegetables.

And many are dairy farmers. They ship large quantities of fresh milk, cream, and butter to market. The cool, moist climate in New England is fine for pastures and growing hay. During the summer, dairy cattle graze in green pastures. In the winter, they can be fed the hay stored in the large barns.

Berries and several kinds of fruit are raised. Many hillsides are lined with rows of apple trees. Apples like the cool climate of this northeastern region.

Some sections of New England are famous for special crops. For example, Ver-

A farm in a New England valley.

mont has acres and acres of sugar maples, sometimes called "sugar orchards." The sap from these trees is used to make maple syrup and maple sugar.

In the early spring, the maple sap moves up the tree trunk toward the branches. At just the right time, the farmer taps the tree, as the picture at the right shows.

After collecting the sap in buckets, it is boiled until most of its water is removed. By this time, it is a sweet tasty syrup. Perhaps you have eaten maple syrup on hot cakes. Some syrup is boiled still longer. When it cools and hardens, it is crunchy maple sugar.

Northeastern Maine grows bushels and bushels of potatoes. For three hundred years, tobacco has been raised in the fertile Connecticut River Valley. Some of Cape Cod's lowlands are covered with cranberry bushes. You may have enjoyed cranberries with your Thanksgiving dinner or on other occasions. Cape Cod is an arm of Massachusetts land that reaches into the Atlantic in a long hook-like curve. Do you see it on the map? What does your Geography Dictionary tell about the word, *cape*?

Turn to the Chief Occupations Map on page 201 and notice where agriculture is important. Locate Vermont's sugar orchards. Find the areas where potatoes and cranberries are raised.

Some river valleys and lowlands in New England have deep rich soil. But most of New England is not well suited to growing crops. Settlers discovered this long ago.

Many early New Englanders were farmers. Remember how they cut down trees and planted crops between the

Maple sap is gathered in early spring. Why is this the correct time to do it?

stumps. But much of the land was too hilly to plow. Also, most of the soil was thin and full of stones. Long, long before, glaciers had scraped away the best soil and left billions of rocks poking up.

Settlers cleared stones from their farms as best they could. They piled them up in "walls" at the edge of their fields. Indeed, miles of low stone walls can still be seen in New England's countryside.

The farmers worked hard and managed to raise enough food for New England. But men on the poorest lands soon turned to other ways of making a living.

Some New Englanders became fishermen. Interest in fishing goes back to the days of the Pilgrims. Remember reading how these people nearly starved during their first winter in the New World? Fortunately, they learned that the waters off their coast were rich with cod. Some men sailed out to fish and brought back a large catch. From that time on, settlers

TRAWLER

TRAWL

BANK

A fishing bank off the coast of Maine. Trawlers drag nets along the ocean floor to catch great quantities of fish.

depended on fish for a part of their food. As time passed, some New Englanders earned their living as fishermen.

Quantities of cod were caught, and dried. Some were sold in the colonies and some were shipped to England. The cod, therefore, was both food and a "money crop" for many New Englanders. Because it meant so much to them, a large wooden cod has been hung in the Massachusetts State House in Boston.

Fishing led to other occupations. Fishermen lived along some of the bays that are carved out of New England's coast. Because these bays reach far inland, they are quite protected from storms. They provide good harbors for fishing boats. Towns grew up along these bays and some became busy seaports. Fishing and trade in fish encouraged shipping and other industries in these towns.

Fishing boats and trading vessels were needed. So a shipbuilding industry developed. Men who were skillful with tools were employed to build these vessels. In time, New England became famous for its strong, handsome ships. Perhaps the most famous were the clipper ships. The graceful clipper ships were so beautiful and fast that they were admired by people all over the world.

It took lumber to build these vessels. But timber was plentiful in New England. Cutting it down and sawing it gave other New Englanders work.

Some men became sailors on trading vessels and others worked on ships called whalers. They hunted whales for their oil. In those days, whale oil was burned in many lamps.

Fishing is still an important industry in New England. Winter and summer, fishing boats make trips to the fishing banks off of New England and Newfoundland. Newfoundland is the large island just east of Canada. Find it on the map on page 376.

A shelf of sunken land follows along the eastern coast of our continent. It is covered by sea waters to a depth of about 600 feet. It is much more shallow than the waters far out in the Atlantic. These shallow coastal waters are the feeding grounds of many kinds of fish. Cod have been among the most plentiful.

Today, most of the fishing boats are trawlers. Trawlers drag nets through the sea and catch many fish at one time. Often trawlers are back with a full load of fish a week after they set out.

Some New England fishermen work near the shores. They catch such "seafoods" as lobsters and clams. The lobsters are captured in wooden traps which the fishermen sink in the water.

The fishing industry provides work for thousands of people besides the fishermen. Some make and repair nets and many are employed in the canneries and freezing plants. The most important fishing ports are Gloucester, Boston, New Bedford, and Portland. Can you locate these cities on the map on page 200? It is interesting to know that Portland and Boston are also busy manufacturing centers.

Manufacturing in New England

New England's manufacturing began long ago. The first factory was built at Pawtucket, Rhode Island about ten years after our Revolutionary War. A picture of it is shown below. The mill contained machines for spinning cotton into thread. They had been built entirely from memory.

You see, Englishmen had invented spinning and weaving machines. They had started the first *textile*, or clothmaking, factories. These factories could make cloth very cheaply. So English merchants were doing a fine business. Parliament passed laws to protect this business. The laws did not allow either machines or drawings of them to be shipped out of England. Neither were trained workmen allowed to leave the country. But one did, just the same. His name was Samuel Slater.

Slater's mill in Rhode Island.

Slater is called the father of New England's factories. He had worked in a cotton mill in England. He tended a new machine that could spin as much thread in a day as one could on a spinning wheel in three months. He learned all he could and became manager of the mill.

Still, young Slater was not satisfied and dreamed of sailing to America. New Englanders wanted to start cotton mills and would pay well to have spinning machines built. He knew he could do this from memory, if he could get to America.

The skilled young workman disguised himself as a poor farm laborer. Then he slipped on board ship. When he arrived in New York, Slater learned of a businessman who wanted spinning machines built. He wrote him a letter offering to build such machines from memory.

Slater's memory served him well. Within a few months, he had set up his machines in a small factory beside a river. Water power would run them.

Years before, colonists had learned how to use the power of New England's swift streams. Millers had built gristmills beside such streams. Falling water turned the big wheel of the gristmill. As the wheel turned round and round, it moved the stones that ground grain into meal.

Men were astonished at how well Slater's machines worked. They were delighted that a way had been found to spin thread so fast. Soon, other machines were built and new cotton mills sprang up.

As time passed, factories of many kinds were started. The picture map on page 209 may give you some ideas of the many products they turned out.

By 1850, New England was the leading manufacturing area of our country. It had plenty of water power. Then, too, it was located near the sea. Ships could bring it tons of raw materials as well as carry away its finished goods. Furthermore, it had many workers. Some were new Americans who had recently come to our shores from other lands.

Manufacturing is New England's Number One industry. The states of Massachusetts, Rhode Island, Connecticut, and southeastern New Hampshire have the chief manufacturing districts. Altogether, hundreds of mills and factories are scattered through these areas.

The map of occupations in New England shows the main manufacturing centers. They produce dozens of the things we use every day. There are some textile mills. They weave cotton, woolen, rayon, and nylon cloth. Rayon goods are woven from rayon fibers made from ground-up wood, specially treated. Nylon is woven from nylon fibers made from coal, air, and water. Some cloth is a mixture of fabrics such as rayon and cotton or nylon and cotton.

Before 1900, New England had more textile factories than any other part of our country. But that is not true today. Now, many textile mills are located in the South near supplies of cotton and other raw materials.

In and around Boston are tanneries where hides and skins are made into leather. In this area, too, are leather goods factories. They manufacture millions of pairs of shoes as well as purses, belts, and other kinds of leather goods.

New England also makes tons of paper goods and publishes many books. This book you are reading was published in Boston. Fine furniture is made in New

England and ships are built there. And all kinds of rubber goods are manufactured. Among these are raincoats, boots, garden hoses, and tennis shoes.

A large number of New England's factories turn out metal goods. Some factories make small articles such as pins, needles, and screws. But others manufacture silverware, tools, kettles, machinery, and many electronic goods. One highway on the edge of Boston has many electronic plants and research centers. So it has been nicknamed "Electronic Highway."

Even today, New England uses water power to help run its factories. Of course, the day of Slater's mill is past. No longer is water power used to turn the wheels of the machines. But now the force of the water power is put to work

to make electricity. This electricity furnishes the power to run the machines just as it furnishes power to run a washing machine in your home.

Modern factories no longer have to be located on a riverbank to obtain power. Power lines can carry the electricity for many miles. Therefore, factories can be located close to shipping points and other business connected with running them.

Today New England has many busy manufacturing towns and cities. Dozens of them are strung through southern New England. In some places they are so close together that a person can hardly

The map below shows the leading manufacturing industries carried on in southern New England in the early 1800's.

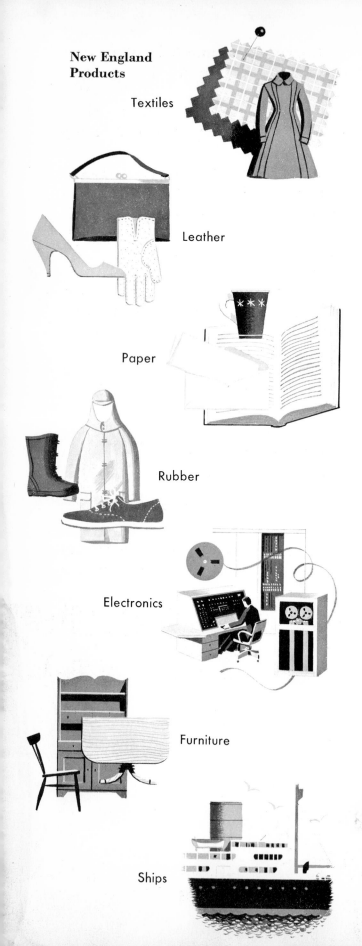

New England Products

Textiles

Leather

Paper

Rubber

Electronics

Furniture

Ships

tell where one city ends and another begins. These parts of New England have a large population.

Turn to the map on page 184. What does it tell about New England's population? Study the key. What color stands for 250 people in one square mile? Find this color on the map. See what a large area of New England this color covers. We know, then, that this area is crowded with towns and cities. Only the larger ones are named on the political map on page 200. The largest one is Boston. What is its population? You can find out if you look in Table 5 in the Tables for Reference.

Boston is the largest manufacturing and shipping center. Indeed, it is one of the most important manufacturing centers in our whole country. One reason is that it has such an excellent location. Point to it on the map. Notice that it is a seaport and looks out on Massachusetts Bay.

Boston has a fine harbor. A view of it appears on page 212. Every day of the year, ships are coming to and going from this port. They bring in raw materials and carry away quantities of manufactured goods to markets all over the world.

Boston is also a land transportation center. Locate it on the railroad map on page 349. Notice how a network of railroad lines fans out in every direction to connect this city with many parts of our land. Fine highways also extend out from Boston, north, south, and west.

These transportation routes are something like the spokes leading out from the hub of a huge wheel. Because these routes lead out from Boston, it is often called the "hub of New England."

Some Other Industries: Lumbering, Quarrying, and Caring for Tourists

Lumbering is carried on in northern New England. You will have a better idea where the lumbermen work, if you look at the Chief Occupations Map on page 201.

Even though the winter is often bitterly cold, it is the busiest season for these lumbermen. Do you know why? After the trees are cut, they are dragged to the rivers. It is easy to pull them over the snow. At the frozen rivers they are piled on the banks. Then in the spring when the ice melts, the logs are floated down to the sawmills and pulp mills.

Some logs are sawed into lumber. But many slender trees are made into pulpwood. Pulpwood is the material from which paper is made. Maine has many pulp mills. Some are also located in New Hampshire and Vermont.

Quarrying is another interesting industry. Quarries are places where building stone is taken from the earth. Look at the quarry in the picture below. The men are quarrying or cutting out the stone.

Much of New England's building stone is granite. This handsome hard stone is used in constructing many large buildings. Marble and slate are quarried in Vermont. Slate is often used in making roofs and for flagstones for walks.

New England is sometimes called "Vacationland." Many people spend their vacations there every year. These visitors are called tourists.

Some tourists enjoy camping in the northern woods, or fishing in the streams and lakes. Others like the seashore. In the winter, whole trainloads of people spend weekends in northern New England where they ski, skate, and go sleighing. But many vacationers also like to visit some of the historic places.

Boston is a fascinating city to see. Some of its buildings date back to the days of the colonies. On one narrow street is

Giant cranes lift huge blocks of granite from a quarry.

An airview showing the Public Garden and Boston Common with the harbor in the background.

This city is very proud of its attractive parks, and fine homes and schools, and also of its interesting Massachusetts State House. There, much government business is carried on. Boston is the capital of Massachusetts, as you know.

Near Boston are other places that attract sightseers. A few miles to the south is the pleasant little town of Plymouth where the Pilgrims landed in 1620. Just west of Boston is Cambridge. There, one can see the grounds and buildings of Harvard University. It was established back in 1636 and is the oldest university in our country. Nearby is the home of Longfellow, the poet who wrote "The Midnight Ride of Paul Revere."

Driving northwest of Boston, one soon comes to Lexington where the first shots of the Revolutionary War were fired.

Altogether, thousands of people take their vacations in New England every year. Providing food, living quarters, and other services for them keeps many people busy. So, caring for the tourist trade is an important industry in this northeast land.

South and west of New England lies another busy industrial region. It is made up of the Middle Atlantic States. As we read about them, think of some ways they are like New England and also some ways they are different.

Old North Church. In its belfry Paul Revere's friend hung a lantern to warn that the British were coming.

The Boston Common was once a pasture set aside for the cattle. It is hard to imagine that now, for today it is a beautiful park, as the picture above shows.

Boston has some old and narrow streets, and some that are broad and new. It has some large handsome new buildings and exciting plans for improving its old run-down areas.

Help Your Class to Remember

1. The names of the New England states.
2. What their lands are like.
3. Why New England is not an important agricultural region. What crops are raised.
4. What kind of climate is found there.
5. What New England's most important industries are.

Some Questions to Talk Over

1. How is New England different from the part of our country in which you live?

2. What is the most important industry in your community?

3. What things that you use at home were unknown to pioneers 100 years ago?

4. If you could vacation in New England, what part would you visit? How would you travel to reach it? What would you take along? What would you do there?

5. Why are computers used today?

Choose the Correct Ending

There are three possible endings given after each of these unfinished sentences. Write the numbers 1 to 10. After each number write the letter (*a*, *b*, or *c*) of the ending which makes that sentence complete and true.

1. Most of New England is (a) hilly. (b) plains country. (c) lowlands.

2. The largest New England state is (a) Massachusetts. (b) Maine. (c) Vermont.

3. The Pilgrims caught many (a) salmon. (b) cod. (c) mackerel.

4. Farmers in northeastern Maine grow quantities of (a) potatoes. (b) wheat. (c) corn.

5. Some lowlands on Cape Cod produce many (a) cranberries. (b) potatoes. (c) vegetables.

6. Vermont is famous for its (a) codfish. (b) maple sugar. (c) sugar beets.

7. The largest river in New England is (a) the Ohio. (b) the Connecticut. (c) the Hudson.

8. Boston is called the Hub of New England because it (a) is large. (b) is interesting. (c) has transportation routes leading from it.

9. Slater built New England's first machines for producing (a) books. (b) leather. (c) textiles.

10. New England manufactures many (a) computers. (b) airplanes. (c) automobiles.

Some Other Things to Do

1. List some things that are manufactured near your home today.

2. See if your class can visit a factory. Be ready to discuss what you see.

3. Use an encyclopedia and other reference materials to learn more about computers and the electronics industry. Plan to share what you find out.

4. Arrange for a class exhibit of several kinds of stone. Label each kind.

5. Use the map on page 200 and: (a) Read its legend. (b) Do what the legend asks. (c) Locate a sound. (d) Tell in which direction the sound is from the city of Hartford. (e) Decide what are the two main ideas which the inset map tells.

6. Turn to the map on page 203, and: (a) Review the legend. (b) Study the key. (c) Tell what part of New England has the shortest growing season. (d) Tell which has the longer growing season, southern Maine or the area in which you live.

Using the "Maps in This Book"

Turn to the page called "Maps in This Book." Notice that the maps are arranged alphabetically under special topics such as *Climate Maps* and *Historical Maps*. When you wish to locate a certain map, decide under which topic it belongs. Under what heading would you look for a rainfall map of New England?

Now look for a landform map of New England. Is one listed under *Landform and Relief Maps*? On what page do you find a map of New England's main occupations? Is dairying shown on this map? If not, what map shows where, in New England, this industry is carried on? On what page is it?

13 · The Middle Atlantic States: Many Cities and Industries

A New Kind of City

The longest city in the world. A new kind of city has grown up along our Atlantic coast. We speak of it as a *megalopolis.*

"A what?" you ask in surprise.

"A meg-a-lop-o-lis," we answer slowly, breaking the word into syllables.

This strange jawbreaker is one of our newest words. It was born so recently that it may not be in your dictionary.

"Megalopolis" means "great city." The one which we are talking about is the longest city in the world. It extends from southern New Hampshire to northern Virginia, a distance of about 500 miles. A little part of it is shown below.

"I can't believe it!" you exclaim. "Who ever heard of a city that long?"

You turn to the map on pages 504–505 to locate the mysterious megalopolis. After a moment, you shake your head and say, "You must be mistaken. This map shows *many* cities between southern New Hampshire and northern Virginia. Some of them are Boston, New York, Philadelphia, Trenton, Baltimore, and Washington, D.C."

You are certainly right. In fact, there are dozens of towns and cities in this Atlantic coastal area. Your map doesn't begin to show them all!

But a megalopolis is not a single city, you see. It is a long cluster of cities of various sizes. They are strung together by highways and throughways.

Many of the cities are linked together by United States Highway 1. In colonial days, it was the main road connecting the colonies and the largest towns, Boston, New York, and Philadelphia.

Gradually these towns grew into bustling cities. So did many new settlements that had sprung up along this route.

For years, the towns and cities were separated by countryside with its farms and patches of "woods." But as they grew, they spread out farther and farther into the country.

Today, this 500-mile-long area is almost solidly built up, as the population map on page 184 shows you. You can hardly tell where one city ends and the next one begins. It seems to be one great city, a megalopolis.

Miles and miles of it extend through the Middle Atlantic States. We'll learn about some of its industries as we study this interesting region.

What These States Are Like

There are seven Middle Atlantic States. Find them on the map on page 217. As you can see, they include New York, Pennsylvania, New Jersey, Delaware, Maryland, Virginia, and West Virginia. Which of these states were among the thirteen colonies?

The District of Columbia is also set in this Middle Atlantic region. But it is not a part of any state. If you study the map, you can see this. Washington, D.C., is located on the banks of the Potomac River between Maryland and Virginia.

The Middle Atlantic region is larger than New England, but it is not very large compared to the other regions of our country. Still, it is a very important one. It has hundreds of cities, large and small, and almost one fourth of all our people. The map on page 222 will show you how thickly settled it is. One reason is that it has many factories and other businesses, and can provide millions of jobs.

This part of our country has an interesting seacoast and some large bays that provide excellent sheltered harbors. One is New York Bay. Find it on the map on page 217. What large city looks out on it? Locate Delaware Bay and see how it is the gateway to Philadelphia on the Delaware River. Now find Chesapeake Bay. It is the largest bay on our part of the Atlantic coast. On the map, it looks like a long crooked finger as it curves deep into the land.

Point to the long tongue of land that spreads out east of Chesapeake Bay. It is

215

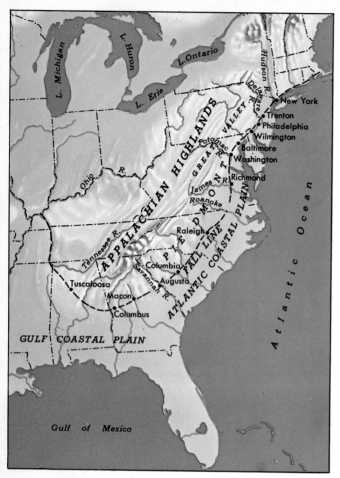

This map shows the fall line where the Piedmont meets the Atlantic Coastal Plain.

almost at sea level. This plain is quite narrow near New York City. But it becomes wider as it spreads southward, as the map shows. It has deep soils and quite a mild climate, so many crops can be grown.

Also, plains follow along Lake Ontario and Lake Erie. Find them on the map. They, too, are good lands for farming.

West of the coastal plain is the hilly Piedmont. Look for the Piedmont on the map on this page. See how it lies between the Atlantic Coastal Plain and the Appalachian Highlands. The word *Piedmont* means "at the foot of the mountains." You can see that the Piedmont lives up to its name. It slopes west to the eastern foot of the Appalachian Mountains.

The Piedmont is really a belt of hilly lands. If you drove through these rolling lands, you would travel uphill and down, through green valleys, and past wooded slopes. You would see many farms. Some of them were laid out long ago by early settlers.

Between the Piedmont and the Atlantic Coastal Plain is the fall line. The map shows that the fall line runs along the boundary between the Piedmont and the coastal plain. "Fall line" is a good name for this imaginary line. Let's find out why.

If you study the map you can see that many rivers start in the Appalachians. Notice those that flow eastward across the Piedmont and the Atlantic Coastal Plain. Finally, they empty into the Atlantic. As they hurry down from the Piedmont, they tumble in rapids and falls over rocky ledges. For this reason the place, or line, where the Piedmont meets the Atlantic Coastal Plain is known as the "fall line."

a peninsula. What three bodies of water wash its shores? What states share this peninsula? Its lands are low and flat, and many fine farms are located here.

Miles and miles of seashore provide this part of our country with inviting wide sandy beaches. In the summer, thousands of city dwellers flock to the shores to picnic on the sand or bathe in the cool ocean waters.

The Middle Atlantic region has some important plains. Find the Atlantic Coastal Plain on the map above. It is almost as flat as a table and in places is

216

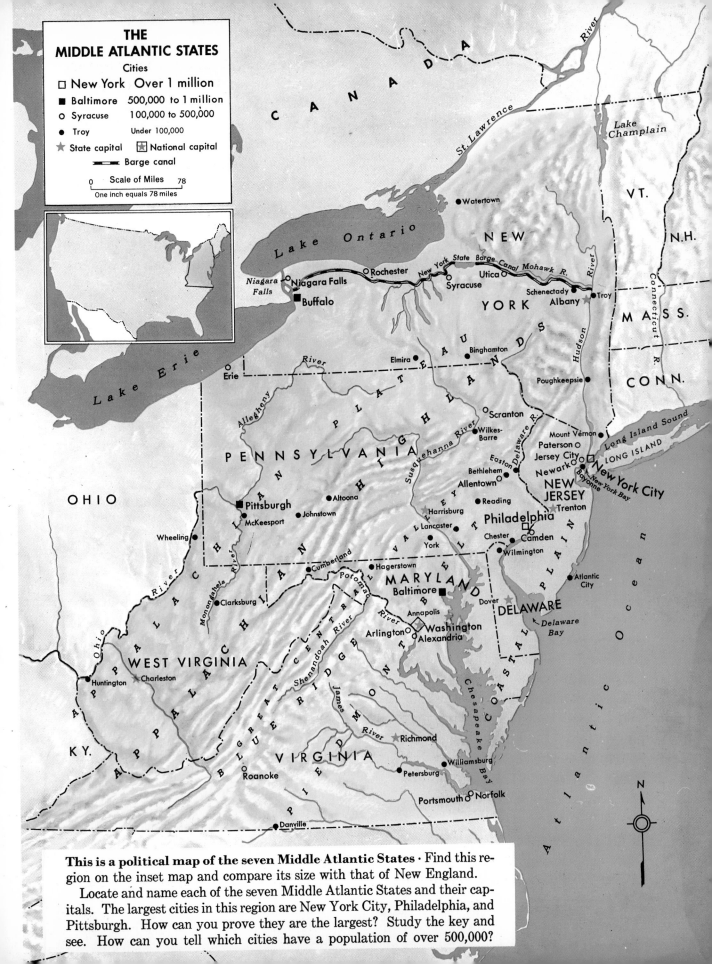

CANADA

Lake Ontario

Lake Erie

NEW YORK

St. Lawrence River

Lake Champlain

VT.

N.H.

MASS.

Connecticut R.

CONN.

● Watertown

Niagara Falls ○ Niagara Falls
■ Buffalo
○ Rochester
New York State Barge Canal
Mohawk R.
○ Utica
○ Syracuse
Schenectady ●
Albany ★
● Troy

Erie ○
Allegheny River
Susquehanna River

● Elmira
● Binghamton
Poughkeepsie ●

PLATEAU
HIGHLANDS

Hudson River

PENNSYLVANIA

APPALACHIAN

○ Scranton
Wilkes- ●
Barre
Delaware R.
Mount Vernon ●
Paterson ○
Jersey City ○
Newark ○ New York City □
Bayonne ● New York Bay
LONG ISLAND
Long Island Sound

OHIO

● Pittsburgh
McKeesport ●
● Altoona
● Johnstown
Harrisburg ★
Lancaster ●
● York
Easton ○
Bethlehem ●
Allentown ○
● Reading
NEW JERSEY
Trenton ●
Philadelphia □ ○
Chester ● Camden ○
● Wilmington

Atlantic City ●

● Wheeling

Ohio River
Monongahela River
● Clarksburg

● Cumberland
Potomac River
● Hagerstown
MARYLAND
Baltimore ■
Dover ●
DELAWARE
Delaware Bay

WEST VIRGINIA

APPALACHIAN

BLUE RIDGE

CENTRAL

GREAT

VALLEY

Annapolis ★
Arlington ● Washington ⬣
○ Alexandria

COASTAL PLAIN

Chesapeake Bay

Atlantic Ocean

● Huntington
★ Charleston

KY.

Shenandoah River

James River

PIEDMONT

VIRGINIA
Richmond ★
● Williamsburg
● Petersburg
Portsmouth ● ○ Norfolk

○ Roanoke

● Danville

N

This is a political map of the seven **Middle Atlantic States** · Find this region on the inset map and compare its size with that of New England.

Locate and name each of the seven Middle Atlantic States and their capitals. The largest cities in this region are New York City, Philadelphia, and Pittsburgh. How can you prove they are the largest? Study the key and see. How can you tell which cities have a population of over 500,000?

The falls have provided a wealth of water power. You already know how the colonists in New England put the power of rapids and waterfalls to work. It ran grain and textile mills. This was also true in the Middle Atlantic region. Many mills and factories were built beside the falls. The towns on the fall line grew into busy manufacturing cities. Three of them are Philadelphia, Baltimore, and Richmond. Find them on the map. What other cities do you see on the fall line? Some of our busiest highways and railroads follow along this fall line to connect the cities.

The Appalachian Mountains rise west of the Piedmont. Glance at the map on page 216 and see how they slant southwestward. They stretch from New England to Alabama. As you know, they have many ranges of rounded, worn-down mountains. They are a part of the Appalachian Highlands, remember.

These mountains are only about five or six thousand feet high. They rise in long ranges, one after another and the slopes are covered with forests. There are few low passes in the ridges, but between the long ridges are deep valleys. One is the Great Valley.

Daniel Boone was one of the first pioneers to venture over the Appalachians, as you know. Do you remember how he and his friends blazed the Wilderness Road? Look back at the map on page 109 and see how this trail led southward through the long narrow Great Valley. Traveling through it was quite easy, but crossing the forested mountains took weeks and weeks.

The Great Valley reaches many miles through the Appalachians. It extends from southeastern New York to the center of Alabama. In some places it is only about twenty-five miles wide. But it is one of the longest valleys in the world. The beautiful Shenandoah Valley is a part of the Great Valley.

The Great Valley is a rich area. It has much fertile soil and its farms produce such fine crops that this valley is sometimes called the Garden of Eden. Some sections are famous for valuable natural resources of coal and limestone. Some iron ore is also mined. The iron ore contains the important metal, iron, from which steel is made. Limestone is also used in making steel.

Long highways reach through the Great Valley. Day and night, trucks rumble over them carrying to markets and mills the products of the farms and mines.

West of the mountains are more high lands. Find them on the map. Through what states do they extend?

These high lands have thousands of farms; but cities are also scattered over them. One of the largest is Pittsburgh in western Pennsylvania. Many people work in the cities, and others earn their living as coal miners. Rich stores of coal are buried beneath the surface of this region.

Some important rivers flow through the Middle Atlantic States. You found several on the map when you looked at the fall line. The largest rivers are the Hudson, the Delaware, and the Susquehanna. Locate them on the map. Notice how each enters the Atlantic Ocean through a large bay. Each one serves as an important water highway.

The Hudson begins in the Adirondacks. It flows south through hills and plains on its way to New York Bay. White men first heard of this river when Henry Hudson explored it in his small vessel, the *Half Moon.*

Many years later, pioneers pushed north on the Hudson and west on the Mohawk River to settle new lands. On the map, you can see that the Mohawk is a branch of the Hudson. Together, the Hudson and the Mohawk River Valleys form a pathway through the Appalachians. From Maine to Georgia, this pathway is the only low one to the West.

In the early 1800's a man-made waterway, the Erie Canal, was built through the Mohawk River Valley. It connected the Hudson River and Lake Erie. Today, it is a part of the New York State Barge System shown on the map on page 217.

South of the Hudson is the Delaware River. In what mountains does it begin? William Penn and his Quaker friends sailed up the Delaware River to found Philadelphia. Today, many ocean-going steamers move up this river to Philadelphia. Some have on board raw materials

for this city's factories and may carry away manufactured goods.

The Susquehanna River also starts in the Appalachians. Winding through Pennsylvania, it flows into Chesapeake Bay, as you can see.

Two great lakes and Niagara Falls face the Middle Atlantic region. The lakes, Ontario and Erie, are a part of the important inland waterway of the Great Lakes. Large freighters steam across the lakes and through the connecting rivers and canals. They carry raw materials like iron ore and wheat to Buffalo, Cleveland, Erie, and other busy lake ports.

In 1955, Canada and the United States began working together to make this useful waterway still more valuable. Parts of

The waters of the Niagara River drop over limestone cliffs to form beautiful Niagara Falls. The American falls are on the left. The Canadian falls are on the right.

the St. Lawrence River were deepened and connecting canals between the lakes were improved. Today, large seagoing vessels can travel from the Atlantic Ocean to any of the Great Lakes. This waterway is now called the St. Lawrence Seaway.

As the map shows, Lake Erie and Lake Ontario are connected by the Niagara River. But ships never dare to take this river route. Mighty Niagara Falls is located on the Niagara River between these lakes. This magnificent falls is pictured on page 219. Its waters spill over rock cliffs and plunge down 160 feet to the river below. The Indians named the falls "Thundering Waters," and no wonder! Their roar is loud and deafening. They are so beautiful that thousands of people go to see them every year.

What kind of climate is found in the Middle Atlantic States? To help us answer this question, let's use two maps. One, the rainfall map is shown below. It tells us that these states receive plenty of rain. The growing season map on page 203 shows that the coastal plains and the Piedmont have quite a long growing season. How long is it? Is it longer or shorter than New England's growing season? Which region has the most favorable climate for growing crops? Why?

This is a rainfall map · Rainfall means both rain and water from melting snow. It is measured in inches. If a section of land gets one inch of rain during a storm, it receives enough rain to cover it with water an inch deep. It takes ten inches of snow to make one inch of rain. This map tells about how many inches of water fall in a year in the different parts of forty-eight of our states.

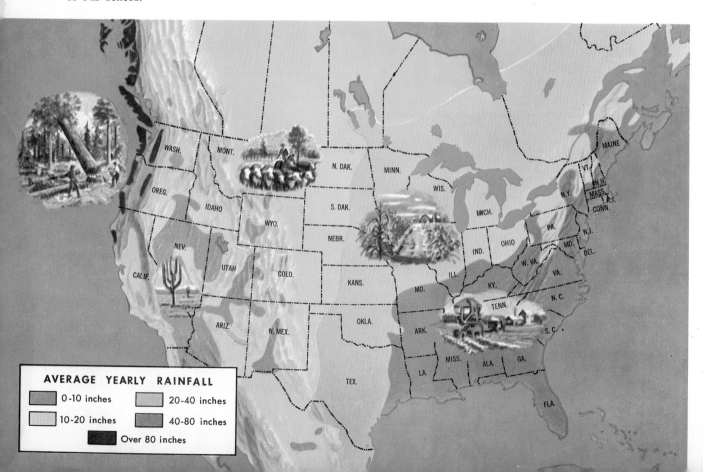

AVERAGE YEARLY RAINFALL

0-10 inches   20-40 inches
10-20 inches   40-80 inches
Over 80 inches

Some Important Cities in the Middle Atlantic States

Our much-loved Statue of Liberty. France gave it to our country in 1884. This huge statue stands on an island in New York Harbor.

The Middle Atlantic States have many cities. The larger ones are named on the political map on page 217. The map key gives you a general idea of their size. Let's make use of it.

Locate Washington, D.C. Is it about the size of New York City or of Baltimore? Look at the key and decide. What other cities seem to have a population about the size of Washington, D.C.?

Of course, the size of the print used for each city name gives us only a general idea of its population. We can get more exact information about a city's population by using Table 5 in the Tables for Reference. Turn to this table and find Washington's population.

On the map, find Albany, the capital of New York. What does the map tell about its size? How many cities in the Middle Atlantic States have a population of more than 100,000? Use Table 5 and count them.

Most cities of the Middle Atlantic States are manufacturing centers. Buffalo is noted for its flour and feed mills, a huge cereal packing plant, and factories making iron-and-steel products. The wheat and iron ore are brought from farther west by boats.

Schenectady makes railroad locomotives, washing machines, refrigerators, and many other kinds of electrical goods. It is sometimes called the City of Magic because amazing new things are being discovered in famous laboratories there. Rochester is known for its cameras and film. Troy has shirtmaking and other clothing factories. Allentown manufactures cement, trucks, and busses. Some cities in eastern Pennsylvania have textile mills. Two New Jersey cities, Camden and Trenton, have enormous canneries for preparing canned soups and vegetables.

The four largest cities in the Middle Atlantic States are New York, Philadelphia, Pittsburgh, and Baltimore. Look for them on the map on page 217. In which state is each located?

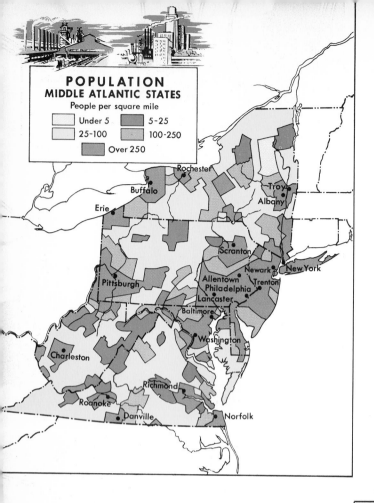

POPULATION
MIDDLE ATLANTIC STATES
People per square mile

Under 5
25-100
5-25
100-250
Over 250

Rochester
Buffalo
Erie
Troy
Albany
Scranton
Newark
New York
Pittsburgh
Allentown
Philadelphia
Trenton
Lancaster
Baltimore
Washington
Charleston
Richmond
Roanoke
Danville
Norfolk

This population map shows how thickly settled some areas of the Middle Atlantic States are · Name some of the largest cities. Notice that many of these cities are either on a river or a lake. How would such a location help a city to become an important manufacturing center? How would such a location help the city to grow? What kind of a location does your city have?

This map shows some of the main occupations in the Middle Atlantic States · Coal mining is one. What are some others? Notice how many manufacturing centers there are in this region. Many people are employed in these centers or cities. In fact, millions of people live in cities in the Middle Atlantic States as the map above shows.

CHIEF OCCUPATIONS
IN THE
MIDDLE ATLANTIC STATES

Manufacturing Center
Agriculture
Coal mining
Fishing

New York is the largest and best known city in the Western Hemisphere. It boasts a population of more than 8,000,000 people. Not all of them live on Manhattan Island, however. New York City is made up of five sections called *boroughs*. Manhattan is the heart of the city and its chief business center. But four other boroughs spread out nearby. They are connected with Manhattan by huge bridges and by tunnels under the rivers. What tunnels are shown on the map on this page?

New York City has many fine homes, apartment houses, schools, and churches. It has famous universities, art centers, and museums. But it is also known the world over for its thousands of businesses and factories.

Hundreds of thousands of people work in Manhattan. Many live in other boroughs or across the Hudson in New Jersey or Connecticut. Crowds of people are rushed to and from their work every day on fast trains, busses, and subways. Subways are electric trains that whizz through long tunnels under the ground. There are more than 500 miles of subways under New York City.

New York City is a fascinating place to visit. Let's take a sight-seeing trip through it. The map on this page will help us keep track of some interesting places we see. The red line on it shows the route we shall take.

We shall start our tour on the southern tip of Manhattan Island near a park laid out by the Dutch, long ago. Before we board our bus, we look across the bay at a small island and see an inspiring sight. There, rising over 300 feet above the sea, is the tall Statue of Liberty given to us by

223

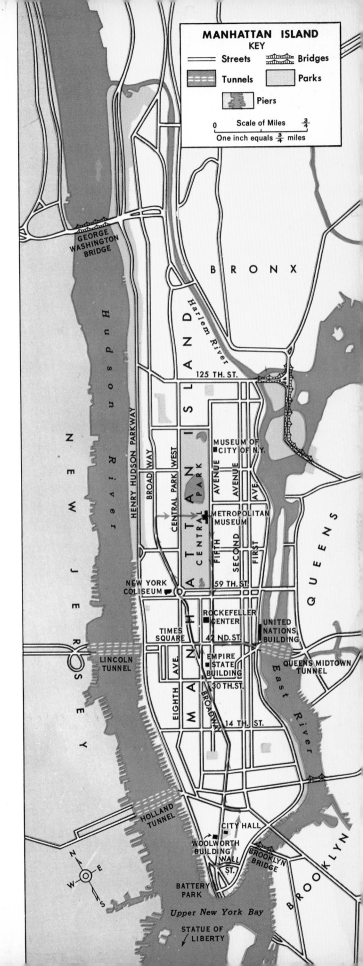

France. Standing at the entrance to New York Harbor, the Goddess of Liberty welcomes travelers approaching our shores. As the picture on page 221 shows, she holds her torch of freedom high. If we had time, we could take a boat trip to the island and climb high in this statue.

Our first stop is in the Wall Street business district with its tall skyscrapers. Find Wall Street on the map on page 223. Our guide tells us that this narrow street was named long ago when the Dutch built a wall there to keep out the Indians. Now, tall buildings almost wall in this district. In them are large banks and other kinds of businesses dealing in money and trade. The Stock Exchange is located here.

Now we ride down Broadway, the longest street in the world. How crowded it is with traffic! Then we turn on to Fifth Avenue and approach another group of skyscrapers. You see, even after the city had used up its land on the island, it continued to grow. So it grew "up" and built taller and taller buildings. Some are from fifty to a hundred or more stories high, so people call them skyscrapers.

Our next stop is at the famous Empire State Building. In New York City only the World Trade Center is taller. We learn that the Empire State Building has 102 stories and is 1250 feet high. About 25,000 people work in offices in this beautiful building. Fast elevators zoom us to its top. There we have a wonderful view of New York City and its splendid harbor.

Leaving the Empire State Building we return to Broadway. We ride through part of New York's famous garment district. Much of the clothing worn in our country is made in this area.

In a few minutes we cross Times Square and enter New York's theater section. At night, electric signs glow above every theater, shop, and restaurant. This part of Broadway is known as the "Great White Way."

Continuing north up Broadway we drive past the New York Coliseum. Then we turn east across Central Park to Fifth Avenue. Locate Central Park on the map on page 223. It is sandwiched in between two of the city's busiest streets. But it has many blocks of green lawns, spreading trees, and inviting walks. It also has a zoo, an outdoor theater for concerts, and a number of playgrounds. So Central Park is enjoyed by many people.

On Fifth Avenue we pass many fashionable shops and finally reach Rockefeller Center. It is made up of a whole family of skyscrapers. Its R.C.A. Building contains about forty broadcasting studios. Soon, we drive east to the United Nations' Building. You read about the United Nations in Chapter 11. Find its buildings on the map. What river do they face?

If we had time, we would visit New York's two immense railroad stations, or its huge airports, or its famous museums. Or we might travel across one of the fine steel bridges leading to highways that fan out from this area. And we would surely visit New York's busy harbor.

New York is our greatest seaport. One reason is because it has one of the best harbors in the world. Its harbor includes Upper New York Bay, parts of Newark Bay, and the lower parts of the Hudson and East rivers. Altogether, New York has more than 600 miles of busy docks and wharves.

Hundreds of ships can tie up at these docks at one time. More than 10,000 ships from many different nations enter or leave it every year. In fact, a ship enters or leaves New York harbor about every 20 minutes. These ships bring many kinds of raw materials and manufactured goods from other lands. Woolen goods and china from Great Britain! Wool from Australia! Tea from India! Coffee from Brazil! Hides from Argentina! Bananas from Central America! All of these products are imports.

When ships leave New York Harbor, they carry many of the goods we export. They haul away cargoes of wheat and other crops from our farms. They also carry machinery, tools, and other kinds of manufactured goods from our factories.

An airview of the southern tip of Manhattan Island.

It is easy to see why New York has grown so large. It can ship goods north and south to ports in our country and to ports in other parts of the world. Also, it is at the end of an inland route from the Great Lakes to the Hudson and south to the Atlantic. Iron, steel, and other raw materials can easily be brought to New York Harbor by this route. Raw materials can also be brought to New York City by railways, highways, and airlines. This giant city has both a favorable location and excellent transportation. It has become a great manufacturing center. Like other industrial cities, it sometimes has air pollution.

Independence Hall and Independence Mall, or park, in Philadelphia. Many old and ugly buildings have been torn down to make this section of the city more beautiful.

Philadelphia is another busy port and important manufacturing city. Although it is located a hundred miles inland, it is one of the chief ports of the United States. Find it on the map on page 217. It spreads out on the banks of the Delaware River, remember. Ships from all over the world sail up this broad river to tie up at its piers and docks.

Like New York City, Philadelphia is also a busy railroad center. Railroads connect it with all parts of the United States. In addition, fine highways and airlines serve it. So this city is also fortunate in having good transportation and an excellent location.

It is not surprising, then, that Philadelphia has become a leading manufacturing city. Ocean liners are built in its shipyards. Its factories turn out thousands of different products. Among them are locomotives and streamliners and fine rugs and carpets.

Philadelphia is partly old and partly new. You have read about its stately old Independence Hall. This famous building still stands and is open to visitors the year round. Here, people can see the Liberty Bell which rang out the news that the states would be free so long ago.

As the years passed, some older parts of Philadelphia became ugly and shabby. In the 1950's, the city began an *urban renewal* program, a plan to clean up and improve such areas. Whole blocks of old buildings were torn down and replaced by new ones. Also, little parks were laid out and some streets were widened.

Above is a view of downtown Philadelphia, and Independence Park. This is in a section where many old and ugly buildings have been torn down.

Pittsburgh is a city of iron and steel. This river port grew up on the point of land where the Allegheny and Monongahela rivers meet. They join to

226

form the Ohio River, as the map on page 217 shows. Clumsy barges crawl up and down these rivers hauling coal, iron ore, and other materials to Pittsburgh's factories and mills. In addition, many freight trains chug along the banks of the rivers. Some cars are loaded with limestone, coal, and iron ore, and are headed for Pittsburgh's steel mills.

There are several reasons why Pittsburgh grew into such a busy city. One is its excellent location. Another is its nearness to valuable raw materials. Pittsburgh is located in the largest coal-mining area in our country. Notice this on the map on page 229. Much of this coal is used in making steel.

Pittsburgh has fine homes, schools, churches, and many businesses. It is well-known for its glass factories. But it is most famous for its steel mills. Steel is important to all Americans. We use it in building our large bridges and tall skyscrapers. Steel is used to make locomotives, steel rails, and the framework for ships. It is used in the manufacture of automobiles, bicycles, washing machines, refrigerators, and even in the pins we need so often. In fact, we depend on steel for making thousands of articles. We will learn more about steel on the next page.

Baltimore is the largest port and factory city on Chesapeake Bay. This city is about 200 miles from the ocean and is on the fall line. It is located on a river that flows into Chesapeake Bay. Baltimore has an excellent harbor, and its port does a thriving business. The business and manufacturing district is near the harbor. But many of the people have homes on hilly land that is part of the Piedmont.

Pittsburgh grew up at the point where the Allegheny and Monongahela rivers meet. Below, part of Baltimore's fine harbor on Chesapeake Bay.

Baltimore's many factories make hundreds of different articles, small and large, from pins and bottle caps to airplanes and enormous battleships. The city is noted especially for its iron-and-steel goods, airplanes, clothing, and food products.

Jobs and automation. Mills, plants, factories, and other businesses in these cities employ millions of employees. Still, today, many employees are losing their jobs because of more and more automation. *Automation* means that machines are doing much of the work people once did. Think, for example, how one computer can do the work of a dozen or more employees.

Automation is increasing in every industry. For this reason, thousands of people every year need new jobs and perhaps more education and special training to get them.

Manufacturing is a leading industry in the Middle Atlantic States, as you know. Notice how many manufacturing centers are shown on the Chief Occupations Map on page 222. The cities have plenty of workers. Also, this region has a web of railroad lines and highways, as well as fine harbors. Raw materials and manufactured goods can be moved quickly and easily.

In addition, these cities are near rich supplies of coal. Much coal is used for making the electricity to run factory machines. It is also used in making iron and steel.

This region is convenient to the other raw materials needed in making steel. It is not surprising, then, that coal mining and steel manufacturing are among the most important industries in the Middle Atlantic region.

Coal Mining and Steel Manufacturing

Much coal is mined in the Appalachians. The coal is found in layers under the ground, as is shown in the pictures at the right. A large area of coal deposits is called a coal field. Find the coal fields on the map at the right. Notice that large fields stretch over western Pennsylvania and West Virginia.

There are several kinds of coal. One looks like soft black rock and is *bituminous*, or soft, coal. When it is burned, a heavy black smoke pours out. Another kind is *anthracite*, or hard coal. It burns with little smoke. Which kind of coal is more plentiful in our country? Look at the map and see.

There are several different ways of mining coal. In some bituminous mines, a tunnel is cut into the layers of coal from the side of a valley. In the tunnel, machines do most of the work of mining. Then coal is loaded on small railroad cars and hauled to the tunnel entrance. There it is sorted and prepared for shipping. The left-hand picture on the opposite page shows this kind of mining.

To mine anthracite, shafts, or deep holes, are usually cut straight down to the layers of coal. Then tunnels are dug out from the mine shaft. An elevator carries the miners to and from these underground tunnels where the coal is dug. This elevator also carries the coal to the surface.

When coal deposits are close to the surface of the earth, strip mining is used. Giant machines remove the earth that

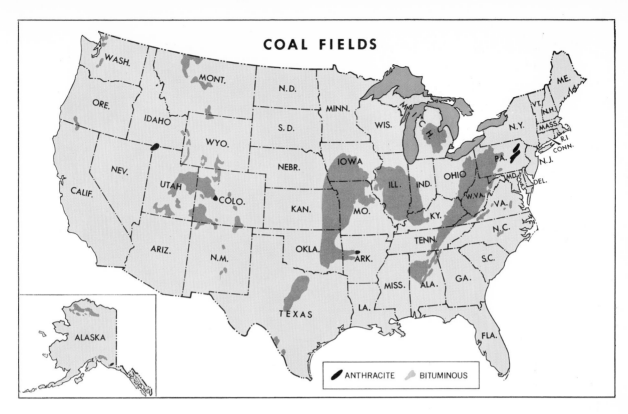

COAL FIELDS

ANTHRACITE   BITUMINOUS

This map shows the most important coal fields in our country. Most of our coal is of what kind?

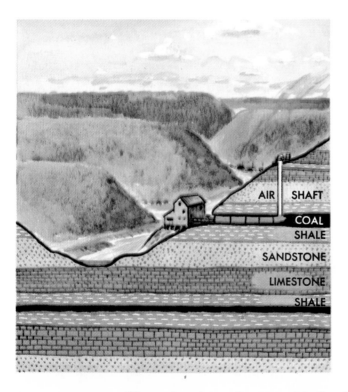

AIR SHAFT
COAL
SHALE
SANDSTONE
LIMESTONE
SHALE

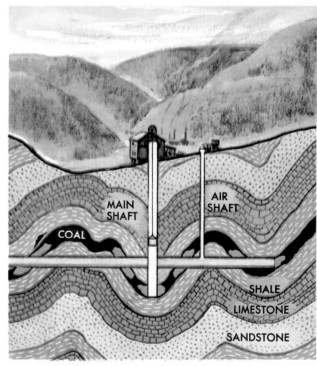

MAIN SHAFT
COAL
AIR SHAFT
SHALE
LIMESTONE
SANDSTONE

These drawings show two kinds of underground coal mines. At the left is a bituminous mine. At the right an anthracite mine.

229

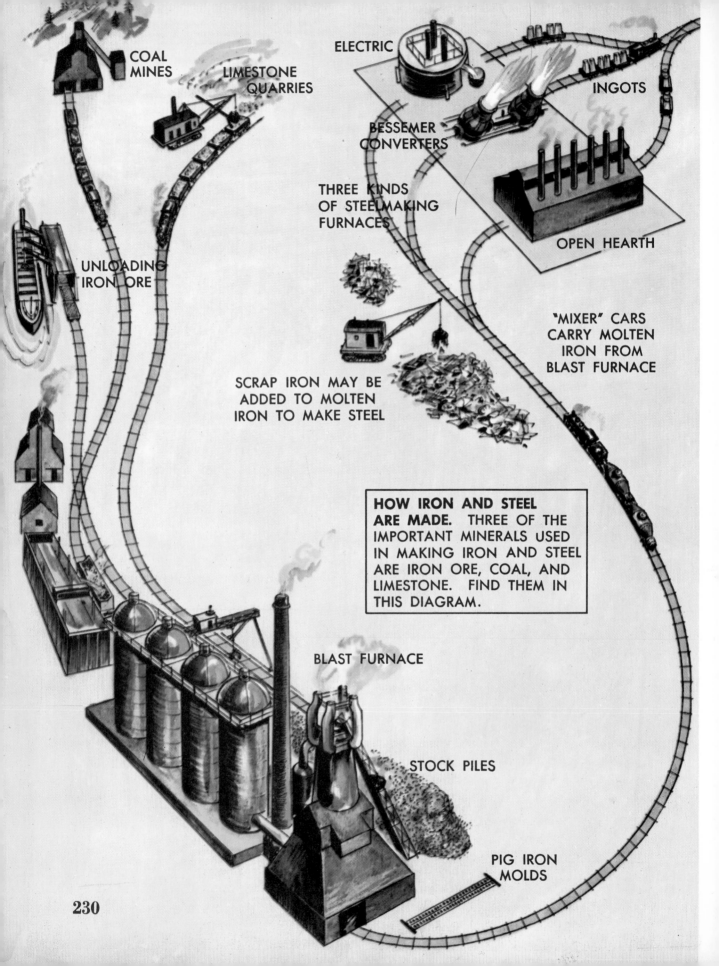

COAL MINES

LIMESTONE QUARRIES

ELECTRIC

INGOTS

BESSEMER CONVERTERS

THREE KINDS OF STEELMAKING FURNACES

OPEN HEARTH

UNLOADING IRON ORE

"MIXER" CARS CARRY MOLTEN IRON FROM BLAST FURNACE

SCRAP IRON MAY BE ADDED TO MOLTEN IRON TO MAKE STEEL

HOW IRON AND STEEL ARE MADE. THREE OF THE IMPORTANT MINERALS USED IN MAKING IRON AND STEEL ARE IRON ORE, COAL, AND LIMESTONE. FIND THEM IN THIS DIAGRAM.

BLAST FURNACE

STOCK PILES

PIG IRON MOLDS

230

covers the coal. Then the coal is broken up and loaded onto trucks. Strip mining is fast and less expensive than other ways of mining. But it ruins the land. Some companies now reclaim the land by planting trees or crops.

Iron ore is brought in by boat. Coal, limestone, and iron ore are used in making iron and steel. You learned that this region has deposits of coal and limestone. The early settlers also found some iron ore in Pennsylvania and New York.

But as the iron and steel industry grew, much more iron ore was needed. Fortunately, one of the largest iron ore deposits in the world was discovered along the shores of Lake Superior. Soon, the iron and steel makers of the Middle Atlantic region began to get their iron ore from this deposit. Your map on page 269 will show you that this iron ore travels most of the way by ship on the Great Lakes. The picture below shows one of the boats.

How iron and steel are made. First the iron ore is melted and the iron is separated from the other rock materials in the ore. This is done in tall round blast furnaces like the one on page 230. Terrific heat is required to melt the iron from the ore. So a remarkable fuel called coke is burned. Coke is made from coal.

Iron ore, limestone, and coke are poured into the red-hot blast furnace. Limestone helps to separate the iron from the waste rock. As the iron ore and the limestone melt, the heavy iron settles to the bottom. The limestone and waste rock rise to the top.

When the iron is removed from the bottom of the furnace, it is a hot liquid called molten iron. Study the pictures on page 230 to help you understand how steel is made. Some molten iron is cooled in molds and is then known as pig iron. But large quantities are rushed to nearby steel mills. There, in fiery furnaces the liquid

iron is combined with scrap metal and some other minerals. This makes the strong, tough metal called steel. A photo of one kind of furnace that makes steel is on page 231. It is an electric furnace.

Thousands of people work in the coal mines and steel mills of the Middle Atlantic States.

Farms and Foods in These States

Many farms are scattered through the Middle Atlantic States. Indeed, farming is the oldest industry. Most of the first settlers were farmers.

Small truck, or vegetable, gardens and dairy and poultry farms are clustered around the cities. Farther away, mixed farming is carried on. Mixed farming means the raising of several kinds of crops and livestock, remember.

New York and Pennsylvania are famous for dairy products and fruit orchards. Large areas are hilly lands, as the map on page 216 shows. But they have fine orchards and pastures for cattle. They also produce hay for winter feed for the cattle. The farms supply city dwellers with milk, cream, and a variety of fruits.

The fertile Lake Ontario plain in western New York grows vegetables and fruit. Its apples and cherries are among the finest in the land. Its pears, plums, and peaches are also of top quality.

Truck, dairy, and poultry farms spread across New Jersey and Delaware. This is one of the most important truck-farming areas in our country. It produces potatoes, cabbages, peas, corn, asparagus, cucumbers, onions, and tomatoes, as well as other crops. The photograph below shows a field of potatoes in this area. Some vegetables are sold fresh, but tons are canned or frozen. These states also raise melons, strawberries, peaches, pears, and apples.

The broad leaves of the tobacco plant are cured, or dried, to make smoking products.

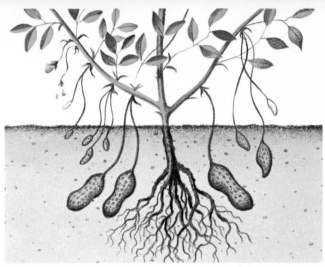

Peanuts grow underground. After the flowers fall off, the stalks push into the soil.

Maryland is another rich farming state. Fruit orchards cover acres and acres of this state. But there are also fields of berries, tomatoes, and vegetables.

Maryland has "oyster farms" hidden in the shallow waters of Chesapeake Bay. Millions of tiny oysters are dropped in the small protected inlets of this salt-water bay. The oysters anchor themselves to rocks on the floor of the bay. They grow there for three or four years. Then, they are ready to harvest. They are loosened with long-handled tongs and gathered into boats. Some oysters are sold fresh, some are frozen, and many are canned.

Virginia raises a variety of crops. If you traveled through eastern Virginia, you would see many truck gardens. They grow cabbages, onions, tomatoes, spinach, and strawberries. On the sandy coastal plain, peanuts are raised.

Peanuts are planted in rows three feet apart. The plants grow about eighteen inches tall and have whitish-yellow blossoms. When they fall off, the flower stalks bend over and push their heads into the soil. Then the nuts begin to grow. In the fall, the nuts are ripe and the plants are dug up and piled in heaps to dry. The nuts are torn from the plants by a threshing machine.

Southern Virginia raises a great deal of tobacco. Remember that many of Virginia's earliest settlers grew tobacco, long ago. It was their money crop, even then. Today, most of Virginia's tobacco is raised in the Piedmont section.

Tobacco leaves are very large. After they are picked, they are hung up to dry in large curing barns. One or more of these curing barns are found on nearly every tobacco farm, and some farms have as many as fifteen. After the tobacco is properly dried, it is sold and stored in warehouses. Later, it is manufactured into cigars, cigarettes, and pipe tobacco.

You have learned that many people in the Middle Atlantic States are engaged in farming. Yet even more people earn their living in agriculture in the South. In the next chapter you will learn about this region.

Some Study Questions

1. Name the Middle Atlantic States.
2. What is the fall line? Why have cities grown up along it?
3. Why have New York City, Philadelphia, Baltimore, and Pittsburgh, become large cities?
4. What is the Piedmont like? What crops are grown there?
5. Describe the Great Valley. In what ways do people earn a living there?
6. Why is steel making an important industry in this region?

Which Belongs Where?

On paper write the numbers 1 to 9. After each number write the word or words needed to complete the following sentences correctly. Use the list of words that follows.

1. A large group of cities extending one after another is called a __?__.
2. The four largest cities of the Middle Atlantic region are __?__, __?__, __?__, and __?__.
3. Lakes __?__ and __?__ border the Middle Atlantic region.
4. Now that the __?__ is finished, ocean-going vessels can travel from the Atlantic to Lake Superior.
5. New York is our largest __?__.
6. Much tobacco is raised on plantations in __?__.
7. __?__ has many orchards and oyster farms.
8. Iron ore and limestone are used in making __?__.
9. Great coal fields lie in __?__ and __?__.

List

Pittsburgh	farms
Maryland	dairy
megalopolis	Baltimore
Ontario	Virginia
West Virginia	Pennsylvania
New York City	Philadelphia
plain	St. Lawrence Seaway
Chicago	Erie
steel	Atlantic Coastal Plain
Huron	seaport

Thinking for Yourself

1. What do you think makes cities grow?
2. Where would you rather live, in a city or in the country? Why?
3. What foods grown in the Middle Atlantic States are raised near your home?
4. What things used in your home are made of iron? What ones are made of steel?

Some Other Things to Do

1. Locate the megalopolis about which you just read on the population map of the United States. To find this map, refer to the list of maps in the front of your text. Locate the megalopolis on the population map on page 222.
2. Take your class on a tour. Use pictures to help you tell about some sights in one of these cities:

New York	Philadelphia
Baltimore	Pittsburgh

3. Find out what products are made from coal. Be ready to share this information.
4. Read in another book about one of these topics:

The Statue of Liberty	How Peanuts Grow
The Steel Industry	Urban Renewal
Automation in the Coal Industry	

Plan to make a written report on your topic. Try to follow the suggestions given in the paragraphs "Preparing a Written Report" across the page.

5. Read the paragraphs on "Interviewing" below. Write some questions you might use if you interviewed one of these people:

A truck gardener   A coal miner
A dairy farmer   A city worker

Preparing a Written Report

Here are some suggestions to help you make good written reports:

1. Look in several books for useful material, using the index to find it quickly.

2. Take careful notes. Write down important ideas but do not copy sentences.

3. Arrange your ideas in the order in which you will use them in your report.

4. Write your report.

Interviewing

One way to find out about things is to *interview*, or talk to, an expert in a field.

Plan for your interview by writing questions to ask. Such questions as these might be asked a farmer:

1. What crops do you raise?

2. Which one is your "money crop"?

3. What is hardest about farming?

4. What do you enjoy most about it?

Begin your interview by introducing yourself. Then say, for example, "Our class is studying about the Middle Atlantic States and its crops. Can you tell me how ____ are raised?"

Be ready to ask the questions you prepared. Listen carefully without taking notes. You cannot write as fast as a person talks. Finally say thank you for the interview.

Let's Talk About the Metric System

There are many kinds of measures. We buy meat by the *pound*, and milk by the *quart*. We measure our height in *feet* and *inches*. Cloth is sold by the *yard*. Cities are *miles* apart. We have used this system since our country began.

But today, most countries throughout the world use a different plan, the *Metric System*. The Metric System is based on a system of tens.

One part of the Metric System is about *length*. It measures length by the meter and members of the meter family. They include millimeters (MM), centimeters (CM), and Kilometers (KM).

A *meter* (M) equals 39.37 inches. It is a little longer than a yard (36 inches).

A centimeter is much smaller. A *centimeter* is 1/100 of a meter, or .39 of an inch. That is a little less than a half inch. One side of your ruler may be marked in centimeters. Also, it may show even smaller parts, *millimeters*.

Kilometers are used to measure long distances. A *kilometer* equals 1000 meters, or about 5/8 of a mile.

Let's measure some distances in kilometers. Turn to your map on pages 504–505 and begin by using the Scale of Miles on page 505. Notice that the distance between New York and Baltimore is about 162 miles. Multiply that number by 1.6 like this: (See the Table on page 498.) Be sure your decimal point is one place to the left.

$$\begin{array}{r} 1\,6\,2 \text{ mi.} \\ \times\ 1.6 \\ \hline 9\,7\,2 \\ 1\,6\,2\,0 \\ \hline 2\,5\,9.2 \text{ KM} \end{array}$$

Now you know that there are about 259.2 kilometers between New York City and Baltimore.

Find the number of kilometers between New York and Chicago. This will be easy if you review the steps above.

There is much more to learn about the Metric System. Some interesting facts are shown in the Table on page 498. Be ready to talk them over with your class and learn how to use them.

14 · The Southern States: From the Old to the New South

Cape Canaveral and Skylab

Skylab and its space pioneers. It was May, 1973. Excitement filled the air at Cape Canaveral, Florida. Another space ship sat high atop a huge rocket, ready for countdown.

This space ship was unmanned. It was a giant compared to its earlier cousins. It was Skylab, a roomy workshop or laboratory. Skylab was twenty-two feet across and thirty feet long. It had a place for cooking and eating, one for sleeping, a bathroom, and work sections. Later, astronauts would work in Skylab out in Space.

Skylab was packed with supplies! Quantities of food, water, and oxygen, and some medicines. There were cameras and computers aboard and far-seeing telescopes.

Countdown went perfectly. The powerful rocket roared upward, pushing Skylab higher and higher. When it was 270 miles high it began to travel around the earth.

Sometime later, the Skylab I astronauts were launched. They caught up with Skylab. Skillfully they connected

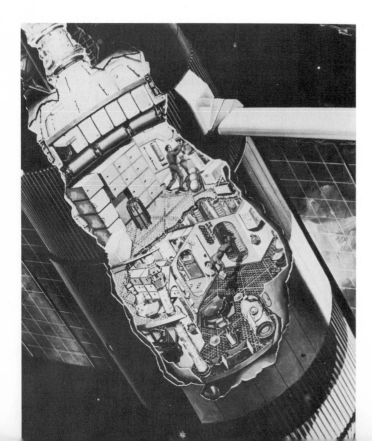

The Skylab has living space below and workshop laboratories above. At the bottom of the capsule is the waste disposal tank.

the two spacecraft. Then they moved into their space home for a four-weeks-stay.

The astronauts followed a daily plan of eating, sleeping, working, and relaxing. They awakened at six in the morning. At seven, they sat down to a breakfast they had prepared. After breakfast, there were chores. Everything was carefully put in place so it would not float around. Lunch was eaten at noon, and dinner at six. Some time each day was spent in exercising. Why was this important?

The space pioneers worked about eight hours a day. They studied and photographed the sun and other bodies. They took pictures of Earth with their cameras. They photographed its pollution. They had ways of "hunting" for new sources of mineral resources, perhaps oil. They also learned much about health problems in space, before they splashed down.

Several weeks later, the Skylab II astronauts began work in this space center. They remained for fifty-nine days, gaining valuable information.

In early winter, the third group of space pioneers occupied Skylab. This Skylab crew and the earlier ones proved that people can live and work in space for many weeks at a time.

Cape Canaveral, from which the Skylab missions began, belongs to the Space Age. But it got its name back in the 1500's. The Spanish explorer, Ponce de Leon, visited the cape when he was searching for the Fountain of Youth. He named it *Canaveral*, a Spanish word meaning "place of reeds." Cape Canaveral is located in one part of the huge region known as the South.

Looking at the South

The South is made up of eleven states. It is one of our largest regions. It stretches from the Atlantic Ocean west to the dry dusty plains of western Texas, a distance of about 1800 miles. Notice, too, that the South reaches from the Gulf of Mexico to the northern boundaries of Texas, Arkansas, and Oklahoma.

The eleven Southern States are North Carolina, South Carolina, Georgia, Florida, Alabama, Mississippi, Tennessee, Louisiana, Arkansas, Oklahoma, and Texas. Find each one on the map on pages 238–239. Which is largest? Point to the peninsula state. Find the states that face the Gulf of Mexico. Which ones look out on the Atlantic Ocean? Name the states that have no coast line.

Three Southern states were among our first thirteen states. They were North Carolina, South Carolina, and Georgia. Which states or parts of them were carved from the vast Louisiana Territory? The map on page 151 will help you decide.

The South is cut almost into halves by the Mississippi River. Point to this mighty river on the map. Notice that it marks a part of the boundary line for several states.

You have already learned some things about the Mississippi. But did you know that it gathers waters from more than 250 branches? The largest ones flowing into it from the east are the Ohio and the Tennessee rivers. Find them on the map on page 90. In what mountains do they rise? The largest branches from the west are the Missouri and the Arkansas. In what mountains do they begin?

237

In the spring the Mississippi's waters are often very high. Then, its branches bring it quantities of water from the melting snows. Sometimes the Mississippi has become so full it has spilled over its banks and flooded the low lands. To help prevent these damaging floods, our Government has constructed miles of strong walls, or levees, along the riverbanks. Also dams have been built on some of the branches. These dams hold back part of the water from melting snows. They store it in *reservoirs* until it is needed.

The Mississippi is a muddy river. For countless ages its branches have stolen soil on their way down mountain slopes and across plains. The giant river has carried some of this soil all the way south to the Gulf of Mexico.

The Mississippi becomes wider as it flows south. It slows down, too, as it winds through the low, flat plains along the Gulf of Mexico. At its mouth the Mississippi divides into several branches. The *mouth* of a river is the place where it empties into a large body of water. Point to the mouth of the Mississippi on the map on this page. Notice the land called the *Mississippi Delta*. Gradually this low swampy plain has been created by the mud the huge river has dumped there. The Mississippi Delta is a tiny part of the *Gulf Coastal Plain.*

Broad plains cover much of the South. Locate them on the map on pages 90 and 91. Find the Atlantic Coastal Plain. It continues all the way south to Florida.

In Florida the Atlantic Coastal Plain joins the Gulf Coastal Plain. Look on the map and see how this plain reaches west along the Gulf of Mexico. It extends north

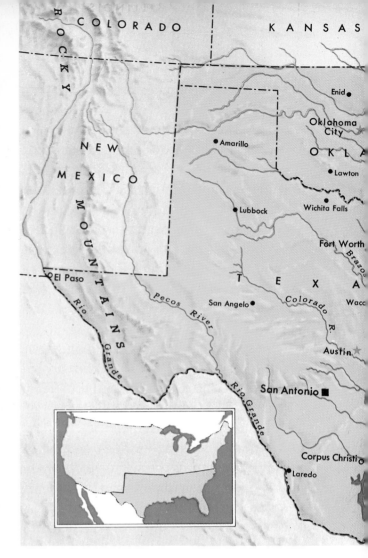

between the Mississippi River and the Appalachians to the Ohio River. Much of it has deep rich soil and is well-suited to growing crops. In fact, the South is one of the two greatest agricultural regions in our country. Agriculture is another word for farming, remember.

Not all of the Gulf Coastal Plain can be farmed, however. In some places the land is so low and flat that the water cannot drain off easily. These low wet places are called swamps, you may recall. One huge swamp in southern Florida is called the Everglades.

The map shows that plains also cover most of Texas and Oklahoma. Along the

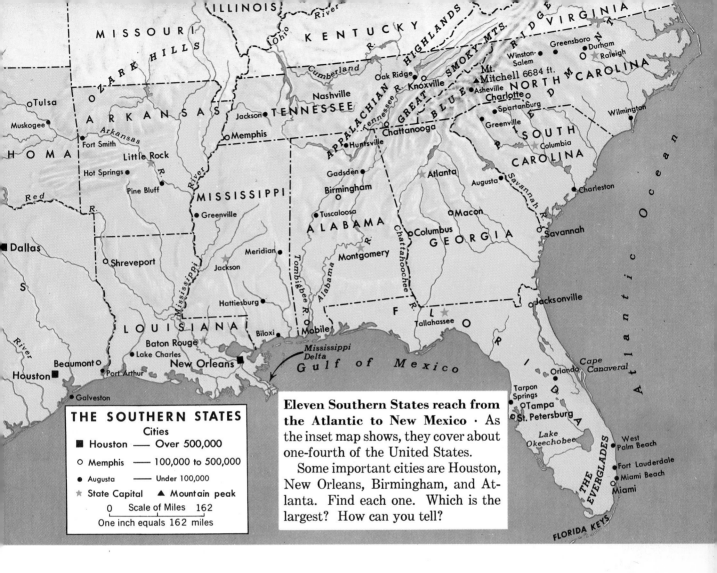

THE SOUTHERN STATES

Cities

■ Houston —— Over 500,000

○ Memphis —— 100,000 to 500,000

● Augusta —— Under 100,000

★ State Capital ▲ Mountain peak

0 Scale of Miles 162

One inch equals 162 miles

Eleven Southern States reach from the Atlantic to New Mexico · As the inset map shows, they cover about one-fourth of the United States.

Some important cities are Houston, New Orleans, Birmingham, and Atlanta. Find each one. Which is the largest? How can you tell?

Gulf of Mexico they are a part of the Gulf Coastal Plain. But the inland plains are much higher than those along the coast.

The South has hills and mountains. Find them on the map on pages 90–91. Notice how the southern part of the Piedmont extends through North Carolina, South Carolina, Georgia, and west into Alabama. Many of the Piedmont hills are clad in forests and others are checkered with orchards and farms.

West of the Piedmont are the Appalachian Highlands. Several ranges of mountains stretch through these high lands. On the east are the Blue Ridge Mountains and farther west are the Great Smokies.

Great Smoky National Park is a favorite vacation spot. A *national park* is land that has been set aside by our Government for all of us to enjoy. What other national parks are located in the South? Look on the map on page 289 to find out.

West of the mountains are other Appalachian Highlands. They reach into Kentucky, Tennessee, and Alabama. Some of these lands have rich deposits of coal and iron ore. More high lands rise in Missouri and Arkansas and extend into Oklahoma.

The famous Tennessee Valley stretches through seven states. It is drained by the Tennessee River and its branches, as the map on page 240 shows.

239

This large area receives a heavy rainfall. Long ago, forests covered the floor of the valley and the surrounding hills and mountains. The roots of the trees and shrubs held the soil and drank in much rain. But alas! Through the years, farmers and town builders chopped down the trees. When the rains fell, the water raced down the slopes. Terrible floods were caused. Farmlands were destroyed, towns were flooded, and lives were lost.

Also, as the water raced down the slopes and over the valley, it washed away the soil. This washing away of soil is called *erosion*. Only poor crops would grow in the thin soil that was left.

Something had to be done to keep this valley from becoming a "waste land." Its rich natural resources needed to be protected, or *conserved*. One dam was built in 1913. You probably know that a dam is a wall of dirt or concrete built across a river to hold back some of the water. This dam did hold back some flood water. So, in 1933, the Government began building a series of dams on the rivers of the Tennessee Valley. The organization in charge of this work was called the *Tennessee Valley Authority*, or TVA.

Today there are more than 25 dams. They can store tremendous quantities of water and have prevented many floods. At the same time, new forests have been planted and farmers have used better methods of farming to prevent erosion. Hillsides have been terraced to hold back water. Crops that protect the soil have been planted on these terraced slopes.

The dams of the valley do far more than prevent floods and erosion. Power plants built below the dams supply electricity for cities and their industries. Many new industries have moved to the Valley to use this cheap, useful electric power.

The TVA has also helped shipping. The Tennessee River was deepened and now boats can travel up it as far as Knoxville. Many boats move along the Tennessee carrying grain, coal, iron and steel, forest and petroleum products, and automobiles.

The TVA has thus helped in many ways to conserve the rich resources of the valley. Many farmers, manufacturing industries, and cities are now using these resources. Conserving our rich natural resources is an important project for all of us, no matter where we live.

Notice how many dams have been built on the Tennessee River and its branches. Why have they been constructed?

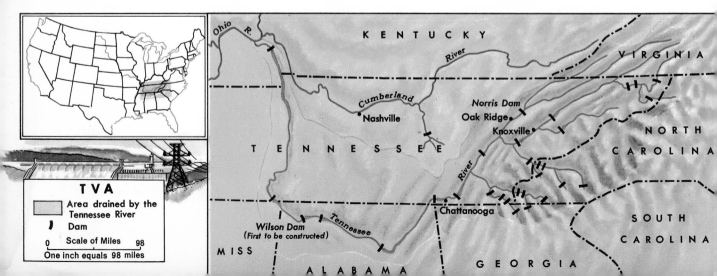

TVA

Area drained by the Tennessee River

Dam

Scale of Miles

0   98

One inch equals 98 miles

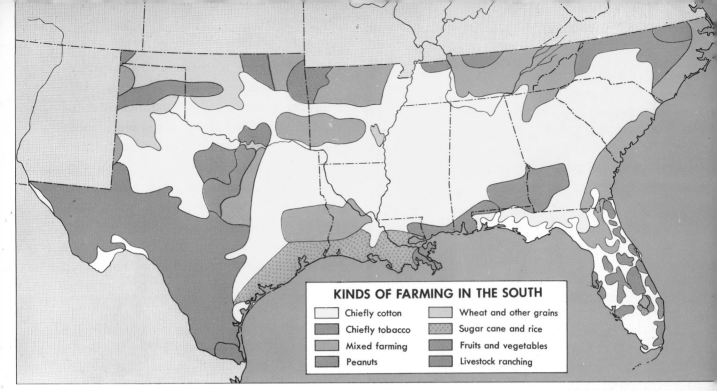

KINDS OF FARMING IN THE SOUTH

- ☐ Chiefly cotton
- ■ Chiefly tobacco
- ▨ Mixed farming
- ▨ Peanuts
- ▨ Wheat and other grains
- ▨ Sugar cane and rice
- ▨ Fruits and vegetables
- ▨ Livestock ranching

Agriculture is one of the South's most important industries · This map tells you some of the main crops grown there. What is the largest crop? Name some crops grown in Florida. Name some raised in southern Texas and southern Louisiana. What is raised in western Texas? Why are few crops grown there? The rainfall map on page 220 will help you answer.

The South has quite a mild climate. It is located closer to the equator than some parts of our country. But there is another reason for this climate. Warm moist winds blow across these states from the Gulf of Mexico. They help to keep the winters mild.

The northern edge of this region is colder than the lands along the Gulf. Some snow falls in the northern part. And sometimes freezing weather visits as far south as Florida. It may come when cold winds sweep south from Canada.

Summers down South are usually hot and damp. The warm weather begins in the early spring and lasts until late in the fall. Therefore the South has a long growing season. Study the map on page 203. What parts have a growing season of more than eight months?

This long growing season helps the South to grow many crops. But still another of nature's gifts is necessary to make agriculture successful. As you know, crops require water. Let's look at the rainfall map on page 220 and see what it tells us.

Notice that the western parts of Texas and Oklahoma are lands of little rainfall. There, even with months of warm weather and good soil, the people have a hard time farming. Herds of cattle and flocks of sheep graze on these lands.

As the map shows, though, most of the South receives plenty of rain. What states receive more than 40 inches a year? They can raise such crops as cotton, tobacco, sugar cane, rice and peanuts.

241

Farmlands in the Piedmont.

Agriculture: A Leading Industry in the South

Even long ago, many crops were grown in the South. The settlers raised corn and vegetables for food and kept meat animals. Livestock could feed in the pastures the year round.

In addition, the South grew some crops that required months of hot sunshine. One was tobacco. Today, North Carolina is still a leading tobacco-growing area.

Rice was another crop raised successfully. South Carolina and Georgia were called the "rice colonies." A third special crop started in the South was cotton.

Eli Whitney helped to make cotton "King" in the South. You read how spinning and weaving machines speeded up clothmaking. Soon cotton cloth could be sold cheaply and the textile business "boomed." Yet the South could not supply enough raw cotton for the mills. There was a good reason why.

The picture on page 243 shows that tiny brown seeds lie half-buried in the raw white cotton bolls. Before the cotton can be used, its seeds must be separated from the fibers. Long ago, this work had to be done by hand. It took a man a whole day to pick the seeds from one pound of cotton. The planters wished with all their hearts for a faster way.

Soon after our country won its independence, Eli Whitney invented a small machine that changed the future of cotton growing. Whitney was a schoolteacher. He had traveled from his Massachusetts home to Georgia to take a job. When he arrived at the school, however, another teacher had been hired.

While Whitney visited friends in Georgia, he learned what a slow task it was to clean cotton. At once he began to plan for a faster way to remove its seeds. He was clever with tools. He succeeded in making what he called a "cotton engine." It had a crank that turned by hand. But it combed the seeds from the cotton fibers surprisingly fast. It could clean over 50 pounds of cotton in a single day.

Soon, others copied and improved the cotton engine, or *cotton gin.* Today's huge gins can prepare enormous quantities of cotton for the mills.

Whitney's cotton gin encouraged many planters to grow more cotton. By the middle 1800's, thousands of acres were being raised across the South. Men in South Carolina and Georgia planted less rice and more cotton. North Carolina gave up some of its tobacco and put in cotton. Other farmers moved west to start cotton plantations in Georgia, Tennessee, Alabama, Mississippi, Arkansas, Louisiana, and Texas. Growing cotton was making some men rich. In fact, this crop was becoming "King" in the South.

Cotton is still the South's leading crop. The South grows a variety of crops, but cotton is the most important. The large area where it is the chief money crop is known as the Cotton Belt. It is shown on the map at the right. What states are a part of this Belt?

Notice that each of the tiny black dots on the map stands for 10,000 acres of cotton. In some places, the dots are so close together that they make a solid black

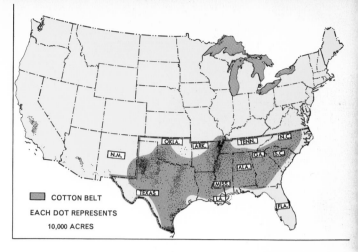

COTTON BELT

EACH DOT REPRESENTS
10,000 ACRES

This map shows the section of our country in which cotton is the leading crop. A section where large amounts of a certain crop are raised is called a *belt*. This map shows the Cotton Belt. Below, a mechanical cotton picker at work. The inset shows how a cotton boll develops. The blossom turns from white to red then drops off, leaving a pod, or boll.

243

Cosmetics · **Upholstery** · **Rope** · **Mops** · **Clothing** · **Soap** · **Phonograph records** · **Paper** · **Explosives** · **Umbrellas** · **Plastics** · **Thread** · **Absorbent cotton** · **Paints**

Some of the many products made from the cotton plant.

area. This tells us that there are many cotton fields in such areas. Altogether, millions of acres of cotton are grown in the Cotton Belt. Texas produces more cotton than any other state.

Look at this map once again. Had you noticed that the Cotton Belt does not include most low lands that fringe the Gulf coast or cover Florida? They receive too much rain for cotton. Neither is cotton raised in parts of western Texas. Its lands do not receive enough rain.

How is cotton raised? It is planted in March or April after the fields have been plowed. Many farmers use a seeding machine, or planter, to plant the cotton. When the plants are a few inches high, the fields are cultivated. In some fields, the weeds are hoed by workers who move up and down between the rows. In other places, the weeds are kept down by cultivators pulled by mules or by tractors.

When the cotton plant is about a foot tall, it bears white blossoms. Within a few days these turn a reddish color. Then they drop off, leaving small green seed pods called *bolls*. The cotton fibers grow in these bolls. The bolls grow larger and larger. By September they begin to ripen and turn brown. Soon they burst open. Then, they almost resemble snowballs.

Cotton picking begins in September. Today most of the cotton is picked by machine. A photo of such a machine at work is shown on page 243.

Loads of raw cotton are hauled to the gins where machines comb out the seeds. Then the cotton is pressed into huge bales, or bundles. They weigh about 500 pounds each. Millions of bales of cotton are shipped to the textile mills.

Though cotton is still the most important crop, it is no longer "King." People realize now that it is wise to raise some other crops on a part of their land. Indeed, some farmers in the Cotton Belt do not raise cotton at all.

What other crops are grown in the South? Parts of Georgia and South Carolina are famous for fine peaches. Peanuts and pecans are raised in many sections throughout the Cotton Belt, but Georgia raises more than any other state.

Florida and southern Texas are famous for grapefruit and oranges. Water from the Rio Grande in Texas is used to grow wonderful groves of orange and grapefruit

244

trees. Settlers from Mexico brought these trees to Texas.

Citrus fruits thrive only in areas with little frost. Orange and grapefruit trees have shiny dark-green leaves and sweet-smelling white blossoms. When the trees are in bloom, the air around them is very fragrant.

Rice is raised on the wet lowlands of the Mississippi Delta and the Gulf coast of Louisiana and Texas. Some is also planted farther north in Arkansas.

When the rice plants are a few inches high, the fields are flooded. They are usually kept under water until just before harvest time. When the grain begins to ripen, the fields are drained. Soon combines move in to cut and thresh it.

A part of Louisiana has enormous fields of sugar cane. This area is often called the "Sugar Bowl" of the South. Find it on the map on page 241. Notice that some sugar cane is raised in Florida.

Tobacco is the main crop in a large part of North Carolina. What other states grow tobacco?

Some farmers raise watermelons or sweet potatoes. Also, acres and acres of soybeans are grown. The soybean belongs to the bean and pea family. It is used as food for us as well as for livestock.

All of the Southern states raise quantities of vegetables. Some are sold in the cities of the South. But many truck farmers in North Carolina, South Carolina, Georgia, Florida, and Texas grow winter vegetables to sell in the North. Because of the mild climate, they can produce vegetables during most of the year.

Much mixed farming is carried on in the South. That means that farmers may raise several different crops and perhaps

Cattle on the Texas plains.

some poultry and livestock. Find some mixed farming areas on the map on page 241. Dairy farming is especially important near the cities. Large wheat ranches spread across the plains of Oklahoma and northern Texas.

Western Texas and Oklahoma raise millions of beef cattle. This industry began on the plains of Texas even before this huge state became a part of our country. These western plains are generally too dry to farm without irrigation. But their coarse grass provides grazing for enormous numbers of cattle.

Beef calves are usually born on a ranch during the spring. They remain on the grazing lands with their mothers for several months. Then in the fall, most of them are sold to farmers who have feed lots. There they are fattened for market.

Huge fenced cattle ranches spread over western Texas. Some ranches extend for miles. Just think! The largest one, the famous King ranch, occupies more land than the whole state of Rhode Island. Oklahoma also has large cattle ranches.

You have read how the South is producing many different crops. This is one reason why we think of it as the "New South." It is no longer just a cotton and tobacco land. Furthermore, its agriculture is becoming more and more mechanized. Machines are being used to do much of the farm work.

Then too, this region is finding new ways to use some of its crops. Think of peanuts, for example. Some are sold as salted peanuts, and some are made into peanut butter. Many are crushed to make a cooking oil, and some are used in manufacturing certain soaps. Peanut vines are excellent for fattening livestock. Indeed, a black scientist, George Washington Carver, discovered about 300 different uses for peanuts.

Most important, the South no longer depends entirely on agriculture. It has developed many other thriving industries.

This pine sap being collected has many uses.

Some Other Industries Using the South's Natural Resources

Lumbering is another important industry. Indeed, the South supplies nearly two fifths of all the lumber for our country. But only a little of its original forests remains. Most of the forests in the South today have been planted.

Many pine trees are raised as a crop. They are grown on hilly lands not suitable for farming. Because of the South's mild climate, long growing season, and heavy rainfall, these trees grow rapidly. As they are cut, new ones are planted. Also the trees are carefully protected from fire and insects.

Some products from the peanut.

Margarine

Cosmetics

Salad oil

Illuminating oil

Cooking oil

PEANUT BUTTER

Medicine

246

Lumbermen are busy winter and summer cutting down trees. Many logs are fed into singing sawmills to be made into lumber. Enormous quantities of pine are used for building purposes. Hardwoods are used for making furniture and woodwork in buildings.

The pine is valuable in other ways. Millions of logs are ground into pulpwood for making paper and rayon goods. The South's woodlands furnish over half of the pulpwood produced in our entire country. Many pine trees are tapped to harvest their thick sticky *resin*, or sap. Notice the gashes cut in them in the picture on page 246. The resin oozes out from the gashes. Resin is used in making paints, varnishes, linoleum, and some soaps. The South has many mills and factories which use the raw materials of its forests.

Some men earn their living fishing. One kind of shellfish, oysters, is plentiful in the warm, shallow waters off the coast in the Gulf of Mexico. Another shellfish,

shrimp, is also caught in the Gulf waters. Fishermen bring in catches of such fish as menhaden, mackerel, flounder, sea trout, and red snappers. Menhaden is an oily fish which is not used for food. Its oil is used in making soap and paints.

Thousands of men work in the South's oil fields. Another name for oil is petroleum. Petroleum is a thick greenish-black liquid. In some parts of the world, this dark oil is stored far below the surface of the ground in layers of rock. Therefore, it has been given the name petroleum, which means "rock oil."

This map shows where our country's leading oil fields are located · Does your state produce some oil? The black lines represent pipelines. These pipelines carry crude oil to refineries. Use the Scale of Miles to find how far some of the pipelines extend.

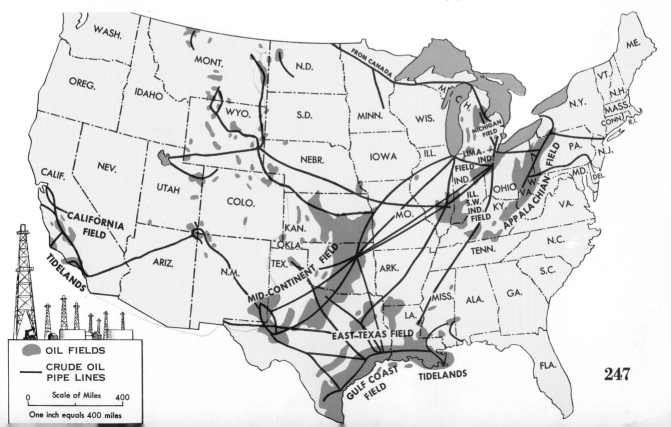

OIL FIELDS
CRUDE OIL PIPE LINES
0   Scale of Miles   400
One inch equals 400 miles

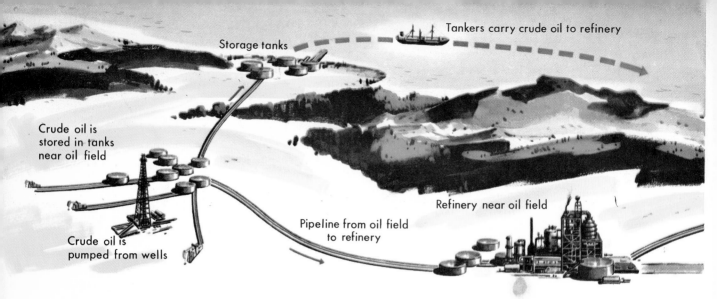

Storage tanks

Tankers carry crude oil to refinery

Crude oil is
stored in tanks
near oil field

Refinery near oil field

Pipeline from oil field
to refinery

Crude oil is
pumped from wells

Follow the crude oil from the well at the oil field to the refineries. The pipelines which carry the crude oil are colored blue. What happens at the refineries? The red arrows show the flow of oil products from the refinery.

The first oil wells in the United States were dug in Pennsylvania about a hundred years ago. At that time some people began to burn oil in their lamps. Today we make many, many products from crude oil.

The South has several large oil-producing areas. Find each one on the map on page 247. Notice how one stretches across the Gulf coast of Texas into Louisiana. What is it called? Another is the East Texas Field. A third, the Mid-Continent Field extends from northern Texas through Oklahoma into Kansas. Another being developed is under water off the coast of the Gulf of Mexico. It is called the Tidelands Field.

The thick dark oil is hidden far beneath the ground. To get it, men drill holes deep into the earth, perhaps a mile or more. Tall derricks are usually constructed to hold the drilling machinery.

Crude oil is pumped up from beneath the ground to huge storage tanks nearby. Then it is sent to refineries. Some is hauled by truck or railroad tank cars, and some is shipped in tankers. Huge quantities are pumped through pipelines. At the refineries the crude oil is separated into gasoline, kerosine, fuel oils, lubricating oils, and other useful products.

Petroleum is so valuable that we call it "black gold." We depend on it to run our automobiles, trucks, busses, airplanes, and farm equipment. It is turned into heating oil and is used for making electricity. It is used in making stockings and thousands of plastic products.

But our supply of this natural resource is running low. After oil is pumped from the earth, it cannot be replaced. We must use this valuable source of *energy*, or power, more wisely.

Natural gas is also a valuable resource in Texas, Louisiana, and Oklahoma. It is used for heating homes and other buildings. Also natural gas runs the machinery in some factories and mills. Perhaps in your home it is used as a fuel in your kitchen stove.

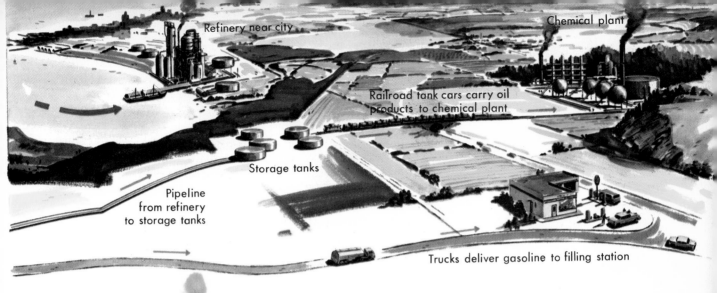

Refinery near city

Chemical plant

Railroad tank cars carry oil products to chemical plant

Storage tanks

Pipeline from refinery to storage tanks

Trucks deliver gasoline to filling station

In many oil fields natural gas comes from the wells along with petroleum. In some places it is found without oil. Pipelines from Texas carry this valuable fuel underground to such far-away cities as Los Angeles, New York, or Boston.

Some men are employed in quarries and mines. Tennessee and Georgia have quarries of beautiful marble and hard gray granite. Florida and Tennessee have rich deposits of phosphate, a mineral used in making fertilizer. Texas and Louisiana mine sulphur, a yellowish material found far underground. Sulphur is used in making paper and matches and in many other industries.

In Arkansas there are stores of a special kind of clay called bauxite. This is the ore from which aluminum is made. Aluminum is used for making pots and pans, parts of automobiles and airplanes, and a thousand other useful articles.

Near Birmingham, in Alabama, there are valuable deposits of coal, iron ore, and limestone. These are the chief materials for making iron and steel, remember. Birmingham has become an important iron-and-steel center. It is sometimes called the "Pittsburgh" of the South. Can you think why?

The Manufacturing, Trading, and Tourist Industries

Manufacturing is one of the main industries. This is not surprising. The South has everything necessary to develop manufacturing industries. It has a wealth of raw materials from its forests, farms, and mines. It has electrical power to run its factories. And it has railways, highways, and waterways for carrying products to and from factories.

Factories of this huge region manufacture textiles, clothing, and paper and furniture and other forest products. They turn out aluminum, iron and steel, metal goods, and dozens of products made of cotton seed oil, soybeans, and peanuts. And they make hundreds of chemical products. Giant plants freeze fruits and vegetables, turn sugar cane into sugar and syrup, and prepare beef for market.

The South has many manufacturing centers. Notice this on the map on page 251. As you know, Birmingham is the center of the important iron-and-steel

An iron-and-steel plant in Birmingham, Alabama. The railroad cars bring in the raw materials used in making iron and steel.

district of this region. Its large steel mills and factories employ thousands of men. Locate Birmingham on the map on pages 238 and 239. Use the key to help you learn about its population.

One of the largest cities in the South is Atlanta, in the Piedmont in Georgia. Use Table 5 in the Tables for Reference to see which is larger, Atlanta or Birmingham. Find Atlanta on the map. It is a "crossroads" for many railroads, highways, and airways, and is a busy transportation center. This is one reason why its mills and factories have grown rapidly. The factories of Atlanta make furniture, machinery, cloth, chemicals, and airplanes.

Find Memphis, Tennessee, on the map. Its fine location as a port on the Mississippi River has helped it to become a busy manufacturing city. Its factories manufacture machinery, chemicals, paper, rubber, cotton cloth, and many useful products from cottonseed oil.

Some cities in Georgia and some in the Carolinas have large cotton and rayon mills. For example, Charlotte, North Carolina, makes cloth, machines for making cloth, and fine furniture.

Some cities in North Carolina and Florida manufacture tobacco products. Several in Tennessee have aluminum plants. Many cities in the South have lumber and paper mills. Some also have aircraft and electronic manufacturing industries.

Two cities with special claim to fame. Oak Ridge is a young city in the Tennessee Valley. It has laboratories for testing and developing peaceful uses of atomic power.

Huntsville, Alabama is called "the Space Capital of the World." Here many scientists worked together to develop guided missiles. Huntsville has immense laboratories and factories for planning and producing engines for giant rockets. These rockets have been used to launch the spacecraft that landed on the moon. In 1950 Huntsville had about 16,000 people. Today it has over 140,000 people.

250

Houston, Texas, is the largest city in the South. Its industries have grown by leaps and bounds. One is a part of our country's Space program. The manned Spacecraft Center is located in this area. It is the control center for our manned spacecraft projects. The Apollo astronauts trained here. They were a part of the "moon program." So it became known as the "moonflight center."

Find Houston on the map on page 238. It is located about 50 miles inland from the Gulf of Mexico. However, it is a busy port because of its remarkable ship channel. A part of this man-made waterway is shown on page 252. The channel connects Houston with the Gulf of Mexico. It has helped the city to become an important manufacturing and trading center.

Houston's location in an area rich in resources has also helped it to grow. Remember that Texas is the leading cotton-producing and cattle state in our country. Houston has become an important business center and port for the cotton and livestock industries. Also nearby are some of our most important oil fields. Houston is a business center for many petroleum and chemical industries. It has oil refineries, chemical plants, and factories that make machinery for the oil industry. Houston is working to get rid of air pollution, as are other industrial cities.

Many Texas coastal cities share the "Golden Crescent." A crescent is shaped like a new moon, as you may know. The Texas "Golden Crescent" is about 370 miles long. It extends along the state's curving coast from Beaumont to Brownsville. Find this area on the map. What cities does it include?

Until recent years, miles of cattle lands and sugar and rice fields faced this coast.

Manufacturing is one of the South's important industries. Notice how many manufacturing centers are located in the region. This map also shows that the South has many natural resources for manufacturing.

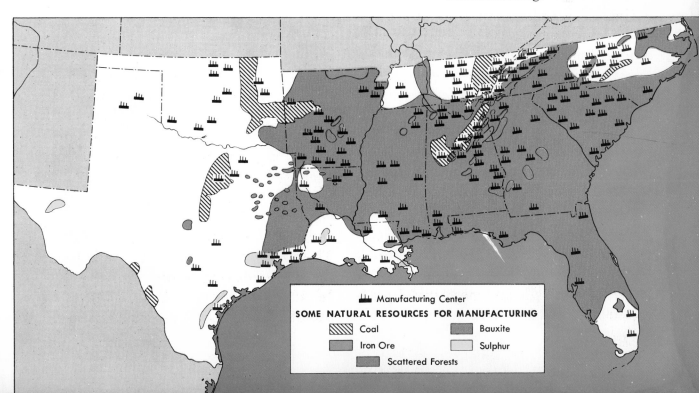

Manufacturing Center

SOME NATURAL RESOURCES FOR MANUFACTURING

Coal Bauxite

Iron Ore Sulphur

Scattered Forests

The man-made Houston Ship Channel.

Today, many acres have been swallowed up by oil refineries, chemical plants, and factories. Indeed, this long curved area is becoming so rich with industry that it is called the "Golden Crescent."

The South has more than a dozen busy ports. Houston is one, of course. New Orleans is another. The map on page 238 shows that it is a seaport for the whole Mississippi River system. About 30 miles of wharves and warehouses stretch along the Mississippi at New Orleans. Ocean-going ships travel up the river and dock at the wharves. Some of these ships bring in such products as coffee, bananas, and cacao. They may carry away such products as corn, cotton, gasoline, and steel.

It is not surprising that New Orleans is a thriving manufacturing center. Materials for manufacturing industries are brought in from many directions. Rice and sugar are prepared for market. There are petroleum refineries and giant chemical plants.

The South has dozens of other busy and important ports. On or near the Gulf of Mexico are Corpus Christi, Port Arthur, Galveston, Mobile, and Tampa. Locate them on the map. Charleston, South Carolina, Savannah, Georgia, and Jacksonville, Florida are bustling ports along the Atlantic coast.

Some cities in the South attract many tourists. One example is Miami, in Florida. Look for it on the map. Miami is one of the most famous winter resorts in the United States. Thousands of people flock to it and other resorts

252

nearby. They like Florida's mild inviting winter climate. And they enjoy swimming, fishing, and sailing.

Miami is a busy city the whole year round, however. It is an important transportation center. Airways that fan out to the south and east connect it with cities in the West Indies and in South America.

Mobile, Alabama, has a beautiful 35-mile long azalea "trail." Every March when these plants are covered with blooms, crowds of sight-seers visit the city. New Orleans is widely known for its interesting old French section and for its Mardi Gras, a festival held every year in late winter. Charleston, South Carolina, is one of our oldest and loveliest cities. Tourists especially enjoy the city's handsome old homes and its famous gardens.

The South has many "vacation" lands. Among them are some national parks. One interesting area is the Florida Keys, a series of tiny islands south of Florida. A fine highway with many bridges connects these islands. One can drive over it all the way to Key West. This city is located on an island about 100 miles southwest of the mainland. By this time, you realize what a large and varied region our South is. You have learned, too, how important it is to our country and how much it helps to make our country strong. Another large region lies to the north. It is made up of the North Central States. Come with us to visit this region.

A beautiful garden near Charleston, South Carolina.

Try to Remember

1. Name and locate the Southern States. Which is the largest? Which is a peninsula? Which border the Mississippi?

2. What are the leading crops of the South? Why can such a variety be grown?

3. Who invented the cotton gin? How did it encourage the raising of more cotton?

4. What is petroleum? How is it used?

5. Why have Atlanta, Birmingham, and Houston become large cities?

6. How has the TVA helped the South?

Match Them

The words in List A describe places or things which are mentioned in this chapter. On a piece of paper write the numbers 1 to 12. After each number write the matching word or words from List B.

List A

1. A leading space center
2. Strong walls to hold back a river
3. Low lands along the Gulf of Mexico
4. A scenic playground in the Appalachians
5. A large Florida swampland
6. An iron-and-steel manufacturing center.
7. Texas' new coastal industrial area
8. An important industry in western Texas
9. Trees tapped for resin
10. An important crop in southern and central Louisiana
11. Grain grown in flooded fields
12. Ore used in making aluminum

List B

Birmingham, Alabama
Great Smoky National Park
Gulf Coastal Plain
Cape Canaveral
Everglades
levees
Alabama
hickory
bauxite
soybeans

maple
rice
sugar cane
pine
peanuts
The Golden Crescent
raising cattle

Some Other Things to Do

1. List the South's main industries. Arrange pictures of some on your bulletin board.

2. Bring samples of cotton, linen, rayon, and nylon goods to school. Be ready to tell how we get each kind and ways these textiles are different.

3. List some important natural resources found in the South. Which ones supply energy?

4. Read the paragraphs on "Choosing a News Item" below. Then, look for a current event about some part of the South.

Choosing a News Item

Your class may wish to spend some time each week reporting interesting news. It is a good idea, then, to discuss how to choose worth-while news items. Talk over the ideas below and decide:

1. What kind of news is worth-while.

2. Where worth-while news items can be found.

3. What special kind of news the class should watch for.

What Do You Think?

1. If you do not live in the South, how is its climate different from that of your state?

How do the growing seasons compare? How does the amount of rainfall received compare? What crops are different?

2. Why is it a good idea to grow many kinds of crops in a region?

3. What causes floods? Levees have been built to help protect river lands from floods. What else can help to prevent floods?

4. How does it help a region to have many kinds of industries? What are some important industries in your state?

5. What do you think the word conservation means?

Using Numbers and Letters to Locate Places on a Map

Have you ever taken a long automobile trip? If so, you may have used a road map. A road map shows highways and locates cities and other important places. To help people use such maps more easily, letters and numbers are often placed along the edges.

Look at the picture map at the right above. It shows one section of a community. Notice the numbers and letters along the edges of the map. Let's learn how to use them to locate places in this section.

Locate the school at C 3. First find C at the northern and southern edges of the map. Then find 3 on the eastern and western edges. Now move one finger down or up from the C in a straight line. Move another finger

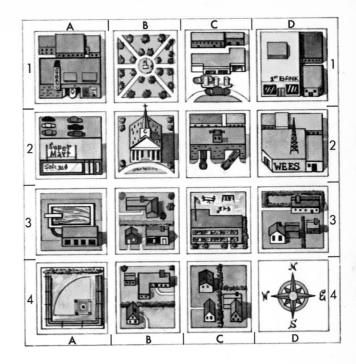

straight across from 3. Notice that your two fingers meet where an imaginary line from 3 crosses an imaginary line from C. The school is located there, as you can see.

Use the letters and numbers on the map above to help you answer these questions:

1. What is at A 1?
2. Where is the church located?
3. What do you find at C 1?
4. What is at A 2?
5. Where is the fire department located?
6. What is at D 2?
7. Which direction is the church from the fire department?
8. Which direction is the school from the market?

15 · The Central States: Farms, Mines, and Factories

A Reaper Helped a Region

A thank you for Mr. McCormick. One evening about sunset, the Gray family drove along the road that led past their wheatfields. The ripened grain was a beautiful sight. It had turned yellow and looked like a sea of gold.

"We should be very thankful," said Mr. Gray, as he stopped to glance at the fields. "Can you children guess why?"

"For harvest-time!" spoke up nine-year-old Ellen.

"I think for our good crop," added Bill, eleven.

"Yes," agreed their father. "But also for the combines that start work tomorrow."

"What's special about them?" asked Bill. "They come every year!"

Mr. Gray smiled. "That's true, son. But if we had lived long ago, they wouldn't have. In the early days, farmers had to harvest their grain by hand. Think of cutting our whole 640 acres that way!"

"We couldn't!" exclaimed the boy. "We'd never finish!"

"Well, hardly," replied the father. "Fortunately, we don't have to worry,

As a boy, Cyrus hated most the slow tiresome work of cutting the grain by hand.

Later he invented a reaper to cut the grain. This shows the successful test of his reaper.

thanks partly to Mr. McCormick. He invented a harvesting machine, the reaper. You might say that his reaper was the grandfather of the combines that will harvest our wheat." Then he told the children the story of the young inventor. Perhaps you'd like to read it.

How a harvesting machine was invented. About 150 years ago, young Cyrus McCormick was growing up on a farm in Virginia. He did many chores but the job he dreaded most came at harvesttime. It was the slow tiresome task of cutting the grain by hand. How he wished for a better way.

Cyrus's father also dreamed of a better way. He liked to tinker with tools and had tried to invent a "harvester." But he had one failure after another and finally gave up. Then Cyrus knew he must make the dream come true.

Several years later, Cyrus completed his reaper. One day, he invited neighbors to watch him test this machine that was pulled by a horse. Curious, they arrived at the field. But they soon shook their heads in disgust and one muttered, "H—m! Only way to cut grain is same as always!" You see, the reaper did not work, after all!

"Never mind!" Cyrus said to himself. "Whatever is wrong can be corrected. I know it!"

As it turned out, the problem was very simple. McCormick had tried out his reaper in a hilly area but had built it for a flat one.

Sometime later, another test was announced. On a flat field, the machine performed perfectly and cut grain much faster than one could by hand. Cyrus's friends and neighbors could hardly believe their eyes. This time, of course, they showered the young man with praise.

In these years, more and more people were moving west. Some settled in parts of what are now the Central States. They found that fine wheat would grow in this fertile plains region. And there was plenty of land on which to start large farms. But, alas! They could plant only a certain amount of grain because it took such a long time to harvest it by hand.

Cyrus saw his opportunity. He moved west to the fast-growing town of Chicago and started a reaper factory. Soon, he was selling a thousand reapers a year.

His reaper encouraged settlers to start large farms on the wide, lonely plains. Indeed, his invention and the improvements on it have made possible the growing of huge crops of grain in the Central States.

Looking at the Central States

The Central States spread across the heart of our country. This region is sometimes called the Middle West. It is a little larger than the South and about 12 times the size of New England. Thirteen states share our fertile central region. Locate each on the map on pages 258–259. Which states reach farthest north? Which are farthest west? Which border the Great Lakes?

Find the states which lie between the Appalachians and the Mississippi River. They were carved from lands which we won from England at the close of the War for Independence. At that time, these lands were called "the West" and were mostly wilderness. Kentucky was the first of these territories to be settled.

The central region west of the Mississippi was added to our country when we bought the Louisiana Territory in 1803. What Central States have been cut from the Louisiana Territory? The map on page 151 will help you decide.

Rolling plains sweep across most of our central region. The lands east of the Missouri River are the Central Plains, remember. The Great Plains stretch west to meet the Rockies. You have already learned that they are higher and drier than the Central Plains.

The Central Plains were settled first. These plains begin just west of the Appalachian Highlands. They have fertile croplands and also rivers which can be used as water highways.

The settlers found the eastern part of the Central Plains covered with forests. They had to cut down trees and clear the land to plant crops. But west of the Mississippi, there were only patches of forest. Stretching farther west were endless prairies covered with tall grass.

For a time, few settlers were attracted to the prairies. They feared that if trees would not grow, neither would good crops. Later on, however, farmers discovered that the prairies had deep rich soil and that fine crops could be raised.

Today, millions of acres of corn, wheat, and other crops are raised in the Middle West. Indeed, agriculture is such an important industry that this region is often called our country's "food basket."

Hills and mountains frame parts of the Central States. On the east the Appalachian Highlands reach down

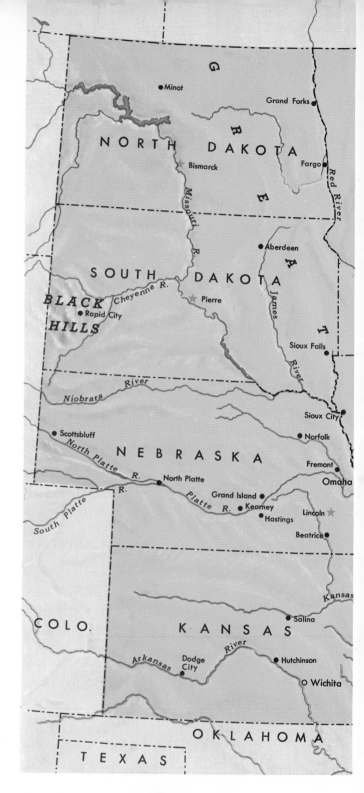

through Ohio and Kentucky. On the west are the towering Rockies.

The wooded Ozark Hills spread over southern Missouri. Find them on the map on page 90. Other areas of hills reach

THE CENTRAL STATES

THE CENTRAL STATES

Cities

☐ Chicago	Over 1 million
■ St. Louis	500,000 to 1 million
○ Toledo	100,000 to 500,000
● Evanston	Under 100,000
★ State capital	

0   Scale of Miles   123

One inch equals 123 miles

Lake of the Woods

Red Lake

MESABI RANGE

Lake Superior

MINNESOTA

Duluth

Sault Ste. Marie

MICHIGAN

Lake Huron

St. Cloud

WISCONSIN

Minneapolis   St. Paul

Richfield

Eau Claire

Green Bay

N.Y.

Rochester   Winona

La Crosse

Oshkosh

Sheboygan

Muskegon

Grand Rapids

Saginaw   Bay City

Flint

Pontiac

Lake Erie

Austin

Milwaukee

Madison   West Allis

Lansing

Dearborn   Detroit

Cleveland

Waterloo

Dubuque

Racine

Kenosha

Battle Creek

Jackson

Ann Arbor

Lorain

Akron   Youngstown

IOWA

Cedar Rapids

Rockford

Evanston

Oak Park   Chicago

Aurora   East Chicago

Kalamazoo

Toledo

PA.

Des Moines

Davenport

Cicero   Gary

Joliet   Hammond

South Bend

Canton

OHIO

Council Bluffs

CENTRAL

Ft. Wayne

Lima

PLAINS

Columbus

Ottumwa

Peoria

INDIANA

Ohio River

St. Joseph

ILLINOIS

Muncie

Springfield   Dayton

WEST VIRGINIA

Leavenworth

Decatur

Springfield

Terre Haute

Indianapolis

Hamilton

Kansas City   Independence

Columbia

Cincinnati

Newport

Topeka   Kansas City

Covington

St. Louis   East St. Louis

APPALACHIAN HIGHLANDS

Jefferson City

VIRGINIA

MISSOURI

Louisville

Frankfort

Lexington

Evansville

Owensboro

KENTUCKY

Springfield

Joplin

OZARK HILLS

Paducah

NORTH CAROLINA

ARKANSAS

Cumberland

TENNESSEE

Mississippi R.

Minnesota R.

Wisconsin River

Des Moines R.

Illinois R.

Wabash R.

Ohio R.

This map shows the Thirteen Central States. Name them · Notice how four of the Great Lakes cut into some of these states. There are many busy cities scattered throughout this region. One, Chicago, is the second largest in our country. Find it. On what lake is it located? What does the key tell about its population? On what lake is Detroit? Find Cleveland on Lake Erie. Which is larger, Cleveland or Detroit? How can you be sure?

Much freight is transported on the Mississippi. It is carried by several different kinds of boats. Barges, pushed by towboats, carry a great deal of the freight.

through parts of Wisconsin and Michigan. The Black Hills rise on the western edge of South Dakota. Locate them on the map. On the granite face of one, Mount Rushmore, are carved huge heads of four of our Presidents, Washington, Lincoln, Jefferson, and Theodore Roosevelt.

Valuable waterways cut into the Central States. As the map shows, there are many important rivers in this region. Most of them finally drain into the mighty Mississippi.

The United States government has deepened the channels of the Mississippi River so that boats can travel far upstream. They dock at Minneapolis and St. Paul in Minnesota, and go up the Ohio River to Pittsburgh. Strings of low, flat barges are the freight cars of the river. They are pushed by small powerful tugboats. The photograph above shows you such a string of barges on the Mississippi. These barges carry heavy loads such as coal and automobiles.

The map also shows that the Great Lakes cut deep into the northeastern Central States. The Great Lakes and the St. Lawrence River are our most important inland waterway, remember.

The Great Lakes and the Mississippi and its branches have helped the Central States in many ways. Most important, they have provided cheap transportation for goods and people. Notice how many cities of this region are either on a river or on one of the Great Lakes.

The Central States have a varied climate. The winters in the northern parts are long and cold. Minnesota and Wisconsin, for example, often have heavy snowstorms. The snow remains on the ground much longer than in Kentucky or Missouri which are next door to the South.

Summers are hot and the weather is often sticky and uncomfortable. Some hot nights scarcely a breath of air stirs. Still, the farmers seldom complain. They know that hot days and nights are good for their crops.

The map on page 203 will show you that most of this region has a shorter growing season than the South. Generally, it lasts from four to six months. This is not long enough for cotton to ripen. But it is long enough to grow many food crops.

As you would expect, summers are longer and hotter in the southern part of the Central States than in the northern sections. For example, crops can grow for a longer time in Kentucky than they can in northern Michigan. Killing frosts may visit northern Michigan quite early in the fall.

Most areas in the Central States receive twenty inches or more of rain each year. Much of this rain comes in the late spring and early summer when growing crops need it.

The western section of the region is the driest part. Notice this on the rainfall map on page 220. See how much less rain falls in the western parts of Kansas, Nebraska, and the Dakotas than falls east of the Mississippi. Farmers in this western section, therefore, grow crops that need less rain, such as wheat. But farther east, the leading crop is corn.

Corn Is "King" in the Central States

Corn is our country's oldest crop. It was being raised by the Indians when Columbus reached America. Friendly Indians taught the Pilgrims how to grow it and also how to grind it into meal, you remember. Soon corn became an important crop in all the colonies. Later, pioneers carried precious seed corn west across the Appalachians and even all the way to Oregon.

But this early kind often had small ears and poor kernels. So farmers and scientists worked hard to produce better varieties. They have succeeded remarkably well. Furthermore, ways have been found to destroy the insect enemies.

Corn is our biggest and most valuable crop. More land is used for producing it than for any other one crop. Some is raised in nearly every state in our country. But our most important corn-growing area is in the heart of the United States. This area is known as the Corn Belt.

Locate the Corn Belt on the map on page 262. Notice that it extends from eastern Ohio to the edge of Colorado. Nearly all of it lies within the Central States.

Most Corn-Belt farmers have some mechanized equipment. There are many kinds of labor-saving machines to help them. One of the most useful is the tractor, today's powerful work-horse.

Spring is a busy time of year on a Corn-Belt farm. There is work to do early and late because it is the planting season. First, a tractor chugs across the field pulling a kind of machine that spreads fertilizer. Later, the tractor pulls

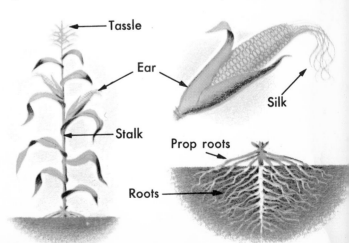

Tassle

Ear

Silk

Stalk

Prop roots

Roots

the plow. If it is a large one, the plow can turn as many as eight furrows at once. Tractors also pull the machines that plant the seeds and at the same time, perhaps, spray on a liquid weed-killer.

Soon, the tender young corn shoots pop through the soil. Hot sunshine, warm, still nights and frequent showers encourage the corn to grow very fast. Generally, it is "knee high by the Fourth of July." Before long, the sturdy green stalks are beginning to show golden tasseled heads. By August, the stalks may be very tall.

In autumn, the corn is ready to harvest. Then, one may see tractors moving down the neat rows of corn, drawing machines called corn pickers. Corn pickers pull the ears of corn from two rows of stalks at a time. They husk the corn and drop the ears into a wagon that follows. A mechanical picker can harvest corn about ten times faster than a man.

A moment ago you read that corn is our most valuable crop. Did you wonder why this is so?

How is corn used? One kind, sweet corn, is a favorite food on our tables in the summertime. How good corn-on-the-cob tastes when you add a little butter and salt to it! Much sweet corn is also canned or quick frozen.

Popcorn is another favorite variety. It has small hard kernels that pop open and become white and fluffy when they are heated rapidly.

Many of our food products are made from corn. Among them are cereals, corn meal, corn syrup, and hominy.

Also corn is used in making many products that we do not eat. The paint on your classroom wall, the chair on which you are sitting, and your clothes may contain corn in some form. Starch from corn is found in certain cosmetics and in some kinds of explosives.

But about nine tenths of the corn crop is used to fatten meat animals, such as cattle, hogs and lambs, and poultry.

The Corn Belt is a mixed-farming area. Most of its farms grow not only corn but also such crops as oats, barley, soybeans, and hay. Furthermore, they have feed lots where meat animals are fattened for market.

Thousands of calves are bought from ranches in Texas or in other parts of the western plains. They are put in feed lots like the one in the picture on page 263.

Our chief corn-growing area is known as the Corn Belt · What states are in this belt? The Central States are outlined in red. About four-fifths of the corn raised in this belt is fed to meat animals. It is not surprising, then, that most meat-packing centers are in or near the Corn Belt.

262

CORN BELT

MEAT PACKING CENTER

CORN

CORN

HAY

MACHINE SHED

CORN CRIB

HOGS

CATTLE

CORN

SOYBEANS

CORN

The Wilson's farm.

They are given corn, soybeans, and other foods for from three to six months. Then they are ready for market.

Large numbers of hogs also are raised and fattened in the Corn Belt. In fact, the Corn Belt has our leading hog-producing states. Hogs, you know, provide us with bacon, ham, and other kinds of pork. Are hogs raised on the farm pictured on this page? Let's visit it.

On a Corn-Belt farm. Mr. and Mrs. Wilson and their family live on the farm in the picture. It is much like many others in the Corn Belt. Their house is modern and comfortable and has a telephone, electricity and much electrical equipment.

Back from the house is a huge barn. The upper part is the hayloft where hay is stored for the winter. Some of it is fed to the dairy cattle which the Wilsons keep. The cows graze in the pasture during the months when the grass is green, however.

Notice the feed lot. See the tall tower-like silos nearby. They store food for fattening beef cattle. You see, the Wilsons earn a part of their living by "finishing" meat animals.

The Corn Belt sends many meat animals to market. When they have been fattened and are ready, they are loaded on trucks or on the special stock cars of a freight train. Then they are rushed to stockyards.

Large stockyards in the Central States are found in Kansas City, St. Louis, Milwaukee, and Omaha. Each of these cities is located in the heart of a busy farming area.

From the stockyards, the cattle and hogs enter packing plants to become meat for market. Some meat is canned and some, like ham and bacon, is smoked. But the largest quantities are sold fresh. Re-

263

Cattle being loaded into stock car. They are being taken to stockyards.

frigerator trucks and railroad cars carry the meat to many parts of our country to be sold in markets, large and small. More and more people are eating more beef. Find the chief meat-packing centers on the map on page 262. Notice that most of them are in or near the Corn Belt. Why would you expect to find a meat-packing center in Texas?

Thousands of people are employed in the meat industry. Every part of the animal is used. Nothing is thrown away. So, many people earn their living making useful goods from hides, bones, and fat. Hides are made into leather for shoes, belts, suitcases, and other leather goods. Bones are ground up into fertilizer, and much fat is used for making soap.

The Corn Belt has also become the Soybean Belt. Soybeans were brought to this country from China about 150 years ago. The Chinese use the bean for food. In our country only a little of it is used as food for people. Most of it is used for its oil and for food for cattle, pigs, and chickens.

The soil and climate of the Central States are just right for growing soybeans. In recent years more and more soybeans have been grown. We are feeding cattle large amounts. Also other countries want more and more soybeans. Other countries are also raising more cattle, pigs and chickens. In 1973 our most valuable export was soybeans.

West of the Corn Belt lies another kind of rich agricultural region. Look at the section title below. Then guess what important crop is raised in this part of the Central States.

Our Nation's "Bread Basket"

The western Central States raise enormous quantities of wheat. They make up a large part of our country's Wheat Belt, as is shown on the map on page 265. This area grows so much wheat that it is sometimes called our nation's "bread basket."

Study the map. What Southern states are a part of the Wheat Belt? What Central States? This belt's fertile soil and fairly dry climate are well suited to wheat-growing. But there are also other reasons for the large harvests of wheat.

One reason is that farmers can now purchase top-grade wheat seed. This seed produces many kernels, or seeds, of wheat. And farmers have learned how to conquer the insects and diseases that are the crop's

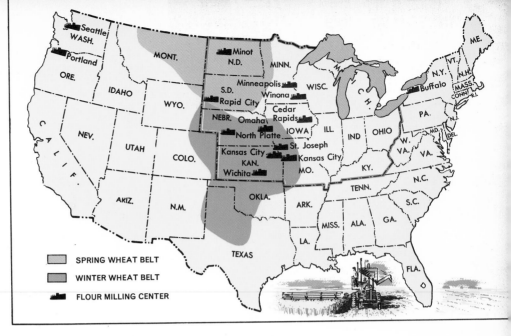

What Central States are part of the Wheat Belt? Which states produce the most winter wheat? Which raise the most spring wheat? Most of this wheat will be taken to flour mills. Find the chief flour-milling centers on this map at the right.

SPRING WHEAT BELT
WINTER WHEAT BELT
FLOUR MILLING CENTER

enemies. Also, they can buy machines that speed up their work and make it possible to farm more land than ever before.

Two different kinds of wheat are grown in the Wheat Belt. Look on the map and find out what they are.

Winter wheat is raised in the southern part of the Wheat Belt. To grow it, farmers prepare their fields in the late summer and sow the seeds in the fall. Within a few weeks the plants are several inches tall. Then, the fields seem to be covered with a coarse green grass. Soon, however, cold weather stops growth and snow blankets the wheat. This covering protects the roots of the small plants. When the warm spring days come, the plants grow very fast. By June the crop is ready to cut.

Spring wheat is raised in the Dakotas and Montana. Find this area on the map. In these states, the winters are too long and cold for wheat to be planted in the fall. Here the wheat must be planted in the spring. It is harvested in the late summer.

Large machines help the wheat farmer, remember. As you know, tractors are used to pull such equipment as plows and planting machines. But the most wonderful machine of all is probably the combine.

Several combines are shown on page 266. The legend, there, tells you what such a machine can do. Why is a modern combine more useful than the reaper which McCormick invented?

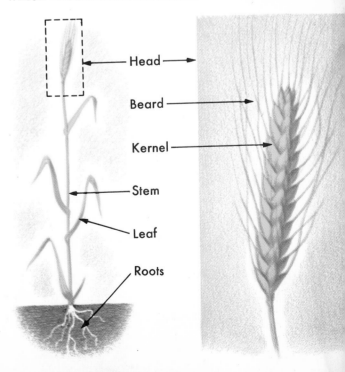

Head

Beard

Kernel

Stem

Leaf

Roots

Combines harvest wheat. They cut and thresh the seeds from the stalks. Compare them with McCormick's reaper on page 256. Below, elevators store the grain. They stand near railroad tracks so that trains can be loaded easily.

Elevators store the wheat. After the grain is harvested, trucks haul it to a grain elevator. You can see a picture of one on this page. Some elevators are very large indeed. One in western Kansas is more than a half mile long.

A grain elevator has equipment for loading, cleaning, storing, and unloading grain. One can see many elevators along the railroad tracks in Wheat Belt towns and cities. They store the grain until it is hauled to the mills. Find the chief flour-milling centers on the map on page 265. In what city in New York State do you find such a center? Why do you think this is a good location?

We use wheat products every day. They are made from the flour manufactured from the small hard wheat kernels. Among them are bread, rolls, cake, pie, cookies, and breakfast cereals. About three fourths of the flour which is milled is used by bakers who sell us bread and other "wheat" foods.

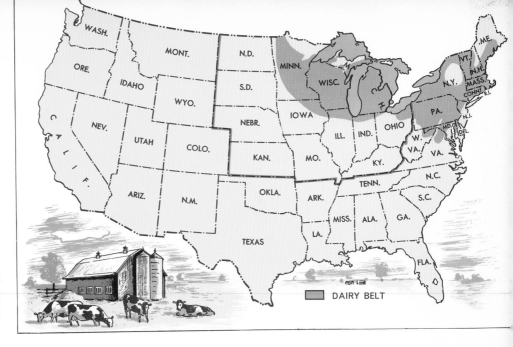

Dairy cattle are raised in every state of our country · They supply people nearby with dairy products. However, the largest amount of dairying is carried on in the northeastern part of the United States. This wide area is known as the Dairy Belt.

DAIRY BELT

The Central States Supply Many Other Foods

Many farms raise vegetables and fruits. Some of them grow such vegetables as peas, tomatoes, sweet corn, and beans, and tons of potatoes. A part of this fresh produce is sold in city markets. But much of it is canned or frozen.

Other farms specialize in growing fruits and berries. Along the eastern shores of Lake Michigan are dozens of neat fruit orchards. Here are grown delicious apples, peaches, grapes, plums, and pears.

Fruit-picking time brings the busy canning season. Then, some housewives "put up" fruit and berries and make jams and jellies. At this season, too, large canneries hum long hours canning fruit to sell in markets.

A wide Dairy Belt reaches across the northeast. As the map above shows, it extends from the edge of North Dakota all the way through New England. You have read about dairy farming in the eastern part of our country.

Much of the Dairy Belt is hilly and rough or swampy and dotted with lakes. This northern area has long cold winters and rather short rainy summers. Such lands are not well suited to most farming. But the summer climate encourages rich green pastures and good hay crops. So this is a fine area for dairy farming.

Milking with machines.

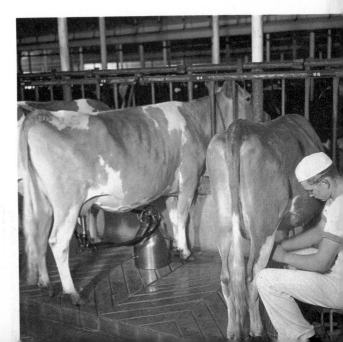

267

Dairy farmers are busy people. In the summer, they raise hay and corn for winter feed for their cattle. The green hay is cut and packed in the haylofts of the huge barns. Much corn is also cut green. Its stalks, leaves, and ears are fed into a chopping machine and blown through huge pipes into a silo. This corn feed is called silage.

Winter and summer, the dairy farmer spends much time tending his cattle. Every morning and evening the cattle must be milked. Also they must be fed and the milking barns cleaned. Everything possible is done to keep the milking quarters spotless and the milk pure, for impure milk can cause disease.

Dairy farmers make a good living selling milk and cream. Much of the milk is sent to dairy plants. There it is pasteurized, or heated, to be certain that any germs are destroyed. Then it is cooled and bottled, or sealed in cartons for delivery to markets and homes.

Some milk is sold to large factories to be made into evaporated or condensed milk. You can buy this kind of milk in cans. "Canned milk" is very thick and creamy. This is because most of the water has been taken out of it.

Some milk is run through machines called separators. Then, from one spout comes rich yellow cream while from another comes the bluish milk that is left. It is called skimmed milk. Much rich cream is sold to factories called creameries to be churned into butter. Some churns are so large that they can make as much as 2000 pounds of butter at one time. There are hundreds of creameries in Minnesota. It is the leading butter state in our whole country.

Large quantities of milk and cream are also used to make cheese. Wisconsin is famous for its cheese manufacturing. Its 3000 cheese factories produce many different kinds of cheese. What kinds have you eaten?

Some Central States also have riches hidden under their soil. So mining is an important industry.

Mining is Important in the Central States

Certain parts of the Central States are rich in iron ore. A hilly area near Lake Superior supplies about four fifths of all the iron ore mined in our country. This area extends from eastern Minnesota through northern Wisconsin and into Michigan. These iron-ore deposits have helped us to lead the world in the manufacture of iron-and-steel products.

Some of this ore is near the top of the ground. It can be scooped out of open pits by large power shovels. Other deposits are buried far underground and are mined from deep shafts.

Freight cars haul the ore to ports on Lake Superior. There it is loaded onto long ore boats and carried to large iron-and-steel centers such as Gary, Chicago, Detroit, Cleveland, and Buffalo. Part of it is then sent on freight cars to other iron-and-steel centers such as Pittsburgh. Follow the journey of an ore boat on the map on page 269.

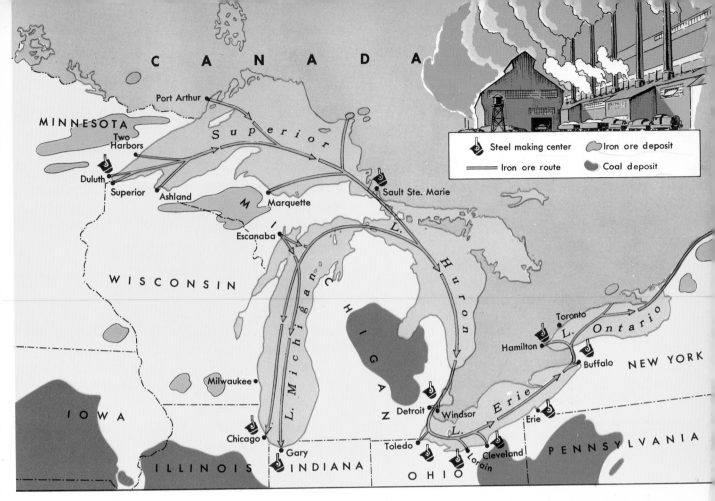

On this map find the map legend:

Steel making center	Iron ore deposit
Iron ore route	Coal deposit

What other mineral resources are found in the Central States? Coal is mined in eastern Kentucky and in Illinois and Indiana. Find these coal fields on the map on page 229. What other Central States have coal deposits?

Deposits of limestone are found in Michigan, Ohio, and Illinois, as well as in several other states. Remember, both coal and limestone are important in the steel industry.

Large quantities of salt are stored beneath the ground in Michigan, Ohio, and Kansas. You probably know how useful it is. Think how unpleasant our food would taste without it. Animals need salt, too. Farmers supply large chunks of salt for their livestock. Salt is also used in many industries.

On this map find the iron ore deposits. Railroads carry the ore to lake ports. There it will be loaded on freighters bound for cities where iron and steel are made. Find some of these cities on this map. Nearby is the coal needed in making this iron and steel.

Missouri mines much lead. It is a soft, heavy metal used for making paint, pipes, and other articles. Some copper is mined in western Michigan.

Many people of the Central States earn their living making the raw materials of farms and mines into manufactured products. Let's visit some cities where these industries are carried on.

Above, St. Louis, Missouri. This city has grown up on the Mississippi near the mouth of the Missouri. Below, an automobile assembly line in Detroit, Michigan.

Important Cities and Manufacturing Centers

The Central States have dozens of busy cities. Most of them are manufacturing centers. There are several reasons why they have many factories. They are located near a variety of raw materials, of course. Also, they are centrally located in our country and have good means of transportation. So goods can be shipped in all directions.

Millions of automobiles are manufactured in Michigan's cities. Some cities in Illinois are famous for their farm machinery, railway cars, and other iron-and-steel products. Akron, Ohio, is called our rubber capital because it manufactures so many rubber tires and other kinds of rubber goods. Certain cities in Ohio have steel mills and make iron-and-steel products. Milwaukee, Wisconsin, is a busy lake port. It manufactures many kinds of goods, including farm machinery. Minneapolis has enormous meat-packing plants and flour mills, as do Omaha, Kansas City, and St. Louis. St. Louis makes shoes, clothing, and electrical products.

The three largest cities in this central region are Chicago, Detroit, and Cleveland. Find each one on the map on page 259. What does the map key tell about their population?

Chicago is the second largest city in our country. More than six and a half million people live and work in or very near Chicago. Yet 150 years ago it was a small frontier fort and trading post.

Locate this city on the map again. It stretches for more than 26 miles along the windy shore of Lake Michigan.

Chicago is our second largest city.

Chicago has an excellent location. It is a crossroads city for railroads, highways, and airways. Then too, it is a lake port, as the map shows. Ships bring in raw materials from other lake ports and carry away manufactured products, grain, and meat. Also, ocean-going ships sail to Chicago from distant ports throughout the world. The St. Lawrence Seaway makes this possible. Furthermore, a canal and river link the city with the important Mississippi System. And don't forget that it is in one of the richest agricultural areas in our whole country.

Chicago is our second largest industrial center. It manufactures food products, iron and steel goods such as transportation equipment and farm machines, and hundreds of other articles. And this city is well-known for its research laboratories.

Tourists like to visit Chicago. They enjoy its shopping areas, museums, libraries, and other fine public buildings. It has lovely parks and wide sandy lakeside beaches. And there are miles and miles of tree-lined streets and attractive homes.

Detroit is the automobile capital of the world. Its giant automobile industry began in the early 1900's. Then, Henry Ford and some other men started to build "horseless carriages." Today, many plants manufacture parts for automobiles. Huge assembly plants put together thousands of cars. If you visited such a plant, you could see an automobile "grow" before your very eyes.

The "skeleton" of an automobile is carried on a belt that moves slowly through an enormous room. Workmen and special machines add parts to the "skeleton" while it travels along. As more parts are added, the car grows. Finally, it rolls off the end of the long assembly line, a shiny new automobile.

Detroit is also famous for manufacturing other products made of steel. Machinery, for instance, and tools and stoves!

271

And it makes chemical and medical supplies, and many other kinds of goods.

Like Chicago, Detroit has a favorable location. It is near steel manufacturing plants and coal fields. It is a port on Lake Erie, as you can see on the map. This means that it is connected with many other cities by the St. Lawrence Seaway. So ships can sail to and from Detroit with raw materials or manufactured goods.

Detroit has some skyscrapers and handsome business buildings. Its parks and museums are among the finest in the land.

Cleveland is another important lake port. Point to Cleveland on the map on page 259. Notice that Cleveland has an excellent location for trade and manufacturing. It is a leading city in the manufacture of iron-and-steel products. It has busy shopping centers and fine public schools and hospitals.

As you know, Cleveland is located on the shores of Lake Erie. In earlier years, the water was clear and sparkling. People fished along the shores. But this is not safe today. Lake Erie became badly polluted. So did two other Great Lakes, Ontario and Michigan.

Pollution was spoiling three Great Lakes. Fast-growing cities and their many factories were mostly to blame. Also pollution came from farmlands.

This pollution has been killing fish. It has been making the lakes sick.

People caused this pollution. Now many people are working together to cure this sad situation. Cities are treating their sewage before it is poured into the lake. Companies are installing equipment to cut down pollution. But the clean-up job is enormous! It can only be done if all of us work together.

Some Questions to Ask Yourself

1. Where are the Central States? Name them.

2. What kinds of climate do they have?

3. What are their leading crops?

4. Where is the Corn Belt? How is most of the corn crop used?

5. Where is the Wheat Belt? What two kinds of wheat are raised there? How are they different?

6. What states make up the Dairy Belt?

7. What important minerals are found in the Central States? Which of these have helped to develop the automobile industry?

8. Why are so many iron-and-steel centers found in the Central States?

9. Why has Chicago become a large city?

Some Other Things to Do

1. Find out what 4-H clubs are, what their members do, and who belongs to them.

2. Prepare a report on corn or wheat. Find out how it grows, how it is harvested, how it is stored, and how it is used. Be ready to present your finished report to your class.

3. Locate the Central States on the map on pages 90–91. Use the elevation sketch to tell which is higher:

a. The Central Plains or the Great Plains.

b. The Central Plains or the Ozark Hills.

4. Read in another book about Cyrus McCormick.

5. Find and share with your class a "worth-while" news item about some part of the Central States.

Think It Over

1. If you do not live in the Central States, how is this region different from your part of the country?

2. How has climate influenced ways of making a living in the Central States?

3. Is it true that iron and steel are necessary to our country? Why, or why not?

4. What do you think this saying means, "It is never wise to put all of your eggs in one basket"?

5. Generally, intelligent planning and looking ahead are keys to success. Why is this true, do you suppose?

Which Are Partners?

Copy the phrases in List A. Write the correct ending for each from List B.

List A

1. The Central States
2. The drier parts of the Central States are
3. Corn is our country's
4. Indians taught the settlers
5. A silo stores
6. Machines such as tractors and combines
7. The western Central States raise enormous
8. Wisconsin makes
9. Most of our corn is
10. Parts of Michigan, Wisconsin, and Minnesota
11. Chicago is
14. Detroit is called

List B

quantities of wheat.
how to grow corn.
cattle feed.
have rich deposits of iron ore.
many kinds of cheese.
the automobile city.
are a rich agricultural region.
the second largest city in the United States.
biggest crop.
the western lands of Kansas, Nebraska, and the Dakotas.
fed to cattle, hogs, and poultry.
help many of the wheat farmers.
have few cities.

Reporting News Items

Here are some ideas to keep in mind when you share news items with your class:

1. Practice telling your news before giving it to your class.

2. Understand it well enough to give it briefly and in an interesting manner.

3. Try to show pictures related to it.

4. Show on a map where it took place.

Fun With Maps

Use the map on pages 258–259 to help you do these things:

1. Tell two main ideas which the inset map shows about the Central States.

2. Tell in what direction:
   a. St. Louis is from Chicago.
   b. Minneapolis is from Detroit.
   c. Cleveland is from Milwaukee.

3. Measure the distance between:
   a. Chicago and Detroit.
   b. Kansas City and Cincinnati.

4. Study the key and the map. Then name the cities which have a population of:
   a. over one million.
   b. from 500,000 to one million.

16 · The Rocky Mountain States: High Lands and Dry Lands

How a Wonderland Became Our First National Park

Some new Americans visit our oldest National Park. Marta and Max had come from Europe with their parents to live in Denver, Colorado. The children's father had an interesting job as a chemist for a big company.

One evening their father said, "Soon it will be vacation time. Then we shall visit the oldest National Park in America."

Max's face shone. "Oh! You mean Yellowstone National Park!" he exclaimed

proudly. "Our teacher showed pictures of it last week. It has pools of boiling hot mud and beautiful geysers."

"What's a geyser?" asked nine-year-old Marta."

"Well,—a kind of on-and-off fountain," Max told his sister. "A kind that nature makes. Geysers are hot water and steam that shoot up from below the ground."

"Very good, Max!" said Mr. Kramer. "And the most famous geyser at Yellowstone is Old Faithful. I will get a picture to show you, Marta."

By July, the Kramers were camping at Yellowstone. They had many interesting experiences, but one Max enjoyed especially was hearing the Yellowstone story. A friendly park ranger told it something like this:

"Long ago, Captain Lewis and Captain Clark led a party of brave explorers across the Rocky Mountains to the Pacific. One of their men was a tall wiry hunter and trapper, John Colter. On the return trip, the restless Colter asked to leave the party. He planned to trap beaver and trade with Indians in the wilds of the Rockies.

"Colter tramped off alone through the rugged wilderness country. One day, he came to a strange land where the earth seemed to tremble under his feet. He saw pools of thick bubbling hot mud. And even more surprising, there were

great fountains of hot water that burst out of the earth.

Colter had never heard of geysers. In fact, few Americans knew what geysers were. He was a very brave man, but this mysterious wilderness frightened him. So he hurried away.

"After wandering here and there, for six years, Colter returned to St. Louis. When he described the breath-taking sights he had seen, people shook their heads. 'Nonsense!' they exclaimed. 'You're just dreaming up tall tales!' Still the land of 'hot' water which he discovered became known as 'Colter's Hell.'

"Then some years later, another Mountain Man visited this astonishing area. Again most people laughed at the stories about this mysterious land. But one young man did believe them. In 1870, he led a party to 'Colter's Hell.' He and his men found the wonders Colter had described and also some other amazing ones. They watched magic geysers shoot plumes of water and steam toward the sky. And they were speechless when they gazed upon a great falls that poured into a deep yellowish stone canyon. Surely this should be called the 'Land of the Yellow Stone.' They knew that some Indians had already given the region that name.

"One night as the explorers sat beside a crackling campfire, a member of their party spoke up. 'This land is so splendid that someone should buy it and charge people to see it. A person could make a fortune doing that.'

"'No!' answered another firmly. 'That wouldn't be right! I think this beautiful region should be set aside as a kind of national park. Then it could be saved for all the people to enjoy!'

"'A splendid idea!' agreed several others. Then they talked far into the night about ways to make this dream come true.

"In time, several of the party traveled about our country telling people about the Yellowstone region. More and more interest was stirred up and in 1872, the park plan was launched. Congress passed a law that made the Yellowstone region our first National Park.

"One of the exploring party was put in charge of the new park. He didn't receive any pay but he kept the job for five years. In fact, he worked so hard to protect Yellowstone from careless visitors that he was nicknamed Mr. National Park."

Yellowstone is our largest National Park as well as our oldest one. It occupies the northwest corner of Wyoming and a bit of Idaho and Montana. It is a part of the grand region we call our Rocky Mountain States. What are they like?

Colter discovers the geysers of Yellowstone.

A Look at the Rocky Mountain States

The Rocky Mountain states are "out West." They make up a large region that begins just west of the Central states. It stretches from Canada to Mexico, a distance of about 1200 miles. The Rocky Mountains extend through the six states of this region. They are Montana, Wyoming, Colorado, New Mexico, Idaho, and Utah. Look across at the map and find them.

Four Rocky Mountain states share the Great Plains. From the Central states, these plains continue into Montana, Wyoming, Colorado, and New Mexico. Many years ago, Indians wandered across these lands hunting buffalo, you'll remember. Daring explorers and hunters crossed them and so did long wagon trains. But times have certainly changed! Gone are the buffalo and the wagon trains. And fine modern highways and railroad tracks have replaced the rutted wagon trails.

These plains are covered with short grass except where they have been plowed. They look nearly as level as a floor, but they are not. They climb steadily as they stretch westward to meet the mountains, as the elevation sketch on page 278 shows.

The snow-capped Rockies rise steeply above the Great Plains. They form a rugged backbone all the way through this grand region. The Rockies include many different mountain ranges, remember. One is the magnificent Teton Range. The picture on page 96 shows some of the mountains in this range. Trees cannot grow on the highest slopes of the Rockies because of the cold. The height at which trees stop growing on mountain slopes is called the timber line, you'll recall. Find the timber line in the picture.

The Colorado Rockies have the loftiest peaks. You have read about one, towering Pikes Peak. But think of this! Fifty others are also more than 14,000 feet high.

West of the Rockies lies plateau country. A plateau, you know, is a high land which is not as level as a plain. The Rocky Mountain region contains a part of the enormous Columbia and Colorado plateaus. Find them on the map on page 90. They have rolling lands, deep valleys, and ranges of mountains here and there.

Notice that Idaho has a share of the Columbia Plateau. The Colorado Plateau extends through parts of Colorado, Utah, and New Mexico. It has some flat-topped "hills," or mesas, that look something like giant tables. In fact, long ago the Spaniards gave them the name, mesas, which means "tables" in Spanish.

Two Rocky Mountain states share the Great Basin. Locate the Great Basin on the map on page 90. It stretches through western Utah and north into Idaho. It has mountains, valleys, and wide thirsty deserts.

Many people think the Great Basin is well named. See if you agree. Probably you know that a kitchen basin is a kind of shallow pan with sloping sides. The Great Basin also has sloping "sides." Its "floor" is surrounded by higher lands. Therefore water cannot run out. Streams that enter the Great Basin never reach the ocean.

"What happens to this water?" you may be wondering.

CANADA

VANCOUVER ISLAND

WASHINGTON

Bellingham
Everett
Puget Sound Seattle
Tacoma
Olympia
▲ Mt. Rainier 14,410 ft.
Yakima

Grand Coulee Dam
Spokane

Eureka

Coeur d'Alene

Moscow

Missoula

MONTANA

Great Falls

Helena

Anaconda

Butte

Billings

Bozeman

Sheridan

NORTH DAKOTA

SOUTH DAKOTA

Fort Peck Reservoir
Missouri River
Fort Peck Dam

Yellowstone River

ROCKY

GREAT

Lewiston

COLUMBIA

Vancouver
Portland
Salem
Eugene

Columbia R.
Bonneville Dam
▲ Mt. Hood 11,245 ft.

PLATEAU

OREGON

IDAHO

Caldwell
Nampa
Boise
Idaho Falls

Snake R.
Pocatello
Twin Falls

TETON RANGE

SOUTH PASS

WYOMING

Casper
North Platte R.

NEBRASKA

Crater Lake
Medford
Klamath Falls

Klamath R.

▲ Mt. Shasta 14,161 ft.

Logan

Rock Springs

Laramie
Cheyenne

Shasta Dam

▲ Mt. Lassen 10,466 ft.

GREAT

NEVADA

BASIN

Great Salt Lake
Ogden
Salt Lake City
Provo

UTAH

Green R.

Ft. Collins
Greeley
Boulder
South Platte R.

COLORADO

Denver
Englewood
Aurora
Leadville
Pikes 14,109 ft. Peak
Colorado Springs
Cripple Creek
Pueblo

Sacramento R.
Reno
Carson City
Oroville Dam

Sacramento
Petaluma
Sonoma
San Francisco
Berkeley
Oakland
San Mateo
San Jose

CENTRAL

SIERRA NEVADA

CALIFORNIA

San Joaquin R.
Fresno

VALLEY

▲ Mt. Whitney 14,495 ft.
Bakersfield

DEATH VALLEY

Las Vegas
Hoover Dam
Boulder City

L. Mead

Colorado R.

Grand Junction

COLORADO

GRAND CANYON
Little Colorado R.

Farmington

Los Alamos
Santa Fe

Trinidad

OKLA.

Arkansas River

Santa Barbara
Glendale
Los Angeles
San Pedro

Burbank
Pasadena
San Bernardino
Long Beach
COACHELLA VALLEY
Salton Sea

MOHAVE DESERT

Colorado R.

PLATEAU

ARIZONA

Phoenix
Roosevelt Dam
Mesa
Globe
Salt R.

Gila

Albuquerque

NEW MEXICO

Clovis

Roswell

Pecos R.

Hobbs

San Diego

IMPERIAL VALLEY

Tucson

Las Cruces

Carlsbad

Rio Grande

TEXAS

Bisbee
Douglas

MEXICO

COAST RANGES

COAST RANGES

Willamette R.

Pacific Ocean

THE WESTERN STATES
Cities

□ Los Angeles	Over 1 million
■ San Francisco	500,000 to 1 million
○ Tucson	100,000 to 500,000
• Las Vegas	Under 100,000
★ State capital	

Name each of the eleven Western States and its capital · Study the key. Name the largest city. Find its population in the Appendix.

Scale of Miles
0 — 173
One inch equals 173 miles

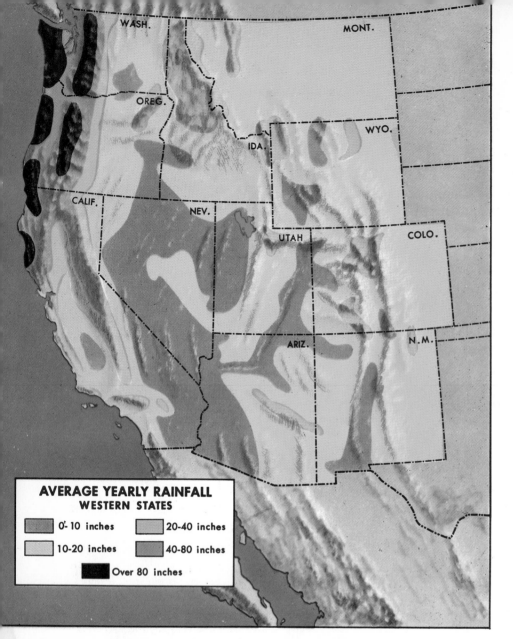

AVERAGE YEARLY RAINFALL
WESTERN STATES

0-10 inches	20-40 inches
10-20 inches	40-80 inches
Over 80 inches	

Study this rainfall map of the West. Where are the wettest lands? Point to the driest lands. On this map find the Great Basin. Notice what a large dry area it is. Why is this so? The drawing below may help you understand. Notice that the colors on this drawing are the same as those used on the rainfall map. These colors are used to show the same things on the drawing and on the map. For example, part of the Great Basin shown on the drawing is colored brown. As the key on the map tells, this means that this area receives 10 inches of rain or less a year.

As you can see, heavy rain clouds blow inland from the Pacific Ocean But the Coast Range and the high Sierra Nevada steal most of this moisture. As the clouds rise to cross the mountains, most of the moisture is dropped on the western side of these mountains as the drawing shows. By the time the clouds reach the eastern side of the mountains, only a little moisture is left. For this reason the Great Basin is a dry land. Indeed, for the same reason, most of the West is a dry land.

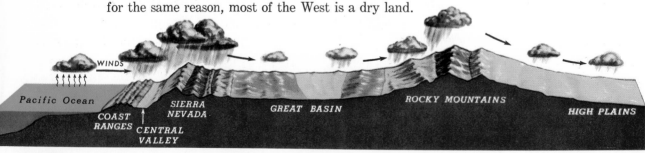

Some of it evaporates, or dries up, in the hot summer sunshine. Some sinks down into the thirsty soil. And some flows into Great Salt Lake.

Great Salt Lake lies along the eastern side of the Great Basin. Point to it on the map. In what state is it? Can you recall what people first settled near it?

This glistening lake is the largest body of water in the Rocky Mountain region, but it is gradually shrinking. For one thing, less water is allowed to flow into it because so much is drawn off for irrigation. Also, some water evaporates during the long hot summers.

Great Salt Lake is too salty to be a helpful body of water. Indeed, it is now five or six times as salty as the ocean. You see, all fresh water has a tiny bit of salt in it. This is true of the streams that feed the lake. When the lake water evaporates, the water disappears, but alas, not the salt! It is left behind. Because no streams flow out of the lake, the salt is never washed away.

Some large rivers begin in the Rocky Mountain region. Among them are the Colorado, Missouri, and Snake rivers and the Rio Grande. Locate them on the map on page 277. Can you find where each one starts? Which of these rivers empties into the Columbia? Which one flows across the Southwest? Name the one which joins the Mississippi. Which one empties into the Gulf of Mexico?

These rivers are far more valuable than all the gold and silver found in this region. Indeed, we might call their precious waters "white gold." Dams on these rivers conserve much water for dry farmlands and for growing towns and cities. They also provide water power to make electricity for farms and cities near and far.

Dams on the Colorado are especially valuable to the Southwest, as you will learn later. Several dams are located on the Missouri River. The largest one is huge Fort Peck Dam. Find it on the map. The reservoir back of it is about 189 miles long. So it can furnish enormous quantities of irrigation water. Below the dam is a powerhouse which manufactures electricity. Dams on the Snake River supply irrigation water for the thirsty farmlands of southern Idaho.

Vast areas in this region are dry. The map across the page shows this quite plainly. Study the legend and key. What color shows the driest lands? Which of the Rocky Mountain states have some of them? But wait! A much larger part of the region can only expect from ten to twenty inches of rain a year. This is not enough to grow most crops.

Why is this region so dry? The diagram and the legend below the map may help you to answer that question. See where the heavy rainclouds from the Pacific drop most of their moisture. Generally, then, only a little remains for the Great Basin and most of the plateau lands. Why are the Great Plains dry lands?

The climate is varied. This should not surprise you when you remember how far these states stretch from north to south. Also, of course, the plains, plateaus, and valleys have a warmer climate than the high mountains.

The northern lands usually have long, bitterly cold winters. Icy winds often sweep across the plateaus and plains.

Sometimes they bring blinding snow-storms called blizzards. It is dangerous to be out in a blizzard. The air is so filled with snow that one can scarcely see.

The high mountains remain extremely cold from fall until late spring. Many areas are half buried under heavy snows. When warm weather comes, much snow melts. But some peaks are snow-capped the year around, as you know.

The mountains have pleasant summers and much cooler weather than the lower lands nearby. But the summers are short! You can see this if you turn to the Growing Season Map on page 203.

The Continental Divide is formed by the main chain of the Rockies.

Where in the Rocky Mountain region can crops grow the longest? Where can they grow from 4 to 6 months? In these areas, summer temperatures may climb to 100 degrees or more. Some weeks, the weather is just as hot on the plains and the plateaus to the north as on those in the south. Day after day, the burning sun beats down. Cooling showers come only now and then. But even in these lands of little rain, farming is important.

Farming and Ranching

Farming is a leading industry in these states. "But what about water?" you ask. "We just read that most areas don't get enough rain for crops."

True, but you see, many farmers have found ways to solve the water problem. One way, dry farming, is used in some areas.

Much dry farming is carried on. Dry farming makes use of all the rain and snow that falls. The farmer plants only one part of his land each year. The rest of his fields are left unplanted, or *fallow*. But the unplanted fields are cultivated. This loosens the soil so that rain will sink in easily. It also kills the weeds that use up moisture. Sometimes the fallow fields are plowed so the furrows will catch and save as much moisture as possible. When seeds are planted, they can use moisture that has been stored in the ground as well as the rain that falls.

The dry farmer must raise only crops that can get along with a small amount of rainfall. Wheat and other grains can be grown by dry farming but wheat is the most valuable crop. Look on the map on page 301 and find the main wheat-growing areas in the Rocky Mountain states.

Immigrants from eastern Europe taught us the secrets of dry farming. They had come from lands where such farming was carried on. They knew that it was a good way to grow certain kinds of wheat where only a little rain falls.

Irrigated farming is also important. Find the irrigated areas in Rocky Mountain states on the map on page 301. What symbol is used to show them?

Rivers flowing down from the mountains provide water for irrigation. As you have learned, this precious water is often stored in reservoirs behind dams that have been built on rivers. The water from the reservoir is then carried by canals to the farmlands. The drawing on page 282 shows you such a dam and canal. Notice the smaller canals that branch off. They carry water to the fields.

It takes careful planning, co-operation, and much money to build these irrigation projects. Most of the larger ones have been built by the United States government. But the farmers who use the water from the Government projects must pay for it.

Many of the smaller irrigation projects have been built by groups of farmers. They share the cost of the work and the water it brings.

What are the main irrigated crops in this region? Idaho is famous for its potatoes and peas. Utah also produces top quality potatoes and tons of crisp celery. One part of Colorado is widely known for its tasty cantaloupes.

New Mexico is the only cotton-raising state in this region. Why, do you suppose? What kind of climate does cotton need? What kind of growing season does it require?

Several states produce sugar beets. Look at the map on page 301 and name them. The sugar beet is a cousin of the beets your mother may serve at your table. But when it is ripe, sugar can be made from its large roundish root.

Sugar beets are planted from seeds. They are ready to harvest in late summer or early fall. Today, this work is often done by an amazing machine, a beet harvester. It loosens the soil, pulls the beets, and cuts off their tops. Then it dumps them on a moving belt that carries them to a truck. The tops are used for cattle feed, but the beets are hauled to a factory called a sugar refinery.

At the refinery, a large machine washes and cleans the beets. Then they are sliced in strips that look something like shoestring potatoes. These are specially treated to remove the "juice." It is boiled and made pure and finally becomes sugar.

Alfalfa is raised in each state. But it is a leading crop in Idaho. Perhaps you know that alfalfa is one of the richest

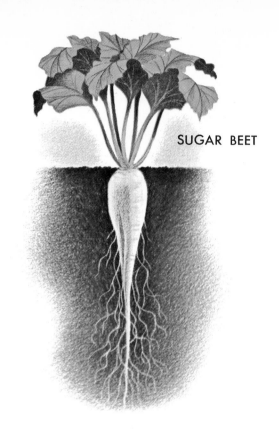

SUGAR BEET

Turning desert into farm land by bringing water by canal from a mountain reservoir.

Reservoir

Dam

Gate controls flow of water into canal

Gate opens to allow water to flow into lateral canals

Main canal carries water from reservoir

Lateral canals carry water to farms

Farm ditches carry water to furrows in fields

Opening gate allows water to flow through farm ditch

Beef cattle on a western ranch. Below, electric shears cut off the sheep's fleece. Find the areas where livestock ranching is important on the map on page 301.

foods given to livestock. Fortunately, it is also a valuable soil builder. It helps to put certain plant foods back into the soil.

In some areas, alfalfa fields are "flooded" with water from irrigation canals. However, alfalfa can push its roots down beneath the surface of the ground to a depth of about 25 feet. So it can find water more easily than shallow rooted plants can. Therefore, it is a good crop for some dry lands. Still, alfalfa is grown successfully in many kinds of climates and in every region of our country.

Stock-raising is another main industry. What color shows livestock ranching areas on the map on page 301? A large part of them are covered by grasslands that are used to graze cattle and sheep.

The cattle industry began long ago, remember. In those days, a man let his cattle graze far beyond his own land. They wandered over wide unfenced areas owned by the Government. This land was known as the *open range*.

The men hired to tend the cattle were called cowboys. They were colorful in

283

their bright woolen shirts, tight pants, and high-heeled boots with spurs. Broad-brimmed hats protected them from the summer's burning sun. Large gay-colored handkerchiefs kept the wind off their necks. And trusty "six-shooters" were ready at their belts to protect them from dangers.

On the open range, one man's herd often became mixed with other herds. Still it was easy to tell the cattle apart, for they had been branded, or specially marked. For instance, Mr. Jones' cattle bore a mark which looked like this, ⊗, or a Circle X. His ranch was known as the Circle-X ranch. Each ranch had its own brand.

In the spring, the cowboys rounded up the cattle. Then each baby calf was branded with its mother's brand.

Thousands of beef cattle are raised today. But now the grazing lands are fenced. From Canada to Mexico, the plains have been cut up into many ranches. One ranch may have several thousand acres. Cattle ranches have to be large for the grass is so thin that many acres are needed for each animal.

No longer does the cowboy ride the open range to keep cattle from wandering away. But he has other work to do. He must be sure the animals are getting enough grass and water. From time to time, he drives them to fresh pastures. He must also inspect the fences and keep them in good repair.

In the autumn or early winter, the cowboys drive some cattle to the nearest railroad station. From there, they are shipped to feed lots to be fattened, as you have read. What part of our country is noted for its feed lots?

Large flocks of sheep graze on some lands. Four states in the Rocky Mountain region have more sheep than people. Sheep can live where the land is too dry or rough to raise cattle. They can feed on shorter and poorer grass.

Each flock is tended by a sheep herder and his faithful dogs. He may live in a truck-drawn "covered wagon" that can be moved from place to place. In the early summer, the shepherd often drives his animals to mountain meadows. Here, they find greener grass and more water than on the hot dry plains. But when fall comes, the sheep are driven back to their ranches again.

Sheep furnish us with meat and wool. Most of those in this region and other parts of the West are raised for their wool. In April or May, experts cut off the thick coats with heavy scissors, or shears. So this work is called shearing. The picture on page 283 shows how it is done.

The fleeces are packed in huge bundles, or bales, and sent to woolen mills. Many such mills are located in Massachusetts and Pennsylvania.

Some years, livestock have damaged grazing lands. They remained in an area longer than was wise. They ate the grass too close to its roots and also tramped it down. This damaged the grass so much that it did not grow back again for a long time.

Today, most ranchers are more careful. They are moving their livestock frequently. They realize that conservation of our grazing lands is very necessary.

In addition to farming and stock raising, several other industries are important in the Rocky Mountain region. Perhaps the most famous one is mining.

Some Other Industries: Mining and Lumbering

Mining opened up some parts of the Rocky Mountain region. You read a little about this in Chapter 11. Gold was discovered in present-day Colorado, Montana, and Idaho about a hundred years ago. Silver was also found in some areas.

Many fortune hunters hurried to the new treasure fields, and mining towns sprang up overnight. They grew so fast that they were called "boom towns." Some had interesting names such as *Last Chance*, and *Rabbit Hole*.

These settlements thrived as long as easy-to-mine gold and silver were found. But when the "supply" gave out, most people moved away. Then the empty camps became ghost towns.

Still, mining has continued to be a leading occupation. Now most of it is done by large companies using various kinds of special machines.

Today, this region "mines" many kinds of treasure. Among them are gold and silver. In fact, Idaho has the largest silver mine in the United States. But the main "mining" industries are concerned with other minerals and with petroleum.

Much copper comes from Utah and Montana. Utah has a giant open-pit copper mine, as the picture below shows. Butte, Montana, is the center of another busy copper-mining area. The copper is blasted from rock, deep in the earth beneath the city. The copper ore is hauled to the surface by little cars run by electricity. Then it is taken to a smelter to be melted and refined.

Butte and other areas also produce zinc. Zinc is a bluish white metal that

This huge open-pit copper mine is in Utah.

has many uses. It is melted with copper to make brass. And because it does not rust, a thin coat of zinc is often used on other metals to protect them.

Quantities of lead are taken from some mines. It is a soft metal but a very useful one. Water pipes are often lined with it, and so are tanks. And it is used in making paints. Leadville, Colorado, is the center of a lead-mining area. It is sometimes called "Cloud City" because it is often hidden in the clouds. You see, it sits high in the Rockies at an elevation of more than 10,000 feet.

Coal is also mined. What Rocky Mountain states have important coal fields? Turn to the map on page 229 and see.

Some "new" metals. Minerals are mined in the Rockies today that the first treasure-hunters did not know existed. Colorado is our chief producer of the rare metal, molybdenum. Molybdenum is used to make hard, tough steel such as is needed in cutting tools and airplane motors. The world's largest molybdenum mine is located near Leadville, and is 11,000 feet above sea level.

Colorado and several other Rocky Mountain states mine uranium. It is used in producing atomic energy and in some other industries.

Another rich resource: "black gold." Five states in this region can boast of rich stores of crude oil beneath the ground. They are New Mexico, Wyoming, Colorado, Montana, and Utah.

The map on page 247 tells more about where these oil fields lie. Turn to it. Notice that it also shows the main pipelines that lead crude oil from the fields to refineries. Wyoming has a number of busy refining centers.

"Green gold." Thick forests grow in some parts of the Rocky Mountain states. One can see especially fine ones in the mountainous areas of northern Idaho and western Montana. There is a good reason why. Trees grow best where there is plenty of rain. Look on the map on page 278 and see how much rain these northern high lands receive.

Lumbering provides many jobs for people who live near the forests. And others are employed at sawmills and factories making wood products. Also some earn their living in the Christmas-tree business.

Millions of Christmas trees are cut in western Montana, every year. One small town, Eureka, ships so many that it boasts of the title, "Christmas Tree Capital of the World." What are some of the larger cities like?

Some Cities: Manufacturing, Trading, and Tourist Centers

The Rocky Mountain region is thinly populated. The map on page 184 shows this. Study it. Then glance at the map on page 277 and notice how far apart the cities are. Of course, towns too small to show on this political map are scattered here and there. But one can ride for miles and miles and not see a single one.

The towns and cities are trading centers for the farms, ranches, and mines nearest to them. Some have become busy manufacturing centers. Their factories, plants, and mills change crops, minerals, and other raw materials into a variety of useful products. Some cities are tourist centers. Many of their people earn a living caring for tourists.

Denver is the largest city in the Rocky Mountain region. It is located in the heart of Colorado "where the mountains meet the plains." Find it on the map on page 277. What does the map key tell you about its size?

Denver is the beautiful capital of Colorado and is sometimes called the "Mile High City." Indeed, the words, "one mile above sea level" appear on the fifteenth step of the handsome Capitol. From its dome, one can enjoy a thrilling view of the Rockies that rise nearby. Denver is especially proud of its handsome Civic Center. You can see a part of it in the picture at the right.

This city is one of the leading cattle and sheep markets of the world. Many meat animals from the Great Plains are shipped to its huge stock yards. Its meat-packing plants prepare large quantities of meat. It has flour mills and beet-sugar refineries and also turns out such products as leather goods and machinery. Much mining business is taken care of here.

Thousands of tourists visit Denver. Because of its elevation, it has pleasant summer weather. And it is the gateway to many inviting vacation lands in the Rockies.

This Colorado city is also the gateway to other parts of the Rocky Mountain region and to the states west of the Rockies. Railways, highways and airways connect it with many other cities. One is Salt Lake City that is located just west of the Rocky Mountains. Find it on your map.

Above, Denver's Civic Center as seen from the Capitol. The Rocky Mountains rise in the distance. Below, the Wasatch Mountains are very important to Salt Lake City. From these mountains comes water for the city and for nearby farms.

Salt Lake City is spoken of as the "Crossroads of the West." It is the second largest city in the region, and is the capital of Utah. Salt Lake City sits in a wide dry basin at the foot of high mountains. Water for the city and nearby farms comes from these snowclad mountains.

Salt Lake City was founded by the Mormons, you'll recall. They used irrigation to raise fine crops. They laid out wide straight streets and built some handsome buildings that are still in use today. One is the Mormon Temple and another the Tabernacle in which the famous Mormon choir sings. You may have listened to this choir, and inspiring organ music from "The Crossroads of the West."

This city began to earn that name during the days of the pioneers. The main trails to the Far West led through or near it. Today, railroads and highways follow these same routes.

Salt Lake City is the chief trading center for miles around. It has canneries, dairies, flour mills, beet-sugar refineries, and plants that prepare salt for market. Like Denver, it is also the headquarters for many mining companies.

A glimpse of some other cities. Pueblo, Colorado is widely known for its steel mills. Most of the steel is used in the city to manufacture mining and farm machinery and steel rails. Cheyenne is a transportation center and Wyoming's capital. Helena, Montana's capital, began when gold was discovered nearby, at Last Chance. It is a busy trading center for mines and farms.

New Mexico has one of our youngest cities and also a very old one. Los Alamos was started in 1943 on a windy mesa. It was the place where scientists did secret work for the first atomic bomb. Santa Fe began way back in 1609 as a Spanish city. It has many attractive Spanish-Indian style buildings built of adobe and is a popular tourist center.

The Rocky Mountain region has dozens of favorite vacation lands. Let's read about several of them.

Some Famous Wonderlands

Magnificent wonderlands are scattered through this region. There are towering mountains crowned with snow! Beautiful canyons! Deserts with strangely-carved and colored rocks! Thick forests! Shining lakes! Tumbling falls! And clear cold streams!

Some of these wonderlands are National Parks. As you know, such parks are controlled by our national government in order to preserve their beauty. The map on page 289 shows our country's National Parks. Which ones are in the Rocky Mountain region? Have you visited any of them?

Yellowstone is the oldest National Park, remember. It was made a park in 1872. As the map shows, Yellowstone is in the Rocky Mountains and spreads over the northwest corner of Wyoming into the edge of Montana and Idaho. Just think! It is two and a half times the size of Rhode Island. Fine paved highways wind through this beautiful park, and hotels, cabins, and camping areas provide quarters for many tourists.

At Yellowstone, one can see dozens of thrilling sights. One is the Grand Canyon of the Yellowstone. It has been carved out by the rushing river which now flows hundreds of feet below. The walls of this canyon are a yellowish stone. At the upper end of the canyon, the Yellowstone River leaps over cliffs to form falls. The water plunges more than 300 feet to the floor of the canyon. The beauty of these falls is breath-taking.

In another part of Yellowstone Park are the amazing geysers about which you read earlier. They spout hot water out of the ground. Some are large and some are small, but the most famous one is known as Old Faithful. Rumbling and hissing, it performs regularly, day and night, about every sixty or seventy minutes. The picture on page 290 shows how it shoots forth a feathery plume of steam and boiling water 150 feet into the air.

At Yellowstone, one can see many kinds of wildlife. The boldest animals are the black bears. Tourists find them amusing to watch and interesting to photograph. The bears come to the roadside and even into the camps to beg for food. But visitors must be careful. Bears are dangerous wild animals and have sometimes injured people seriously. Some distance from the tourist centers are fenced meadows where shaggy buffalo feed. In the forests are deer, antelope, and sometimes moose. Big horn sheep feed on some lonely high cliffs.

Several other National Parks are set in the Rockies. Another in Wyoming is Grand Teton with its beautiful sharp high peaks. Look for it on the map.

This map shows our national parks · Some people call them vacationlands. Have you visited any of them? Which ones are near your home?

National Parks

Old Faithful geyser thrills crowds in Yellowstone Park.

collects year after year, layer upon layer, and some of it never melts. Gradually, the lower layers have changed to ice and have formed glaciers.

Rocky Mountain National Park is in Colorado. It has 65 peaks that are more than 10,000 feet high. The tallest ones wear caps of snow through the summer. This park is dotted with deep sparkling lakes and threaded with silvery streams. Well-kept camps and miles of trails attract many vacationers.

Bryce Canyon and Zion Canyon are located in southwestern Utah. Point to them on the map on page 289. Bryce Canyon is shaped something like a huge horseshoe. It is filled with bright-colored, strangely-shaped rocks. Some tower several hundred feet above the floor of the canyon and resemble pillars of stately temples.

Zion Canyon is also a colorful land. A river has carved out this deep narrow canyon, leaving beautiful high walls and towers of stone.

Southwestern New Mexico has Carlsbad Caverns National Park. It is a chain of immense caves several hundred feet underground. Each one is like an enormous room. In fact, one cave, called Big Room, is nearly two thirds of a mile long. Amazing stone "icicles" hang from the ceilings of these caves. Other strange column-like rocks rise from the floors. Perhaps you have visited Carlsbad Caverns. If you have, you know that this "fairyland" has a strange beauty all its own.

There are also wonderful vacation-lands in the next region that we shall visit. Chapter 17 will tell us about our fascinating Northwest.

Glacier National Park spreads over mountainous country in western Montana. Locate it. See how it reaches to the northern border of our country. It has many interesting trails and some fine roads. One that tourists enjoy especially is known as the "Going-to-the-Sun-Highway."

This National Park is famous for the glaciers that creep very slowly down the slopes of some of its mountains. They feed streams and lakes. Altogether, there are sixty glaciers. You see, much snow falls in the mountains of this park. It

Bryce Canyon in Utah.

Carlsbad Caverns, New Mexico.

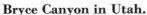

Questions to Help You Review

1. What are the Rocky Mountain States? Which ones share the Great Plains? Which ones have some plateau country?

2. Why are rivers so important to this region? How are they used?

3. What are the main industries in the Rocky Mountain States?

4. What are the leading crops? What are some main natural resources?

5. Why is this region famous as a vacationland? What National Parks are located in it?

Which Will You Choose?

Find the ending that makes each of the following sentences true. On a sheet of paper, write the correct letter of the word or words after each sentence number.

1. The Rocky Mountain States region lies just west of (a) New England. (b) the Central States. (c) the Middle Atlantic States.

2. Dry farming is used to raise (a) wheat. (b) corn. (c) sugar cane.

3. A leading industry in this region is (a) fishing. (b) stock raising. (c) shipping.

4. Many ranches raise large numbers of (a) horses. (b) dairy cattle. (c) beef cattle.

5. Utah and Montana mine much (a) lead. (b) copper. (c) silver.

6. Five states have rich deposits of (a) petroleum. (b) gold. (c) iron ore.

7. The largest city in this region is (a) Salt Lake City. (b) Denver. (c) Santa Fe.

8. Our oldest National Park is (a) Glacier. (b) Zion Canyon. (c) Yellowstone.

Some Other Things to Do

1. Draw pictures to illustrate the stock-raising industry.

2. Use an encyclopedia or another reference book to learn more about one of the National Parks in this region. Take notes on what you read. Write a report and be ready to share it with your class.

3. Study the map and diagram on page 278 and answer the questions in each legend.

4. Make a list of articles which are made from each of these natural resources:

   a. Petroleum   c. Lead
   b. Copper   d. Zinc
         e. Coal

What Do You Think?

1. Why is water important to a region? Why may lack of it keep an area thinly populated?

2. Where does the water for your community come from?

3. How can a fifth grader help to conserve water?

4. Why is it wise for our Government to establish National Parks? If these areas were not made National Parks, what might happen to them?

5. How can visitors help to take care of a National Park?

Learning About East-West Lines, or Latitude

On page 255 you learned how to use letters and numbers to locate places on a map. Many maps have north-south lines and east-west lines. These lines help people to find the exact location of places. You will read about north-south lines later. We shall begin now to learn about east-west lines.

East-west lines run between east and west on a globe or map. Turn to the pictures of the globe on page 24. Find the equator. Notice that it is an east-west line. The equator is an imaginary east-west line around the center of the earth. It is exactly halfway between the north and south poles. Now turn to the map of the United States on pages 504–505. Point to its east-west lines. Find the east-west line that runs south of New York City. Is Denver just north or south of an east-west line? What city in New Mexico is located almost on an east-west line?

Notice that these east-west lines are numbered. The line that runs through Florida is numbered 30°. The ° stands for degrees. The numbers help you locate places on the map. For example, you can quickly find the city of Provo, Utah, if you know that it is located a little north of the east-west line numbered 40°. All east-west lines are called lines of latitude, or *latitude*.

Fun with Maps

Use the map on page 184 to help you decide which is more thinly populated:

1. Colorado or Wyoming
2. New Mexico or Texas
3. Utah or Illinois

Why is the Rocky Mountain State region thinly populated? The map on pages 90–91 can give us some clues. Turn to it.

1. What kinds of lands does this region have mainly? Are they easy to farm? Can roads and railroads be built across them easily?

2. Does this region have any seacoast? Any inland waterways? How does a port location help manufacturing?

17 · The Pacific Northwest: Farms, Forests, and Fish

Using the Left-overs

Why Big Burners are idle. The Northwest has vast green forests. It can boast of many busy sawmills.

Until recently, each mill had a huge hungry partner nearby. It was an enormous outdoor "stove." Some people called it "the Big Burner."

Big Burners worked day and night when the mills were running. They were fed tremendous quantities of left-overs. Sawdust! Chips! And odd scraps of wood! Their job was to destroy this "waste material." So, smoke and flames poured from Big Burners, hour after hour around the clock.

But times have changed! Scientists have found ways to use the left-overs. And modern machines make such uses possible. Therefore, most Big Burners are idle and the "waste" is being conserved.

Sawdust is put to work. In some mills, it is burned as a fuel. Thus it helps to manufacture electrical power for running the giant saws and other equipment.

A paper mill.

Also, sawdust is turned into certain products. Much is pressed into small solid logs for fireplaces.

Wood chips and odd scraps are extremely useful. They can be ground up, mixed with a special material, and pressed into hard board. Its tough firm sheets make remarkably good counter tops.

And think of this! Wood scraps can be changed into dozens of paper products.

"But how?" you ask.

That story is too long to tell here. But again, scientists, chemicals, and special machines make this modern-day magic possible.

Machines chop or grind the wood scraps into small bits. They are cooked with chemicals in an enormous cooker. After a time, the liquid is drained off. This is valuable in making some medicines and plastics.

The material that remains is pulpwood. It can be used for making rayon, remember, and some other products. But mainly, paper goods are manufactured from it. Paper for newspapers, magazines, and books! Paper towels and napkins and picnic plates! Milk cartons, too! And boxes and heavy cartons, large and small! What other products can you name?

Everyday, we use things made of paper. So we might say that pulpwood is one of our best friends. How fortunate, then, that Big Burners are idle and that mills are conserving wood scraps.

Of course, forests give us far more than the things we have just read about. We depend on them especially for lumber, as you know. Indeed, forests are so valuable that we sometimes call them our "green gold," you'll recall. The Northwest is rich in green gold.

Our Northwest

Three states share our Northwest. They are Oregon, Washington, and Alaska. Point to each one on the map on page 178. Which two are next-door neighbors? What ocean do they face?

Alaska is our largest state. Locate it. Notice that it occupies the northwestern part of our continent. It is about one-fifth the size of the rest of the United States.

Oregon became the first state in the Northwest. It was once a part of the *Oregon country*, remember. What other states have a share of this immense region?

Oregon became a state more than a hundred years ago. You read how pioneers traveled westward over the Oregon Trail to settle on its rich lands.

Washington was named in honor of our first President. In fact, George Washington's picture appears on its flag.

Washington's first pioneers were the missionaries about whom you read earlier, Dr. and Mrs. Whitman. George Bush, a black pioneer, is not as famous. But he helped many half-starved newcomers get a start, and gave them food from his farm.

Alaska is one of our newest states. It joined the Union in 1959, you know. But it had become an American land nearly ninety years before that.

Alaska was discovered long ago by a daring sea captain, Vitus Bering. He claimed it for Russia, the country that had hired him. The map on page 295 shows how close Alaska is to Russia.

Both the Bering Sea and the Bering Strait are named for this explorer. A *strait* is a narrow channel of water that connects two larger bodies of water.

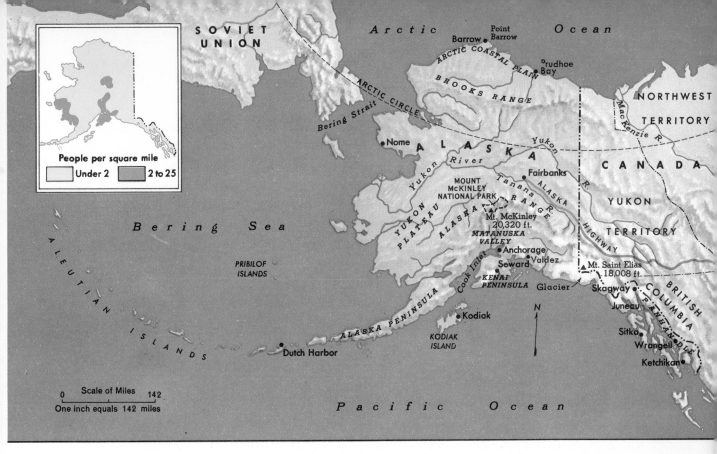

This political map of Alaska also shows how mountains and glaciers
cover a large part of this state. What does the inset map tell?

In time, the Russians built several fur trading posts in Alaska. But they were not very successful. Soon, therefore, Russia lost interest in this faraway northern land and offered to sell it to the United States. Our country bought it for $7,200,000. So, in 1867, the American flag was raised above Sitka, the old Alaska capital.

You remember how a search for gold brought many Americans to California and to the Rocky Mountain states. The same thing happened in Alaska a little over sixty years ago. Thousands of people went to Alaska when gold was discovered in several parts of the territory.

Alaska is rich in other natural resources as well. So are its two sister states, Washington and Oregon. Let's take a closer look at these Northwest lands.

A freighter steams through the Inside Passage on its way to Skagway. Find this Alaskan town on the map above.

The three states have miles and miles of seacoast. Oregon's beautiful rugged coast is famous for its scenery. A winding highway follows this coast for over 300 miles. Travelers who take it can enjoy grand views of the Pacific and the rocky cliffs that rise above pounding waves.

Washington's western coast also faces the Pacific. But its northern shores look out on a long strait. This water pathway leads to Puget Sound, the "front porch" for a number of Washington cities. Find Puget Sound on the map on page 277.

Alaska has the longest seacoast, as the map on page 295 shows. But then, most of this huge land is a peninsula. The icy Arctic Ocean lies north of Alaska. To the west are the Bering Strait and the Bering Sea. What ocean stretches to the south?

Southern Alaska has a long tongue of land, the Alaskan Peninsula. Point to it. See how it leads southeastward to the string of Aleutian Islands. This chain curves across the Pacific for more than a thousand miles.

Southeastern Alaska is bordered by a very ragged coastline. It is known as the Panhandle. It is embroidered with so many inlets that our map cannot show them all. These arms of the sea reach deep into the mainland. They were cut out by glaciers long ago and are called *fiords*.

Hundreds of forested islands are scattered off the shores of the Panhandle. Between them and the mainland is a natural waterway, the *Inside Passage*. The islands shelter it from storms that sweep across the open sea. Many ships sail on this protected route. Some are crowded with tourists on their way to and from Alaska. But the main business of other ships is carrying on trade between ports in the Northwest.

Washington and Oregon share the Coast Ranges. They are chains of hills and mountains that extend along the Pacific. In places, they slope gently down to meet the shore. But generally, their slopes are steep and many end suddenly with rocky cliffs that plunge down to the sea.

Trees grow close together on the western slopes of these mountains. They have the kind of climate trees like best, a rainy one. Just imagine! They may receive as much as 150 inches of rain a year. They are among the wettest lands in our country, as the map on page 220 shows.

The rocky coast of Oregon.

Beautiful Mount Rainier rises high in the Cascades.

East of the Coast Ranges are some fertile lowlands. Find the areas that extend back from Puget Sound in Washington. Now locate the long Willamette Valley in Oregon. Many pioneers started homes in this rich-soiled region.

The Cascades rise farther east and have some magnificent scenery. These high mountains can expect long cold winters with one snowstorm after another. In places, the snow piles up until it is thirty or forty feet deep. Some of it never melts and the highest peaks are clad in white the year around.

The tallest peak, Mount Rainier, is located in Washington. It wears such a thick cloak of snow and glaciers that it resembles a giant frosted cake. This majestic peak is a part of Mount Rainier National Park.

Mount Hood is one of Oregon's loveliest peaks. It, too, is a widely-known vacation land. Indeed, skiing is popular on its glacier-clad slopes summer and winter.

Many peaks in the Cascades were formed by volcanoes, long, long ago. A *volcano* is an opening in the earth's surface through which steam, ashes, and lava are forced out. *Lava* is rock that has been melted into red-hot liquid by tremendous heat deep within the earth.

When a volcano is pushing out materials through its opening, it is *erupting*. It may pour out so much lava that it builds up a high mountain. Study the drawing on page 298 and find out how this happens. Notice that some of the lava piles up around the mouth of the volcano. When it cools, it becomes hard and rock-like. When the volcano erupts again, more lava piles up and the mound grows taller and taller.

Volcanoes that erupt now and then are *active* volcanoes. Mount Rainier and Mount Hood are quiet now. They have not been active for a long, long time.

The Cascades in southern Oregon are also volcanic lands. A beautiful lake occupies the top of one quiet volcano.

Crater Lake is another wonderland. Many ages ago, a volcano caved in. This left a giant bowl-like crater about six miles across. Gradually it filled with

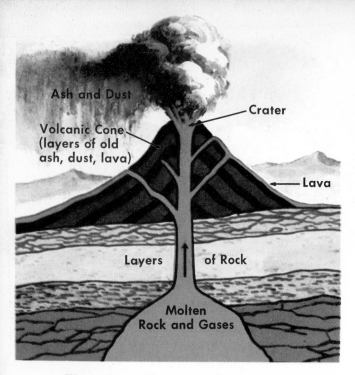

This shows how a volcano erupts and builds up a cone.

water, to form Crater Lake, one of the deepest lakes in North America.

Crater Lake seems to be colored dark blue. From a plane, it looks like an enormous blue jewel. It is surrounded by reddish lava cliffs that tower about a thousand feet above the water. This lake is a part of Crater Lake National Park.

The Columbia Plateau begins beyond the Cascades. Do you see it on the map? It covers much of eastern Washington and Oregon. Only a little rain falls on this rolling, sun-baked land. Nevertheless, parts of it produce excellent crops and grazing for livestock. A large river is helping this thirsty area.

The Columbia is the most important river in the Northwest. Find it on the map. It tumbles swiftly down through mountains to the plateau which bears its name. Then it zigzags west and south in a half circle, as the map shows. Just after the Snake joins it, the Colum-

bia heads westward. From then on, it marks the boundary between Washington and Oregon. It rushes on through the splendid canyon which it has worn away through the Cascades. Finally it empties into the Pacific.

In the past, the Columbia has caused damaging floods. But now a number of dams control its flow. One is the Bonneville Dam located just west of the Cascades. The powerhouse below it supplies electricity for many farms and cities in the surrounding area.

Grand Coulee is the largest dam on the Columbia, and indeed, the largest concrete dam in the United States. It is more than 4000 feet wide and about as high as a 46-story building. It holds back a lake 150 miles long. So there is plenty of water for irrigating many farms. Just as important, the huge powerhouse below the dam manufactures a great deal of electrical power. This provides electricity for industries and homes near and far.

Like Oregon and Washington, Alaska has range after range of mountains. Actually, mountains cover more than one third of our largest and northernmost state.

In the Panhandle, forested mountains rise from the ocean. Also, the islands which are scattered off this coast are the tops of mountains resting in the sea.

Glaciers fill the high valleys of these coastal mountains. Find this glacier area on the map. Strangely enough, one of these slowly-moving rivers-of-ice extends for fifty miles.

The long narrow Alaska Peninsula has a range of volcanic mountains. Certain areas have active volcanoes and some "peaks" are still smoking.

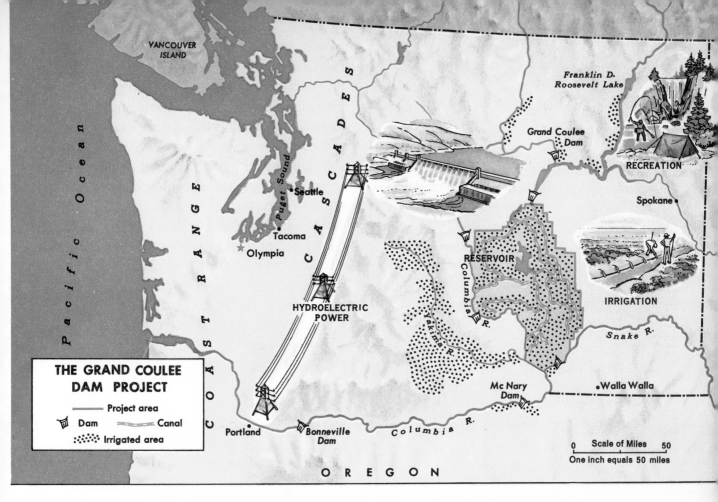

THE GRAND COULEE DAM PROJECT

—— Project area

⚒ Dam   Canal

⋰⋰⋰ Irrigated area

HYDROELECTRIC POWER

VANCOUVER ISLAND

Pacific Ocean

COAST RANGE

CASCADES

Puget Sound

• Seattle

• Tacoma

★ Olympia

Portland

Bonneville Dam

Columbia R.

Yakima R.

Columbia R.

RESERVOIR

Franklin D. Roosevelt Lake

Grand Coulee Dam

RECREATION

Spokane •

IRRIGATION

Snake R.

• Walla Walla

Mc Nary Dam

OREGON

0   Scale of Miles   50

One inch equals 50 miles

Grand Coulee Dam serves us in many ways.

The snow-covered Alaska Range is a part of the Rockies, the mountain chain that stretches through North America. Locate the Alaska Range. Mount McKinley is its highest peak. It soars to a height of 20,320 feet, or nearly four miles, above the level of the sea. It is the highest mountain in the United States and even in North America.

This mighty peak is a part of McKinley National Park. If you visited it, you might see caribou, moose, bears, and many other kinds of wild game.

To the north is the Brooks Range. In what direction does it extend?

Alaska also has rolling hills, valleys, and flat lands. On the map find the Yukon Plateau in Middle Alaska. Through it flows Alaska's largest river,

the Yukon. Use the map and see how it begins in Canada, the country to the east. During the summer, the Yukon serves as a useful highway for boats that deliver supplies to scattered villages. But alas! Many months of the year, it is frozen over because of the very cold winters.

North of the Brooks Range are rolling uplands and flat coastal plains. The Arctic Coastal Plain lies north of the Arctic Circle. This plain has winter for about nine months. Much of it is *tundra*, or frozen plain, where no trees grow. The tundra is frozen solid many feet below the surface during the long bitterly-cold winters. It thaws out a little during the

299

A glacier creeps down a valley.

summer but not enough for trees to grow. Still, at that time grasses, moss, and bright-colored wildflowers pop up and carpet the land.

The Northwest has a variety of climates. As you would expect, the Alaska tundra has the coldest winters. Snow blankets the land for many months. Another thing, the sun shines very little during mid-winter. Then, night lasts almost two months.

Summers in the far north are very short but sunny. In fact, for many weeks the sun shines both day and night. One can read a newspaper by daylight all night.

Find Fairbanks farther south in inland Alaska. The people in this area prepare for long fiercely-cold winters. But often their weather is quite similar to that in

North Dakota and Montana. Fairbanks has many hours of summer daylight, too, of course. And this is interesting! The longest day of the year, June 21st, is celebrated with a baseball game that is played at midnight without lights.

Southeastern Alaska and the western parts of Oregon and Washington have a rather similar climate. They can expect cool pleasant summers with some showers and fog. Their winters, except for the high lands, are fairly mild. Almost no snow falls. Yet some of these lands are located farther north than New England. You read about New England's long icy winters and heavy snows.

What protects this coastal Northwest? The Pacific helps a great deal. The ocean water stays about the same temperature throughout the year. So winds blowing from off the ocean cool these lands in summer and warm them in winter. The Cascades and other ranges also play a part. They shut out the icy winds that sweep down from the Arctic region.

The areas west of these mountains have extremely rainy winters. In fact, people living in some areas there, need to keep raincoats and umbrellas handy about 200 days of the year.

East of the Cascades, the rainfall story is very different. Notice this on the map on page 278. Rains almost forget the plateau lands. Why? Study the diagram below the map and try to find out.

In these inlands, winter temperatures dip far below freezing. You see, they are too far inland for ocean breezes to help. Also the mountains cut off these lands from such ocean breezes. Still agriculture is the main industry, as you will read in the next section.

Farming and Stock Raising

Mixed farming is carried on in parts of Oregon and Washington. Notice this on the Farming Map on this page. It is especially important along a fertile strip that extends from southern Oregon through Washington. The map on page 91 shows that this strip stretches through the Willamette Valley and the lowlands around Puget Sound.

Huge quantities of vegetables and potatoes are grown. And some farms raise acres of bulbs for producing such flowers as daffodils, gladiolas, and iris.

These two states raise carloads of fruit. Berry farms grow strawberries, loganberries, blackberries, and raspberries. Some are hurried to market, but quantities are frozen or made into jam and jelly at special plants.

Water for irrigation has turned some of the dry valleys of eastern Washington into fruit-growing areas. Apples are the most important crop of these valleys. But

Farming is a leading industry in the West, as this map shows · In what part of this region is dairying important? What have you learned about the climate here that helps to explain why dairying is successful? Compare this map with the map on page 278. Why is livestock ranching an important industry in such a large part of the West? Find the irrigated areas on the map at the right. Why is it possible to grow cotton in southcentral California, where there is so little rain?

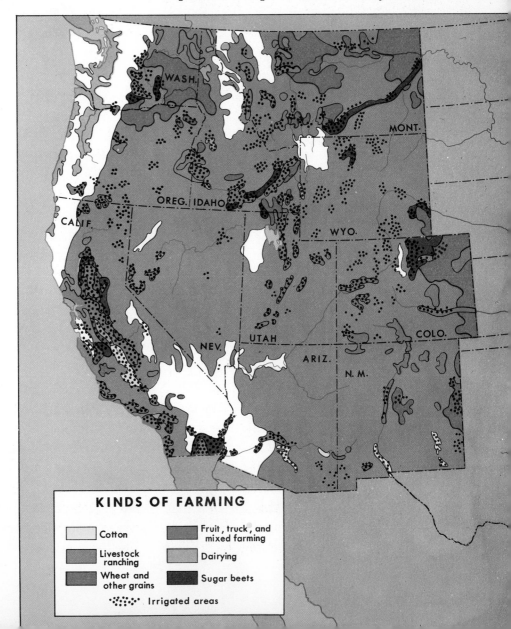

KINDS OF FARMING

- Cotton
- Livestock ranching
- Wheat and other grains
- Fruit, truck, and mixed farming
- Dairying
- Sugar beets
- ·:·:· Irrigated areas

301

other fruits and vegetables are also grown. Washington produces about a fourth of the apples eaten in our country.

When the fruit trees are in bloom, they are a beautiful sight. But they are also handsome at harvesttime. Then, the orchards are as busy as beehives.

Pickers gather the fruit at just the right time and handle it carefully to prevent damage. Much of it is rushed to canneries, but some is shipped to market in refrigerator cars to be sold fresh.

Dairying is a thriving industry near the coast. The coastal lands are cut up by hills and mountains, remember. So farmers do not try to make a living raising crops. But the rainy climate and mild winters provide grass for year-round grazing.

Some farmers ship dairy products to nearby cities. But many sell milk and cream to cheese factories and creameries.

Wheat and other grains are raised on the Columbia Plateau. Indeed, wheat is Washington's biggest crop.

The picture below shows a view of a plateau wheat ranch. As you know, the plateau gets little rain. Therefore, wheat and other grains are grown by dry farming.

Some other crops such as sugar beets are raised where lands are irrigated. Where does this water come from?

Above, picking black raspberries on a farm in the Willamette Valley. Below, a large farm on the rolling hills of the Columbia Plateau. Grain fields and fallow fields lie side by side. Rain that falls on the fallow fields will be used by next years's crop.

Eastern Oregon has immense cattle and sheep ranches. They spread over thousands of acres. But they lack enough water and grass during the hot summers. So, late in the spring, the animals are driven to grazing areas in the mountains.

Alaska has only a few farms. One of its best farming areas is the fertile Matanuska Valley.

Only a few years ago, this valley was covered with forests. But modern-day pioneers moved in. They cut down trees and laid out farms. Today, most of these farmers have comfortable houses with electric lights and other conveniences.

Some dairy cattle are raised to supply milk and cream for the busy city of Anchorage not far away. Also, farmers grow crops of oats, peas, cabbages, and potatoes. Strawberries thrive too, and sometimes grow as big as plums.

The growing season this far north is very short indeed. But the summer months are quite hot and provide about twenty hours of daylight. So plants shoot up very fast. Almost like magic!

Nature produces a very different "crop" in southern Alaska. And millions of acres of it are found in Washington and Oregon. It is timber.

Harvesting Green Gold

Lumbering is a main industry in the Northwest. Some timber is cut in southeastern Alaska. Oregon and Washington, however, are among the leading lumber-producing states of our entire country. In fact, Oregon produces more lumber than any other state.

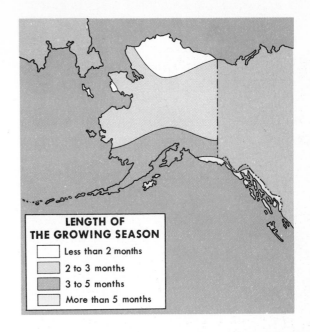

LENGTH OF THE GROWING SEASON

- Less than 2 months
- 2 to 3 months
- 3 to 5 months
- More than 5 months

Most of the trees are evergreens and include pines, hemlocks, cedars and spruces. But the Douglas fir is the largest and most valuable tree in this region. It grows straight and tall to a height of 250 feet or more. Its huge trunk can produce an immense amount of lumber.

How is lumbering carried on? The pictures on page 304 will give you some ideas. Study them carefully.

Trained experts decide which trees shall be cut. Douglas firs are harvested in patches as is shown in the picture. But most other trees are selected here and there through the forest. The expert may mark, for cutting, trees that are crowding young timber. And he chooses some "old" trees that are ripe and ready to cut.

Soon, the fallers, or cutting crew, move in with their power equipment. They cut a notch in the direction the tree should fall. Then they move to the opposite side and start their power saw. When the green giant begins to lean, a logger shouts "Tim-ber-r-r!" What does this warning mean, do you suppose?

A logger's saw bites out a wedge
that will direct the tree's fall.

A huge "heel-boom loader"
swings giant logs onto a truck.

After the branches are sawed off, the tree may be cut into several logs. Then the logs are taken to a loading place. Some are dragged by tractors. Others are carried by cables. These are worked by a pulley and an engine.

At the loading place the logs are lifted by machinery onto powerful trucks or perhaps onto the flat cars of a train. Some may be towed to the mill by a boat.

When the logs reach the mill, they are dumped into a pond. This wet "store-

In the mill some of the logs
are cut into boards.

Unrolling a log in thin strips
for making plywood.

house" prevents drying out and damage by insects.

In the mill enormous saws rip the big logs into long slabs. Other electrically-powered saws slice the slabs into boards, perhaps as many as twenty at a time.

Special equipment turns some short lengths of logs into shingles, or fence posts, or material for making boxes. Many small trees and wood scraps are cut into chips to make pulpwood.

Indeed, today a large variety of useful products are made from trees. So we say that the "lumber business" has grown into the "forest products industry."

Who owns the forests? Millions of acres belong to our state or national governments. There are such forests in every region of our country.

Lumber companies pay to cut down timber in these forests. And they agree to obey certain rules and orders of the rangers. Probably you know that rangers are specially-trained men in charge of state and national forests.

Some forests are owned by lumber companies. In many cases these forests are TREE farms! Yes, today trees are being grown as a crop, not only in the Northwest but also in other parts of our country.

Many tree farms are located in hilly or mountainous areas where the land is not suited for ordinary crops. Usually, forests are already growing on such lands. But the tree farmer takes over to guard the woodlands. He plants new trees in the bare open spots. He may have his "crop" sprayed from a plane to fight harmful insects. He also keeps watch especially for another kind of enemy— fire.

FIRE is the forest's worst enemy. This is true in every part of our country,

particularly during dry seasons. Immense forests have been wiped out by this cruel villain. Many fires have started because campers or sightseers were careless.

The hot dry season is the most dangerous time. Then, one spark may be fanned into flames within minutes. Such flames can spread with frightening speed. It takes a lifetime to grow a tree but only minutes to turn it into a black skeleton.

Wild life may die for lack of food and shelter

Valuable soil is washed away

When forests are destroyed a whole region may be harmed

Rain, snow, and water races down bare slopes, causing floods

Fire also causes other costly damage. It eats away the forest's *humus* carpet of needles, twigs, and dead leaves. Humus can act like a sponge. It soaks up rain water and melting snows, as do the roots of trees. But alas! When it is destroyed, the water rushes down slopes and washes precious top soil away. This causes floods, and the runaway soil may choke reservoirs, or do damage elsewhere.

Another thing, forest fires burn the seeds nature has scattered and scorch the soil. And they are terribly cruel to wildlife. A fire can race through a forest faster than a deer can run. Many animals and birds are trapped in flames and blinding smoke.

"Well! If fire does all of these dreadful things, why do we let them start?" you exclaim.

This is a question that all of us should ask ourselves. Certainly we should help to prevent fires in every way possible.

Protecting our forests from fire. Our leaders are trying to keep our forests green. Special laws have been passed. Signs are posted in many forest areas to tell us what people may do. One says, "No Smoking," and another forbids camp-fires except in certain outdoor stoves that are provided.

One way to help conserve our forests, then, is to obey the fire laws. Also, when we are in these green areas, we should

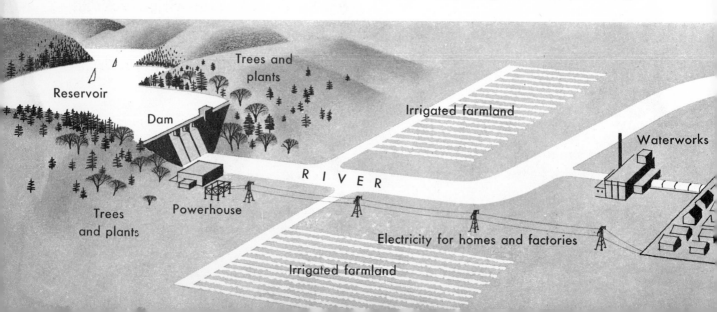

Reservoir

Trees and plants

Dam

Irrigated farmland

Waterworks

R I V E R

Trees and plants

Powerhouse

Electricity for homes and factories

Irrigated farmland

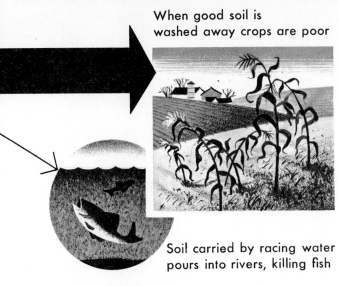

When good soil is washed away crops are poor

Soil carried by racing water pours into rivers, killing fish

Other Natural Resources: Fish, Minerals, and Furs

keep our eyes open for fires. If one starts, we should report it at once.

Forest rangers are on duty all summer in high lookout towers. If they spot a wisp of smoke, they check in a hurry. They have two-way radio phones on which they can call firefighters, if necessary.

Forests give us so much! Lumber and a variety of other kinds of products! Protection for our water supply! And help for preventing floods. But they also furnish homes for wildlife. And they provide us with pleasant places to hike and camp, and perhaps to hunt and fish. So all of us should guard this precious natural resource—green gold.

Fishing is the main industry along some coastal areas. Shellfish such as shrimp, clams, and crabs are taken from the waters along some of the shores of Washington and Alaska. Quantities of oysters are harvested from shallow waters in Puget Sound. And halibut, herring, and salmon are caught. But salmon provide the largest and most valuable catch.

Many people in the Northwest earn their living in some part of the salmon business. A number are fishermen and others are employed in the canneries. Most of the salmon are canned, though some are frozen, smoked, or sold fresh.

Men who earn their living as fishermen catch salmon in the oceans. But "sport fishermen" catch them in the rivers.

The summer months are the busiest ones for the salmon industry. Then, thousands of salmon can be caught in a short time. Salmon spend most of their lives in the ocean. But from May until October, millions of them are moving toward the mouths of rivers. They are on their way "back home" to the place where they began life. Many are caught at the beginning of this long journey.

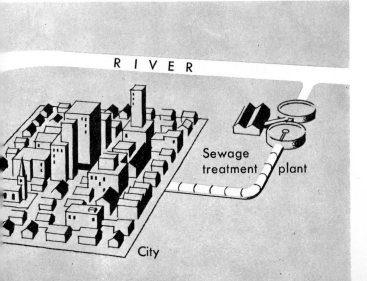

R I V E R

Sewage treatment plant

City

How man can both take care of and use natural resources. Trees and plants hold back water to prevent floods. Dams also prevent floods and store water for many uses.

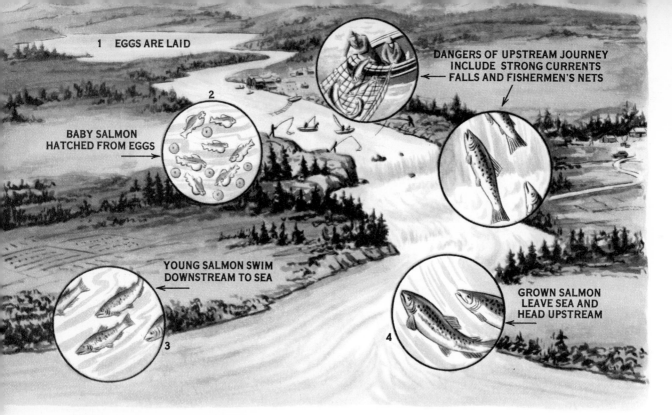

1 EGGS ARE LAID

BABY SALMON
HATCHED FROM EGGS

2

DANGERS OF UPSTREAM JOURNEY
INCLUDE STRONG CURRENTS
FALLS AND FISHERMEN'S NETS

YOUNG SALMON SWIM
DOWNSTREAM TO SEA

3

GROWN SALMON
LEAVE SEA AND
HEAD UPSTREAM

4

Salmon spend most of their lives in the deep ocean. But when it is time to lay their eggs, they start back to the place where they were born.

"But how do salmon know where to go?" you ask.

Many people are puzzled about this. No one understands for sure. But we have learned *why* they head upstream. You can find out, too, if you study the salmon's interesting story.

The salmon's life story. Salmon eggs are laid on the sandy floor of streams or in quiet lakes. Baby salmon hatch from these eggs. While they are still small, they start drifting downstream toward the sea.

These fish may travel several hundred miles. And dangers lurk all the way. The salmon may be gobbled up by bears or raccoons that wade into the streams. Or they may be snatched by birds or swallowed by larger fish. They may be poisoned by dirty water from mills or fac-

tories. Or perhaps they will stray into irrigation ditches or be killed by powerhouse machinery below a dam.

Still, many salmon finally reach the ocean. There, they feed on smaller fish and grow larger and larger. After several years, they are fully grown and may weigh twenty pounds or more. Then they know it is time to find their way upstream.

The salmons' journey back to their birthplace is extremely dangerous. It may end in a fisherman's net almost before it begins. Those that escape must swim upstream against swift currents. They must leap over rocks and perhaps waterfalls. They may be killed trying to climb over dams.

However, fish ladders have been built beside some dams, as at Bonneville. Fish ladders are a series of pools built in steps. Salmon can easily "climb" a step at a time and thus make their way safely to the river above the dam.

At last, some salmon reach their goal. They lay their eggs, and then die.

Indians and other Americans of Japanese ancestry helped to build the fishing industry. The Indians were the first expert fishermen in the Northwest. They were skillful at spearing and trapping salmon that swam up the rivers. Indians are still allowed to fish much as their ancestors did long ago. But this is against the law for other people.

Some Americans whose ancestors came from Japan have had a very important part in the fishing industry. They have brought their special "know-how fishing skills" to it. So have some Italian and Greek Americans.

Salmon are a precious natural resource. But they are becoming less plentiful. Some years, too many have been caught so not enough were left to lay eggs upstream. But also, many salmon have died because of our dirty rivers and dams that have blocked their way.

Today, we are trying to conserve more salmon. A number of fish ladders have been built. Ways are being found to make wastes harmless before they are dumped into rivers.

Laws also help us to protect salmon and other fish. Nearly all states have the kind of fishing laws about which you read in an earlier chapter.

Some mining is carried on in the Northwest. Each of the three states has deposits of coal, and gold has been found in each one. But gold mining has been especially important in Alaska.

Alaska had an exciting gold rush, as you have learned. Just before the 1900's began, glistening bits of this metal were discovered on its lonely cold west coast.

Pipes to carry oil are driven through a mountain pass in Alaska.

News of this treasure spread far and wide. As a result, many men rushed to the region. They pitched their tents or put up rough shacks, and thus the "gold rush" town of Nome was born. Later, gold was found farther inland on the Yukon Plateau. The miners helped to start the city of Fairbanks. Gold mining is still an important industry near Fairbanks.

Rich oil deposits have been discovered in the far north near Prudhoe Bay. The oil will be brought south, through a pipeline nearly 800 miles long. At Alaska's port city, Valdez, it will be loaded on tankers. They will haul it to refineries.

Some people in the Northwest earn a living in the fur industry. Many fur-bearing animals are trapped in Alaska.

Among them are foxes, minks, muskrats, ermine, otters, and beaver. Their coats grow long and thick because of the sharp cold winters. Thousands of muskrats are also caught in the back country of Oregon.

Some fur-bearing animals are raised on special farms. They are kept in pens and fed certain foods until they are grown.

But sealskins from the Pribilof Islands bring in the largest amount of money. Find these Alaskan islands on the map. If you could sail near them in the summer, you would hear many seals roaring at each other. They are amusing to watch as they argue and play.

When the weather turns cold, the fur seals and their pups swim away. But the next summer, thousands return. The Government has passed laws to protect these animals. To conserve them, only a certain number may be killed each year.

Furs and skins are shipped to furriers in cities to be made into stylish wraps. What are some of the main cities in the Northwest?

Juneau is crowded on a narrow strip of land at the foot of steep mountains.

Some Cities and Their Industries

Most of the Northwest is thinly settled. Notice how the map on page 184 tells this. Which of the three states has the most people? Where in Washington and Oregon do more people live, east or west of the Cascades?

Alaska has the smallest population even though it is our largest state. Some of its people are Eskimos. They live chiefly along the western and northern coastal lands. Some of them earn their living working for the United States government on defense projects.

Many Indians are found in central and southeastern Alaska. Some are employed in the fur trapping and fishing industries.

Also, Alaska has thousands of people who once lived in other parts of the United States or in Europe.

Alaska's largest cities are modern and busy places. Juneau, the capital, is near the northern end of the Inside Passage. It nestles on a narrow strip of land between the sea and forest-covered mountains. Freighters steam away from its harbor carrying lumber, fish, and other products from southern Alaska.

Fairbanks is an important trade and business center. Trucks and railroad freight cars bring in goods from ports along the coast. It sits at the northern end of the Alaska Highway. Find this highway on the map on page 376. This is the only highway that links Alaska with highways in Canada and the rest of the United States. The University of Alaska is near Fairbanks.

and trading posts. Anchorage is the center of a "spider web" of air lines. They connect it with cities and towns throughout Alaska. Then, too, Anchorage is on one main route connecting the Far East with the United States. But just as important, many planes carry passengers and cargo between Anchorage and Seattle.

Seattle is the largest city in the Northwest. Look for it on the map. In what state is it? A little over a hundred years ago it was started on a sheltered bay of Puget Sound.

Seattle's favorable location has helped it to become a leading shipping center. It is the chief port for carrying on trade with Alaska. And it trades with the Far East. Railroads also connect the city with the eastern part of our country.

Seattle is famous for its enormous airplane and missile producing industries. It has turned out many jet liners and has a large share in our country's space program. So, scientists, space engineers, and expert workmen have come to live in the city.

Anchorage is Alaska's largest city. Find it on the map on page 295.

Anchorage is Alaska's largest city. It looks out on a narrow arm of the Pacific. Beautiful mountains rise behind it. This booming city has many businesses, fine homes, schools, and two universities. Near it is one of our country's defense air bases.

Alaska depends largely on air transportation to link its widely-scattered towns

A part of the beautiful harbor of Seattle on Puget Sound. The map on page 277 shows that this long body of water leads to the Pacific Ocean. To the east are the mountains of the Cascade Range.

The Eskimo and Indians were the first Americans in the Northwest. Above an Eskimo mask in the form of a sea bird.

This helmut was worn by an Indian leader over 150 years ago. It shows a raven and a frog.

Seattle also produces large quantities of lumber and paper products. And it has furniture factories and fish and vegetable canneries, as well as other food-processing plants.

As the city grew it spread out along Puget Sound and over nearby hills. It has a beautiful location as the photo on page 311 shows. To the west, across Puget Sound, are the Olympic Mountains. To the east are the Cascades. Seattle is proud of its lovely lakes and parks and tree-lined streets. And it can boast of fine schools, churches, and public buildings.

Portland is Oregon's leading city. Portland is also a busy shipping and trading center. It has grown up on the Willamette River near where the Columbia and Willamette rivers join. It is located more than a hundred miles inland. Still, ocean-going vessels can sail up the broad, deep Columbia to its docks. Portland is near one of the few gateways through both the

Cascade and Coast ranges. Why is this a wonderful location for a trading center?

Some of the raw materials and products that come to Portland are used by its factories. Among the chief products of these factories are lumber, furniture, woolen goods, and chemicals. Portland also has flour mills and food canneries.

Spokane is the Northwest's largest city east of the Cascades. It was started about 100 years ago beside falls on the Spokane River. This was a fine location because it was near a pass through the Rocky Mountains. Several railroads and highways have been built through this pass. Today four transcontinental railroads go through Spokane.

Spokane is in a rich lumbering, farming, and mining region. It has become the trading and business center for this area. It uses the products of the region in its many factories. Spokane has immense woodworking plants for making doors and window frames. It has a huge flour mill and plants that pack fruits and vegetables and canned meats. It also turns out many different aluminum products.

Power from the falls on the river is used to make electricity to run some of these factories. The electricity from the powerhouse at Grand Coulee Dam on the Columbia is also used.

The people of Spokane are proud of their clean city with its wide streets and attractive homes. Nearby are many lovely vacation areas—beautiful lakes, forests, and high mountains.

And now, thinking back! In what ways are parts of the Northwest like the area where you live? How are they different? The next chapter takes us into another region of our country, the Southwest.

Let's Review

1. What states make up our Northwest? Which one is the largest? Which was named for a President of our country? Which one joined the Union first?

2. What important ranges of mountains rise in this region? What important rivers drain it?

3. How did Alaska become a part of our country?

4. What are the main industries in the Northwest?

Some Other Things to Do

1. Read in another book about one of the following topics and be ready to share the new information you learn.

Grand Coulee Dam   The Alaska Highway
salmon   Portland
Seattle   Anchorage
            volcanoes

2. Help the class to make a large picture map of the Northwest. Project a map slide on a large piece of paper. Trace the outline of the map with a heavy pencil or crayon. Draw pictures of the Northwest's chief products and industries and put them on the map in the correct locations. Decide what other things you might show.

3. Make a poster about protecting our forests. Choose the best posters to display in the halls of your school.

4. Arrange a picture exhibit on your bulletin board to tell the story of lumbering.

What Is Your Idea?

1. How do forests help to protect our soil? How do they help to prevent floods?

2. How can fifth graders help to conserve our forests?

3. What do you think the word "litterbug" means? How can you keep from being a litterbug? Where can you prove you are litter-careful every day?

4. How does climate affect people's ways of living? How does it affect their ways of earning a living?

Fun with Maps

1. Refer to the map on page 277 to help you answer these questions:

a. Is this a political map? What are the reasons for your answer?

b. Does it show relief?

c. Does it show the four main kinds of landforms?

d. Which of the three Northwestern states are shown?

e. Which of these cities have a population of from 100,000 to 500,000?

Portland   Salem   Seattle
Medford   Spokane   Eugene

Which one has more than 500,000 people? About what is its population? (Refer to Table 5 on page 501.)

2. Using the two maps on pages 278 and 301, try to answer these questions:

a. Where in Oregon and Washington is dairying carried on? Why is this a good area for such an industry? Why isn't wheat raised there?

b. About how much rain falls a year in eastern Oregon and Washington? Is this enough for most crops? If not, how can some crops be raised in parts of this region? What other important agricultural industry is carried on in this area?

3. Use the map on page 295 to help you name and locate:

    a. a strait
    b. a long peninsula
    c. Alaska's largest river
    d. a famous northern highway
    e. a northern coastal plain
    f. a plateau

Learning More about Latitude

East-west lines on maps and globes are called lines of latitude, remember. Notice these lines on the global map above. They show distance north and south of the equator. Notice that the equator is numbered zero. The other latitude lines are numbered north *and* south from the equator. There is a line of latitude numbered 20°, *north* of the equator, and one with the same number *south* of the equator, for example.

The latitude lines with the lowest numbers mark the east-west lines near the equator. So the region close to the equator is sometimes called the *low latitudes*. The low latitudes are

between the lines of latitude marked 23½. These two lines have special names, the Tropic of Cancer and the Tropic of Capricorn. Find them on the global map above. Therefore the low latitude region is also known as the *tropical region*.

Find the latitude lines with the highest numbers. They are near the north and south poles. The regions near the poles are therefore known as the *high latitudes*. The high latitudes are between the lines of latitude marked 66½ and the poles which are marked 90°. The lines marked 66½ are known as the Arctic Circle and the Antarctic Circle. Find them on the global map above. Locate Alaska on the map on page 334. What part of Alaska is in the high latitudes?

The regions between the low latitudes and the high latitudes are known as the middle latitudes. They are between the latitudes numbered 23½ and those numbered 66½. Point to the middle-latitude regions on the map above.

There are two other important regions known as middle latitudes. Is the state of Washington in the middle latitudes or the high latitudes?

18 · Our Southwest:
A Region of Rapid Change

Saving and Sharing Water

Water's long journey to Lake Perris. One day, Ann's aunt took her to Lake Perris. This lake is seventy miles southeast of Los Angeles. "What a lovely lake!" exclaimed Ann. "But it's so dry around here. Where does the lake's water come from?"

"A good question, Ann" her aunt replied. "It comes from northern California 600 miles away! Perhaps from snow melting from mountain slopes last spring. Perhaps from a rainstorm during the north's long rainy season. Once, such a rainstorm often caused terrible floods. Now much of this water is saved and held behind the highest dam in our country. Huge Oroville Dam! Lake Oroville is back of it. You're looking at water from this large lake, 600 miles north of us."

"Really? I can't believe it!" said Ann. "How does it get here?"

"I'll show you on this map I brought along," her aunt answered. "After water leaves Lake Oroville, it flows south. It flows 110 miles down the Feather and Sacramento rivers to the Delta region. See, the Delta is east of San Francisco. There the water is pumped into the *California Aqueduct*. The California Aqueduct is a cement-lined canal about 200 feet wide. The water travels south to the end of the San Joaquin Valley. Then powerful pumps lift it many hundreds of feet over the mountains. Finally it reaches Lake Perris. It will irrigate crops and help cities in this dry region. Also Lake Perris is a recreation area. People can enjoy swimming, boating, fishing and camping here.

"Lake Perris receives only a small part of Lake Oroville's outflow, however. The California Aqueduct has several branches.

Water for dry lands comes from the mountains.

They feed about twenty lakes and reservoirs. Each one serves cities, farms, and vacationers. This *California State Water Project* is supplying water in the San Joaquin Valley for nearly a million acres of once-dry crop lands."

Like California, the other states of the Southwest have vast dry lands. They, too, are seeking ways to save and share their precious water.

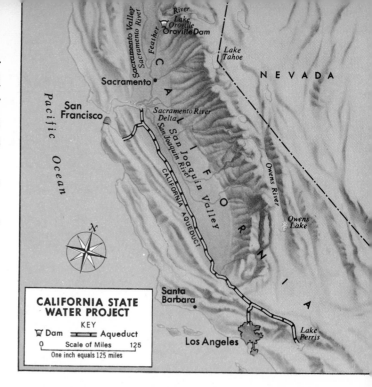

CALIFORNIA STATE
WATER PROJECT
KEY

Dam ▭▭▭ Aqueduct
0   Scale of Miles   125
One inch equals 125 miles

Our Southwest

Our Southwest includes four states. They are California, Nevada, Arizona, and Hawaii. Locate each one on the map on page 178.

California is the largest state and has the most people. It has the largest population of any state in our country.

California faces the Pacific. Its shores are washed by the ocean for more than 1,190 miles. Southern California has some wide sandy beaches. But farther north, there are miles of rugged cliffs and grand scenery.

Hawaii sits far out in the Pacific, remember. It is made up of a string of islands, as the map on page 317 shows. The largest one is Hawaii. However, another island, Oahu, is the richest and most thickly-settled one. It has the city of Honolulu, the capital of the state.

California, Nevada, and Arizona were part of the Spanish Southwest. Probably you recall reading how our country gained this huge region.

You learned about California's Gold Rush, and that many Forty-Niners stayed to settle in this western land. A few years later, gold and silver were also discovered in Nevada and Arizona. Miners were among the early settlers in this part of the Southwest. And what about Hawaii?

An Hawaiian chief gives Captain Cook a cloak of feathers.

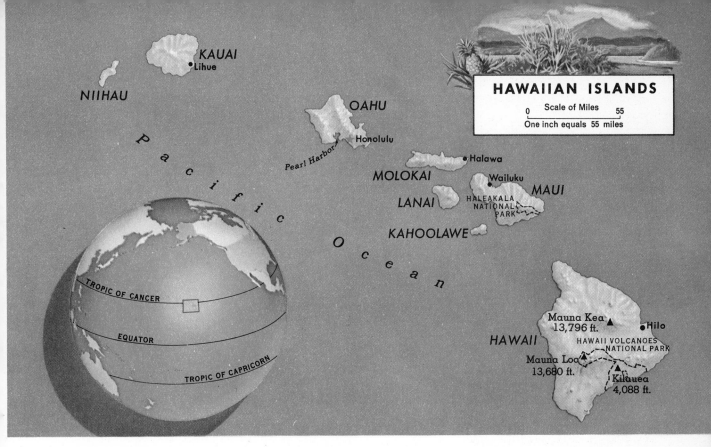

MAP LABELS:
NIIHAU
KAUAI
•Lihue
OAHU
Pacific Ocean
Pearl Harbor
Honolulu
•Halawa
MOLOKAI
•Wailuku
LANAI
MAUI
HALEAKALA NATIONAL PARK
KAHOOLAWE
TROPIC OF CANCER
EQUATOR
TROPIC OF CAPRICORN
Mauna Kea 13,796 ft.
•Hilo
HAWAII
HAWAII VOLCANOES NATIONAL PARK
Mauna Loa 13,680 ft.
Kilauea 4,088 ft.

HAWAIIAN ISLANDS
0 Scale of Miles 55
One inch equals 55 miles

This map shows only the larger islands.

How did Hawaii become a part of our country? In a way, that story begins in 1778 when the English explorer, Captain James Cook, discovered the islands. He found living there tall, handsome, brown-skinned people.

These islanders had never seen white men. They supposed that the visitors were gods. They welcomed them with gifts and treated them splendidly. But later on, when Cook's party returned, feelings had changed. Fighting broke out. Captain Cook and several sailors were killed.

Cook's visit marked the beginning of change. Soon, trading ships were calling at the islands. One American ship sailed away leaving two sailors behind. In time, they married members of the king's family and became his advisors. They taught this king of the islands many of the white man's ways.

Later, missionaries from New England arrived to teach the islanders about Christianity. They started schools and showed the people new ways of living. Other Americans and people from many parts of the world settled on the islands. They planted new crops and took part in trading and other businesses.

Then in 1898, the United States went to war with Spain. Some battles were fought in the Philippine Islands, far to the west of Hawaii in the Pacific. Therefore, Hawaii was used as a stopping place for American ships on the way to the Philippines. Soon, Hawaii was made a territory of the United States. Finally, in 1959, Congress voted Hawaii a state.

317

Lava pours out of a crack in the huge crater of the volcano, Kilauea. Find Kilauea on the map on page 317. It is on the island of Hawaii.

Today, we can think of it as a part of our Southwest.

The Southwest is a region of contrasts. It has some very high lands, but also the lowest ones in our country. Some parts face the sea, but others are located far inland.

The mountains and the ocean have an enormous influence on the climate of this region. There are some very rainy lands, but also some of our driest ones. You can understand this climate story better after we look at the geography of the Southwest.

The Southwest is a mountainous region. The map on page 90 tells some things about the mountains in California, Nevada, and Arizona. But use the map on page 317 to locate Hawaii's ranges.

The Hawaiian Islands are really the tops of mountains. You could see this very plainly if you could drain away the ocean around them. The highest peak, Mauna Kea rises on the island of Hawaii and has an altitude of 13,796 feet. Find

it on the map. Some miles away on this same island is another lofty peak, Mauna Loa. It is an active volcano.

Actually, the islands were formed by volcanoes. Long, long ago, some volcanoes erupted through the floor of the Pacific Ocean. Gradually they built up the mountainous Hawaiian Islands.

California also has some volcanic mountains. They are a part of the Cascade Range you read about in Chapter 17. Use the map on page 90 and notice how the Cascades extend through northern California.

Two famous Cascade peaks in California were formed by volcanoes. One is Mount Shasta which is wrapped in snow and ice nearly the whole year round. The other is handsome Mount Lassen.

California also has a share of the Coast Ranges. They are chains of low mountains and hills as in Washington and Oregon.

The Sierra Nevada is the highest range in the Southwest. Locate it on the map. It extends for more than 400 miles along

318

the eastern boundary of California and into the edge of Nevada.

This great thick wall of mountains has no low passes. So roads and railroads that cross the Sierras zigzag back and forth to climb through them.

The Sierra Nevada Range has much beautiful scenery. Sharp snowy peaks! Sparkling lakes! Tumbling streams and splendid green forests. One famous area, Sequoia National Park, has some enormous trees called giant sequoias. A number are said to be more than 3000 years old. They climb over 300 feet toward the sky. Another wonderland in the Sierras is Yosemite National Park.

Towering Mount Whitney is the highest peak in the Sierras, and also the loftiest one in the entire Southwest. It soars to a height of 14,495 feet. Other fairly high mountains rise in Arizona on the Colorado Plateau.

The Colorado Plateau occupies a large part of Arizona. Its wide tablelands have some volcanic peaks and also some wonderful deep canyons. The most thrilling one is beautiful Grand Canyon.

Grand Canyon extends through Arizona for about 200 miles. It was carved out by the Colorado River many ages ago. One view of its colorful steep rock walls is shown below.

The Great Basin spreads across most of Nevada. Use the map to prove this is true. We think of this area mainly as desert country. But don't picture it as just a flat sandy region. Not at all! It has some rolling hilly country, and mesas, and even ranges of mountains scattered through it.

Some basin lands extend into eastern California and southeastern Arizona. One wide area in California is the Mojave Desert. It is dotted with various kinds of thorny cactus and gray-green sage brush.

Another area is Death Valley. It stretches along the southeastern border of California. It was given its name by a party of Forty-Niners who were on their way to the Gold Fields. They turned off the main trail to take what they believed was a short cut. But they wandered into this lonely dry wasteland. The travelers suffered terribly in the low valley and some died. The survivors gave the valley the sad name it bears to this day.

Death Valley is a sun-baked desert and has scorching hot summers. It has the lowest lands in the United States. Just think! A part of it is 280 feet below the level of the sea.

The Southwest has fertile valleys, large and small. The great Central Valley stretches through the heart of California for more than 400 miles. Do you see it on the map between the Sierra Nevada and the Coast Range? It is a rich-soiled valley. Thanks to irrigation, more than 200 different kinds of crops are raised on its lands.

There are two well known desert valleys in California. They are the Coachella and Imperial valleys. Parts of Imperial Valley are about 200 feet below sea level.

This lowland can expect only about three inches of rain a year. Nevertheless, agriculture is the leading industry in both it and the dry Coachella Valley. The magic of irrigation makes this possible.

"But where do the farmlands get their irrigation water?" you ask. "Where does the water come from?"

Melting snows and rainfall provide it, of course. The high mountains receive very heavy snows. And rainfall is quite heavy in these mountains, also. Much of this precious water flows into rivers. Huge quantities are stored in reservoirs back of the dams built on rivers.

What large rivers drain the Southwest? The Colorado is the mightiest one. As you read earlier, it starts as a small stream high in the Rockies. Use your finger to trace its course across the Southwest on the map on page 277. On a part of its journey, it races along the floor of the Grand Canyon, nearly 2000 feet below the canyon's rim. See how the Colorado River forms California's southeast boundary.

In earlier years, the Colorado River spilled over its banks and caused damaging floods every spring. But today, it has been tamed. Now, large dams hold back enormous "lakes" of water.

Hoover Dam is a giant and one of the tallest dams in the world. Locate it on your map on page 277 and then look at the picture on page 321. The huge body of water behind it is known as Lake Mead. Below the dam is an immense power house that manufactures electricity for many cities in the Southwest.

Much Colorado River water is used to irrigate thirsty farmlands in Arizona and southern California. But tremendous

Hoover Dam holds back water from the Colorado River to form Lake Mead.

quantities are carried to southern California cities for homes and industries.

Two large rivers flow through the Central Valley. They are the Sacramento and San Joaquin rivers. Look for them on the map. Both begin in the snowfields of the Sierra Nevada, but they start hundreds of miles apart. Which one flows southward?

Shasta Dam extends across the Sacramento River and holds back a large reservoir of water. Immense Oroville Dam is on a branch of the Sacramento. Its thick wall reaches more than a mile across a deep canyon. Canals and aqueducts carry water stored by this dam all the way south beyond Los Angeles, remember. Thus, water from the rainy parts of northern California is shared with drier areas in the state.

The Southwest's climate story is especially interesting. Along the California coast, breezes from the ocean cool the land in summer and keep the weather mild in winter. These breezes also bring rainclouds, as the drawing on page 278 shows. Turn to this drawing and review the legend information above it. Then study the rainfall map on this same page. Which "Southwest" areas receive the most moisture? Northern California's coastal lands have very rainy winters. They have a climate much like the coastal lands in the Northwest.

However, our Southwest region is mainly a dry thirsty land. See how plainly this fact is told on the rainfall map. No wonder water is precious! No wonder men are searching for more and better ways to provide it.

The desert areas have a sunny climate winter and summer. Thousands of vacation seekers enjoy the delightful winters but only a few care for the summers. Then, the days are blistering hot and temperatures may soar to 115° or higher. Even lizards and snakes hide from the daytime heat. They wait until night to hunt for food.

Much of California has a long growing season, a fact shown on the map on page 203. In some places crops can be raised nearly the whole year. This is true in parts of Arizona, also. Where, in the Southwest, is the growing season the shortest? What kinds of lands are found there?

Hawaii has a climate story all its own. One reason is that it is located in the low latitudes and therefore is in the tropics. Notice this on the map on page 317. This means that these islands have a *tropical climate*, a climate that is warm all year long.

In Hawaii, however, the weather is seldom hot. Sea breezes cool the islands, day after day. The winds come mostly from the northeast. They have blown across thousands of miles of ocean and have gathered a great deal of moisture. As they approach Hawaii's mountains, they rise and become even cooler. So they dump most of their moisture on the northeastern sides of the island.

The northeast slopes of the mountains have a dense tangle of trees, vines, flowers and ferns. But the southwest areas are much drier. So farms and plantations there are usually irrigated.

How important the mountains and the ocean are in influencing the climate of our Southwest!

At the left below, a forest of tree-ferns on the northeastern slopes of Hawaii's mountains. Below, planting pineapples on Kauai. The paper keeps in the moisture.

Agriculture: Farming and Stock Raising

The Southwest is a rich agricultural region. Yet less than one twentieth of its land is suitable for growing crops. Think of that! The main kinds of farming are shown on the map on page 301. As you read earlier, the largest fertile area in California is the Central Valley.

Many farms in the Southwest are huge, extending over thousands of acres. Generally, the large ones are owned by a company or a group of men. But there are also hundreds of smaller "farms," some of which have only five or ten acres apiece. Some small ones are poultry ranches and others may be orange ranches. In the Southwest, "farms" are usually called ranches, no matter what their size or crops.

Most crops must be irrigated, remember. Notice how this is shown on the farming map on page 301. Canals or aqueducts carry the water from reservoirs to croplands.

At the right is a picture of one very important aqueduct. It is about eighty miles long and leads water from the Colorado River to the thirsty Imperial Valley. It provides enough water to irrigate more than 500,000 acres.

Ditches and pipes laid underground, guide the water from the main canals into fields and orchards. These ditches have small water gates. When it is time to irrigate, the farmer opens the gate and lets the water into the furrows. Furrow irrigation is the most widely used way of watering fairly flat lands. But sprinklers are often seen in rolling country.

A machine picks cotton bolls on a farm in the Central Valley of California.

The All-American Canal carries water about 80 miles to the Imperial Valley.

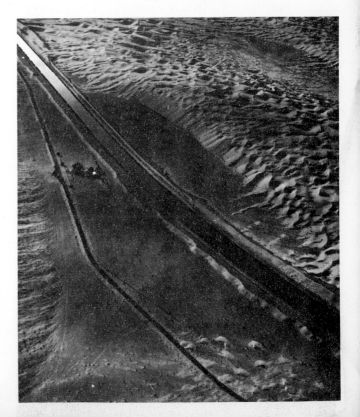

323

Raisin grapes are spread out
to dry in the sun.

When raisins are ready, they
are rolled up in their papers.

The ranchers use many kinds of machines. Among them are tractors, combines, tree shakers, cotton pickers, and even airplanes. As in other parts of our country, agriculture is becoming more and more mechanized.

Cotton is one of the leading crops. Thousands of acres of it are grown in the Southwest. In what states? Use the map on page 301 to find out.

Many of the cotton ranches are very large. One reason is that expensive machinery is needed to raise this crop. A man could not afford to buy such machines for a small farm.

You have learned how cotton is planted and grows. By September, the fields are dotted with cotton snowballs, and picking season is near. But first, an important job must be done. Small planes fly low above the fields. As they speed back and forth, they spray the cotton with a special powder. This makes the green leaves die. As soon as they drop off, the cotton is harvested. Today, much of this work is done by cotton-picking machines.

California has miles of fruit orchards and vineyards. Oranges, lemons, and grapefruit are grown in suitable areas that have a mild climate. Citrus fruits cannot stand much frost.

Parts of the Central Valley produce huge amounts of such fruits as peaches, plums, cherries, apricots, figs, and grapes. They are often called "Fruit Salad Lands." Some fruits are sold fresh. But millions of pounds are canned, frozen, or dried. The hot summer air is just right for drying fruits. Tons of grapes and prunes are dried. Dried grapes, of course, are raisins.

Raisins are the biggest dried fruit crop. After the raisin grapes are harvested, they are spread out to dry. After several days, they are turned to make sure they will dry evenly.

Finally, the raisins are hauled to a packing plant to be prepared for market. By this time, they have lost most of their moisture so they are smaller and look quite wrinkled. It takes about four pounds of grapes to produce one pound of raisins.

324

Harvesting the cane

Rollers press out the juice from cane stalks

What are some other California crops? Much rice is raised in the northern part of the Central Valley. It is planted by plane. A skilled pilot can sow about thirty acres of rice an hour.

Some ranches produce sugar beets, and others raise alfalfa. Many truck gardens specialize in vegetable crops. Among these are artichokes, asparagus, broccoli, carrots, cauliflower, peas, beans, lettuce, celery, tomatoes, potatoes, and onions.

Crops can be grown for about 300 days of each year in the desert valleys. So Imperial Valley supplies quantities of winter vegetables for markets. Coachella Valley is famous for its dates and grapefruit.

Arizona produces a variety of crops. One is cotton, as you know. Others include citrus fruits, cantaloupes, vegetables, and alfalfa. In what part of the state are the main farming areas? Turn to the map on page 301 and see. Notice that most of these croplands are irrigated.

Sugar is Hawaii's largest crop. The islands have a tropical climate well suited to growing sugar cane. Thousands of acres are raised.

Sugar cane is a kind of giant grass, as you may know. It looks something like a tall thick cornstalk. When the stalks are

Waste is removed from the juice

Sugar crystals are formed by boiling the juice

ripe, they are full of sweet juice. Sugar is made from this juice.

Sugar cane is planted differently from most crops. Large planting machines dig furrows and place pieces of stalk deep in them. Soon little plants sprout and grow from the stalks. In many fields the plants are irrigated as they grow. By harvest-time, the tall thick stalks may be from twelve to fifteen feet high.

To begin the harvest, the fields are set afire. This destroys the leaves of the plants but it does not damage the stalks or the sweet juices within them. After the stalks are cut, they are gathered up and hauled to a mill. There they are made into sugar. The pictures on page 325 tell how this is done.

In earlier years, many workers were needed to lay out and care for sugar plantations. Men came from such faraway countries as Japan, China, and the Philippines. Most of them stayed on in the islands. Today, many of Hawaii's people can trace their ancestors back to those who came to work in the sugar industry, long ago.

Golden pineapples are another famous crop in Hawaii. Millions of them are grown on pineapple plantations. Large companies own most of these plantations. Like sugar cane, pineapples are raised from shoots called slips.

The picture above gives you an idea of how they are harvested. Some are shipped away to be sold fresh, but most of them are canned or crushed for their juice.

Each state in the Southwest raises much livestock. Nevada and Arizona have huge cattle and sheep ranches. Some also spread over the hilly back country of California. The grazing lands are usually

Pickers place pineapples on a moving belt to be carried to a truck.

found in the rolling areas not suited to farming or where there is not enough water for growing crops.

Hawaii has several large cattle ranches. One occupies more than 300,000 acres and is among the largest cattle ranches in the world. It was started by a New Englander who arrived in the Islands soon after the War of 1812. Its first cowboys came from Mexico. It and the other cattle ranches nearby furnish much of the beef used on the islands.

California has an enormous dairy business and also many poultry ranches. Indeed, the Petaluma area north of San Francisco calls itself the "Egg Capital of the World." It produces millions of eggs and also hatches and ships away many chicks that will grow up to be laying hens.

By now, you may think that most people in the Southwest earn their living in some kind of agricultural occupation. But no! It is just one of many important industries carried on in this region. What are some others?

Other Industries: Fishing, Lumbering, and Mining

Some people are employed in the fishing industry. The chief kinds of fish caught off the California coast are barracuda, halibut, sardines, and tuna. Tuna is the largest and most valuable catch. The tuna that brings the best price is albacore. It has white meat and tastes something like chicken.

Canneries prepare tuna for market. After the fish are cleaned, they are cooked in enormous ovens. Next, skilled workers remove the bones and pack the tuna in cans. The cans are sealed tightly and cooked for more than an hour. Finally they are labeled and prepared for shipping.

As you would expect, the waters around Hawaii have many kinds of fish. Fishing has long been an important industry. Indeed, the catching and canning of tuna provides jobs for many people.

Fishing for tuna.

Lumbering is a leading industry in northern California. Redwoods, pines, and Douglas firs are among the main kinds of trees cut.

Redwoods are magnificent trees that like very damp air. They grow in the wet coastal lands of northern California. Actually they are one kind of sequoia, and are among our tallest and oldest trees. Some redwood forests have been set aside as parks.

Like the Rocky Mountain region, the Southwest has rich mineral treasures. Arizona produces more copper than any other state in our country. Its cities of Globe, Bisbee, and Douglas have grown up chiefly because of the valuable copper mines nearby.

Nevada also mines copper. Both it and its neighbor, Arizona, mine some gold and silver as well as certain other minerals.

Gold mining is still carried on in a number of California areas. But the easy-to-find gold on the surface is gone. Strangely enough, today such quantities of cement, sand, and gravel are "mined" that they bring in far more money than do the gold mines.

But black gold is California's most valuable mineral treasure. This state has a number of rich oil fields, as is shown on the map on page 247.

Electric pumps send much of the crude oil through underground pipes to refineries. One of the largest refining centers is at Los Angeles. Another is located near San Francisco.

The rich natural resources of the Southwest provide plentiful raw materials for much manufacturing. The next section will discuss several important manufacturing and trading centers in this region.

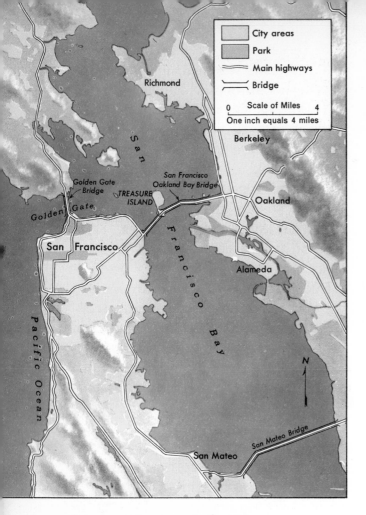

A map of part of the San Francisco Bay district.

Some Cities and Their Industries

Some areas of the Southwest are thinly populated. The map on page 184 shows this. Notice how far apart the cities are in Arizona and Nevada. Which parts of California are thinly populated? What are some reasons for this, do you suppose?

What areas are thickly populated? Look at the map and decide. If you could drive through these areas, you might say,

"These cities run together. I can't tell where one stops and the next one begins."

The Los Angeles and San Francisco areas are very thickly settled. Strings of cities reach out from each one. We can almost think of each great area as a megalopolis. What does that big word mean? Do you remember? If you have forgotten, turn back to page 214 and see.

San Francisco is the busiest city of northern California. Find it on the map on page 277. Now point to it on the map at the left. See how it is located at the north end of a peninsula. On the west, this city faces the Pacific, but on the north and east it looks out on a large bay. Locate this bay on the map.

San Francisco Bay provides one of the best harbors in the world. Its deep waters are well protected from ocean storms by many hills. They are a part of the long chain of coastal mountains.

There is a break through these mountains at San Francisco. It is the famous Golden Gate. Where is it on the map? Notice how it forms the entrance to sheltered San Francisco Bay from the Pacific. A huge bridge has been built across Golden Gate. It reaches from the edge of San Francisco to the hills on the north.

Countless ships sail through Golden Gate into San Francisco Bay. They carry passengers and freight from near and far. They bring imported goods from all over the world. They take away such exports as lumber, sugar, canned goods, and many kinds of manufactured products from the factories of San Francisco and of other "bay" cities. The busy seaport of San Francisco carries on much trade with the Orient, Australia, and Hawaii, as well as with cities up and down our coasts.

San Francisco is a hilly city in a beautiful setting. It has many handsome buildings, lovely homes, and splendid schools and churches. Visitors enjoy its fine museums and lovely parks.

One of the longest bridges in the world connects San Francisco with several large cities across the bay. Look for the Bay Bridge on the map on page 328. It connects San Francisco with such cities as Berkeley and Oakland. Because they, too, share San Francisco Bay, shipping is one of their important industries.

All of these "bay" cities are trading centers for the Central Valley. The map on page 277 shows that the Sacramento and San Joaquin rivers flow out of the Central Valley into San Francisco Bay. Highways and railroads follow these rivers to the bay. Therefore goods that come into San Francisco Bay can be easily sent to the cities and farms of the Central Valley. Five hundred miles to the south is another megalopolis, Los Angeles.

Los Angeles is the giant city of the West. It was started by Spaniards in 1781 even before our country became the United States. They gave their little pueblo a long name which meant "The Town of Our Lady, Queen of the Angels." Soon, though, the pueblo became known by a much shorter name, just Los Angeles.

Find Los Angeles on the map. It has grown very fast and is our third largest city. Near it are Pasadena, Long Beach, and dozens of other cities. All of them have needed more water for their growing population and industries.

Los Angeles built a huge aqueduct all the way from a mountain basin in the Sierra Nevada, 330 miles away. It and some neighboring cities also banded together to bring water from the Colorado River, 300 miles to the east.

The Los Angeles area forms one of our leading industrial centers. It has large aircraft, missile, and electronics industries. There are also automobile-assembly plants, oil refineries, food-packing plants, and many other kinds of factories.

Air pollution is often a problem. Smog is caused by its factories, busy automobile traffic and certain weather conditions.

Golden Gate Bridge makes a graceful span across the entrance to San Francisco Bay. Find the bridge on the map on the opposite page.

An air photo of "downtown Los Angeles." The tall building with the pointed tower is City Hall in the Civic Center.

In some ways, Los Angeles resembles an enormous octopus. It seems to reach out in every direction. Indeed it does spread out over more land than any other city in our country. One long narrow strip extends nearly twenty miles to the ocean and San Pedro Harbor. This harbor has been deepened and widened and provides Los Angeles with a fine port. Ships from all over the world tie up at its wharves.

A map of Los Angeles.

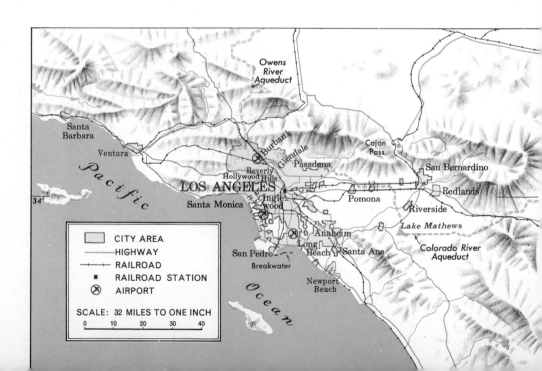

CITY AREA
HIGHWAY
RAILROAD
RAILROAD STATION
AIRPORT

SCALE: 32 MILES TO ONE INCH
0   10   20   30   40

Los Angeles has excellent stores, shops of every kind, and miles of attractive homes. Its schools and churches are among the finest in our land.

Thousands of people visit Los Angeles and other parts of California every year. Many spend the winters in southern California because of its mild climate. So caring for tourists is one of its main businesses.

San Diego and Sacramento are two other well-known California cities. Locate each one on the map. Which one is the capital of California? Which one has a deep harbor?

San Diego is the center of aircraft and space industries. Sacramento is the leading manufacturing and trading city for the northern part of the Central Valley. Both cities have grown rapidly in recent years.

Phoenix is Arizona's fastest growing city, and also its capital. It is located in the heart of a rich agricultural area. Many of its people are employed in canneries and food-packing plants. Phoenix is also a shipping center for these goods and for the beef cattle raised nearby. But it, too, has much manufacturing. Some plants turn out aircraft, and others air conditioning and electronic equipment.

Phoenix is a city that grew up in a desert. Water for it and for irrigation is stored at Roosevelt Dam on the Salt River and in other nearby reservoirs.

Both Phoenix and its sister city, Tucson, attract many tourists during the winter. Easterners enjoy the dry sunny climate and relief from the cold.

Honolulu is Hawaii's beautiful capital and its main seaport. Over half of the people of our 50th state live in this fast-growing modern city. Ocean liners and freighters from all over the world tie up at the docks of its fine harbor. Freighters unload manufactured goods, gasoline, and foods. Some departing ships carry away cargoes of fresh and canned pineapples, canned pineapple juice, and sugar.

Honolulu is a modern city in every way, but it is also different from some other large cities in our country. Tall palm

An irrigation canal brings water to farmlands near Phoenix, Arizona.

trees line many avenues and its parks and gardens are bright with lovely tropical flowers. One of its main businesses is taking care of tourists. So there are many fine hotels and apartment houses as well as stores, markets, and office buildings. There are blocks and blocks of homes, also, and public schools and churches.

A huge airport is located near Honolulu. It is the landing place for many large planes which fly the airways of the Pacific. The air route map on page 355 will show you why Hawaii is sometimes called "the crossroads of the Pacific."

A short distance from Honolulu is Pearl Harbor, a strong United States naval base. In an earlier chapter, you read how it was attacked by Japan in 1941. Do you remember?

Thousands of people visit Hawaii every year. They land at Honolulu's large airport or its harbor. They are often greeted with the lovely song, *Aloha Oe.*

Honolulu's Waikiki Beach with Diamond Head in the background.

Sometimes, fragrant chains of flowers, or *leis* are hung about their necks.

Tourists find many interesting things to do on the islands. They like to visit the fine sandy beaches, and especially the wide sun-baked sands of Waikiki. A picture of this lovely beach appears on this page. At Waikiki, one is sure to see some Hawaiians riding flat, narrow surfboards on the rolling waves. They paddle their surfboards far out from shore and race in on the waves.

Sightseeing is fun, too. One may fly to other islands and take drives through the countryside. Some highways lead past sugar or pineapple plantations and some to beautiful mountain scenery. Also, one can travel to see Mauna Loa, the exciting volcano on the island of Hawaii. In fact, it would take many pages to describe all the beautiful and interesting things to see in our newest state.

When vacations are over, visitors are given a happy sendoff. Again they are presented with leis and hear the music of

Daniel Inouye was the first man to represent Hawaii in the House of Representatives. He is a Japanese-American. Hiram Fong, right, was one of Hawaii's first two Senators. He is a Chinese-American.

"Aloha." This time, "Aloha" means "Farewell until we meet again."

Americans all! Visiting Hawaii reminds us again that the people of our country are of many different backgrounds. Hawaii has a mixture of people whose ancestors have come from every continent. They have brought to Hawaii their skills, arts, and music. They are proud Americans all—citizens who are

Our country is great largely because of its ambitious, hard-working people. But we have had plenty of natural resources to help us. Which ones have you read about in Unit Three? Which ones should we use more wisely? The United States will stay strong and beautiful only if all of us do our part.

Some Questions to Test You

1. What states make up the Southwest? What are some of its important mountain ranges? What are its main rivers?

2. How is the climate along the coast of northern California different from the climate in Arizona, Nevada, and the rest of California?

3. How would you describe the climate of Hawaii? Is it the same throughout the islands? Give reasons for your answer.

4. How did Hawaii become a part of our country?

5. What are the leading farming industries in the Southwest?

6. What other industries are also important in this region?

7. What are some of the most famous vacationlands in this region?

Some Other Things to Do

1. Read a book about early life in one of the Southwest states.

2. Find and share a worth-while current event about some part of the Southwest.

3. List several main reasons why one of these cities has grown large:

Los Angeles   San Francisco   Honolulu
Salt Lake City

4. Be ready to tell at about what latitude each of these cities is located:

Los Angeles   Seattle   San Francisco
Honolulu   Portland   Anchorage

You may want to refer to a large wall map of the World.

5. Learn more about a water project in one of the Southwest states.

6. Sing the song *Aloha Oe* with your class.

7. Make a lei.

8. Find out from what lands your ancestors came. Help members of your class to show this information on an outline map of the world. Pin strings leading from your ancestors' countries to your community.

What Would You Say?

1. What is meant by these words, "Water is King in the Southwest"?

2. How has modern transportation helped to develop the Southwest?

3. What are some ways in which Hawaii is different from Nevada?

4. What can we do to better understand those whose background or race is different from ours?

A Choosing Game

Decide on the correct ending for each of the following incomplete sentences.

1. The largest state in the Southwest is (a) Nevada. (b) California. (c) Arizona.

2. The newest state in this region is (a) Arizona. (b) Nevada. (c) Hawaii.

3. Hawaii was discovered by (a) Cook. (b) Cabrillo. (c) Columbus.

4. Mount Shasta and Mount Lassen are in the (a) Cascades. (b) the Sierra Nevada. (c) the Coast Range.

5. Central Valley and Imperial Valley are famous for their (a) winter sports. (b) mineral resources. (c) farm products.

6. California raises huge quantities of (a) corn. (b) wheat. (c) cotton.

7. Hawaii is famous for its pineapples and (a) alfalfa. (b) sugar. (c) oranges.

8. The giant city of the Southwest is (a) San Francisco. (b) Phoenix. (c) Los Angeles.

9. The largest city in northern California is (a) Sacramento. (b) Oakland. (c) San Francisco.

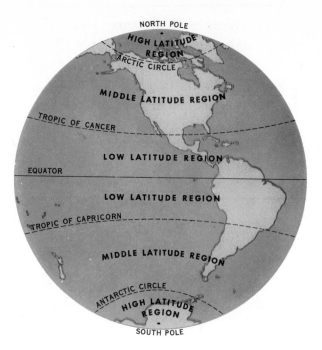

Latitude and Climate

You have learned that we often use latitude lines to divide the earth into regions. These are the low latitude, or tropical, region; the middle latitude regions; and the high latitude regions.

Let's look for these regions on the map at the right. Find the middle, or mid-latitude, regions. Notice that one of these regions is north of the tropics and one lies to the south. In which one do you live?

Point to the high latitude, or polar, regions. As you can see, one is near the north pole. The other is near the south pole.

The region near the equator is hot while the regions around the two poles are cold. So, as you travel from the equator toward the poles, the climate becomes colder. Therefore, if you know the latitude of a place or the region in which it lies, you will know something about its climate.

In the low latitude, or tropical, region the weather may be warm the year round. There is no spring, summer, fall, or winter as we think of them. Which one of our states is in the low latitudes, or tropics?

In which of the regions would you expect to find the coldest and longest winters? The high latitude, or polar, regions have very short summers and cold weather for most of the year. Which state is partly in the high latitudes?

Most parts of our country are in the middle latitudes. They generally have warm summers and cold or cool winters. What kind of climate does your part of the country have?

UNIT FOUR

Binding Our Huge Nation Together

19 · Transportation: How We Travel and Exchange Goods

A Glance at Transportation Today

How did you travel to school this morning? Did you walk? If so, you depended on man's first means of going from one place to another. You went on foot.

But perhaps you traveled some other way. Perhaps you depended on some kind of "machine" to take you. You may have ridden a bicycle, or your mother may have taken you in an automobile. Or perhaps you were a passenger on a bus.

Bicycles, automobiles, streetcars, and busses furnish us with a part of our transportation. *Transportation* means the way we travel and carry goods.

We have many kinds of transportation. One kind, the automobile, is owned by millions of Americans. But some kinds belong to large companies. Among them are busses, trains, steamships, and planes. They travel over certain routes day and night and in all kinds of weather. They run at regular times and charge fares for carrying passengers and goods.

Most modern kinds of transportation are rapid. The drawings across the page show how the speed of travel has in-

How changing ways of travel have made our country seem smaller.

1856—a traveler could cross the United States by railroad and stagecoach in 29 days.

1869—the same distance was traveled by the first transcontinental train in 7 days.

TODAY—we can fly across our country by nonstop airplane in 5–6 hours.

creased. Notice how much faster we can cross the United States than pioneers could in 1856.

Airplanes are our newest and fastest means of transportation. Giant jet passenger planes can travel more than five hundred miles an hour. They can speed from New York to San Francisco in a few hours. Even faster jet planes streak through the air at eight hundred or more miles an hour. They can race to any part of the world in about thirty hours.

Railroad trains are another important means of transportation. Our swiftest trains can travel about eighty miles an hour.

Large steamships carry many people across the world's oceans. Water travel is slower than most travel on land. Still, a modern steamship can cross the Atlantic Ocean in less than five days. Long ago, such a voyage took weeks and weeks.

Large busses roll along the main streets and highways. Some carry people within a city, and others make long cross-country trips. Trucks also share our boulevards and highways. They serve us in many ways. Those which haul goods are sometimes called the "freight cars" of the highways.

Our modern ways of transportation are very important to us. We depend on them so much that we cannot imagine doing without them. But long ago, our people were not so fortunate. How did they travel?

From Dirt Paths to Superhighways

The earliest colonists depended mostly on water transportation. They settled along the seacoast and on rivers so they could use waterways. They counted on ships to bring them goods and mail, and to take their crops to markets.

Some colonists traveled by water when they went on certain journeys. Canoes, rafts, and flatboats were used on the rivers. Small sailing ships made trips along the coast from one seaport to another.

But a journey along the coast was often quite dangerous. In some places, sharp rocks and sand bars caused shipwrecks. Such a journey was slow, too, for ships were at the mercy of the wind. When the wind died down, vessels drifted about for days helplessly. Still, traveling by water seemed easier and safer than going long distances through the lonely forest wilderness.

Early settlers walked or rode horses when they traveled on land. At first there were no roads. There were only the narrow twisting trails that the Indians or wild animals had worn down through the woods. Few early colonists dared to venture very far along these lonely paths.

In time, paths connected settlements and farms. But they were only suitable for traveling on foot or on horses.

By 1775, however, one could travel on horseback all the way from Boston to Charleston, in South Carolina. New York and Philadelphia were on this road. Though this was an important road, it was rough and narrow. In rainy weather it was dotted with mud puddles. And in dry weather it was bumpy because of deep holes and also very dusty.

On rainy days stagecoaches often got stuck in the mud. What happened then?

As time passed, people made longer journeys on horseback. Riders carried the mail from one settlement to another. Indeed, many of the delegates to the Continental Congresses rode to Philadelphia on horses. But, by that time, people were beginning to travel on "wheels."

Some colonists began to use carriages and coaches. A few people could afford handsome carriages drawn by teams of fine horses. And many settlers owned some kind of cart or buggy.

By 1776, some large carriages, or coaches, were carrying passengers between the main cities. One coach line ran between New York and Philadelphia. In good weather, it could complete the ninety-mile trip in two days. It made stops at inns along the way. Because such stops were called stages, the coach became known as a stagecoach.

Passengers were not very comfortable on the early stagecoaches. Furthermore, they could expect some strange experiences along their journeys, as is shown in lines from this diary:

We left New York in a bright red-and-yellow coach pulled by two fast teams of horses. Our coach had hard benches without backs. Some of us sat on our bundles and two of the party sat high up on the outside with the driver.

A part of our baggage and much mail skated around on top of the flat roof of the coach. A metal railing kept these articles from sliding off.

We traveled only by daylight. When night came, we stopped at inns. They were quite pleasant places where we got good meals and plenty of hot tea.

It rained during much of our journey. Those who rode with the driver were soaked and spattered with mud. They were a sight, and uncomfortable, too.

Twice our coach was stuck in deep mud. Then the coachman asked us all to get out. While the three women watched, we men pushed and pulled trying to get the coach moving again.

How 'glad we were when we finally reached Boston. Our journey had taken us six days!

After the Revolution, more roads were built. Some were *toll* roads constructed by companies. To use these roads, one paid a small amount of money, or *toll*. In the picture above, a toll is being collected from the driver at the tollgate. People also paid a fee to cross *toll bridges*.

Some stretches of road were covered with logs, as is shown in the picture above. These *corduroy* roads were often built

Travelers were stopped at a long spiked pole. After the toll was paid the pole was turned aside. So toll roads were called turnpikes.

across low places that remained muddy long after a rain. They prevented coaches and wagons from getting stuck. A ride over a corduroy road was rough and bumpy, however. Such a trip shook a coach so much that it sometimes broke down, spilling out passengers and bundles. No wonder people wished for better roads!

Then some *macadam* roads were started. They were named after their inventor, John McAdam, a Scotsman. They were slightly higher in the center so that rain and snow would drain off. Macadam roads were made with layers of broken stone topped with sand. Heavy rollers pressed these layers together into a hard solid road.

Our first highway was built by the United States Government. It was started in 1811 and led across the Appalachians to the West. It began at Cumberland, Maryland, on the Potomac River and went to Wheeling on the Ohio River. This was called the *Cumberland Road*, or the *National Pike*. You can find this route on the map on page 109.

Engineers planned this freeway carefully. How have they solved the problem of roads crossing one another? Why are such roads needed today?

The National Pike was a macadam road covered with crushed rock. At that time, it was the finest road in our country. It became one of the most important, too. Many covered wagons passed over it on their way to the West. Stagecoaches used it. And cattle, sheep, and hogs were driven over it to markets in the East.

From macadam roads to modern freeways. In time, miles and miles of macadam roads were built. Yet, by the early 1900's, still better roads were needed for automobile travel. Men planned for smoother, wider roads. They began to use concrete and other improved mate-rials for the newer highways. In addition, stronger bridges were built.

Today, our country has more than 4,000,000 miles of fine highways. Some are wide enough for six or even eight lines of cars. They are sometimes called *superhighways* or *freeways*. Some that are being paid for by charging tolls are also known as *turnpikes*. These highways often lead around a town or city or go above part of it. On them, one may drive for miles without being stopped by a traffic signal.

Look above at the picture of a modern highway. Notice the cloverleaf-like pat-tern of the roads, or *off ramps*, which lead from the main highway. They may go to a nearby town or connect with some other highway.

Though much of our travel today is on land, water transportation is also impor-tant. Suppose we learn more about it.

Travel on Water

For many hundreds of years ships carried man's heaviest loads. Indeed, transportation by water was the easiest way to carry goods long distances. It is still the easiest and cheapest way to carry heavy loads.

In early times men depended on oars, poles, and paddles to move their boats. They could also use sails when the wind blew in the right direction. Then, men learned how to tack, or sail against the wind. This meant that ships could sail to distant places without carrying oarsmen.

Later, the steam engine was invented and men began to dream of making it drive ships over water. Two American inventors who worked on this problem were John Fitch and Robert Fulton.

The first usable steamboat in our country was built by John Fitch. He was an ambitious watchmaker who lived in Philadelphia. His steamboat had six paddles on each side and a steam engine to work them. He tested his vessel on the Delaware River.

Many people stopped to watch this strange-looking boat. Some were members of the Constitutional Convention.

People could hardly believe their eyes as they saw the steamboat slowly churning up and down the Delaware. "An interesting toy," said some as they shook their heads. "But surely Fitch does not expect steam to move a boat very far."

Sometime later, however, Fitch's surprising steamboat began regular runs from Philadelphia to Trenton, New Jersey. For a time it made this twenty-five mile journey quite successfully; but one day it was wrecked. The unhappy Fitch could not raise enough money to build a new boat so he gave up. After several years, another inventor turned his attention to steam-driven ships.

Robert Fulton built an improved steamboat, the *Clermont*. One August day in 1807, Fulton's *Clermont* was ready to move up the Hudson River. It was to travel from New York City to Albany. These cities are about 150 miles apart.

A large crowd gathered to watch the *Clermont* leave. As its big paddle wheels began to turn, it crawled slowly away from the docks. Soon it was chugging along at a speed of about five miles an hour. Some onlookers cheered; but others laughed and called the boat "Fulton's Folly." "Folly" means something that is very foolish. Many men thought it fool-

A steamboat race on the Ohio.

ish for a boat to attempt a long journey without sails. But surprise was in store for them.

The *Clermont* reached Albany in thirty-two hours. On its long run, it had proved that steam could drive boats for miles. This success encouraged men to build other steamboats.

Soon, many steamboats were chugging up and down rivers. Some traveled on the Hudson and others steamed up and down the Mississippi and the Ohio. Others were used on the Great Lakes. These steamboats furnished cheap transportation for crops, lumber, and coal.

But alas! There was no waterway connecting the rich Great Lakes region with eastern cities. Pioneers needed such a water route to send their crops to markets. And New York City wanted a water route to the West. To help provide it, some leaders said, "Let us make a river. Let us dig a canal."

The Erie Canal was built. This big "ditch" connected the Hudson River with Lake Erie, as the map on this page shows. The Erie Canal was more than 360 miles long. Look at the map and trace its route. What two cities did it connect?

Building the Erie Canal took eight years. In those days men had no large machines to help them. Digging it through miles and miles of thick forests and swamps was a long tiresome job. The canal cost more than seven million dollars; but as the years went by, people realized that it was money well spent.

The Erie Canal provided a good route west to the lands around the Great Lakes. Boats on it carried tons and tons of settlers' crops to markets. Indeed, the canal brought so much new business to New

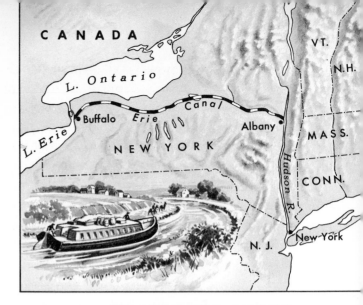

How did the Erie Canal help New York City? What two bodies of water did it connect? It is now a part of the New York State Barge Canal.

York that it soon became the largest city in the United States. At the same time, many towns and cities grew rapidly along the canal route.

Many boats traveled up and down the Erie Canal. They carried freight and passengers. They were not steamboats, however. They were slow flat-bottomed boats pulled by horses or mules walking along footpaths beside the canal.

During these years, Americans were using another kind of water transportation,—fast, graceful, sailing ships.

Handsome American sailing ships were crossing the oceans. They were sailing near and far carrying goods and passengers. Some of these vessels were called packet ships. They had earned that name because they hauled many packets, or letters. Packet ships also carried freight and some passengers. The people who paid well had comfortable quarters; but those who could afford only a small fare had to share crowded sleeping rooms.

The most famous of all American sailing ships were the *clippers*. They won their name because they clipped through the water very swiftly. They were long, handsome vessels like the one pictured on page 157. Clipper ships needed a large crew to manage their huge snowy sails.

Many clipper ships traveled back and forth to Europe. Some made the long voyage around South America and up along the Pacific coast. Clipper ships, you may remember, took many gold seekers to California during the Gold Rush. Some clippers sailed to China and other distant lands in the Orient.

By 1840, however, men were beginning to build another kind of sea-going vessel. Steamships had been used so successfully on rivers that finally men turned to them for sea travel.

Iron steamships gradually replaced wooden sailing ships. As early as 1819, a kind of steamship had crossed the Atlantic. It was named the *Savannah*, and had sails as well as a steam engine. But the *Savannah* needed its sails most of the way across the ocean. So people hooted at the idea that steam would ever work on the sea.

About twenty years later, however, an improved steamship made a remarkable voyage across the Atlantic. Then men began to realize that a steamship could be more dependable than a sailing vessel. A steamship need never worry about poor weather conditions or lack of wind. In time, many iron steamships were built.

Today, thousands of steamships travel over the sea. Some are known as *freighters*. Our freighters carry American products to nearly all the seaports of the world. They also bring back goods that we need from other countries.

Other steamships called *ocean liners* carry many passengers. One huge liner is the *France*, owned by the French. It can carry more than 2000 passengers and a crew of 1000. Our large liner, the *United States*, crossed the Atlantic in less than four days. It no longer makes the trip.

Modern ocean liners are like luxurious floating hotels. They have beautiful dining rooms and fine lounges which are furnished like elegant living rooms. They have hundreds of bedrooms as well as smaller cabins. They also have pleasant libraries, game rooms, and swimming pools. Passenger liners take people to ports in many parts of the world. Some ocean liners and many cargo ships follow routes that lead through a remarkable canal.

Tugs guide the *United States* into a berth in New York Harbor. Columbus' ships were no larger than these tugs.

343

The Panama Canal: A Water Highway Connecting Two Oceans

The Panama Canal cuts through the Isthmus of Panama. An *isthmus* is a narrow strip of land which connects two larger bodies of land.

The Isthmus of Panama joins together the continents of North America and South America. Notice this on the map on page 345. See what a narrow bridge of land it is. At its narrowest point, it is only about twenty-eight miles wide.

For hundreds of years, men dreamed of making a waterway through this isthmus.

You see, ships had to sail all the way around South America to travel from the Atlantic to the Pacific. Just think! Ships that sailed from New York to San Francisco had to travel over 11,000 miles. Such a voyage took weeks and weeks and was also dangerous. No wonder, then, that men wished for a shortcut from ocean to ocean. Finally, in the early 1900's their dream came true.

In 1914, the United States completed the Panama Canal. It was built across the middle of the isthmus through a strip of land our government rented from the country of Panama. Locate this Canal Zone on the map. Notice that it extends from the Caribbean Sea to the Pacific. The Caribbean Sea joins the Atlantic Ocean.

Building the canal was a difficult task and required years of planning and hard

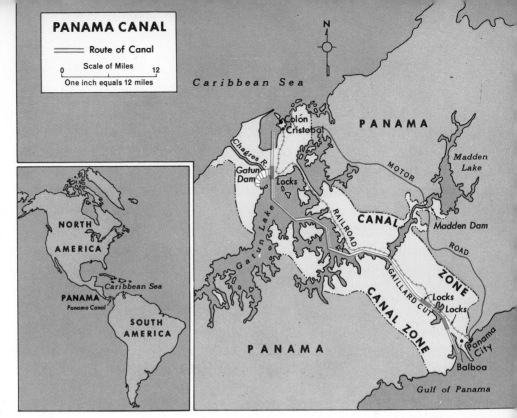

Route of Canal

Scale of Miles

0   12

One inch equals 12 miles

Find the three sets of locks on this map of the Panama Canal. The voyage from New York City to San Francisco by way of Cape Horn was about 11,000 miles. The voyage between these two cities by way of the Panama Canal is about 5,000 miles.

work. Thousands of men had a part in this. Many helped carve out the pathway for the new waterway. Some cleared the land of its jungle—the tangled growth of trees and vines often found in hot rainy tropical lowlands. Others helped to slice through hills and mountains that blocked the way.

Some workers dammed up a river to form Gatun Lake. Find it on the map.

This picture diagram shows how ships are raised in the canal locks of the Panama Canal.

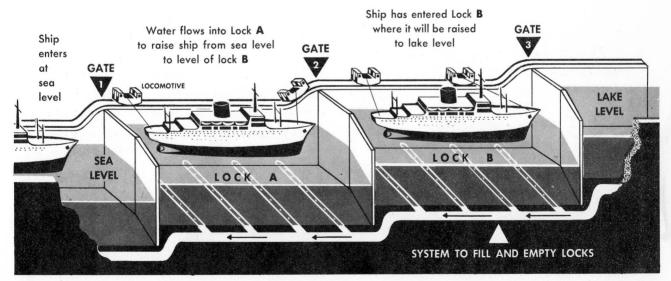

Also large numbers were employed to build the locks. The Panama Canal has three sets of locks, as the map on page 345 shows. A *canal lock* is a kind of giant water elevator. It lifts or lowers a ship to the water level of the next lock or of the waterway beyond.

You may be wondering how such a lock works. Imagine that you have a toy boat in a bathtub which contains a little water. Then you decide that you want to raise the boat. You do this by turning on the faucet and adding more water. As the water rises, your boat is lifted to a higher level. The water has acted as an elevator to raise your boat. On the other hand, you can lower your boat by letting the water out of the tub.

The canal locks are giant tubs. Each one is about 1000 feet long, 110 feet wide, and 70 feet deep. By adding or letting out water in them, ships can be raised or lowered. You can learn more about how this is done if you study the picture on page 345. This drawing shows how a ship is raised by canal locks.

This is a profile of the Panama Canal. Engineers constructed locks to raise and lower ships to and from the high lands across the center of the Isthmus of Panama. They also dammed a river to form Lake Gatun. Find this lake on the map on page 345.

"But why did they *need* locks along the Panama Canal?" you may ask.

That is a good question. The answer has to do with geography. As you have learned, the canal was dug through a range of mountains. But it was not cut through at sea level. Indeed, the middle part of the canal is eighty-five feet above the sea. To cross the Isthmus, therefore, ships must climb up to this higher level and descend on the other side. The locks are the elevators that make such a journey possible.

The United States shares the Panama Canal with many nations. Thousands of vessels pass through it every year. Among them are large passenger ships and freighters, as well as some small boats.

Each ship is charged a *toll*, or fee, to go through the canal. The amount depends on the size of the ship. A large one may pay several thousand dollars but a small one is charged only a little.

The Panama Canal has been especially valuable to the countries of North and South America. Perhaps it has helped our country most of all. It has encouraged much shipping from one coast of the United States to another. Also it has been important in defending our country. It saves the ships of our navy many days of travel between our east and west coasts.

The railroad is another important means of transportation. But of course, it takes us over land.

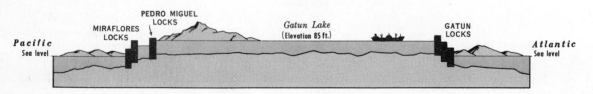

346

Travel on Rails

Men began to use rails long before the steam engine was invented. According to one story, some Englishmen were digging stones from a hillside late in the 1500's. One man said, "This stone will make the wagon very heavy. Let us put down rails for the wagons to travel on. Then the horses can pull larger loads."

The idea of using rails spread. Some men laid rails in shipyards. Others used them in coal mines and in quarries where blocks of stone were being cut. After the steam engine was invented, men thought of making steam move loads on rails.

The first successful trains were introduced in the early 1800's. One is pictured on this page. It looked much like a series of small stagecoaches. They were pulled by a little engine called a locomotive, followed by a small wood or coal fuel car.

One famous early train was the *Tom Thumb*. It ran a race with a horse-drawn coach. At first the *Tom Thumb* dashed far ahead. But it broke down, and in the end, the gray horse won.

Many people were afraid of the first trains. They were noisy and had clumsy brakes. When the train jerked to a stop, passengers were thrown to the floor.

These early trains had no cushions on their seats nor glass at their windows. Smoke, and red-hot cinders poured in on the passengers. The cinders burned holes in clothing and the black smoke covered travelers with grime. On windy days, umbrellas and hats were apt to sail out of the windows. On rainy days, train travel was even more disagreeable. Then, the leather curtains were pulled and the unlighted cars were dark and stuffy.

The first trains had no regular schedules. They made trips when they could, but did not travel at night. They had no conductors, so the engineers took the fares at the beginning of the trip.

Railroad service improved. More miles of track were laid and more trains began to run. They traveled on regular schedules. Some even dared to travel at

An exciting and dangerous ride on an early train. Why was travel as such on a train uncomfortable?

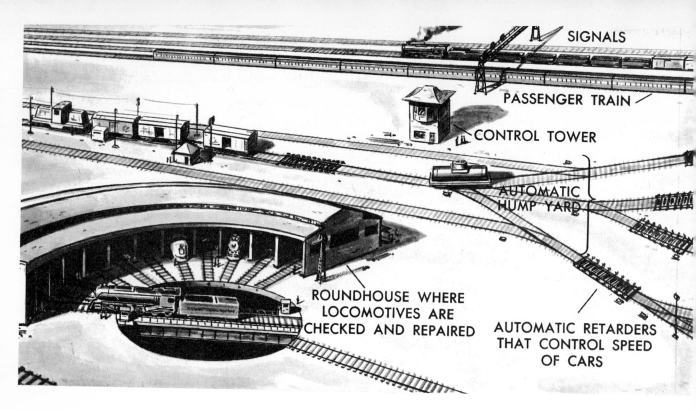

SIGNALS

PASSENGER TRAIN

CONTROL TOWER

AUTOMATIC HUMP YARD

ROUNDHOUSE WHERE LOCOMOTIVES ARE CHECKED AND REPAIRED

AUTOMATIC RETARDERS THAT CONTROL SPEED OF CARS

Railroad yards are busy places · The tracks at the top of the railroad yard are for the trains that are going through. In the hump yard trains are broken up and their cars are sorted out to make up new trains. A yardmaster in the control tower controls the switching of the cars. How many kinds of freight cars are in the hump yard?

night and provided straw-covered shelves where passengers might sleep. Later, larger and more comfortable trains were built. They were safer and faster, too, and were pulled by more powerful engines.

By 1860, hundreds of miles of railroad tracks extended across eastern United States. Some led west to St. Louis, but none reached to the Pacific coast.

In 1863, two companies started a railroad for the Far West. One began to lay tracks west from Omaha, Nebraska, and another started building eastward from Sacramento, California.

In 1869, the two railroads met at Promontory in Utah. There, an excited crowd watched a train from the East chug toward a train from the West. As the two trains stopped, facing each other, spikes were driven in the last rail. One was silver and one was gold. At last, a railroad reached across our continent.

Today, hundreds of trains thunder across our country. They speed over shining rails which stretch like narrow silver ribbons in every direction. As the map on page 349 shows, they crisscross much of our country. They go through or near most of our towns and cities.

Freight trains carry goods to all parts of our land. Some freight trains have dozens of cars. There are steel and wooden boxcars with center doors. One of these cars may carry 100,000 pounds of furniture or clothing. Or it may haul flour, canned fruits, and packaged foods.

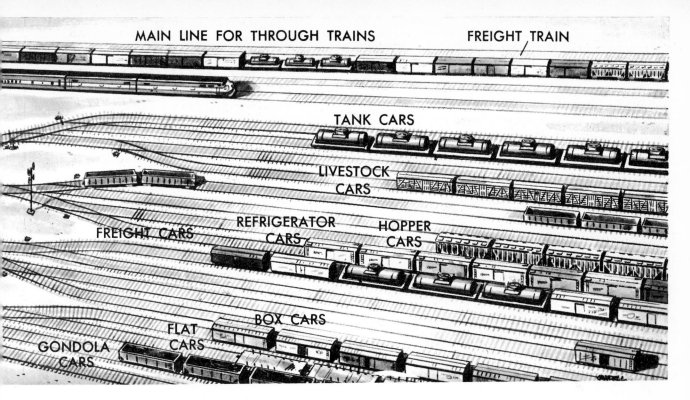

MAIN LINE FOR THROUGH TRAINS   FREIGHT TRAIN

TANK CARS

LIVESTOCK CARS

FREIGHT CARS   REFRIGERATOR CARS   HOPPER CARS

GONDOLA CARS   FLAT CARS   BOX CARS

Thousands of miles of railroads stretch across most of the United States in a vast network · This map shows the most important ones. What part of our country has the most? Can you tell why? Look at the population map on page 184 and see what part of our country is most thickly settled. Why are more railroads needed for areas where many people live?

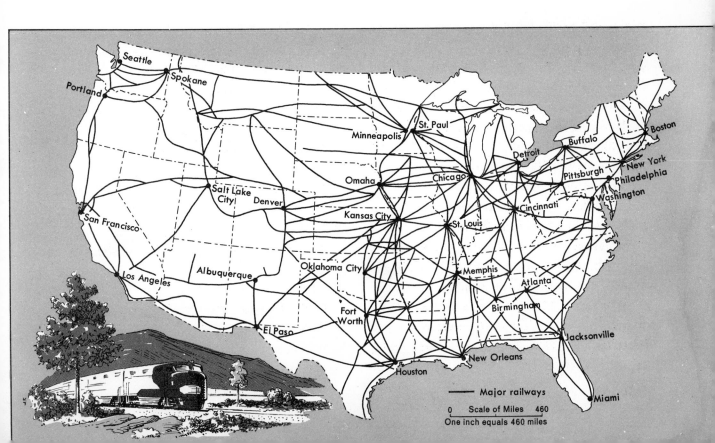

Seattle • Spokane • Portland • Minneapolis • St. Paul • Detroit • Buffalo • Boston • Omaha • Chicago • Pittsburgh • New York • Philadelphia • Salt Lake City • Denver • Cincinnati • Washington • San Francisco • Kansas City • St. Louis • Los Angeles • Albuquerque • Oklahoma City • Memphis • Atlanta • Fort Worth • Birmingham • El Paso • Jacksonville • New Orleans • Miami • Houston

—— Major railways

0   Scale of Miles   460
One inch equals 460 miles

Flatcars are open platforms on wheels and move such freight as lumber, logs, and heavy machinery. Tank cars carry gasoline and oil, and refrigerator cars are traveling refrigerators. They keep meats, milk, fruits, and vegetables fresh on the way to distant markets.

Special stock cars have feed and water troughs and carry cattle, sheep, and hogs to meat-packing houses. Gondola cars move coal, ores, and other resources from mines. A freight train usually has an end car called a caboose. It serves as office and headquarters for the train crew.

Streamliners are our newest and fastest trains. Many are pulled by giant diesel-electric locomotives which manufacture their own electricity. Streamliners are usually made of steel and aluminum.

Modern trains are air-conditioned. They are cool in summer and warm in winter. They have dining cars where meals are served. Pullman cars have seats which can be made into beds. Most passenger trains today are a part of our country's Amtrak system. *Am* is for American, *tr* for transportation and *ck* for track.

Streetcars and subways are the trains of the city. The first streetcars were used more than a hundred years ago. They were small coaches pulled on rails by horses. Modern streetcars are run by electricity. Today most streetcars have been replaced by busses.

Subways are electric trains which run through tunnels built under the ground. One of the most famous subways serves New York City. The newest is in the San Francisco area. Subways are so expensive to build that only the largest cities can afford them.

Other Kinds of Travel on Land

Bicycles: Old and New. Today more bicycles than automobiles are made. In the United States, nearly 100,000,000 people ride bicycles. Streets in many cities are now marked with bikeways. Parks also have bike trails.

The earliest bicycles were invented in Europe. They were heavy and clumsy and had no pedals or chains. The rider pushed himself along with his feet. These bicycles had iron tires and no springs so they were very uncomfortable. Some people called them "boneshakers."

Soon, a bicycle with pedals was introduced. Its front wheel was about five feet high, but its back wheel was very small. The rider's seat was high over the front wheel. It took real skill to stay on it.

Later on, men developed the "safety" bicycle. It had good brakes and rubber tires, as well as a comfortable spring "saddle" seat. The bicycles of today are improved "safety" bicycles.

In the late 1800's, people heard about a new kind of transportation, the "horseless carriage." It was the "grandfather" of our modern automobile.

From horseless carriages to modern automobiles. After the invention of the steam engine, men tried to move carriages by steam. But steam-driven carriages were large and clumsy and were not successful.

Then a gasoline engine was invented. It could run a horseless carriage. As the years passed, such a carriage became known as an "automobile." The word *automobile* means something that runs by itself.

Early in the 1900's, several companies in Detroit began to make automobiles. But only a few people could afford them.

Riding in an early automobile was a real adventure. The auto was started by turning a crank outside on the front of the car. As the engine coughed and wheezed, the driver jumped into the car and moved handles and pedals. This sent the roaring auto on its way with a jerk. Once started, it could sometimes travel at the frightening speed of twenty miles an hour.

Most roads were rough and sometimes shook automobiles so hard that they broke down. Then people would shout, "Get a horse! A horse will go when you want him to."

The roads were often dusty. The early automobiles had no glass windows or windshields, as you can tell by looking at the picture at the right. People protected themselves from the dust and wind as best they could. The driver usually wore special glasses, or goggles, to protect his eyes. Women wore large hats tied down with long veils and coats called "dusters."

In time, thousands of people could afford automobiles. This was because companies developed a better and cheaper way of making them. Automobile parts were made by machines and put together on an assembly line.

Millions of cars, buses, and trucks crowd our streets and highways. We are, indeed, "a nation on wheels."

Trucks are the workhorses of the automobile family. There are specially built trucks to perform every kind of hauling job. There are refrigerated trucks for carrying food and giant vans for moving furniture. Cattle trucks! Gasoline tankers! Heavy trucks for hauling rock or gravel! What others can you name?

Only a small number of our families own trucks. But about three-fourths of us have one or more automobiles. We depend on our cars to take us to work and on vacation trips. We drive them to shopping centers and to baseball games and restaurants.

Automobiles use gasoline. Large cars may need a gallon of gasoline for every eight or ten miles they travel. Small cars may go twenty or more miles on a gallon.

Because our population is increasing, there are more people to use cars. So more gasoline is needed. But we are running short of this energy fuel. How can we solve this problem. What can each of us do?

An early automobile gets stuck in a deep mud puddle.

The Wright's airplane flies!

Travel by Air

Wanted: Wings! An old legend tells us how man first tried to fly. Long ago, a skilled artist named Daedalus, and his young son, Icarus, were thrown into an island prison. But they escaped from the prison and then sought a way to leave the island.

"Perhaps we could fly," said Daedalus. He studied the wings of birds and gathered many feathers. Next, the two made wings for themselves and fastened them on with wax. Then they started off. Daedalus was able to fly to another island. But Icarus sailed up so high that the hot sun melted the wax from his wings. He plunged into the sea.

Of course this is just a story. Actually, men did not fly for hundreds of years after the days of this legend. But, in time, inventors in Europe and the United States began to experiment with ways to fly. The hard work and testing of these men helped two clever and ambitious Americans. They were the Wright brothers. Early in the 1900's the Wright brothers were able to build a "flying machine."

The Wright brothers proved that men could fly. They built an airplane that looked something like a large box kite with a gasoline motor in it. At the left is a picture of it. Notice how very different it was from the planes which we use today. It had only one small motor. Its pilot had to lie flat on the lower wing which held that motor.

The Wright brothers first flew their plane on a windy December day in 1903. They tested it above the sand dunes of Kitty Hawk, North Carolina. They had invited many people to watch their flight. But nearly everyone thought it was just a foolish stunt and only a few bothered to go.

However, this "foolish stunt" made Wilbur and Orville Wright famous. Their airplane flew! It rose ten feet and moved ahead for more than a hundred feet before it came to rest on the ground. It had stayed in the air twelve seconds. This was the first successful flight in a motor-driven plane.

In time, thousands of airplanes were built. More and more people became interested in this new way of travel. Inventors in both the United States and Europe helped to improve airplanes. Some men started companies for building them, and brave pilots tested them over land and sea. Airline companies were organized to carry passengers and mail. So the *aviation* industry was born.

Today, many planes are fast and powerful. The largest ones carry dozens of passengers, mail, and some freight. They fly well-planned routes on regular schedules, day and night. Some roar across our country and some speed to other lands. Airlines now link every continent but Antarctica. Study the map on page 355 and locate some main routes.

Large planes may have a crew of five or more specially-trained people. The pilot and co-pilot are in charge of a flight. They guide their plane by watching and working the proper dials and controls. Women called stewardesses serve meals and help passengers in many other ways.

Some planes perform special jobs. They may deliver mail, medicines, and other supplies to areas where they are needed. Some rush firefighters to burning forests. Some skim just above the ground to plant certain crops or dust some with insect-killing powder. Others are small planes used by business men or doctors, perhaps. And thousands of specially built planes are used by our air forces. Among these are the very fast jet planes.

A helicopter to the rescue!

A helicopter is a special kind of "flying machine." It is sometimes called a "whirlie" because its blades whirl round and round. A helicopter has no wings and usually travels less than a hundred miles an hour. But it is a very useful machine. It can fly backwards and forwards and straight up and down. So, it can land on a vacant lot or the flat roof of a large building. Furthermore, it can "stand," or hover, in the air for a short time. Some helicopters are used for rescuing people in "hard to get at" places. Others carry mail and passengers on short hops of a few miles. Some haul passengers to the large airports.

Loading a cargo plane · Compare it with the airplane on the opposite page.

Our country has thousands of airports and landing fields. One or more can be found in or near almost every city. Large cities have enormous ones with many special buildings.

An airport is shown in the picture on this page. Notice how it is crisscrossed with wide, paved runways. They extend in different directions so that planes can take off and land into the wind. Runways are marked with boundary lights to help the pilot land safely at night. But the "brain" of the airport is the control tower. Find it in the picture.

The control tower is a lookout for directing planes which are leaving and arriving. The men in the tower direct all the airplane traffic on the ground and in the air near the airport.

Before a pilot comes in to land, he calls the control tower on his radio. Then he learns what the weather is like at the airport, when he may land, and on what runway. *Radar* is often used to guide a plane to a safe landing, particularly in bad weather.

Our transportation system is very important to us. It helps us to move goods quickly and easily from one place to another. It delivers farm products and raw materials to the cities and factories. It carries manufactured goods to shops and stores. It also helps us to trade with other countries.

And of course, our transportation system makes it possible for us to travel. Because of it, we can go quickly and easily from one place to another. Another thing, it provides millions of jobs for our people.

Equally important to us are our ways of keeping in touch with one another. We call this *communication*. We shall learn about communication in the next chapter.

An airport covers a large area. Why? Runways used by jets may be more than two miles long. Find the control tower.

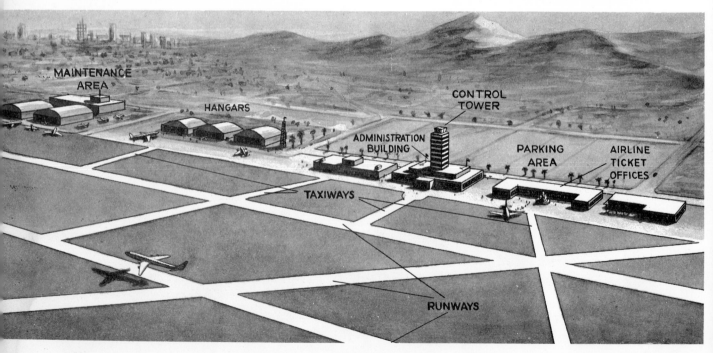

354

As you look down on the "top of the world," notice how air routes connect our country with faraway places. Such routes leap over continents and oceans to follow the shortest routes possible from city to city. These shortest routes are known as GREAT CIRCLE ROUTES.

Some Questions about This Story

1. How did the early colonists travel?

2. What are corduroy roads? toll roads? macadam roads? What kinds of highways do we have today?

3. What kinds of ships sailed the seas a hundred years ago?

4. How are modern trains different from those of a century ago?

5. What improvements have been made in automobiles during the past forty years?

6. How did the Wright brothers help to conquer the air?

7. Why is the Panama Canal important to the United States?

Yes or No? You Decide

Write the numbers 1 to 13 on a paper. Read the sentences below. If a statement is true, write *yes* after its number. If it is not true, write *no* after its number.

1. The early colonists found roads leading through the wilderness.

2. John Fitch built the first American steamship.

3. The *Clermont* proved that steam could move boats.

4. The Clippers were iron steamships.

5. The United States built the Panama Canal.

6. The railroad connecting the East and the West was finished in 1869.

7. Some freight trains are a mile long.

8. Subways are city trains.

9. "Boneshakers" were much like our bicycles of today.

10. Some of the first automobiles were built in Detroit.

11. The Wright brothers were pioneers in the aviation industry.

12. Helicopters can fly long distances.

13. Airplanes have helped to make all nations our near neighbors.

Some Questions to Think About

1. How can good roads help a country?

2. Try to imagine what our country would be like without railroads or automobiles. How would your life be different without them?

3. How have airplanes changed our ways of living? How have they helped us?

4. Why do we say that airplanes make the world seem smaller?

5. Why are we running short of energy fuel? What are some ways we can be more saving of it?

6. Should another canal be built across some other part of Central America someday? Give reasons for your answer.

Some Other Things to Do

1. Sketch as many different road signs as you can and tell what each means.

2. Discuss "road courtesy" with your class. Decide what makes a good automobile driver.

List things good drivers remember.

3. Plan an exhibit of model airplanes, automobiles, and trains.

4. If you live near a harbor, try to visit it. Learn what cargoes are being loaded and unloaded. Share what you learn with your class.

5. Find out what is being done to provide new sources of energy fuel in our country. Share what you learn with your class.

Using Pictures

Use pictures to help you compare *our* ways of transportation with some earlier ways. Study the pictures in this chapter and others which you have collected.

Talk over these comparisons in class. Then plan a mural to show some of them. The title of it might be *Yesterday and Today in Transportation.*

Fun with Maps

1. Bring to school a highway map which shows your community. Tell in what ways this map is something like the Town Map on page 255. Use the letters and numbers on the highway map to locate some places.

2. Tell what the map on page 349 shows and do the things asked in its legend. Use the scale of miles on this map to help you measure the distance by railroad from: (a) Cincinnati to Memphis, (b) Denver to Fort Worth, (c) Houston to Albuquerque, (d) Salt Lake City to Los Angeles, (e) San Francisco to Portland.

3. Turn to the global map on page 434 and find the Isthmus of Panama.

a. Is it north or south of the equator?

b. Is it in the low, middle, or high latitudes?

c. What kind of climate could you expect to find in this region?

20 · Communication: How We Keep in Touch with One Another

What Is Communication?

Communication means sending and receiving messages. It includes all the ways we have of telling things to each other. You use some of these ways at school. When you say hello, you are using a spoken word to communicate. When you write a story, you are putting words on paper to communicate with your teacher, perhaps. If you wave good-by, or nod your head, you are communicating with gestures.

When you read a book, you are receiving messages from printed words. Through them, the author is telling you a story and thus communicating with you.

Talking, writing, and telling a story on a printed page are old ways of communication. They have been used for many centuries. But we also have some remarkable new ways of keeping in touch with others. We can send messages by fast air mail, or by telephone, or telegraph. We can even send and receive messages and information by radio and television.

Man has not always had our remarkable new means of communication. In the earliest days of the colonies, there was scarcely any way to get the news. Of course there were no radios or television, nor even any telephones or telegraph, or daily newspapers. There was not even a dependable mail system.

An old and a new way of communicating.

Sending Messages by Mail

The earliest colonists sent mail any way they could. Ships brought letters from England. But there was no satisfactory plan of sending mail from one colony to another, or even from one village to another. So a letter was delayed sometimes a month or more as the following story explains.

In 1650 the Williams family lived in a little Connecticut settlement. One afternoon in the spring, Mrs. Patience Williams finished writing a letter to her sister whose home was fifty miles to the southwest.

Then she said to her daughter, Joy, "I cannot think how to send this. Your father is busy with the planting. Even if he could leave, I would fear for him on the long trail through the forests."

Postriders carried mail from one town to another in the Thirteen Colonies.

"There'll be less danger when several men can ride south together," said Joy.

"True," replied her mother. "I hear that Postmaster Franklin has plans to improve the mail service. I must not fret. The message to my sister can wait for a time."

A week passed! Four weeks! Six weeks! Still the letter lay on the mantle above the fireplace. Then one day a traveler and several hunters were leaving for the southwest. They agreed to carry the letter to Delight Smith.

As was the custom, Mrs. Williams' letter was sent "collect." To pay for his trouble, a traveler usually collected a small amount of money from the person who received the letter. The sender felt more certain of delivery if the money was paid at the end of the journey.

Sometimes, a traveler carried a letter part of the way and left it at a village to be carried on by another traveler. To make sure that an important letter arrived, several copies were made and sent at different times. Then surely one copy would be delivered. This way of sending mail was not dependable, of course. People were glad when, later on, better arrangements were made.

By 1700, many colonies had begun some kind of mail service. In most towns, the mail was left at a central place called the *post*, or *post office*. Sometimes this place was in a home or in the corner of an inn.

Travelers still carried some of the mail to and from smaller settlements. But men were hired specially to take it from one large town to another. They rode horses and were called postriders. You can see a postrider in the picture on this page.

Postriders faced many dangers. They had to ride through dark forests and over rough trails. They braved all kinds of weather. Pouring rains! Icy winds! Blinding snowstorms! And the heat of summer!

As the years passed, some colonial leaders insisted that a better mail system was necessary. One such man was Benjamin Franklin. He was Philadelphia's leading citizen and its postmaster for a time.

Franklin did much to improve the mail system in the colonies. He arranged for three mail trips a week between Philadelphia and New York. He also encouraged faster handling of the mail between Boston and Philadelphia. He started the plan of sending newspapers through the mail. And he found ways to help pay for sending mail.

In colonial days, the cost of sending a letter depended on how far it was going and how much it weighed. It cost about forty cents to send a letter from Boston to Philadelphia. But only about eighteen cents was charged for a letter traveling from New York to Philadelphia. Why was there this difference? If you locate these cities on the map on page 504, you can tell. Which two are farther apart?

Franklin helped people to realize that mail should be rushed on its way quickly and safely. As the mail system was improved, more people exchanged letters. This helped the colonists to know and understand each other better.

Carrying the mail in the new United States was a huge job. In those days, transportation was slow and there were few good roads. Furthermore, thousands of people had moved west to settle frontiers, remember. These areas were difficult for mail to reach.

In time, stagecoaches carried much mail over the Cumberland Road. Steamboats hauled some on the rivers and along the Great Lakes. Then, by 1840, railroads were carrying a large share.

Sending mail to the far West was a big problem for a long time. No railroad reached across this vast part of our country until 1869, as you may recall. So people had to depend on ships or stagecoaches for hauling mail. Neither of these ways was very satisfactory.

Ordinary sailing ships required six months or more to make the journey around South America. Clipper ships sometimes made this voyage in three months. But they charged high prices.

A Pony Express rider reaches a station where he will change horses.

The journey overland was made by stagecoach. However, the route was long and dangerous. It led west across wide sweeps of lonely plains. It wound through high mountains and across dry empty deserts. There were weeks of raw, bitterly cold weather and other weeks of burning hot days. Sometimes there were prairie fires and buffalo stampedes! There were bands of angry Indians and sometimes desperate robbers hiding along the way. So only the bravest men had the courage to drive stagecoaches.

In 1860, the Pony Express runs began. Its route was two thousand miles long and reached from St. Joseph, Missouri, to San Francisco, California. Eighty daring young riders and five hundred swift ponies were used for this mail service. Ponies could travel much faster than stagecoaches.

A noisy send-off was given the first Pony Express riders as they sped away. One left from San Francisco and the other from St. Joseph. Bells rang joyously and cannon boomed as the people cheered loudly. The people in both towns were just as excited about ten days later. Then the Pony Express riders were arriving from the other end of the route. In San Francisco a parade and bands honored the rider. One woman welcomed him by placing her own fancy bonnet on his pony's head.

The Pony Express was a kind of relay race, run from one station to another. The stations were from ten to fifteen miles apart. A rider galloped swiftly to a station. There he mounted a fresh pony and tossed the mail bags over its back. Each man covered several stations or a distance of about seventy-five miles. At the end of his run, a weary rider stopped to rest and a fresh one raced on.

The long trip across the West took the Pony Express about ten days. The fastest trip ever made was covered in about eight days. That time, the riders carried a copy of Lincoln's First Inaugural Address as well as many letters.

Sending a letter by express was very expensive. Even the thinnest one cost as much as five dollars. Still, the Pony Express lost money for its owners. It was given up in 1861 when California was connected to the East by a new way to exchange messages, the telegraph. After 1869, the transcontinental railroad carried mail west.

The early 1900's brought many changes in transportation and each one helped to speed up mail service. Today, we can boast of a very fine mail system.

Our mail today. Fast trains, trucks, and airplanes haul mail from place to place. Indeed, it can be sent to any small village in our land as well as to our big cities. It can be carried to distant mountain resorts and to lonely farms. Actually, there is scarcely an area in our whole country without some regular service.

Taking care of the mail is a tremendous job. So of course it provides employment for large numbers of people. The men who deliver the mail in cities usually wear blue-gray uniforms and are called postmen. Those who carry the mail in farm areas are known as rural, or country, mail carriers. They place mail in boxes that stand near the edge of the road.

Each home in the country has a box on the main road nearest to it. The delivery service is known as R.F.D. or Rural Free Delivery. When a letter is being

sent to the country, the letters R.F.D. and a special route number are usually on the envelope.

Postage stamps help pay for sending mail. Some kind of postage stamps are now in use in nearly every country in the world. They have been used in our country for over a hundred years.

A stamp for sending an ordinary letter costs just a few cents. Such a stamp allows a letter to take a train ride to any place in the United States. An "air mail" letter is rushed on its way by plane. How much does its postage cost? Still more expensive stamps are used on special kinds of letters and packages.

Our postage stamps are printed by a department of the Government, the Bureau of Engraving and Printing. Each stamp has a picture on it. Some stamps bear the pictures of great statesmen, such as Washington or Jefferson. Others have pictures of great events or interesting places. Stamps are interesting to study and are collected by many people.

Our mail service has made it possible for millions of people to communicate with each other. Newspapers provide another important means for keeping in touch with people and events.

From Town Crier to Modern Newspapers

The town crier "broadcast" the news in some early colonial villages. He walked about ringing a bell and shouting important information. After dark, he served as a kind of watchman. For instance, one might hear him singing out, "Ten o'clock and all's well." When there was special news, he added that to his call.

Often during the Revolutionary War, there was exciting news to announce. The happiest news of all, perhaps, was that called out by one crier at three o'clock in the morning. He wakened people out of a sound sleep, shouting, "Cornwallis has surrendered to General Washington and all is well."

In a small way, town criers took the place of a daily newspaper. But, as villages grew into larger towns, a few colonists began to publish newspapers.

Franklin's printing shop looked much like this. The man in the back is working hard to turn the screw which causes the paper to be pressed against the inked type.

By the early 1700's, some newspapers were being printed in the colonies. The first successful paper was the *Boston News Letter*, begun in 1704. It had four pages of articles in small print.

Later, another newspaper was started by Benjamin Franklin's brother. Young Ben was put to work in the print shop. The picture above shows what such a shop was like. Compare it with the modern one pictured on the opposite page.

Young Franklin liked being a printer but enjoyed even more writing for the paper. Still, he wanted to keep this fact a secret. So he signed his articles with a woman's name, Mrs. Silence Dogood.

A few years later, Franklin began to publish a newspaper of his own in Philadelphia. In it he wrote many articles about Philadelphia's problems. Often, he

signed a made-up name so he could complain freely about the rough streets, lack of fire protection, and poor mail systems. He also suggested ways to solve these problems. His stories were clever and interested many people. Through his paper, Franklin did much to improve conditions in Philadelphia. But printing in Franklin's day was not easy. The press was operated by hand, so turning out the newspaper took a long time.

The first *daily* newspaper in America was started in Philadelphia in 1774. But, like Franklin's paper, it contained more articles about problems than news stories. Word of news traveled very slowly in those days. Can you think why?

Today, many daily newspapers are printed in our country. A daily paper in a large city may have from twenty-four to fifty pages. Its front page usually contains the most important state and national news as well as news about other countries. Such a newspaper also prints much news about its community as well as sports stories, comics, radio and television news, and special articles. Its editorials are often about important problems.

Every newspaper fills much space with advertising. Merchants and other businessmen pay well to advertise what they have to sell. This payment helps a newspaper pay for the very latest equipment and well-trained people for obtaining the news.

A daily newspaper usually employs many men and women. Some work in its business office and some run its presses. Others distribute and sell the newspaper. But perhaps the most fascinating work is done by its reporters and photographers. They gather and write news stories and take its "news" pictures. Some reporters and photographers travel to distant parts of the world to obtain important news. They send back some news over telegraph wires. How did this wonderful means of communication begin?

Sending Messages by Wire

The telegraph was invented by Samuel Morse. Morse had already won fame as an American artist and had sailed to Europe for further study. While he was in Europe, he became interested in electricity. One day, as he was returning home on board ship, he and several friends began to discuss electricity. Morse suggested that messages might be sent over wires by means of an electric current. But his fellow passengers shook their heads. "Impossible!" declared one.

"Not at all!" insisted Morse. "I'll show you how it could be done." Then he made drawings of a machine for sending messages by electricity—a telegraph.

A huge modern press.

When Morse arrived home, he decided to give up his career as an artist. Instead, he turned to making a telegraph. He rented a small shop. Because he had little money, this workshop also became his home. In one corner was a stove where he could cook his own meals. In another corner was his sleeping cot.

Morse sometimes went hungry to save money for the materials he needed. But he also used ordinary materials that could be gathered easily—pieces of cotton thread, parts of old clocks, and frames that he had once used for paintings.

This very determined inventor worked month after month and year after year. Often he was discouraged and no wonder! His closest friends scolded him for wasting so much time on a "foolish dream." Still, Morse would not give up.

At last, the clumsy telegraph was finished. Then Morse asked a friend to help him test it. Together, the two men strung a long wire through the shop. They

Morse taps the first message to be sent over telegraph wires.

placed the sending set in one corner and the receiving set as far away as possible. Then Morse tapped out a message that traveled over the long wire.

"Hurrah! Your message came through clearly!" the friend exclaimed joyously.

"Very good!" answered Morse. "Now I must persuade others that this telegraph will work!"

Morse showed his invention to many friends. Then, he took it to Washington, D.C., to explain it to Government leaders. He hoped that Congress would agree to build a telegraph line from Washington to Baltimore. This was a distance of about forty miles. Messages sent over such a line surely would prove that the telegraph was a success and could be useful to our country.

At Washington, some government leaders were interested in the new invention. But others made fun of the mysterious equipment. They doubted that it would actually work. So the discouraged inventor returned home.

Several years passed. Then one day Morse heard that Congress was ready to discuss his telegraph. He hurried to Washington with high hopes. Still, once again men shook their heads. "We cannot consider your invention yet," they said. Months passed and finally Morse gave up and made plans to return home.

The next morning, though, a knock brought surprising news. At Morse's door stood young Annie Ellsworth, the daughter of an old friend. "Father has sent me to tell you something wonderful," she said as her eyes sparkled. "Late last night, at Congress's last meeting it agreed to build a telegraph line. Father was there and heard all about it."

Morse could hardly believe his ears. This was the most thrilling news he had ever heard. He asked Annie to choose the first message to be sent over the wires. She selected a verse from the Bible, "What hath God wrought?"

In May, 1844, crowds gathered at the Capitol in Washington to watch Morse tap out his first telegraph message. Would you like to know how this was done?

An electric current was traveling through the wire between Washington and Baltimore. By tapping on a key at one end of the wire, Morse caused a bar at the other end to make a clicking sound. He had worked out signals for each letter of the alphabet. These signals are known as the *Morse Code*. Using this code, Morse tapped out his message, as the picture on page 364 shows.

Morse's helper in Baltimore changed the tapped code into letters and then into the words, "What hath God wrought?" So the people soon realized that the telegraph worked.

As the years went by, Morse and other men made many improvements on the telegraph. Before long, telegraph wires were strung from city to city in the east-ern part of our country. Indeed, by 1861, a line reached all the way to the Pacific coast. Fortunately, Morse lived to see his invention serving people in many ways.

The telegraph is very important to us. It carries messages to millions of people every day. It brings the latest news from near and far. It controls the movement of trains and so helps prevent accidents. It helps people in businesses.

Today, our country has a network of more than 2,000,000 miles of telegraph wires. They extend in every direction. They connect nearly every town and city of any size. Because they can carry messages so speedily to all parts of our land, they help to bind our people together.

Samuel Morse suggested that messages could also be sent across the Atlantic Ocean by underwater cable. Such a cable could be specially made to protect the wires from salt water. A wealthy American became interested in this idea.

Cyrus Field and the message-carrying cable. Field was a paper manufacturer. In 1857, he made plans to lay a

How the Atlantic Cable was laid.

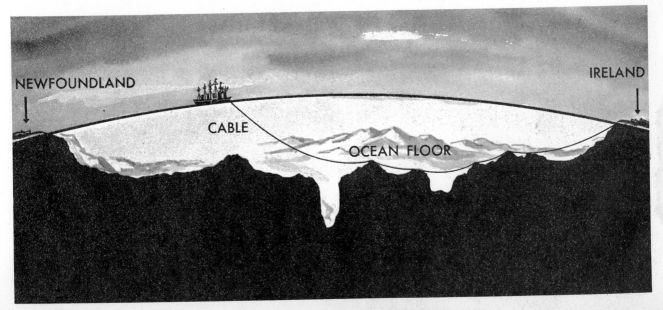

NEWFOUNDLAND

IRELAND

CABLE

OCEAN FLOOR

heavy telegraph line, or *cable*, across the floor of the Atlantic Ocean. It was to connect Newfoundland and Ireland. Find them on the map on pages 188 and 189.

Field and his men began to lay the cable from Ireland. Sailing slowly west across the Atlantic, they dropped the cable to the ocean floor. As the picture on page 365 shows, the ocean floor has plains, mountains, and valleys.

At first the laying of the cable went very well. But four hundred miles out at sea, the valuable line broke and sank. Still, Field was not discouraged, and soon tried again. But there were more failures. Then people said, "You are wasting time and money! A cable just can't be laid across an ocean!" Still Cyrus Field would not give up. Finally, after nine years, he was successful.

This cable across the Atlantic was more than 2000 miles long. It was made of copper wires woven together. They had been soaked in oil, pitch, and wax and covered with waterproof material.

Bell and Watson worked month after month trying to make a telephone.

This was the first cable to be laid across an ocean. But today there are more than 400,000 miles of such cables. They connect our country with most of the important seaports of the world.

About thirty years after the telegraph was invented, another kind of remarkable communication was developed. Another inventor found a way to talk over wires.

Alexander Graham Bell invented the telephone. He was born in Scotland where his father taught deaf people how to speak. Bell became a teacher of the deaf in Boston, Massachusetts. During his spare time, young Bell learned all he could about how the voice makes sounds and how the ears hear. These studies helped him become interested in making an instrument that would send a voice by wire across distances. We call this instrument a telephone. The word, telephone, means "speak from afar."

Bell and a friend, Thomas Watson, spent many months working on this telephone. Finally it was ready to test. He and his friend strung wire from Watson's workbench in the basement to Bell's study, two floors above. Then Bell talked over the telephone. But alas! Watson could not understand what the inventor said.

The inventor and his friend were disappointed but they did not give up. Instead, they worked harder than ever.

Then one day when Watson was busy in the basement, Bell called over the transmitter, "Mr. Watson, come here! I want you!"

The surprised Watson ran up the stairs, shouting, "I heard you! I heard you!" Indeed, on that March evening in 1876, Watson had heard the first message ever sent over a telephone successfully.

In time, Bell's telephone won many friends. In 1876, Bell took his invention to Philadelphia to show it off at a World's Fair. This fair was held to celebrate a hundred years of our country's independence. Bell thought that many visitors would be interested in his telephone. But he was sadly mistaken. Those who did examine it considered it just an amusing toy.

Then one afternoon, a dignified dark-eyed stranger stepped up. He was the Emperor of Brazil. "What is this?" he inquired of Bell.

"A telephone, sir," answered Bell. Then he began to explain how his invention worked. "If you will listen on this wire, I'll speak into the transmitter."

When the Emperor heard Bell's voice over the telephone, he was amazed. "It talks! It talks!" he exclaimed. Then others crowded around. From that moment on, many people began to ask questions about the strange new invention. Soon, there were even long reports about it in the newspapers.

Bell was not entirely satisfied with his telephone, however. He and other inventors continued to make improvements on it. Meanwhile, he and several friends formed the Bell Telephone Company to make telephones and build telephone lines. Soon, dozens of telephone lines were put up over our country. Before long, many telephones were being installed in homes and offices. By 1915, a line reached all the way to the Pacific coast.

Today, the telephone is very important to our way of life. We depend on it to help run our homes and businesses. It calls policemen, firemen, and doctors when we need them. It works day and night in the services of our government. It helps us to keep in touch with people near and far.

The telephone and the telegraph required wires to carry voices and messages. Some scientists believed, however, that messages could also be sent through the air without wires.

Sending Messages without Wires

The wireless telegraph and the wireless telephone. In the 1890's, a young Italian, Guglielmo Marconi, found a way to send messages without using wires. He flashed the dots and dashes of the Morse code through the air. He called his invention the wireless telegraph.

After several years, Marconi could flash wireless messages all the way across the Atlantic, from England to Newfoundland.

The wireless telegraph has proved very valuable to ships at sea. Many a ship has sent out an S.O.S., or distress signal, by wireless. In this way, it has summoned help.

A wireless telephone was also developed. Many men helped us to have it. One who worked on it was Lee de Forest. He invented a kind of tube which helped to send a person's voice or music long distances without using wires.

The wireless telephone is called the radiophone. It can send messages through the air by means of electrical waves, or radio. The radiophone can be used to talk to moving trains, to ships at sea, and to airplanes. And it is successful across whole continents and oceans.

As time passed, men made many improvements in the wireless telegraph and radiophone. They also worked on ideas which led to the development of our modern radio.

By 1920, the radio was coming into use. Lee de Forest is sometimes called the "father of radio." It was his special kind of tube that first made it possible to broadcast voices and music. However, no one man invented the radio. It was the result of a series of inventions, the work of many different scientists.

The first radio sets looked like queer little boxes. Each one had a long wire attached to it. Also, there was a headphone which the listener clamped over his ears in order to hear a program.

Mary's family owned one of these early radio sets. Mary and her sisters and brother called it a magic box. And indeed it was! Unfortunately, Mary was never able to listen to an entire program. You see, she had to share the headphones with other members of her family. You can imagine how disturbing it was to give up the headphones in the middle of an exciting broadcast. No wonder she wished someone would invent a better magic box.

As time went on, Mary's wish came true. She is grown up and married, now, and has four children of her own. But none of them depend on headphones to hear a broadcast. Like you, they simply turn on a dial. Then a program can be heard as clearly as if it were produced in their home.

Radios bring us news, weather reports, other valuable information, and entertainment. Indeed, the radio has become a powerful means of communication, as has its cousin, television.

Television is our newest means of communication. Television cameras and sound equipment telecast, or send out, pictures at the same time they send sound. So, on our television sets, we can see and hear programs at the same time, as you know.

By watching our television screens, we can learn to cook, or to draw, or to play some game. We can see sports events such as football and baseball games as they are happening, or later from films. Television brings us pictures and reports of news events. It entertains us with plays, movies, concerts, and other kinds of interesting programs. Like a magic carpet, television whisks us off to adventures everywhere.

Many television sets bring us only black and white pictures. But some programs are telecast in color. People who own color sets can see "colored" television in their homes. Today, many families own "color" television sets.

There are not as many television stations as radio stations. But our largest cities have a number of channels. What television channels can you get on your set?

Television has done a great deal to help people learn about and understand other people. And, like the radio, television is having so much influence on us that it is changing many ways of living.

In 1962, men found a thrilling new way to send television programs. They put Telstar to work.

Telstar was our first communications satellite. This unmanned satellite was a kind of radio-and-television station in space. It could send messages and pictures thousands of miles to powerful ground stations. It could also receive them.

Telstar's first program was sent from the United States to Europe. It showed pictures of Americans at work and a minute of a Chicago baseball game. It included a short visit with our President. This program lasted only seventeen minutes. But it proved that man-made satellites could flash clear sounds and pictures long distances.

Several communications satellites work for us in space today. They and their helping ground-stations link us with about fifty countries. And they keep us in touch with our space explorers and pioneers.

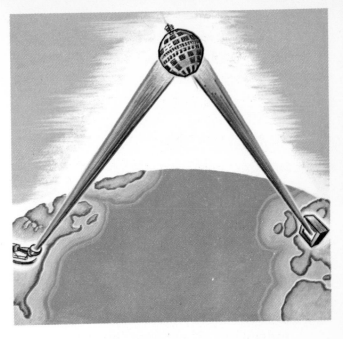

This diagram shows Telstar, our communications satellite, sending television signals to Europe.

These satellites made it possible for astronauts and ground engineers to talk to each other. They brought us pictures of the astronauts exploring on the moon. They flashed views of the Skylab pioneers at work.

We have a remarkable system of communication. It provides up-to-the-minute news of events in our country, around the world, and even in Space.

Some Study Questions

1. What is communication? What means of communication do we have that the colonists did not have?

2. In what ways has mail been carried in our country? What is air mail?

3. What is postage? Why must we pay it?

Who prints our postage stamps?

4. How are our newspapers different from the one Franklin published?

5. Who invented the telegraph? In what ways does the telegraph help us?

6. Who invented the telephone? How does it help us today?

7. What is a submarine cable? How has it improved communication?

369

8. What kinds of wireless communication do we have? How do radio and television serve us?

Test Yourself

The following sentences are incomplete. Write the sentence numbers, 1 to 12. After each number copy from the list which follows the word, words, or dates needed to complete the sentence correctly.

1. By __?__ many colonies had begun to hire men to carry the mail.

2. The __?__ are now the chief carriers of mail in the United States.

3. The Pony Express began to carry mail in __?__.

4. The Pony Express carried mail from St. Joseph to __?__.

5. Mail delivered to rural communities is addressed __?__.

6. The town __?__ used to spread the news long ago.

7. __?__ invented the telegraph.

8. __?__ laid the first cable to span an ocean and connect continents.

9. __?__ invented the telephone.

10. __?__ discovered how to send messages by wireless.

11. __?__ makes it possible to hear and see programs at the same time.

12. Some television programs have been sent by a communications satellite called __?__.

Cyrus Field	1860	Massachusetts
continents	R. F. D.	California
San Francisco	1847	crier
television	Morse	airplanes
railroads	Marconi	expensive
1700	Bell	Telstar

370

Some Other Things to Do

1. Compare the ways of communicating in colonial days with our ways today.

2. Look in the encyclopedia for more information about one of these inventors:
Alexander Graham Bell   Cyrus Field
Samuel Morse   Guglielmo Marconi

3. If you collect stamps bring your stamp album and show it to the class. Tell your class about several interesting stamps.

4. Dramatize scenes about Alexander Graham Bell and his telephone.

5. Arrange to visit one of these:
A newspaper office   A telephone office
A radio broadcasting station

6. Interview someone who can tell you more about one of the following topics?
a. How news is gathered.
b. How telegrams are sent.
c. How programs are televised.
Have your list of questions handy to ask at your interview. Report what you saw.

7. Review with your class the important standards for choosing a news item.

8. Find and share a news item about some topic related to communication.

Some Questions to Talk Over

1. It is sometimes said that "communication has conquered distance." What do you think this means?

2. How has communication helped our country grow strong?

3. Have you ever tried to do a very difficult task? Were you discouraged? Did you give up? Or did you keep on trying until you succeeded, as Bell and Field did? What other people have you read about who worked for a long time to complete a job successfully?

4. What kinds of radio and television programs do you think are most worth while?

UNIT FIVE

Our North American Neighbors

21 · Canada: Our Neighbor to the North

Canada Has a Colorful History

Vikings discovered Canada about a thousand years ago. The Vikings lived in northern Europe along the shores of Norway, Sweden, and Denmark. They built the sturdiest ships of the times and were bold and fearless sailors.

Some sea-roving Vikings ventured far out on the Atlantic Ocean. Even before the year 1000, they had discovered the islands which we call Iceland and Greenland. A few daring settlers started a colony on Greenland's southern coast.

One day, a bright-sailed Viking ship, like the one shown below, set out for this colony in Greenland. Skilled seamen manned its long, thick oars behind large carved shields. Their captain was tall, bearded Lief Ericson.

Ericson and his men journeyed farther and farther west. But there was no sign of Greenland's bare shores. A stiff wind had driven the sailors off course and they were lost. Finally, though, they sighted an unknown land.

When the adventurers went ashore, they found trees, and also vines that bore clusters of small purple grapes. Because of the grapevines, Ericson named the land Vinland.

Cabot's men enjoyed the fishing grounds off Newfoundland.

Stories tell us that other Vikings sailed to Vinland. However, no permanent settlements were established and soon Vinland was forgotten. About five hundred years later, John Cabot "discovered" it all over again.

John Cabot claimed Canada for England in 1497, remember. As you learned in Chapter 1, he sailed west from England in search of a shorter route to the Far East. He failed to find one, but he did accomplish other important things. His explorations gave England a strong claim to Canada. Also, he found the rich fishing grounds, the Grand Bank.

This discovery was good news, especially to the French. Fish were a main food in Europe, and many Frenchmen earned a living in the fishing industry.

Fishermen led the French to Canada. These hardy "sailors" found plenty of cod at the Grand Bank. They dried and salted down the fish on shore. There,

they began to trade kettles, knives, and trinkets for the Indians' furs and skins. Such trade meant extra money for the fishermen, for furs were eagerly sought in Europe.

In time, France sent Cartier to Canada. He sailed far up the St. Lawrence River to hunt for a waterway to the Pacific, you may recall. Find this river on your map on page 19. Finally the journey was halted by a dangerous stretch of rapids.

Cartier and his men climbed a steep hill above an Indian village on this river. They named the hill *Mont Real*, the French words for Mount Royal. Today, Canada's largest city, Montreal, spreads out around this place.

Cartier claimed a vast region for his king, and called it New France. He tried to start settlements, but failed. Then the king lost interest and turned his back on the Canada wilderness.

Still, French fishermen continued to sail to and from the Grand Bank. Furthermore, some of their countrymen had become successful fur traders and trappers. They were venturing far back in the wilderness of New France.

Champlain started the first permanent settlement in New France. By the late 1500's, the fur trade had increased greatly. It was bringing in so much money that English traders were moving in. This worried the new King of France. Surely now it was necessary to establish a strong colony to occupy New France.

Wise and able Samuel de Champlain was asked to start the new colony. Champlain was a respected leader and a trained explorer.

After several failures Champlain built a settlement at the foot of a high cliff on the St. Lawrence. He named it Quebec. As you learned earlier, this tiny village was the first successful settlement in New France. From it has grown the large busy city of present-day Quebec.

As the years passed, more French colonists settled along the St. Lawrence. There were fur traders and trappers, of course, but farmers also came. They laid out long, narrow "strip" farms that faced the St. Lawrence. On such

Quebec is Canada's oldest city.

farms, neighbors could live close together and help each other in time of danger. Also, each strip farm had its own piece of river front. This was important, for the St. Lawrence was the main "highway" in those early days.

At first, life was hard and discouraging, as it was for all pioneers about whom you have read. Families had to provide nearly everything for themselves or do without. So they worked from sunrise until dark, or later, day after day.

The worst problem of all, though, was how to get along with unfriendly Indians. There was always fear of dreadful Indian attacks.

Gradually conditions improved. The settlers learned how to manage on the frontier. They were able to raise more food and build more comfortable homes. There was less worry now, too, for French soldiers had forced the Indians to make peace.

Still, there were quarrels with the English. Some had started over the rich fur trade. For one thing, an English company had built trading posts on Hudson Bay and was doing a thriving business. France was not happy about that.

Early in the 1700's, the French and English settled their differences. England gained the Hudson Bay region and a fine area in eastern Canada. But later on more trouble developed.

France and England fought a war. You have already learned some things about this war. Several battles took place west of the Appalachians. At that time, George Washington and other colonists served with the British army, as you learned in Chapter 3. There was also heavy fighting in Canada.

An airview of the Parliament Buildings at Ottawa. They are on a hill overlooking the Ottawa River.

In 1763, France lost the war, and had to give up New France. Then England took over the French-Canadian lands.

England ruled Canada for a number of years. Most of the French settlers remained on their farms or in their villages, even under English rule. They were allowed to speak their own language, and continued to follow their own customs.

Meanwhile, more English settlers arrived to make their homes. Gradually, the Canadians became more independent and helped to govern themselves. Indeed, as time passed, England gave Canada more and more self-government.

Today, Canada is a democracy. Its people govern it. A *prime minister* serves as the head of the government. His duties are something like those of the President of the United States.

Canada's Parliament makes the laws of the land. This Parliament is divided into two groups. The most powerful one is called the House of Commons. Its members are elected by the people.

Canada still has close ties with England, or Britain, and belongs to the Commonwealth of Nations. The *Commonwealth* is a family of free nations which are loyal to the King or Queen of England. Great Britain's Queen, Elizabeth, is also Canada's Queen.

Ottawa is Canada's beautiful capital. As the map shows, it is located in southeastern Canada, not far from Montreal.

The stately government buildings rise on a hill above the Ottawa River near the heart of the city. The picture on this page shows their fine location.

The Mounties help Canada's government to keep law and order. Today, more than 4,500 Mounties serve their country as members of the Royal Canadian Mounted Police. No doubt you have heard of this organization. It is famous the world over for heroic deeds. Some Mounties work in the cities but others are on duty on the plains or in the wilderness of the far north.

The Mounted Police was organized in 1873. At that time, the men were required to be skilled horsemen, for they traveled mainly on mounts, or horses. But present-day Mounties may use automobiles, or motorcycles, or planes, or even motorboats or dog teams, depending on what area they serve.

Mounties are trained to perform a variety of tasks, especially when they are on duty in the back country. They may use "first aid" to help sick or injured people. They may act as judges and settle quarrels, or decide how to punish lawbreakers. And they track down criminals. But whatever the job, a Mountie does his best to keep law and order in his country.

Now let's get better acquainted with this wide and exciting land of Canada.

Canada is divided into ten provinces and two territories. Locate each one and name its capital. Point to Ottawa, the capital of Canada.

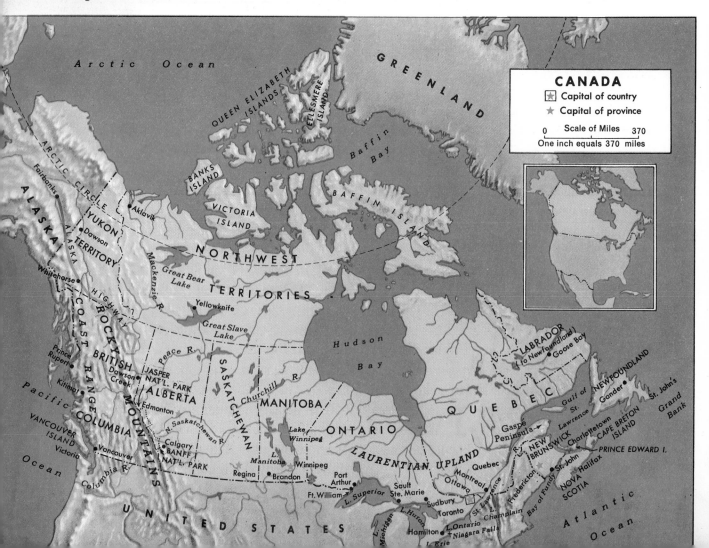

A Closer Look at Canada

Canada is an enormous country. It has more land than the United States. It is the largest of the eight nations which share our continent. Indeed, it is the second largest country in the world.

Study the map on page 376. Notice that Canada extends from the large island of Newfoundland in the Atlantic to Vancouver Island in the Pacific. It stretches north to the frozen waters of the Arctic Ocean and south to the borders of the United States.

And had you realized that Canada reaches farther east than the United States? It does! Glance at the map and prove this for yourself. Point to some areas that are located farther east than New England.

Canada has many kinds of lands. Large parts of it resemble landform areas in the United States. You see, land forms may not end at the man-made borders of a country. They may extend on and on.

Eastern Canada has hilly lands and low mountains. Some of them are a part of the Appalachian Mountains, and are thickly forested. Lowlands follow along the St. Lawrence River and also around the Great Lakes.

Wide grassy plains sweep across central Canada. They are the Canadian section of our central plains.

North of Canada's plains are immense stretches of evergreen forest and swamplands. They are dotted with thousands of quiet lakes. Many kinds of wild life have homes in this wilderness.

Banff National Park in the Canadian Rockies of Alberta.

Still farther north are flat, marshy treeless plains known as tundra. The empty tundra reaches to the lonely shores of the Arctic Ocean. During most of the year, it is a frozen land. But when warm summer days come, the soil thaws out a little. Then, much of the tundra is wet and marshy.

West of the central plains rise the sharp, snow-covered peaks of the Canadian Rockies. Locate them on the map on page 376. They are a part of the great chain of mountains that extends north and south through North America. The Canadian Rockies are usually topped with snow. The Indians call them the "Shining Mountains" because their snowy peaks sparkle in the sunlight. Along the Pacific

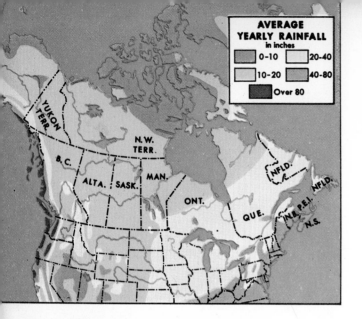

AVERAGE YEARLY RAINFALL
in inches

0-10	20-40
10-20	40-80
Over 80	

What parts of Canada have the most rainfall? What parts usually receive from 10 to 20 inches a year? Where there is less than 15 inches of rain, trees will not grow, and only a few crops will grow.

coast are other mountains. They resemble the coastal ranges found in Oregon and Washington. In some places, they slope down to the very edge of the Pacific.

Many people spend their vacations in Canada's mountains. Two of its most beautiful national parks are in the Canadian Rockies. They are Banff National Park and Jasper National Park. They have some of the grandest scenery in the world.

Canada has many rivers. Among them are the Saskàtchewan, the Churchill, and the Peace rivers. Find them on the map. Where does each empty? The Mackenzie is Canada's longest river. Point to it. Notice how it flows northward to dump its waters into the Arctic Ocean.

The long St. Lawrence is Canada's most valuable river. It is often called Canada's "Main Street" because it is such an important water highway.

Trace the St. Lawrence on the map. Notice how it flows northeast and widens as it reaches the Gulf of the St. Lawrence. This gulf is a "front door" to Canada. Ocean-going ships enter it and sail up the St. Lawrence River to Montreal, a distance of nearly a thousand miles.

Even more remarkable, ships can now travel over 1,200 miles farther inland. They can take the St. Lawrence Seaway which begins at Montreal and extends to Lake Ontario. Then they can steam on as far west as Lake Superior. Turn to the map on page 389 and see how the seaway connects the Atlantic Ocean and the lower St. Lawrence with the Great Lakes.

The Great Lakes are the largest and most important lakes in Canada. Four are shared by Canada and the United States. Use the map on page 376 to help you name them.

Niagara Falls is located between Lake Erie and Lake Ontario, remember. Niagara's thundering waters have tremendous power as they crash to the river below. Some of this power is turned into electricity for homes and industries.

Three of Canada's other lakes are also immense. They are Great Bear Lake, Great Slave Lake, and Lake Winnipeg. Just think! Each one is larger than our state of Massachusetts. Locate them on the map. Which one is farthest north?

Canada has many kinds of climate. That is because it is a large country and has many different kinds of lands. The weather in southern Canada is much like that in the northern parts of the United States. Winters are cold and summers are warm. In southern Canada, the growing season is long enough to raise such crops as wheat, hay, vegetables, and fruits.

378

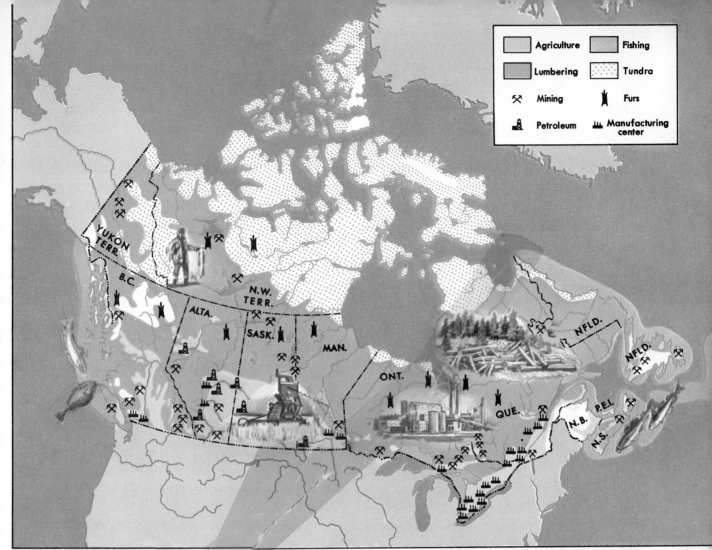

Farther north, the weather is very cold most of the year. There, in the wide belt of lonely forests, snow blankets the ground month after month. The winters on the tundra are so bitterly cold and long that neither trees nor crops can grow.

Study the rainfall map on page 378. As you can see, eastern Canada receives from twenty to forty inches of rainfall a year. Its lands have enough rain for growing many kinds of crops.

But the central plains are drier lands. Notice this on the rainfall map. About how much rain do they receive? The southern plains grow huge quantities of wheat. Wheat does not require as much rain as other crops, remember.

What are some important ways of making a living in Canada? Find the chief farming regions. Where is most of the wheat grown? Where are most of the manufacturing regions? Notice how much of Canada is covered by forests.

Heavy rains fall in the lands along the Pacific coast. Here the climate is mild and damp much of the year. It is similar to that in western Oregon and Washington.

Canada has a small population for such a large land. Can you think of some reasons why? What facts have you learned about Canada's lands and climates that help to explain this?

The population map on this page shows that most of the people live in southern Canada. It has a friendly climate, fertile soil, water power for its factories, and the easiest routes for transportation.

More than half of the Canadians speak English. Many people in eastern Canada are French-Canadians. A large number are descendants of early French settlers.

Canada has over 320,000 Indians. Many of them live on reservations, but others live and work in cities. Eskimos occupy small villages that are widely scattered along the shores of the Arctic Ocean.

Canada also has many new citizens. More than a million immigrants have come from Europe in recent years.

Canada is divided into ten provinces and two territories. A *province* is a large division of land which is governed something like one of our states. Canada's territories are large areas of northern land and have only a very small population. What are these provinces and territories like?

This population map tells some important facts about Canada · Where do most of Canada's people live?

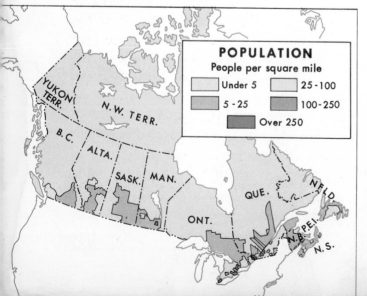

Canada's Provinces

Newfoundland is Canada's far eastern province. It has two parts, the large rocky island of Newfoundland and Labrador on the eastern coast of Canada. Locate them on the map. Both of these cool, lonely regions are often blanketed with fog or swept by cold ocean winds. In both lands, most of the people live in towns along the rocky coasts.

As the map shows, the island of Newfoundland seems to guard the entrance to the Gulf of the St. Lawrence. St. John's is the capital of the province and the largest city of the island. It is located on Newfoundland's east coast and has a fine harbor.

Newfoundland is sometimes called the "Crossroads to Continents." It is a front door to Canada, and even to parts of the United States. Airplanes stop at its two largest airports on their way to and from New York, the British Isles, and northern Europe. Its airfield at Gander is very large. Gander is on the east coast of Newfoundland. Do you see it on the map? Another huge airfield is located on the shores of Labrador's Goose Bay.

You may think that Gander and Goose Bay are "out-of-the-way" places. But wait! Let's look at a globe and find out if they really are. Suppose we stretch a string on the globe from England to New York. Notice how Gander lies in the path of the shortest route to New York City. Gander is a convenient "half-way" point for taking on fuel after the long sea hop across the Atlantic. Cut another piece of string long enough to reach from England to Montreal. Goose Bay is on this main air route.

Newfoundland's location was important long before the days of airplanes, however. Almost a hundred years ago, the first Atlantic cable was laid between Newfoundland and Ireland, in Europe. In 1910, the first wireless messages were sent from England to Newfoundland. You see, Newfoundland is the part of America which is closest to Europe.

Fishing, mining, and lumbering are leading occupations in Newfoundland. Nearly half of the people earn their living in some part of the fishing industry. Some men fish for cod at the Grand Bank off the coast of Newfoundland. Others catch salmon in the Gulf of the St. Lawrence or gather lobsters close to shore. Some build and repair boats or make nets. And many people are busy preparing fish for markets.

Most of the fisherfolk live in villages which nestle on the small sheltered bays. In these quiet towns, one can see cod being dried on long tables and idle fishing nets spread out on fences to dry. At times, fishing boats ride at anchor in the bays.

Some men work in the mining industry. One of Newfoundland's newest and richest mines is located deep in the lonely Labrador wilderness. There, much valuable iron ore is now being mined. It is hauled out on a new railroad that winds through rugged mountains and across bridged canyons. The ore finally reaches the Gulf of the St. Lawrence where it is loaded on to ore boats. Much of this ore is delivered to steel mills in the United States.

The map on page 379 shows that Newfoundland is also a forest land. In many places, loggers cut trees for Newfoundland's large paper mills.

Fishing on the Grand Bank off the coast of Newfoundland.

Three other Atlantic Provinces. Nova Scotia, Prince Edward Island, and New Brunswick are also Atlantic Provinces. Like Newfoundland, they border the Atlantic. They are located south and west of Newfoundland. Find them on the map.

These provinces have ragged, rocky coasts similar to those in New England that are beautiful to see. Inland there are rocky hills clad in thick forests. They are a part of the Appalachians. They almost cut off these provinces from the rest of Canada.

Halifax is the largest city in these provinces. Locate it on the map. It is the capital of Nova Scotia and an important seaport. In the winter, the ports on the St. Lawrence River are closed because the river is blocked with ice. But the harbor at Halifax is open the year round.

Charlottetown is the capital and largest city of Prince Edward Island. St. John, New Brunswick's chief city, is on the Bay of Fundy. Do you see these cities on the map?

381

Logs are steered from a river into a narrow waterway. A conveyor belt will then carry them to the lumber mill.

Most of the people in these sister provinces work in the cities. But others get their living from the sea or the soil.

Fishing, farming, lumbering, and mining. As in Newfoundland, fishing is one of the chief industries. Some of the catch is canned and some is frozen, salted, or smoked. Huge quantities are prepared for market. One company alone markets about 50,000,000 pounds of fish in a single year.

Much farming is carried on in the moist, cool, fertile valleys. Crops of grain, hay, vegetables, and fruits are grown. Nova Scotia is famous for its sweet, tasty apples. New Brunswick and Prince Edward Island are widely known for their fine seed potatoes. Some farmers raise dairy cattle and sell milk and cream to the towns and villages nearby.

Lumbering is an important occupation in Nova Scotia and New Brunswick. In the winter, many sturdy spruce and hemlock trees are cut down. They are sawed into short lengths and dragged over the snow to frozen streams. When the ice melts in the spring, the logs float down the river to the pulp mills. Nova Scotia harvests thousands of "Christmas trees," late each fall. Many of them are shipped to the United States.

Nova Scotia and New Brunswick have rich deposits of coal. Some coal and iron from Newfoundland are used in Nova Scotia's busy steel mills.

Quebec is Canada's largest province. Find it on the map. As you can see, a part of it joins New Brunswick. This part is a long arm of land that reaches out to sea and is called the Gaspé Peninsula. Another part of Quebec stretches along the shores of Hudson Bay. On the east, Quebec borders Labrador.

Glance at the map on page 87 and see how much of the province of Quebec is covered by the Laurentian Upland. This upland extends for hundreds of miles to the north and a thousand miles across Quebec into the Province of Ontario. Uplands are lands that are *up* fairly high above sea level.

Use the landform map to locate the Laurentian Upland. Notice that this region is very hilly. Long ago, enormous glaciers spread over it. They scraped away so much topsoil that it is not suitable for farming. But it is rich in minerals.

Many mineral treasures are found in Quebec. Indeed, Quebec's share of the Laurentian Upland has valuable deposits of silver, gold, iron ore, copper, and nickel.

Southern Quebec is famous for another kind of rock, one that contains tough *asbestos* fibers. Such fibers do not burn so they are useful in making a number of remarkable products. Asbestos boots, gloves, and suits for special fire fighters! One kind of shingles for roofing buildings! And linings for furnace pipes, to mention a few uses.

Canada has the richest asbestos mines in the world. It sells much of this valuable material to the United States.

Southern Quebec has many farms. Fertile plains border both sides of the St. Lawrence River, as you learned earlier. The soil is rich and receives plenty of rain. So good crops of hay, oats, fruits, and vegetables are raised. Some farmers grow sugar beets and others tend sugar maple trees.

Dairying is another profitable kind of farming carried on in southern Quebec. Much cream and milk as well as fruits and vegetables are sold to markets in nearby towns and cities. One of these cities is Montreal.

Montreal is Canada's giant city. It is located in southern Quebec on the St. Lawrence River. You have read how far inland Montreal is. It is one of the largest inland seaports in the world.

Montreal has an excellent location. Land, water, and air routes extend out of it in all directions. But it is especially fortunate in being a crossroads port on the St. Lawrence. The St. Lawrence River links it with the Atlantic Ocean and the ports of the world, of course. Also remember that the St. Lawrence Seaway leads far inland from Montreal to the Great Lakes and central Canada and central United States.

This city has become a leading manufacturing center. More than half of its people are employed in factories, mills, or refineries. One of the main industries is refining petroleum, and another is turning out iron and steel. Among the products manufactured are electrical equipment, clothing, foods, aircraft, and railroad cars. Much wheat brought in from the west is made into flour.

Montreal has many modern stores and some towering office buildings. Attractive homes, schools, and churches face some of its broad tree-lined avenues. It also has two universities, one French and one English.

Quebec is the capital of Quebec Province and Canada's oldest city. It was founded in 1608. What explorer started it? Do you recall?

If you visited Quebec, you would discover that it is made up of two towns, "upper" and "lower" town. Upper town spreads out above the St. Lawrence. Lower town sits at the foot of cliffs along the water's edge. Many ships load and unload cargo at this busy water front.

Quebec is partly old and partly new. Its oldest streets were laid out long ago and are very narrow. Still standing is a part of the ancient fort and high stone wall which once protected the city. In recent years, many modern stores and office buildings have been built.

Next door to Quebec Province is another large province, Ontario. Look on the map for it. See how it stretches westward toward the center of Canada. Notice that Ontario touches four of the Great Lakes. From its back door, it looks out on the bleak shores of Hudson Bay.

A part of Montreal's large and busy harbor · Notice the grain elevators, the warehouses, and docks. See how many ships are tied up at these docks. At the right are huge piles of coal. This coal has been brought in by ships from Nova Scotia and from the United States.

The Laurentian Upland reaches across Ontario. Notice this on the map on page 87. Now study the map on page 379 and see how much of this region is covered by forests. During the fall and winter, many trees are cut down and sawed into logs. At the mills they are made into lumber or pulpwood.

The southern part of Ontario's Laurentian Upland is also rich in such minerals as gold, silver, copper, and nickel. Indeed, more nickel is mined in this region than anywhere in the world. *Nickel* is a tough metal which does not rust. When it is mixed with steel, it makes a very strong metal. Some is used in building bridges and for making certain automobile parts.

Nickel is also used for making our five-cent coin called a nickel. Quantities of Canada's nickel is bought by the United States.

Ontario has more people than any other single province. Most of them live in the southern part. One thickly-populated area is the neck of land which separates Lake Erie and Lake Huron. Point to this region on the map.

Much farming and manufacturing are carried on in southern Ontario. Here, the soil is rich and the climate suitable for growing many kinds of crops. This region is well-known for its fine apples, peaches, pears, plums, and grapes. Much tobacco is grown. Here, too, are many vegetable gardens and dairy farms.

384

Southern Ontario has Canada's leading manufacturing region. It has plenty of water power for making electricity to run factories. It is close to a rich supply of raw materials from mines and forests and is convenient to shipping and railroad centers. Transportation lines connect it with trading centers in Canada as well as in parts of the United States.

Many iron-and-steel products are manufactured. Among them are automobiles, farm machinery, and airplanes. Large quantities of pulpwood and paper goods are also produced.

Toronto is the chief city of southern Ontario. It is the second largest city in Canada and the capital of the province. As the map shows, Toronto is located on Lake Ontario. It has an excellent harbor and a water front ten miles long. Because of its fortunate location, it has become a leading manufacturing and shipping center.

Toronto is also a very attractive city. It has beautiful parks and many fine streets. It is proud of its handsome modern stores and other business buildings as well as its friendly churches and well-kept homes. In addition, it has very good schools and a famous university.

West of Ontario stretch the "Prairie Provinces." They are Manitoba, Saskatchewan, and Alberta. Do you see them on the map? Which one is Ontario's nearest neighbor? Which one lies farthest to the west?

Wide, flat, grassy plains sweep across these provinces for hundreds of miles. They are a part of the plains region that reaches across the central part of our country, remember. Canada's plains stretch from the Laurentian Upland on the east to the Rockies on the west. You have already learned that thick forests grow to the north of these grassy plains.

The Prairie Provinces are the wheatlands of Canada. Like our central plains, they have the dry climate and fertile soil needed for growing grain.

Wheat ranches are so large that they require many men and machines. In fact, wheat is the main crop of the Prairie Provinces. Farther west, on the drier plains stock-raising is the chief industry. Also, where there are lakes or rivers, some farmers raise crops by irrigation. In these irrigated fields sugar beets, peas, corn, hay, and clover are grown. Does this remind you of some of our western farms?

Cities are far apart on the central plains. Winnipeg is the largest city of the prairies and the capital of Manitoba. It is sometimes called the "Chicago of Canada." Much of the business of buying and selling wheat and cattle is carried on there. Also, it is an important manufacturing center. Its most important indus-

Harvesting wheat on Canada's prairies. Compare this with the photo on page 266. How are the two photos alike?

tries prepare the foods that are raised on the prairies. They include meat packing, flour milling, and the making of butter and cheese.

Winnipeg is often called "the Gateway City." The map will show you that it is near the western end of the Laurentian Upland. This location makes it a gateway between central Canada and eastern Canada. The railroads that cross Canada from the Atlantic to the Pacific pass through bustling Winnipeg.

Coal, oil, and gas are found in some parts of this central region. Alberta mines so much coal that it is sometimes called Canada's "coalbin." It also has rich stores of oil deep underground. Quantities of this "liquid gold" are now being pumped from wells near the city of Edmonton. Locate Edmonton. Long pipelines carry the oil both to the east and to the west.

An oil refinery at Regina. The crude oil is brought in from nearby oil fields.

Natural gas is another of Alberta's valuable resources. Much gas is now being drawn from beneath the earth. Some is piped to cities hundreds of miles away.

Saskatchewan also has oil and gas fields. Regina, the capital of this province, has become an important manufacturing center partly because of the wealth of nearby oil fields.

West of Alberta is mountainous British Columbia. The map on page 376 shows it reaches to the Pacific and is Canada's far western province. Notice how much of this land is covered by the rugged Canadian Rockies. The forested Coast Range rises along the Pacific.

British Columbia has a ragged coastline with thousands of sheltered bays and inlets which have been carved out by glaciers and streams. A long chain of islands marches along this coast. The grand scenery one sees here is much like that

Winnipeg's railroad yards are the largest in Canada. Find this city on the map on page 389.

along Alaska's Panhandle. It is so beautiful that it is breathtaking.

Lumbering is a leading industry in British Columbia. This province produces more lumber than any other part of Canada. As you already know, the western slopes of its Coast Range are rainy lands. The mild, moist climate encourages the growth of thick forests.

Fishing, farming, and mining are also important industries in the west. Cod, herring, and halibut are caught; but salmon are the largest catch. From May until September, millions of silvery salmon are captured in nets as they leave the sea and swim upstream to lay their eggs. During this season, canneries and freezing plants are very busy.

Farming and stock-raising are carried on in parts of British Columbia. Some farms are hidden in river valleys and others spread out on Vancouver Island. Find this island on your map.

Large cattle ranches are scattered over British Columbia's dry inland plateau. It extends from north to south through the center of the province. This region has long, sharply cold winters.

Mining provides work for many men. Some dig coal and others are employed in mines that produce gold, silver, copper, lead, and zinc.

British Columbia has several busy cities. The largest one is Vancouver, Canada's leading seaport on the Pacific coast. Find Vancouver on the map. It is located near the mouth of the Fraser River. About three fourths of the people of British Columbia live in the Lower Fraser Valley.

Vancouver is quite a young city but it has grown very fast. Today, it is the

Vancouver is surrounded by mountains, ocean, and forests.

third largest city in all of Canada. Vancouver is the western "end of the line" for Canada's transcontinental railroads. Its port has warehouses, cold-storage plants, grain elevators, oil refineries, fish canneries, and lumber yards. No wonder it is often called "Canada's western gateway."

Victoria is the capital of British Columbia, and is located on Vancouver Island. Victoria began as a tiny trading post, many years ago. But it is now a large and beautiful city. Flowers thrive in Victoria's mild climate. This area is warmed by ocean breezes which blow across the warm current of water that flows north along the northern Pacific coast. So, even though Victoria lies quite far north, one can often pick garden flowers until Christmas.

387

Canada's Territories

The aluminum smelter at the new town of Kitimat. The town lies at the end of a fiord on the Pacific coast. The ore for the smelter is shipped from Jamaica.

The Yukon and Northwest Territories reach across northern Canada. Parts of these empty lands have never been explored. Indeed, they have some of the loneliest areas in the world.

As the map on page 87 shows, the Yukon Territory is a mountainous region. Only a few people live there. The town of Whitehorse is its busiest community. It is an important supply center on the Alaska Highway which winds through the southern part of the territory. Trace the Alaska Highway on the map.

The Northwest Territories spread across nearly a third of Canada. The map shows how they stretch north to the Arctic Ocean. A part of these lands are frozen islands within the Arctic Circle. One is only about five hundred miles from the north pole.

North of Victoria are several fast-growing communities. One is the seaport, Prince Rupert, a lumbering and mining center. Locate it. Near this seaport is the new town, Kitimat. Do you see it on the map? A huge aluminum manufacturing plant has been built in this faraway area. You see, manufacturing aluminum requires a tremendous amount of power. Waters rushing down from high mountain lakes furnish the power for making electricity to run this plant. The aluminum plant employs many people, even though it is located in a distant northern wilderness.

The southern part of the territories is covered with forests. If you traveled north through these woodlands, you would discover that the trees get smaller and smaller. Far to the north, they grow only a few inches high and are like little dwarfs. They cannot grow taller because the weather is extremely cold and the soil is frozen most of the year.

The region north of the forest is tundra. Here, a blanket of snow remains on the ground much of the year. The winters in northern Canada last about nine months.

A number of mines are tucked away in the northlands. Some are just west of Hudson Bay and others are scattered farther west.

Gold has been mined for many years in the Yukon Territory. Also, gold mining is now carried on near Yellowknife, a new town that has sprung up in the Northwest Territories. Yellowknife is located at the edge of Great Slave Lake.

Deposits of uranium and radium have been discovered near Great Bear Lake. Uranium is used for making atomic energy, remember. Radium is helpful in treating certain diseases. Silver, lead, zinc, and copper are among the other minerals found in northern Canada.

This vast northland is sometimes called "the land of tomorrow." You see, its rich natural resources have scarcely been touched.

At present, it costs fortunes to establish settlements and "harvest" and ship away products. There are no good through roads or railroads to link the faraway settlements with Canada's busy cities. So they depend largely on planes to fly in supplies, mail, and even machinery. This is expensive! Think, then, how important transportation is in helping a region develop its resources and market its products.

Binding Canada Together

Modern means of transportation bind Canada's provinces together. Just as in our country, the most thickly-populated areas are connected by airways, railways, and highways. Notice this as you compare the map below with the population map on page 380.

The first transcontinental railroad was completed in the 1880's. It linked the eastern provinces with British Columbia in the far west. It encouraged many settlers to move to the central plains to lay out farms. Furthermore, trading centers grew rapidly along its route. Winnipeg was one of these, and another was Regina.

Building this railroad across the West was a difficult task. There were miles of

Railroads and highways help to bind together this wide country.

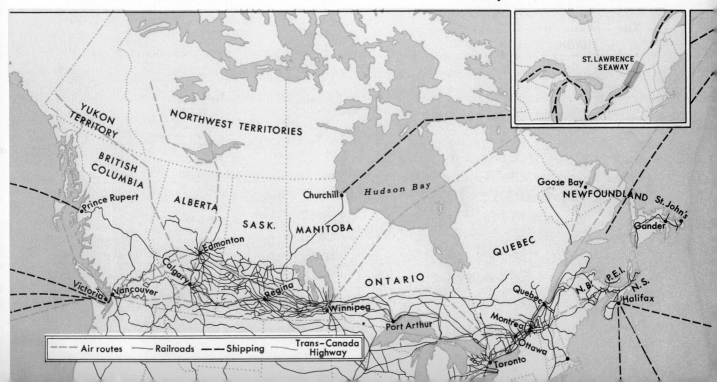

mountains to cross, and almost endless prairies. It was hard to get supplies, and there were problems with the Indians.

The Indians complained that the railroad would frighten away the buffalo on which they depended for food. Often they tried to drive the workmen off the job.

For example, one day a large band of Indians galloped up to the railroad workers. "We hate white man's steam horses!" shouted their chief. "Leave our hunting grounds."

Then the Indians slid from their ponies. They set up tepees on the new track and shot arrows into the air.

The workmen fled in terror, but soon they returned. Mounties stationed nearby had rushed to the scene to take command.

The Mountie leader spoke sternly to the chief. "Take your tepees down and move on!" he ordered. "This railroad must be built!"

"No! We stay!" declared the chief.

"Leave here at once!" commanded the Mountie. "I shall give you just fifteen minutes to move your belongings!"

Still the Indians paid no attention to the order. Therefore, when the time was up, the Mountie marched to the chief's tepee and jerked its heavy buffalo hide to the ground. Then he pulled down another tepee and another.

The Indians were astonished at such courage. Because this leader was fearless and meant business, they gave in. Sadly, they gathered up their things and left. The Mountie had won his battle without firing a single shot, and the railroad building continued.

Today, Canada has thousands of miles of railroads and highways. Its most thrilling highway is a new one that extends from sea to sea.

The Trans-Canada Highway was completed in 1962. It took twelve years to build and cost an enormous amount of money. But it is nearly 5,000 miles long. It begins at St. John's in Newfoundland and ends at Vancouver, in British Columbia. It was Canada's first transcontinental highway, and a dream come true. Trace it on the map on page 389.

The Indians were astonished at the Mountie's courage.

Canada:
A Good Neighbor

Canada and the United States are friendly neighbors. Our two countries border each other for more than three thousand miles. Yet nowhere on this long border is there a single fort. Neither country needs to guard this boundary, for Canada and the United States trust each other. They have proven that neighboring countries can live together in peace and friendship.

Several stately monuments have been built in honor of this friendship. One is the beautiful Peace Arch at Blaine, Washington. On the American side are carved the words "Children of a Common Mother." As you know, both countries once thought of England as their mother country. On the Canadian side of the monument are the words "Brothers Dwelling Together in Unity."

Canada and our country co-operate with each other. They have worked together to build bridges and dams and the Alaska Highway. They have made plans for defending our continent together if it should be attacked. Also, our two countries co-operated to build the costly St.

The new Trans-Canada Highway winds through a pass in the mountains of British Columbia.

Lawrence Seaway, as you read earlier. Doing this immense job together is one more proof that Canada and the United States are good neighbors.

Another country, Mexico, is our friendly next-door neighbor on the south. Chapter 22 will tell about this land south of our border.

Can You Remember?

1. What people first visited Canada?
2. Who Cabot and Champlain were?
3. How large Canada is? How it compares with the United States in size? In landforms?
4. The names of Canada's ten provinces and two territories and where each is located?

5. Why most of Canada's people live in the southern part?

Using Maps to Find Out

1. Turn to the map of the Chief Regions of the Earth on page 334. In which two

regions does Canada lie?   In which region is southern Canada located?

2. Find Canada on the map of North America on page 87. What east-west line crosses Hudson Bay? Would you expect the climate near this latitude to be colder or warmer than at latitude 50? Why?

3. What large area of plains sweeps across both Canada and the United States? Are these plains in the eastern, western, or central part of the two countries?

4. What part of Canada has about the same length of growing season and rainfall as North Dakota? Look on the maps on pages 203, 220 and 378 and see.

A Matching Game

On a paper, match the items in List B with the phrase which describes it.

List A

1. A city founded by the French long ago
2. Two vacationlands in the Canadian Rockies
3. Fire proof fibers from rock
4. The head of Canada's government
5. Canada's long water highway
6. The capital of Canada
7. The largest city of Canada
8. The hilly high lands stretching across Quebec into Ontario

List B

prime minister
Quebec
Laurentian Upland
Montreal
The Royal Canadian Mounted Police
Jasper National Park
Banff National Park
Ottawa
asbestos
St. Lawrence River

Some Other Things to Do

1. Help your class make a large picture map of Canada. On it, place pictures to show the main industries, and the leading farm and mineral products.

2. Interview someone who has lived in Canada or visited there. Share what you learn with your class.

3. Find and give a worthwhile current event about Canada.

4. Discuss with your class the paragraphs on "Summarizing."

5. Read in an encyclopedia about one of these topics:

Nickel   Asbestos   Ottawa
The British Commonwealth of Nations
The Royal Mounted Police

Summarize what you learn.

6. List ways you think the people of the United States and Canada are alike.

What Is Your Opinion?

1. Why were rivers especially important in Canada's early days?

2. Why do we say that fish and fur encouraged Canada's exploration?

3. How has climate influenced ways of living in Canada? the location of cities?

4. Why have railroads been so important to Canada?

Summarizing

Perhaps you know that a *summary* is a very short "story" of the main facts. A summary may be written or told. When we give one, we are *summarizing*.

Summarizing is very useful. It helps us choose and remember the most important facts we have learned.

22 · Mexico: Our Next-Door Neighbor on the South

Long Ago in Mexico

The Aztecs ruled Mexico long, long ago. These Indians once lived in northern Mexico. But this was a dry land and food was very scarce. So the Aztecs made their way southward, searching for a better place in which to live. After many years, the wanderers reached a wide green valley surrounded by towering mountains. It was an inviting land except that stronger tribes already occupied the best areas. The Aztecs were run out every time they attempted to settle.

Years passed. Then one day, according to a legend, Aztec leaders were resting beside a shallow lake in the valley. Suddenly, they saw an eagle with a snake in its beak swoop down on a small island in the lake. It perched on a thorny cactus and began to devour the long snake.

The great Aztec city of Tenochtitlán.

Then one leader said, "Surely this is a sign from our gods to settle here. But we must have courage. If we are as brave as the eagle, we can conquer our enemies."

They built a village on the swampy island. They named it *Tenochtitlán*, which means "cactus growing on a stone."

Though the island was small, the Aztecs thought of a clever way to make more land. They wove rafts of reeds and twigs and piled on mud scooped up from the lake. They planted vegetables and trees on their rafts. When the trees pushed their roots deep into the shallow lake, the little floating islands became anchored. Some spaces separating the "man-made" islands were filled with twigs and mud to build more land. But other spaces were used as waterways in place of streets.

Certain Aztecs were farmers, but others worked at such occupations as stone cutting, building, and weaving. The strongest young men were trained as warriors and served in the armies.

In time, the Aztecs ruled a mighty empire. Their armies conquered one neighboring tribe after another. When a group of people conquers and rules other lands and peoples, it is said to have an *empire*. At the time Columbus discovered America, the Aztec empire spread over all of the central part of what is now Mexico.

The Aztecs demanded enormous payments from the defeated tribes. Soldiers of these tribes were held as prisoners or forced to work as slaves. Quantities of food were seized. And load after load of gold, silver, jewels, and other treasures was carried to the storehouses at Tenochtitlán.

By the 1400's, Tenochtitlán had grown into a rich and beautiful city. It was the capital of the Aztec Empire. It had many handsome buildings surrounded by lovely gardens. There were immense stone temples and stately palaces.

The largest palace was magnificent, indeed, and had more than a hundred rooms. It was the home of the proud Aztec ruler, the *Montezuma*.

The Spaniards heard that the Aztecs possessed great wealth. True stories had spread that the Montezuma ate from gold plates and drank from gold cups. Furthermore, some untrue stories told of gold palaces facing streets paved with silver.

Cortés led a party to Mexico to hunt for gold. Cortés was a daring Spanish leader, you may recall. In 1518, he sailed from the West Indies with several hundred men.

One day, Aztec soldiers discovered these visitors on their shores. Who were these strangers who carried fire-spitting weapons and rode prancing animals, they wondered? The Indians did not know. But they were frightened and hastened to Tenochtitlán to warn their ruler.

The Montezuma was puzzled. Still, he believed that a god had come to visit and made plans to welcome him. He sent presents of beautiful cotton robes and hats decorated with bright feathers.

Cortés was furious when he saw these gifts and flung them to the ground. "I want gold and silver!" he shouted angrily. Then he handed one messenger a soldier's helmet and demanded that it be filled with gold.

You can imagine how troubled the Montezuma was when he heard how rudely the stranger had acted. But he tried to make peace. He ordered the helmet filled with gold and also had other costly gifts assembled. One was a huge gold plate as large as a wagon wheel. Another was a large silver plate. There were also beautiful gold and silver figures, a bow with gold arrows, and glittering necklaces set with sparkling jewels.

Messengers rushed to the coast carrying these precious offerings. This time Cortés was delighted. But his smile vanished when he learned that the Montezuma wanted him to leave Mexico.

"No!" declared the Spanish leader. "We shall march inland!" Now he was determined to reach the rich Aztec city.

"On to Tenochtitlán!" commanded the bold captain. Soon, the Spaniards set out on the long journey to the rich valley in the mountains. They chopped their way through dense jungles in spite of hot, steamy weather and millions of mosquitoes. When they reached the mountains, they had to climb miles of steep winding trails.

Montezuma and his nobles shared with the Spaniards their beautiful palaces, rich clothing, and fine food.

Finally, many weeks later, the Spaniards moved into the valley and approached Tenochtitlán. They had come to the heart of the Aztec Empire.

The Spaniards conquered the Aztecs. The Montezuma rode forth to meet the strangers. Politely, he provided his guests with quarters in a stately palace and served them a fine banquet.

Cortés was pleased, but already he was plotting against the Indian leader. In an unguarded moment, the Montezuma was tricked and taken prisoner. Bitter fighting followed and the Montezuma lost his life.

Terrible battles continued for many months. Heavy guns pounded Tenochtitlán until it was almost destroyed. At last, the Aztecs surrendered and this brought an end to the Aztec Empire.

From Spanish Rule to Present-day Mexico

After Tenochtitlán fell, Spain took over Mexico. Cortés became governor of this land, now known as New Spain.

Cortés decided to build the capital of New Spain where proud Tenochtitlán had once stood. He ordered the ruins cleared away and the canals filled in. Then work began on a splendid new capital, Mexico City.

In time, many Spaniards settled in New Spain. Among them were Spanish officials, soldiers, and pioneers. Missionaries arrived to work among the Indians and teach them the Christian religion and Spanish ways of living.

Many settlers received large grants of land for *haciendas* for raising crops and cattle. Indians were forced to grow the crops and care for the cattle on these haciendas.

Spain ruled Mexico for about three hundred years. Its government was in charge of the *viceroy*, the king's special representative. He had enormous power and sometimes was a cruel ruler. His main jobs were to please the king and enforce the laws Spain had made for the colony.

These laws were harsh and unfair. The colonists had no say in their own government. They were not allowed to have factories of their own. Instead they had to buy "manufactured goods" from their mother country. Furthermore, they were not permitted to trade with any country but Spain, and were required to pay a high tax on all goods bought.

Most people disliked such laws. As time passed, they became more and more unhappy with Spain's rule and longed for a change.

By 1800, word had spread that the Thirteen Colonies had won independence from England. Could not Mexico also gain its freedom? Spain was no longer a powerful nation and now had problems in Europe. Surely this was the time to act!

National Palace in Mexico City.

Fearless Father Hidalgo helped Mexico to become a free country. This kind priest served in the small Indian village of Dolores. His people were farm workers and were extremely poor. He tried to help them earn a better living but angry Spanish officials stopped his work.

Then Father Hidalgo began to worry, not only about his discouraged villagers, but also about the large number of poor people scattered over Mexico. What miserable lives they lived under Spanish rule!

Early on September 16, 1810, Father Hidalgo rang the bells of his church and called the people together. He told them it was time to overthrow their cruel Spanish officials. He urged them to fight for independence from Spain.

Father Hidalgo's daring call to arms was quietly passed from one village to another. Before long, thousands of people had become his followers. But alas! Father Hidalgo's soldiers were no match for the trained, well-equipped Spanish troops. In time, the priest was captured and put to death.

This sad event made the people still more determined to fight. Other brave men led the revolt. Then in 1821, Mexico was freed. At last, Father Hidalgo's dream had come true. The church bell which he rang is known as "Mexico's Liberty Bell." It now hangs in the National Palace in Mexico City.

A free Mexico faced many problems. For one thing, it needed a plan of government and wise leaders. Unfortunately, though, a Spanish officer took command of the government. He had himself declared the Emperor of Mexico. He became a dictator.

Meanwhile, a group of leaders decided that Mexico should be a republic. The dictator was run out of the country. A constitution was drawn up and a president and a congress elected. Actually, though, only a few people could vote or have a part in the government. Most Indians and mestizos had almost no "say" in making or enforcing the laws. *Mestizos* are those who have both Indian and Spanish ancestors. You see, some Spaniards had married Indians and their children grew up as mestizos.

Leaders often quarreled. Some years the government was taken over by military men who were greedy for power. Other years wealthy landowners ran it. Both groups were selfish and mainly interested in building up their own fortunes. They did not have the interest of their country or its poor people at heart.

Then one day, a different kind of leader became President of Mexico. He was an Indian lawyer, Benito Juárez.

Juárez worked hard to improve conditions in his country. He remembered what it was to be poor. He had been a penniless orphan. Friends helped him to get an education. He had studied long hours to make the most of his opportunities. Finally Juárez had become a lawyer, and later on, a judge.

Juárez served as a governor of a part of Mexico. Then about the time that Lincoln was elected President of the United States, Juárez became the President of his country.

Juárez urged many improvements, or reforms, in the government. But the one for which he is especially remembered was land reform. He wanted to improve conditions of land ownership in Mexico. He hoped that many large haciendas could be broken up into small farms which the poor people could own. Wealthy landowners fought this idea. So Juárez could not carry out his plans for land reform. Still, his work was not forgotten. Later on, other leaders helped to make this dream come true.

Today, Mexico has a government which is much like ours. A president serves as its chief executive and its Congress makes the laws.

Our southern neighbor is often called the "United States of Mexico." Indeed, it is divided into twenty-nine states. In addition, it has two territories.

The capital, Mexico City, is located in a separate federal district. You may recall that our national capital is in the District of Columbia.

We often think of Mexico as a Latin-American country. You see, Spanish is still the official language in Mexico as it is in nearly all of the lands south of the United States. The people of Brazil speak Portuguese. Spanish and Portuguese come from the old Latin language which was used in Europe many centuries ago. So most countries to the south of us are called *Latin-American* countries.

The people of present-day Mexico are being helped in many ways. The government has built hundreds of new schools and miles of roads and highways. It has carried on a health program to wipe out malaria and some other diseases and improve living conditions.

Land laws have been passed to break up many of the haciendas. Furthermore, more than two million acres of land in dry areas have been opened up for farming.

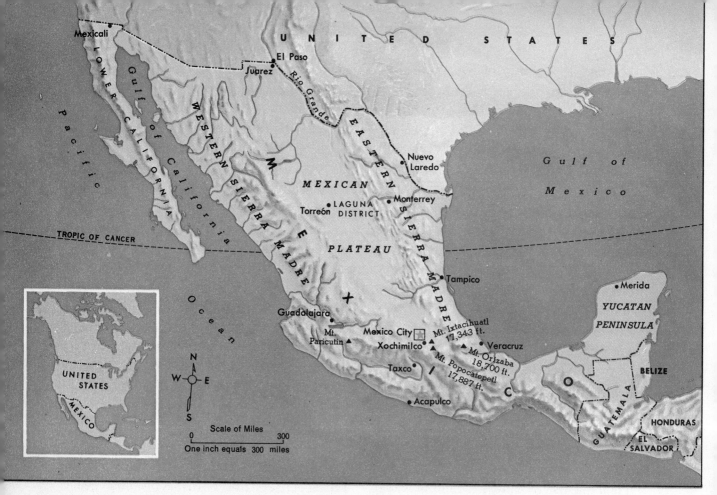

This is a political map of Mexico. What country borders it on the north? What country lies to the south?

Water is supplied by irrigation projects which the government has completed recently.

Young farmers are being taught better ways of raising crops and livestock. They are learning how to fertilize the soil and wise ways of plowing hilly lands. And they are being taught how to use and care for modern farm machinery.

Changes are taking place in the cities, also. More manufacturing is being developed and new industries started. Many Mexicans have moved to the cities to work in these industries. Handsome modern buildings have been put up in these cities.

Suppose we get better acquainted with this fascinating neighbor country.

A Closer Look

As you know, Mexico is located south of the United States. It borders our country for hundreds of miles. A part of this boundary is marked by the Rio Grande. Find this river on the large map above.

Strangely enough, one part of Mexico is called Lower California. Point to this long narrow peninsula. The Spaniards named it several centuries ago.

Mexico is a large country. It is a little more than a fifth of the size of the United States. But it is the largest Latin-American country on our continent.

Mexico stretches a long distance from north to south. Its northernmost city is located about as far north as Savannah, Georgia. On the south, Mexico extends to the borders of another Latin-American country, Guatemala. Notice this on the map. What parts of Mexico are in the tropics? How do you know this is true?

Another thing the map helps us realize is how far Mexico stretches from east to west. A part of its low Yucatán Peninsula lies farther east than Chicago. But a town in Lower California is located about as far west as our city of San Diego.

Mexico has many kinds of lands and climates. It has very wet lands and extremely dry deserts. It has hot steamy lowlands and towering snow-capped mountains.

A wide plateau stretches through the heart of Mexico. Find it on the map.

Two ranges of mountains separate the plateau and the coastal plains. As the map shows, they are the Eastern Sierra Madre and the Western Sierra Madre. They are a part of the long chain of mountains which reaches through North and South America.

South of Mexico City, the two ranges meet. Three of their loftiest peaks rise in this region. They have Indian names as you will notice if you locate them on the map. Which one climbs the highest? Which is taller, it or Mount McKinley in Alaska?

The Sierra Madre have many cone-shaped peaks. They are old volcanoes. Some of them have not erupted for years and are said to be asleep. One quiet volcano is beautiful snow-capped Mount Orizaba. The Indians call it the "Mountain of the Star."

Parícutin is Mexico's youngest volcano. It was born in a cornfield one winter afternoon in 1943. That day, while a farmer was plowing, he felt the soil grow hot. In a short time, the earth began to spit out hot rocks and smoke. Thus began a new volcano, Parícutin. Find Parícutin on the map.

Parícutin's lava shot hundreds of feet into the air. Most of it piled up to create a new cone-shaped mountain. But some lava buried two villages and the fields for twenty miles around.

Mexico's mountains are rich with minerals. From them come such minerals as gold, silver, copper, lead, zinc, coal, and some iron ore. The miners live in small villages which cling to the steep mountainsides. One charming little village named Taxco is located near a famous old silver mine. A large city, Monterrey, is located farther north near coal and iron ore deposits. Do you see Monterrey on the map?

Only a few roads and railroads have been built through the mountains to the low plains along the coast. Still, these coastal plains are very important.

Hot, low plains extend along the eastern coast. They border the Gulf of Mexico, reaching all the way from the Rio Grande to the southern edge of the Yucatán Peninsula. In the north, they are grasslands, but farther south they are covered with tropical forests and thick jungles.

These plains are generally quite level, but they rise slightly as they run inland to meet the mountains. Look on the map on page 87 and notice how they reach inland for many miles just south of the Rio Grande.

Fine crops can be grown on the hot, wet southeastern plains. These lands receive much rain, as the rainfall map below shows. Plentiful showers and long days of hot sunshine provide fine growing conditions for many tropical crops. So, some of the jungle has been cleared to make room for plantations.

Today, thousands of acres of sugar cane, bananas, and rice are grown on these fertile lands. Henequen is raised on the Yucatán Peninsula. The strong string called twine is manufactured from the fibers in henequen's long tough leaves. You can see henequen drying in the picture above.

The henequen fibers shown drying above come from the cactus plant shown at the left above.

Several busy seaports sit on the eastern coastal plains. Veracruz is the most important one. It is sometimes called the "front door" to Mexico. Many goods are shipped to and from this port. It is connected by railroad to Mexico City. Therefore, among the goods exported from Veracruz are products and minerals from the southern part of the plateau.

Veracruz is also the port through which the products of the coastal plantations are sent to other countries. But this city has

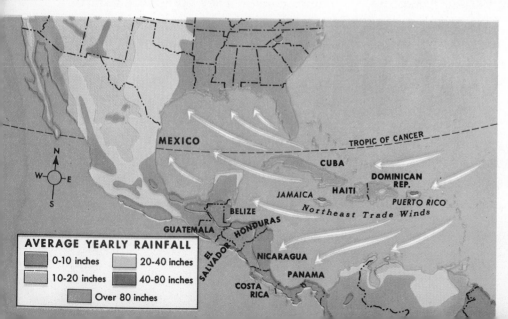

This is a rainfall map of Mexico, and the countries of Central America · Find the regions with the heaviest rainfall. The arrows on the map show the winds that blow across the Atlantic from the northeast, bringing rain clouds. Which regions have the least rainfall?

MEXICO

TROPIC OF CANCER

CUBA

DOMINICAN REP.

JAMAICA   HAITI

PUERTO RICO

Northeast Trade Winds

BELIZE

GUATEMALA   HONDURAS

EL SALVADOR   NICARAGUA

PANAMA

COSTA RICA

AVERAGE YEARLY RAINFALL

- 0-10 inches
- 10-20 inches
- 20-40 inches
- 40-80 inches
- Over 80 inches

a small population. Like other places along the east coast, its climate is hot, sticky, and disagreeable.

Tampico is Mexico's chief oil-shipping center. Point to it on the map. Much oil is pumped from the lands along the Gulf coast near Tampico.

The western coastal plains face the Pacific. The northern part of these plains is a desert, as the map on page 400 shows. However, irrigation is now making it possible to grow fine crops of cotton, sugar cane, rice, wheat, and winter vegetables in some areas.

The United States and Mexico have worked together to build a mighty dam on the Rio Grande. Its waters are used for irrigation and are shared by farmers on both sides of the border. Also, the Mexican government has built dams on three other rivers in this region.

On the coastal plains farther south are some lonely cattle ranches and small farms. Halfway down the coast the mountains crowd out the plains. There, high cliffs rise close to the sea.

Beautiful Acapulco lies at the foot of steep mountains. It is one of the chief ports on Mexico's Pacific Coast. Near Acapulco is a strip of fertile lowlands where cotton and citrus fruits are grown.

The Mexican Plateau reaches through central Mexico. The map on page 87 shows how it stretches from the Rio Grande to Mexico City. It occupies about a third of the country. Three sides of this plateau are hemmed in by the Sierra Madre. Here and there, mountains and hills run through the plateau, breaking the land into many valleys.

The Mexican Plateau is a high land. In the north, it is about 3,000 feet above sea level. As it reaches southward, it climbs steadily, and at its southernmost part is about 8,000 feet above the sea.

The northern part of the plateau is a dry land. Much of it is covered with thorny cactus, sagebrush, and thin coarse grass. This land looks brown and thirsty. The brief showers generally beat down so hard that most of the water runs off. Then it may not rain again for several months. As in our country, these dry lands are used chiefly for cattle ranching. Thousands of beef cattle wander over them, but grass is scarce. It takes hundreds of acres to feed a large herd, so some cattle ranches are enormous.

This is a population map of Mexico and of the surrounding areas · Locate the most densely-settled regions. Do any of these have less than 20 inches of rainfall a year? Do any have more than 80 inches of rainfall a year? Locate the least densely settled regions.

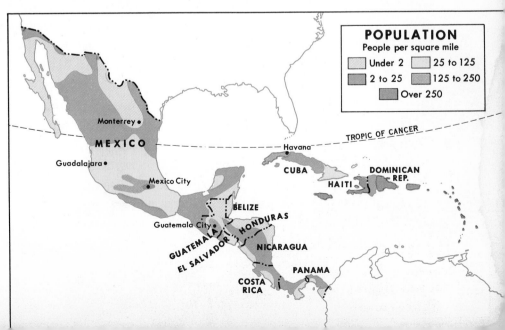

POPULATION
People per square mile
Under 2
2 to 25
25 to 125
125 to 250
Over 250

TROPIC OF CANCER

Monterrey
MEXICO
Guadalajara
Mexico City
Havana
CUBA
DOMINICAN REP.
HAITI
BELIZE
HONDURAS
Guatemala City
GUATEMALA
EL SALVADOR
NICARAGUA
PANAMA
COSTA RICA

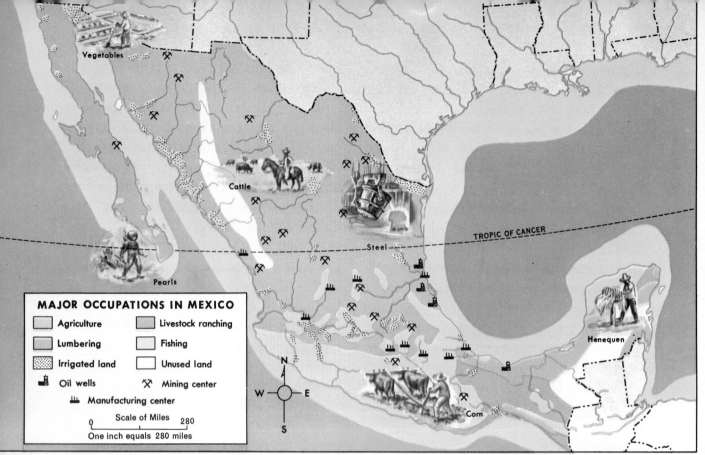

MAJOR OCCUPATIONS IN MEXICO

- ▢ Agriculture
- ▢ Lumbering
- ▨ Irrigated land
- ⛴ Oil wells
- ⛰ Manufacturing center
- ▢ Livestock ranching
- ▢ Fishing
- ▢ Unused land
- ✕ Mining center

Scale of Miles
0 ————— 280
One inch equals 280 miles

Vegetables

Cattle

Steel

TROPIC OF CANCER

Pearls

Henequen

Corn

N W E S

Though Mexico is building many factories, most of her people are still farmers. Name some of the products they raise. Mexico also has large mines, as the map above shows.

In certain areas, such as the Laguna District, men have been able to irrigate the land. Locate Laguna on the map on page 398. At Laguna, irrigation water from two rivers has helped men develop prosperous cotton and wheat farms. Indeed, about half of Mexico's cotton is raised here.

The southern part of the Mexican Plateau has many farms. The rainfall map shows that this part of the plateau receives more rain. Here many kinds of crops can be grown. Wheat, hay, vegetables, and fruit are raised; but corn is the biggest crop. It is Mexico's chief food.

The largest farms are called haciendas, as they were long ago. They usually belong to wealthy people. But the work is done chiefly by poor farm workers.

Today, however, many farmers who once worked on the haciendas care for their own land. Their farms are usually from three to fifty acres in size. Though some of these farmers are poor, they like working for themselves. They are happier than the other farm workers.

Many Mexican farmers still tend their fields much as their ancestors did. Some use sharp sticks to cultivate the soil. They sow their seed by hand and tramp it into the soil with their bare feet. Others use homemade plows pulled by oxen or mules. These people are too poor to buy modern tools and fertilizer.

But the future looks brighter for some of Mexico's young farmers. They are learning better ways of farming, as you read earlier. Which picture below tells this?

With these improved ways of farming, more crops are being raised. Also, as you have learned, new lands have been opened to farmers by irrigation projects. Mexico now raises almost all the food its people eat. Also, it sells to other countries cotton, sugar, coffee, and vegetables.

The southern part of the plateau has a fortunate location. It can grow a variety of crops and has a pleasant climate. So it is thickly populated. It has many villages and several large cities. One is Mexico City.

Mexico City is the largest city in all of Mexico. It has more than eight million people and is one of the oldest cities in North America. As you know, it was started on the ruins of the old Aztec capital. A part of it, therefore, is more than four hundred years old. Its famous cathedral and its university were founded long before the Pilgrims came to New England.

At the left below, a Mexican raises crops as his ancestors did hundreds of years ago. The other farmer uses more modern methods and tools.

Locate Mexico City on the map. It lies in a high, bowl-like region and is almost surrounded by mountains. It is about 7,500 feet above sea level. So, even though it is located in the tropics, its weather is mild throughout the whole year. In the tropics, the temperature does not change much with the seasons.

Mexico City is a beautiful and interesting city. Some ancient thick-walled churches and old Spanish homes still remain. Several are located near the central *plaza*, or square, in the heart of the city. Facing this plaza is the Cathedral of Mexico with its twin bell towers. On another side of the plaza is the National Palace pictured on page 396.

Mexico City also has many new buildings. So, this famous old city is also a very modern one. It has tall office buildings and attractive stores. Fine hotels and handsome apartment buildings rise along some of its broad paved avenues.

Thousands of tourists visit Mexico City every year. Those who travel by plane can land at the beautiful modern airport located just outside of the city.

Mexico has several important manufacturing centers. You can locate them on the map on page 402. Mexico City is the largest. It has a number of

Handsome business offices, apartment houses, and hotels line one of Mexico City's avenues.

cotton mills as well as flour mills, sugar refineries, and factories turning out leather goods. It manufactures some iron-and-steel goods.

Mexico's second largest city is Guadalajara. Its busy factories produce such goods as textiles, flour, and steel. But it is especially well-known for its fine pottery and glass products.

Monterrey, in northern Mexico, is the center of the iron-and-steel industry. So it is called the "Pittsburgh of Mexico." Also, it has more than 500 factories and makes textiles, cement, and plastics as well as many other kinds of goods.

Manufacturing is one of Mexico's newest industries, but it is a growing one. More and more people are finding work in factories in the cities.

Hundreds of villages are scattered over the southern part of the plateau. Some nestle in the valleys, and some cling to the lower slopes. Most families raise small patches of corn, beans, and chili peppers, and perhaps a few chickens and goats. The men may work in the mines or make articles to sell at the market. And, of course, many of these settlements are farm villages. In these villages most of the men earn their living as farmers.

A village is called a *pueblacito*. In the center of the pueblacito one may see the church and perhaps a school facing the plaza. Nearby is the market place. And lined up along the narrow streets are adobe houses. Some have red-tiled roofs and are painted in gay colors. Flowers bloom beside nearly every doorstep.

Eleven-year-old Juan Garcia lives in one pueblacito that clings to a rocky hillside on the Mexican Plateau. Let's visit Juan and his family.

Juan welcomes us with a friendly "Buenos días!" These are Spanish words that mean "Good morning" or "How do you do." Juan invites us to visit his home.

Juan and his family live in a small adobe house. His home has only one room. Look below at the picture of it. Most of its furniture has been built by Juan's father. Juan's mother has made the pottery and baskets which you see and has also woven the bright rugs. From the garden she has brought orange-red peppers and strung them up to dry. Dried peppers are used to season some foods.

Notice that one part of the room pictured below is used as a kitchen. Do you see the stove and the large stone for grinding corn into meal? This stone is used very often, for much cornmeal is needed for Mexican foods.

Juan's favorite foods are probably different from yours. He eats tortillas as often as you eat bread, toast, and sandwiches. *Tortillas* are made of cornmeal mixed with water and patted until they are very thin. They are baked on a thin sheet of iron set over the fire and look something like flat pancakes. Tortillas are used for making many other Mexican foods. *Enchiladas* are tortillas with meat and vegetables cooked in them. *Frijoles* are eaten almost as often as tortillas. Frijoles are beans.

How do Juan's people dress? He and his father wear white cotton suits. Neatly folded sarapes are carried over their shoulders. A *sarape* is a kind of blanket which serves as an overcoat when the weather is cool. Sometimes they go barefoot and sometimes they wear woven leather sandals.

Boys and men often wear enormous hats called *sombreros*. They provide shade from the hot sun and protection from the rain.

Juan's mother wears a long full skirt and an embroidered blouse. Out of doors she likes a scarf-like *rebozo*, or shawl, over her long black braids. In the cities, many of the people dress about as we do.

Thousands of Mexicans earn their living by making articles to sell. They do this work by hand in their homes. They fashion beautiful pottery, baskets,

Juan lives in a one-room adobe house.

jewelry, and other articles. The special know-how for each trade has been handed down from father to son.

Juan's village is near a silver mine, so some of its men are silversmiths. They hammer silver into fine vases, bowls, or trays, or shape it into jewelry.

In some villages, the men are glass-blowers and make delicate glass figures or beautiful glass vases. Villagers who live near forests may make wooden trays or other useful wooden articles.

Many Mexicans carry their handmade goods to the nearest market to sell. Let's go to market with Juan.

To market! We discover that market day is a happy, gay occasion. The people sell some things and buy some things. But they do not rush about. Everyone has plenty of time to visit with his friends.

The picture below shows a Mexican market. Some people sell their goods from small booths which face the market place. Others sit on the pavement with their wares piled around them. One woman has

carefully arranged home-grown vegetables. Another woman sells fruit and a third offers tortillas. Several men are peddling interesting toys. There are whistles made of clay and straw animals.

In this market, there are no price tags. Instead, people bargain for goods. *Bargaining* is a kind of buying and selling. The seller offers one price and the buyer suggests a lower one. After the two argue about a price for a time, they may agree on a "middle" price.

Mexicans and tourists alike visit Xochimilco's Floating Gardens. They are located in a shallow lake just southeast of Mexico City. They are on small islands said to have been built up by the Aztecs long ago. All kinds of flowers and vegetables are raised on the islands. Canals shaded by graceful trees wind between the islands. It is fun to go boating on the canals.

Our ride on a flower-trimmed boat is a delightful experience. Boatloads of musicians pass by, playing and singing gay Spanish tunes. There are flower vendors too, offering flowers for sale from their gaily decorated canoes.

An open-air market in a village of Mexico.

Mexicans and tourists enjoy Xochimilco's floating gardens.

Another trip takes visitors to some ancient pyramids. They are located about twenty miles from Mexico City. They were built more than 3,000 years ago by Toltec Indians, even before the Aztecs.

The Pyramid of the Sun is very large and covers eleven acres of ground. Its huge blocks of stone form steps that rise more than two hundred feet. Nearby is the smaller Pyramid of the Moon.

Adios, Mexico. As our visit to Mexico comes to an end, Juan says, "Adios, amigos mios." He is saying, "Good-bye, my friends." Fortunately, increasing numbers of tourists are visiting Mexico every year. This is helping Mexicans and Americans to understand each other better.

South of Mexico are the Latin-American countries of Central America. The next chapter will tell about them.

Help Your Class to Recall

1. Where Mexico is and how its size compares with that of our country.

2. What mountains extend through Mexico. Some ways they have hindered Mexico's development.

3. What central Mexico is like.

4. The main facts about the Aztecs, and how they were conquered.

5. How Spain ruled Mexico and how Mexico finally won independence.

6. What problems a free Mexico faced.

Using Maps

1. Find Mexico on the Regions Map on page 334. In what two regions does it lie? Which part of Mexico is in the low latitudes?

2. The map on page 398 can help you answer these questions: (a) What river is a part of the boundary between the United States and Mexico? (b) What city is Mexico's capital? In which direction is it from Veracruz? from Monterrey? from Acapulco? (c) Name and locate Mexico's two peninsulas. Which extends farthest east?

3. Use the rainfall map on page 400. (a) Which region receives more rain, southern Mexico or Lower California? (b) Which of Mexico's peninsulas receives enough rain to grow crops? (c) What parts of Mexico have very dry areas?

4. Study the map on page 402. (a) What are the chief crops raised? (b) Is cotton grown mainly in the north or the south? (c) What kind of symbol shows that cotton is chiefly an irrigated crop?

Which Ending Will You Choose?

There are eleven beginnings of sentences in List A. Write 1 to 11 on a paper. After each number write the ending from List B which correctly completes that sentence.

List A

1. Mexico is divided into
2. A huge plateau extends
3. The rich eastern lowlands
4. Twine is manufactured
5. Monterrey is a busy
6. Spain ruled Mexico
7. Juarez was one of
8. Some Mexican foods are
9. Mexico City is the
10. Guadalajara is famous
11. Xochimilco is well known

List B

for three hundred years.
across the heart of Mexico.
grow bananas, sugar cane, and rice.
from henequen fibers.
for fine pottery and glass products.
largest manufacturing center.
twenty-nine states and two territories.
Mexico's most famous presidents.
iron and steel center.
tortillas, frijoles, and enchiladas.
for its floating gardens.

Some Questions to Think About

1. What do you think this statement means? "We can learn much from the cultures of other people." What are some things we can learn from the Mexicans?

2. How can we encourage more understanding of people in other lands?

Some Other Things to Do

1. Have an exhibit of Mexican pottery and other Mexican handcrafts.

2. Help to plan a program about Mexico. It might include a dramatization of a market scene, Spanish songs, and folk dances.

3. Summarize what the pictures on pages 396 and 404 tell about Mexico City.

Pronouncing Difficult Words

Turn to the Index and Pronouncing Vocabulary in the back of your text. Notice the pronouncing helps after the hardest words.

Look for the word Cortés, for example. See how it is followed by this pronouncing help, *kôr tez'*. The mark above the o shows that this letter has a special sound. The o sounds like the o in *order*. The e is pronounced like the e in *let*.

These letters also have other sounds. Think of the o in *hot*, for example. Study the key on page 506 to review more about the sounds of letters.

Many words have two or more parts or *syllables*. How many syllables are in the word Cortés? Notice the small slanting accent mark over the second syllable. It tells us to stress the second syllable.

However, in most words, you will find the accent mark after the syllable to be stressed, as in *Mex' i co.*

23 · Central America: Shared by Seven Countries

Yesterday and Today in Central America

The Maya Indians settled in Central America long, long ago. They wandered to this region south of Mexico long before the Aztec Empire began.

Ancient records prove that the Mayas were a very intelligent people. They invented an excellent calendar and a remarkable system of writing. The stories they carved on stone have lasted more than a thousand years.

The Mayas built great pyramid temples and cities. The earliest of these were built at about the time of the birth of Christ.

The Mayas had some schools. Sons of leaders attended them and studied such subjects as writing, astronomy, arithmetic, and history. History lessons were taught in songs or chants. The songs and certain tribal legends had to be learned by heart.

Many boys were trained at home and became what their fathers were—farmers, potters, or weavers, perhaps. Other boys grew up to be stone workers or builders or sculptors. The sculptors carved pictures on stone to decorate the palaces and temples.

The Mayas built a number of cities. Ruins of these cities have been found in Guatemala and also in Yucatán. Large palaces were put up for the rulers. Giant terraced pyramids were also erected. They looked something like the one in the

picture on page 409. Each pyramid had a flat top and was crowned with a temple that was used for religious ceremonies. Some ancient pyramids are still standing today.

As time passed, the Mayas became less prosperous. They were no longer a powerful tribe by the time the Spaniards arrived.

Spain conquered Central America. Very early in the 1500's, Spain's explorers reached this region. Columbus sailed along its Caribbean coast. He visited Central America on his fourth and last journey to the New World.

Later on, Balboa and other Spaniards came. Like Columbus, they were searching for a water passageway to the Pacific. But they were also claiming land for Spain and keeping their eyes open for gold.

By 1522, Cortés was interested in Central America. He had just conquered Mexico, you remember. Now he dreamed of winning more land and riches for his king and more glory for himself.

Cortés sent soldiers to Guatemala to conquer the Indians. The natives fought fiercely. But their bows and arrows were no match for the white man's guns and cannon and they were defeated.

Spain ruled Central America for about three hundred years. But finally Spanish control came to an end.

In 1821, Central America declared its independence. This happened about the same time that Mexico won its freedom from Spain.

Five different provinces, or "states," were formed. They joined together in a kind of "United States of Central America," with one government over all. This union lasted only nineteen years, for it was not a happy one. The leaders of the states quarreled with each other and disagreed on how to solve the problems they faced.

Finally, in the middle 1800's, the union was broken up. Its states became five separate countries: Guatemala, El Salvador, Costa Rica, Honduras, and Nicaragua. At that time, Panama was part of Colombia, a country in South America, and Belize was the colony of British Honduras.

Today, seven countries, one a former British colony, share Central America. Use the map on the opposite page to locate each one.

Which two countries border Mexico? What small country lies just south of Guatemala? Name the two countries that look out on both the Caribbean Sea and the Pacific. What other countries have two coastlines? Point to Costa Rica and Panama. Through which one does a famous canal extend? Locate it on the map.

Like Mexico, six of the Central American countries are a part of Latin America. Their official language is Spanish. In Belize, however, English is the official language.

An Over-all Look at Central America

Central America is the narrow southern part of our continent. It is the region which is colored buff on the small inset map on page 411. See how it forms the bridge of land which connects North and South America.

Central America lies wholly in the tropics. You can prove this for yourself if you'll turn back to the map on page 11.

Gulf of Mexico

MEXICO

Caribbean Sea

Belize
BELIZE

GUATEMALA
Puerto Barrio
Guatemala City

HONDURAS
Tegucigalpa

San Salvador
EL SALVADOR

NICARAGUA
Lake Managua
Managua
Bluefields
Lake Nicaragua
San Juan R.

Pacific Ocean

COSTA RICA
San José
Puerto Limón
Panamá Canal
CANAL ZONE
PANAMA
Panamá City
Gulf of Panamá
COLOMBIA

CENTRAL AMERICA

Scale of Miles
0   225
One inch equals 225 miles

N

Find Central America on this map. Do you see how it is located in the low latitudes south of the Tropic of Cancer?

Because of this tropical location, you might expect all areas in Central America to have hot weather the year round. But they don't! Remember that the climate of an area depends partly on the elevation of its lands.

Much of Central America is mountainous. This is shown very plainly on the map on page 87.

The highest ranges are near the Pacific coast and have many volcanic cones. A few volcanoes are still active. One of the most famous rises in El Salvador, a small country on the west coast. Sailors have nicknamed it the Lighthouse because they can see its flames or white smoke from far out at sea.

This map shows the republics of Central America · They are sometimes called countries of Middle America because they lie between North America and South America.

Which is smallest? Through which is the Panama Canal cut? Find the one colony. To whom does it belong? Which country borders Mexico on the north?

Lands near volcanoes often have earthquakes. Central America has had many very damaging ones. Some have killed large numbers of people and left whole cities in ruins.

The Indians of this region have an interesting legend about what causes earthquakes. According to this tale, the Bad Spirit sleeps in the high mountains. When he turns over in his bed, he shakes the land for miles around.

411

Of course, that story is only a legend and therefore not true. We know that earthquakes are caused by changes that take place deep within the earth.

Strangely enough, these oft-disturbed lands are the most thickly-populated areas in Central America.

Cities, villages, and farms are located in the high valleys. One reason is that such valleys have a pleasant and comfortable climate.

But there is another reason. The high valleys and mountain slopes of Central America are good places to farm. Long ago, they were covered with a thick blanket of volcanic ash and lava. After hundreds of years, this ash and lava helped to form rich soil. The fertile soil and the mild climate make it possible to grow many kinds of crops in these valleys. In addition to food crops, a great deal of coffee is raised.

Coffee is the chief "money" crop in the highlands. Most of it is grown on the lower slopes of the mountains. Here, the growing season lasts the whole year, with never a touch of frost. Coffee needs weather that is balmy and mild, never too hot or too cold. Because the highlands of Central America are in the tropics, they have about the same pleasant temperature all the year round.

The mountain slopes also receive plenty of rain for growing coffee. Yet the extra rain drains away, so the soil does not remain wet and muddy. Coffee demands well-drained soil. Because the highlands have just the right climate and soil for coffee, it has become their most important money crop.

Tegucigalpa is located more than half a mile above sea level. How can you tell from these pictures that it is "a city of hills"?

As coffee berries ripen, they turn dark red.

Jungles and banana plantations spread over the low, hot plains. Hot, wet low lands face the Caribbean Sea. Locate these plains on the map on page 87. These are lands of the trade winds, winds that blow almost steadily toward the equator.

Month after month the trade winds blow from across the Atlantic. By the time they reach Central America, they are heavy with moisture. They bring drenching rains to the low plains on the eastern side of the mountains. When the showers are over, the hot sun beats down fiercely and the air becomes so steamy it is almost unbearable.

Because of the heavy rains and hot sunshine, thick tropical forests grow on the eastern low lands. In these jungles are many wild parrots and other bright-feathered birds. Monkeys chatter and howl as they swing from one tree to another. Lizards and snakes hide in the damp undergrowth. Lazy alligators and sleepy turtles live along the muddy rivers.

As the low plains run inland, there are fewer swamps. On the drier plains, wild pigs roam about and cat-like pumas slink through the forests. Here, the beautiful blue and green birds called quetzals nest in the trees.

Thousands of acres of jungles have been cleared in order to grow bananas. In some places, banana plantations spread over many miles. We shall learn about them later.

The map shows that the low plains along the Pacific are much narrower than those along the Caribbean Sea. Bananas are also grown on the western plains. But not enough rain falls west of the mountains, so crops are irrigated there.

Jungles and mountains cause many transportation problems. It is difficult and expensive to build roads and railroads through rain-drenched jungles and swamps. It costs a fortune just to keep them in good repair. Heavy rains wash them out almost as fast as they are built. Nor is it easy to build roads through rugged mountains.

Central America is mostly mountains and jungles. It is not surprising, then, that for years this region had almost no good transportation routes. Neither did it have a good communication system. So the people could not keep in touch with one another or understand one another's problems. Indeed, geography played a large part in breaking Central America up into several separate countries.

Today, airplanes are helping to solve Central America's transportation problem. Air lines link its cities and connect them with other parts of the world. Too, each country is building some roads and railroads. Guatemala, El Salvador, and Costa Rica recently constructed several important new highways.

413

Looking at Guatemala, Honduras, and El Salvador

Guatemala is Central America's northernmost country. Notice this on the map. What countries are its neighbors? It is about the size of our state of Tennessee. The name Guatemala means "full of trees." Certainly, much of this country is thickly forested.

More than half of Guatemala is covered by mountains, valleys, and plateaus. Find the plains on the map on page 87.

Guatemala is largely an Indian country. Over half of its people are Indians. In fact, the ancient Mayas were their ancestors. Many other Guatemalans are part Indian, or mestizo.

Guatemala City is the capital and largest city of this colorful country. It is set in a high valley near a winding river. Earthquakes have sometimes caused great damage in this city. One in 1917 left so many buildings in ruins that the whole city had to be rebuilt. Today, therefore, Guatemala City looks quite new and modern.

This city has many Spanish-type homes. They are generally low one-story buildings with thick adobe walls. They are often painted light colors and have red-tiled roofs. These homes face directly on the sidewalks so they have no "front yard." Instead, their rooms are built around a large open-air *patio* like the one pictured below.

Most of Guatemala's Indians live in small villages. Their homes are often tiny one-room adobe huts. They may be roofed with palm branches and have only the ground for a floor.

The Indians usually raise their own foods. As in Mexico, corn and beans are their most important foods. Corn is used for tortillas as flour is to bake our bread. So nearly every family has a patch of corn. Some families also keep goats and chickens to provide milk, meat, and eggs.

Each Guatemalan village has its own market. Many people earn a part of their living by making articles to sell on market day. Some weave beautiful cloth or rugs or blankets. And some make articles of leather, or other goods.

Indian families carry their wares to market. The father straps his load on his back. But the mother may balance her share in a large basket on her head.

People for miles around come to enjoy market day.

Market day is a pleasant one for the whole family. People sell some things and buy others, but also have a good time visiting.

Guatemala has many farms and plantations. The small farms grow food crops and cotton. Acres and acres of sugar cane and bananas are raised on the low coastal plains. Guatemala is a leading banana-growing country.

Coffee is another important product. Much coffee is raised on plantations that spread over the lower mountain slopes.

Coffee grows on small bush-like trees that have shiny dark-green leaves. When the coffee berries are ripe, they look much like polished red cranberries. Inside each berry are two small beans. It is from them that coffee comes.

Stock-ranching is being developed in parts of Guatemala. Large herds of cattle and sheep graze on the grasslands.

And you may be interested in this! One of Guatemala's most famous products comes from its forests.

The tall "chewing-gum tree" grows in the Guatemalan forests. Its real name is the *sapodilla,* or *chicle* tree. Chewing gum is made from dried chicle sap. With long sharp knives, workers slash crisscross cuts on the tree trunk. Then the white sticky sap flows slowly down into a heavy bag. Later, this sap is boiled to make it thick and hard. Then it is flown to factories to be made into gum.

South and east of Guatemala is the country of Honduras. Point to it on the map. Columbus landed on its shores. Because he found deep water off the coast, he named the new land Honduras. *Hondo* means "deep" in Spanish.

Honduras is a little larger than its neighbor, Guatemala. Its capital has a long jaw-breaker name, Tegucigalpa, which means "silver hills." Indeed, it is set on lovely hills in a high valley near silver mines.

415

Workman lowers the bananas
on to his partner's shoulder.

Honduras is mostly a mountainous
country. But it also has some low coastal
plains. They are famous for their banana
industry.

A railroad takes bananas to a
port to be put on refrigerator
ships.

Honduras is sometimes called Banana Land. And no wonder! It is the
second most important banana-growing
country in the world.

Miles and miles of banana plantations
stretch across its hot coastal plains. Most
of them are owned by large American
fruit companies. You see, it is very expensive to grow large quantities of bananas. It takes a great deal of money to
clear the jungles and plant, care for, and
market this tasty fruit.

Whole villages have been laid out for
the plantation workers. Each one has
modern homes, a store, a hospital, a
school, and a church and are nicknamed
"banana towns."

Bananas grow on tall plants. Small
pieces of banana root are planted about
twenty feet apart. Soon, green spongy
stalks shoot up. Within a few months,
they may be from twenty to twenty-five
feet tall. Near the top of each stalk,
enormous bright green leaves unfold.

After about ten months, a huge cluster
of finger-like blossoms appears at the top
of the banana stalk. When the blossoms
drop off, tiny bananas are seen pointing
toward the earth. As the fruit grows
larger, however, the bananas point upward. Each plant produces only one
bunch of fruit, but a single bunch may
hold a hundred or more bananas.

The banana plants grow very rapidly
in this hot tropical land. Twelve to fifteen months after they are planted, the
fruit is ready to harvest.

"Banana Land" is a busy place at
harvesttime. The fruit is gathered while
it is still quite green so that it will keep
well on its way to market. Many pairs
of workmen move through the rows of

plants. One man cuts the tall banana stalk so that it will bend down. Then he lowers the bunch of bananas onto the shoulder of his partner.

Waiting oxcarts or trucks take the bananas to the nearby railroad cars to be hauled to ports. Fast refrigerator ships rush the fruit to the United States and other countries.

Mahogany trees like the hot, wet plains of Honduras. Mahogany is a hardwood used in making fine furniture. When it is polished, it looks very rich and shiny. You may have some mahogany furniture in your home.

Mahogany trees are found in the jungle. Though many kinds of trees crowd around each one, usually no other mahogany tree grows close by. Each one stands like a proud king of its part of the tropical forest. Just think! The mahogany tree is two hundred years old before it is full-grown. By that time, it towers a hundred feet high and has a sturdy trunk that may be thirty feet around.

Because mahogany is very valuable, men are willing to work hard to obtain it from the hot jungles. After a tree is cut down, it is sawed into logs. Powerful oxen drag the heavy logs to the nearest river. Then they are floated to seaports to be shipped to other countries.

El Salvador is tucked in between Guatemala and Honduras. Find El Salvador on the map. This smallest country of Central America is about the size of Maryland. Its capital is the busy city of San Salvador.

As the map on page 87 shows, El Salvador is a mountainous land. But its people have made good use of its pleasant fertile valleys. Nearly every foot of good soil outside of its towns and villages is used to grow crops. Cotton, wheat, corn, and coffee are raised, but coffee is the biggest crop. Strangely enough, this small country grows nearly a fourth of the world's finest coffee.

In some of the mountains, there are rich deposits of minerals. Among those which are now being mined are gold, silver, lead, and zinc.

El Salvador is an ambitious country. It is doing many things to help improve the living conditions of its people. It has built schools for children and night schools for adults. It is working to stamp out yellow fever and malaria. In addition, it is building modern hospitals and improving its transportation system.

A Glance at Nicaragua, Costa Rica, and Panama

Nicaragua sits in the middle of Central America. Locate it. It is a little larger than our state of New York. Its capital, Managua, is built on the beautiful shores of Lake Managua. Do you see this city on the map? Unlike most other capital cities of Central America, Managua has a hot climate. It is located on low plains near the west coast. Most of the people live on the western plains. Here farmers raise corn, cotton, beans, rice, and sugar cane.

Nicaragua also has mountains and hills. Gold is mined in parts of these mountains.

Inside the seed pods of the cacao tree are the chocolate beans.

Some lumbering and cattle-ranching are carried on. But the chief industry is raising coffee. Fine coffee is grown on the hilly lands and mountain slopes west and northwest of Managua.

Miles of low plains extend along the Caribbean. This eastern region is one of the wettest lands on earth. As much as 300 inches of rain may pour on these plains in a year. Dense jungles crowd over the land except where banana and cacao plantations have been laid out.

Nicaragua is famous for its cacao trees. Chocolate beans grow on cacao trees. After a tree is about five years old, it begins to bear blossoms. As the blossoms drop off, purplish yellow pods form.

When they are ripe, they are filled with many chocolate beans. The beans are harvested and dried. Then they are shipped to factories to be crushed and made into cocoa and chocolate.

Nicaragua may have an ocean-to-ocean canal some day. The route for it would probably lead up the San Juan River and across Lake Nicaragua. Continuing westward it would cut through the mountains to the Pacific. Trace such a route on the map. It was this route which dozens of gold seekers took on their way to California in 1849. Cutting across Central America saved a long sea journey around South America.

South of Nicaragua lies Costa Rica. Locate Costa Rica on the map. Its name means "rich coast." Its attractive capital, San José, is located near the center of the country in a wide valley, or basin, in the mountains.

Many people live in this beautiful high valley. Its soil is very rich, and its climate is well-suited to growing crops. Nearly every farm family has its own patch of corn and beans to supply its table. Dairy cattle provide milk, cheese, and butter for the farmers and the people of the towns. Sugar cane and pineapples are also raised. And of course bananas are grown on the low plains. But coffee is the chief "money" crop.

Costa Ricans are very proud of their country. And they have a right to be. They have provided fine schools for their children. Indeed, all those between the ages of seven and fourteen are required to attend school.

Costa Rica is a nation of farmers. It wants all of its people to share the land. So no one is allowed to own an enormous plantation. The land is divided into many small farms, and the people are encouraged to use the best and most up-to-date ways of farming. In fact, farming is one of the subjects taught at school.

Costa Rica has a strong and united government. Because so many of its people can read and write, they take an active part in voting and helping to run the affairs of their country.

Panama is the narrowest country of Central America. It also reaches the farthest south, as the map shows. It occupies the long crooked bridge of land known as the Isthmus of Panama. This country is a little larger than the state of West Virginia.

Like the other countries of Central America, Panama has a backbone of mountains reaching through it. They are highest in the north but shrink in size toward the south. At the foot of the mountains are low forested hills, broad valleys, and sizzling hot low plains. Pouring rains often soak these plains.

Bananas, coconuts, sugar cane, and cacao are grown on the plains. On the small farms, the people raise corn and beans and other food crops.

Panama has had an exciting history. As long ago as 1519, a group of Spaniards settled on the Pacific coast of this isthmus. They found so many fish that they named their settlement Panama, meaning "many fish."

In the next unit, you will learn how Spaniards conquered many lands in South America. From some of these lands, they took large quantities of gold, silver, and other valuable treasures. This loot was shipped to the settlement of Panama. Then it was carried by donkeys and Indian slaves over rough trails across the isthmus. Finally, it reached the Atlantic side of the isthmus. There, it was loaded on ships bound for Spain. During these years, Panama became known as "the crossroads of the New World."

For a long time, Panama was a part of Colombia. Then, in 1903, it won its independence. Today, the ten-mile-wide Panama Canal Zone runs through the center of the country.

Many of Panama's people have jobs connected with the running of the canal. Furthermore, Panama receives a large sum of "rent" money for the use of the Canal Zone.

The old village of Panama no longer stands. But large, modern Panama City is located nearby. It is the capital and largest city of this long, narrow land.

Summing up. The Central-American countries have many problems to solve. Among these are how to improve their health conditions and provide better transportation and communication systems. They need also to help more of their people get an education and work for better ways of living.

But these countries have come a long way. Central America was held down by Spain for many years. Then, most of its people were very poor and had no chance to improve their lot. They also had no chance to learn how to govern themselves. Today, each country is working to help its people. Furthermore, these countries are co-operating with the countries of North America as good friends and good neighbors.

Other Latin-American countries share the continent of South America. We shall read about them later.

Some Review Questions

1. Where is Central America? Name and locate its countries.

2. What have you learned about the Mayas' ways of living? How were the Mayas conquered?

3. How are the Central-American republics alike? How are they different?

4. What are the chief products of each of the Central-American countries? Which are grown on the low plains? Which are grown in the high lands?

Play Detective! What's Missing?

On paper write the numbers 1 to 8. After each number, write the missing word or words from the list below to complete the sentence correctly.

1. _?_ is Central America's newest country.

2. The _?_ were among the earliest people to live in Central America.

3. Most of the capitals of the Central-American countries are in _?_.

4. The tall _?_ tree is sometimes called the "chewing gum tree."

5. The chief crop of Honduras is _?_.

6. The _?_ tree is sometimes called the "king of the tropical forests."

7. _?_ is raised on the lower mountain slopes by many Costa Rican farmers.

8. _?_ is the long, narrow republic cut in half by a large canal.

bananas	coffee	mahogany
cacao	Panama	mountain valleys
chicle	Mayas	Belize
Aztecs	Costa Rica	corn

Using Maps

Refer to the maps on pages 87, 334, and 411 to help you answer these questions:

1. Which of these maps show relief? Which is a political map? Which is a landform map?

2. Is Central America north or south of the equator? Is it in the low, middle, or high latitudes?

3. What country has the most plains? What country is an isthmus? What sea do most of these countries face?

4. Study the inset map on page 411. What two main ideas does it tell you?

Thinking Together

1. Why is air transportation so important to Central America?

2. How has climate influenced ways of living in Central America? How have landforms influenced them?

3. What things do we import from Central America? What do we export there?

4. What can you do to encourage more understanding of Central Americans?

Some Other Things to Do

1. Read in an encyclopedia about one of the following and summarize what you learn.

Mayas   cacao   chicle   bananas

2. Collect and arrange pictures showing the banana industry.

3. List the main products of Central America.

4. Be ready to help your class pronounce these words correctly:

Tegucigalpa   mestizo   Caribbean

24 · The Caribbean Region: Islands Large and Small

The West Indies Story

How sugar cane came to the New World. Manuel and Pedro were Spanish colonists. They had sailed to the West Indies with Columbus on his second voyage to the New World.

This time, the ambitious captain had led seventeen ships. They carried more than a thousand colonists and soldiers as well as horses and cattle. Also on board were foods, seeds, plants, and tools.

It took hours and hours to unload the large quantities of supplies, and some men complained. "This task is endless!" grumbled Manuel, wearily.

"Aye, but necessary!" reminded his older friend, Pedro. "Everything we've brought will help our new colony."

"Nonsense! What good are these sticks anyway?" Manuel pointed to bundles and bundles of cuttings.

"They're pieces of sugar-cane stalks," explained Pedro. "Columbus told me so. We're to guard them carefully. Columbus says we'll plant them soon. They'll grow into tall stalks full of sweet juice, in this warm climate. They'll produce sugar! Think of that!"

"Sugar!" exclaimed Manuel. "Well! That is good news!"

Both Manuel and Pedro knew that sugar was very expensive. Only the rich could afford it because it was so scarce. In those days, sugar cane was grown in large quantities only in certain hot, far-away lands of Asia and Africa. No wonder, then, that Columbus dreamed of raising it in the new colony.

The treasured cane cuttings were planted in a part of the West Indies now

Columbus brought sugar cane to the West Indies on his second voyage to the New World.

THE VOYAGES OF COLUMBUS

——— First voyage, 1492
············ Second voyage, 1493
– – – – Third voyage, 1498
ooooooo Fourth voyage, 1502

Spanish lands

Portuguese lands

This map shows Columbus's four voyages to the New World. Which one took him to South America? On this map you can see what lands Spain and Portugal claimed in the New World. Which country claimed the most?

occupied by the Dominican Republic. Look on the map on page 423 and find this republic. Before long, a sugar mill was built. Thus, more than 400 years ago, the West Indies' sugar industry began.

For a time, Spain controlled the West Indies. As you learned in Chapter 1, Columbus discovered and named this region in 1492.

During the early 1500's, a number of Spanish colonies were started. The Spaniards tried to force the Indians to raise their sugar cane and other crops. But this plan was not successful. Later on, slaves were brought from Africa to work in the fields.

Three other European countries seized lands in the West Indies. In the early days, as you know, gold and silver were being shipped from Panama to Spain. The treasure ships sailed across the Caribbean Sea past the West Indies and out into the Atlantic. Several European countries watched with longing eyes as this valuable cargo headed for Spain. They, too, wished for riches.

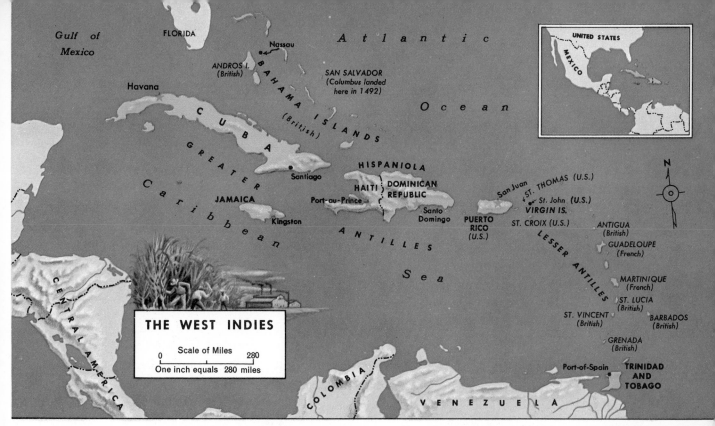

Gulf of Mexico

FLORIDA

Nassau

ANDROS I. (British)

Havana

SAN SALVADOR (Columbus landed here in 1492)

Atlantic

Ocean

BAHAMA ISLANDS (British)

CUBA

GREATER

Santiago

JAMAICA

Caribbean

Kingston

HISPANIOLA

HAITI DOMINICAN REPUBLIC

Port-au-Prince

Santo Domingo

PUERTO RICO (U.S.)

San Juan ST. THOMAS (U.S.)

St. John (U.S.)

VIRGIN IS.

ST. CROIX (U.S.)

ANTIGUA (British)

GUADELOUPE (French)

MARTINIQUE (French)

ST. LUCIA (British)

BARBADOS (British)

ST. VINCENT (British)

GRENADA (British)

ANTILLES

LESSER ANTILLES

Sea

CENTRAL AMERICA

COLOMBIA

VENEZUELA

Port-of-Spain TRINIDAD AND TOBAGO

N

UNITED STATES

MEXICO

THE WEST INDIES

Scale of Miles

0   280

One inch equals 280 miles

Daring English, French, and Dutch pirates sailed to the Caribbean Sea. They hid in certain quiet harbors of the islands, ready to pounce on Spanish treasure ships and rob them. Sometimes fierce battles were fought over the shiploads of precious gold.

After a time, England, France, and the Netherlands seized some of the West Indies for themselves. England took the Bahamas, Jamaica, and an island called Trinidad, far to the south. Find these islands on the map. France and the Netherlands got only a few small islands off the coast of South America. Later, the western third of Hispaniola became a French colony.

For many years, Spain kept a firm hold on the West Indies. It governed Cuba, the eastern two thirds of Hispaniola and Puerto Rico for over three hundred years. Locate these islands. During these

This is a political map of the West Indies. What island is shared by two countries? Find the islands which are a part of the United States.

years, the people of the islands had no share in their government.

Today, most of the islanders run their own governments. In 1898, the Spanish-owned islands gained their independence. Freedom was also won by Haiti on the island of Hispaniola. Today each of these lands governs itself. As you know, one of them, Puerto Rico, is a part of the United States.

In 1962, Jamaica, Trinidad, and Tobago were given their independence by Great Britain. Like Canada, these three islands are members of the Commonwealth of Nations. As you learned earlier, the Commonwealth is a family of free nations that are loyal to the King or Queen of England.

423

A Glance at
the Islands' Geography

The West Indies are a group of large and small islands. They are scattered through the Caribbean Sea. They extend in a long curve for more than 2,000 miles. One end of this curve begins near Florida, as the map on page 422 shows. Notice that the southern end almost touches the South-American country of Venezuela.

Most of the islands in the West Indies are the tops of a sunken chain of mountains. The four largest islands are Cuba, Hispaniola, Jamaica, and Puerto Rico. Which one is quite near Florida? Which one is closest to Central America?

The West Indies are densely populated. Many of their people are descended from the early Spanish settlers. Spanish is still the official language in some islands. A much larger number of people are blacks, however.

The West Indies have a tropical climate. Like the lands of Central America, the West Indies are in the trade-wind belt. The northeast trade winds bring plenty of rain to most of the islands. As these winds rise to cross the mountains, they are cooled and drop heavy showers on the lands below. The rains are heaviest on the northeast side of the islands. This is the side facing the winds.

As the air goes down the other side of the mountains, it is warmed and drops little moisture. So the southwest side of the islands is drier. Some islands like the Bahamas have no mountains and are quite dry. Can you tell why?

From August to October, terrible storms called hurricanes sometimes whip across the West Indies. *Hurricanes* are mighty whirling winds that are often hundreds of miles across. They can uproot trees, smash buildings, and leave whole towns in ruins.

Hurricanes begin over the Atlantic Ocean and usually travel northwestward. They may whirl across the Gulf of Mexico and on through the states of the gulf, or across Florida and north over states along the Atlantic coast. Drenching rains often follow hurricanes.

The West Indies have a warm climate, winter and summer. There, flowers bloom all the year round. But then, these islands are in the tropics, as the map on page 314 shows. Winters are especially pleasant, with never a touch of frost. The balmy mid-winter weather attracts many vacationers to islands such as the Bahamas.

A Closer Look
at Some Islands

The Bahamas are coral islands. Corals are small creatures that live in the sea. Certain corals are found mainly in warm tropical waters such as those of the West Indies region.

For thousands of years, coral skeletons have piled up, layer upon layer. The huge masses that collected in one area have formed the islands known as the Bahamas. Find them on the map.

The Bahama islands were a British colony for about three hundred years. The capital and largest city is Nassau. Some

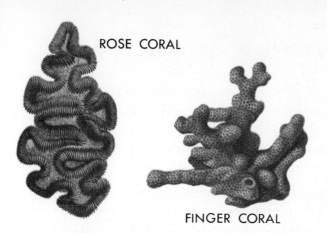

ROSE CORAL

FINGER CORAL

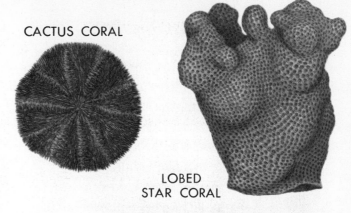

CACTUS CORAL

LOBED
STAR CORAL

Some of the many kinds of coral.

of the people make their living fishing, or by farming. But the chief business of the islands is caring for the tourist trade.

The United States has been allowed to build a large naval base on one of the islands. It helps to protect our southern coasts as well as the Panama Canal.

Cuba is the largest island in the West Indies. Look for it on the map. Notice how this long, curved island sits at the entrance to the Gulf of Mexico. Cuba is more than 700 miles long and is about the size of Pennsylvania. A rugged backbone of mountains covers about a fourth of the island. But the rest of the land is a rolling plain.

Havana is Cuba's capital and chief seaport. It looks out on a fine harbor on the north coast of the island.

Havana is partly old and partly new. In the oldest sections are narrow streets and thick-walled churches built by the Spaniards long ago. But the newer parts of the city have wide avenues and modern buildings.

Cuba gained freedom from Spain in 1898. In 1895, bitter revolt broke out. The Spanish governor punished the rebels by ordering their homes burned and their crops destroyed. Their leaders were thrown into prison and left to die. Such cruel treatment shocked many Americans.

In 1898, however, an event occurred which angered the United States still more. An American battleship, the *Maine*, was anchored in the harbor of Havana on a friendly visit. Suddenly, one February night, a terrible explosion rocked the ship. Within minutes it sank, carrying several hundred officers and men to their deaths. Many people blamed Spain for this tragedy. They believed that Spaniards had planted explosives beneath the ship.

Soon, our Congress declared war on Spain. American soldiers and sailors were rushed to Cuba to fight—not to gain the island but to help it become free. The war lasted only a short time. After Spain's defeat, Cuba became an independent nation.

Meanwhile doctors and workmen from our country were fighting battles against another enemy, the deadly disease of yellow fever. Thousands of American and Cuban soldiers had died of yellow fever. But its cause had not yet been discovered.

Doctors and their helpers made many tests and experiments. Finally, they learned that mosquitoes were spreading the disease. The big job, then, was to get rid of millions of these insects. Americans and Cubans worked together to drain swamps and clean up the mosquitoes' breeding places. Thus living conditions were improved in cities and on farms.

For many years, the United States and Cuba had close ties. There were friendly feelings between the two countries. Today, however, this has changed.

In 1959, Cuba was taken over by Fidel Castro. He made himself a dictator and took away much freedom from the Cuban people. As you have learned, a dictator has complete power over the people of a country. Later, the Soviet Union and other Communist countries became friendly with Cuba. They increased their trade with this island country and sent it money, soldiers, and arms.

Cuba became a Communist country. Then all trade between it and the United States stopped.

The Communist government in Cuba has caused many problems. The United States and the Latin-American countries are concerned that Communism will spread to other parts of Latin America. Indeed, the fact that Soviet arms are in Cuba may threaten the peace of the Western Hemisphere and even of the entire world.

Agriculture is Cuba's main industry. It is easy to understand why. Cuba's year-long growing season, rich soils, and plentiful rains make it possible to raise many kinds of crops. Sugar cane is the most important one.

The busiest time of the year is the harvest season. The sugar-cane stalks are cut close to the ground. The tops are cut off and the stalks stripped of leaves. Then they are rushed to the mill where raw sugar will be made. Oxcarts carry the

stalks from the fields to nearby railroad cars. The cars haul them on to the sugar mill. The picture on page 427 tells much about the interesting story of sugar.

Tobacco is grown on many hillsides. In some fields, the plants are covered with thin white cheesecloth. This protects them from the burning sun. When dried, the tobacco leaves are used to wrap cigars.

Coffee plantations stretch across some hilly lands. There, too, are citrus orchards, fields of pineapple, and patches of cassava plants. Tapioca is made from cassava roots.

South of Cuba lies beautiful Jamaica. Find it on the map. Here, the language spoken is English. Jamaica is famous for its scenery. In fact, long ago Columbus was charmed by its beauty. It has many lovely mountains. Some of its peaks rise more than a mile above sea level.

Agriculture is Jamaica's chief industry. At one time, sugar was the only important crop. But now, fields of coffee and cattle ranches stretch over the higher lands. On the plains along the coast are banana and sugar plantations. Here, too, are farms which grow vegetables and fruits for the island.

Haiti occupies the western third of Hispaniola. Locate Hispaniola on the map. As you can see, this large island lies southeast of Cuba. Hispaniola is a mountainous land. Indeed, some of its peaks rise 10,000 feet above the sea.

Look for Haiti on the map. Notice how close it is to Cuba. Haiti's capital, Port-au-Prince has a French name. But this is not surprising, for western Hispaniola was once a French colony. Though Haiti is now an independent nation, French is

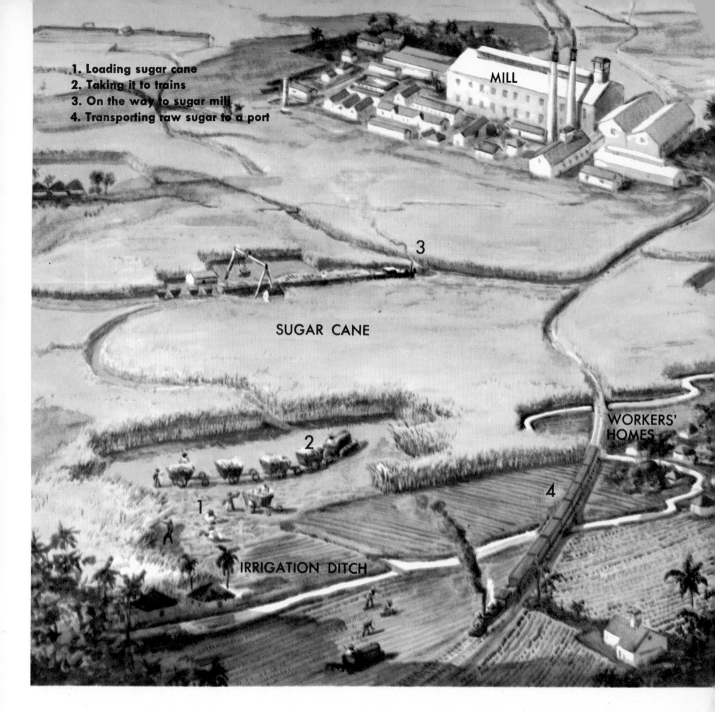

1. Loading sugar cane
2. Taking it to trains
3. On the way to sugar mill
4. Transporting raw sugar to a port

MILL

SUGAR CANE

WORKERS' HOMES

IRRIGATION DITCH

still its official language, Haiti is the only French-speaking country in Latin America.

Haiti is thickly populated. Most of its people are blacks whose ancestors were brought by the French to work on sugar plantations. Farming is the main industry. Such crops as sugar cane, tobacco, cotton, and coffee are raised.

The Dominican Republic reaches across eastern Hispaniola. It, too, is an agricultural land. On its plains are sugar, cotton, and tobacco plantations as well as smaller farms. Farther inland are cattle ranches.

The capital and chief city of the Dominican Republic is named Santo Domingo. It was started just four years

after Columbus first visited the West Indies and is the oldest city in the New World. One of its churches was built in 1512. It is said that Columbus is buried beneath this church.

East of the Dominican Republic is Puerto Rico. It is a hilly land about the size of our states of Delaware and Rhode Island added together. It is nearly a hundred miles long and about forty miles wide. Low mountains and hills cover the central part, but low lands extend along the coast.

For a long time, Puerto Rico was governed by Spain. Columbus had claimed it when he landed there on his second voyage to the New World. He gave it its name, which means "rich port." As time passed, many Spaniards settled in Puerto Rico. Spain ruled it for four centuries; but in 1898 it became an American territory.

Puerto Rico manages its own government. It elects its governor and the representatives who make its laws. The people of Puerto Rico are citizens of the United States; but it is not one of our states. So its people do not vote for the President of our country nor members of our Congress.

The United States government has helped the Puerto Ricans in many ways. It has shown them better ways of farming and how to make their island a healthier place. Also, it has guided them in improving their roads and opening more schools.

Puerto Rico has a large population for a small land. More than 2,400,000 people are crowded on this island. Many live in its capital, San Juan.

428

Puerto Rico's most important industries. Farming is the main industry on this tropical island. The warm moist climate is well-suited to growing crops such as tobacco, coffee, citrus fruits, pineapples, and bananas. Most farmers also raise corn and beans for their families. Beef and dairy cattle are kept on some farms. But sugar cane is the biggest crop.

Many people are employed on the farms and plantations. And others work in the cities. But because Puerto Rico has such a large population, there have not been enough jobs to go around. Recently, however, many new businesses have been started to provide more jobs.

Manufacturing is Puerto Rico's newest industry. Some factories are using the products of the island. Pineapples are canned or made into juice. Cigars and cigarettes are manufactured from tobacco grown on the island. Other factories make textiles, clothing, pottery, chinaware, and cement. Some of these goods are sold to other lands.

The lovely Virgin Islands are neighbors of Puerto Rico. They lie about forty miles east of Puerto Rico. Look for them on the map on page 423. Notice how small they are. There are about fifty in all, but only a few have people living on them. The three largest and most important of the Virgin Islands are St. Thomas, St. Croix, and St. John.

For many years, the Virgin Islands belonged to Denmark, a country in Europe. Then in 1917, they were sold to our country. The United States has built strong defense bases on the islands to help protect the Panama Canal.

Our study of the West Indies brings Unit Five to an end. It has told you about the Latin-American republics of North America and the Caribbean region. The next unit will take us to the Latin-American republics of South America.

Let's Review!

1. Where are the West Indies?
2. What are the main islands in this group? Why were they given the name *Indies*?
3. What country first claimed the West Indies? Why? What industry did it start in the islands long ago?
4. What are the chief industries today in Cuba? Puerto Rico? Haiti? the Bahamas? Jamaica? the Dominican Republic?

Test Yourself

Try to complete the sentences below.

1. The four largest islands of the West Indies are __?__, __?__, __?__, and __?__.
2. Puerto Rico is a part of the __?__ __?__ but it is not a state.
3. A dictator named Fidel Castro rules the island of __?__.
4. Terrible storms called __?__ sometimes whip across the West Indies.
5. Because the West Indies are in the __?__, they have a mild climate the year round.
6. The Bahamas were formed by millions of little sea creatures known as __?__.
7. Tapioca is made from the roots of the __?__ plant.
8. The two countries of __?__ and __?__ share the island of Hispaniola.
9. The __?__ Islands belong to the United States. They lie south of __?__.

Some Questions to Think About

1. If you were planning to visit the West Indies, when should you go? Why?

2. What are some ways in which people might protect themselves from hurricanes?

3. What does it mean when we say an area is over-populated? What are some problems this causes, do you think?

4. We name winds for the direction *from* which they come. In the northern hemisphere the trade winds blow toward the southwest. Since they blow *from* the northeast we call them the northeast trades. In the southern hemisphere the trades blow toward the northwest. What are they called?

Things to Do

1. Use the pronouncing helps in the Index and prove that you can pronounce the following words correctly:

Jamaica	Bahamas	Tabago
Puerto Rico	Havana	Trinidad

2. On a large map of the West Indies help your class point out these places:

Caribbean Sea	Havana
Cuba	Hispaniola
Haiti	Dominican Republic
Jamaica	Puerto Rico
Bahamas	the Virgin Islands

3. Share with your class an illustrated report on one of these topics:

Coral   Sponges   The cassava plant

4. Bring samples of different kinds of sponges to exhibit.

5. Read how men have conquered yellow fever. Some members of your class may wish to dramatize this story.

6. Look in your newspaper and news magazines for interesting items about the West Indies. Bring them to school and tell your class what you have learned.

In What Order Did These Events Happen?

Below are listed some important events about which you have just read. Number each one in the order in which it happened.

—?— The United States bought the Virgin Islands.

—?— Cuba lost its freedom.

—?— Columbus landed at San Salvador.

—?— Cuba gained freedom from Spain.

—?— Columbus made his fourth voyage.

—?— Jamaica, Trinidad, and Tobago were given their independence.

—?— England took a share of the West Indies.

Fun with Maps

Use the map on page 422.

1. Is this a global map or a flat one?

2. How many voyages did Columbus make to the New World? Which helps you identify each voyage, the key or the map's legend.

Now refer to the map on page 423.

1. What is the title of this map?

2. Is this a political map or a landform map? What are the reasons for your answer?

3. Name and locate each of the main islands which are a part of the United States.

4. Which island is shared by two countries?

5. Which faces the Caribbean Sea, Jamaica or Trinidad? Which one is closer to South America?

6. Use the scale of miles and measure the distance from the tip of Florida (a) to Havana. (b) to the island on which Columbus landed.

UNIT SIX

Our South American Neighbors

25 · South America: Our Sister Continent

South America's Story

South America was discovered by Columbus in 1498. As you know, he had found and claimed the West Indies for Spain. But this had not satisfied the king. The Spanish ruler still dreamed of finding a waterway to India. So in 1498, Columbus set out on a third trip west. Turn back to the global map on page 422 and trace this journey.

The brave explorer reached the continent now known as South America. On its northeast coast, he found a wide waterway leading inland. Hopefully, Columbus helped his men lower small boats to explore it. The sailors rowed several miles upstream, but when they tasted the water it was not salty. That proved the waterway was only a river. Today, this river is known as the Orinoco.

Columbus was bitterly disappointed, but he planted the Spanish flag on the new land. He did not know that he had discovered a large, rich continent.

In time several European countries claimed lands in South America. But Spain won the largest share. Its explorers and soldiers followed Columbus to new lands on this continent.

Most of South America became a part of a huge Spanish empire. Use the global map on page 422 again and see how the Spanish Empire extended over much of South America. Indeed, it also stretched over a large part of North America.

Portugal claimed the part of South America now called Brazil. It had been discovered by a Portuguese explorer. Portuguese settlers started settlements along its coast.

Several other European countries were interested in South America. England, France, and the Netherlands wanted tropical lands for growing sugar cane and tobacco. South America's hot, wet northeast coast had the right climate for such crops. A few Europeans sailed to this coast. They started settlements in areas now known as Guyana, Surinam, and French Guiana. Surinam governs itself now. But it still has some ties with the Netherlands. French Guiana has some ties to France. British Guiana is now the independent country of Guyana.

Spanish adventurers and settlers arrived in South America. Some of them reached fascinating Indian cities and

South America is an exciting place to visit. 1. At the left, ruins of an Inca city in the Andes of Peru. 2. An Indian village on a hillside. 3. The busy port of Santos, Brazil. 4. Caracas, Venezuela, one of the continent's large, modern cities. 5. Jungle in the Amazon region. 6. Gauchos round up cattle on a ranch in Argentina.

The Western Hemisphere · In which direction is South America from our continent?

stores of gold and silver which the natives had mined. Much treasure was seized and shipload after shipload of gold and silver was sent to Spain.

Some Spaniards started cities and farms. They did not intend to do the work themselves, however; so they settled in areas where many Indians lived. As in Mexico, the Spaniards took the best lands for themselves. They forced the Indians to put up buildings, raise crops, and tend cattle and sheep.

Farming became an important business in Spanish South America. Food had to be raised for the Spanish settlers and their Indian workers. Hides and wool were needed for clothing. Sugar, cotton, tobacco, and cacao were raised to be sold to Spain.

Spain ruled its South American empire for nearly three hundred years. During this time, the colonists could take no part in their government. They had to obey many harsh laws and pay high taxes. Indeed, they were as unhappy and dissatisfied as the other Spanish colonists about whom you read in earlier chapters.

Independence and many new countries. In 1809, fighting broke out between the colonists and Spanish officials and soldiers stationed in South America. During the next fifteen years, many bitter battles

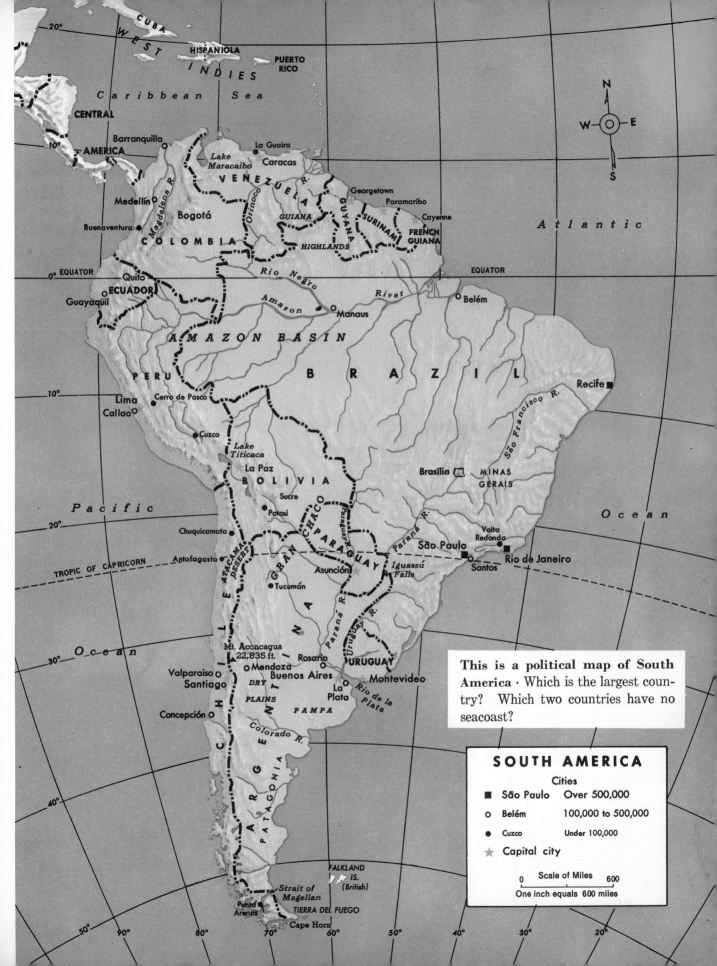

20° W E S T

CUBA

HISPANIOLA

PUERTO RICO

I N D I E S

C a r i b b e a n   S e a

CENTRAL

10°

AMERICA

Barranquilla

La Guaira

Caracas

Lake Maracaibo

V E N E Z U E L A

Georgetown

Paramaribo

Atlantic

Medellín

Bogotá

Orinoco R.

GUIANA

GUYANA

SURINAM

Cayenne

FRENCH GUIANA

Buenaventura

COLOMBIA

Magdalena R.

HIGHLANDS

0° EQUATOR

Quito

ECUADOR

Rio Negro

River

EQUATOR

Belém

Guayaquil

Amazon

Manaus

A M A Z O N   B A S I N

Ocean

P E R U

B R A Z I L

10°

Lima

Cerro de Pasco

Recife

Callao

São Francisco R.

Cuzco

Lake Titicaca

La Paz

Brasília

MINAS GERAIS

Pacific

B O L I V I A

Sucre

Potosí

CHACO

Paraguay R.

Paraná R.

20°

Chuquicamata

GRAN

PARAGUAY

Volta Redonda

São Paulo

Ocean

ATACAMA DESERT

TROPIC OF CAPRICORN

Antofagasta

Asunción

Iguassú Falls

Santos

Rio de Janeiro

Tucumán

Paraná R.

Uruguay R.

Mt. Aconcagua 22,835 ft.

Rosario

30°

Ocean

Valparaíso

Mendoza

A R G E N T I N A

URUGUAY

Santiago

DRY

Buenos Aires

Montevideo

La Plata

Rio de la Plata

Concepción

PLAINS

PAMPA

This is a political map of South America · Which is the largest country? Which two countries have no seacoast?

Colorado R.

PATAGONIA

40°

C H I L E

SOUTH AMERICA

Cities

■ São Paulo   Over 500,000

○ Belém   100,000 to 500,000

● Cuzco   Under 100,000

★ Capital city

FALKLAND IS. (British)

Strait of Magellan

TIERRA DEL FUEGO

Punta Arenas

0   Scale of Miles   600

One inch equals 600 miles

50°

Cape Horn

90°   80°   70°   60°   50°   40°   30°   20°

TROPIC OF CANCER

20°

Caribbean Sea

A landform map of South America · What mountains stretch through the continent from north to south? Where are most of the plateau lands? Find the low plains of the Amazon Basin.

SOUTH AMERICA SHOWING LANDFORMS

Chiefly plains

Chiefly plateaus

Chiefly hills

Chiefly mountains

0   Scale of Miles   600

One inch equals 600 miles

Lake Maracaibo

ORINOCO BASIN

Orinoco R.

GUIANA HIGHLANDS

Magdalena R.

Río Negro

Amazon

Amazon River

0°

EQUATOR

A t l a n t i c

AMAZON BASIN

A N D E S

BRAZILIAN HIGHLANDS

10°

El Misti 19,167 ft.

Lake Titicaca

PLATEAU OF BOLIVIA

MINAS GERAIS

O c e a n

P a c i f i c

ATACAMA DESERT

GRAN CHACO

Paraguay R.

20°

M O U N T A I N S

O c e a n

TROPIC OF CAPRICORN

Paraná R.

Uruguay R.

Iguassú Falls

30°

Mt. Aconcagua 22,835 ft.

DRY PLAINS   PAMPA

Río de la Plata

Colorado R.

Study the small population map · Notice how much of South America has under 2 persons to a square mile.

PATAGONIA

VENEZUELA

GUIANA

SURINAM

FR. GUIANA

COLOMBIA

ECUADOR

PERU

BRAZIL

BOLIVIA

PARAGUAY

40°

CHILE

ARGENTINA

URUGUAY

POPULATION
People per square mile

Under 2   25 to 125

2 to 25   125 to 250

Over 250

436

Strait of Magellan

50°

Cape Horn

90°   80°   70°   60°   50°   40°   30°   20°

were fought. Finally the brave colonists won their independence.

Nine republics were carved out of Spanish South America. They were Argentina, Chile, Bolivia, Peru, Ecuador, Colombia, Venezuela, Uruguay, and Paraguay. Soon Brazil also gained its independence. Locate these ten countries and the new one, Guyana, on the map on page 435. What colonies occupy a small part of South America?

A Look at the Geography of South America

Comparing two sister continents. North and South America bear the same "last" name. And they share the Western Hemisphere, as the map on page 434 shows. They also have other things in common; yet in some ways the two continents are very different. Let's compare them.

South America is not *directly* south of North America. Most of South America lies *east* as well as *south* of our continent. You can see this if you lay a ruler on the map in a north-south direction so that it passes through New York City. Notice what a large part of South America lies east of our east coast.

South America is smaller than North America but both continents are somewhat similar in shape. Look at the map and notice how both are wider toward the north and become narrow in the far south.

Both Americas have a backbone of high, young mountains stretching in a north-south direction through their western lands. Find South America's western ranges on the map on page 436. Both continents have ranges of old, worn-down mountains in the east. Both continents are blessed with broad, rich plains and some large rivers. Find South America's immense plains region on the map. Try to think of further comparisons as you continue with your study of South America.

Most of South America lies south of the equator. Point to the equator on the map on page 436. Through what countries does it pass? The equator, remember, is a line which map-makers draw on maps midway between the north and south poles. It is the east-west line marked 0° that divides the earth into the Northern and Southern Hemispheres. Because most of South America is south of the equator, this continent is said to be in the Southern Hemisphere.

About three fourths of South America is located in the tropics. As you have learned, the tropics extend north and south of the equator from the Tropic of Cancer to the Tropic of Capricorn. Find the tropics on your map. What countries are in the tropics?

The tropics have about the same temperature winter and summer, you'll recall. But not all of the lands in the tropics have the same kind of climate.

The tropical low lands are hot, wet lands. Their climate is very disagreeable. But the valleys and the plateaus have a cooler and more pleasant climate. You know the main reason why. High lands have a cooler climate than low lands in the same region. It is important to remember, then, that the temperature in the

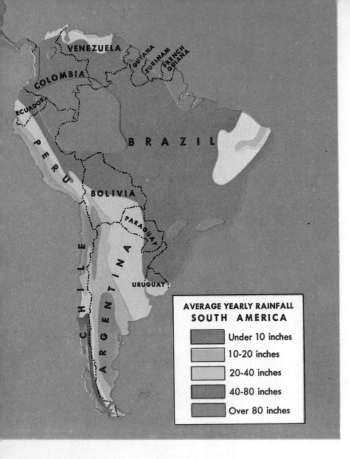

AVERAGE YEARLY RAINFALL
SOUTH AMERICA

	Under 10 inches
	10-20 inches
	20-40 inches
	40-80 inches
	Over 80 inches

This map shows how much rain falls in the different parts of South America in a year. Below are photographs of the tropical plains of the Amazon Basin. Notice how dense the foliage is in the closeup.

tropics depends on how high the land is above sea level. Except for the seaports, most cities in the tropics are located in the high lands.

Nearly a fourth of South America lies in the region of the mid-latitudes. In the Southern Hemisphere, the mid-latitudes are located between the Tropic of Capricorn and the Antarctic Circle. Use the map on page 435 to find out what countries are in the mid-latitudes.

These mid-latitude countries have a cooler climate than the tropical lands. They have changes in temperature from season to season. As you may recall, our country is in the mid-latitudes in the Northern Hemisphere. Like most of the United States, Argentina and Chile have four seasons, winter and summer, and spring and autumn.

In the Southern Hemisphere, however, the seasons are the opposite of ours in the Northern Hemisphere. When the people there are having summer, our people may be shivering through winter. When we are having hot summer days, they are having cool winter weather. Their spring-time and corn-planting season comes with

our autumn and back-to-school days. And in our spring, they are having autumn. What kind of weather might they have at Christmastime?

Our sister continent has many kinds of lands and climates. You will learn more about them in later chapters.

South America has miles and miles of plains. In fact, about half of the continent is low plains, as you can see on the map on page 436. In the tropics, most of these plains are covered with dense jungles. Some of these thickly forested plains lie along the northeast coast. Others reach about 2,000 miles inland through the heart of Brazil. This vast region is known as the *Amazon Basin.* Study the rainfall map on page 438 and find out how much rain pours down in the Amazon Basin.

Broad plains also sweep over much of Argentina. Because they are in the mid-latitudes, they have a much cooler climate than the plains in the tropics. In fact, Argentina's plains have a climate much like that of our Central Plains.

The rainfall map shows that Argentina's plains receive much less rain than do plains in the tropics. This drier, cooler region is not covered by jungles but by tall grasses. It has rich farms and pastures where cattle graze. Argentina's plains have more people than do Brazil's steaming hot plains. Look at the population map on page 436. Notice how many more people live on the plains near Buenos Aires than on the plains of Brazil.

Many ranges of mountains rise in South America. The highest and longest ones are the Andes. Glance at the map and see how they follow close to the Pacific coast as they stretch through the continent. They begin on the hot Carib-

Compare these mid-latitude plains in Argentina with those on the opposite page.

bean coast and march south to the lonely wind-swept island of Tierra del Fuego.

The Andes climb very high and are crowned with snow all the year round. Just think! Many peaks are higher than our loftiest one in North America. The Andes are very hard to cross. Their towering ranges rise up like wall after wall. Nowhere are there low passes, so only a few roads and railroad lines cross these unfriendly mountains.

Many Andes peaks are volcanoes. The lands near them often have earthquakes. Dozens of cities and villages have suffered earthquake damage from time to time.

Lower, worn-down mountains, hills, and plateaus are scattered through some eastern parts of South America, as the map shows. In some places, the wooded slopes remind us of our Appalachians.

Some fertile valleys and rolling plateaus extend between the mountains. Though they are much lower than the mountains, they are still high lands. A number of narrow valleys are tucked in between the Andes. They have rich soil and a pleasant climate and farming is their chief industry.

On the map on page 436, find the plateau lands among the Andes. The largest area is in Bolivia, as the map shows.

Mighty rivers drain parts of South America. One is the giant Amazon. It starts high in the Andes Mountains where it is fed by melting snows. As it races swiftly down the steep slopes, it collects more and more water. A thousand muddy streams pour into it and make it one of the mightiest rivers of the world. It is so broad and deep that ocean-going vessels can steam up its channel for more than 2,000 miles. Still, the Amazon is not a very busy waterway. You see, it wanders across tropical plains that are so hot and rainy that few people live on them.

The Orinoco is the second largest river in South America. It flows east and north across 1,600 miles of high lands, plains, and swamps. Finally, it dumps its waters into the Atlantic. Far to the south are three other important rivers. They are the Paraná, the Paraguay, and the Uruguay. Locate each one on the map. Notice that all three empty into a kind of "bay" called the Río de la Plata. What large Argentina city sits on this bay?

Many busy cities are scattered through South America. They are an interesting mixture of the old and the new. Old buildings built by early Spanish settlers are surrounded by new office buildings, hotels, and apartment houses. In some places, houses face narrow streets and are crowded close together. In other sections, beautiful homes look out on broad tree-lined avenues.

Most of South America's cities are far apart. Some are separated by high mountains or jungles or rugged plateaus. Roads and railroads are very expensive to build through such lands. So there are few highways and railroads connecting the cities. People who travel long distances usually go by airplane.

What people live in South America? Many are Indians. Thousands of Indians were living in South America long before the white man came.

South America also has many *Mestizos*. Mestizos have both Spanish and Indian, or Portuguese and Indian, ancestors. Spanish and Portuguese settlers married Indians. Their children became known as Mestizos.

Thousands of South America's people are blacks. Their ancestors were brought from Africa to work on plantations. Large numbers of people are from Europe and the Far East.

Altogether, about 153,000,000 people live in South America. This is a small population for such a large continent. Indeed, South America is almost twice the size of the United States; yet our country has over 190,000,000 people.

There are many reasons for South America's smaller population. Some are a result of geography. For example, only a few people live in the enormous Amazon Basin. Why? What have you learned that would help to explain this?

The next chapter will take us to the country in which this basin is located, the exciting land of Brazil.

Help Your Class to Remember

1. Where South America is and who discovered it.
2. Why the Spanish colonies rebelled.
3. What countries and colonies share South America today.

What Is Your Idea?

1. How does elevation affect climate?
2. Why is so much of South America thinly populated?

Some Other Things to Do

1. Study the paragraphs about Latitude and Longitude across the page. Talk them over with your class.
2. List and locate on a map the places mentioned in Chapter 25. Check those you cannot find and get help from your class.
3. Be ready to pronounce these words correctly: Andes, Chile, Venezuela, Uruguay, Rio de Janeiro, and Buenos Aires.

Using Maps

1. Use the global map at the right above to help you answer these questions:

a. Which extends farther east, North America or South America?

b. Find the meridian which marks 40° West Longitude. Does it pass through a part of North America or a part of South America?

c. Look for the meridian which marks 80° West Longitude. Is it closer to New York City or New Orleans? Does it cross the equator near the east coast of South America or the west coast?

2. Study the maps on pages 434 and 435 and discuss their legends with your class.

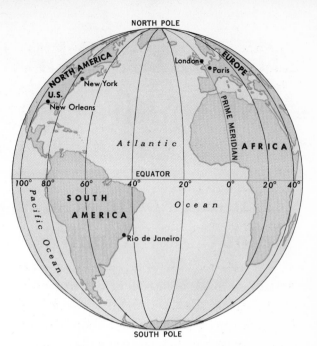

Latitude and Longitude

You have already learned some things about latitude. Remember that lines of latitude are east-west lines that circle the globe. Some lines of latitude are shown on the map on page 434.

The global map above shows only one line of latitude. Point to it. What is it called?

Notice that this map shows a number of north-south lines. They are known as *meridians of longitude*. They are half circles. See how they extend from one pole to the other.

Both latitude and longitude help us to locate places. They are also useful in helping us measure distances.

The equator is the starting point for measuring latitude, as you know. It is the 0° line of latitude.

Find the starting point of 0° meridian of longitude on the map above. It is called the *prime meridian*. What large city in England does it pass through?

Notice how the other meridians are numbered both east and west of the prime meridian. Do you live east or west of 0° Longitude? Which of these cities is west of 0° Longitude: Paris, New York, Rio de Janeiro?

26 · Brazil: The Giant Country of South America

From a Portuguese Colony to a Republic

How Brazil became a Portuguese land. In 1497, a bold Portuguese explorer, Vasco da Gama, sailed from Lisbon, Portugal, around Africa to India and back. News of his remarkable voyage set many people in Lisbon to talking.

"Captain da Gama is a great man," said twelve-year-old Henri to his father, as they strolled along the waterfront.

"Yes, my boy," agreed his father. "He has made our king and country very proud."

"Will other ships follow his route to India?" asked Henri.

The older man nodded. "Aye. Even now, the king is collecting a fleet of ships to send on Da Gama's route. Captain Cabral will be in command."

Cabral led thirteen ships south along the coast of Africa. But strong winds blew them westward to the part of South America that reaches farthest east. It is now a part of Brazil and sometimes is called Brazil's bulge. Find it on the map on page 435.

Cabral knew he had not reached India. Still, he and his men went ashore and made friends with some "Indians." They

Indians load brazilwood and water on Cabral's ship.

set up a large cross and claimed the land for Portugal. Then, well-supplied with fresh food and water, twelve ships sailed on to India. The other ship returned to Portugal with reports about the new land.

Soon, other Portuguese visited this land. They called it "Land of the Brazilwood," because brazilwood trees grew in its dense forests. This wood was used to make a rich red dye for coloring cloth. In those days good dyes were very scarce, so brazilwood was considered valuable.

Portuguese adventurers crossed the Atlantic to obtain this brazilwood. Also sailors began to stop along the bulge on their way to India. By sailing with the winds, they were carried southwest to Brazil. There, they obtained fresh food and water and then journeyed on. But it was not until the middle 1500's that the first permanent Portuguese settlement was established.

The Portuguese colony grew slowly. Some of its early settlers hoped to become rich planters. They knew the hot, wet northwest coast had just the right soil and climate for growing sugar cane. Sugar could be sold for a high price. But the planters did not care to do the farm work themselves. In their homeland they had never worked in the fields. They tried to force Indians to raise their crops, but the Indians were not used to farm work. Neither did they want to serve the white men.

Then planters began to buy slaves from Africa. Thousands were used on Brazil's plantations. Large numbers of blacks still live in the hot coastal regions of Brazil, but now they are free.

As time passed, more plantations and farms were laid out along the coast. And here and there, villages sprang up.

Some of Brazil's early settlers came to search for gold. None was found along the northwest coast, so they ventured south. Late in the 1600's, some bits of the shining metal were discovered near the small seaport of Rio de Janeiro. Find this city on the map on page 435.

News of the exciting discovery soon caused a "Gold Rush" to southeastern Brazil. Some treasure hunters were planters, but others were adventurers from Europe. A few men roamed west all the way to the Andes but they did not find gold. Still, their explorations gave Brazil claim to a huge area of land.

In the early 1700's, diamonds were found in the hilly lands northwest of Rio de Janeiro. This news also stirred up much excitement and many people hurried to these high lands.

The discovery of gold and diamonds helped Rio de Janeiro to grow. Strangely enough the name Rio de Janeiro means River of January. Long ago, on a New Year's Day in Brazil's mid-summer, a Portuguese explorer reached a lovely bay. It curved between mountains, as the picture on page 444 shows. The explorer thought the bay was the mouth of a river so he called it River of January, or Rio de Janeiro.

Later, a settlement was started on the shores of the bay. It also took the name of Rio de Janeiro. The settlement grew slowly at first, for it was hemmed in by mountains and the sea. The mountains almost cut it off from the farms and plantations farther north. During the Gold Rush, however, many gold seekers landed at Rio de Janeiro. From that time on, the village grew steadily. By 1800, it had become quite a busy little city.

An airview of Rio de Janeiro and its large island-dotted harbor.

For a time, Rio de Janeiro was the capital of Portugal. You see, in the early 1800's, the French ruler, Napoleon, tried to conquer Europe. When his armies marched toward Portugal, its king and many wealthy Portuguese fled to Brazil.

The king and his people landed at Rio de Janeiro. But my how disappointed they were! It was neither up to date nor splendid enough to serve as the capital. So work was begun at once to make it "a city fit for kings." Workmen built stately palaces and fine public buildings. A bank and a library were established and wide avenues and new parks laid out. New industries were started and trade was begun with other lands.

Later on, Napoleon's armies were defeated. Then, King John and his court returned to Portugal. But the king's son, Pedro, was left behind to rule Brazil.

In 1822, Brazil gained its independence. The Portuguese government soon sent ships to carry Pedro back to his homeland. But the young ruler refused to go. Remaining in the land he had come to love, Pedro announced Brazil's independence from Portugal. He was crowned the first Emperor.

For a time, all went well. But later, Pedro began to quarrel with his advisors. He even had some of them put in prison. This turned many Brazilians against him. Indeed, some men began to plot against the Emperor's life.

Because Pedro feared for his safety, he made plans to escape to Portugal. But he arranged to leave his five-year-old son, Pedro, at the palace. The boy was to be educated in Brazil and then crowned emperor.

444

As Pedro said good-bye to his son, he spoke solemnly, "You, my boy, will some-day be the Emperor of Brazil. Be a good ruler and not as foolish as I."

Dom Pedro II ruled Brazil for almost fifty years. He grew up to be wise and kind, and was friendly with rich and poor alike. In his palace, poor, barefoot Indians were as welcome as important leaders.

While Pedro II was Emperor, he visited many different countries. Everywhere he went, he was eager to learn things that would help Brazil. Indeed, it was he who had shown such keen interest in Alexander Graham Bell's telephone. You read about that in Chapter 20.

During Pedro's long rule, he did much to help his people and make his country strong. He encouraged the building of railroads and trade with other lands. He also freed the Negro slaves in his country. This act, however, caused many wealthy planters to dislike him. They finally forced Pedro to give up his throne.

Today Brazil is a republic. It has twenty-two states and five territories. Its full name is the The United States of Brazil. Its government is something like that of our country. A president serves at its head and a congress makes its laws.

Portuguese is the official language in Brazil. This nation is the only Latin-American country in which Portuguese is the chief language.

Brasília is the new capital. It is laid out on a plateau about 600 miles north-west of Rio de Janeiro, as the map shows on page 435. Find Brasília. It became the capital of Brazil in 1960 in place of Rio de Janeiro. Because Brasília is located in high lands, it has a more comfortable climate than the former capital.

Brasília is a brand-new city, and a fascinating one. It has many handsome modern buildings and is bordered on three sides by a man-made lake.

Brazil's new capital, Brasilia. Government workers moved here from Rio in 1960. Below, the President's Palace. At the left, some of the government office buildings.

An Over-all Look at Brazil

Brazil is the largest country in South America. You can see this if you study the map on page 435. Notice that this huge country stretches from Venezuela and the Guianas on the north to Uruguay on the south. In fact, Brazil touches the borders of all but two of South America's countries.

Most of Brazil lies in the tropics. In these latitudes, the low plains have a hot climate the year round. A large part of them receives heavy rains, as the map on page 438 shows. However, many parts of Brazil are fairly high. Even though they are in the tropics, they are high enough to have a cooler and more pleasant climate. They may even have a little frost in the winter.

The iron and steel plant at Volta Redonda is about fifty miles from Rio. In recent years Brazil has built many industrial plants.

Brazil has a small population for its large size. Look on the population map on page 436 and locate the most thickly-settled areas. Now find them on the large map on page 435. Notice that most Brazilians live on the coastal plains or on the eastern edge of the high lands nearby. The main cities are in one of these areas as is shown on the map on page 435. Why are so few cities located far inland, do you suppose?

Brazil's high lands rise sharply from the narrow plains along the coast. The high lands reach across southern Brazil, the map on page 436 tells us. A part of them are mountains. In which direction do they extend? See how much of the land is hills. Notice how far the plateau region stretches.

Coffee is grown on the hills east of the mountains. The hilly lands and rolling plateaus west of the mountains are dotted with small thorn trees and cactus. Here are grasslands where cattle graze. In some areas near rivers, crops are grown. They must be irrigated, for the summers are hot and dry.

A part of the southern high lands is rich in minerals. This region is called Minas Gerais. Find it on the map. It was the area of the Gold Rush. It is not far northwest of Rio.

Minas Gerais is a good name for this land, for it means "general mines." It is rich in many minerals. Gold has been mined for about 300 years and the iron deposits are among the largest in the world. Some of this iron is now being used by a large iron-and-steel plant at Volta Redonda near Rio de Janeiro.

Minas Gerais is also famous for its diamonds and other precious stones. Some diamonds are sold as jewels, but many are used in manufacturing and for cutting glass.

The northern part of Brazil has another hilly region which is rich in mineral deposits. Valuable stores of silver, copper, tin, and iron are buried there, but little mining has been done.

The Amazon Basin spreads over an immense area. It is located in the heart of the tropics. The hot sunshine and heavy rains make it a steamy land. This wet tropical climate causes trees and plants to grow very rapidly. So thick jungles have crowded across the Amazon Basin. The trees, vines, and undergrowth grow so close together that only a little sunshine sifts through to the ground.

Much wildlife lives in this jungle. There are hundreds of kinds of bright-feathered birds. Among them are the brilliantly-colored parrots and macaws that screech from perches high in the trees. Monkeys chatter and scream as they swing from one branch to another. The large, cat-like jaguar and the sloth are two other kinds of animals that have homes in this region. Also, beautiful giant butterflies flit about and mosquitoes seem to be everywhere. Snakes creep through the dark undergrowth and some kinds often swim in the rivers.

The Amazon River drains this enormous basin. As you already know, the Amazon is one of the largest rivers in the world. Point to it on the map on page 435. This map has room to show only the Amazon's main branches. But actually, there are more than 200 of them. Why are there so many? Let's study the rainfall map on page 438 and hunt for a clue.

See how much rain the Amazon Basin receives in a year. So much pours down that the water cannot soak into the ground fast enough. Much drains off into the streams that feed the Amazon. Altogether, they drain huge quantities of water into this long river. No wonder, then, that the Amazon is a mighty giant!

Only a few people live in the vast Amazon Basin. Most of them are Indians. They live in small villages near rivers. Some of the men gather Brazil nuts to sell to traders. But no important industries are carried on. Because of its jungles, poorly drained soil, and hot, wet climate, this region is not a good land to farm.

The Indians live very simply. Their homes are usually small one-roomed huts made of palm branches fastened over a framework of poles. The Indian women

An Indian village on the Amazon River.

447

Bulldozers clear a way for part of the Trans-Amazon Highway.

do most of the work. They gather wild nuts and fruits, and grow some corn, beans, sweet potatoes, peppers, and cassava. They pound the cassava roots into meal for making their "bread." The men fish and hunt.

There have been no roads or railroads through the thick jungles. The rivers are the highways in this part of Brazil.

In the late 1800's, much rubber was taken from the Amazon jungle. By this time, men had begun to make erasers, rubber boots, and waterproof clothing. They used the rubber from the sap of the *hevea* tree. Many of these trees were scattered through the forests in the Amazon Basin.

Gashes were cut in the hevea trees so that the milky white sap could flow down into a container.

The rubber gatherer dried the sticky white juice over a smoky fire. After dipping a long paddle into the juice, he turned it over and over above the fire. By dipping and drying, and dipping and drying, the worker soon had a large ball of rubber on his paddle. When he had dried many balls of rubber, he took them to the nearest trading boat.

After automobiles were invented, more rubber was needed. To get it, traders steamed far up the Amazon. Many of them stopped at the little Indian village of Manaus. Find it on the map on page 435. Notice how far inland it is located.

Manaus became a busy trading center for collecting and shipping rubber. Some of the rubber traders became rich and built fine homes there. Stores, a cathedral, and even an opera house were erected. Manaus became an important city, though it had a hot, disagreeable climate and was surrounded by jungles.

By 1913, however, Brazil began to lose much rubber business. Some years before, seeds from the hevea tree had been shipped to the East Indies and planted. Thousands of rubber trees were being grown there in neat rows on plantations.

This plantation rubber could be bought more cheaply than that supplied by Brazil. You see, plantation rubber could be gathered more easily than that from the scattered trees in the jungles. However, this inland city continues to be the chief trading center on the upper Amazon.

The Amazon region has become a frontier. Some scientists are working to find crops that will grow well there. Other experts have found tin, iron ore, gold, and other valuable minerals in the region.

The government is building a highway through part of the Amazon basin. As the road is built some settlers are building homes beside it. This region is a "Land of Tomorrow."

Farming and Manufacturing

The coffee business is one of Brazil's leading industries. In fact, Brazil produces nearly three fifths of the world's coffee. The coffee served in your home may have come from this country.

Most of the coffee is grown on huge plantations called *fazendas*. They spread out over the eastern slopes of the hills which rise from the coastal plains. There, the well-drained reddish soil and the mild tropical climate are just right for this crop. Plenty of rain falls from October through March while the coffee is growing. But the rest of the year, the weather is sunny and dry.

The fazendas are owned by wealthy planters. But thousands of poor people do the work. They live in small houses clustered together on each fazenda.

Above is an airview of a coffee fazenda. At the left below, workers are picking the berries · After the shells and pulp are removed, the coffee beans are washed. Then they are laid out to dry. The workers shown below are spreading them out. They also stir them with rakes so that the sunshine can dry them evenly.

Coffee comes from berries which grow on small trees eight to twelve feet tall. Coffee trees bloom in Brazil's springtime. What months are these? The fragrant star-shaped coffee blossoms are snowy white. It is a beautiful sight to see thousands of trees covered with these pure white blossoms. When the blossoms drop away, tiny green berries begin to form. They grow very fast during the warm tropical summer. After a few months, they begin to turn yellow. Then they darken and soon resemble shining red cherries.

Coffee-picking season is the busiest time of year on the fazendas. During these weeks, thousands of men, women, and children move down between the rows of trees to strip off the berries. Each tree produces about enough berries to make a pound of coffee. Railroad cars haul the berries to the drying yards. There, they are washed and sorted and the pulp is removed from the seeds. The coffee bean is the seed. With cherries, we eat the pulp and throw away the seeds. But just the opposite happens with coffee. The pulp is removed and the seeds are used. Each berry has two seeds, or beans. These beans are dried, roasted, and ground to make the coffee your parents drink.

Brazil's chief coffee port is Santos. Millions of sacks of coffee are hauled by railroad and trucks to the port of Santos. Over half of these sacks then are shipped to the United States.

But Santos does not depend entirely on its coffee business. About half of Brazil's exports are shipped from its docks. Among these exports are manufactured goods from São Paulo, 40 miles away.

São Paulo has become Brazil's largest city. Coffee helped it to grow, for São Paulo is in the high lands in the center of the coffee-producing region. Find it on the map on page 435.

São Paulo is much more than a center of the coffee business, however. It has become the greatest manufacturing city in South America. It has over six thousand factories. They turn out food products, textiles, refrigerators, furniture, and many other manufactured goods. The city also has plants where cars and trucks are assembled to be sold throughout Brazil and to neighboring countries.

The picture at the left shows you that São Paulo is a modern city with many skyscrapers. The people of this city are also proud of its good schools and university, museums, and handsome homes.

São Paulo.

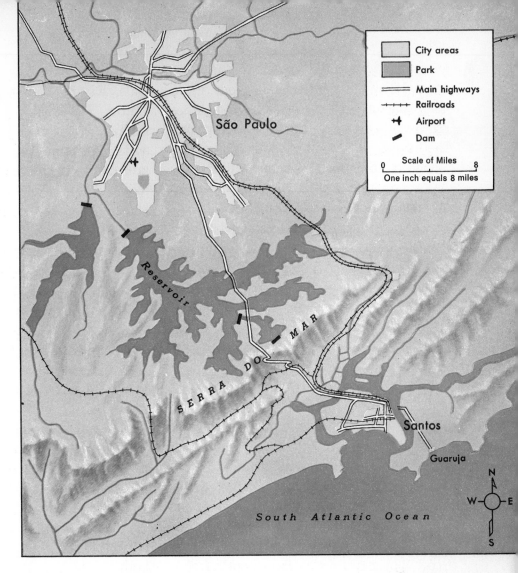

Legend:
- City areas
- Park
- Main highways
- Railroads
- Airport
- Dam

Scale of Miles
0   8
One inch equals 8 miles

São Paulo

Reservoir

SERRA DO MAR

Santos

Guaruja

South Atlantic Ocean

N
W   E
S

What does this map tell you about the location of the city of São Paulo? How many miles is it from São Paulo to the port of Santos?

What other crops are raised in eastern Brazil? Much cotton is grown in the southeastern high lands near São Paulo. Some is also raised near Recife, the seaport on Brazil's bulge. Enough cotton is produced to supply Brazil's textile mills and also to ship to other countries. Some farmers in the high lands raise cattle and hogs, and such crops as corn, wheat, vegetables, and fruits.

Rice, cacao, and sugar cane are the chief crops cultivated on the hot, wet low lands along the coast.

Manufacturing is increasing in Brazil. So many new factories and mills have been built that Brazil has more industry than any other country in Latin America. Some of the swift rivers of Brazil's high lands supply many factories with electric light and power.

Brazil's textile mills now produce all the cotton cloth needed at home. They also weave silk, rayon, and woolen cloth. Other factories make shoes and clothing.

São Paulo and Rio de Janeiro are Brazil's busiest industrial cities. But São Salvador and Recife far to the north also carry on some manufacturing.

Rio de Janeiro is Brazil's most famous city. Some people call it the most beautiful city in the world. It is set along the blue waters of a huge bay which is

451

surrounded by rugged mountains and forested hills. One peak stands out more than the others. On its top is a large statue of Christ, 130 feet tall, or about the height of an eight-story building.

Rio de Janeiro, sometimes called Rio, has many fine modern buildings. Some are tall skyscrapers like those in our largest cities. Many are attractive apartment houses or hotels, or perhaps fine stores and office buildings. Most of the business buildings are crowded together on the level land near the bay. But thousands of homes are perched on hillsides or sit in the valleys that run back between the mountains.

Rio has some grand old homes, churches, and palaces that were built in colonial days. And this is interesting! Some of the sidewalks are very wide and paved in early Portuguese fashion. They have many tiny colored stones fitted together in designs. Tourists like to stroll along these colorful sidewalks. They also enjoy visiting the tall island called Sugar Loaf. This mass of rock has smooth, steep sides and soars to a height of nearly 1,300 feet above the sea. From its top, visitors have a wonderful view of Rio as well as of the island-dotted bay. However, getting to Sugar Loaf's summit is quite an adventure. One must travel through the air in a box-like car which moves on strong cables, or ropes.

Rio de Janeiro is the third largest city in all of South America. It has grown large mainly because of its excellent location and immense, deep harbor. It is located in one of the richest sections of Brazil. Nearby are many valuable mineral resources as well as miles and miles of prosperous coffee plantations and farms.

Because it is near plentiful raw materials, Rio has become a busy industrial center. It has flour mills, textile mills, oil refineries, and many factories, large and small. Among the goods manufactured are clothing, shoes, textiles, furniture, foods, and iron and steel products.

Rio depends largely on railroads to bring raw materials to its factories. They also haul quantities of farm products to its harbor to be shipped overseas. You see, Rio is at the hub of most of Brazil's railroad lines. From it, railroads reach out in many directions. Notice this on the map on page 453.

Only a small part of Brazil has railroads. No railroad line reaches across the vast interior. You learned why when you read about this region.

Rio is also one of Brazil's leading ports. Several thousand ships a year tie up at its docks. They unload such goods as oil, machinery, and automobiles. They carry away loads of coffee, cotton, cacao, and other products from Brazil's rich lands.

Looking ahead. Brazil has many problems. One is its lack of a good transportation system. Roads and railroads serve only a small part of the country. Even important coastal cities are not connected by highways and railroads.

Another problem is that most of its people are very poor. And most of them have few opportunities to improve their ways of living. More schools are needed and more job-training must be done.

Still another problem is how to help more people move to Brazil's wide frontiers. There are vast inland areas waiting for settlers to start farms and to open mines. But pioneering requires large sums

The black lines show the routes of South America's main railroads. Notice how many areas lack railroads.

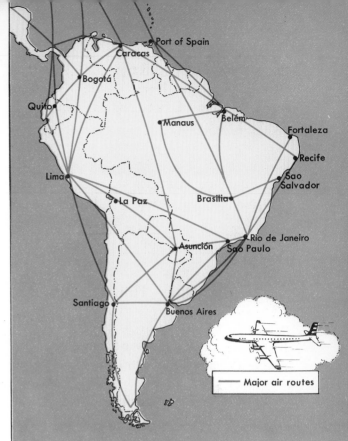

This shows South America's main airways. Compare it with the railroad map. How can you travel from Rio to Belém?

of money, wise leaders, and courageous workers. Solving all these problems may take a long time.

Another large country is Brazil's neighbor to the south. Chapter 27 will tell us about this land, Argentina.

Some Review Questions

1. How was Brazil discovered?

2. How did Brazil gain its independence? What is its new capital like?

3. What kinds of lands does Brazil have? How are they different?

4. What are Brazil's leading industries? What and where are its main cities?

5. What are some of the problems the people of Brazil need to solve?

A Test about Brazil

On a paper, write the numbers 1 to 9. Then read the descriptions below. After each number write the word or words from the list which best fit each description.

1. The explorer who discovered Brazil

2. The country that claimed it

3. The capital today

4. The largest city

5. The beautiful city on a deep bay

6. The leading industry
7. The largest river
8. The most famous mining region
9. A vast jungle

List

São Paulo	coffee	Cabral
Brasília	Amazon	Rio de Janeiro
Orinoco	Portugal	Amazon Basin
Pedro II	oranges	Minas Gerais

Some Other Things to Do

1. Help your class make a mural to tell the story of the coffee industry. Prepare reports to explain your mural.

2. Read more about animals and birds that live in Brazil's jungles. Be ready to share what you learn.

3. Find and give a worthwhile news item about some topic related to Brazil.

4. Be ready to pronounce correctly:

Brasília   São Paulo   Manaus

Let's Think Together

1. Why are Brazil's inland areas thinly settled?

2. What makes cities grow? What things helped Rio de Janeiro to grow? São Paulo? Manaus? your city? Do cities sometimes shrink? If so, why?

Fun with Maps

A. Use the List of Maps in the front of your text. On what page would you look to find a map showing:

1. Brazil's high lands and plains?
2. Rainfall in the Amazon Basin?
3. Brazil's thickly-settled areas?
4. Brazil's railroads?
5. Air routes to Brazil?
6. Brazil's neighbors?

B. Use the map on page 435 to help you answer these questions:

1. Is most of Brazil north or south of the equator?

2. Lines of latitude are sometimes called *parallels*. Parallels of latitude which are south of the equator are called South Latitude. Find the parallel of 20° South Latitude. What countries in South America does it cross?

3. Is South America in the West Longitudes or the East Longitudes? What are the reasons for your answer?

4. Look for the parallel of 40° South Latitude. Now find the meridian of 60° West Longitude. Notice where they cross. Is this closer to Brazil or to Argentina?

C. Study the Occupations Map on page 490 and summarize what it tells about Brazil.

27 · Argentina: Land of the Pampa

Early Days in Argentina

Magellan visited South America in 1519. He had been hired by Spain to sail to the "Spice Lands" in the Far East. He hoped to find a short cut to these lands. Did a waterway lead through South America? To find out, Magellan headed west across the Atlantic.

After many weeks at sea, Magellan's five ships reached South America. Sailing southward along its coast, the explorers hunted patiently for the "magic waterway." But they did not find it.

Magellan's ships sail through the strait now named after him.

Finally, the men reached the shores of lands now known as Argentina. Locate Argentina on the map on page 435. As they sailed south along the coast, the weather became cold and stormy. It was winter in this land. Sharp winds whistled across the snowy plains.

The explorers discovered that tall dark-skinned Indians lived in the chilly southland. For shoes they wore enormous bundles lined with straw and fur. They appeared to have very large feet. So Magellan's men called the land Patagonia, or "Place of Big Feet." To this day, southern Argentina is named Patagonia.

Journeying on, Magellan's ships finally reached a strait near the southern tip of South America. The winding waterway near the southern end of the continent is now known as the Strait of Magellan.

Find it on the map. Its dangerous waters lead from the Atlantic to the Pacific.

Skillfully, Magellan guided his ships through this strait's rough waters and then led them on across the Pacific. Although he was killed in the Philippine Islands, one of his ships did reach the "Spice Lands." Some time later, it returned to Spain. It was the first ship to sail all the way around the world.

In 1526, Spain sent Sebastian Cabot west. He was the son of brave John Cabot, who had discovered Newfoundland for England. Like Magellan, Sebastian Cabot was hoping to find a short route to the rich lands of the East.

Far down the coast of South America, Cabot came to a wide body of water that seemed to cut inland for a long distance. Could it be a strait leading to the Pacific, he wondered? Eagerly Cabot and his men sailed into the bay and far upstream; but finally they decided they were just traveling up a river. They were interested in the surrounding lands, however, and went ashore to make friends with the Indians. Some of the Indians were wearing silver necklaces, so Cabot believed he had discovered lands of silver. He did not know that this silver had come from mines far to the west.

According to a story, Cabot named the wide body of water Río de la Plata, or "River of Silver." Do you see the Río de la Plata on the map on page 435? Actually, it is a broad bay into which two large rivers flow. They are the Paraná and Uruguay rivers, as the map shows you.

Soon, Spanish colonists began to settle near the Río de la Plata. The first large settlement was in charge of proud Pedro de Mendoza. In 1535, he led eleven ships across the Atlantic. On board were 1250 men and many horses. Some distance up the Rio de la Plata, the Spaniards anchored and waded ashore. There on the flat, muddy banks they began to build a fort and a group of small huts. They named their village Buenos Aires which means "good air."

Pedro de Mendoza had ambitious plans for his colony. Some men were to push inland to bring out silver and gold. Others were to manage large farms called *estancias*, and captured Indians were to raise the crops. But alas! These plans did not work out.

There was no gold or silver except that in the Andes hundreds of miles away. Neither were successful estancias established. The Indians in this region were hunters and would not tend crops. Still, the Spaniards refused to work in the fields. Many had come from wealthy families and had had servants to wait on them.

The Spaniards nearly starved to death. Also there were frequent attacks by Indians who lived on the plains west of Buenos Aires. Miles and miles of these treeless plains, or *pampa*, swept back from the Rio de la Plata. The pampa was covered with grasses. In some places the grass was as tall as a man, so it was easy for the Indians to hide.

These Indians became angry as they watched their lands being taken away by the strange settlers. One day they decided to try to stop the Spaniards. They swooped upon the settlement and destroyed it, killing many Spaniards. Those who survived decided to move far up the Paraguay River. Find the Paraguay River on the map on page 435. Notice that it empties into the Parana River.

were turned loose. Free to roam the plains, they became "wild." They were the ancestors of thousands of wild horses that came to wander over the Pampa.

The Spaniards settled at the village of Asunción. By this time, they realized that they must work to survive. So they began to raise or make the things they needed.

More than twenty-five years later, some of Asunción's settlers returned to the Río de la Plata and started the second settlement of Buenos Aires. This time the village fared better. Its people knew how to protect themselves and how to raise crops. Also, they brought along hundreds of "farmer" Indians to help them.

More Spanish settlers came to this part of South America. The colony grew and became known as Argentina. This is Spanish for "Land of Silver." Although little silver has ever been found in Argentina, it still bears the name which the Spaniards gave it by mistake, long ago.

Spain ruled Argentina for more than two hundred years. But the Spanish governors were not interested in helping the colony. They wanted to make money for themselves and for the king. The colonists were given little freedom and no part in their government.

Finally, some leaders decided that Argentina must break away from Spain. One was a brave and unselfish soldier, José de San Martín.

San Martín led Argentina's soldiers against Spain. At first his job looked hopeless. He had to collect money for ammunition and supplies and train a brand-new army. But he was not discouraged.

San Martín had a very bold and clever plan. He knew that the most important

This monument in Buenos Aires was built in 1936 to celebrate the city's 400th birthday.

Spanish armies were stationed on the west coast of South America, beyond the towering Andes. He realized that Argentina could not be free until these western armies were defeated. So he made up his mind to lead his army west across the high mountains and surprise the enemy.

You have already learned how high the Andes are, and how hard they are to cross. You can imagine, then, what a difficult task San Martín was undertaking. He made careful plans. He began by having his army camp at a town on the eastern side of the Andes. Day after day, for almost three years, the men were trained in mountain climbing as well as in soldiering.

Meanwhile, San Martín rode about arousing the people and persuading them to help. Some gave him money and others brought their jewelry to be sold. Hundreds worked without pay to make shoes and uniforms for the soldiers, and guns and ammunition.

San Martín and his brave army cross the Andes to surprise a large Spanish army. For three years San Martín has trained his army for this journey. Why was this march so difficult?

One January day, San Martín and his large army set out. Why do you think they started at this time of year? What have you learned about the seasons in the Southern Hemisphere?

The journey across the steep Andes was an exhausting one. In spite of their leader's careful plans, the men suffered terrible hardships.

The rough, narrow trails led up through passes 13,000 feet high. The weather was bitterly cold and the snow was deep. Indeed, the air was so thin that the men could hardly breathe.

At last, San Martín's army crossed the Andes and looked down on Chile's low hills where the large Spanish army was camped. The Argentine troops surprised and defeated the enemy. Then they went on to win other victories.

In time, Argentina gained its freedom. When San Martín returned to Argentina, however, sad news awaited him. Some jealous men accused him of planning to seize the powers of government.

These people treated him so badly that he could not stay in Argentina. He sailed away to France, and never returned to the land he had served so bravely.

Today, however, Argentina honors San Martín as a national hero and as the "father of the country." Almost every village has a street or plaza named for this great leader.

Argentina as an Independent Country

Freedom brought Argentina many disturbing problems. You remember that the people in the Thirteen Colonies in our country had learned to govern themselves while they were still colonists. This helped them build a successful democracy. But in Argentina, the people had had no experience in carrying on the affairs of government. Furthermore, the leaders of the new country could not decide what kind of government they wanted or who should be its head.

There were many quarrels and some bitter fighting. For years the leaders disagreed. Finally, a wealthy cattle-owner seized the powers of government and decided to rule in his own way. This cattleman was Juan de Rosas.

Rosas became a powerful dictator. As you may know, a *dictator* decides by himself how his country shall be governed. His people are not allowed to choose leaders or help to make any laws.

Rosas was hard-hearted and cruel. Anyone who disobeyed him was put to death or thrown into prison. He made many bitter enemies. Still, people feared him so much that they put up with his rule for twenty years. Finally, Rosas was driven out of the country.

Since that time, many different leaders have headed Argentina's government. Some have been wise and helpful. One, for instance, encouraged education and established many new schools. Others, however, have been heartless dictators and have added to Argentina's problems.

One problem with a happy ending began when Argentina and Chile quarreled over the boundary line that separated them. Both countries claimed some of the same lands in the Andes. Because neither was willing to give up any part of its claim, the two neighbors made plans to fight. Guns and ammunition were collected and soldiers were prepared for battle.

Then a wise leader reminded the people that war costs many lives and much money. Surely it would be better not to fight but to talk things over.

Representatives of the two countries agreed to meet. They decided on a new boundary line. They did even more! They made a solemn promise that they would never go to war against each other again.

The "Christ of the Andes."

A statue for peace: the Christ of the Andes. Argentina and Chile celebrated their promise by building a beautiful monument. They melted their cannon and used the metal to build an enormous statue of Christ. This famous statue is known as the Christ of the Andes. It stands on a high pass in the lofty snow-covered Andes on the border between Argentina and Chile. Beneath it are carved these words:

Sooner shall these mountains crumble to dust than the Argentines and Chileans break the peace sworn at the feet of Christ the Redeemer.

Argentina has twenty-two provinces and one territory. Its provinces are something like our states. Each province has its own governor and legislature. Spanish is the official language throughout these provinces. A president heads Argentina's government and a congress helps to make its laws.

Buenos Aires is Argentina's capital and largest city. In fact, it is the second largest city in South America and the fourth largest in the western hemisphere. Only New York, Chicago, and São Paulo are larger. About one fourth of all the people of Argentina live in Buenos Aires or its suburbs.

Buenos Aires is located about 160 miles up the Plata. The map on page 435 shows that this city stands on the northeastern edge of the Pampa. Now study the map on page 453. See how railroads connect Buenos Aires with other parts of Argentina, and with other countries. Because of its level lands, railroads have been easy to build in Argentina.

Beautiful Buenos Aires is as modern as our American cities and is often called the "New York of South America." In some ways the two cities are alike. Both have tall skyscrapers and fine stores. And each one has a subway system connecting the different parts of the city.

Many of Buenos Aires' older streets are too narrow for today's traffic. One, the main shopping street, is pictured on page 461. It is closed to automobiles for several hours each day so people may walk safely from store to store. This city also has lovely plazas and some handsome wide avenues.

Buenos Aires is Argentina's chief manufacturing center. Huge meat-packing

One of Argentina's shopping streets during the rush hour.

the Plata and to build wharves and warehouses. Thousands of ships visit this harbor every year. They bring in coal, iron machinery, and many kinds of manufactured goods. Some carry away cargoes of frozen and canned meats, hides, and tons of corn and wheat.

The location of Buenos Aires helped it become an important manufacturing and shipping center. Its excellent harbor and transportation system to all parts of the land have helped it to grow. But one of the most important reasons for its growth is that the city is located on the edge of the rich agricultural region of the Pampa. What are Argentina's lands like?

houses and flour and textile mills are located in or near it. Some of its factories make paper, clothing, and shoes and other leather goods. An assembly plant puts together American-made automobiles.

This city is also Argentina's most important seaport. At its front door stretches a fine man-made harbor. Millions of dollars have been spent to deepen

A Look at Argentina

Argentina is the second largest country in South America. As the map shows, only Brazil is larger. Argentina is about a third of the size of the United States and is much longer than it is wide. Study the map and see how Argentina extends from Bolivia on the north to the islands of Tierra del Fuego. This is a distance of almost 2,000 miles.

Man-made harbor of Buenos Aires. These docks were dug from land along the Plata.

Argentina's wheat belt is much like our winter wheat lands.

The map on page 435 will show you that most of Argentina is in the south mid-latitude region. So, much of the country has mild or cool winters and warm or hot summers. How does this differ from the climate of central Brazil?

The steep Andes Mountains rise like high walls along western Argentina. One snow-clad peak, Mount Aconcagua is taller than any other in the Western Hemisphere. It soars nearly 23,000 feet into the sky.

Several large rivers flow through Argentina. Two, the Paraná and the Uruguay, empty into the Río de la Plata. They are deep enough for ocean steamers to sail upstream hundreds of miles. They have many branches, but the largest is the Paraguay. The Paraná, Paraguay, and Uruguay are a part of the Plata River System. Which one marks the boundary between Argentina and the small country of Uruguay?

Argentina has several different kinds of regions. Far to the north is the Gran Chaco. As the map on page 435 shows, it reaches into Bolivia and Paraguay. The Gran Chaco is a fertile plain but few people live there because of its disagreeable climate. Its hot, rainy summers change the low plains into steamy swamps. Its hot, rainless winters burn up the land and dry up many streams.

Stretching south from the Colorado River to the end of the continent is Argentina's southern region, Patagonia. This is an area of cool, windy plateaus. Patagonia is thinly populated, but its cool, dry climate is largely to blame. Look on the rainfall map on page 438 and see what a dry land it is. Only a little of it is suitable for farming.

North of Patagonia and west of the Pampa are the Dry Plains. Locate them. They extend far west into the Andes. In some ways these Dry Plains remind us of our Great Plains. Both rise gently as they stretch west to meet high mountains. Both have fertile soils; but both are drier lands than the plains to the east. The rain-bearing winds from the Pacific spill most of their moisture on the western slopes of the towering Andes. So there is little left for the eastern slopes and the nearby plains. Many crops grown on these rich plains are irrigated with water from mountain streams.

The Pampa is Argentina's most useful region. The Pampa covers over a fifth of the country. Its low, level plains extend west, northwest, and south of Buenos Aires. This region is somewhat like our Central Plains. Both areas have fertile soil, a good growing season, and plenty of rain for raising many kinds of crops.

Cattle raising is Argentina's oldest industry. It dates back to the days of the early colonists. The Spaniards turned their cattle and horses loose to graze on the plains. In those times, there were no fenced lands, so many animals wandered away. They soon became wild and no longer belonged to anyone.

Some horses were caught and tamed by Indians and young Spaniards. On these fast ponies the men hunted wild cattle. The "hunters" became known as *gauchos*, or cowboys.

A gaucho was proud of his colorful dress. He usually wore a loose-fitting blouse and baggy trousers tucked into high leather boots. From his wide belt hung a long sharp knife. On his head he wore a stiff-brimmed hat that fastened under his chin. During chilly weather he used a woolen blanket, or poncho, to keep him warm. A poncho usually had a hole in the middle and could be slipped over a man's head.

Gauchos raced fearlessly across the plains in all kinds of weather to catch the wild cattle. They killed the animals for their hides, not for their meat. The "meat" was left to rot. You see, there

were no refrigerators to keep it from spoiling nor good roads or railroads for rushing it to markets.

Later, large farms were laid out on the Pampa. Their owners raised cattle for meat as well as for hides. To prevent

Skillful gauchos round up cattle on the Pampa. Above, a gaucho wears his poncho.

the meat from spoiling some was smoked, some was dried, and fresh meat was kept very cold. By the late 1800's, there were refrigerator railroad cars and ships to carry fresh meat to markets. This encouraged the people of Argentina to raise still more beef cattle.

Millions of cattle are now raised on the Pampa. A large part of the world's beef comes from this region. Indeed, Argentina exports more beef than any other nation in the world.

Today, the cattle graze in fenced pastures. Animals produce better meat when they are not allowed to wander too far. As in our country, the cattle are fattened on corn and alfalfa before they are shipped to the stockyards.

Herds of dairy cattle are raised on farms near Buenos Aires. They furnish milk and other dairy products for the

Loading freshly-picked grapes into a truck at a vineyard in Mendoza. Most of them will be used to make wine.

many people who live in and near this large city.

Wheat, corn, and flax are among the Pampa's chief farm crops. Large fields of wheat stretch across the central part of the Pampa. This rich wheat belt is sometimes called the Bread Basket of South America. It ships huge quantities of grain to other countries.

Corn is raised in the northern part of the Pampa. The busy planting season comes during the months of September, October, and November. South of the equator the seasons are just the opposite of ours, remember.

Flax fields spread over some areas. The flax fields are a sea of blue when their flowers are in bloom. After the blossoms fall, seeds begin to grow. When they are ripe, they are harvested and crushed to make linseed oil, used in making paint.

Many other kinds of crops are grown in Argentina. Sugar plantations are located near Tucumán. This region is in the higher lands northwest of Buenos Aires, as the map on page 435 shows. Tucumán has a fairly warm climate winter and summer.

The lands surrounding the city of Mendoza have many grapevines and fruit orchards. Most of the people who care for the vineyards are descendants of Italian immigrants. These immigrants had been "grape farmers" in Italy. As you may know, Italy has many vineyards.

Alfalfa also thrives in the Mendoza area. It is fed mainly to beef cattle. Like Tucumán, Mendoza is in the hilly lands at the edge of the Dry Plains. The Mendoza region is very dry indeed. Because less than ten inches of rain fall a year, crops must be irrigated.

Sheep graze on the grasslands
of Patagonia.

Tucumán and Mendoza are busy cities partly because they are trading centers for the rich farmlands around them. But they have also grown because they are near passes through the Andes. They are transportation centers on the main routes that connect the east and west coasts of South America. It was at Mendoza that San Martín trained his soldiers before leading them across the Andes into Chile.

The Gran Chaco region in the north has only a few people, as you have learned. But this region does have some cattle ranches. Also, some of its eastern and southern lands are used for growing cotton and sugar cane.

Thousands of sheep are raised in southern Argentina. Some flocks feed on the lonely windswept lands of Patagonia. Others graze far to the south on the islands of Tierra del Fuego. Point to these islands on the map. Those to the east belong to Argentina, but those to the west fly the Chilean flag.

The weather in these southern lands is usually windy and cool. So the sheep grow long, thick coats. This fine wool is the "money crop" of the thinly populated southern region.

Manufacturing is becoming more and more important. Argentina's chief wealth comes from cattle, sheep, and grain. But most of the people live in cities. There are more than forty cities in Argentina with over 20,000 people. Many of them are centers of manufacturing as well as of trade.

Most of this manufacturing uses the products of Argentina's farms, as you

465

This highway winds over the Andes to connect Mendoza, Argentina and Santiago, Chile. Why is it difficult to build highways in much of South America?

would expect. There are meat-packing plants and flour mills. Many plants also use the other parts of the cattle and sheep to make such products as leather, shoes, tallow, and fertilizer. Textile mills make woolen, cotton, and rayon cloth for the people of Argentina.

Argentina also has oil fields. Petroleum is used to make some gasoline, and new plants are being built to produce many valuable chemicals from petroleum. Some iron and steel is manufactured for making ships and machinery. But Argentina must now import much of the iron and coal that she uses.

Summing up. Argentina has become a rich and important country. It sells large quantities of farm products to other countries. It has factories which make many of the goods it needs. It provides schools for most of its children, and is building more roads and railroads. Actually, it already has more railroads than any of its sister countries. Turn to the map on page 453 and notice this.

Yet Argentina has difficult problems. Its people long for more freedom and more opportunity to take part in the affairs of their government.

West of Argentina is a long, narrow country, Chile. In the next chapter, we shall visit this land beyond the Andes.

Let's Review!

1. Where is Argentina?
2. What early explorers visited it?
3. How was Argentina settled? How did it win independence?
4. What are Argentina's leading cities? What are the main industries?

Put On Your Thinking Cap!

1. What products are grown in Argentina that are raised near your home?
2. Think again about the qualities needed by a good leader. What do the words "strong leadership" mean? Why is strong leadership necessary to win a difficult struggle?

Be an Expert

Prove you can locate some places by using latitude and longitude.

1. Find the meridian of 60° West Longitude. Is it closer to Rio or to Buenos Aires?

2. Point to the parallel of 40° South Latitude. Does it cross the Chaco or Patagonia?

3. Where is the parallel of 30° South Latitude on the map? Where would it cross 60° West Longitude, in Brazil or in Argentina?

Describing Places

On paper write 1 to 8. After each, write the name in List B which fits the description.

List A

1. A cold, dry, windy plateau
2. A hot, swampy plain in northern Argentina
3. A main city in western Argentina
4. Cattle- and wheat-raising lands
5. Argentina's chief sheep-raising region
6. Largest city in Argentina
7. A range of high mountains
8. The capital of Argentina

List B

Gran Chaco   Mendoza
The Pampa   The Andes
Buenos Aires   Patagonia

Some Other Things to Do

1. Use a globe. On it locate (a) the equator, (b) the prime meridian, (c) the parallel of 40° North Latitude and (d) the meridian of 80° West Longitude. Notice where 40° North Latitude crosses 80° West Longitude. Is this nearer San Francisco or Washington, D. C.?

2. Write and illustrate a story about an adventure as a gaucho on the Pampa, or as a sheepherder in Patagonia.

3. List ways in which Buenos Aires is like New York City. Make another list of ways in which the two cities are different.

4. Be ready to share a news item about Argentina.

Let's Compare Argentina and Brazil!

Refer to the maps on pages 434, 435, 438, and 453 to help you answer these questions.

1. Which country is larger?
2. Which has more high lands?
3. Which has rainier lands?
4. Which is mainly in the Mid-Latitudes?
5. Which has more land north of 20° South Latitude?
6. Which is crossed by railroads?
7. Which has the longest river?

28 · Chile: The Shoestring Republic

How Chile Became a Republic

Long ago, bold Valdivia led soldiers to Chile. Valdivia grew up in Spain. One day, as he was strolling down a Spanish street, two girls peered out of their window.

"Who is that handsome soldier?" asked Maria.

"Ah, Pedro de Valdivia," whispered her friend. "Soon he will sail to Peru to join Pizarro's forces. Pizarro has captured the rich Indian ruler of Peru."

Santiago was the first Spanish settlement in Chile. Compare this drawing with the photograph on page 474.

"How exciting!" exclaimed Maria. "What thrilling adventures Valdivia will have!"

But neither Maria nor her friend dreamed that tragic experiences awaited the young soldier.

Valdivia was appointed to lead a band of soldiers south into Chile. His orders read, "Conquer the proud Araucanian Indians. Seize their gold and start Spanish settlements."

Valdivia made careful plans for this difficult task. He spent a whole year training his soldiers and preparing for the trip. He gathered together farm animals, tools, seeds for crops, arms, and a great deal of food. He also arranged for more than 1000 Indians to carry supplies on the long journey.

The trip to Chile led southward through miles and miles of mountains. The trails

were narrow and rough and the high passes were blocked with snow and ice. So travel was slow. After many weeks, the adventurers finally left the mountains and entered the vast Atacama Desert.

Look for the Atacama Desert on the map on page 435. If you use the scale of miles, you can see that it extends through Chile for more than a thousand miles. Imagine crossing such a desert on foot!

Beyond this immense desert were more mountains to climb. But finally the men crossed the last range. To the south was a promising green land. It was the fertile valley that stretches through Middle Chile.

Valdivia's men built settlements in Middle Chile. The first one was called Santiago. It was laid out in a green valley by a river. Quickly, the men put up a fort and some huts with grass roofs. The picture on page 468 may give you some idea of what this first Santiago was like.

The Spaniards were so anxious to get crops planted that they did not build sturdy houses. A few months later, the fierce Araucanians attacked and the Spaniards had to flee for their lives. When they returned, their buildings had been burned to the ground. Most of their animals had been killed and only two handfuls of corn were left.

Still, Valdivia did not give up. He and his men planted the corn and rebuilt their town on a rocky hilltop above the blackened village. This time, the buildings were constructed of thick adobe bricks and had tile roofs that would not catch fire easily.

In time, other settlements were built in Middle Chile. And more crops were culti-vated on the rich fertile lands. But the Spaniards had to be alert, day and night, even after they drove the Indians south. Trouble was brewing. Thousands of Indians were ready to return to fight to get back their lands.

A great Indian leader, Lautaro, defeated the Spaniards. He had been captured soon after the Spaniards arrived in Middle Chile. He had become a trusted caretaker for Valdivia's horses. One morning he did not appear at the stables. He had run away.

Ten years later, the clever Lautaro led the Indians in a bitter battle against the Spaniards. The Indians won and Valdivia was captured.

A story tells us that Valdivia was tied to a tree. Then Lautaro spoke out boldly, "You have stolen our lands! You are greedy for gold. Now, gold we have brought you. Drink, Valdivia, drink!" As the Indians poured hot melted gold down Valdivia's throat, the courageous leader died.

It was true that some Spanish leaders had conquered the Indians in order to seize their gold. But Valdivia had been interested, chiefly, in establishing new settlements. Still, the Indians had suffered much from the white man's greed. Furthermore, they were angry because they had been driven far to the south. It is little wonder, then, that they hated the settlers.

Gradually, more Spanish settlers came to live in Middle Chile. Large haciendas were laid out and settlements were started. From time to time, trouble broke out afresh between the pioneers and the Indians. But slowly these people learned to live in peace with one another.

Some Spaniards married Indians. Their children were Mestizos, but when they grew up they called themselves Chileans.

For many years, Chile was a Spanish colony under Spain's stern rule. Like other Spanish-governed lands, Chile longed for freedom. By the early 1800's, there was growing unrest in the land.

In 1810, Chile rebelled against Spain. One of the greatest Chilean leaders in this rebellion was Bernardo O'Higgins. He was part Irish and part Spanish and a very proud Chilean.

O'Higgins took command of the Chilean army. His soldiers and San Martín's troops joined together to drive the Spaniards from Chile. In 1818, Chile finally gained its independence.

Chile became a new nation. General O'Higgins served as the head of the country for five years. During this time, he worked for the people in many different ways. He sent soldiers north to help Peru gain its independence from Spain. He started schools and had roads built. He freed Chile's Negro slaves.

O'Higgins also tried to help the other poor people of the haciendas. But his plans were disliked by wealthy Chilean planters, and within a few years he was forced to resign.

In time, Chile became a republic. After a number of stormy years, a new government was organized. It had a president at its head. In 1925, another constitution was drawn up. It provided for a republic. In a republic the citizens choose representatives. The representatives run the government.

Chile has a president and a congress. Santiago is the capital and Spanish is the official language.

A Picture of Chile

Chile is a long, narrow country. This is the reason why some people call it the "Shoestring Republic." It is almost 2,700 miles long but nowhere is it more than 250 miles wide. Look at the map on page 435 and notice how it stretches from Peru to the tip of South America. If it were placed along the west coast of North America, it would stretch from Canada into Mexico.

A country that extends so far from north to south is certain to have several different kinds of climate. Northern Chile is in the tropics and is burned by a hot tropical sun. Southern Chile reaches into the colder parts of the mid-latitude lands.

Mountains and hills cover about three fourths of Chile. The Andes rise like high walls along the entire eastern border. They separate Chile and Argentina. Some peaks rise more than 20,000 feet. Many are volcanic peaks but most of the volcanoes are quiet now.

Low mountains and hills extend close along the Pacific coast. Locate them on the map. They seem to get lost in the sea as they reach south. Only their tops show and these tops appear as islands. The islands are strewn along the coast for hundreds of miles.

Chile has three main regions. In the north is the long desert which Valdivia crossed. It lies between the low bare mountains on the west and the high Andes on the east. Day after day, it is scorched by the burning sun. Huge clouds of dust blow across it. Not a single blade of grass can be seen for miles. Years may go by without even a sprinkle here.

470

The early Spaniards thought that the Atacama Desert was a worthless wasteland. But they had not discovered its secrets. They had not learned of its rich deposits of copper, nitrate, and other minerals. They could not guess that some day men would endure the unpleasant dry heat to mine in this area.

Southern Chile is a cold rainy region. It is often blanketed by fog. Parts of it are drenched with rain, as is shown on the rainfall map on page 438. Southern Chile is almost wholly mountainous. Because of this and the cool rainy climate, this region is thinly populated. Little of it is suitable for growing crops, but some sheep are raised.

In some ways, Southern Chile reminds us of western British Columbia and the Alaska Panhandle. Deep bays and inlets cut into its coast. Also, this Chilean coast is fringed with tree-covered islands.

Between Chile's hot desert and its rainy southern region is the rich and fertile central region, Middle Chile. As the population map on page 436 shows, Middle

Chile is the most thickly-populated part of this long country.

Middle Chile is the most important region. Chile's largest cities are located here as are most of the haciendas and many smaller farms. A variety of crops are raised in this fertile valley.

Middle Chile extends for about seven hundred miles. Because this valley is so long, its northern and southern sections have different kinds of climate. The northern part is closest to the tropics and has warm, dry summers and mild, rainy winters. Its climate is similar to that found in southern California.

The southern part of the valley begins near the city of Concepción. Southward from Concepción, the valley has a climate more like that of western Oregon. The weather is cool and rain falls the year round. As in Oregon, so much rain falls that thick forests have grown up.

Chile's Central Valley has fertile soil and climate well-suited to many kinds of farming.

Farming and Stock Raising

Farming is one of the leading industries in Middle Chile. Many large haciendas spread over the land. Other haciendas are being broken up into farms of 50 to 100 acres in size. These smaller farms are run by the people who own them.

The owner of a large hacienda does no farming. He may be a government official or run a business in a city. He usually hires a manager to direct his farm workers. The largest haciendas need many workers to care for crops and livestock.

The haciendas in the northern part of the valley have fine fruit orchards. The fruit trees are especially beautiful during September and October, Chile's springtime. Then, the peach and apple trees are in bloom. So are the orange trees with their fragrant snow-white blossoms. During that season, too, acres of melons, grapes, and vegetables are beginning to grow.

These crops have to be irrigated during the long, dry summer. The water is brought in canals and ditches from rivers that rush down from the snowfields of the Andes.

Large crops of grain are raised on some haciendas. Wheat is the chief grain crop but oats and barley are also grown. In the springtime, the grain fields are green. But by late summer, they turn a golden yellow. This means that harvesttime has come. What are the late summer and early autumn months in Chile?

Some hilly lands are used as pastures. During the winter, they have plenty of green grass for the cattle. But they are brown and dry in the summertime. Then, the beef cattle are driven to meadows high in the Andes.

Thousands of sheep are raised in southern Chile. Some flocks graze on the coastal hills and lower slopes of the Andes. But the famous sheep-raising region is far to the south on the cold plains near Tierra del Fuego. Do you see this southern tip of the continent on the map? Because cold winds sweep across these lands, the sheep grow heavy wool coats. The wool brings an excellent price. Some of the animals are slaughtered for their meat and skins.

The business and shipping center for the sheep industry is located at Punta Arenas. Find it on the map on page 435.

Punta Arenas is farther south than any other city in the world. Even so, it is a modern one and has a busy harbor. Ships load bundles of wool and skins from its warehouses and lamb and mutton from its freezing plants.

The Chilean government is helping farmers in a number of ways. In the last few years, it has granted land to about 10,000 farmers. These farmers had been working for others; now they have their own land. Certain government organizations are helping these farmers. They are encouraging them to use better seeds, more fertilizers, and chemicals that fight insects and plant diseases. Our country has worked with some Chilean organizations to improve living conditions in the farming areas. Better houses and roads are being built and health centers are being set up.

Mining and Manufacturing in Chile

Parts of Chile are rich in minerals. Vast deposits of whitish nitrate are scattered through hard layers of sand and gravel in the dry Atacama Desert. Nitrate is used for making a kind of fertilizer for the soil. It is also used in the manufacture of explosives and for making a kind of medicine called iodine.

In certain places on the Atacama Desert, deposits of borax are found. Borax, too, is a whitish mineral. It is useful in softening water. Your mother may add borax to the water when she launders clothes or washes the dishes.

Large stores of copper are buried in some of Chile's mountains. In fact, Chile has the largest known deposits of copper in the whole world. Iron is mined near the edge of the desert in northern Chile. A railroad carries the iron to the coast.

Chile also has coal. Actually, about two thirds of all the coal mined in South America is taken from Chilean lands. Deposits of silver and lead have been discovered in some mountainous areas.

Rich oil fields have been developed in the part of the island of Tierra del Fuego that belongs to Chile. Wells drilled in these fields now supply almost two thirds of the petroleum used in Chile.

Mining nitrate. Nitrate is found in gravel beds close to the surface of the ground. Dynamite is set off to loosen and break up the mixture of gravel and nitrate. Large steam shovels load this mixture onto mule carts or railroad cars and haul it to plants nearby. There, the nitrate is removed from the gravel and sand and sacked to ship away. The clean nitrate looks as white as snow.

Open-pit copper mine at Chuquicamata, Chile.

The nitrate lands are very dry and have no grass or trees. Years go by without a single drop of rain. Workers often tire of this hot rainless climate, but they know their jobs depend on it. Rain could wash away the valuable nitrate beds.

Some copper mines are located in the Andes of northern Chile. One of the largest is near the busy village of Chuquicamata. Find it on the map. It has a whole mountain of copper ore. The copper can be mined from the surface of the ground.

The earth and rock are loosened from the side of the mountain. As the chunks tumble down, they are scooped up by large machines and dropped into railroad cars. The ore is then hauled to a smelter where the copper is removed. Much of this copper is sent to the seaport of Antofagasta and shipped to other countries.

Chile's manufacturing industries are growing. In recent years, hundreds of factories have been built. They are providing jobs and goods for many Chileans. Today, over one fifth of the Chileans earn their living in manufacturing.

Santiago, Chile's capital.

Among the products manufactured are leather goods, textiles, paper, chemicals, clothing, and iron-and-steel goods. And of course, some plants prepare foods from Chile's farms for market. There are factories in many cities, but Santiago is the leading industrial center. It is near the source of many of Chile's raw materials.

Two Busy Cities

Santiago is Chile's capital and largest city. It is located in the northern part of Middle Chile, as you may remember. Point to it on the map. Back of it rise the beautiful Andes.

Santiago has many large and handsome buildings. Its widest street is stately tree-lined Bernardo O'Higgins Avenue. Down the center of this street is a wide sidewalk with lanes for automobile traffic on either side.

Santiago has many attractive homes, schools, and churches. Some were built long ago and some are modern. A railroad and a highway connect Santiago with Chile's chief seaport, Valparaiso, about ninety miles away.

Valparaiso is Chile's busiest seaport. Look for it on the map. It is the largest seaport on the western coast of South America. It faces a fine curving bay which is visited by the ships of many nations. They bring in manufactured goods and food to exchange for citrus fruits, wines, wool, and minerals.

Geography has helped Valparaiso become an important seaport. In addition to its excellent harbor, it is located at the entrance to the most heavily-populated part

Valparaiso is Chile's largest port.

of Chile. It is the gateway city to a rich fertile farm region.

The business district of Valparaiso is crowded on a narrow plain along the shore. Farther back, are homes clinging to steep hills. Large elevators and cable cars carry people up and down the hillsides.

Chile is now doing much to help its people. It has free schools. It is developing new industries and improving its transportation systems.

Because of its long coastline, Chile has depended largely on water transportation for shipping goods in and out of the country. To aid this shipping, large sums of money have been spent to improve its harbors.

Many miles of roads and railroads have been built. Some cross the high Andes Mountains. One railroad runs to Argentina, another to Peru, and a third into Bolivia. You can find these routes on the railroad map on page 453.

Chile has also built modern airports. Some of the largest ones are visited regularly by planes which link Chile with many other countries.

Some Study Questions

1. Where is Chile? Why is it called the "Shoestring Republic"?

2. How did Chile become a Spanish colony? How did Valdivia help its settlement?

3. What are the three main regions of Chile? What kind of climate does each have? What are the chief products of each?

4. Name two of Chile's main cities and tell some interesting things about them.

5. What products are made from nitrate?

6. Name other minerals found in Chile.

7. What are some ways Chile is helping its people today?

Choose for Yourself

Three possible endings are given for each of the incomplete sentences below. Write the numbers 1 to 7 on paper. After each number write the letter of the ending which completes the sentence correctly.

1. The Spanish settlement of Santiago was established by (a) Pizarro. (b) San Martín. (c) Valdivia.

2. In Chile the Spaniards had to conquer (a) the Mayas. (b) the Araucanians. (c) the Aztecs.

3. The high mountains running through eastern Chile are (a) the Sierra Madres. (b) the Andes. (c) the Rockies.

4. The capital of Chile is (a) Santiago. (b) Valparaiso. (c) Lima.

5. Southern Chile is famous for its (a) wheat. (b) nitrate. (c) sheep.

6. Nitrate looks something like (a) salt. (b) gold. (c) crude oil.

7. Chile has some of the world's richest deposits of (a) silver. (b) copper. (c) oil.

What Would You Say?

1. It is sometimes said "to the victor belongs the spoils." What do you think this means? Do you think this practice is fair? What spoils did the Spaniards take when they settled Chile? Can you remember what spoils they took in Mexico?

2. Do you think it is a good idea for a few people to own most of the land in a country? Give reasons for your answer. How is most of the land in our country owned?

3. Why can we tell some things about climate if we know the latitude of a region?

Some Other Things to Do

1. Read *Robinson Crusoe* and learn about a sailor's adventures on an island near Chile.

2. Use the map on page 490 to help you make an outline. Show the leading industries and products in each of Chile's three regions. The outline might begin something like this:

Chile's Leading Industries and Products
    I. In Northern Chile
      A. Main industries
        1. _____ etc.
      B. Main products
        1. _____ etc.
    II. In Middle Chile   etc.

Complete your outline and talk it over with your class.

3. Use pictures and a map together. Study the pictures in this chapter which tell you something about Chile's kinds of lands. On the map on page 436, try to find the general area in which each picture might have been taken. Talk over with your class what you decide and why.

4. Compare the Central Valley in California with the great valley in Middle Chile. Be ready to tell in what latitude each is, some ways the two regions are alike, and some ways they are different.

Using Latitude and Longitude

1. Locate Chile on the map on page 435. Is it east or west of 80° W. Longitude?

2. Discuss with your class how to find the latitude or longitude of a spot not on one of the circles marked on your map.

3. Notice that Chile extends from about 18° S. Latitude to 55° S. Latitude. About how many degrees is this?

4. Turn to the map on pages 504–505 and locate California. About how many degrees latitude does it extend? Which extends a longer distance north and south, our state of California or the country of Chile?

5. Find as nearly as possible the latitude and longitude of the following cities:

Santiago   Antofagasta   Punta Arenas

29 · Seven South American Neighbors

The George Washington of South America

Simón Bolívar is one of South America's greatest heroes. He was born in 1783, in Caracas, Venezuela. His parents were very wealthy.

In those days, families of wealth usually hired tutors, or private teachers, for their children. Simón's first teacher found him quite spoiled.

The next teacher would not stand for rudeness. He insisted on dependable citizenship and plenty of study, though Simón was only five. But he was also a friendly companion and often took the boy swimming, riding, and hiking. He gave Simón many new ideas, especially about justice and freedom. This tutor believed that all people in the world should be free. But they weren't—certainly not in Venezuela.

When Simón was seventeen, he was sent to Spain for further education. While in this country, he met and married a beautiful girl. He brought his bride back to Venezuela; but before long she died of yellow fever.

Bolívar was heart-broken and returned to Europe. His favorite tutor decided that a long vacation would help the young man forget his sorrow. And soon the two close friends set out on a hiking tour.

Bolívar talked over many things with his tutor. But the subject which interested him most was freedom. The people of Venezuela had little freedom and no say in their government. Bolívar knew that the Thirteen Colonies had fought a war to win their freedom from England. Could not his people, the Venezuelans, free themselves from Spain?

"Freedom is precious!" Bolívar declared. "And I shall help my people gain it!"

One afternoon while the two men rested in the shade, they discussed Spain's unfair treatment of Venezuela. Suddenly, Bolívar leaped to his feet. "Freedom *is* precious!" he declared. "And I shall help my people gain it! It is time to act!"

"Splendid words, my friend!" replied the older man. "But do not speak hastily! Think! This struggle for freedom might take years! Spain has large armies in South America. Most people will be afraid to side against them. If you lead a revolt, you may lose your entire fortune. Perhaps even your life!"

Bolívar nodded. "I know! But whatever the cost, I am ready. I promise you that!"

On his way back to Venezuela, Bolívar visited the United States. He talked with Thomas Jefferson and learned much about how George Washington and other leaders had worked for freedom. He studied our plan of government and dreamed of the day when Venezuela could establish a democracy.

Bolívar helped five countries win their independence from Spain. Simón Bolívar never forgot his promise. He served his people bravely for more than sixteen years. He traveled about, arousing the people to fight for freedom. He spent most of his fortune to make his dream come true. He raised armies and indeed, led troops in more than 200 battles.

The daring young general won some battles and lost others. Sometimes his soldiers were so discouraged that they turned against him. Several times he had to flee for his life. Still he did not give up. Instead he made new plans.

The long struggle dragged on for years.

But finally Bolívar's armies won. He had led in freeing from Spain the countries now known as Venezuela, Bolivia, Colombia, Ecuador, and Peru. No wonder, then, that Simón Bolívar is called the *Great Liberator!* The word, *liberate*, means to free.

One new republic chose Bolívar as its president. His name was given to another, Bolivia. He urged the new countries to work together and hoped they would form a "United States of South America." He often talked about ways such a union might co-operate on certain matters with our United States.

But Bolívar was far ahead of his times. The countries could not even govern themselves and wars broke out. Bolívar traveled from one area to another to try to stop them. Other leaders were jealous of his power and spread ugly rumors. Sadly enough, some of his friends also turned against him.

By this time, the brilliant statesman was weary and sick. He thought the people had lost faith in him. Was this the reward for his years of hard work and sacrifice? Feeling he was a failure, the heart-broken forty-seven-year-old leader gave up his work. Soon afterward he died.

Today, South Americans honor Simón Bolívar as one of their greatest leaders. Many cities have erected fine statues of him. He is often called the George Washington of South America.

The people of Caracas are especially proud. Their city was Bolívar's birthplace, remember. They enjoy showing visitors the stately old stone house where their famous patriot was born. To honor Bolívar, the flag of Venezuela always flies above his home.

Three Neighbors: Venezuela, Colombia, and Ecuador

Venezuela is in the northern part of South America. Point to it on the map. Spanish explorers named it long ago when they were exploring along the shores of Lake Maracaibo. They saw houses built on stilts above the shallow waters. This reminded them that houses were also built above the waters of canals in Venice, Italy. So they called the new land Venezuela, which means "little Venice."

Venezuela is about one third larger than our state of Texas. It looks out upon the warm tropical waters of the Caribbean. Venezuela lies entirely in the tropics. In the west are the Maracaibo lowlands. They have a miserable, hot, sticky climate. They are covered by steamy jungles and swamps.

To the east is Venezuela's share of the Andes. Most of the people live in basins in these mighty mountains. Such areas have a pleasant climate. Remember that the climate of lands in the tropics depends on their elevation.

Farther east between the Andes and the Orinoco River are low, nearly level plains. They are mainly cattle-grazing lands. Dams are being built on some of the rivers to irrigate the pastures during the dry months.

The Guiana Highlands rise in the southeast. They have some of the richest deposits of iron ore to be found anywhere.

Venezuela has very rich stores of oil and iron ore. Large pools of black gold lie in the rocks beneath the shallow waters of Lake Maracaibo. As the map shows, an arm of the Caribbean Sea bends inland to form this wide protected body of water. Rising above the water are many oil derricks. They are built on high platforms set on poles driven into the lake.

Oil is Venezuela's most important product. In fact, petroleum and petroleum

Oil from the derricks in Lake Maracaibo is pumped through pipelines to oil tankers.

products make up about nine tenths of the country's exports. The oil industry has been developed by foreign oil companies. This industry pays a great deal of money to Venezuela. So the country has been able to build many schools and some fine modern highways.

Some of the mountains of the Guiana Highlands contain many, many millions of tons of iron ore. First one United States company and then another, discovered an "iron mountain" in this wilderness region. Each company agreed to pay the government of Venezuela for the right to mine the iron ore.

Trained men and much money were needed to develop these mines. Indeed, it took years of hard work before any iron ore could be shipped out of the wilderness. Roads and railroads had to be built. One company built a completely new port on the Orinoco River. Ore boats from the Atlantic Ocean now come up the Orinoco to the port to get the iron ore. Most of it is shipped to the United States.

Today, the government of Venezuela is developing its own iron mines in this region. It has built a huge iron and steel plant to use this ore.

Caracas, La Guaira, and Maracaibo are Venezuela's most important cities. Caracas is its beautiful capital. It sits in a high inland valley and has a comfortable climate the year round. It has some magnificent buildings and a number of tall skyscrapers.

Steep slopes separate Caracas from the seaport of La Guaira, nine miles away. The four-lane highway which connects the two cities leads through several tunnels and over bridges above deep canyons.

Maracaibo, on the shores of Lake Maracaibo, is the center of the petroleum industry. It is also a "coffee port." Coffee and cacao are the most important exports from Venezuela's farms.

The open mine of Cerro Bolívar. A railroad then carries the iron ore to a port on the Orinoco River.

Caracas is in a high inland valley more than 3,000 feet above sea level. Below, the highway from Caracas to the coast.

Colombia is also in the northern part of South America. It faces both the Pacific and the Caribbean Sea, as the map on page 435 shows. Only one of Colombia's important ports is on the Pacific, however. The others are on the Caribbean. Let's find out why this is so.

Colombia's lands along the coast are hot lowlands covered by tangled tropical jungles. Farther inland are the towering Andes. In Colombia, these mountains divide into three ranges. In the valleys between these ranges flow rivers which are fed by heavy rains and melting snows. East of the Andes are hot plains which make up more than half of the country.

Many of Colombia's people live on the northeastern plains or in the valleys leading into them. Others dwell in high mountain basins in the Andes. Mountains cut off these regions from the Pacific coast.

481

An Indian village.

The best natural highways are the northward-flowing rivers. They empty into the Caribbean Sea. They are useful highways during the rainy season. But during the dry season, the water level is so low that boats may get stuck on sand-bars. In some places, short railroads have been built around swirling rapids and falls.

Colombia's chief occupations are mining and farming. Gold and platinum are taken from the mountains. Precious green stones known as emeralds are dug from some places in the jungles. And oil is pumped from underground in several areas.

Colombia has many farms. Bananas, rice, and cacao are among the chief crops on the warm low lands. But coffee is Colombia's most important farm export. The coffee is planted on the lower slopes of the high lands.

Buenaventura and Barranquilla are Colombia's leading seaports. In recent years, Colombia's coffee has been shipped out of the country's one important Pacific port, Buenaventura. This is because a railroad and highway have been built to this port from the upper mountain valleys where coffee is grown. Bogotá, the capital, is also connected with Buenaventura by this railroad and highway.

The port of Barranquilla is located on the Magdalena River. What kind of climate would you say these cities have? Think whether or not they are in the tropics and whether or not they are in the low lands.

Most of the ships from these cities sail to ports of the United States. People in

Loading coffee on a freighter at the port of Buenaventura.

our country buy coffee, oil, bananas, and other products from Colombia's farms and mines. In return, we ship all kinds of manufactured goods to Colombia.

Bogotá and Medellín are Colombia's busiest cities. Find them on the map. Bogotá is located in the high lands and therefore has a pleasant climate. But it is about 600 miles inland from the ports on the Caribbean. Because of the lofty Andes and marshy plains, good transportation routes have been very difficult to build. In 1961, a railroad connecting Bogotá and the Pacific coast was finally finished. It had taken nine years to build.

More than a million people live in Bogotá. As in many other cities of South America, Bogotá is partly old and partly new. Modern apartment houses stand beside homes built by the Spanish colonists. Broad, paved avenues are crossed here and there by narrow cobblestone streets. These little streets were laid out hundreds of years ago.

Medellín is Colombia's largest industrial center and is growing rapidly. The map shows you that it is located high in the mountains. It has become one of the main textile manufacturing cities of South America.

Colombia has many problems. It needs to build more highways and railroads. The long rivers are still used to transport quantities of goods. But they are not satisfactory during the dry season when they become very low.

Like her sister countries, Colombia needs more schools and more help for its poor. It needs more industries and especially more manufacturing. At present, it has to buy most of its factory-made goods from other countries.

Ecuador is the equator country. Its name which is Spanish for equator suits it well. The equator runs through it, as the map on page 435 shows.

Ecuador is a small country; but it has three main regions. One plains region stretches along the Pacific coast. It is mainly a hot, rainy area clothed in dense forests. Where the land has been cleared, crops such as cotton, rice, sugar cane, bananas, and cacao are grown. Some of these products are shipped to other countries. Cacao is probably the most important export. Much of it is shipped to our country and Europe to be made into chocolate.

Ecuador's other plains lie in the east and are covered with jungles. Few people live on them.

Separating these two plains regions are the high lands of the towering Andes. Between the ranges are deep valleys and a plateau. Here one finds a delightful spring-like climate all year long. It is not surprising, then, that about three fourths of the people live in this region. As the map shows, Quito, the capital of Ecuador, is located here.

Quito and Guayaquil are Ecuador's largest cities. Quito spreads out on the floor of a high mountain basin. It is located fifteen miles south of the equator but it is more than 9,000 feet above sea level. So its climate is never hot. Quito has many modern buildings and some which were erected by the Spaniards long ago.

Guayaquil is the country's chief seaport. Actually, it sits on the Guayas River fifty miles inland. But the river is deep, so ocean vessels can visit Guayaquil's docks. Because this city is in the heart of Ecuador's farm region, ships take

Highland farmers walk along
a railroad track on their way
to market.

on cargoes of cacao and other crops. They
also carry to markets tagua nuts and
"Panama" hats.

Buttons and hats from trees. Tagua nuts are made into such articles as
buttons and umbrella handles. These nuts
come from the tagua palm tree which
grows wild in the forests. It bears giant
"pods" which weigh about fifteen pounds
each. Inside each pod are hard white nuts
which look something like ivory.

In a way, Panama hats also come from
palm trees. They are fashioned from
strips of fan-shaped palm leaves which
have been treated in boiling water. The
picture on this page shows Indian women
weaving such hats. The name "Panama"
was given to these hats during the California Gold Rush. In those days, they were
sold in Panama to gold seekers who were
crossing the Isthmus.

484

Ecuador owns the Galapagos Islands. They are located more than six
hundred miles off the Pacific coast. Rare
birds, huge lizards, and giant turtle-like
tortoises live on these islands. Some tortoises are said to weigh about five hundred pounds and are about two hundred
years old. Part of the Robinson Crusoe
story happened on these islands.

Ecuador's outlook. Ecuador lacks
mineral wealth. But it exports many
farm products, as you know. One of its
chief problems, however, is getting them
to markets. There are few roads, even on
the coastal plain. But the most densely-populated part of Ecuador is in the high
lands. There, the high, rugged Andes
make it difficult to build roads.

Like its sister countries, Ecuador has
many poor people who have not had a
chance to attend school or learn modern
ways of living. Because many live in
out-of-the-way places in the high lands,
it is difficult to help them.

South of Ecuador is Peru, a famous
old Indian land. The next section will
tell you about it.

Women weaving Panama hats
in Ecuador.

Peru: Center of the Inca Empire

An Inca official travels on one of the roads that connected all parts of their huge empire.

Peru is called the land of the Incas. The Incas were ambitious Indians who built cities and temples along the west coast of South America long, long ago.

A legend tell us that the first Inca rulers were Manco Capac and his sister. The Sun gave them a golden staff. He told them to settle where this staff disappeared into the earth. Their golden staff led them to the Valley of Cuzco, high in the Andes. There, where the shining staff entered the earth, the city of Cuzco was started. It became the capital of the Inca nation. Find Cuzco on the map on page 435.

The legend says that Manco Capac, was kind and wise. He taught the Indians how to farm and mine gold and silver in the mountains. He also helped them erect buildings and make roads. His sister showed the women how to weave and sew and keep their homes neat and clean.

The Incas built a large empire. As the years passed, the Inca Indians conquered many other Indian tribes and became very powerful. In time, their empire reached for almost 3,000 miles along the western coast of South America. It spread across most of Peru and Ecuador, and also dipped into parts of Bolivia, Colombia, northern Argentina, and northern Chile.

For five hundred years, the Incas prospered. Then they began to quarrel among themselves. While they were battling with each other, gold-seeking Pizarro and his soldiers landed on Peru's shores. They climbed the narrow, twisting trails that led high into the heart of the Inca Empire.

Gold-hungry Spaniards conquered the Inca Empire. The Inca, or ruler, had thousands of warriors, but he did not try to drive out the Spaniards. When they arrived he treated them kindly and provided them with a place to stay.

Sly Pizarro planned a cruel trick in order to seize the Inca's gold. He invited the ruler to be his guest. Then, as the Inca approached, Spaniards rushed from their hiding places and captured him. He was held prisoner while Pizarro demanded an enormous price for his freedom.

The unhappy Inca agreed to pay a large ransom. He promised to fill a room with gold and also two rooms with silver. This probably was more than $10,000,000 in our money. Pizarro was delighted and accepted the offer. So the Inca ordered messengers to hasten through the empire collecting treasure.

But when the gold and silver were piled high before him, Pizarro was not satisfied after all. Greedily he declared, "I must have all of the Inca wealth. I shall rule the empire myself." Then he ordered the Inca put to death.

In time, the Spaniards conquered Cuzco and the rest of the Inca Empire. Then Spain began to govern this vast region.

Cuzco's location was not convenient for the Spaniards. It was in the high mountains away from the coast and they could not keep in touch with Spain. So a new capital was planned close to the sea.

Lima: the capital of Peru yesterday and today. Pizarro chose the place for the new city. It was laid out just eight miles from the Pacific and the good, natural harbor at Callao. Furthermore, this location was in a beautiful fertile river valley where many crops could be grown.

The new capital was begun in 1535 and was known as Lima. In time, Lima became the most important city in all of South America. This was partly because Spain's governing officials lived there. It was the capital of Spain's vast lands on the continent.

But another reason was that enormous riches poured through Lima. Millions of dollars worth of gold and silver were hauled down to this city from Peru's mountains. Much treasure was shipped to Spain. But some was used to build handsome palaces and beautiful churches in Lima.

Today, Lima is still an important city. It is the capital of Peru and its largest city. It has many fine modern buildings and some older ones dating back to the colonial days. The oldest university in the Western Hemisphere is located at Lima. Its sister city, Callao, is Peru's largest port.

There are really three Perus. Near the coast are strips of desert plain and low hills and mountains. Find this coastal region on the map on page 436. Here, little rain falls, but the soil is rich. Also many small rivers and streams flow down from the Andes to the Pacific across this region. Water from these rivers is used to grow crops of cotton, rice, and sugar cane. Farming is Peru's leading industry and this coastal region is its most impor-

A copper mine and smelter in the Andes of Peru. Why do you think it took much money to develop this mine?

tant agricultural area. Here also are the country's leading cities.

Another region spreads out east of the Andes. The map shows that its plains are a part of the Amazon Basin. These hot steamy lands have a very uncomfortable climate and are almost covered with tropical forest. Few people live in this region. Indeed, some of this wild area has never been explored.

Separating these two regions are Peru's high lands, where the lofty Andes rise. Find them on the map. Tucked in between the towering ranges are narrow little valleys, deep canyons, and high basins. They are in the tropics but they have a cool and pleasant climate. Can you explain why? About half of Peru's people live in these high lands. Most of them make their living by farming. Corn and potatoes are their main crops.

Peru's mountains are rich with minerals. They have deposits of gold, silver, lead, zinc, iron, and copper. But today, the stores of copper are the most valuable.

Peru's most famous copper mine is located near Cerro de Pasco nearly 15,000 feet above sea level. You can see a picture of this mine above. The miners are Indians who are used to living in the high lands. Other people cannot stand to do hard work so high above sea level.

When this mine was first developed, mule-pack trains carried the copper down the twisting mountain trails to the seaport. But today it can be shipped in freight cars. Now, a remarkable railroad climbs from Lima to Cerro de Pasco. On its way, it passes through dozens of tunnels and crosses more than sixty bridges reaching over canyons.

487

Peru's future. Providing good transportation routes has been one of Peru's problems. More than two fifths of the country is high lands and another large part is tropical low lands. It is difficult and expensive to build roads through such lands. In fact, a country cannot afford to build roads and railroads unless important industries can use and help pay for them. Except for its large copper mines, Peru's industrial centers are located on the west coast.

Peru has other problems because many of its people are very poor and can neither read nor write. More schools are needed as well as opportunities for learning better ways of farming and living.

Bolivia: The Land of the Sky

Bolivia is a landlocked country. Do you see it on the map? We say it is landlocked because it has no seacoast. So it is shut off from most of the world. To reach Bolivia, one must either fly in or travel from Chile or Peru by train. The railroad lines hug steep slopes as they wind and twist around the mountains on their climb over the Andes.

Ranges of high Andes parade across western Bolivia, as the map on page 437 shows. Some peaks tower more than 20,000 feet high and are always capped with snow and ice.

Bolivia has two main regions, its high lands and its low plains. Notice that more than half of the country is low plains.

But this area is thinly populated. In the northeast are hot steamy jungles reaching into the Amazon Basin. In the southeast, the low plains are a part of the Gran Chaco. They share its miserable hot wet summers and very dry, hot winters.

Three fourths of Bolivia's people live in the high lands. Their homes are on the high, wind-swept Plateau of Bolivia and in the valleys of the mountains to the east of this plateau. They work on farms, in mines, and in cities.

Where is this plateau? Do you know? When you looked at the map, you found that western Bolivia was covered by mountains. But notice that a large plateau stretches through the heart of them. It is a wide, hilly land and so high that it is often called the "Land of the Sky." Indeed, most of it is more than 12,000 feet above the level of the sea. Rising still higher are the lofty mountains that surround it.

Because this plateau is so high, it is cool the year round and nights may even be sharply cold and frosty. This is a dry land. Look at the rainfall map on page 438 and find how much rain it receives a year. This chilly dry climate is suitable for only a few kinds of crops. The chief one is potatoes.

The valleys in the mountains to the east are lower and warmer than the plateau. In these valleys, corn, wheat, and many kinds of fruits and vegetables are raised.

The northern edge of the plateau has a large lake with an Indian name, Lake Titicaca. It is the highest large lake in the world. If you visited it, you could sail across its blue waters in a modern steamship. On your sightseeing tour, you would see Indian villages along the shore. You would also notice Indians skimming over the lake in queer little boats called balsas. Balsas are made of long tough reeds and grasses which grow along the shores of Lake Titicaca. Look at the balsas in the picture on this page.

Most of Bolivia's people are Indians. Many are farmers and are extremely poor. Thousands work on the large ranches owned by wealthy people and many spend some time cultivating their own small patches. Most Indians farm much as their ancestors did, centuries ago.

Every family who can, raises a few sheep in order to have warm woolen clothes. Women card the wool and spin it into thread. Then they dye it in bright colors, weave it into cloth, and sew garments for their families.

Indian women often wear gay-colored blouses and ten or twelve skirts, one on top of another. When the weather is coldest, they may bundle up in warm shawls. Men use blanket-like ponchos for their "overcoats." Most of these Indians go barefooted no matter how chilly the days are. They sometimes wear

A llama train on the Plateau of Bolivia.

home-made sandals, but they are too poor to afford shoes. Both men and women usually wear stiff-brimmed hats like those in the picture on this page. What other interesting things does the picture tell about how the people dress?

Balsas on Lake Titicaca. Indians have used such boats for hundreds of years.

SOUTH AMERICA
CHIEF OCCUPATIONS

- Agriculture
- Fishing
- Lumbering
- Livestock ranching
- Petroleum
- Mining
- Manufacturing center

Some of the important ways of making a living in South America. Find the manufacturing centers. Are there many?

Most Bolivian Indians live in small homes made of adobe brick. Because they live at such a high altitude, there are few trees. So there is not enough lumber to build houses. The cooking is done over a small fire built on the dirt floor.

Many Bolivians own one or more useful animals called *llamas*. Look at the picture of the llamas on page 489. Though they are small cousins of the camel, llamas have no humps. They are sturdy pack animals and can go without water for several days.

A llama can carry a load of about a hundred pounds. If he is treated well, he is usually gentle and friendly. But if he is abused or overloaded, it is a different story. Then he may hiss and stubbornly refuse to move until his load is lightened.

Bolivians love their llamas and like to decorate them. They hang bright-colored tassels on their ears and silver bells around their necks. Llamas are valuable animals. Their thick coats can be sheared much like sheep's wool and used to make warm clothing. If necessary, llamas can be killed for meat. But they are chiefly used as pack animals. They are sure-footed and can carry goods over steep cold mountain trails. Often, visitors to Bolivia's high lands can see long trains of llamas on their way to market.

A farm high in the Andes.

La Paz is in the Andes. Notice the tree-lined boulevard which runs through the city.

Bolivia has several important cities. The largest one is La Paz. The map will show you that it is at the eastern edge of the plateau. It is sheltered in a deep valley with steep canyon walls rising above it. They help to protect the city from the cold winds that sweep over the plateau.

La Paz is a busy city, for it is the most important business center of the country. It has some up-to-date buildings but many homes and churches are quite old. The streets in the center of the city run along the bottom of the valley and are fairly wide. But those which climb the sides of the valley are too narrow even for carts and wagons. They are used by people travelling on foot and by the llama trains.

La Paz is one of Bolivia's two capitals. Sucre, the other capital, is in a valley in the eastern Andes. Do you see it on the map?

South of Sucre is the interesting old city of Potosí. It is located near a once-famous silver mine. Long ago, this mine had one of the richest deposits of silver in all of South America. The Spaniards forced Indians to work it.

As more and more silver was mined, Potosí grew. Some Spaniards made fortunes and built handsome homes and other buildings there. Later on, though, the supply of silver gave out and gradually the rich people moved away.

Potosí's wealth was nearly forgotten until about fifty years ago when tin ore was discovered nearby. Today, mining tin ore is the chief industry of this high city. Tin has many uses. One of the most important is for coating steel cans known as "tin" cans. Because of this coating, food keeps well in such cans.

491

Indians sort tin ore from a mine 15,000 feet above sea level.

Bolivia is rich in many minerals. It has mined gold and silver for centuries. And today, it mines about a fifth of the world's tin. It also has rich stores of such minerals as lead, zinc, and copper.

But these minerals are in the high mountains. They must be dug at altitudes of from 13,000 to 15,000 feet above sea level. In such high altitudes, the air is thin and hard to breathe. So it is difficult for people to work. Still, many Indians are employed in the mining industry. Indeed, mining is the "money" crop of this high "Land of the Sky."

About Bolivia's problems. What have you learned about Bolivia that suggests some problems? For one thing, it has a serious transportation problem. Why? Remember that it has no seacoast and that most of its people live in the high lands. It needs good roads and more railroads to serve its mines and towns.

Then, too, Bolivia has almost no manufacturing. So its people cannot produce enough goods for themselves. Manufactured products must be bought from other countries.

Mining is the one "money" industry. When other countries buy Bolivia's minerals, times are fairly good. But when Bolivia cannot sell her minerals the mines have to close and the employees are out of work. To prosper, a country needs a variety of industries and many kinds of crops.

Finally, we remember that Bolivia's people are very poor. Most of them can neither read nor write. Neither do they have the advantages of communication with other areas. So they hardly know what is going on in their own country or in the world.

Paraguay: An Inland Country

Paraguay is another inland country. Find it on the map on page 435. Paraguay has the smallest population of any country in South America. In some ways, it has been the least-developed nation of the continent. It has not traded much with other nations and has been slow to adopt modern ways of doing things. This is partly because of its out-of-the-way location.

Like Bolivia, Paraguay has no seacoast. Its ships use the Paraná River as a water highway to the outside world. Look on the map for this river. From Paraguay it leads through Argentina for hundreds of miles to the Argentine ports of Rosario and Buenos Aires.

Paraguay has had a stormy history. It was ruled by cruel dictators for many years. Several times it was led into long costly wars. During these years, the strongest men were killed or wounded. Therefore, this inland nation has lacked enough men and money to develop its resources.

Paraguay is divided into two parts by the Paraguay River. To the west are the grassy plains of the Gran Chaco. They extend across Paraguay and on through northern Argentina.

The Gran Chaco has such a disagreeable climate that only a handful of people try to live there. Some of them raise cattle. In the summer, the pastures are green because heavy showers pour down. But during the hot dry winters, there is neither grass nor water for the livestock.

A belt of forest follows along the Paraguay River. Here valuable hardwood quebracho trees grow. Quebracho wood is cut into chips which are soaked in water. The liquid which is drained off is used to tan leather. Yerba maté trees are also found in the forests. Yerba maté leaves are gathered to make a kind of tea called *maté*.

East of the Paraguay River is a rolling fertile land of farms and cattle ranches. There gauchos tend thousands of cattle. Other men grow such crops as corn, rice, sugar cane, oranges, and cotton. Millions of acres of cotton are now being raised near the Paraguay River.

Asunción is the interesting capital of Paraguay. This small, quiet city sits on the high banks of the Paraguay River, almost a thousand miles from the sea.

Like many other capital cities in South America, Asunción was founded long ago. Visitors are reminded of this when they see its old thick-walled churches and colorful Spanish-style homes.

If we visited in one of these homes, we would probably be served maté. The Paraguayans are so fond of maté that they drink it several times a day. It is often served in hollow gourds. Paraguayans like to sip maté through straw-like tubes called *bombillas*. Point to the bombilla in the picture on this page.

Asunción has some modern stores and government buildings, and a few factories. But as yet it is not an important industrial center.

Paraguay is waking up. Its leaders realize that its location and costly wars have prevented it from keeping step with other nations. It needs more schools for its children. It needs better ways of farming and more factories to provide jobs and goods for its people. It needs increased trade with other nations.

Southeast of Paraguay is the busy little country of Uruguay.

A gaucho sips maté through a bombilla.

Little Uruguay: A Forward-Looking Country

Uruguay is the smallest country in South America. Find it on the map on page 435. Notice how it borders the Río de la Plata and is tucked in between its two big neighbors, Brazil and Argentina.

Uruguay is a pleasant mid-latitude country. Its summers are somewhat warm but its winters are quite cool. In general, it has a comfortable climate all the year round.

Many people think of Uruguay as a large stock ranch. You see, stock raising is its most important business. Its rolling grasslands receive plenty of rain and provide good pastures for millions of cattle and sheep.

A sheep market in Uruguay. Sheep and cattle can graze outdoors the year round.

Looking down on the harbor of Montevideo from the rolling grasslands behind it.

Uruguay's stock ranches send whole trainloads of cattle and sheep to the stockyards to be killed. Some of the meat is frozen and some is smoked or canned. Enormous quantities of meat, hides, and wool are exported.

Some crops are raised, too. The rich soil and mild climate make it easy to grow wheat, corn, oats, and flax. Vegetables and other food crops are also produced.

In Uruguay, it is easy to ship products to market. A fine system of roads and railroads connects the large ranches with Uruguay's chief seaport, Montevideo.

Montevideo is the capital and industrial center of Uruguay. Locate it on the map. See how it faces the Río de la Plata. Ships from many countries visit its excellent harbor. Montevideo is a modern city with skyscrapers, attractive stores, hotels, and apartment houses. It has over one third of Uruguay's people. Many are employed in the meat-packing houses, flour mills, or tanneries. A tannery is a place where hides are treated to be made into leather, remember.

Montevideo is also a popular vacation resort. Its wide, sandy beaches stretch for miles along the Rio de la Plata. During the summer, from December to April, they are crowded with visitors.

Uruguay was a forward-looking country. In the past the government did much for its people. It built good roads and railroads. It provided fine schools for its children and improved working conditions for its citizens.

But Uruguay has been a "one-industry" nation. Many of its people have jobs which are related to the stock-raising business and exporting meat, wool, and hides. When foreign trade in these products is poor, some people lose their jobs. Today, many people are without jobs. Some have used force to try to overthrow the government. They failed. But there is little freedom now in Uruguay.

Neighbors Working Together

A part of Bolívar's dream has come true. In the late 1800's, many delegates from the two Americas met in Washington, D. C. They talked over problems that Latin America had in common with our country, and agreed to meet every four years.

In 1910, a permanent organization was set up. It was called the *Pan American Union*. Today, it is a part of the *Organization of American States*. This name was chosen in 1948 when the delegates from twenty-one American nations gathered together at Bogotá, Colombia. They represented the United States and twenty Latin-American nations. One of the main purposes of OAS is to work for the peaceful settlements of any trouble or disputes that break out among its member countries. Its headquarters is in the Pan-American Union in Washington, D. C.

This organization is doing much to encourage better understanding and cooperation in the Western Hemisphere. It meets regularly to discuss matters of trade, health, education, transportation, and defense. Thus, these American neighbors, large and small, talk together and try to help each other solve their problems.

The Peace Corps is helping in many parts of Latin America. Several thousand Americans from our country are serving in the Peace Corps. Some are teachers and some are nurses, mechanics, or farmers, perhaps, or are trained in another special field.

Members of the Peace Corps are volunteers. They work without pay for two years in countries where they are needed. They usually live and serve among the poor people. They have been so helpful and friendly that they have spread much goodwill. A newspaper in Colombia has called them "soldiers of peace."

Our country is also sharing its surplus food crops. You see, our farmers produce enormous crops—more than they can market. We call the extra that is left over the surplus. This surplus is helping many poor, unfortunate people in the world. In Latin America, it is provid-

At the left above, a Peace Corps worker from New Jersey teaches in a school he built in Peru. Above, a worker from Florida has started this nursery in Santiago, Chile. At the left, other workers from our country build a new village in Bolivia.

ing more than eight million children with school lunches, for example.

Probably you have plenty of lunch every day. But many poor children in South America do not and are half-starved and sickly. This is one reason why some don't go to school.

The United States has developed a *Food for Peace* plan with Latin American leaders. It shares our surplus food but asks that the communities that are helped do their part. Many have. The men have built school lunchrooms and the women cook and serve the meals.

In Bolivia, there weren't nearly enough schools. But recently villagers have erected new ones. They are plain and

built of hand-made bricks formed from a mixture of mud and straw. The builders have been paid in beans, flour, cornmeal, and powdered milk furnished by our *Food for Peace* plan.

There is not enough room here to tell all the remarkable things that the *Food for Peace* program has accomplished. But two of its main benefits are helping people to help themselves, and building goodwill.

All of the people of our two continents are Americans. All of our countries were started as colonies by people from Europe. All of our countries have fought and worked for independence. We buy many useful products from each other. And we sell many products to each other. We are neighbors and need to work together in solving certain problems we all have. Let us try to understand and help our neighbors as best we can.

Some Questions to Answer

1. Who was Simón Bolívar? Why is he sometimes called the George Washington of South America?

2. Where is Venezuela? What are its main industries? its busiest cities? How have rich natural resources helped to develop this country?

3. In what area is Colombia? What are its main occupations and leading products? What have you learned about its chief cities?

4. How would you describe Ecuador? What have you learned about its name? its main cities? its leading industries?

5. Why is Bolivia called the "Land of the Sky"? How does its location affect people's ways of living?

6. Where are Paraguay and Uruguay located? What are some ways in which these countries are different?

Thinking Together

1. Why has there never been a United States of South America, do you suppose?

2. Some countries in South America are said to be backward. What does this mean? What would help them?

3. Are there frontiers in South America? Where? Would you like to pioneer on one of them? Where? Why?

4. How has the Andes influenced ways of living in the countries of South America?

5. How do you think we can help the people of South America? In what ways can they help us?

Reviewing with Maps

Let's use maps to review some important things about South America. The maps on pages 435, 436, 438, and 453 will help you answer these questions.

1. Which is the largest country?
2. Which countries face the Atlantic?
3. Which ones face the Pacific?
4. Which ones have no seacoast?
5. Through which country does the Amazon flow?
6. Uplands are lands that are "up" or high. They may include hills, plateaus, and mountains. Which country has the largest region of uplands?
7. Which receives the most rainfall, the Pampa or southern Chile? Which region has the best climate for growing crops?
8. Which is more thickly settled, southeastern Brazil or the Amazon Basin? What kind of climate does each region have? How does climate affect man's choice of a place to live and ways of earning a living?
9. Which has a larger population, Patagonia or Middle Chile? Why?
10. Which country has the most miles of railroads? What is one reason for this?
11. No railroads reach across the interior of Brazil. Why?
12. Which countries lie partly in the mid-latitudes? How is their "plains" climate different from the "plains" climate in the lands near the equator?

Using Latitude and Longitude

A. Study the map on page 435. Which countries lie entirely within the South Latitudes? Which colonies? Which country is located in the North Latitudes? How can you be sure your answers are correct?

B. Following is a list of South American cities which are located in the South Latitudes. Copy this list. Then find as nearly as you can the latitude and longitude at which each city is located. Use the map on page 435.

	Latitude	Longitude
1. Montevideo	___?___	___?___
2. Asuncion	___?___	___?___
3. Sao Paulo	___?___	___?___
4. Brasilia	___?___	___?___
5. Lima	___?___	___?___

C. Refer to the global map on page 441 to answer these review questions:

1. Is the United States in the North Latitudes or the South Latitudes?

2. Is our country in the East Longitudes or the West Longitudes?

D. Use the map on pages 504–505 to help you tell the approximate latitude and longitude of these cities:

1. Seattle
2. Philadelphia
3. Los Angeles
4. Boston
5. New Orleans

E. Use the map on pages 504–505 and its scales of measurement on page 505 to help you measure some distances. Find about how many miles and how many kilometers Washington D.C. is from the following cities: (See Table across the page)

	Miles	Kilometers
1. San Francisco	___?___	___?___
2. Phoenix	___?___	___?___
3. Atlanta	___?___	___?___
4. Buffalo	___?___	___?___
5. Salt Lake City	___?___	___?___
6. Minneapolis	___?___	___?___

Some Other Things to Do

1. Use an encyclopedia to learn more about one of the topics below. Take notes on what you read and prepare a report. Be ready to share it.

The Incas	The OAS
Simon Bolivar	Pizarro
Llamas	Yerba mate
The Food for Peace Plan	

2. Look for the countries you have just studied on the map on page 490. In which ones is manufacturing not a chief industry? Write some reasons why and discuss them with your class.

3. Help your classmates pantomime a story about the Incas.

4. Find and give a helpful news item about one of the countries which you read about in Chapter 29.

5. Learn more about what the Peace Corps is doing in one of the South American countries. Talk this over with your class.

Compare Some Common Measuring Units

The Table below shows how to change some common ways of measuring *length* into metric ways.

When you know:	You can find:	If you multiply by:
inches	millimeters	25.4
feet	centimeters	30.48
yards	meters	0.9
miles	kilometers	1.6

Tables of Reference

Table 1 · The United States

No.	State	Date of Admission	Abbreviation	Nickname	Area in Square Miles	Population 1970	Capital
1	Delaware	Original Thirteen States	Del.	Blue Hen	2,057	548,000	Dover
2	Pennsylvania		Pa.	Keystone	45,333	11,794,000	Harrisburg
3	New Jersey		N.J.	Garden	7,836	7,168,000	Trenton
4	Georgia		Ga.	Empire State of the South	58,876	4,590,000	Atlanta
5	Connecticut		Conn.	Nutmeg	5,009	3,032,000	Hartford
6	Massachusetts		Mass.	Bay	8,257	5,689,000	Boston
7	Maryland		Md.	Old Line	10,577	3,922,000	Annapolis
8	South Carolina		S.C.	Palmetto	31,055	2,591,000	Columbia
9	New Hampshire		N.H.	Granite	9,304	738,000	Concord
10	Virginia		Va.	Old Dominion	40,815	4,648,000	Richmond
11	New York		N.Y.	Empire	49,576	18,191,000	Albany
12	North Carolina		N.C.	Tar Heel	52,712	5,082,000	Raleigh
13	Rhode Island		R.I.	Little Rhody	1,214	950,000	Providence
14	Vermont	1791	Vt.	Green Mountain	9,609	445,000	Montpelier
15	Kentucky	1792	Ky.	Bluegrass	40,395	3,219,000	Frankfort
16	Tennessee	1796	Tenn.	Volunteer	42,244	3,924,000	Nashville
17	Ohio	1803	Ohio	Buckeye	41,222	10,652,000	Columbus
18	Louisiana	1812	La.	Pelican	48,523	3,643,000	Baton Rouge
19	Indiana	1816	Ind.	Hoosier	36,291	5,194,000	Indianapolis
20	Mississippi	1817	Miss.	Magnolia	47,716	2,217,000	Jackson
21	Illinois	1818	Ill.	Prairie	56,400	11,114,000	Springfield
22	Alabama	1819	Ala.	Cotton	51,609	3,444,000	Montgomery
23	Maine	1820	Me.	Pine Tree	33,215	994,000	Augusta
24	Missouri	1821	Mo.	Show Me	69,686	4,677,000	Jefferson City
25	Arkansas	1836	Ark.	Wonder	53,104	1,923,000	Little Rock
26	Michigan	1837	Mich.	Wolverine	58,216	8,875,000	Lansing
27	Florida	1845	Fla.	Sunshine	58,560	6,789,000	Tallahassee
28	Texas	1845	Tex.	Lone-Star	267,339	11,197,000	Austin
29	Iowa	1846	Iowa	Hawkeye	56,290	2,825,000	Des Moines
30	Wisconsin	1848	Wis.	Badger	56,154	4,418,000	Madison
31	California	1850	Calif.	Golden	158,693	19,953,000	Sacramento
32	Minnesota	1858	Minn.	Gopher	84,068	3,805,000	St. Paul
33	Oregon	1859	Oreg.	Beaver	96,981	2,091,000	Salem
34	Kansas	1861	Kans.	Sunflower	82,264	2,249,000	Topeka
35	West Virginia	1863	W.Va.	Mountain	24,181	1,744,000	Charleston
36	Nevada	1864	Nev.	Silver	110,544	489,000	Carson City
37	Nebraska	1867	Nebr.	Corn Husker	77,227	1,484,000	Lincoln
38	Colorado	1876	Colo.	Centennial	104,247	2,207,000	Denver
39	North Dakota	1889	N.D.	Flickertail	70,665	618,000	Bismarck
40	South Dakota	1889	S.D.	Coyote	77,047	666,000	Pierre
41	Montana	1889	Mont.	Treasure	147,138	694,000	Helena
42	Washington	1889	Wash.	Evergreen	68,192	3,409,000	Olympia
43	Idaho	1890	Ida.	Gem	83,557	713,000	Boise
44	Wyoming	1890	Wyo.	Equality	97,914	332,000	Cheyenne
45	Utah	1896	Utah	Beehive	84,916	1,059,000	Salt Lake City
46	Oklahoma	1907	Okla.	Sooner	69,919	2,559,000	Oklahoma City
47	New Mexico	1912	N.M.	Land of Enchantment	121,666	1,016,000	Santa Fe
48	Arizona	1912	Ariz.	Grand Canyon	113,909	1,772,000	Phoenix
49	Alaska	1959	none	none	586,400	302,173	Juneau
50	Hawaii	1959	none	Aloha State	6,424	770,000	Honolulu

Table 2 · Our Lands Beyond Our Boundaries

Place	Date of Annexation	Area in Square Miles	Population 1970	Capital
American Samoa	1900	76	27,770	Pago Pago
Guam	1899	206	86,926	Agana
Pacific Islands under U.S. Trusteeship	1947	8,475	101,592	
Panama Canal Zone	1904	553	44,650	Balboa Heights
Puerto Rico	1899	3,435	2,690,000	San Juan
Virgin Islands	1917	133	63,200	Charlotte Amalie

Table 3 · Our North American Neighbors

Country	Year of Independence	Area in Square Miles	Population 1970	Capital	Political Divisions
Belize (Br. Hon.)	1969	8,867	130,000	Belize	
Canada		3,851,809	21,641,000	Ottawa	10 Provinces 2 Territories
Costa Rica	1821	19,575	1,800,000	San José	7 Provinces
Cuba	1898	44,218	8,553,000	Havana	6 Provinces
Dominican Republic	1844	18,703	4,325,000	Santo Domingo	26 Provinces
El Salvador	1821	8,260	3,534,000	San Salvador	14 Departments
Guatemala	1821	42,042	5,189,000	Guatemala City	22 Departments
Haiti	1804	10,714	4,867,000	Port-au-Prince	5 Departments
Honduras	1821	43,277	2,582,000	Tegucigalpa	18 Departments
Jamaica		4,411	2,000,000	Kingston	
Mexico	1821	761,602	48,313,000	Mexico City	29 States 2 Territories
Nicaragua	1821	53,938	1,984,000	Managua	16 Departments
Panama	1903	29,209	1,464,000	Panamá	9 Provinces
Trinidad and Tobago	1962	1,980	1,070,000	Port of Spain	

Table 4 · Our South American Neighbors

Country	Year of Independence	Area in Square Miles	Population 1970	Capital	Political Divisions
Argentina	1816	1,072,070	24,352,000	Buenos Aires	22 Provinces 1 Territory 1 Federal District
Bolivia	1825	424,163	4,931,000	La Paz, Sucre	9 Departments
Brazil	1822	3,286,478	92,238,000	Brasília	22 States 4 Territories 1 Federal District
Chile	1818	292,257	9,780,000	Santiago	25 Provinces
Colombia	1819	439,513	21,100,000	Bogotá	19 Departments 3 Intendancies 5 Commissaries 1 Special District
Ecuador	1822	109,483	6,093,000	Quito	20 Provinces
French Guiana		35,135	51,000	Cayenne	
Guyana	1966	83,000	763,000	Georgetown	
Paraguay	1811	157,047	2,386,000	Asunción	13 Departments
Peru	1824	496,223	13,586,000	Lima	24 Departments
Surinam		55,144	403,000	Paramaribo	
Uruguay	1828	72,172	2,890,000	Montevideo	19 Departments
Venezuela	1811	352,143	10,400,000	Caracas	1 Federal District 2 Territories 20 States

Table 5 · Cities in the United States Having 200,000 or More People (1970 Census)

(Greater Metropolitan Area Figures Used)*

City	Population	City	Population	City	Population
Akron, Ohio	679,000	Grand Rapids, Mich.	539,000	Phoenix, Ariz.	968,000
Albany-Schenectady-Troy, N.Y.	722,000	Greensboro, N.C.	604,000	Pittsburgh, Pa.	2,401,000
Albuquerque, N.M.	316,000	Harrisburg, Pa.	411,000	Portland, Ore.-Wash.	1,009,000
Allentown, Pa.-N.J.	544,000	Hartford, Conn.	664,000	Providence, R.I.-Mass.	911,000
Anaheim, Calif.	1,420,000	Honolulu, Hawaii	629,000	Richmond, Va.	518,000
Atlanta, Ga.	1,390,000	Houston, Tex.	1,985,000	Rochester, N.Y.	883,000
Bakersfield, Calif.	329,000	Indianapolis, Ind.	1,110,000	Sacramento, Calif.	801,000
Baltimore, Md.	2,071,000	Jacksonville, Fla.	529,000	St. Louis, Mo.-Ill.	2,363,000
Baton Rouge, La.	200,000	Jersey City, N.J.	609,000	Salt Lake City, Utah	558,000
Beaumont, Tex.	316,000	Kansas City, Mo.-Kan.	1,254,000	San Antonio, Tex.	864,000
Binghamton, N.Y.-Pa.	303,000	Knoxville, Tenn.	400,000	San Bernardino, Calif.	1,143,000
Birmingham, Ala.	739,000	Lancaster, Pa.	320,000	San Diego, Calif.	1,358,000
Boston, Mass.	2,754,000	Lansing, Mich.	378,000	San Francisco-Oakland, Calif.	3,110,000
Bridgeport, Conn.	389,000	Little Rock, Ark.	323,000	San Jose, Calif.	1,065,000
Buffalo, N.Y.	1,349,000	Los Angeles, Calif.	7,032,000	Seattle, Wash.	1,422,000
Canton, Ohio	372,000	Louisville, Ky.-Ind.	827,000	Springfield, Mass.	530,000
Charleston, S.C.	304,000	Memphis, Tenn.-Ark.	770,000	Syracuse, N.Y.	637,000
Charlotte, N.C.	409,000	Miami, Fla.	1,268,000	Takoma, Wash.	411,000
Chattanooga, Tenn.-Ga.	305,000	Milwaukee, Wisc.	1,404,000	Tampa-St. Petersburg, Fla.	1,013,000
Chicago, Ill.	6,979,000	Minneapolis-St. Paul, Minn.	1,814,000	Toledo, Ohio-Mich.	693,000
Cincinnati, Ohio-Ky.-Ind.	1,385,000	Mobile, Ala.	377,000	Trenton, N.J.	304,000
Cleveland, Ohio	2,064,000	Nashville, Tenn.	541,000	Tucson, Ariz.	352,000
Columbia, S.C.	323,000	Nassau-Suffolk, N.Y.	2,553,000	Tulsa, Ariz.	477,000
Columbus, Ohio	916,000	New Haven, Conn.	356,000	Utica-Rome, N.Y.	341,000
Dallas, Tex.	1,556,000	New Orleans, La.	1,046,000	Washington, D.C.-Md.-Va.	2,861,000
Davenport, Iowa-Ill.	363,000	New York, N.Y.	9,019,000	West Palm Beach, Fla.	349,000
Dayton, Ohio	850,000	Newark, N.J.	1,857,000	Wichita, Kans.	389,000
Denver, Colo.	1,228,000	Norfolk, Va.	681,000	Wilkes-Barre, Penn.	342,000
Detroit, Mich.	4,200,000	Oklahoma City, Okla.	641,000	Wilmington, Dela.-N.J.-Md.	499,000
El Paso, Tex.	359,000	Omaha, Nebraska-Iowa	540,000	Worcester, Mass.	344,000
Flint, Mich.	497,000	Orlando, Fla.	428,000	York, Pa.	330,000
Ft. Lauderdale, Fla.	620,000	Oxnard, Calif.	376,000	Youngstown, Ohio	536,000
Ft. Worth, Tex.	762,000	Patterson, N.J.	1,359,000		
Fresno, Calif.	413,000	Peoria, Ill.	342,000		
Gary, Ind.	633,000	Philadelphia, Pa.-N.J.	4,818,000		

*These tables are revised more frequently than the statistics and maps in the body of the Text.

A Little Geography Dictionary

altitude: The height above sea level. (See picture at right.)

antarctic: The region around the South Pole. (See picture of globe below.)

arctic: The region around the North Pole. Also an ocean. (See picture of globe below.)

bay: Part of a large body of water which reaches into the land. (See picture on page 503.)

branch: A river which flows into a larger river. Also known as a **tributary**. (See picture on page 503.)

canyon: A deep, narrow valley with high, steep sides. (See picture at right.)

cape: A point of land reaching out into a body of water.

cliff: A high, steep wall of rock. (See picture at right.)

climate: The kind of weather a place has year after year.

continents: The largest bodies of land on the earth. (See globe picture below.)

current: The flow of a stream of water.

delta: Land built up of soil deposited at the mouth of a river. (See picture on page 503.)

desert: A very dry land where few plants can grow.

divide: A high ridge of land which separates river systems. (See picture on page 503.)

downstream: The direction in which a river flows. (See picture, p. 503.)

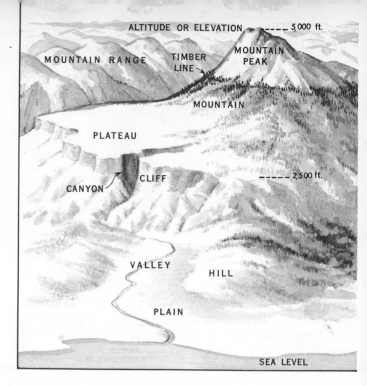

elevation: The height above sea level. (See picture above.)

equator: An imaginary line around the earth halfway between the North and South poles. (See picture of globe below.)

falls: A fall of water from a high level to a lower level. Also a waterfall. (See page 503.)

fiord: A long, narrow arm of the sea which reaches inland and usually has steep sides.

glacier: A large body of ice moving slowly over land.

globe: A small model of the earth which usually has a map of the world on it.

growing season: The number of days when the weather is warm enough for crops to grow without damage from frost.

gulf: Part of large body of water reaching into the land, larger than a bay.

harbor: A sheltered body of water where ships may anchor safely.

hemisphere: One half of the earth.

high latitudes: The regions of the earth close to the North and South poles where the degrees of latitude have high numbers. (See picture of globe at left.)

highlands: High or mountainous lands.

hill: A raised and somewhat rounded part of the earth's surface, smaller than a mountain. (See picture above.)

iceberg: A floating mass of ice which has broken off a glacier.

island: Land entirely surrounded by water, smaller than a continent.

isthmus: A narrow strip of land connecting two larger bodies of land. (See picture below.)

jungle: Land thickly covered with bushes, vines, and trees.

lake: An inland body of water.

latitude: Distance north or south of the equator, measured in degrees. (See globe picture on page 502.)

low latitudes: The regions of the earth nearest to the equator where the degrees of latitude have low numbers. (See globe picture on page 502.)

middle latitudes: The regions of the earth between the low and the high latitudes—that is, between the tropics and the Arctic and Antarctic circles. (See page 502.)

mountain: High rocky land with rather steep sides and with a sharp, pointed peak or a rounded top; higher than a hill. (See picture at top of page 502.)

mountain peak: The pointed top of a mountain.

mountain range: A long row of mountains.

mouth (of a river): The place where a river empties into a larger body of water. (See picture below.)

North Pole: The point on the earth which is farthest north. (See globe picture on 502.)

oceans: The earth's largest bodies of water.

pampas: The vast, treeless plains around and west of the Río de la Plata in Argentina.

peninsula: A body of land almost surrounded by water. (See picture below.)

plain: A region which is mostly level and may be low land. (See picture at top of page 502.)

plateau: A region which is not as level as a plain and which is high land. (See picture at top of page 502.)

port: A city with a harbor where boats load and unload cargo.

prairie: A large area of level or rolling grassland.

river: A stream of water flowing through the land. (See picture below.)

river basin: The land drained by a river and its branches. (See picture below.)

river valley: Low land through which a river flows. (See picture below.)

sea: A large body of salt water, smaller than an ocean, partially or entirely enclosed by land.

sea level: Level with the surface of the sea. (See picture at top of page 502.)

season: A part of the year when the weather from day to day is somewhat alike. Winter is a season.

sound: A long, narrow body of water separating one or more islands from the mainland. (See picture below.)

source (of a river): The place where a river begins. (See picture below.)

South Pole: The point on the earth which is located the farthest south. (See it on the globe on page 502.)

strait: A narrow body of water which connects two larger bodies of water. (See picture below.)

tide: The regular rise and fall of ocean water which occurs about every twelve hours.

timber line: The line on a mountain above which trees cannot grow because of the cold. (See picture on page 502.)

tropics: The warm region which lies on both sides of the equator. (See globe picture on page 502.)

tundra: The vast, level, treeless plains in the cold Arctic regions.

upstream: The direction from which a river flows. (See *downstream* on page 502.)

valley: Low land between hills or mountains.

volcano: A mountain with an opening through which steam, ashes, and lava are forced out.

125°　　　120°　　　115°　　　110°　　　105°　　　100°

C · A · N · A · D · A

P a c i f i c

Olympia ■ ★ ● Seattle
○ Tacoma
WASHINGTON
Spokane ●
Portland ○
Columbia River
★ Salem
Eugene ●
O R E G O N
Great Falls ●
Helena ★
Missouri River
MONTANA
Butte ●
NORTH DAKOTA
Bismarck ★
SOUTH DAKOTA
Pierre ★

★ Boise
I D A H O
Snake River
Pocatello ●
W Y O M I N G
Casper ●
Great Salt Lake
Ogden ●
★ Salt Lake City
Provo ●
Cheyenne ★
N E B R A S K A

Reno ●
Richmond ●
★ Sacramento
Carson City ●
N E V A D A
San Francisco ●
Berkeley ●
○ Oakland ● Stockton
San Mateo ●
San Jose ●
Fresno ●
U T A H
Denver ★
Colorado Springs ●
C O L O R A D O
Pueblo ●
Abilene ●
K A N S A S

O c e a n

Las Vegas ●
River
Colorado River
C A L I F O R N I A
Burbank ● Glendale ●
Inglewood ○ ○ Pasadena
Los Angeles ★ ● Alhambra
● Compton
Santa Monica ● ● San Bernardino
Long Beach ○ ● Riverside
● Santa Ana
San Diego ● ● Lakeside
A R I Z O N A
Phoenix ★
Tucson ●
Santa Fe ★
Albuquerque ○
N E W   M E X I C O
El Paso ○
Amarillo ○
Lubbock ○
Wichita Falls ○
Fort Worth ●
Abilene ●
San Angelo ●
O K L A
Oklahoma City ★
T E X A S
Austin ★

M E X I C O

Rio Grande

San Antonio ★ ■

Bering Strait
U.S.S.R.
170°　180°　170°　160°
ARCTIC CIRCLE
70°
140°
INTERNATIONAL DATE LINE
60°
B e r i n g   S e a
Fairbanks ●
160°
22°30′
KAUAI
NIIHAU
OAHU
157° 30′
Honolulu ★ MOLOKAI
LANAI
KAHOOLAWE MAUI
20°
155°
Hilo ●
HAWAII

Anchorage ●
60°
Juneau ●

504

ALASKA
Scale of Miles
0　　　500
Scale of Kilometers
0　　　800

HAWAII
Scale of Miles
0　　　150
Scale of Kilometers
0　　　240

P a c i f i c   O c e a n

A L E U T I A N   I S L A N D S

Corpus Christi ●
Laredo ●

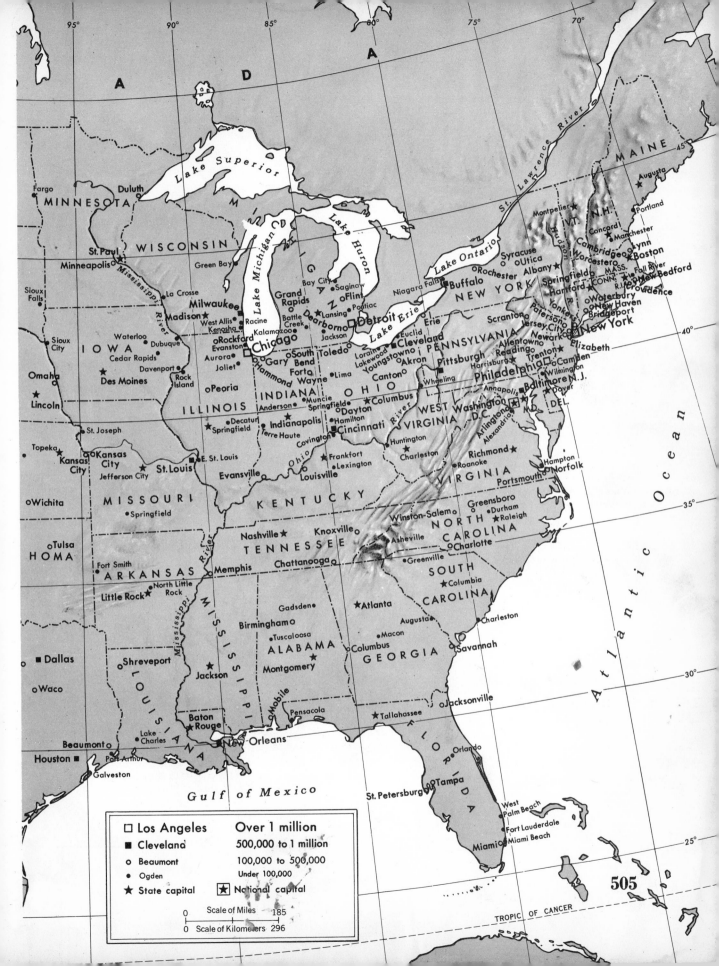

Index and Pronouncing Vocabulary

KEY

Edmonton, Alberta, 386
Electric power, 209, 240, 279, 298, 312, 320, 378; atomic power and, 193; Canada, 385, 388; South America, 451
Electronics industry, 198-199, 209, 329, 331
Elevations, 88
Elevator, grain, 266
El Salvador (el sal'və dôr), 410, 411, 413, 417
Emancipation (ē man'sə pā'shən) Proclamation, 169
Employee, 181; employer, 181
Employment: automation and, 228; Unions and, 181-182
Energy, 248, 351
England: Canada and, 373, 374-375; colonial revolution against, 43, 45-66; colonial war with France, 47-48, 56-57, 120, 374-375; colonization by, 32-41; Florida and, 118-119; land claims by, 23, 56, 373, 432; New World and, 21; Oregon Territory and, 129, 138; South America and, 432; textile manufacturing in, 207; and War of 1812, 120-121; West Indies and, 423
English colonies, 26-66; *See also* Colonies
Equator, 437
Ericson (er'ik s'n), Leif (lāv), 372
Erie Canal, 219, 342
Erosion, 240, 306
Eskimos, 310, 312, 380
Estevanico (este vä nee'cō), 17
Europe, 10, 12; slavery in colonies of, 160; World Wars in, 190
Everglades, 238
Executive (eg zek'ū tiv) branch of government, 71; state, 79
Exports, 186

Factories, *see* Manufacturing
Fairbanks, Alaska, 300, 309, 310-311
Fall line, 216
Farming: Canada, 382, 383, 384, 387; Central America, 412-413, 414, 415, 418-419; Central States, 258, 261-266; colonial, 27, 29, 31, 35, 36, 40, 42, 102; income from, 181; by Indians, 12; in Mexico, 397-398, 400, 401, 402-403; in Middle Atlantic States, 232-233; in New England, 204-205; in the North, 161; in Northwest, 113, 115, 302-303; in plains, 179-180; in Rocky Mountain States, 281-

283; slavery and, 162-163; in Southern States, 162-163, 238, 241, 242-246; in Southwest, 323-326; in South America, 434, 449-451, 464, 465, 471, 472, 482, 483, 486, 487, 488, 493, 494; tree, 305; West Indies, 426, 427, 428, 429
Field, Cyrus, 365-366
Finland, colonists from, 39
Fiords (fyôrds), 296
First Continental Congress, 51-52
Fishing: in Canada, 373, 381, 382, 387; colonial, 32, 37-38, 46; by Indians, 12; in New England, 161, 205-207; in North America, 23; in Northwest, 307-309; in Southern States, 247; in Southwest, 327
Fitch, John, 341
Flags: American, 59; Continental Army, 59; state, 80
Flatboats, 111, 116
Flatcars, 350
Flax, 464, 494
Flood control, 298, 307, 320
Florida, 66, 236, 237, 238, 244, 245, 249; acquired from Spain, 119-120; De Soto in, 16-17; discovery of, 15; England and, 118-119
Florida Keys, 253
Flour mills, 266, 288
Flord, Henry, 271
Forest rangers, 305, 307
Forests, 96; Canada, 377, 379, 381, 382, 384, 387, 388; Central America, 413, 414, 415; Central States, 258; conservation of, 305-307; Mexico, 399; New England, 199, 202; Northwest, 293-294, 297, 303-307; Rocky Mountain States, 286; South America, 439, 443, 447, 448, 471, 483, 487, 493; Southern States, 239, 246; Southwest, 327; United States, 37, 136. *See also* Lumbering
Forts: Duquesne (dü kān'), 56-57; Kaskaskia (kas kas'ki ə), 64; McHenry, 120; Mandan, 125; in Northwest Territory, 108, Pitt, 110; Sumter, 168; West Point, 63
"Forty-Niners," 155-156, 320
France, 85; Canada and, 373-375; colonial war with England, 47-48, 56-57, 120, 374-375; explorers from, 18-20; land claims of, 18, 20, 56, 116, 373, 432; Louisiana Purchase and, 117-118; in Revolutionary War 62-63, 66; South America and, 432;

Statue of Liberty and, 223-224; trade 186; West Indies and, 423; in World Wars, 186, 187
Franklin, Benjamin: in Constitutional Convention, 70, 71; in Continental Congress, 55, 58; mail service and, 359; opposed to slavery, 160; as printer, 362; in Revolutionary War, 62-63
Freedom: Bill of Rights and, 71; colonists fight for, 52-66; of colonial government, 27, 43, 46, 49; Cuba loses, 426; of Negroes, 168-169, 175; of religion, 32, 33, 34, 40, 71; in United States, 191
Freeways, 340
Freight trains, 348, 350
Freighters, 343
French-Canadians, 375, 380
French Guiana (gē ä'nə), 432
French and Indian War, 56-57, 374-375
Frontier: pushed across Appalachians, 101-112; space, 193-194
Fulton, Robert, 341-342
Fur trade, 21, 39, 41, 46, 129-130, 138; Alaskan, 309-310; Canadian, 19, 373, 374

Gadsden Purchase, 151
Gage, General, 46, 49, 50-51, 53, 55
Galapagos (gə lä'pə gəs) Islands, 484
Galveston, 252
Gander, 380
Gary (gār'i), 268
Gasoline, 194, 351
Gaspé (gas pā') Peninsula, 382
Gatun (gə tün') Lake, 346
Gauchos (gou'chōz), 463, 493
George III, King of England, 46
Georgia, 17, 237, 242, 243, 244, 249
Germany: immigrants from, 180; trade, 186; in World Wars, 186-187, 190
Gettysburg, Battle of, 170
Gettysburg Address, 170
Geyser (gī'zėr), 274-275, 289
Glacier National Park, 290
Glaciers (glā'shėrz), 36, 93, 202, 290, 299, 382
Glass making, 227, 404, 406
Glenn, John, 192
Globe, Arizona, 327
Gold mining: Alaska, 295-296, 309; California, 155-157, 178; Canada, 382, 384, 387, 388-389; Central America, 417; Mexico, 399; search for gold, 15, 16, 17, 28, 410, 443; South America, 446, 482, 487, 492; Western states, 179, 285, 327

Montevideo (mon′tə və dā′ō), 494-495

Montezuma (mon′tə zü′mə), 394-395

Montreal (mon′trē ôl′), 373, 383

Moonflight Center, 251

Mormons, 151-153, 288

Morse, Samuel, 363-365

Mount Ranier National Park, 297

Mount Vernon, 57, 71, 73

Mount Whitney, 88, 319

Mounties, 376

Napoleon (nə pō′lē en), 117, 118, 444

Nassau (nas′ô), 424

National Cemetery, 170

National parks, 239, 274-275, 288-290, 297, 298, 299, 319; *map*, 289

Natural gas, 248-249, 386

Natural resources, 96, 97, 194, 246-249, 303-310

Navy, 74, 78; bases of, 425; in Revolutionary War, 64-65

Nebraska, 261

Netherlands (neTH′ėr ləndz): American colonies of, 39; New World and, 20-21; Pilgrims in, 32; slave trade and, 159; South America and, 432; West Indies and, 423

Nevada, 151, 179; described, 316, 318, 320; mining, 327; ranching, 326

New Amsterdam, 21, 39

New Brunswick (brunz′wik), 381, 382

New England: climate, 36, 42, 203-204; colonial life in, 32-33, 34-38; geography, 89, 199-202; industries, 204-211; maps, 200, 201; missionaries from, 317; population, 210; in Revolutionary War, 60, 61; settlement of, 32-38; tourist trade, 211-212

New France, 19, 373, 374, 375

New Hampshire, 35, 38, 202, 208, 211

New Jersey, 38, 40, 215; farming, 232; in Revolutionary War, 60

New Mexico, 17, 136, 150, 151, 179, 276, 281, 286, 288, 290

New Netherland, 21, 39

New Orleans (ôr′lē ənz), 112, 115, 116-118, 252, 253

New Spain, 18, 395

New World, 10; discovery of, 14; exploration of, 9, 14-23

New York, 38, 74, 151, 215, 231, 266; Canal System in, 219; cities, 221; farming, 232; in

Revolution, 61, 63; settlement, 39

New York Bay, 215, 218

New York City, 39, 46, 185, 215, 221, 338, 341, 342, 359; British tea tax in, 46; described, 223-225; first national capital, 71-72; Revolutionary War and, 60, 61, 63; seaport of, 225; size of, 183, 223; United Nations in, 192, 225

Newfoundland (nū′fənd land′), 206, 366, 380-381

Newspapers, 361-363

Niagara Falls, 220, 378

Nicaragua (nik′ə rä′gwə), 410, 417-418

Nickel, 382, 384

Nitrate (nī′trāt), 473-474

Nome, Alaska, 309

North America, 9, 10, 11, 85; compared with South America, 437

North Carolina, 17, 23, 100, 237, 242, 245

North Dakota, 125, 261

Northwest, 293-312; cities, 310-312; climate, 300; dairying, 302, 303; explored by Lewis and Clark, 123-128; farming, 301-303; fishing, 307-309; geography, 294-300; lumbering, 293-294; manufacturing, 311-312; mining, 309; population, 310

Northwest Territories of Canada, 388-389

Northwest Territory, 63-64, 109-113

Norway, immigrants from, 180

Nova Scotia (nō′və skō′shə), 381, 382

Nylon, 208

Oahu (ō ä′hü), 316

Oak Ridge, 250

O'Higgins (ō hig′inz), Bernardo (ber när′THō), 470

Ohio, 110, 112, 258, 269

Ohio River, 20, 47, 56, 63, 93, 108, 111, 115, 227, 237, 260, 342

Ohio Valley, 56, 110-111

Oil industry, 194, 247-248, 251, 252, 286, 309, 327; Alaska, 309; Canada, 386; Mexico, 401; South America, 466, 473, 479-480, 482

Oklahoma, 150, 237, 238, 245, 248

Old World, 10

Omaha (ō′mə hô), 263, 270, 348

Onate, 144

Ontario (on tār′i ō), 382, 383-385

Oregon, 129, 294, 296, 297, 298, 300; industries of, 301, 303; Territory of, 123-128

Oregon Territory: claims to, 128, 129, 138; explored, 127-128, 129-130; settlement of, 131-132, 138; trade in, 129

Oregon Trail, 132

Organization of American States, 495

Orinoco (ōr′ə nō′kō) River, 432, 440, 479, 480

Oroville (ōr′ō vil) Dam, 315, 321

Ottawa (ot′ə wə), 375

Oyster farming, 233, 247

Pacific Ocean, 11, 125, 296; effect on land climates, 300, 322; reached by Lewis and Clark, 127; in Second World War, 190

Pampa (pam′pə), 456, 457, 460, 461, 462, 463-464

Pan American Union, 495

Panama (pan′ə mä), 344, 410, 419; Isthmus of, 344

Panama Canal, 344-346, 419

Panama hats, 484

Paper industry, 208, 247, 294, 385, 474. *See also* Pulpwood

Paraguay (par′ə gwī), 437, 492-493

Paricutin (pä rē′kü tēn), 399

Parliament, Canadian, 375; English 47-49

Pasadena, 329

Patagonia (pat′ə gōn′yə), 455, 462

Pawtucket, Rhode Island, 207

Peace Corps, 495

Peanuts, 233, 244, 246

Pearl Harbor, 188, 190, 332

Pedro I and II, Emperors of Brazil, 444-445

Penn, William, 40, 219

Pennsylvania, 38, 39, 110, 215, 228, 231; farming, 232; in Revolutionary War, 60; petroleum in, 248; settlement of, 40

Peru (pə rü′), 437, 470, 478, 485-488

Petaluma (pet′ə lü′mə) area, 326

Petroleum, *see* Oil industry

Philadelphia (fil′ə del′fi ə), 46; Constitutional Convention in, 70; Continental Congress in, 51, 55; described, 226; first daily newspaper in, 362; founded, 40, 219; importance of, 221, 338, 341, 359; manufacturing in, 218, 226; national capital, 73; World's Fair in, 367

Philippine (fil′ə pēn Islands, 188, 317

Phoenix (fē′niks), 331

Piedmont (pēd′mont), 216, 227, 239

Map and Picture Credits

The maps on the pages listed were made by the following artists:

Norman C. Adams, 184, 229, 316. Norman Greenawalt, 329. Christie A. McFall, 243, 247, 262, 265, 267.

All the other maps were made by Edward A. Schmitz, Inc.

We wish to express our appreciation to the following for permission to reproduce the paintings listed below:

Page 22, *John Cabot*, courtesy of the Confederation Life Association. Page 64, *Wabash* scene at the *George Rogers Clark Memorial*, W. M. Cline Company. Page 141, *Discovery of Pike's Peak*, courtesy of Missouri Historical Society. Page 156, *Gold Mining in California*, Currier and Ives lithograph, courtesy of the California Historical Society. Page 256, *Reaper Demonstration*, painting by N. C. Wyeth, courtesy of The International Harvester Company. Page 136, *The Homesteader's Wife*, painting by Harvey Dunn, South Dakota Memorial Art center.

The drawings on the pages listed were made by the following artists:

John Ballentine, 30-31, 37, 43, 135, 163, 210, 233 (both), 244, 246 (bottom), 261, 263, 265, 282 (top), 306-307 (both), 336. Merrill Bent, 32, 70. Edward Bradford, 351, Foster Caddell, 206, 248-249, 282 (bottom), 298, 348-349 (top), 365, 403, 418. Robert Doremus, 197, 335, 371, 431. Bernard Friedman, 425. George Garland, 84, 110-111, 119, 161, 167 (both), 171, 174, 180. Herman Giesen, 448. Denver Gillen, 207. Ray Granai, 59, 369. David Hendrickson, 45, 99, 101, 103, 104, 105, 106, 108, 230, 338, 341, 347, 357 (left), 372, 393, 395, 409, 421, 468, 477. Tom Hill, 33, 38 (bottom), 39, 149, 152, 159, 160, 169, 173, 177, 179, 274, 275, 405, 414. Russ Hoover, 7, 15, 165. Charles Kerins, 458-459. Robert Lambdin, 47, 60, 62, 66. Brendan Lynch, 8-9, 18, 23, 26, 29, 35, 48, 50 (both), 51, 52, 54-55, 55 (top), 58, 132-133, 144, 182 (both), 183. Charles Naugle, 2-3, 4-5, 13, 68, 73, 83, 99, 125, 141, 143, 157, 161. William Reusswig, 38 (top), 115, 123, 124, 127, 145, 146-147, 170, 359, 362, 364, 366. Milburn Rosser, 373, 390, 406, 455, 493. Harve Stein, 162, 187, 352, 485. Shannon Stirnweis, 69, 72, 121, 128, 129, 131, 137, 315, 316, 325. Darrell Sweet, 20, 40, 41, 256 (left), 353, 358, 442. Visual Services, Inc., 74, 337, 345. John Wonsetler, 154, 157, 339, 427.

The photographs on the pages listed were obtained from the following sources:

Paul Almsay, 439, 489 (top). American Airlines, 89, 219, 353 (bottom). American Forest Products Industries, Inc., 246 (top). American Hereford Association, 245. Amon Carter Museum of Western Art, 312 (both). Anaheim City Schools, 357 (right). Associated Photographers Inc., 227 (top). David H. Bergamini, 433 (center right). Bernadine Bailey, 475, 484 (top). J. D. Barnell, 382. Charles J. Belden, 283 (top). Mildred Berman, 400 (left). Bethlehem Steel Corporation, 231 (right). Black Star Publishing Co., 412 (both). Bliss Aerial Surveys, 330. The Boston Globe, 97 (both), 194 (right). Herb Brinkman, 327. California Division of Highways, 79 (bottom). Courtesy of the California Historical Society, San Francisco/Los Angeles, 156. California Raisin Advisory Board, 324 (both). State of California, Resources Agency, 315. Canadian Government Travel Bureau, 387. Canadian Pacific Railway, 385. J. I. Case Company, 243. Caterpillar Tractor Company, 304 (top right). Cerro de Pasco Corp., 487. Chamber of Commerce of St. Louis, 270 (top). Charles Phelps Cushing, 77 (top right), 461 (top), 491 (left, James Sawders; right, Carl S. Bell), Chicago Association of Commerce and Industry, 271. Chicago Public Schools, 81. Coca Cola Export Corp., 461 (bottom). Community Relations Service, 194 (left). Compannia Siderurgicia Nacional, 446. Library of Congress, 112. A. Devaney, 185, 250. Dole Corporation, 326. Eastern Photo Service, 361. Ecuadorean Consulate, 484 (bottom). Embassy of Venezuela, 481 (bottom). Elizabeth Eiselen, 448. Fairchild Aerial Surveys, 96, 214. Ford Co., 270 (bottom). Free Lance Photographers Guild, Inc., 205 (Griffin), 253 (P. Gendreau), 266 (bottom, Kronfeld, 267 (bottom, Bond), 283 (bottom, Packard), 290 (Jack Breed), 311 (bottom, Ellis-Sawyer), 318 (Camera Hawaii), 322 (left, Werner Stoy), 377 (Jarrett), 445 (left, Dana Brown). Ewing Galloway, 462. Phillip D. Gendreau, 374. Galaxy, 396. William A. Garnett, 102. Laura Gilpin, 144. Greater North Dakota Association, 88. Rapho-Guillumette Pictures, 463 (bottom). Hamilton Wright Organization, Inc., 481 (top). Grant Heilman, 96 (bottom). Walter Hendricks Hodge, 413. House of Photography, 416. Houston Chamber of Commerce, 252. George Hunter, 384, 388. Imperial Oil, Ltd., 386 (top). Copyright © 1972 by F. L. Kennett, London, 43. Life Time, 449 (top, Life Copyright 1957, Time, Inc.), Los Angeles County Chamber of Commerce, 340. Lowry Aerial Photo Service, 202, 212, 242, 280. Mac's Photo Service, 300. Magnum Photos, Inc., 473 (Cronell Capa), 194 (Burke Uzzle). Steve McCutcheon, 309, 311. Mexican Tourist Bureau, 404. Monkmeyer Press Photo Service, 266 (top, Block Townsend), 489 (bottom, Linares). Josef Meunch, 92, 94, 153, 291, 296, 319, 322 (right), 407, 415. National Aeronautics and Space Administration, 191, 192, 198, 236. National Cotton Council, 323 (top). National Film Board, 375, 381, 386 (bottom), 391. Pan American Society of New England, 400 (right). Peace Corps, 496 (all). Philadelphia Convention and Visitors Bureau, 226. Photo Art Commercial Studios, 302 (top). Photo Researchers, 449 (bottom right and left, John and Bini Moss), 460 (Litwin), 471 (Tom Hollyman), 490 (John Louis Stage), 494 (top, Thomas B. Hollyman; bottom, Ewing Kranin). Pix Publishing, Inc., 295 (Don Horter). Puerto Rico News Service, 428. Charles Rotkin, 310 (courtesy of Fortune Magazine © Time, Inc.). Salt Lake City Chamber of Commerce, 287 (bottom). Dr. Richard Evans Schultes, 438 (both), 447. Scott-d'Aragien, 363, 464. Shostal Press Agency, 57 (Paul Hogan), 77 (top, left, Hal Neilson; bottom, Robert Leahey), 96 (top left, Jack Zehrt; bottom right, Ray Manley), 204 (Edward Gockeler), 211, 221 (Timothy Sheehan), 232 (Grant Heilman), 260 (Gordon Lord), 285 (Winston Pote), 287 (top), 291 (left, Robert W. Chase), 302 (bottom, Ray Atkeson), 321 (Willard Luce), 329 (George Hunter), 331 (Ray Manley), 332 (top, Irving Rosen), 344 (Herbert Lanks), 432 (Ray Manley), 433 (top left, George Hunter; top right, Ace Williams; bottom, Art D'Arazien), 444 (Goegr Hagopian), 445 (right, Ace Williams), 450 (Ace Williams), 465 (L. B. Messens), 466 (Ace Williams), 474 (Nelson G. Shawn), 482 (bottom, Robert Leahey). Standard Oil Co. of New Jersey, 479 (right). South Carolina State Commission of Forestry, 305 (top). The Texas Co., 433 (center left). Three Lions, Inc., 264, 463 (top), 479 (left). Thomas Airviews, 225. Mort Tucker, 93. United Fruit, 416 (top). U.S. Army Photograph, 190. U.S. Bureau of Reclamation, 323 (foot). U.S. Forest Service, 297, 305 (foot). U.S. Post office, 361 (both). U.S. Lines Co., 343. U.S. Steel, 231 (left), 480 (both). Charles Perry Weimer, 482 (top). Weyerhaeuser Company, 293, 304 (top left, bottom right and left). Wide World Photos, 79 (top), 191, 332.

DEFG   09876

PRINTED IN THE UNITED STATES OF AMERICA